k is

Trends in Outdoor Recreation, Leisure and Tourism

Trends in Outdoor Recreation, Leisure and Tourism

Edited by

William C. Gartner

Department of Applied Economics and Tourism Center
University of Minnesota
St Paul
USA

and

David W. Lime

Department of Forest Resources and Tourism Center
University of Minnesota
St Paul
USA

CABI *Publishing*

CABI *Publishing* is a division of CAB *International*

CABI Publishing
CAB International
Wallingford
Oxon OX10 8DE
UK

Tel: +44 (0)1491 832111
Fax: +44 (0)1491 833508
Email: cabi@cabi.org
Web site: http://www.cabi.org

CABI Publishing
10 E 40th Street
Suite 3203
New York, NY 10016
USA

Tel: +1 212 481 7018
Fax: +1 212 686 7993
Email: cabi-nao@cabi.org

A catalogue record for this book is available from the British Library, London, UK.

Library of Congress Cataloging-in-Publication Data
Trends in outdoor recreation, leisure, and tourism / edited by W.C. Gartner and D.W. Lime.
     p. cm.
  Includes bibliographical references and index.
  ISBN 0-85199-403-2 (alk. paper)
     1. Outdoor recreation. 2. Leisure. 3. Tourism. I. Gartner, William C. II. Lime, David W.

GV191.6.T74 2000

99–087665

ISBN 0 85199 403 2

Typeset in 9/11pt Melior by York House Typographic Ltd, London.
Printed and bound in the UK by Biddles Ltd, Guildford and King's Lynn.

Contents

Contributors

Biosketches (alphabetical listing):

Dr Dorothy H. Anderson is Professor in the Department of Forest Resources at the University of Minnesota. She coordinates the Recreation Resource Management undergraduate and graduate programme and the planning, policy and law concentration in the Natural Resources Environmental Studies undergraduate programme. Dr Anderson has 25 years experience in conducting research with federal and state agencies including the US Department of Agriculture (USDA) Forest Service, US Department of the Interior (USDI) National Park Service, Bureau of Land Management and the Minnesota Department of Natural Resources Division of Parks and Recreation. Her research has focused on developing and testing management frameworks to better plan, manage and monitor recreational use on public lands. Dr Anderson's research has also looked at ways in which management frameworks, such as the benefits-based management framework, can be extended beyond recreational use as landscape level management tools.

Carter J. Betz is an Outdoor Recreation Planner with the Outdoor Recreation and Wilderness Assessment Research unit of the USDA Forest Service, Southern Research Station, Athens, Georgia. His speciality is database development, management and analysis. He contributed to both the 1989 and 1998 Forest Service Renewable Resources Planning Act (RPA) Assessments of Outdoor Recreation and Wilderness, including authorship of the chapter on recreation resources in the 1998 Assessment. Currently, he provides research support for the multi-agency National Survey on Recreation and the Environment (NSRE) 2000. Betz has an MS in recreation resources from North Carolina State University and previously served as a Research Associate in NCSU's Office of Park and Tourism Research.

Dr Rita J. Black recently finished a 2-year postdoctoral appointment with the Institute for Tourism and Recreation Research at the University of Montana–Missoula. Her research interests include sport tourism and the social dimensions of sport and recreation, especially as they relate to gender.

Dr Tommy L. Brown is a Senior Research Associate and Leader of the Human Dimensions Unit at Cornell University. His research in outdoor recreation, tourism, and human dimensions of fish and wildlife management over the past 30 years has been diverse. Long-standing research interests include recreation participation trends and associated factors, attitudinal studies, market segmentation of recreation user groups and other stake-holders, incorporating human dimensions information into management decision making, and survey research methods. A recent major effort has been coediting a text on human dimensions of wildlife management with colleagues D.J. Decker and W.F. Siemer, sponsored by The Wildlife Society. Tommy is a member of The Wildlife Society, American Fisheries Society and Rural Sociological Society. He has been an active participant in each of the 5-year Outdoor Recreation and Tourism Conferences.

Dr Dimitrios Buhalis is Senior Lecturer in Tourism at the Department of Tourism, University of Westminster in London. Dimitrios is also Adjunct Professor at the Institut de Management Hotelier International (Cornell University–Ecole Superieure des Sciences Economiques et Commerciales ESSEC) in Paris. Other professional activities include: Reviews Editor of the *International Journal of Tourism Research* and Books Editor of the *IT and Tourism: Applications-Methodologies and Techniques* journals; Associate Editor for the *Encyclopaedia of Tourism*; Mediterranean Editor for *Anatolia International Journal of Tourism and Hospitality Research*; Books Editor for *Tourism*, the Tourism Society journal; and Board Member of the *Journal of International Hospitality, Leisure and Tourism Administration*. Dimitrios is Chairman of the Association of Tourism Teachers and Trainers; Executive Committee member of the International Federation of Information Technology and Tourism and the Tourism Society; and Chairman of the ENTER 1998, 1999 and 2000 conferences on Tourism and Information Technology.

Dr Henry Campa III is an Associate Professor of Wildlife Ecology in the Department of Fisheries and Wildlife at Michigan State University (MSU). His research interests are in the areas of wildlife–habitat relationships, wildlife nutrition and ecosystem management. He teaches courses in upland ecosystem management, conservation biology, and wildlife nutrition. Prior to working at MSU, he was a Wildlife Research Biologist with the Michigan Department of Natural Resources. Dr Campa has received a Lilly Endowment Teaching Fellowship and the Teacher-Scholar Award at MSU. He holds a BS in wildlife management from the University of Missouri–Columbia, MS and PhD degrees in wildlife ecology from MSU, and is a Certified Wildlife Biologist with The Wildlife Society.

Dr Nevenka Čavlek is Assistant Professor and faculty member of the Department of Tourism at the Faculty of Economics, University of Zagreb, Croatia. She joined the Faculty after 9 years experience working in the field of the tour operating business. Dr Čavlek belongs to the younger generation of Croatian tourism experts and is well known as a result of a large number of articles and papers published by her on the topic. Her latest book (1998) focuses specifically on tour operators and international tourism. She is also editor of the scientific journal *Acta Turistica*, has worked since 1992 on the *Croatian Tourism Magazine* as a columnist dealing with international tourism, and edits the International Tourism News Programme on Croatian Television. Dr Čavlek's discipline and expertise includes: Tourism Economics, Multinational Corporations in Tourism and Management of Tour Operators.

Dr David N. Cole is research biologist with the Aldo Leopold Wilderness Research Institute (ALWRI), Missoula, Montana. He has degrees in geography from the University of California, Berkeley, and the University of Oregon. He has conducted research related to the management of wilderness, especially on the biophysical impacts of recreation use for the past 25 years for the USDA Forest Service's Wilderness Management Research Unit, Systems for Environmental Management and ALWRI. His recent work has been diverse, addressing ecological restoration visitor education and factors that influence the quality of recreation experiences. He is married, with two young children, and spends as much time as possible whitewater rafting and hiking.

Dr H. Ken Cordell earned his PhD degree in economics and forestry at North Carolina State University. As a USDA Forest Service scientist, he has worked on the application of social science theory and methods in outdoor recreation, wilderness, and, generally, natural resources management. Recently, Dr Cordell directed an ongoing series of national studies, including the US National Recreation Study. He is a national authority on recreation demand and supply trends and serves as adjunct faculty at several major universities.

Dr John L. Crompton is Professor of Recreation, Park and Tourism at Texas A&M University. Dr Crompton's primary interests are in the areas of marketing and financing public leisure and tourism services. He is author or coauthor of seven books and more than 350 articles and monographs which have been published in the recreation, tourism, sport and marketing fields. He is past recipient of the National Recreation and Park Association's National Literary Award, the NRPA Roosevelt Award for outstanding service; the Society of Park and Recreation Educator's Distinguished Teaching Award, the Travel and Tourism Research Association's Travel Research Award and the Texas A&M Vice-Chancellor's Award in Excellence in Graduate Teaching. He is a past president of the American Academy of Park and Recreation Administration; a past president of the Society of Park and Recreation Educators; and a current member of the NRPA Board of Trustees.

Dr Graham M.S. Dann obtained his PhD from the University of Surrey in 1975. Graham spent the next 21 years lecturing in sociology at the University of the West Indies in Barbados. In 1996 he was appointed Professor of Tourism at the University of Luton. A founder member of the International Academy for the Study of Tourism, and of the Research Committee on International Tourism of the International Sociological Association, he has research interests in tourist motivation and the semiotics of tourism promotion.

Dr Daniel J. Decker is a professor in the Department of Natural Resources at Cornell University, where he is co-leader of the Human Dimensions Research Unit. He received his PhD from Cornell University. His research of 25 years has focused on the human dimensions of wildlife management, especially improving understanding of diverse stakeholders in management and using that insight for wildlife programme planning, implementation and evaluation. Research during the 1990s targeted stakeholder involvement in wildlife management, especially stakeholder expectations for participation in decision making and the role of community-based management in a vision of 'next-generation wildlife management'. A feature of this pursuit is the articulation of a model of wildlife management and policy making that integrates human and biological dimensions in wildlife management and policy making, and considers how human attitudinal and behavioural considerations can be addressed effectively in these endeavours.

Dr Sara Dolnicar is assistant professor at the Institute for Tourism and Leisure Studies of the University of Economics and Business Administration, Vienna. Her research interests are centred on consumer psychology, tourism market segmentation and adaptive techniques in analysing tourist data. Dr Dolnicar is a participant in the Joint Research Programme on 'Adaptive Modelling and Information Systems in Economics and Management Science' which is sponsored by the Austrian Research Foundation. Dr Dolnicar is the current Secretary General of the Austrian Society for Applied Research.

Dr William R. Eadington is Professor of Economics and Director of the Institute for the Study of Gambling and Commercial Gaming at the University of Nevada, Reno. He is an internationally recognized authority on the legalization and regulation of commercial gambling, and has written extensively on issues relating to the economic and social impacts of commercial gaming. Professor Eadington has edited or coedited a number of books, including *The Business Of Gaming* (1999), *Gambling: Public Policies and the Social Sciences* (1997); *Gambling and Public Policy: International Perspectives* (1991); *Gambling and Commercial Gaming* (1992); *Gambling Behavior and Problem Gambling* (1993); *Gambling and Society* (1976); *Indian Gaming and the Law* (1990); and *Tourism Alternatives* (1992). Dr Eadington has served as a consultant and adviser for governments and private sector organizations throughout the world on issues related to gaming laws, casino operations, regulation, gambling legalization and public policy. He is a founding member of the International Academy for the Study of Tourism, and a former Associate Editor of the *Annals of Tourism Research*.

Dr Jody W. Enck is a Research Associate in the Human Dimensions Research Unit at Cornell University. He received a BS in wildlife biology from the University of Vermont, an MS in environmental and forest biology from the State University of NY at Syracuse, and a PhD in resource policy, management and human dimensions from Cornell University. His research interests include investigating recreationists' motivations and satisfactions, exploring factors affecting the social feasibility of restoring extirpated wildlife species, and analysing hunting policies as they relate to wildlife management. He also teaches an upper level undergraduate course in the human dimensions of natural resource management.

Dr Daniel L. Erkkila is a tourism and travel specialist with the University of Minnesota Extension Service and serves as associate director of the University's Tourism Center. He is also an adjunct associate professor within the University's College of Natural Resources, Department of Forest Resources. Dr Erkkila has more than 20 years of experience in natural resources and tourism, with positions in private business as a natural resource consultant, as well as in the public sector, including USDA Forest Service positions as an operations research analyst at the forest level and policy analyst in Washington, DC. His extension work for the University's Tourism Center includes development of a tourism business retention and expansion programme and his research interests include regional economic impacts from tourism and travel, nature-based tourism, sustainable development, and tourism and travel transportation systems.

Dr John Fletcher is Professor of Tourism and Head of the International Centre of Tourism and Hospitality Research, Bournemouth University. He received his doctorate from the University of Wales in economics and was Director of the Institute of Economic Research, University College of North Wales, Bangor. Before moving to Bournemouth, he was leader of the tourism group at the University of Surrey. His research interests have been in the development of interactive software for tourism impact and forecasting models. He has undertaken numerous tourism impact and development studies in the Caribbean, the South Pacific, the Indian Ocean and throughout Europe. He works closely with the World Travel and Tourism Council and is on the editorial board of leading academic journals.

Dr William C. Gartner is the Director of the Tourism Center and Professor of Applied Economics at the University of Minnesota. Bill has conducted numerous research studies in the area of tourism image, development, seasonal home impacts, tourism marketing and methods for tourism research. He is active regionally, nationally and internationally, having served as secretary, vice-president, president and Chairman of the Board of the CenStates chapter of the Travel and Tourism Research Association, on the editorial board of many tourism journals, and as secretary, vice-president and president for the International Academy for the Study of Tourism. He has also been involved in international development work including major projects in Ghana and Israel. He is the author of numerous tourism articles published in professional journals and most recently a book, published by Van Nostrand Reinhold, entitled *Tourism Development: Principles, Processes and Policies*.

Dr Donald Getz is Professor of Tourism and Hospitality Management, Faculty of Management, at the University of Calgary. He also holds a visiting professorship at the Australian International Hotel School in Canberra, and has strong research links with Edith Cowan University in Perth, Western Australia. He teaches, conducts research, writes and consults in the area of recreation and tourism planning and destination management. Don has authored two books on events: *Festivals, Special Events, and Tourism* (1991) and *Event Management and Event Tourism* (1997). He is co-founder and coeditor of *Festival Management and Event Tourism: An International Journal*. Don has coedited and contributed to a third book, entitled *The Business of Rural Tourism* (Thomson International Business Press, 1997), and has worked with several colleagues to produce a workbook entitled *Planning For Sustainable Tourism*. Reflecting his interest in rural development and wine, Dr Getz recently completed a book entitled *Wine Tourism*. Other current research themes include family businesses in tourism and hospitality, and event evaluation concepts and methods. Increasingly, Don is examining global leisure and tourism trends and giving speeches with a 'futurist flavour'.

Dr William E. Hammitt is Professor of Wildland Recreation in the Departments of Parks, Recreation and Tourism Management, and Forest Resources at Clemson University. He has been at Clemson since 1990, teaching and conducting research in the area of wildland recreation. His research speciality is recreation behaviour and visitor management. He was previously employed at the University of Tennessee for 12 years. Dr Hammitt is an author and/or coauthor of more than 150 papers and articles in professional and trade publications in his field. He is a past associate editor of the *Journal of Leisure Research*, *Leisure Sciences* and currently is an associate editor for the *Journal of Human Dimension of Wildlife and Fish Management*. He is a senior author of the text, *Wildland Recreation: Ecology and Management*, 1987, 1998. He is the recipient of two Fulbright Awards, Peru and Norway, and The Theodore and Franklin Roosevelt Award for Excellence in Recreation and Park Research (1998).

Dr Karla A. Henderson is professor and chair in the Department of Recreation and Leisure Studies at the University of North Carolina at Chapel Hill. She is the author of several books and numerous articles addressing gender and leisure as well as research methods. Karla has over 20 years of experience in higher education and has served the profession in a number of capacities including being president of the Society of Park and Recreation Educators, president of the Research Consortium of the American Alliance of Health, Physical Education, Recreation, and Dance, and president of the Academy of Leisure Sciences. She has been on the Board of Trustees of the National Recreation and Parks Association, the Board of Directors of the World Recreation and Leisure Association and the American Camping Association.

Dr Ray Hutchison is Professor of Sociology and Urban and Regional Studies at the University of Wisconsin–Green Bay. He received his MA and PhD in sociology from the University of Chicago and has taught at DePaul University, the University of California–San Diego and the University of Nevada–Las Vegas. His research on ethnic, racial and immigrant groups has been supported by funding from the USDA Forest Service, the W.T. Grant Foundation, and the University of Wisconsin Institute on Race and Ethnicity. He is coauthor with Mark Gottdiener of *The New Urban Sociology* (McGraw-Hill) and series editor of *Research in Urban Sociology* (JAI Press). Dr Hutchison's discipline and expertise includes urban sociology, race and ethnicity, immigrant and refugee populations, and the leisure and recreation activity of urban populations.

Dr Peter F. Keller is Director for Tourism at Switzerland's Secretariat of State for Economic Affairs (SECO) and Professor at the School for Economics and Management of the University of Lausanne, where he is in charge of the Tourism Research and Education Unit. Professor Keller is a member of the board of the Swiss Tourism Industry Association, the Council of Switzerland's National Tourism Office, and various other organizations of his country which he represents in the network of international organizations. Since 1991 he has been president of the Commission for Europe of the World Tourism Organization (WTO) and since 1994 president of the International Association of Scientific Experts in Tourism (AIEST). He is also in charge of the relaunch of the Tourism Committee of the OECD, which groups the world's highly developed countries. He is the editor of the AIEST publication *Globalisation and Tourism* (1996, St. Gallen).

Dr Bernard Lane is Director of the Rural Tourism Unit at the University of Bristol, responsible for a programme on rural and sustainable tourism development issues. He has been a consultant on rural tourism for the Paris-based Organization for Economic Coopera- tion and Development (OECD), for the government of Australia, for development agencies and tourist boards in Canada, France, Ireland, Japan, New Zealand, Norway and Poland and for many communities and local authorities throughout Britain. He also works with a range of private sector tourism enterprises. In 1992 he founded and is coeditor of the international *Journal of Sustainable Tourism*.

Dr Will F. LaPage teaches parks, recreation and tourism in the Department of Forest Management at the University of Maine. He has taught at the University of New Hampshire, University of Wyoming and Colorado State University. Prior to coming to Maine, he served as the director of the Wolf Education and Research Center, in Idaho, director of New Hampshire State Parks, and as a senior recreation research scientist with the USDA Forest Service. His current research focuses on noneconomic and nontraditional uses and benefits of public parklands. Dr LaPage has been a consultant on parks and tourism in South Africa, Bulgaria, Jamaica, and with Croatian National Park directors; and he served as a member of President Reagan's Commission on American's Outdoors from 1985 to 1987. Dr LaPage has authored numerous technical reports on outdoor recreation trends and partnerships; and is completing his third book of outdoor poetry.

Dr Martha E. Lee is an associate professor in the School of Forestry at Northern Arizona University. Dr Lee teaches undergraduate and graduate classes in the human dimensions of ecosystem management, including wildland recreation management and planning. Her current research interests include documenting the benefits that users and nonusers receive from forest and park resources and understanding the relationships between the benefits of recreation and the wildland settings in which they occur. Dr Lee's discipline and expertise include: motivations for recreation behaviour, outcomes of recreation and leisure, visitor use management and attitudes and perceptions of wildland use and management.

Dr David W. Lime is a senior research associate and faculty member in the Department of Forest Resources at the University of Minnesota. He serves as the social science programme leader and unit leader for the Cooperative Park Studies Unit, a research partnership between the University of Minnesota and the National Park Service and US Geological Survey, Biological Resources Division. He also is a staff member with the University's Tourism Center. Dr Lime has over 30 years experience conducting research and other services with the USDI National Park Service, USDA Forest Service, Bureau of Land Management, and other federal and state land management agencies. Dr Lime's discipline and expertise includes: human geography, human behaviour concerning recreation and tourism, social science research methods, recreation resource management, resource-based tourism and visitor use management for parks and protected areas.

Dr Patrick Long is a Professor of Business at the University of Colorado at Boulder (UCB) where he teaches and conducts research in tourism. He also served as CEO/president of the

National Rural Tourism Foundation and is a faculty affiliate with the Center for Sustainable Tourism at UCB. Dr Long works primarily on issues related to tourism impacts, policies and planning, with particular focus on community-based tourism development.

Dr John B. Loomis is a Professor in the Department of Agricultural and Resource Economics, Colorado State University. During his 20-year career he has worked as an economist for the Bureau of Land Management and US Fish and Wildlife Service, as well as being an Associate Professor at UC–Davis. Dr Loomis has published extensively on recreation economics, including coauthoring a book entitled *Recreation Economic Decisions*. Dr Loomis has been involved with the USDA Forest Service in estimating the economic value of recreation on national forests since 1984.

Dr Stephen F. McCool is Professor, Wildland Recreation Management at the School of Forestry, The University of Montana. He received his PhD from the University of Minnesota during the Cretaceous Period. Dr McCool is currently interested in various paradigms of planning as they are applied to protected areas and tourism development. His work encompasses the concept of sustainability as applied to tourism and recreation planning, public participation in planning processes and use of systems such as Limits of Acceptable Change in developing planning frameworks for protected areas.

Dr Maureen H. McDonough is a Professor of Social and Community Forestry in the Department of Forestry at Michigan State University. She holds a BS degree in biology from Baldwin-Wallace College, a MSF in Wildlife Ecology from the University of Florida, and a PhD in Forest Resources from the University of Washington. She has been a faculty member at Michigan State University since 1980. Her work focuses on the interactions of people and natural resources and currently includes community forestry projects in Thailand and Detroit. She has studied public participation in natural resource decision making in the US, Thailand, Taiwan, Jamaica and the Dominican Republic. She is currently involved in projects to expand participation by underrepresented groups in both ecosystem planning and urban and community forestry in the USDA Forest Service and the Michigan Department of Natural Resources. She serves on the Michigan Urban and Community Forestry Council, the technology transfer committee of the Urban Forestry Center for the Midwestern States and was an invited panellist at the *Community Futures Forum: Building an Urban Natural Resource Agenda for the 21st Century* sponsored by the USDA Forest Service.

Dr Robert E. Manning is Professor of Natural Resources at the University of Vermont where he chairs the Recreation Management Program. He teaches courses and conducts research on the history, philosophy and management of parks, wilderness, and related areas. He conducts a programme of research with the US National Park Service on carrying capacity, crowding and management of outdoor recreation, and has spent year-long sabbatical leaves at Grand Canyon and Yosemite National Parks and the Washington Office of the National Park Service. Dr Manning is the author of *Studies in Outdoor Recreation*.

Dr Josef A. Mazanec has been full professor of business administration in tourism and director of the Institute for Tourism and Leisure Studies of the Vienna University of Economics and Business Administration (WU Wien) since 1981. He was a visiting scholar at the Alfred P. Sloan School of Management, MIT, Cambridge, Massachusetts, during the spring term 1992. Since 1997 he also functions as the Vice-rector for Research of the WU Wien and as the Speaker of the Joint Research Programme on 'Adaptive Models and Systems in Economics and Management Science'. His research interests are in hospitality and tourism management, explanatory models of consumer behaviour, strategic marketing, multivariate methods, decision-support systems and management science applications in leisure and tourism.

Dr Norma P. Nickerson is an associate research professor and Director of the Institute for Tourism and Recreation Research (ITRR) and faculty member in the School of Forestry at the University of Montana–Missoula. As ITRR director she is responsible for the legislatively funded travel research programme for the state of Montana which conducts market, economic and environmental research on travel and tourism in the state. Dr Nickerson serves as the research workshop co-coordinator of the Travel and Tourism Research Association (TTRA) annual conference and is the incoming president of the Greater Western Chapter of TTRA representing the states of Alaska, Montana, Washington, Idaho, Oregon, Nevada and California. Dr Nickerson's discipline and expertise includes: strategic planning, travel behaviour, tourism marketing, outdoor recreation impacts, economic impacts of travel and nature-based tourism.

Dr Ron Nickerson is an assistant professor in the Department of Recreation, Parks and Leisure Services at Minnesota State University (Mankato). His primary teaching responsibilities include outdoor recreation planning, commercial recreation and tourism, park administration and park and recreation policy. Dr Nickerson had 19 years of state government experience as a business manager and senior state park planner with the Minnesota Department of Natural Resources and a fiscal analyst with the Minnesota House of Representatives prior to his appointment to the Minnesota State University (Mankato) faculty. He has also served as an adjunct assistant professor in the Department of Forest Resources at the University of Minnesota with responsibilities for natural resource planning and management courses. Dr Nickerson's research interests and expertise include: benefits-based management, human behaviour concerning recreation and tourism; outdoor recreation planning, social science research methods, recreation resource policy and management, and park and recreation curriculum design.

Dr Michael E. Patterson is currently in his second year as an assistant professor on the Wildlife Biology and Recreation Management faculties in the School of Forestry at the University of Montana. He was previously an assistant professor in the Department of Parks, Recreation, and Tourism Management at Clemson University for 3 years. He received a PhD from Virginia Polytechnic Institute and State University in 1993 with a dissertation focusing on the nature and meaning of recreational experiences in wildland settings. His research interests focus on human dimensions of natural resource management. He is especially interested in research that explores human wildlife interactions and how these shape people's perceptions of and values toward wildlife; the nature of environmental beliefs, values, and philosophies that shape how people interpret and respond to wildlife conflicts; and approaches to conflict resolution.

Dr Richard R. Perdue is a professor and coordinator of the tourism management curriculum in the University of Colorado College of Business and Administration. He is an active researcher who has published extensively in the tourism research literature. He currently serves as coeditor of *Tourism Analysis* and on the editorial boards of the *Journal of Travel Research* and the *Journal of Travel and Tourism Marketing*. Additionally, he has served on the editorial boards of the *Journal of Leisure Research* and *Leisure Sciences*, on the board of directors of the Society of Park and Recreation Educators, on the tourism research review board for the National Coastal Resources Institute, and on the US Travel and Tourism Administration task force on accountability research. He has conducted tourism research and development projects for state tourism offices in North Carolina, Tennessee, Nebraska and Colorado, for the National Oceanic and Atmospheric Administration, for the National Marine Fisheries Service, and for numerous local and regional tourism development authorities. His current research is focused on service quality and marketing in the Colorado ski industry.

Dr George L. Peterson is a senior-level Scientist and Project Leader with the Rocky Mountain Research Station of the USDA Forest Service in Fort Collins, Colorado. The first 18 years of his 35-year career were in academic positions, first in Environmental Systems and Resources at the University of California at Los Angeles and then at Northwestern University, where he served as Assistant, Associate and Full Professor of Civil Engineering specializing in urban and regional planning, environmental resource management, and impact assessment. Dr Peterson's publications include numerous scientific and technical papers on outdoor recreation research, environmental psychology, impact analysis and natural resource economics, as well as five edited books. Since joining USDA Forest Service Research in 1982, he has worked primarily in nonmarket valuation, outdoor recreation research, and environmental resource damage assessment. Professional assignments and activities have included forest health policy, forest planning, road policy reform, USDA representative on the Economic Steering Committee for the Exxon-Valdez damage assessment, Leader of Economic Evaluation of Multifunctional Forestry for the International Union of Forestry Research Organization (IUFRO), Human Dimension representative on the IUFRO Task Force on Management and Conservation of Forest Genetic Resources, the UNEP Global Biodiversity Assessment, the Board of Research Advisors for the National Outdoor Leadership School, Associate Editor of *Leisure Sciences* and the *Journal of Leisure Research*, the Editorial Review Board of *Environment and Behavior*, and the Editorial Advisory Board of *Advances in Environment, Behavior, and Design*. He is also a Fellow of the Academy of Leisure Sciences.

Dr John J. Pigram is Director of the Center for Water Policy Research at the University of New England. He has widespread research interests in resources management, in particular, tourism, water resources, recreation and parks management. Current research interests include policy issues arising from resource allocation, environmental auditing, and impediments to the adoption of best management practice in the water and tourism industries. Professor Pigram is the author of several publications in resources management including *Outdoor Recreation and Resource Management*, *Outdoor Recreation Management* and *Issues in the Management of Australia's Water Resources*. Dr Pigram is a charter member of the International Academy for the Study of Tourism. He is also a member of the Universities Council on Water Resources, and the American Water Resources Association, vice-president of the International Water Resources Association, a member of the Board of Governors of the World Water Council and Chair of the Organizing Committee for the 10th World Water Congress in Melbourne, Australia, March 2000.

Anna Pollock has worked as a researcher, consultant, facilitator and entrepreneur in the tourism industry. As a researcher she has been instrumental in identifying trends associated with the development of new adventure and health tourism products in Canada. As a consultant, she has played a key role in the development of more systematic approaches to the delivery of tourism education in Western Canada. Her role as a facilitator has focused on the creation of an effective industry-driven tourism association for British Columbia, Canada. Currently she resides in England, where she manages an information technology enterprise. Her company, the Pembridge Group, develops and markets database management systems to tourism destinations in Europe and North America. She is a recognized leader in Canada's tourism industry.

Dr Dennis B. Propst, a native of the Shenandoah Valley (Virginia), is an Associate Professor in the Department of Park, Recreation and Tourism Resources at Michigan State University, where he has been a faculty member since 1983. His degrees are in biology (BS), outdoor recreation management (MS), and forestry (PhD). His academic interests include the economic impacts of recreation and tourism, human/natural resource interaction, leisure and recreation behaviour, and natural resource management and planning. He has 15 years of research experience with various federal and state agencies pertaining to the economic impacts of outdoor recreation and has authored or coauthored numerous publications stemming from this work. He has also conducted 10 years of research and authored several journal articles related to perceived control, participation and choice in outdoor recreation. He teaches undergraduate and graduate courses in behaviour, environmental attitudes and natural resources policy and serves as an Ingham County (Michigan) Parks Commissioner.

Dr Greg Richards obtained a PhD in geography from University College London in 1982, and entered market research with RPA Marketing Communications. He worked on a number of travel and tourism projects, including surveys of the UK conference and exhibition industry, hotel feasibility studies and tourism development and marketing consultancy for local government. In 1984 he became a partner in Tourism Research and Marketing (TRAM), a consultancy specializing in tourism and event marketing. With TRAM he has worked on projects for the British Tourist Authority, the English Tourist Board, the Scottish Tourist Board, and numerous local authorities. Greg is coordinator of the European Association for Tourism and Leisure Education (ATLAS) and has directed a number of ATLAS projects for the European Commission on topics including cultural tourism, sustainable tourism and tourism education. He is currently directing a second European Cultural Tourism Survey, which covered some 30 cultural attractions and events in 12 European countries in 1997. ATLAS is also undertaking a project for DGXVI of the European Commission on crafts tourism, aiming to support local crafts and regional cultures through the promotion of craft products to tourists.

Dr Ingrid E. Schneider is an Assistant Professor at Arizona State University in the Department of Recreation Management and Tourism where she teaches undergraduate and graduate courses in leisure behaviour and outdoor recreation management. Her academic training includes a BS degree in technical communication from the University of Minnesota, a MS degree in forest resources, specifically outdoor recreation management, from the University of Minnesota, and a PhD from Clemson University, Department of Parks, Recreation and Tourism Management. Her research interests include visitor behaviour, recreation conflict and response to conflict, stress, diversity and sustainable tourism.

Dr George H. Siehl is adjunct staff with the Institute for Defense Analysis in Alexandria, Virginia, and principal in Capitol Research and Strategies, a consultancy operated from his home in Gaithersburg, Maryland. Projects include ongoing work on stewardship of military lands, and compilation of *Outdoor Recreation: A Reader for Congress*. Previously he served as specialist in natural resources policy in the Environment and Natural Resources Policy Division (26 years) and Foreign Affairs and National Defense Division (4 years) at the Congressional Research Service, Library of Congress until his retirement in 1997. His areas of specialization include parks, recreation, tourism, and military land use and construction issues. His recommendation led to the establishment of the President's Commission on Americans Outdoors, on which he served as associate director for trends and forecasts.

William F. Siemer is a Research Support Specialist with the Human Dimensions Research Unit at Cornell University. He holds an MS in the human dimensions of wildlife management from Michigan State University and a BS in wildlife management from the University of Missouri, Columbia. Since coming to Cornell in 1987, he has conducted human dimensions studies on a wide range of topics, including wildlife-related activity involvement, attitudes towards wildlife, wildlife-related risk perception, wildlife damage management, hunting access, and educational programme evaluation. He is a Certified Wildlife Biologist and is currently serving as coeditor of an undergraduate wildlife management text, *The Human Dimensions of Wildlife Management in North America*.

Dr Stephen L.J. Smith is Professor of Recreation and Leisure Studies, University of Waterloo, Waterloo, Ontario. He earned his PhD in 1973 at Texas A&M in Recreation and Resources Development. Stephen consults for Canadian government agencies and tourism businesses. He has served as a Special Projects Officer with Tourism Canada and with the Canadian Tourism Commission and currently serves as Chairman of the Research Committee of the Canadian Tourism Commission. Steve is an elected Fellow of the International Academy for the Study of Tourism, a member of the Travel and Tourism Research Association International, and is active with regional and local tourism destination marketing organizations. He has given guest lectures and seminars at numerous universities throughout the world. His specialities are tourism measurement, product development strategies, and geo-economic analysis of tourism development. Steve publishes frequently in journals and is the producer of a video on tourism development and the author of several books.

Dr Taylor V. Stein is an Assistant Professor in Natural Resources Management – Ecotourism for the School of Forest Resources and Conservation at the University of Florida. He has conducted research and assisted in natural resource planning in Florida, Minnesota, Utah and Colorado on state, USDA Forest Service, Bureau of Land Management and private lands. With expertise in benefits-based management, nature-based tourism, landscape values, and wildland recreation management, his research efforts focus on the market and nonmarket benefits of natural or near-natural landscapes with an emphasis in the social sciences. Dr Stein completed his PhD in Forestry at the University of Minnesota in 1997. He received a BS in Recreation Resource Management from Utah State University and a MS in Forestry from Northern Arizona University.

Dr Patricia A. Stokowski is an Associate Professor with the Recreation Management Program, in the School of Natural Resources at the University of Vermont, where she teaches and conducts research on topics related to outdoor recreation and tourism planning. Before moving to Vermont in 1998, she was a faculty member at Texas A&M University and the University of Colorado–Boulder. Her PhD (1988) is from the College of Forest Resources at the University of Washington. Dr Stokowski is the author of two books: *Riches and Regrets: Betting on Gambling in Two Colorado Mountain Towns* (1996, University Press of Colorado) and *Leisure in Society: A Network Structural Perspective* (1994, Mansell Press). Her current academic interests centre on rural community development, social impacts research, and rhetorical issues in sense of place studies. Beyond the halls of academia, Dr Stokowski is also a gold-medallist figure skater and professional ice dance coach.

Gregory R. Super is an economist and programme manager in the Recreation, Heritage and Wilderness Resources Staff at the USDA Forest Service national headquarters in Washington, District of Columbia. His USDA Forest Service career has included forest planning, strategic planning, campground management, firefighting and the development of recreation fee systems. Mr Super is a graduate of Colorado State University (BS) and Utah State University (MS). He lives in Arlington, Virginia, with his wife, Sue, and son, James.

Jon Teigland is a Senior Social Scientist at Western Norway Research Institute. He was responsible for Norway's first national holiday and recreation surveys in the early 1970s. Trends and processes influencing consumer behaviour and travel demand internationally have been a major research interest since then. Applying research findings to decision making processes both at policy, planning and at project level is another issue of interest. For the past 10 years, Teigland has done impact assessments of the effects on tourism and recreation from major projects, including hydro power and highway developments, mega-events such as the Olympic Games and the designation of national parks. Jon has done impact assessments and planned regional tourism developments on several continents, among them two pilot tourism and recreation regional plans in Saudi Arabia.

Dr Gail A. Van der Stoep is an Associate Professor at Michigan State University (MSU) in the Department of Park, Recreation and Tourism Resources. For the past 15 years, much of her professional work has focused on interpretive communications, and has included serving as president of the National Association for Interpretation. She also is an adjunct faculty member with the MSU Museum. Her current research, outreach and training efforts are integrative in nature and include work in community-based tourism development, heritage and nature-based tourism, use of communications as a resource management tool, human dimensions of resource management, and integrated maritime resource management. As Faculty Liaison with MSU's Center for Maritime and Underwater Resource Management (CMURM), these areas of expertise are applied in coastal and marine park areas, including international work in Anguilla.

Dr Salah E.A. Wahab is Professor of Tourism at the University of Alexandria School of Tourism and Hotel Management. He is also chair of the Tourism Division of the National Council on Productivity and Economic Affairs in Egypt, chair of ESSET, Egyptian Society of Scientific Experts on Tourism, and founder and chair of Tourismplan, and a member of the Advisory Council of the World Tourism Organization. Formerly Dr Wahab was chief of the State Tourist Administration, first under Secretary of State for Tourism, chair of the National Organization of Tourism and Hotels in Egypt, and chair of investment companies in the public and private sectors. Dr Wahab is author, coauthor and coeditor of more than 15 scientific books on tourism in Arabic and English as well as author of more than 100 research papers and chapters published in international journals. Dr Wahab is a member of ten international associations including the International Academy for the Study of Tourism, the International Association of Scientific Experts on Tourism, and the Travel and Tourism Research Association in the US.

Dr Stephen Wanhill is Travelbag Professor of Tourism at the School of Service Industries, Bournemouth University, and Head of Tourism Research at the Research Centre of Bornholm, Denmark, where he is involved in a multi-annual programme, funded by the Danish Social Science Foundation, researching tourism in the peripheral areas of Europe. His experience as a practitioner and as an academic in the field of tourism spans more than 25 years and he has previously held professorial posts at the University of Surrey and the University of Wales, Cardiff. He has been a parliamentary Specialist Adviser on tourism to the UK House of Commons and a board member of the Wales Tourist Board. His research interest lies in the area of tourism development and he has published on development policy, tourism projects, investment incentives and the impact of tourism. He is editor of *Tourism Economics* and has collaborated with John Fletcher as author of *Tourism: Principles and Practice.*

Dr J. Douglas Wellman was a member of the Forestry faculty at Virginia Tech from 1976 until 1990, during which time he taught courses in natural resources policy and outdoor recreation behaviour and pursued scholarly work in outdoor recreation policy, public involvement in natural resource planning, urban forestry and professional education. In 1990, he joined the College of Forest Resources at North Carolina State University as Associate Dean for Academic Affairs, in which position he helped develop innovative interdisciplinary undergraduate and graduate programmes in natural resources management. In 1998, he became the founding director of the Faculty Center for Teaching and Learning, a university-wide faculty development office at North Carolina State. Dr Wellman is author/coauthor of more than 100 publications and presentations.

Dr Peter Williams is a strategic planner, researcher and educator who has worked for more than two and a half decades on projects related to the tourism industry. As a strategic planner, he has worked around the globe for clients on issues related to the development, marketing and on-going management of tourism destinations and businesses. As a researcher, he is Director of the Centre For Tourism Policy and Research at Simon Fraser University in Vancouver, Canada. Located in super, natural British Columbia, this leading edge tourism institute focuses its research on projects which encourage more sustainable forms of tourism development. As an educator, Dr Williams is a professor in the University's School of Resource and Environmental Management, where he teaches graduate courses in tourism policy and planning. He is also a past president and former Chairman of the Board for the International Travel and Tourism Research Association – an organization dedicated to encouraging excellence in tourism research and strategic planning.

Dr Peter A. Witt is Professor and Head, Department of Recreation, Park and Tourism Sciences at Texas A&M University. Besides departmental administration, Dr Witt's major interests are in the area of evaluating outcomes of recreation programmes being offered by recreation and park departments for at-risk youth. Dr Witt is also involved in efforts to identify best practices and characteristics of successful programmes in the recreation and parks field. Much of this work is based on models of risk, resiliency and protective factors. Dr Witt is the coordinator of the At-Risk Youth Recreation Consortium, a joint effort of eight universities, some 14 cities and the National Recreation and Park Association, who are jointly seeking to improve available information about the impact and value of park and recreation services for at-risk youth. Dr Witt has written or edited five books and authored more than 75 articles on the social psychological aspects of leisure involvement and recreation services for a variety of different user groups.

1

The Big Picture: a Synopsis of Contributions

William C. Gartner and David W. Lime

How will we choose to travel and recreate in 20 years time? Will we still be content to squeeze into an airline seat and endure hours of uncomfortable travel to do the things we want to do in the place where we want to do them? Will we still recreate in ways that our mentors taught us or will we find new forms of recreation to challenge our skills? Will technology enable us to travel to all the places and do all the things that we can vicariously experience now using the Internet, or will new communication and virtual reality devices substitute for old-fashioned recreation and travel? How will public and private sector providers of leisure opportunities and services adjust to the numerous forces with which they will have to contend and, often, only peripherally control? These are only some of the many questions being asked today regarding the future of recreation and tourism.

As we enter the new millennium hardly anyone expects that how we select or participate in our chosen leisure and travel activities today will be the same in 20 years time. Certainly, most people will still be drawn to challenge themselves physically and mentally in the outdoor environment, but increasingly people may be doing this with equipment that is unheard of today. Twenty years ago no one, outside the military, was even thinking about global positioning systems. What else is out there waiting to be released and sold to the mil-

lions of travellers and recreationists who make up today's active leisure society? Not only will the equipment we use change, but how we select where we do what we want will also change. How we choose where we want to travel and recreate is now in the throes of a major transformation as the Internet becomes an even greater force in our daily lives.

This book is about trends in recreation, leisure and tourism. It attempts to detail where we are today in relation to some of yesterday's events. In other words, where are we now and how did we get here? It also attempts to take us into the future by discussing the 'so what' of where we are now. Implications related to the trends discussed tell us, as a society, what we should expect to contend with in the coming years.

This is not a book about predictions. Trends are based on documented historical precedents. Predictions are based on anything, including the alignment of Jupiter's moons! What we hopefully have delivered in this book is an analysis of some of the more interesting trends of today shaping how people travel and play. We also hope to inform the reader about what these trends mean for the foreseeable future. Given the immensity of the literature regarding recreation, leisure and tourism this book provides only a fraction of the multitude of relevant trends which one could argue are operational in today's world. We recognize this but feel that readers will find trend convergence as they read through the chapters.

Trends are not isolated occurrences. There are discernable patterns that affect numerous aspects of recreation, leisure and tourism, and many of the trends addressed in this book are variants of other related trends. This will become evident to the reader as he or she progresses through the 37 chapters of this book.

Putting the trend information in this book into perspective requires a review of the mega-trends that affect how all of us live and play. Once this is done, the specific trends detailed in this book will become clearer and more understandable.

Mega-trends

Mega-trends are those forces that affect almost everyone in the world. Individually no one person can initiate, control, or manage a mega-trend. They can only be dealt with through collective action. It is important that society understands how mega-trends affect certain aspects of life. Only through understanding this can informed collective decisions occur. The next section of this chapter examines one mega-trend that affects us all – population growth. We then discuss ancillary outputs of that mega-trend and eventually move on to more specific trends relevant to understanding what forces are affecting recreation, leisure and tourism.

Population growth

The mother of all trends is simply population growth. At the beginning of 1900, the world population was estimated at 1.6 billion. Thirty years later, the world population had increased by 25% to more than 2 billion. Today it is estimated to have surpassed 6 billion and is still growing at an annual rate of 1.4% (Brown and Flavin, 1999). One could argue that population growth is under control, as the percentage increase has slowed from its record annual rate of 2.2% in 1964. Thirty-two countries now report relatively stable populations

with no appreciable growth except from immigration. The annual growth rate of the world population is expected to decline shortly after the new millennium begins (Evenson, 1999). All this is good news for a world that has only known increasing rates of population growth and all the implications associated with it. However, statistics can be deceptive. While it is true that many countries have achieved population stability most of these can be considered as developed countries, with China being the notable exception. In addition new medicines and medical techniques have more than doubled life expectancy in the last 100 years. We live longer and are healthier. This applies to people in all parts of the world, although in many regions one would be hard pressed to conclude that people are better off today. What this means, with special emphasis on developing countries, is that overall population growth is still very high, resulting in extreme pressure on environmental and other resources.

Some people argue that more people in the world means more consumers and greater economic opportunity for all. How true is this statement? Can the world afford millions more consumers if they consume at the same rate as those of us in the developed world? Can our stressed environment support these growing millions of consumers? How will we cope with millions more vehicles contributing greenhouse gases to an atmosphere that, by many indications, has already exceeded its carrying capacity?

Concomitant with the growth in population is the increasing urbanization of the world's people. Mega-cities (population more than 10 million) now number 14 where none existed in 1900. Urban populations around the world are expanding with some very undesirable results. Shanty towns with unsanitary conditions are common in places like Mexico City and New Delhi. In Cairo one of the popular taxi tours is through the City of the Dead, where squatters have moved into the open spaces of mausoleums. Traffic jams are everyday occurrences in large cities throughout the world and more vehicles will not only contribute to atmospheric pollution but make cities even more undesirable as living spaces for residents and visitors alike.

The mega-trend of population growth has led to decreasing environmental quality. Part of the blame for declining environmental quality results from the travel age we find ourselves in today. In 1900 only a few thousand automobiles were in service, today there are more than 500 million (Brown and Flavin, 1999). Jumbo jets routinely carry thousands of passengers millions of miles each day. Jet vapour trails have been associated with destroying ozone and contributing to the greenhouse gases affecting world climate. The travel age has made it easier not only to move people but to move other sentient life forms, deliberately or unwittingly. The importation of exotic species to areas previously geographically isolated has caused enormous harm to many of the world's ecosystems. Darwin's theory of evolution may no longer be operable as it becomes harder and harder to find places untouched by the introduction of exotic species. Slow evolutionary change has been replaced by rapid environmental transformation.

Technology change

Counterbalancing the relatively dark picture painted above is an almost religious faith in the power of technology to overcome many of today's problems. Hardin (1968) in his classic work, *Tragedy of the Commons*, paints a picture where all members of a society eventually lose as individuals act to maximize their individual return from a productive enterprise based on communal resources. If we assume the world's stock of environmental resources is more or less a communal resource to be divided among the world's citizens based on relative purchasing power, it becomes clear the world will eventually consume all that it needs for continued survival. One need only look at the state of the world's tropical forests or major fishing grounds for validation of this statement. Recognition of limited resources has not stopped or appreciably slowed consumption of these precious resources. Why? Because many people believe that technology will solve the problem.

Once scientists discovered and convinced decision makers that chlorofluorocarbons (CFC) were destroying the earth's ozone layer, substitute chemicals were developed. Technology is praised for helping clean up water and air emissions. Some bodies of water, previously thought of as 'dead', are now able to support a more diverse selection of species. Sometimes, as with Lake Erie (one of the five US Great Lakes), a clean-up is so successful that it leads to a major tourism boom as the environment once again becomes conducive to leisure pursuits.

There is theory behind the belief in technology to solve most problems. The theory of induced innovation (Runge, 1999), initially confined to the microeconomics of the company, has been expanded to institutions (Binswanger and Ruttan, 1978). Simply stated, the theory rests upon decisions being taken to find the 'right' mix of inputs in the production process. For example, at the firm level, if one input (e.g. labour) becomes scarce with a commensurate increase in the price of the input, a search for substitutes will take place. By rearranging the production process, firms found they could increase output and at the same time lower costs. This extends the 'innovation possibilities frontier' for the firm. If one examines the different production processes, for essentially similar products, utilized by different cultures in the world it becomes clear that factor substitution is operable.

At the institutional level, the theory is not as straightforward, as the production process is subject to forces such as policy decrees that are usually not tied to measurable output (e.g. profit). However, there are forces operating at the institutional level that will change inputs and ultimately how these organizations do business.

Since the theory of induced innovation is based on the relative abundance or scarcity of inputs, measured by market- or policy-imposed values, how inputs change in value is an important consideration. Most economists accept the basic argument for Engel's Law which, simply stated, is that each product will have a consumption level associated with it for a certain level of income. When income changes, superior goods will capture additional shares of income whereas inferior goods will claim a smaller percentage of the total income available. Food consumption was the basis for Engel's Law and is still used as the primary example today. When income increases, less of the total budget will be allocated to food purchases after a certain level of consumption has been reached. Certainly there will be substitutes for more expensive food items but other goods, previously unattainable, will now be purchased and consumed. Extending this theory into the realm of environmental decisions was the intent of Ruttan's work (1971). He intended to show that after society reaches a certain level of affluence, nonmarket goods, such as the environment, assume value. Runge (1987) termed the extension of Engel's Law to environmental considerations the 'Ruttan principle'. Simply stated, Ruttan's principle claims that as societies advance and acquire wealth, the environment assumes value. This is reflected in policy decisions intended to protect certain environmental values (e.g. US Endangered Species Act) or prohibit certain actions (e.g. toxic waste discharge). Policy decisions that protect or enhance the environment effectively raise environmental input costs, thus forcing input re-allocation or productivity increases brought about by using new technology.

So where are we today with respect to solving some of the world's problems? For example, technology has not yet advanced to the point where tropical forests, in general, are being preserved or conserved instead of exploited. It is easy to argue that developing nations have yet to reach a level of economic security where they have enough income to value their environment (i.e. invoke Ruttan's principle). Thus, environmental degradation will continue. Yet tourism has the ability to change the factor input mix in the production process. Regardless of how one feels about the term ecotourism, travel based on an attraction to certain environmental values has been growing in popularity. Successes in saving environmental systems and their inhabitants are well documented. Countries such as Costa Rica, Tanzania, Kenya and Botswana have substantial tracts of land set aside in national parks and preserves. The reason for their creation and their continued existence has been due, in part, to tourist expenditure, thus giving value to environmental resources. Tourists' expenditures are a form of income redistribution. One could argue that citizens of developed countries are paying for the environmental inputs in the tourism product production process. If this is the case, why then does the world still lose vast tracts of fragile environmental resources each day? Is it because we still do not have enough tourists to provide value to these exploited resources?

Two questions that must be asked are: will technology and its progenitor, induced innovation, be able to overcome some of the most pressing environmental stresses of today? And if so, at what cost? These questions are critical as we discuss recreation, leisure and tourism trends. As will be shown shortly, this growth has been phenomenal since the end of World War II. Looking at the travel patterns of today, it can be argued that the number of tourists, of all types, counted on a daily basis may exceed the total number of tourists recorded since the very beginning of touristic activity through World War II. Surely it already exceeds the total number of tourists up until 1900.

Population growth leading to urbanization and decreasing environmental quality is the mega-trend of the 21st century. Even though the rate of population growth has levelled off and shows signs of a gradual decline, world population is still growing rapidly. Will the theory of induced innovation manifest itself in ways that will protect resources, now exploited to provide short term relief, for future generations? How important will tourism, recreation and leisure be in invoking induced innovation and extending the frontiers of innovation possibilities? Attempting to answer these questions requires us to look at some of the most salient trends relevant to recreation, leisure and tourism.

Tourism, Recreation and Leisure Trends

Against the backdrop of the population growth mega-trend and its ancillary outputs we analyse recreation, leisure and tourism trends. As will be argued, we are now in a period of leisure affluence. In spite of the concern throughout most of the world over longer working hours and less leisure time, people are still travelling more than ever before. Tourism and its resulting recreation and leisure activities have become so important to many economies that any disruption in demand will have serious implications. We are now at a point in world history in which we have achieved global dependencies. Travel to maintain global trade is essential and the future of the world economy is now tied, for better or worse, to tourism.

Tourism, as defined by Smith (see Chapter 20) or Gartner (1996b) is a product of technological and economic advances since the end of World War II. Travel before World War II was almost the exclusive activity of the leisure and trading classes. Turner and Ash (1975) named the new wave of tourists appearing since the end of World War II the 'golden hordes'. It is easy to see how this name was coined. In the 1970s and into the 1980s, annual tourism growth was regularly in double figures, pausing only in the recession years of the late 1970s and early 1980s. In terms of percentage increases, international tourist arrivals are expected to grow well into the new century at rates of around 4–5%. Although this rate of increase is very impressive, it is below the percentage increases of 10–20 years ago. What is more impressive, however, is the amount of money spent. Worldwide, tourism receipts stood at US$445 billion up from US$221 billion only 10 years ago, an increase exceeding 100% (WTO, 1999). At the same time, international arrivals stood at 625 million in 1998 up from 426 million in 1989, or less than a 50% increase. What this tells us is that although percentage increases for total travel will remain at pretty constant levels for the foreseeable future, receipts continue to show impressive gains. People are finding more ways to spend money while they travel, and the industry is finding even more ways to entice them to spend money. A review of some ongoing development activity indicates that even more expensive and amenity-laden leisure properties are soon to be competing with properties considered the 'ultimate' a few short years ago (Tourism Development Report, 1999).

Tourist distribution

Where is all the tourist money going? It is apparent from reviewing worldwide travel patterns that tourism remains an economic activity that primarily benefits developed countries. Travel today from Europe to North America and vice versa accounts for approximately 79% of all travellers and 78% of all tourism receipts (WTO, 1999). A few countries in Asia, in particular Japan, have entered the picture as major recipients and generators of tourists. In most cases tourism growth is tied to level of development. Those countries that show economic growth are most likely to be the ones to generate and benefit from tourism. Countries in Africa and South America, with few exceptions, are not yet major tourism generators or receivers. For example, Africa, which has great resource wealth, especially in primary commodities such as timber, gold and tropical agricultural products, attracts only 4% of all world travellers (WTO, 1999). Given Africa's burgeoning population, its tourism adds very little to the Gross National Product (GNP) of many countries.

Reasons for low levels of travel to the world's developing countries are numerous and include political instability, medical fears, poor facilities and inadequate levels of service. However, the major reason tourism growth has been retarded has to do with inadequate distribution channels. Travel to remote parts of the world is not easy or inexpensive. Government policies, such as overflight charges (fees airlines pay for flying over sovereign air space) add to the cost of travel. The infrastructure needed for moving people around a country is in many places so poor or nonexistent that many regions appeal only to the most resilient adventure traveller. Added to the structural problems of travel encountered in many developing countries are policies that restrict travel. Edgell (1988) details many of the barriers making travel time-consuming and expensive. Included in his list of barriers are restrictive and relatively expensive visa entry regulations, exit taxes and a host of other travel-sector specific taxes. One could add regulations, still mandatory in some countries, that require people to register their movements within the country. The result of these and other barriers is that for most people travel becomes too much of a hardship for any rewards that may be gained. In an age where globalization is a common word, many of the travel barriers that countries face are self-imposed. This is very surprising, especially when developing countries have been advocating more open trade policies with their major trading partners.

Consumption centres

The tourism of today increasingly takes place in areas that look nothing like they did 20 years ago. When tourism was still experiencing double-figure increases, many travellers were new to the travel scene and appeared to be content simply to see what the world had to offer. However, many communities began to realize that tourism is the perfect consumption activity. Whether travelling on business or pleasure, goods and services must constantly be purchased. Most travellers are in consumptive mode from the very beginning of their trip. For this reason new consumption centres are being built and older industrial cities are being redesigned. In the US, for example, Las Vegas (Nevada) and Orlando (Florida) are at the forefront of new consumption centre design. Older European cities can still count on their historical development as an attraction, but increasingly more consumption activities are being added to the mix of what is already available. Even single purpose touristic activity (e.g. shopping) can be developed using a consumption centre model. Such is the case of the Mall of America in Bloomington, Minnesota. The focus of

development for consumption cities is to reduce the distribution channel barriers by making attractions available in a centrally located district or finding ways to move people, efficiently and with little extra cost, between consumption centre zones.

Travel patterns

The next decade is bound to show a shift in travel patterns. Large groups of consumers, 'baby boomers', for example, are nearing the end of their child-rearing years and are beginning to enter their retirement years. There are some indications that common short holidays will decrease in favour of long-haul, long-stay destinations. A recent Delphi study of experts in the travel and tourism industry (Obermair, 1998) indicates that long-haul travel is expected to increase markedly in the next 5–15 years, with most of this travel headed to developing countries. The US and Canada are expected to be the sole exceptions to the trend away from travel to developed countries. Traditional European destinations are expected to remain unchanged or be the big losers. To facilitate this trend, developing countries will have to spend large sums of money to improve their infrastructure and internal distribution channels. Because many of these long-haul countries are in Asia, their ability to capitalize on this trend depends in large part on their ability to rebound from the most recent economic recession they have experienced and achieve sustained economic growth.

Consolidation

Tourism businesses worldwide have for the most part been independently owned and operated. Depending on the sector, the percentage of small businesses has been estimated to be greater than 90% with most sectors having more than 50% of the businesses classified as small businesses. The major exception to this is the airline industry which, because of the cost of the equipment, is heavy on large corporate ownership. Other sectors, such as tour operators, lodging and resorts, have increasingly merged into larger and larger corporations.

For example, the major ski resorts in Colorado recently merged to form one of the world's largest alpine skiing corporations. Tour operators and travel agents have also been going through a period of consolidation. This is more apparent in Europe than in the US, even though US airlines were at the forefront of the consolidation trend starting in 1978 with the passage of the Kennedy-Pearson Act. This act essentially deregulated the airline sector in the US. The first wave of consolidation was primarily brought on by mergers as airlines purchased other airlines, not so much for the acquisition of their equipment but, more importantly, to secure bases for their hub-and-spoke systems.

Recently, mergers have taken second place to the formation of strategic alliances. These partnerships allow for the consolidation of many airline operations without the risk and cost involved in outright acquisition. One of the most successful strategic partnerships between international carriers has been that of KLM and Northwest Airlines (and recently Continental Airlines), extending the reach of each carrier (Gartner, 1996b). European airlines, many supported by government, are now experiencing the wave of deregulation experienced by US carriers.

Consolidation has its advantages and disadvantages. On the one hand, large corporations can use economies of scale to offer services at a reduced price, something that most tourists agree is a good thing. On the other hand, product lines may be eliminated and consumer choice may be restricted. Some would argue that this is already happening in the Mediterranean basin where control of travel by a few operators has forced destinations to either lower prices or suffer loss of business to other destination areas which are more willing to accept lower returns in exchange for bookings. In the long run this has serious implications for the condition of the physical plant which may not receive enough revenue to maintain the facility. It also raises the issue of maintaining the environmental integrity of the destination if revenues are not even sufficient to support

basic business operations. Since consolidation for tourism enterprises is still in its early stages, many of the long-term consequences of this trend are still unknown.

Energy

Tourism has moved beyond the 'golden horde' period described by Turner and Ash (1975) and is now in the 'platinum' stage. Since tourism requires travel and most travel is carbon powered, we are now at a period in history where the price of travel may never be lower. There is no doubt that the number of travellers will continue to grow, but at what cost? Energy is still relatively cheap but with increasing attention being paid to global warming and the emission of greenhouse gases, it is inevitable that things will change. Even with the advances in fuel-efficient planes and motor vehicles, projected increases in tourist numbers will more than offset the saving in energy usage. The concern now is not that the world will run out of fossil fuels, as it was during the 1970s and early 1980s, but that the consumption of carbon-based fuel will irreparably damage the environment before a solution can be found. Automobile companies are investing millions of dollars in finding alternatives to carbon fuels. Most of their attention is being directed to developing solar or electrically powered vehicles. Might alternative fuels for boats and aeroplanes also be developed?

Governments are reluctant to impose further restrictions on the use of fuel or even to raise taxes on its consumption, in part because of the fear that large increases in energy costs may have a drastic effect on all aspects of their economy including those tied to tourism. Even in Europe, where petroleum prices are approximately four times those in the US, the 4 : 1 ratio has remained relatively constant for the last decade or more. The wildcard in the energy-use equation is technology. Will technology reach a level that will not only support the level of tourism we now enjoy but also allow it to grow at the expected rate of 4–5% a year? Even if technology comes to the rescue, who will pay for these new technological innovations? The answer is simply the tourists. The question then becomes how elastic is the demand for travel? Will it continue to increase in the face of increasing costs? When all this happens, the question of how much we are willing to pay for environmental values (i.e. Ruttan's principle) will take centre stage. Many parts of the world are so dependent on tourism now that the answers to these questions will ultimately determine whether the platinum age of tourism continues or whether we retreat to a point where tourism growth eventually levels off and/or declines.

Communications

Communication technology is a mega-trend affecting all aspects of life. Its importance to recreation, leisure and tourism is only now beginning to be revealed. Traditional tour operators and travel agents will find themselves at risk as individuals bypass the wholesaler and book travel directly with the providers (Obermair, 1998). Individual mass tourism is projected to be the outcome of all the positioning now taking place on the Internet. Since it is such a new phenomenon, and changing on a daily basis, many of its implications are yet unknown beyond the belief that it will dramatically change how people select and book their travel arrangements.

A few years ago, in the early days of communications technology, much was heard of virtual reality systems and how these would become substitutes for travel. Experiencing remote places without leaving home was viewed as a distinct possibility. Given the extent of travel today, it can be argued that either the technology does not yet exist to simulate a travel experience or that there is simply no substitute for the real thing.

Societal change

Throughout much of the world, particularly in developed countries, a widening segment of society is participating in leisure and travel activities. Reasons for this continuing trend include: (i) more discretion in when people can take holidays, such as more flexible work schedules; (ii) a greater desire to build travel, leisure, recreation and physical fitness into our lifestyle and routine; (iii) the reduction in pollution associated with many resources (e.g. waterways) near where people live and improved access to these resources; (iv) growth in the number of commercial sector providers offering relatively inexpensive service; (v) the increased marketing and advertising of various outdoor settings as places to have a good time; and (vi) growth in the manufacture of a variety of both inexpensive and expensive high-tech equipment that attracts new consumers as well as creating the impression that anyone can enjoy leisure pursuits.

These and related societal trends have witnessed a growing demand by women, for example, to partake in leisure activities traditionally dominated by men (e.g. Kelly, 1987; Henderson, 1996b). Members of many ethnic groups who have not traditionally participated in outdoor recreation activities are also entering the leisure and travel market in increasing numbers. Such activity will create new opportunities for commercial sector providers and for public land management agencies concerning interpretive and information materials.

Because age is closely linked with outdoor recreation and tourism pursuits, it is particularly important to speculate on possible changes that might result as the age structure changes in many countries. The general ageing of the population in many developed countries significantly influences what goods and services are purchased.

The growth in the number of mature-market adults pursuing travel and outdoor recreation will be one result of the general ageing of the population. Many of yesterday's parents were introduced to leisure activities in their youth, and they will have considerable experience with and knowledge of available resources and the people that provide the services. Many of these mature adults will continue to buy the latest equipment, but commercial sector providers will still have excellent opportunities for growth.

In general, people will participate in their chosen activities longer because of improved physical fitness and previous experience in their preferred activities. Better public health programmes, increased emphasis on fitness and early exposure to leisure activities and increased marketing aimed at older people will all come to encourage more people to participate longer. This should entice some commercial sector providers to experiment with trips and activities designed for 'older' people. The trend toward a greater proportion of older people being healthier may be offset, in part, by another trend in which more travellers will have physical problems and be less physically fit. As such, training and safety programmes will have to adjust to accommodate a wider distribution of age groups.

A proportionally older, more experienced, and knowledgeable leisure and travelling public will generate new opportunities for learning and education to become important components of travel and outdoor recreation. Increased levels of demand for educational products and services will fall on both public and private sector providers. The trend also will result in increasingly significant challenges to land-management agency decision makers. For example, a more diverse public will want to learn about available leisure opportunities and to express their feelings about important issues in the planning and management process.

Public involvement

As a wider segment of the world's population seeks to engage in recreation and leisure pursuits, ages, gains first-hand experience and demands higher quality experiences, all sectors of the tourism community will be challenged to find innovative ways to involve these people in decision making. With more and changing clientele groups there undoubtedly will be more conflict among user groups and between recreation and nonrecreation tourism interests. Some seemingly homogeneous groups will be displaced and others may be excluded altogether from gaining access to their preferred settings. A regional, drainage basin or systems approach may be useful in addressing some conflicting demands. In such an approach, public land managers, interest groups and commercial sector representatives could be brought together to communicate with one another and to come up with a mix of opportunities within a region that is politically acceptable. Not all uses and activities can necessarily be accommodated in any given region and some users may have to seek what they want in other locations.

Collaboration and coordination among government bodies are essential to improve public rapport, to implement regional planning and management strategies, and to meet other goals. Partnerships also can be formed with commercial sector providers and organizations (Howe *et al.*, 1997; LaPage, see Chapter 33). For many outdoor recreation pursuits (river running, for example), a large proportion of visitors (if not most) have direct contact with outfitters, livery operators and outing groups. They seldom interact with area resource managers. As a result, these business people and organization representatives are in a favourable position to aid public land managers in getting information to users before their visits and in educating their clients about appropriate river etiquette and expected visitor behaviour (Lime, 1985).

To accommodate a rapidly changing traveller, all segments of the public and commercial sector community can benefit from continuing education programmes aimed at upgrading the knowledge base and technical skill levels of their professional staff (Anderson *et al.*, 1995; Propst *et al.*, see Chapter 35). Such programmes seem especially necessary because the number of years since many key officials received formal training continues to increase and many managers, at least among public land managers in the US, are tending to stay in one job or location longer.

Fees for using public lands

Public land managers worldwide who are responsible for park and recreation resources have experienced a trend in reduced budgets to finance their programmes. Budgets have not kept pace with inflation, government budget priorities have changed, costs have risen and the backlog of repair and maintenance projects continues to grow. All this is coupled with more people in search of the out-of-doors, who demand more and more services, programmes and facilities.

New expanded user fee programmes are seen as one alternative to help finance public recreation. In the US, for example, Congress recently (1997) authorized federal agencies (including the USDA Forest Service, Bureau of Land Management, National Park Service and US Fish and Wildlife Service) to increase or establish new recreation user fees on a trial basis in some of their park and recreation areas (Public Law 104–134). This 3-year recreational fee demonstration programme allows individual areas to keep 80% of all the increased revenue, with the remaining 20% retained by the agency for distribution among other areas. Such funds are earmarked to address the huge backlog of repair and maintenance of existing buildings and trails. This currently stands at about US$8 billion for the National Park Service. These funds cannot be used to build new facilities.

In spite of the evidence that current visitors generally accept the concept of paying a user fee, if all or most of the fees collected remain in the area where collected or with the agency to improve visitor services or protect resources, many questions remain concerning the appropriateness and long-term benefits of fee programmes (e.g. Lundgren and Lime, 1997). To what extent might new fees lead governments to reduce appropriations for individual park and recreation areas or agencies? Can and should public resources be income generators and perhaps become self-sufficient? With expanded or new fees will visitors expect additional facilities, services and programmes? Will visitors accept that the new income will be spent primarily on the large and growing backlog of repair and maintenance projects – not on new facilities and development? Over time to what extent will increased user fees deny access or be a barrier to some users or user groups – lower income people and minorities, for example? Might user fees make public resource man-agement agencies too dependent on visitor use and promote agendas to solicit higher levels of visitor use to generate more income?

The Purpose of this Book

Most experts (e.g. Obermair, 1998) expect tourism to continue to grow by at least the 4–5% annual rate projected by the World Tourism Organization (WTO). In the short term there is no reason to suspect otherwise. However, the mega-trend of population growth and its ancillary trend of declining environmental quality is one of the big unknowns in the equation. Will increasing numbers of people translate into a larger tourism market, or will the crush of humanity lead to accelerating environmental damage resulting in governments, reluctantly, imposing energy taxes to dampen demand? Will technological advances be able to overcome and reverse the trend of environmental damage brought on by the increasing use of carbon-based fuels? How will the consolidation movement already under way affect the supply and price of tourism products? Will communication technology lead to more travel or simply make purchasing travel products easier? Will distribution channels evolve to move more people to developing countries, as predicted, or will there simply be more travel from developed to developed nations? Some answers to these and related questions, derived from documented trends, are addressed, in part, by the authors in this book. You are encouraged to read on and see how what is happening today will affect how we live and play in the 21st century!

Structure of the book

This book has an introductory and a concluding chapter, enclosing six sections, each with a variable number of chapters. It is the intention of the editors to lead the reader through a logical sequence in order that the trends and implications can build on each other. This introductory chapter, 'The Big Picture: A Synopsis of Contributions', is intended to introduce the reader to some of the more pervasive issues and related debate surrounding how the identified trends affect our lives.

Part I, 'Society', will examine some of the forces shaping the demand for and use of resources. In this section Henderson examines how gender issues affect recreation choice and provision. Nickerson and Black look at demographic changes in society but also concentrate on how women in the workforce affect recreation choice and provision of services. Teigland addresses broader issues of societal changes, especially those affecting how societies organize themselves politically. With the ascendancy of market-based societies and the decline of centrally planned and controlled economic and social systems has come a reconsideration of what effect this will have on travel and recreation. Buhalis discusses the ever-increasing influence of information and communication technology on tourism systems and operations. Hutchison ends this section by reviewing the literature on ethnicity and subcultures. He concludes that very little attention, in the provision of leisure services, has been given to groups in developed countries, outside the mainstream Caucasian majority.

Part II examines the supply of resources that attract tourists and provide recreation and leisure pursuits. Cordell and Betz explore recent trends in the supply of federal, state, local and private sector outdoor recreation opportunities. While the supply of opportunities continues to grow in the US, patterns of growth differ between certain types of natural or undeveloped settings and developed recreation opportunities. Also from a strictly US perspective, Siehl examines not only the pieces of policy which provided for the plethora of travel and recreation resources now available to US residents and guests but the times in which the policies originated. Wahab discusses policy as well but from a developing nation's point-of-view: the role of national agencies is a focus of his chapter. McCool and Patterson then review planning issues as they affect the creation and/or development of resources needed for recreation and tourism. Finally, Manning addresses an

altogether different topic related to understanding how resources are utilized for leisure pursuits and focuses on a review and synthesis of social science research in outdoor recreation. He highlights the diversity of research activity over time and characterizes some of the significant theoretical and methodological directions this research has taken.

Part III reveals how people use the resources available to them for recreation and travel purposes. Cordell and Super discuss the current situation in the US with respect to many different recreational activities. Because of their long-standing work in the area of recreation use, it is possible to see which forms of recreation are on the upswing and which are stagnating or declining. This chapter is followed by some in-depth looks at specific types of recreation/tourism options. Brown et al. detail what is happening to hunting participation in the US over time. Especially revealing in this chapter is the implication that even though a sport may not show participation growth over time, this does not mean that expenditures are stagnant. Eadington examines a recent growth activity, gaming, which provides an excellent contrast to the more traditional recreational pursuit discussed by Brown et al. Pollock and Williams focus on a specific trend, health tourism, which is important to a population interested in extending the number of years they can enjoy the good life. Travel to participate in organized health care activities appears to be on the increase and Pollock and Williams reveal why. Getz examines another growth activity of recent years, festivals and events, with respect to where this trend may be in its product life cycle. Richards also discusses what has been a growth activity in recent years and sounds a note of caution to communities relying on their heritage to sustain a tourism industry. He reveals that even though there is increased interest in heritage tourism, there are a number of indications that supply is growing faster than demand. Finally Anderson et al. round off this section by examining the benefits, in a sociocultural context, that people gain from recreational pursuits. While Anderson *et al.* recognize benefits under four general categories – personal, societal, economic and environmental – they focus their discussion on the personal benefits that can be obtained both on and off site.

Part IV is dedicated to understanding how valuable the recreation/tourism resources are and what is happening to them in the way of human induced impacts. Peterson and Loomis review the history of attempts to value nonmarket recreation resources. What we do with resources in the future has a great deal to do with this body of work regarding nonmarket valuation. Smith looks at another tricky valuation exercise by examining the work currently under way to provide a form of industry classification to tourism. The focus of his work deals with tourism satellite accounts and their relationship to traditional input–output analysis. Erkkila dissects economic impact methods and discusses the advantages and disadvantages each brings to understanding tourism's economic value to a region. Often the valuation techniques discussed by Peterson *et al.*, Erkkila and Smith do not include some of recreation and tourism's dark side which is the creation of externalities (i.e. pollution). Moving away from discussing specific activity trends, Dolnicar and Mazanec discuss new methods for categorizing and understanding tourists. Increased competition requires new marketing research methods. Cole addresses the biophysical impacts created by recreation use. As pressure mounts on public recreation resources, the work of Cole takes on even greater importance. Stokowski examines impacts from a sociocultural, community-based perspective. Her appraisal is not upbeat, indicating that too often sociocultural assessment is too superficial and fails to account for the complexity inherent in social systems.

Part V focuses on how resources are organized for use or, in other words, how resources may be developed to achieve their recreation and tourism potential. Fletcher and Wanhill provide the overall development picture by discussing development theory and applying it to national and multinational tourism development issues. Keller examines tourism from a developing versus developed country perspective. His conclusions are optimistic for developing countries but suggest some concern for tourism in developed countries. Long and Lane investigate rural development issues which are becoming increasingly important to communities that may be losing manufacturing and agricultural jobs. Van der Stoep brings the issue of development into the community and examines various concerns that must be addressed to have successful recreation/tourism development at the local level.

Part VI focuses on tools to get the job done. Čavlek reviews the recent history of the tour operation business in Europe. Her chapter deals with the consolidation trend discussed earlier in this chapter. Dann reviews marketing issues from a semantics and image development perspective. The use of words to influence personal behaviour is a focus of his work. Hammitt and Schneider address an age-old human dilemma; conflict resolution and management. As recreation and tourism activities are expected to expand, conflict management will take on even greater importance. Perdue returns to the issue of technology and shows how it is being applied to increase customer satisfaction. At a time, especially in the US, where it is becoming harder and harder to find labour, improving service while reducing the workforce is a goal of many companies. LaPage continues with a review of the role of partnerships in creating synergy to improve product availability and quality. LaPage, a practitioner and researcher of the subject, examines the partnership issue as it has come of age. Pigram discusses how businesses are rethinking their operational standards to make them more environmentally sustainable. This reaction supports the Ruttan principle addressed earlier in this chapter.

Part VI also addresses education and training issues. It has already been mentioned that a lack of employees poses a problem for the expansion of tourism and related recreation activities. What is being done to prepare individuals to work in the recreation/tourism sectors of the global economy? Probst *et al.* review the increasing role of public participation in resource-related decision making. They discuss the need for practitioners to gain the skills necessary to integrate citizen input more fully into planning and management activities. Witt and Crompton deal with an issue germane to many communities which is what do we do with our youth to keep them from idleness and its sometimes severe consequences. Are community recreation programmes part of the answer and has the time come round again for revisiting this issue?

The book closes with a concluding chapter, 'So What? Implications of Trends for Management, Public Policy, Marketing and Planning', from the trends revealed in earlier chapters. Instead of providing a short synopsis of what that section contains, we advise the reader to give it a thorough review. It is in the implications section that the question posed earlier in this chapter, 'How will we choose to travel and recreate in 20 years time?', will be addressed. After reading this book, the reader may even change the question from how we will choose to travel and recreate to one that addresses how we will adjust to the changes that may be thrust upon us by forces we can only peripherally control.

Part I

Society: Factors/Forces Shaping Demand For and Use of Resources

2

Gender Inclusion as a Recreation Trend

Karla A. Henderson

Kelly (1987) predicted that by the year 2000, women would be participating in recreation activities in greater numbers than ever before. Statistics suggest that women are participating more than previously in recreation, adventure and tourism activities (Simmons Market Research Bureau, 1994; State of the Industry Report, 1998). For example in the US, women are currently one-third of the participants in fresh water fishing, one-quarter of the hunters, more than half the hikers, and have surpassed males in the percentage of cross-country skiers (Simmons, Market Research Bureau 1994). The most significant determinant of participation in outdoor recreation, and most likely in other recreation activities, is whether or not one participated as a child. With the passage of major legislation, not only have girls been given opportunities to participate in organized sports, but the variety of recreational opportunities has expanded. This involvement has translated into increasing numbers of women continuing their active participation in a variety of activities as they get older.

Because of the visible increase in recreation and tourism among women, one might assume that problems regarding demand and use have been solved. Gender equity is a common idea in North America today. Most people would agree that women and men ought to have equal opportunities in the workplace and in their leisure. Despite this general attitude, however, gender issues have not been resolved in all aspects of everyday life. Recreation professionals must continue to address ongoing gender concerns. Not to acknowledge and confront these issues may mean that little further progress occurs in the new century. The overall goal of gender inclusion is that all individuals, regardless of their sex, will have opportunities to find identity and interaction through socially responsible recreation and leisure opportunities.

This chapter identifies some of the issues addressed during the past 30 years through the contemporary women's movement and through the recreation field's ongoing focus on gender inclusion. These interpretations emanate from my feminist philosophy. Research on women's experiences and the issues of gender from feminist perspectives addressing equity, liberation and integrity have provided the foundation for social change not only for women, but also for men. These perspectives also permit the redefining of some of the questions recreation professionals are asking about inclusion. Inclusion means addressing the experiences of girls and women and other traditionally marginalized groups to facilitate their recreation needs and interests.

© CAB *International 2000. Trends in Outdoor Recreation, Leisure and Tourism*
(eds W.C. Gartner and D.W. Lime)

A Brief History

A brief analysis of how research concerning gender and recreation has evolved from the past to the present day is useful to reconsider (Henderson, 1994b). Research about and the provision of recreation activities in the first two-thirds of this century were generic. Mostly males were visible in recreation, and therefore they were studied with the assumption that females were like them or should be like them. In reality girls and women were involved in many aspects of recreation, but their efforts were often not seen as being as noteworthy as those of boys and men (Bialeschki, 1992; Henderson, 1996a).

In the past 25 years, a focus on gender differences emerged. In this situation, the gender differences in recreation are described and studied with the male model of recreation experience generally compared with female ways of being. Although these studies have made girls and women visible, they have not always helped to understand the meanings of gender. The problem with this approach is that the differences become the conclusions rather than the starting points for understanding the experiences of both males and females regarding recreation. A number of problems occur when people begin to identify what constitutes 'differentness'. For example, how much difference makes a difference? Different from what? Who determines what different means? How much is difference a function of culture and not chromosomes? An examination of gender differences has been, and probably will continue to be, useful in understanding recreational behaviour. Recreation professionals, however, must be careful in making gender differences simple answers to the complex issues of gender inclusion. Differences may exist, for example, between men and women and their recreation participation but greater differences may also exist between women regarding age, class, ethnicity and other characteristics. Some women and some men may share more similarities than some women do with other women. Generally most individuals want the same outcomes in their recreation experiences such as choice, enjoyment and social interaction. Individuals, however, may desire and/or learn to access those benefits in different ways. Recreation involvement by diverse groups may be a function of what exists and not necessarily what they would really prefer if greater choices were available (Dwyer and Gobster, 1992). This research determining that differences exist, therefore, is just the initial step towards making recreation opportunities available to all populations.

Another approach to understanding girls and women that may occur concomitantly and as a reaction to the gender differences phase, is research about the experiences of female participants. These studies are useful, particularly when related to understanding the value of women as leaders and in relation to all-female groups. Understanding the needs of women, in particular, is useful but it does not give the complete picture of what gender inclusion means.

The newest emerging phase related to understanding the interface of gender and recreation takes into account the great diversity that exists in society, not only related to gender but to other aspects such as race, class, disability, age and sexual orientation. Recreation professionals are moving towards a greater understanding of gender and its meanings in recreation including the diversity that exists. Today, the best way to examine gender is from an inclusion perspective. This outlook recognizes both males and females and broadens our understanding of how gender expectations relate to recreation choices and opportunities. Gender refers to the cultural expectations that occur as a result of one's biological sex. Although gender and women are not synonymous, the impact of gender has been most often felt by women and has had constraining effects on their recreation. An application of the philosophy of gender inclusion, however, will also ensure that boys and men are not disadvantaged or constrained in their recreation involvement either.

Trends into the 21st Century

When discussing gender inclusion for the coming century, several trends emerge for consideration. Each of these emerging ideas builds upon previous scholarship to lead to more meaningful recreation opportunities.

Just recreation

As the millennium changes, the discussion of recreation programming and management requires a continuing focus on ethical dimensions. Just recreation is not intended to mean 'mere' recreation, which implies a devaluation of the contribution that activities and leisure pursuits make to people's lives. Rather, it relates to the notion that leisure and recreation contribute to social justice (Henderson, 1996b). Recreation professionals must ensure that recreation is not unjust nor a contributor to the devaluation of girls and women, or to any other group.

To illustrate this idea of just recreation, a rather crude metaphor described several years ago by a sociologist named Molotch (1988) will be used. This example provides a basis for examining gender and just recreation:

> In many public buildings, the amount of floor area dedicated for the men's room and the women's room is the same. The prevailing public bathroom doctrine in the US is one of segregation among the genders, but with equality the guiding ideology ... Such an arrangement follows the dictum that equality can be achieved only by policies that are "gender-blind" (or "color-blind" or "ethnic-blind") in the allocation of a public resource ... Women and men have the same proportion of a building to use as rest rooms.
>
> The trouble with this sort of equality is that, being blind, it fails to recognize differences between men as a group and women as a group ... (such differences include hygiene needs, different physiological functions, and the use of toilets versus urinals) ... By creating men's and women's rooms of the same size, society guarantees that individual women will be worse off than individual men. By distributing a resource equally, an unequal result is structurally guaranteed
>
> (Molotch, 1988, pp. 128–129)

Molotch goes on to describe the specific situation of intermission time at a theatre where long queues for women and no queues for men are usual. The 'liberal' policy or solution is to make women's rooms larger than men's. An alternative solution (which he calls 'conservative') would be for women to be like men and to change the way they do things, rather than for society to change the structuring of rest room space. In other words, a conservative approach would say there is no need to overturn the principle of equality of square footage between the genders. Instead, women need to use their allotted square footage more efficiently. This conservative argument, however, discounts the role that men play in the problem. For example, most men expect women to look demure and beautiful so they need more time and privacy in the rest room. What if the problem is not because women primp and gossip in the rest room, but that men expect them to be beautiful? Another possible solution might be called a 'radical' approach where women decide for themselves what they will need for rest room space and how they will use it. This approach will also enable them to resist dominant views about how women use rest rooms.

Molotch (1988) concluded that figuring out equality is not a matter of arithmetic division, but social accounting and justice. The equal treatment of groups may create unequal opportunities for individuals. This rest room analogy prompts us to think about what is 'just', who is going to change and in what ways, and who makes the decisions. It provides a foundation for examining the outcomes of gender inclusion in the new millennium.

Just recreation is not likely to occur until recreation managers begin to delineate the important, but often subtle, differences between equality and equity (Henderson, 1997). Equality and equity are widely confused. Equality is a matter of fact (e.g. women have as many rest rooms as men, or women have the same access to programmes as men), and is basically objective. Equity is a matter of ethical judgment (e.g. women need more rest rooms than men because of the way they use rest rooms, or women need more outdoor skills development opportunities than men because they have not had the same learning opportunities when younger) and it takes subjective assessments into account. Recreation provision is an intentional act deliberately designed to bring about the development of worthwhile states of mind and the development of character in participants. This act assumes that if equity is to occur in recreation, then recreation managers must intentionally frame their aims and not leave matters to chance (Henderson, 1997). Thus, issues of equity and not merely equality will be critical trends related to gender inclusion in the coming years.

Negotiating constraints and resistance

Linked to the evolving visibility of gender is the way in which people define their recreation and leisure. The leisure that all individuals experience may be personal (autonomous) or social (relational) leisure (Henderson et al., 1996). Within those two contexts, both social and personal constraints also exist for women and men. The literature in the past decade has focused on constraints. These constraints may not relate so much to females or males but to gender roles, as Jackson and Henderson (1995) found in their research. When these researchers controlled for childcare and household work responsibilities, they found similar constraints for both men and women. These gendered constraints, however, do not mitigate the institutionalized sexism that is omnipresent in women's lives. Some of the recent visibility of women in recreation activities may relate to their conscious and unconscious resistance to sexism as well as to gender expectations. Many women are attempting to claim personal leisure as an entitlement in their lives.

Resistance and the resulting empowerment are emerging as important aspects that all recreation professionals may benefit from using. Philosophically and practically, recreation is a place where gender discrimination can be resisted. Shaw (1995) argued that leisure and recreation is a domain where gender is resisted or reinforced. This idea opens the door for further equity discussions. Both women and men have used recreation and leisure as a way to find identity and interaction over the years, but a greater awareness of how leisure shapes our gendered lives is a trend going forward into the 21st century.

Individual women sometimes use leisure activities to resist or challenge traditional roles. When a woman undertakes a non-traditional role such as playing ice hockey, she presents herself as a strong, independent person not swayed by social norms. When people step out of their expected social roles, growth is most likely to occur (Henderson et al., 1996). Resistance, however, is not without potential negative impacts. If an individual can work through that negative aspect, then leisure is empowering. Whether she deliberately sets out to challenge those traditional norms does not make any difference. The more that previously held stereotypes are addressed and resisted, the more likely it is that opportunities are going to be available for all, regardless of biological sex.

Gender is created, resisted and transformed in human practices, including leisure. Women's resistance embodied in leisure as a source of empowerment manifests itself in other aspects of their lives. Through resistance, people force themselves and others to re-examine hegemonic assumptions. The resistance of individuals to gendered roles can result in institutions, such as recreation organizations, questioning some commonly held assumptions about behaviour. For example, if women comprise more than half the individuals who go fresh water fishing, then agencies should find out what they want and need. Resisting stereotyped roles may lead individuals and recreation providers into new opportunities in the future.

Targeting specific (i.e. all-women) groups

Gender inclusion in the future will necessitate the examination of the value of specifically targeted groups. The visibility of gender-specific groups has been primarily about all-women groups. In one way, these targeted groups may be more exclusionary than inclusionary. On the other hand, they may provide a safe environment in which to encourage greater involvement by the targeted group. Although all-women groups are not for everyone and may not be needed as much in the future, they offer an important way for some women to experience recreation and adventure activities.

To examine the efficacy of gender-specific groups in recreation, the literature from educational research offers some insights. The educational literature consistently suggests that, overall, coeducational experiences are better for boys, but gender-specific opportunities (given equal resources) are generally better for girls (K.A. Henderson, 1999). Although the passage of Title IX in the US in 1972 ensured that educational institutions should have equal resources for male and female students/participants, it also mandated that all public programmes that were previously segregated must now be coeducational. In recent years, particularly in some sports and outdoor programming, recreation providers may deliberately attempt to keep girls and women separate from boys and men for a number of reasons.

Girls and women continue to make similar statements about why gender-specific groups are good for them. McClintock (1996) described several themes emerging from reasons given: (i) emotional and physical safety; (ii) the freedom to throw out gender role stereotypes; (iii) opportunities to develop close connections with other women; (iv) a comfortable environment for beginners or for individuals practising advanced skills; and (v) opportunities to have or be a role model or leader.

Outcomes of recreation experiences may also reflect these reasons not only for girls and women but also for other targeted groups such as men, particular age cohorts or ethnic groups. The implication that gender-specific programming has for the future relates to how it parallels other broad questions about diversity and social justice. Some individuals would argue that all-woman programming is a regressive step. Civil rights legislation has pushed for ending segregation of any type. Unfortunately,

research is not conclusive in suggesting that ending any type of segregation necessarily results in better educational or social outcomes, given that resources are equal (Riordan, 1990). Are mixed-gender or gender-specific groups best? Under what circumstances? Most people today agree that the answer is 'it depends'. To move this question farther, recreation providers need to address two issues: (i) How can people be given choices in what they want to do? and (ii) Once given a choice, how can providers ensure that the leadership is such that all individuals get an opportunity to gain the most from the experience? No one programme structure is always going to be the best. Opportunities to choose, however, provide the means for greater inclusion.

Skills development

Skills development is necessary to enable both boys and girls to grow up feeling comfortable with different aspects of recreation. The effects of Title IX are only now beginning as a new generation of young women has had the opportunity to participate in various physical activities. Recent research also suggests that the most significant determinant in outdoor participation is whether or not one participated in outdoor recreation as a child. About two-thirds of those individuals who recreate outdoors were introduced to their favourite outdoor activity before the age of 17, and half of those before the age of eight (Widdekind, 1995). These trends in outdoor involvement are likely to continue as people get more experience in the outdoors. Researchers have confirmed the same finding among women of colour in the outdoors. Those individuals who have had previous positive outdoor experiences as young people, whether with the family or other youth groups, were likely to continue to be active in the future (Roberts and Henderson, 1997). For those individuals, however, who did not receive the training as young people, opportunities must continue to be developed so that recreation can be more enjoyable. Skill development can be learned at any age. A recent example of skill development that has exploded in the US is involvement in

hunting and fishing. These skill development classes are open to all women who
want to gain skills that they did not get when
they were growing up. The trend to provide
these opportunities, especially for women
and other previously under-served groups,
is likely to continue in the future.

Diversity is an issue that also must be
addressed through skill development. For
example, Roberts and Drogin (1993) described the lack of participation of African-
American women in outdoor activities and
identified such potential factors as: historical oppression and racism, stereotyping by
race and gender, lack of role models, insufficient exposure to activity options, limited
accessibility to outdoor recreation areas and
oppressive economic conditions. In another
study, Roberts and Drogin (1996) found that
most women of colour believed that they
had not been socialized to participate in
outdoor activities, often due to their race.

Safety issues are also linked to skill
development. These issues have always
been around but the impact of issues of
feeling physically and psychologically safe
is becoming more obvious. Fear and safety
are omnipresent for both women and men,
but women are more likely to report fear as
subconscious in their minds (Whyte and
Shaw, 1994). For skill development to occur
and a recreational experience to be meaningful, most girls and women in the coming
years will seek experiences and places
where they do not have to face overt fear.

Ecofeminism and concern for the environment

Many recreation and tourism activities take
place outdoors. Therefore, environmental
issues must not be ignored. The interaction
between social and environmental concerns
will continue to provide important philosophical underpinnings for the work that
recreation managers do and the ways the
outdoors is preserved into the new millennium.

A number of ecophilosophies exist that
can guide the thinking of participants in
recreation as well as managers. One philosophy that has been useful is ecofeminism.
The hypothesis of ecofeminism is the belief

that the oppression or domination of women
is connected with the domination of the
earth (Plant, 1989; Henderson and Bialeschki, 1990–91; Warren, 1990). No one
form of ecofeminism exists, but all the views
share a common commitment to making visible the ways in which patriarchy dominates
women and nature. Ecofeminists suggest
that all acts (including recreation activities
and recreation management) should focus
on respect for, and the diversity of, human
beings and the life enhancement of natural
environments. Applying aspects of ecofeminism can help us consider what
recreation managers do, why they do it, and
how it contributes overall to ending the
domination of people *and* of nature.
Although the environment and its preservation are not issues for only one gender to
consider, a variety of philosophical approaches will be necessary. Without clean air
and clean water, the continued existence of
recreation is a moot point in the coming
century. No discussion of trends regarding
gender inclusion would be complete without an ongoing connection being made with
impacts on the natural environment.

Recreation and health issues

As the millennium changes, the relationship
of recreation to physical and mental health
will be a basis for ongoing work. The
benefits-based recreation movement has
helped us to begin to identify the potential
multitude of values associated with recreation (Driver *et al.*, 1991a). Recreation will
still be fun and enjoyable, but people will
also be seeking ways to maximize the health
advantages. People will look consciously to
recreation for stress relief and for therapeutic benefits.

The therapeutic benefit of the outdoors
for women is an area that has assumed great
significance in the past 10 years. Therapeutic benefits range from dealing with stress on
a daily basis to examining how recreation
might be a major therapeutic treatment. Mitten (1986) suggested that women do not like
to be under stress and that outdoor activities
might provide a way of counteracting the
negative effects of stress. Survivors of violence have also found great solace in the

outdoors (Mitten and Dutton, 1996); for example, Pirfman (1988) confirmed that a 3-day wilderness course as a supplementary treatment for victims of rape resulted in a decrease in overall levels of fear, fear of rape and fear of failure.

Roberts (1995) explained how wilderness therapy may be beneficial for women in general, but ethnic minorities less comfortable with the outdoors might need nurturing. Women of colour may not seek an educational opportunity to find energy and healing in the wilderness when traditionally the outdoors has signified a foreign concept to them. Outdoor researchers are just beginning to address the issues of women of colour and the benefits of the recreation and leisure for all women. Clearly more empirical research is needed in this area. Nevertheless, the results gained so far are compelling regarding the value of outdoor recreation for addressing health issues in both women and men.

Professional development

The emergence of women in recreational activities parallels their rise in the recreation workplace. Therefore, the recreation field must acknowledge the growing potential for women to be involved in leadership roles in providing recreation opportunities. To enable women and men to perform at their highest level, however, also requires that professionals balance their careers and personal lives. Career development is an area that has implications for gender inclusion in the coming century.

A number of factors enter into career development for women employed in recreation and leisure services. Some of these career development factors have more salience for certain women than for others. For example, Henderson and Bialeschki (1995) found that many women perceived that discrimination continues to exist in leisure services in both conscious and unconscious ways. Women in the traditionally male-dominated area of parks said they experienced more sexual harassment than did women in other areas of leisure services. Fortunately for women, laws now protect them from harassment and conscious discrimination; organizations, however, must enforce these laws. Unconscious discrimination is more difficult to identify and to remedy. Some women feel isolated and internalize their experiences by thinking they are all alone. More importantly, many women feel their equity problems, or the lack of them, are a result of their personal history and fail to see that the social system has sometimes discriminated against anyone who is not white, middle-class, able-bodied, heterosexual and male. The acknowledgement of legislative and equity issues by individual women as well as employers is the first step in addressing how to overcome them. All aspects of professional development in the future will be dependent on the joint efforts of individuals and organizations.

Additional research is needed to understand how to enhance the lives of women employed in recreation organizations. Women have come a long way in establishing themselves as contributing members in all areas of employment at all levels. Although some variability exists among the women within employment areas and employment levels, the factors important for career development appear to be similar for women in the field of recreation, parks and leisure services. Recreation employers must acknowledge that career development may differ between males and females and among females because of the traditional family and work expectations of women, the cultural and organizational barriers that may affect women's advancement and the socialization that women experience (Rose and Larwood, 1988). Understanding professional development and how different women may attach meaning to their work can lead to strategies to help individuals, organizations and associations enhance the contributions that both women and men can make to the field of recreation, parks and leisure services.

Policy Implications

None of these preceding trends have any practical meaning unless connected to policy issues. The US Bill of Rights guarantees life, liberty and the pursuit of happiness for all. This premise ought to underlie all policy issues in recreation organizations. Recreation opportunities for all cannot occur without acknowledging the power of privilege and the diversity among people. Differences between men and women are one aspect, as are differences among women and among men. Even if women and men were to obtain 'equal rights', the diversity that exists due to race, class, physical ability, sexual orientation, age and other issues of privilege needs examination.

Just recreation requires that 'gender inclusivity', 'race inclusivity', 'class inclusivity', and 'ability inclusivity' rather than 'neutrality' related to any of these diverse situations ought to be the policy of recreation providers (Henderson, 1997). Ignoring gender differences or any kind of differences, and suggesting they are not important, as Molotch (1988) described in the bathroom story, does little good. Arguing that no differences exist, however, draws attention away from actual differences in power and resources between groups (Rhode, 1990). Ignoring gender differences does not challenge the existing structure and assumes that women have no special needs. Affirming the similarity between women and men, black and white, gay and straight, or any groups, may inadvertently validate the norms of the dominant social groups. These norms often have not addressed diverse interests, experiences and perspectives for groups participating in recreation activities. On the other hand, the basic values for all groups may be similar and ways to address them must be examined as the essence of public policy.

To change anything about recreation opportunities, policy makers must know what differences they seek to address. For example, are more opportunities for sports participation for women (e.g. making the opportunities equal to men's in recreation departments) warranted if women do not feel safe going out in a particular neighbourhood to play sports at night? Are the differences such that different scheduling or different accommodation may be needed for

certain groups of people? Claiming and acknowledging differences are not enough without exposing, challenging and disrupting previous understandings of the divisiveness of differences. The challenge to recreation professionals lies in considering differences and adopting a policy inclusive of gender, race, class and other potentially divisive characteristics.

Management Implications

Policy issues shade into aspects of management pertaining to gender inclusion. Management includes both the management of participants involved in recreation activities and the supervision of professionals who assist in facilitating those activities.

Providing recreation areas and programmes that are 'equal' for everyone may result in disadvantaging some individuals as Molotch (1988) illustrated. For example, a recent American Association of University Women (1991) study found that as young girls reach adolescence, their self-esteem plummets. Most girls enter first grade with the same aspirations as most boys, but by the time they reach high school their attitudes have changed. They emerge from adolescence with reduced expectations of life, and with much less confidence in themselves and in their abilities than boys. Because of these facts, recreation programmes for adolescent girls should not be equal to that of boys if for no other reason than boys and girls are not equal in other ways. Recreation professionals must struggle with how to teach and provide recreation opportunities for girls and women, as well as other groups, that will enable them to become empowered not only in their leisure time but also in other areas of their lives (Henderson *et al.*, 1996).

A management model for gender inclusion in the future should have as its foundation gender equity. Achieving gender equity means recognizing and addressing the needs and interests of females and males equally. In education, this model means that:

a wider range of choices will be genuinely available to girls only when an equally wide and nontraditional range of choices is available to boys as well

(Bailey, 1993, p. 322)

The model also seeks to counter stereotypes and behaviours that diminish the value of education and/or recreation. Equitable recreation means that managers address common stereotypes. Frequently when a person does not perform in some way, attributions are made to that person's group affiliation. For example, if a woman does not shoot an arrow well, the assumption is that females cannot shoot well. If a man cannot shoot an arrow well, then he is simply not a good shot.

Managing for recreation in the future using gender inclusion would result in recreation and leisure opportunities that provide a wider range of choices for all individuals. A number of steps will be necessary in implementing these recreation programmes. For example, clearly worded, widely distributed and strictly enforced policies requiring fair treatment of all participants and staff must be established. Criteria must be developed for what an equitable situation is. Furthermore, promotional material and training materials must be reviewed to ensure that no gender or racial biases exist. In future, all participants must have an opportunity to learn a variety of skills with the focus on the process and not necessarily the outcome. Professionals can facilitate inclusive recreation by encouraging individuals to feel emotionally and physically safe trying various activities, being supportive of differences in participants' needs, supporting the belief that individual needs vary, recognizing that individual accomplishments are different and special to each person, and encouraging individuals to set their own standards. The personal power available to both males and females is based on participation and involvement, and not history or gender expectations. Along with this notion of power would be the desire to allow all participants to experience expertise so that they might assume leadership positions. A diversity of role models is also a step towards this inclusive recreation (Henderson, 1996a).

Management not only includes providing opportunities for participants but also having a gender-inclusive workplace. The professional responsibility of recreation managers is to create an atmosphere of integrity, excellence, and performance reflecting ethical standards within the organization. For recreation managers concerned about the workplace, several issues relate to the treatment of employees. Affirmative Action is one of those issues. This is the generic term that describes policies intended to remedy the effects of past discrimination. It is a fair and equitable policy when it considers the extra effort women have to make to surmount systemic barriers resulting in distributive equity. A second issue in the workplace pertaining to gender and other aspects of diversity relates to how employees are treated holistically inside and outside the workplace. Gender roles may result in different opportunities and levels of energy that women contribute in the workplace when forced to balance, or more appropriately 'juggle', their work and family commitments. According to Salem (1986), women who work often pay with their time, energy and increased levels of stress for a system that gives them primary responsibility for domestic affairs but offers minimal institutional support to help alleviate that burden. Managers in leisure service organizations must at least recognize the quandaries of some working women as well as working men regarding their lives outside the workplace. Thus, managing for gender inclusion will require that supervisors within organizations are aware that managing areas, facilities and programmes is one dimension of work along with managing a more diverse workforce.

Marketing Implications

Marketing is the human activity directed at satisfying needs and wants through some type of exchange. Marketing textbooks generally describe the marketing mix as including the four Ps of marketing: Product,

Place, Price and Promotion. These principles must continue to be considered for females and males as gender inclusion is addressed in the coming years.

The product or the product-service of recreation consists of carefully planned programmes that result in benefits to people. People seek benefits or positive outcomes when they recreate. The product marketed is not activities *per se*, but experiences and benefits. In a service field like recreation, providers are really marketing the intangible aspects of involvement. Thus, the product-services of recreation, regardless of gender or any other characteristic, include such outcomes as friendships, safety and security, relaxation and happiness.

Market segmentation is determining who wants the product recreation managers have to exchange. Psychographics, or an examination of values and lifestyles, are useful in identifying market segments. Recreation managers are beginning to pay more attention to the issues of gender regarding what girls and women want and need as well as how decision-making about recreation occurs. Thus, in the future providers may be better able to target the market towards particular groups of women based on geographic (i.e. a neighbourhood, county, region or country), sociodemographics (including such characteristics as age, income, education, ethnicity) and/or behavioural (i.e. ability, interests, values) foci.

Price, as an important aspect of the marketing mix, relates to the attractiveness of recreation experiences. Although women today have more spending power, they still do not have the same wage-earning capability as most men. Each recreation manager must carefully consider price related to the recreation opportunity as well as target markets. Because the product-service can never be disconnected from the price, perceived price/value is an essential part of the presentation mix.

The communication mix involves all the aspects of promotion used to tell people about recreation opportunities. The challenge in communication is to make sure that their meaning reflects the product-service that is being promoted. The best communication is going to be information which attracts attention, is stated clearly and is relevant in fitting the audience's frame of mind and their everyday experiences. Women are a growing new market for a variety of recreation activities. Managers, however, must examine more than just an economic potential. Programmes and services ought then to be based on what recreation managers know about issues such as the ethics of care, safety and family concerns.

Conclusions

When examining these ideas about gender inclusion and recreation, a body of knowledge appears to be evolving. Data exist that describe what girls and women want and how the concept of gender inclusion works for males as well as females. These data can be applied directly to recreation programming and management. Further, the basic concepts of equity and inclusion and the issues identified relate to policy, management and marketing regardless of the recreation or tourism entity. Yet, as some answers emerge, other questions arise. No simple answers exist.

When all individuals are confronted with comparable life, leisure and employment choices, there will be no need for discussions about equity and inclusion. Society is a long way from that point, as are providers of recreation and tourism services, despite the gains made by women and other underrepresented groups in the past three decades. Eventually it is hoped that people in organizations will reach gender blindness or gender neutrality. Yet, it has been this very blindness that has made women, as well as other disenfranchized groups, invisible. A silence surrounding women and diversity issues implies consent. By making gender visible, recreation managers focus on improving programmes for all individuals. Focusing on gender issues can help to reexamine the way that recreation occurs. The models that have worked for boys and men in the past may not be as effective for girls and women. Additionally, however, those models may not work perfectly for all males either. Therefore, gender inclusion and empowerment have implications for all individuals in their recreation choices. More discussion and additional perspectives are needed to ascertain alternatives for inclusive recreation today and into the new millennium.

3

Changes in Family and Work: Impacts on Outdoor Recreation and Tourism in North America

Norma P. Nickerson and Rita J. Black

Life is not composed of theme parks and cruises. It is composed of dinner table talk, holidays together, getting the house and garden in shape, fooling around, caring for each other, relaxing, day-dreaming and all the minutiae of the day and the hour. That is the real life in real conditions that is important to us all (Kelly, 1997, p. 134).

Family changes in the past quarter century are increasingly viewed as a major contributor to work-related concerns and challenges. When family life changes or brings additional responsibilities such as care for children, stepchildren, or elderly relatives, personal home-life stress tends to increase, causing more employers to recognize 'family' within the work environment. The separation between family and work is slowly becoming closer and more balanced. This chapter will focus on changes in the family and changes in the work environment. These changes are then discussed in terms of implications for outdoor recreation and tourism into the 21st century.

The Changing Family

Nearly everywhere one looks today, the institution currently recognized as 'the fam-ily' is changing. Dad, the breadwinner, Mom, the homemaker, and two kids at home has almost become a thing of the past. In 1960, more than 70% of Americans lived in such 'traditional' family units; today, less than 15% of Americans fit into that family structure (Brock, 1994, p. 64).

While predictions are that married famil-ies will remain the ideal living arrangement (Crispell, 1996), what is changing is the fam-ily structure. There are first marriages, stepfamilies/blended families (which are the products of remarriage and/or cohabita-tion), single-parent households and other families (e.g. multigenerational families, solo householders).

First marriages

Statistics indicate that attitudes toward mar-riage are changing. According to Furstenberg and Kate (1996), women still tend to marry at least once by age 45, the figure declining slightly since 1960. How-ever, both men and women are delaying the age of first marriage, and the proportion of women who have never married by their late 20s has tripled. The average age of first mar-riage is correlated with an increase in the proportion of college-educated women (Schwartz, 1992). According to Blum (1991), the education gap between men and women is beginning to close worldwide.

Stepfamilies/blended families: products of remarriages and cohabitation

In 1992, only 58% of American children lived with both biological parents (Cherlin and Furstenberg, 1994). According to the US Bureau of the Census (1994), American children in 1990 lived in the family structures shown in Table 3.1.

Table 3.1. Family structures of American children, 1990.

Type of family structure	% of all US children
Lived with both biological parents	58
Lived with one biological parent	25
Lived with a step-parent	11
Lived with neither parent	6

Source: US Bureau of the Census (1994, The diverse living arrangements of children).

More than 20% of married couples raising children under 18 years old include a step-parent (US Bureau of the Census 1994). Approximately 80% of stepfamilies are custodial mother–stepfather families, 13% are custodial father–stepmother, and the rest are stepfamilies with two custodial parents marrying each other (Mason and Mauldon, 1996). The prevalence of stepfamilies/blended families should remain constant or even increase. Two forces are at work: (i) divorce rates are remaining stable (not decreasing), and (ii) an increasing number of children are born to unmarried women. For example, in 1993, 30% of all births were to unmarried women, more than double the percentage in 1973 (Mason and Mauldon, 1996).

Remarriages

Cherlin and Furstenberg (1994) stated that divorce and remarriage rates are higher in the US than in other developed countries. Almost one-third of all Americans will marry, divorce and remarry. However, the rate of remarriage has fallen since 1960, despite a rising divorce rate. Roughly two-thirds of divorced women currently remarry, compared to three-quarters in 1960. A similar trend is seen for divorced men as three-quarters currently remarry, compared with four-fifths in 1960. There are definite racial differences in these trends. Non-Hispanic whites are far more likely to remarry than are Hispanics or African Americans. About half of non-Hispanic whites remarry, compared to one-third of Hispanic Americans and one-fifth of African Americans.

Cohabitation

According to Wu (1996), cohabitation has become an increasingly popular lifestyle choice for heterosexual couples in postindustrial countries including the US and Canada. In the US the estimated number of cohabitating couples has increased fivefold from 0.5 million in 1970 to 2.5 million in 1988 (Revolution in Family Life, 1990).

Bumpass et al. (1995) further speculate that if the definition of 'stepfamily' is broadened to include people who cohabit (e.g. single parents who live together for a long time but do not marry), an estimated 40% of all women and 30% of all children will spend time in a stepfamily situation. These percentages will vary depending on cultural group and other variables such as income.

Single-parent families

In 1996, 28% of children lived in one-parent families compared to 12% in 1970 (US Bureau of the Census, 1997). Another estimate states that approximately half of all of today's children will spend part of their childhood in a single-parent home (New Families, 1993). Although the number of single fathers continues to grow, single mothers outnumber them in a ratio of 4 : 1 (Crispell, 1996).

Single-mother households

The proportion of children under 18 years old living in single-mother families increased from 11% in 1980 to 20% in 1990 (US Bureau of the Census, 1993, 1994).

These proportions vary substantially when looking across racial lines. For example, 13% of non-Hispanic white children, 49% of African-American children and 24% of Hispanic children live in mother-only families (US Bureau of the Census, 1993). However, Manning and Smock (1997) warn that these figures may be misleading because the complete household context is not usually considered. For example, of the children living in single-mother families, 57% live with their mother only, 8% live with a cohabitating couple, 32% live with extended families and 3% live with nonfamily members. These proportions also vary substantially across racial lines. Manning and Smock (1997, p. 539) continue:

> In particular, theories purporting to explain the association between family structure and children's life chances (e.g. socialization, family stress, social control, and residential stability) tend to be conceptualized without acknowledging the complexity of children's living arrangements.

The number of unwed mothers (either never married or divorced) is also on the increase. In 1970, one-in-ten babies was born to an unwed mother. Currently, one-in-four babies is born to an unmarried mother (New Families, 1993). According to Thomas *et al.* (1996), most white single-mother families form through divorce or separation while their African-American counterparts form through mothers who have never been married. Families headed by single mothers have an approximately 50% chance of living in poverty (US Bureau of the Census, 1993).

Absentee fathers

Since the majority of single-parent families are headed by single mothers (i.e. single mothers outnumber single fathers 4 : 1), the question of absentee fathers has become a hotly debated topic in the last decade. Mason and Mauldon (1996) estimate that approximately one-quarter of all stepchildren have no contact at all with their biological father and receive no child support, one-quarter see their biological father once a year or less and receive no child support, one-quarter have periodic contact and receive some child support, and one-quarter see their father once a month or more but may or may not receive child support. In studying the determinants of postdivorce contact between noncustodial fathers and their children, Stephens (1996) suggests that contact decreases over time as fathers develop new relationships, regardless of the characteristics of the children, the mothers or the former marriage.

According to Fost (1996), the National Fatherhood Initiative and the Institute for American Values estimate that nearly 40% of today's children do not live with their biological fathers. The repercussions of such a statistic include the following: 70% of juveniles in state reform institutions grew up with one or both parents absent; 43% of incarcerated adults grew up in single-parent homes (mostly with absent fathers); and 30% of children living with never-married mothers and 22% living with divorced mothers repeat a grade in school, compared with 12% of children living with both biological parents.

The Changing Work Environment in North America

In the 1950s, the father worked outside the home while the mother stayed at home and raised the family. By 1997, the majority of families are working couples who 'assume their employers should address their needs, offering informal flexibility or a wide range of advancement options' (Employers, 1998, p. 17). By 2010 the dual-working couple will expect company benefits and policies geared toward the family. Successful employers cannot ignore the home-life any longer. These and many changes are occurring throughout the workforce in developed countries. With increased dual-career families and single-parent families, home-life is forced upon the employer.

According to a study conducted by the Families and Work Institute (the National Survey of the Composition of the Workforce, 1997), job and family conflicts have emerged. Among the findings (Americans, 1998, p. 39) are:

- Among workers with a spouse and/or children, 54% reported having 'some or a lot' of interference between their job and family life, versus only 38% in 1977.
- Seventy-eight per cent of married Americans reported they have an employed spouse (up from 66%, 20 years earlier).
- The mean hours worked per week (paid and unpaid) climbed to 47.1 h from 43.6 h in 1977.
- Twenty per cent of respondents report working at job-related tasks at home occasionally, versus 14% 20 years earlier, while 31% work at home once a week or more, up from 21%.
- The average age of the workforce is 39.9 years, up from 37.3 in 1977.
- Twenty-seven per cent of respondents said they are managers or professionals, down from 34% 20 years earlier.
- Women composed 47% of the workforce, up from 42% two decades ago.

Compared with 20 years earlier, the marriage between work and family is now beyond the honeymoon and is into the mid-life crisis. Working women, dual-career families and changes in family structure appear to be the catalysts for change. This has brought about a new focus in balancing work and family, home workers and alternative work arrangements.

Until employers are willing to share in the family concerns of their employees, profits will decrease, turnover will increase and job satisfaction will plummet. The need for employers to become more family friendly is in the forefront. The following pages will highlight some of the changes taking place and why these changes are occurring.

Women in the work force
In the last decade of the 20th century, 59% of US married women with preschool children and 75% of married women with children between the ages of 6 and 17 years were employed (US Bureau of the Census,

1992). By 1995 in Canada, 57% of women aged 15 and older were in the paid labour force (Statistics Canada, 1996). The likelihood of a mother working increases with the age of her youngest child.

According to the US Census Bureau, 85% of all new workers will be women and/or members of minority groups by the year 2000. In 1960, 36% of 25–34 year-old women were working. In 1995, that proportion had jumped to 75%. In 1960, 50% of 45–54 year-old women were in the workforce. By 1995 that percentage had increased to 74% (Troland, 1997). There appears to be no decline in the number of women in the workforce, and women are expressing dissatisfaction with the increased demands they face from work and family roles (Hoffman, 1989). Employers will need to look positively at the needs of women and families in order to remain successful.

Balancing work and family
Three of every four US employees are parents. In 1994 these parents had 1.7 million children in childcare schemes before and after school (Lozada, 1997). With dual-career households, the division between paid work and work at home has become harder to separate. Family and work responsibilities have created tension in the workplace, the home and the marriage. It has become a balancing act.

In a survey conducted by William M. Mercer, Inc., 64% of increased employee morale was attributed to family-friendly programmes. Eighty-six percent of the employers surveyed agreed that 'a company cannot remain competitive in the 1990s without addressing the issue of the balance between an employee's work and personal life' (Lozada, 1997).

For businesses and government agencies to succeed into the 21st century, more attention will need to be paid to the job satisfaction of employees which inherently means dealing with family issues.

A good example is Hallmark Cards Inc., who supports a balance between work and family through such offerings as family care assistance, counseling and education, and alternative work arrangements that enable employees to fulfill their work and family responsibilities without sacrificing one or the other. In 1995, Hallmark celebrated its 10th year on *Working Mother* magazine's "Best Companies for Working Mothers' list" (Flynn, 1996)

The balance between family and work does not simply refer to childcare. The lack of care policies for elderly relatives within companies is becoming a big issue. In a Canadian study on workplace policies, it was found that companies have a childcare bias in family-friendly policies, a gender bias in policy formulation and a focus on workplace productivity rather than employee well-being. The research found that workplace policy generally expected that:

> ... care provision for elderly kin, like other caregiving, continues to be regarded as a private issue to be resolved within the family, that is by women. As such, it is unpaid, undervalued, individualized, and unrecognized. In this context, workplace policy does not regard women's private labor within the home as having legitimacy (Medjuck *et al.*, 1998)

Home-based offices

According to the US Bureau of the Census (1998), 'The decade of the 1980s marked a rebirth of work at home in the US'. The number of home workers jumped 56% between 1980 and 1990. Although estimates vary widely, and it is difficult to ascertain the numbers in part-time versus full-time employment, some 30–40 million people in the US are purportedly either telecommuters or home-based workers (Apgar, 1998) (Table 3.2). Certainly, the advances in personal computers and Internet technology have been instrumental, but this does not give the whole picture.

The differences found between home workers and on-site workers indicate that home-based workers are more likely to live in rural areas, are more likely to work non-standard hours, and are far more likely to be women, to be white, and to work in the service industries and occupations. Home workers generally earn less than those who

Table 3.2. Types of worker in 1990.

	Office worker (%)	Home worker (%)
Private wage and salary	77	36
Government	17	6
Self-employed	5	54
Unpaid family	1	4

Source: US Bureau of the Census (1998, Increase in at-home workers reverses earlier trend).

do not work at home (US Bureau of the Census, 1998).

In addition to the self-employed, home-based worker is the ever-increasing number of telecommuters. According to International Data Corporation's (1996) market research study, approximately 7 million of the 30 million telecommuters are corporate employees who work from home. The remainder are either self-employed or government workers. A growing number of both private and public employers are implementing telecommuting programmes to reduce costs, minimize environmental problems, improve employee retention and morale, and enhance performance (Reilly, 1997).

During the 1996 Summer Olympic Games, Atlanta city officials promoted telecommuting as a way to help keep city workers from adding to the crowds and traffic. Now, to reduce ozone-forming air pollutants, the governor of Georgia is recommending that all state departments and agencies – covering a total of 26,000 employees – reduce solo trips to and from work by 20% on so-called Ozone Action Days between May and September (Girard, 1998). Telecommuting is how Georgia employees are dealing with this mandate.

While telecommuting seems to be the answer for some people, it appears to have a negative side that employers need to address. One example is the housebound research analyst who was not among those chosen when his boss was awarding promotions; 'It seemed like you weren't around much', the boss explained (Warner, 1997).

Another issue identified by home-based workers is work that is never done. It is too easy to work late into the evenings, at weekends and through meals. Since the work is right there, it does not go away. According to Morris (1997), the expected advantages for family life are therefore not always apparent. Additionally, home workers miss their friends and resent having to maintain and fix complicated office equipment like computers and fax machines. According to Tanaka (1997), telecommuting works best as an adjunct to the office, not a replacement for it.

Flexitime, part-time and temporary workers

Flexibility, adaptability and responsiveness are crucial to business success in a constantly changing environment (Resnick, 1997). Flexitime is a system that allows the employee to choose either their arrival and departure times or their days of work. This system has been shown to increase productivity, decrease absenteeism, decrease turnover and reduce employee stress (Dalton and Mesch, 1990; Mogelonsky, 1995; Solomon, 1996). In Canada, a recent study showed that almost two-thirds of the employees surveyed combined their job responsibilities with caring for a child, an older relative, or both. These employees recognized that greater flexibility in their work schedules such as flexitime, compressed work weeks, part-time hours, job sharing and leave options helped them to coordinate their jobs and family responsibilities (Barham et al., 1998).

While flexitime has been a solution for employee satisfaction, nonstandard work arrangements (NSWAs) are other solutions to which businesses and governments have turned. NSWAs refer to independent contractors (e.g. freelancers or consultants); contract workers (e.g. janitors or computer specialists employed at janitorial or computer service firms that contract to provide services to other firms); the self-employed who own and run their own business; and workers employed in a regular employer–employee relationship who work fewer than 35 h per week (Rasell and Appelbaum, 1998). By 1995, at least 29% of workers in

the US (about 37 million people) were in nonstandard jobs (34% of all female workers and 25% of all male workers). Of these NSWAs, 47% were in regular part-time jobs, 41% were independent contractors or were self-employed, and 5% were on-call workers. Most observers expect to see the number of NSWAs rise in coming years (Rasell and Appelbaum, 1998).

Implications

With the above-mentioned changes in the family and the work environment, many implications for the outdoor recreation and tourism fields can be identified. While the social forces identified in this chapter reflect North American concerns, most developed countries are dealing with similar issues.

The common thread holding society together is the family. The other common denominator is work. Although traditionally these two social forces have been treated separately by both the public and private sectors, the trends indicate that we have been in the midst of a paradigm change.

The change is most readily evidenced by the economic necessity of both parents working. Time at work is time away from home. This creates stress on the family and on the marriage. Based on the accepted notion that recreation benefits the individual, the family and society, we ask the following questions: How do family and work influence the fields of outdoor recreation and tourism? What role can recreation and tourism play in helping families cope?

Family change: implications for outdoor recreation and tourism

Single-parent families may find it more difficult to take time to enjoy the out-of-doors regularly. In addition, since many one-adult households have lower income levels, their ability to travel to national parks, wilderness areas and the like could be limited. With the majority of single parents being female and many fathers absent from their children's lives, the male influence for sports and outdoor activities will not be available.

Ultimately, the US will see fewer children growing up to learn fishing, hunting, hiking and other outdoor activities.

Women opting for college and a career first rather than marriage have the opportunity, desire and time to explore the outdoors and to travel. The positive correlation between education and travel will lead to more young, single women experiencing the out-of-doors and worldwide travel excursions which were unheard of in the previous century.

While some stepfamilies are cohesive units blending together for recreation and travel experiences; some are divided, with too many 'parents' for the children. One thing can be said about stepfamilies, their lives are complicated. If the absent biological parent has an active part in the child's life, spending quality time with that child will probably take the form of long weekends or a week's holiday. Activities and outdoor excursions by this subfamily group will therefore be headed by one parent rather than two.

Work change: implications for outdoor recreation and tourism

With the average working week increasing to slightly more than 47 h and both parents working, people are finding their free time is taken up with family and household chores. Recreation will be allocated to fewer hours per week. On the other hand, when holiday time rolls around, these families are ready to head out of town. Outdoor activities and travel provide people with the needed change from their daily routine. Escaping 'home' relieves their stress and outdoor recreation or travel provides this outlet. These opportunities, however, will only come during holidays and long weekends. Regular monthly or weekly outings will be less likely to occur.

Individuals who choose flexitime or part-time work usually do so to provide themselves with more time for family or other obligations. When a spouse has the 'extra' time to perform the daily household chores, the family usually has more time for other types of activities. This provides them with the opportunity for weekend trips and more outdoor adventures, probably more so than most families.

People who work at home are generally self-employed or telecommuters. This lifestyle choice can free up time (no commuting) for daily outdoor activities such as walking or hiking. Many who choose this lifestyle live in rural areas with easy access to the outdoors and are thus more likely to partake in outdoor activities just beyond their backyard.

Implications for public policy

Work policies will need to change to be more family friendly. It may require government intervention (i.e. laws enacted in Congress directed at businesses and government offices) to allow for guilt-free care of children and elderly parents. Tax breaks could be provided to businesses with family-friendly policies such as on-site childcare. Recreation opportunities and holidays are only one component of helping to reduce family stress. The workplace needs to step forward to assist in this issue. For example, the European model which allows 4–6 weeks of paid holidays could be adopted by North American employers. While many state and federal government employers provide up to 4 weeks of holiday, most private sector employers do not.

Some government agencies have already been leading the way in terms of flexitime, telecommuting and the use of contract work. These ideas need to be encouraged throughout the workforce as these are generally family-friendly policies, have been shown to increase profitability and can help reduce air/noise pollution on our highways.

Implications for planning

Outdoor recreation planners will see more people living where they want to live (e.g. next to scenic and recreational opportunities) since telecommuting and self-employment are providing these options. Rural areas will experience population growth without the typical growth in visible job sites within a community. These new and regular recreationists will become the users and spokespersons for management of public lands. They will view these lands as their backyard and will fight to protect the rights they feel are theirs. Management plans for outdoor recreation lands need to consider the interests and opinions of their neighbours. Public agency managers will need to be in the forefront of conflict resolution to be able to work through the differences between local concerns and agency directives. Otherwise, implementing the plan and gaining much-needed public support will be difficult.

Implications for marketing

We no longer have masses of people who can be stereotyped and placed into easy-to-programme recreational bins. The splitting apart of our mass culture will mean that leisure is increasingly defined within smaller and smaller subgroups of people. Not only will such groups define what is and is not acceptable behaviour during leisure, but they will increasingly dictate the style of participation for those within the group (Godbey, 1997, pp. 76–77).

By not compartmentalizing people, market niches are created. For example, while approximately 25% of all households in the US consist of people living alone, 15% of these solo householders are elderly women and 10% are single men under 45 years of age. Clearly these two groups of people will have differing recreation and travel needs. Another market niche is the young single adult who has delayed marriage. On the surface, this group appears to have more available time and less monetary responsibility than their married counterparts. However, this excess time may be used to advance careers (i.e. working long hours) and the cost of higher education may have significantly increased debt load. Clearly, we cannot look at young singles as one homogeneous market with the same needs.

Tourism is business. Knowing the customer and marketing to the customer is the primary means of business survival and, in general, tourism businesses have been successful. On the other hand, public agencies have typically not operated in this manner. A fundamental operational change within public agencies is needed. One way to implement this philosophical change is to incorporate marketing classes into all recreation management curricula, not just into commercial recreation programmes. Additionally, knowing the needs of the visitor will help structure the recreation approach taken on public lands. Research and public input into management plans are marketing tools for land managers. To do this well, land managers need knowledge and understanding of the social sciences.

Conclusion

As illustrated, there is no 'everybody' any more! What we are seeing is a dissolution of mass culture. Planning, policy making and marketing to the masses are ill-advised. Traditionally, public agencies have tried to be all things for all people which simply will not suffice in the 21st century. Given the increased revenue-generation obligations of public agencies, understanding and knowing the customer/client/visitor/user is more important today than ever before. Survey research, focus group discussions, public meetings and written public comments provide the required knowledge of the visitor. The key to 'listening', 'understanding', and 'providing' the outdoor recreation and tourism experiences desired by people is reaching all the audiences, not just one 'clumped together' group of people. The changing family and work situation requires planners, policy makers and marketers to know their users' various needs.

4

The Effects on Travel and Tourism Demand from Three Mega-trends: Democratization, Market Ideology and Post-materialism as Cultural Wave

Jon Teigland

A trend is a trend is a trend
But the question is, will it bend?
Will it alter its course,
Through some unforeseen force
And come close to a premature end?
(Cairncross, 1969)

Introduction

It is a common phenomenon that the demands for recreation and travel do not always develop as investors or policy makers expect. But when investments or policies are failures, it is rarely a coincidence. Misjudgements are most usually based on a lack of understanding of the forces shaping consumer behaviour in time and space.

One reason for failures is a tendency to believe that earlier trends will continue unchanged. But technological or organizational change can shift demand to new levels, up or down. Trends may also turn if travel habits change more fundamentally. A problem for investors and policy makers, therefore, is to foresee major shifts or turning points in the demand and especially long-term changes in direction. 'Heavy

trends' may be a term for more fundamental but stable long-term changes in travel and recreation behaviour. 'Mega-trends' refer to major changes in society in general (Smeral, 1994), which can cause new heavy trends in travelling to emerge.

This chapter focuses on social forces and ideas shaping three mega-trends in Western societies and the effects on travel and tourism behaviour of

- long-term democratization of tourism and travel consumption,
- the recent dominant influence of market system ideology, and
- post-materialistic trends and modernization of value systems.

In the past, leisure travel and recreation activities were only available to the few, but today are a reality for many inhabitants in

industrial societies. It has been a social evolution that has 'democratized' travel
consumption. Western Europe has in many
ways led this development and become a
'leisure continent' with a higher degree of
democratization and different leisure systems than other continents (Clark, 1999).
Industrialized countries in other parts of the
world have focused more on other ideas and
led the way toward the growing importance
of market system ideology. That mega-trend
has influenced economic systems. One
effect is polarized consumer behaviour with
growth in demand for luxury goods and
cheap bargains simultaneously. The third
mega-trend in post-modern society is major
changes in value systems, especially in the
interest in material belongings and conspicuous consumption. All three mega-trends
have major implications for recent and
future trends in travel and tourism.

Basic Concepts: Stability, Change and Interaction Effects

Effects of mega-trends can emerge gradually
or be hidden for a long period if short-term
or preliminary processes affect demand in
the opposite direction at the same time. A
cause and its visible effect also can be separated and by substantial time lags. Heavy
trends and major turning points are, therefore, not always easy to identify.
Interactions between short and long-term
changes cause interpretation problems, too.
The tourist industry in northeastern USA
realized, for example, a misinterpretation
some years ago. A declining tourist demand
at the beginning of the 1990s was not preliminary and caused by a business cycle, as the
industry believed, but was a long-term effect
of reduced relative attractiveness (Kuentzel
et al., 1996).

A substantial change in tourism demand
may come quickly if short-term processes
start to move demand in the same direction
as long-term heavy trends. In Switzerland
during the first half of the 1990s, short-term
economic problems reduced demand for
tourism in general and this interacted with a
long-term trend towards a greater domestic

demand for holidays abroad. This interaction effect forced a new Swiss hotel to close
down every 62 h on average for 5 years
(Kaspar, 1995, p. 140).

Stability in recreation and travel behaviour, rather than change, may be the most
prominent feature in many industrialized
countries. However, few comparative longitudinal studies are available. The US and
Sweden are the only countries having comprehensive and longitudinal travel studies
covering both day and overnight trips. These
studies show that several of the main structures of travel behaviour have been
remarkably stable in the 1990s. Leisure-
oriented travel has been the main
component (60–80%) of total travel volume
in both countries (NTS, 1995; Nyberg, 1995).
Most trips (80–90%) were domestic and
85–95% of total volume was overnight trips,
if volume is measured in travel-days. The
majority of overnight leisure trips (55–65%)
in both countries represented visits to relatives and friends or were based on the use of
private second homes, recreation boats, caravans or trailers. Longer leisure trips, or
holidays, tend to be concentrated in a few
summer months. In addition, 75–80% of
overnight trips abroad were leisure trips
both in Western Europe and the US.

This structural stability is most probably
no coincidence, but indicates established
consumer habits and mature markets in
many industrialized countries, if Sweden
and the US can be used as examples. The
similarity in major structural elements also
indicates that important forces forming
travel behaviour are not very different.
Among the stabilizing factors are the institutionalized (legal) rights to leisure, including
4–7 weeks of paid holidays in western European countries, but less on other continents.
A substantial volume of private leisure capital that is 'locked up' in second homes,
caravans, leisure boats, etc., and different
kinds of skills (such as foreign languages or
skiing), also stabilize the volume and structure of leisure behaviour. The large volume
of visits within social networks, reflecting
the continuing importance of relatives,
friends, and work colleagues also acts to
stabilize the structure of leisure behaviour.

The travel market in the US between 1985 and 1997 was characterized by a 44% growth in total travel volume (NTS, 1997). Business travel increased, however, less than pleasure and holiday travel (47%). Visits to relatives and friends were the fastest growing segment in the US (up 87%). Travel volume in Sweden showed a very different pattern during the same period, going from substantial growth to a strong decline, with a partial recovery later. Leisure visits to relatives, friends and to second homes were stabilizing elements during the most turbulent years in Sweden at the beginning of the 1990s (Nyberg, 1995; Sahlberg, 1996). A variety of substitution processes took place, with effects both in time and space. Among the most important were shifts between domestic and foreign destinations (external substitution) and between domestic types of travel (internal substitution).

One reason for turbulence in general, or major shifts and turning points, is unexpected events that partly or totally change the assumptions on which a project or policy are based. Such events include unexpected and rapid changes in macroeconomic conditions (as in the Swedish and Swiss cases), natural disasters (e.g. earthquakes or hurricanes) and major shifts in a political system (such as the break-up of the Soviet Union). A major war or terrorist action also can give an unexpected and strong shock to recreation and travel demand, with short- and long-term effects throughout a large influence zone.

The effects from such impulse-processes can be especially strong if several events occur at the same time. That was the case when the Gulf War reduced air traffic in most parts of the world for a short period. But the main problem then for the travel trade was that the Gulf War came during a slowdown in the North American economy. Many bankruptcies were, therefore, an interaction effect between a war going on far away and a relatively small downturn in the business cycle, which changed demand in the same direction. The drastic changes in Sweden in 1991 and 1992 were interaction effects, too. A major devaluation, a business cycle influenced partly by the earlier break-

down of the Soviet Union (a lagged effect) and a major change in taxation system interacted during a relatively short period with large cumulative effects on travel demand among Swedish citizens.

Some events are not unexpected, but planned and well-known years ahead. A major policy change such as the deregulation of the air transport market in the US and Europe, a new tax system, or a mega-event such as the Olympic Games, should not come as a totally unexpected happening. But if investors and policy makers do not understand what is going on, or have a poor theory of the effects from the planned event itself and their interactions, they may find themselves in major trouble. The 1994 Winter Olympic Games in Norway was one example. Instead of the expected boom in tourism and recreation demand afterwards, the reality was different. The divergence between high growth predictions based on poor impact theory and the lower reality explain why 40% of the full-service hotels in the Norwegian host town (Lillehammer) have now gone bankrupt (as measured at the end of 1997).

The Olympic failure relates partly to a lack of understanding of long-term megatrends in many high-income countries and especially in Germany, the most important tourist-generating country in the world. Concepts such as democratization processes and roof effects increase our understanding.

Democratization Processes

At the beginning of the 20th century, travelling for pleasure was something that only the very rich did. Today the majority of people in many industrialized countries take holidays each year. That process has 'democratized' the possibility of travelling as a consumption phenomenon. However, democratization as a concept can also be used about processes that in general tend to reduce differences in society; politically, economically and socially. According to Minogue (1985), democracy, in classical Greek, was the name of a constitution in which the poorer people exercised power in their own interests as against the interests of the rich and aristocratic. The struggle for racial and sexual equality is also a democratization process, which is treated in other chapters in this book.

French scientists claim that the lower classes of society copy the consumption of the upper classes and also their recreation and travel patterns (Monteiro and Rowenczyk, 1992). Social diffusion and lag mechanisms affect development among rich and poor countries alike. The rich countries in Europe have, for example, in many ways led the democratization of travel behaviour. A large majority of the inhabitants (70–80%) of rich countries like Sweden and Switzerland travelled on holidays abroad as early as in the 1970s. Many other countries, especially in southern Europe were far behind with much lower participation rates (30–40%) at that time.

In Europe 'holiday' is often defined as a leisure trip away from home lasting at least 5 days or 4 nights. Leisure trips that last 1–3 nights are referred to as 'short holidays' (Schmidhauser, 1992). Travel surveys from the US do not define trips in the same way, but measure journeys according to distance travelled (NTS, 1995). A 'holiday trip' in the US can, therefore, be different from a European 'holiday'. In fact, most 'holiday trips' (approximately 50–60%) in the US last only 1–4 days, indicating that half the total leisure travel volume consists of day-trips or short holidays according to European definitions. It is important to be aware of conceptual and methodological differences when transferring information on trends between the two continents.

An important trend in the US and parts of Europe during the last 10–15 years has been a substantial growth in the demand for short holidays, mostly having effects at the local and regional level. On the international level, however, the most important process has recently been the democratization of holiday habits in the largest country in Europe, Germany. One effect of this process was a huge increase in German tourists abroad between 1986 and 1994. During those 8 years the number of German visitors to other countries for holidays (lasting at least 5 days) almost doubled (Aderhold, 1996), making Germany the most important source of international tourists.

The strong growth of German tourists to most parts of the world was an interaction effect between internal democratization of consumption and a major external political event in the Soviet Union. The political democratization of East Germany and the reunion with West Germany in 1989 added, in 1994, at least 3 million to the many German tourists travelling abroad on holidays. But more important for other countries was democratization of travel behaviour in West Germany during the same period. Only 57% of West Germans went on holiday in 1986 compared with 78% in 1994. The number of West Germans on holiday increased, therefore, by nearly 12 million during those 8 years. As the majority (64–71%) of them travelled abroad, the effect was nearly a 100% increase internationally in German holidaymakers (Aderhold, 1996). The growth measured in travel days on holidays to foreign countries was probably more than 100 million days, as Germany introduced a 6-week holiday with pay early in that period (Nahrstedt, 1993). Only 4% of West Germans had 6-weeks holiday in 1980 compared with 70% in 1990 (Grümer, 1993).

In theory, the upper limit to holiday making is that 100% of the inhabitants in a country will participate. But some inhabitants will lack the money, free time, be too sick or too old to travel away from home on holidays. In practice, therefore, the upper limit for participation rates is perhaps around a level of 75–85% in many countries (Edwards, 1985, 1992). If participation approaches such levels, then growth in holiday volume may level off. The strong democratization of holiday making recently in Germany and other European countries, with participation rates above 70–75%, indicate that holiday making is approaching an upper limit or roof. In such countries, increased holiday participation will not be a major driving force behind growth in travel demand. The roof-effect in itself reduces growth rates and stabilizes demand more and more the closer participation approaches 100%.

The growth in travel demand in a country does, however, not depend only on participation rates. Travel volume measured in days (or in monetary terms) can grow even with stable participation rates, if the volume of free time (or money) increases by the introduction of an extra week of holidays or higher incomes, for example. Volume also can grow if the inhabitants use more of their available free time (or money) on travelling. That will be the case if nearly 100% of paid holidays are used for travelling (as in Austria and Switzerland), instead of the 50% that is a more normal upper limit or roof, according to Edwards (1992). Limits on the volume of free time, and the degree that free time is used for travel can, therefore, act as two other types of upper limits influencing the volume of travel demand.

Leisure systems are very different among industrial countries. The European Union introduced a common minimum 4-week paid holiday from 1999 in all member countries, although some European countries have more. The average volume per year of holidays with pay among industrial workers is much higher in Europe (4–7 weeks) than for example in the US and Japan (2.5 weeks). Available leisure time creates a 'ceiling' for the volume of holiday travel at a much higher level in Europe than in the two biggest industrial countries in the world. The different leisure systems and free time volume are not a coincidence, but reflect different history, cultures and ways of thinking.

Leisure systems in western Europe are linked to the history of organized labour unions. The sociodemocratic unions decided in the 1920s that a revolution as in Russia should not be their strategy in the struggle for a fair share of economic development. The organized workers in western Europe decided instead to negotiate common (collective) wage agreements with the owners of productive means. The negotiations focused on more pay and improved working conditions. More time free from work obligations was also an important requirement, with shorter working days and

weeks, lower retirement ages and longer holidays. The struggle for more free time was based on the view that work is a burden, which workers would like to reduce (in combination with higher pay).

One effect of this century-long social struggle is a significant reduction in the number of paid work hours, both on a yearly and on a (theoretical) lifetime basis. A 'normal work-year' in a rich country such as Norway has been reduced from 3000 h in 1900 to 1750 h in 1997. Reduced retirement ages and more years spent in the education system have reduced the 'theoretical lifetime work' by 55%, from 165,000 h in 1900 to 75,000 h in 1997 (Landsorganisasjonen, 1998).

The volume of organized free time has increased slowly, although steadily in many European countries. The introduction of 1–2 weeks holidays with pay before World War II was followed up with demands for 3 weeks during the 1950s. When that became a reality, the labour unions asked for a 5-day working week (and longer weekends). A 4-week holiday was introduced in several countries during the 1960s, with a strong increase in travel demand in the following years. Countries with good economies and strong labour unions led the way, with a diffusion of ideas and demands to labour unions in other European countries the following years. If one union got a 5-week holiday or lower retirement ages, then other unions wanted the same (and quickly, to keep up with the 'neighbours').

A major shift in thinking came during the 1970s, as high unemployment in many western European countries became a long-term phenomenon. Labour unions reasoned that if it is not possible to increase the number of jobs by increasing the economic activity, and in that way reducing unemployment, then alternative solutions should be found. One alternative would be to reduce the number of people looking for a job, by reducing the retirement age or keeping young people longer in the education system. Another way would be to share the available jobs by increasing the number of paid holidays or reducing the number of weekly work hours. The changed thinking reflects that jobs are

Table 4.1. Days per year with paid holidays for industrial workers according to wage agreement, 1995.

Country	Paid holidays (days)	Holiday weeks (5 days = 1 week)
Japan	11	2.2
USA	12	2.4
Europe		
Finland	37	7.4
Italy	35	7
Netherlands	32	6.4
West Germany	30	6
Austria	26	5.2
Denmark	25	5
Sweden	25	5
France	25	5
Great Britain	25	5
Spain	24	4.8
Switzerland	24	4.8
Greek	22	4.4
Portugal	22	4.4
Ireland	21	4.2
Norway	21	4.2
Belgium	20	4

Source: Opaschowski (1996).

not only a necessary burden, but also a good (having variable quality) which should be shared according to sociodemocratic ideologies.

During the last 10–15 years, European labour unions have implemented such ideas. One effect is that 5-, 6-, and even 7-week paid holidays have been introduced in some countries according to laws or wage agreements for industrial workers (Table 4.1). Other countries have reduced retirement ages and hours worked per week. It is, however, a fundamental difference inside Europe as countries emphasize equality in the way that all (or most) workers have a right to the same volume of free time (even farmers have 3 weeks holiday paid by the state in Norway). Egalitarian conscious countries like France and the Nordic countries have, therefore, the same number of paid holidays for 'everyone,' reflecting inspiration from the French revolution and its concept of equality. European Union members today have a 'minimum rule' of at least 4 weeks holiday for nonindustrial employees. However, employees in coun-

tries such as the UK and Germany who have worked for some years in the same organization, or are at a high level, may be given (much) more than the minimum. Non-egalitarian systems are also common on other continents (as in the US).

One effect in Europe of the many new, but different collective agreements is that the volume of institutionalized free time has increased during the past decades. Leisure time limits that have restricted leisure travelling in the past have, therefore, been lifted to higher levels. But there is a question whether the forces behind this social evolution can sustain an upward trend for much longer. Some governments seem to think so, and France has recently introduced a 35-h working week (with no reduction in salaries). Italy has reduced the working week as well.

Europe has, however, also signed world trade agreements recently that are opening their economies to global competition. Most European countries also have a growing imbalance between people in work and those out of the work markets. A strongly growing number of elderly people makes it necessary to reverse the reduced pension age (OECD, 1998a) and restrict growth in leisure in general. It may not be possible for Europe to increase or even keep the existing free time volumes, if competition increases with countries that have much less free time. Increasing global competition and economic problems may reduce some 'time-roofs' again, and stabilize or reduce leisure travel, too. A new study published by the World Tourism Organization revealed a reduction in free time in developed countries worldwide (Clark, 1999). In all the leading outbound countries, in Europe, the US and Japan, there was little hope of an increase in paid holidays in the near future. The reason is that the competitiveness of the world economy will act as a brake against more leisure time.

Polarization Trends as an Effect of Market System Ideology

A driving force behind stronger competition globally is the increased faith in market economies and free trade. This constitutes another recent mega-trend in many countries.

The end of the Soviet Union was a turning point for market theory as an international guideline for the organization of society. But the trends towards commercialization and the privatization of public services had started earlier. The core idea is that more competition would make the private and public sectors more efficient and reduce the wasteful use of resources. The resources available for other use should, therefore, increase. Reduced costs and prices should also contribute to higher living standards generally.

Use of 'market fundamentalist' guidelines is a controversial ideological issue. The fact is, however, that several countries are increasingly organizing their public and private sectors according to market theories. Countries such as the UK, New Zealand and the US have led this process, which affects many sectors in society. One effect for the travel industry is reduced public responsibility and support for travel policy issues, and a trend toward privatization, for example, of the budgets for national tourist organizations.

Few studies have clarified the direct and indirect effects of market ideology trends on consumer behaviour and travel demand, but European research shows a polarization of consumption in general. The affluent members of society have generally increased their incomes substantially during the last 10–15 years, while low-income families have had relatively small or almost no pay increases. One effect in Europe is strong growth in the demand for expensive goods and luxury holidays; such as trips to other continents and expensive special events, high cost adventure travelling and the purchase of high quality second homes and yachts. At the same time there has been a strong increase in demand for cheap bargains, such as 'mass-produced' charter flights, as consumers increasingly seek value for money. The simultaneous growth in demand for both high- and low-priced products on the poles (or at each end) of the price scale is a polarized consumption phenomena (Nilsson and Solgaard, 1995).

Similar changes in consumption patterns have most probably taken place in the US, as income differences have increased there, too. The 20% most affluent Americans increased their real incomes by 20% from 1984 to 1994, while the 20% poorest inhabitants had only achieved a 0.1% increase during the same period (Kacapyr, 1996). More uneven income distribution is, according to Kacapyr, a characteristic of market economies, because markets will mostly reward resourceful inhabitants who make use of new opportunities.

A more skewed income distribution in the UK has influenced travel demand in several ways during the last 10–15 years (Prentice, 1993). The UK experience indicates that higher incomes among low and middle-income groups should increase travel demand volume in general by democratizing the participation in travelling. Increased income for the affluent increases demand, too, but mainly in the form of additional trips to the main holiday destination or by selecting more expensive trips. If international trends toward the use of market theory continue, with increased affluence as the expected effect, then trends in the most affluent European countries such as Switzerland and Norway may indicate future travel trends for other countries as well. A major long-term trend both in Switzerland and Norway has been increased travel abroad, especially long distance travel.

Comparative studies show that trips abroad are a luxury with an average income-elasticity above one in general and 1.76–1.86 in western countries (Crouch 1994, 1995; Crouch and Shaw, 1994). Which means that if incomes increase by 1% in western countries, trips abroad will increase by 1.76–1.86%. The more advanced countries in Asia, such as Japan, have very high elasticities for travel abroad. However, the income level in developing countries has to reach a certain threshold before trips to foreign countries become commonplace. If the income level is high, as among the affluent, then higher income will not increase the number of trips abroad but instead more expensive travel options will be chosen (Crouch, 1994).

Such trips are partly a substitution for 'inferior' domestic holidays to more attractive ones abroad. One effect in European countries, where relatively short distances to go abroad are common, is a decline in domestic demand for holidays in the homeland, especially during the summer. Extended trips to other continents increased among Swiss inhabitants by 178% from 1980 to 1992 at the same time as the number of Swiss holidays in Switzerland declined 4% (Schmidhauser, 1995). The reduction in Swiss demand for domestic holidays would have been even greater if a growing number of winter holidays in Switzerland had not been a compensating factor. The flow of holidaymakers abroad from (oil)-rich Norway increased so much during the same years that Norwegian demand for domestic holidays decreased by 30% measured in days (Teigland, 1990). Such changes create problems for the tourist industry as the consumers can change spatial travel patterns quickly, but the tourist supply is not

mobile in the same way. Short- and long-term external substitution processes combined with the immobility of most tourist supply contributed to many bankruptcies both among Swiss hotels during the 1990s, and after the 1994 Winter Olympics in the Norwegian host region.

Affluence is only a partial cause of the external substitution from domestic to foreign destinations. A comparative study from several continents shows that the demand for travel to foreign countries followed a strongly growing trend, independent of other factors such as increased economic growth. This independently growing time-trend or 'trend of our times' was 4.5% per year for travel abroad in general and 7% for long distance trips (Crouch, 1994). The time-trend for travel to Europe from other continents was negative (−2%), but strongly positive (14% per year) for trips to countries in the Pacific Rim.

Interactions between 'time-trends' and growing incomes, especially among the affluent, may explain the increased demand for high quality and especially 'luxury' travel. Luxury is, however, a dynamic concept that varies over time, and between countries and cultures.

Germans make a distinction between 'old' and 'new' forms of luxury. Enzensberger (1996) claims that the new luxury for the privileged 10 million Germans who have more than they need of material luxury objects, is represented by life qualities, such as:

- time to do what you choose yourself,
- privacy, including enough space and escape from unwanted attention,
- security from violence and crime,
- high environmental qualities; such as pleasant surroundings, quietness and clean air and water.

Such 'post-materialistic' changes in value orientation have been predicted in industrial countries in general (Ingelhart, 1977, 1990). Basic value systems that oscillate over time can be viewed as cultural waves that create new trends also in travel behaviour.

Post-materialistic Trends

Post-materialistic theories focus on a differ-ence in value systems among the old and young generations in the Western world. The older generations that grew up with high unemployment in the 1930s and the hardships during World War II have been marked by those experiences for most of their life. A core value for them is security and material prosperity. Such values are more taken for granted among later genera-tions. The new generations are, therefore, more interested in 'post-materialistic' values and life qualities like personal devel-opment, co-determination and environ-mental issues, according to post-materialist theory (Inglehart, 1977). Inglehart predicted that generation replacement would create a clear trend from materialistic to post-materialistic value systems. This process, which was to take place gradually and almost unnoticed, was called the silent rev-olution.

Longitudinal studies have confirmed a trend toward post-materialism in 18 of 20 societies on five continents for which we have comparable data from 1981 and 1990/91 (Becker, 1995). The European/World Values Surveys covering 70% of the world's population indicate that this value shift has occurred in societies that have experienced sufficient economic growth in recent decades so that the pre-adult experi-ences of younger generations were more secure than those of the older ones. A study of work values indicates at the same time that evaluations of North Americans and Europeans became more similar during the 1980s (Zanders and Harding, 1995). Con-vergence is also the overall pattern of change in a comparison of Canadian and US values, but in many domains Canadian values appear to 'lead' the American ones (Nevitte and Inglehart, 1995). The value systems at the individual level have, however, became more pluralistic or fragmented and less sim-ilar according to a study of four Europe and North American regions (Halman and Pet-tersson, 1995).

Post-materialistic values have so far not become a dominant force and interest in material belongings, conspicuous consump-tion and economic development has grown in countries like Norway, especially among the young (Hellevik, 1996). High material living standards does, therefore, not neces-sarily reduce the interest for more material belongings. It is still important among 'mate-rialistic' oriented inhabitants to get more, or the right, brands, as they do not 'have enough' (Hellevik, 1996). This trend is prob-ably not only a phenomenon in northern parts of Europe, but helps explain why 'shopping tourism' is the top activity among domestic travellers in the US (NTS, 1997) and is strongly growing also in Asia.

Implications

Democratization of free time, polarization of consumption patterns and post-materialism as a cultural wave are the three mega-trends discussed in this chapter. They have impli-cations both for public policy and for planning and investment in the private sec-tor. Consumer behaviour also depends, however, on other types of mega-trends. Women's struggles worldwide for equality represent another important democratiza-tion process taking place that has effects both on leisure and business travel. The polariza-tion of the population into physically active and passive groups is a mega-trend, too, showing effects such as increased over-weight problems and increased passive recreational use of nature. The percentage of adults who are obese increased, for example, in the US from 24% in the 1960s to 35% in 1994 (Dortch, 1997). Physical fitness is declining in Europe too. This partly explains why the trend among tourists in the Euro-pean Alps is that everybody wants to experience nature – but not on foot.

Our understanding of the dynamic pro-cesses shaping demand is, alas, limited. But we do know that mega-trends will interact also with other short-term processes to shape travel demand. Unexpected events, such as the economic crisis in Asia or the war in Jugoslavia, in combination with major changes in international policies such as the introduction of the new European money system or world trade agreements, make tourism and recreation trends less predictable. Decision-makers should, therefore, plan for a more dynamic world and more uncertainty. It is increasingly important to be flexible and to invest accordingly. To keep options open may be one of the most important strategies for long-term survival for tourist investments or policies.

If the trend toward more international competition continues, and the effect is higher economic growth globally and regionally (as predicted by market theory), then travel demand will increase. In this case, it is probable that travel demand among the affluent parts of society will grow most strongly. Higher incomes, but not much more free time, may change demand toward products costing more per time-unit such as short and expensive breaks, or toward other forms of luxury or high quality experiences. Substantially higher income among the affluent may explain why a strong demand exists on several continents for very expensive leisure capital such as deluxe yachts or second homes at high quality destinations or resorts.

A development toward higher incomes, in general, but not more free time or even less, would change the way in which holidays are taken (Clark, 1999). Holidays would tend to be shorter, more frequent and more intense forms of recreation. To stay at home will then be an increasingly important alternative for consumers, especially if they continue to buy more and more leisure equipment for home-based recreation. Destinations that want to compete on the market for the more frequent, shorter and more intense holidays will most probably need to supply more diversity and higher quality than before. One reason is that improved home-based recreation possibilities will be a cheap alternative, making the consumers more price sensitive towards tourism supply close to home. One important implication is that there will be a growing demand for quality at a lower price.

If globalization is a brake not only against more leisure time, but also against higher incomes for large population groups, that mega-trend will contribute to increased demand for quality at a lower price. No surprise then that the European and North American markets show a growing interest in organized holidays and short breaks (Freitag, 1999) as these are a way for producers to standardize and deliver quality and lower prices to a higher volume of consumers.

Roof effects will continue to restrict growth potentials in the total volume of holiday travel, especially in north and central Europe where the volume of leisure travel will probably stabilize during the coming years. However, the introduction of a minimum 4 weeks holiday with pay in all of the European Community from January 1999 will increase travel demand especially in the southern parts of Europe, in the years to come. It may need a long period of strong and stable economic growth, perhaps 30–40 years, before the inhabitants of eastern Europe in general reach the same level of holiday demand as that found in the West today.

The European and Japanese experience indicate that higher incomes will particularly increase the volume of trips abroad and to long-haul destinations. When incomes reach the same high level as in Norway and Switzerland, then the demand for some of the traditional domestic holidays may decline. Substitution effects can reduce demand on a regional level but also in large countries, if domestic supply is of a common or 'inferior' type. The flexibility of the cruise industry in delivering new experiences to consumers, combined with a predictable travel quality, make cruise products an increasingly attractive and affordable luxury.

In this paper, many examples have been provided of recent developments showing that tourism and recreation are influenced by mega-trends. Democratization, polarization and changes in value systems are among them. How they affect travel for specific destinations is not easily understood. However, a number of global examples have been provided so that some understanding of where we are headed can be gained. Against the backdrop of the above-mentioned mega-trends, destination areas will be able to analyse their own situation and make significant adjustments. Travel will increase but travel patterns will also change.

5

Trends in Information Technology and Tourism

Dimitrios Buhalis

Introduction

Information is the lifeblood of the travel industry, and therefore the effective use of Information Technology (IT) is crucial to its competitiveness and prosperity. Tourism is inevitably influenced by the business process re-engineering experienced due to the technological revolution.

> A whole system of ITs is being rapidly diffused throughout the tourism industry and no player will escape its impacts
> (Poon, 1993)

Timely and accurate information, relevant to consumers' needs, is increasingly the key to satisfaction of tourist demand and to the ability of tourism enterprises to offer suitable products. Therefore, IT provides the information backbone that facilitates tourism. Effectively, IT empowers the emerging globalization of tourism demand and supply experienced worldwide, and at the same time propels it by providing effective tools both to consumers for identifying and purchasing suitable products and to suppliers for developing, managing and distributing their offerings on a global scale. IT therefore becomes an essential partner which increasingly determines the interface between consumers and suppliers globally (Vlitos-Rowe, 1995; Sheldon, 1997a; Buhalis, 1998a,b; O'Connor, 1999).

However, IT is currently far from providing perfect, reliable tools which can deliver the entire range of functions promised in their specifications. Technological deficiencies are often coupled with organizational inefficiencies and incompetencies, frequently due to the inability of top management to appreciate the emerging capabilities of IT and the unparalleled opportunities emerging for the tourism industry. As a result, the usage of IT in tourism is often less than satisfactory and cost effective. However, by analysing the emerging trends it is quite evident that over 5 years (1995–2000) IT has enabled the tourism industry to advance its offering and delivery mechanisms more than in the previous three decades. The re-engineering of business processes in tourism has generated a paradigm shift, altering the structure of the entire industry and developing a whole range of opportunities and threats for all stakeholders. Therefore, developments in IT represent a revolution for the tourism industry, comparable only to the introduction of the jet engine. This chapter illustrates the progress of the tourism industry in the last few years due to IT and also develops a framework for future developments.

Factors of Change: Synergies between IT and Tourism

To understand IT's impacts, it is critical to demonstrate the changes it has brought. To do so requires examining the factors of change, which illustrate the major trends. As these developments are closely interrelated, it is often difficult to identify whether IT generates or simply facilitates changes in tourism demand and supply. Perhaps the reality is somewhere in between. IT provides the tools and enables the evolution of tourism demand and supply by facilitating existing needs and business prospects. Similarly, the tourism industry increases its requirements from IT by expanding its needs and users' requirements and by sponsoring technological developments which facilitate its functions.

The continuous development of information and communication technologies during the last decade has profound implications for the whole tourism industry. IT incorporates not only software and hardware, but also information, management and telecommunication systems to enable the processing and flow of information within and between organizations, as well as all the equipment utilized for the production of commodities and the provision of services. IT should be regarded, therefore, as a synthesis of electronics, computing and telecommunications technologies (Poon, 1993).

The eras of IT development

The major developments in new information technologies can be classified into four main eras. In the first, *data processing*, the main objective was to improve operational efficiency by automating information-based processes. This era happened from the 1960s onwards and mainly used mainframes and mini-computers. The second era was that of *management information systems (MIS)*, where the aim was to increase management effectiveness by satisfying organizational requirements. This era commenced in the 1970s. Information systems were used primarily to address the needs of internal management and coordination. Emphasis was placed on administrative and clerical functions, especially accounting or inventory. In the early 1980s, the *strategic information systems (SIS)* era aimed to improve competitiveness. This can be achieved mainly by changing the nature or

conduct of business. Integrated networks were developed in order to: achieve organizations' strategic objectives; enhance performance and efficiency; coordinate activities of functions and business units; facilitate interaction with external entities; and ultimately achieve a competitive advantage. The proliferation of personal computers and the development of suitable software, which supported decision making and managerial activity, facilitated this era. Since the early 1990s a fourth and more profound era has been emerging: *the network era*. Intra- and inter-organizational networking is proliferating by using local and wide area networks. The development of the Internet, Intranets and Extranets revolutionized this era and the way that communication and business function. This enables efficient communication and multi-level integration. More importantly, this era alters the competitiveness of both firms and governments in the global marketplace and reduces the significance of location and size in the product delivery processes. The consequences are therefore paramount for both the private and public sectors globally (Peppard, 1993; Lord, 1997; Robson, 1997).

The evolution of hardware, software and networking

Several technologies are already available while others are expected to come on to the market in the future. Technological development in terms of hardware, software and networking has enhanced the capabilities of organizations by providing robust tools for management and marketing. As far as hardware is concerned, faster and more reliable computers and other equipment enable the performance of processes at a fraction of the time and cost required in the past. Increasingly computers are becoming smaller, faster and less expensive, providing affordable tools to larger segments of society. In addition, the development of other devices (such as advanced portable computers, mobile phones, intelligent work stations, palmtops) make it possible to have access and function in conjunction with powerful databases and networks. Software developments enable a much more integrated management of data as they enable the integration of all enterprise functions. In particular, they support the automation of both front and back office operations and thus empower the decision-making process. Increasingly software applications use embedded artificial intelligence and learning facilities to predict users' behaviour and desires and to provide suitable solutions and services. Through knowledge management, enterprises can enhance their organizational understanding of issues. Data warehousing and data mining enable enterprises also to understand their market segments and support the development of suitable marketing and management strategies. The development of user-friendly interfaces and multimedia provide data and media-rich applications. Organizations can therefore distribute a greater wealth of information at a fraction of the cost and at the same time enhance their efficiency and performance. As a result, they can develop suitable opportunities to interact with their customers and partner organizations. They can also reduce their training costs, as employees are guided by software applications and do not need to memorize complicated procedures (O'Connor, 1995; Buhalis et al., 1998; Buhalis and Schertler, 1999).

Perhaps networking is the most important element of the contemporary information technology revolution. Synergies and interoperability between processes, departments and functions enable enterprises to reduce their labour costs, to increase efficiency and to make better informed decisions. Developments in software and integration of entire processes reduce work duplication, while enhancing transparency of information and decisions within organizations, empowering employees to improve their performance. Networking is experienced within organizations, between organizations and their partners as well as between the entire world of individuals and organizations. The proliferation of the Internet, Intranets and Extranets supports communications between employees, units, organizations, as well as with external partners and consumers. As a result, the efficiency and effectiveness of networks are revolutionized.

The Internet uses the World Wide Web (WWW) as a distribution multimedia protocol to enable the instant dissemination of media-rich documents (such as textual data, graphics, pictures, video and sounds). The Internet effectively revolutionizes the interactivity between computer users and servers. As a result, an innovative and user-friendly platform for the efficient, live and timely exchange of ideas and products was established. It also provided unique opportunities for interactive marketing to all service providers. Similarly, Intranets operate as closed or secured networks within organizations, using standard protocols to harness the needs of internal business users. By using a single controlled, user-friendly interface to provide relevant data to all employees in the organization, this empowers their function and supports the formulation of close partnerships with other members of the value-chain for the production of goods and services. More recently, Extranets use the same principles and computer networks to enhance the interactivity and transparency between organizations and their trusted partners. By linking and sharing data and processes, they formulate low-cost and user-friendly electronic commerce arrangements. Automation of standard procedures supports the effectiveness of business networks and empowers closer collaboration.

Applications of information technology in tourism

The tourism industry already uses a wide range of IT systems as illustrated in Box 5.1. Several tailor-made, internal-management applications facilitate the management and marketing of tourism organizations. These systems use databases as well as office automation software for inventory control and generic administration purposes. Knowledge management systems enable organizations to gain information about their functions and to build knowledge about approaches to resolve problems and emerging issues. Increasingly Intranets and Extranets are used to offer user-friendly

---

Box 5.1. Information technology (IT) applications used currently.

Internal management and ad hoc relationships with external partners
- Tailor-made internal management applications
- Databases
- Office automation
- Knowledge management systems
- Intranets/Extranets

Networking and open distribution
- Dedicated internal management and distribution systems
- Computer Reservation Systems (CRSs)
- Global Distribution Systems (GDSs)
- Switch applications for hospitality organizations (e.g. THISCO and WIZCOM)
- Destination Management Systems (DMSs)
- Internet in general
- New Internet-based travel intermediaries (e.g. Expedia, Travelocity, Preview Travel, Internet Travel Network, Priceline.com, etc.)
- Mobile devices (PDA, WAP, GPRS, etc.)

Traditional distribution technologies supporting automated systems
- Calling centres
- CD-ROMs
- Kiosks

---

access to employees of organizations as well as their authorized partners to use company data to perform their tasks.

The World Tourism Organization (WTO) acknowledges that computerized networks, and in particularly airline Computer Reservation Systems (CRSs) have been leading dramatic structural changes since the early 1970s (WTO, 1994a, 1995d). Tourism principals realized that their presentation on travel agencies' desktop screens was critical for their ability to attract bookings. Hence, they developed interfaces to enable them to communicate directly with intermediaries through CRSs. Principals use CRSs to manage their inventory and distribute their capacity as well as to manage their expansion of tourism globally (Emmer *et al.*, 1993). The evolution of CRSs to Global Distribution Systems (GDSs) in the early 1980s effectively allowed them to become electronic travel supermarkets. GDSs gradually expanded their geographical and operational coverage by integrating both horizontally, with other airline systems, and vertically by incorporating the entire range of principals, such as accommodation, car rentals, train and ferry ticketing, entertainment and other provisions (Truitt *et al.*,

1991; WTO, 1994a, 1995c,d; Kärcher, 1996; French, 1998). Switch companies such as THISCO and WIZCOM emerged also to facilitate interconnectivity between dedicated or internal hotel systems and GDSs (Emmer *et al.*, 1993; O'Connor, 1995, 1999). In addition, Destination Management Systems emerged to provide integrated solutions for destinations and small and medium tourism enterprises which were excluded from the major systems, as well as to amalgamate all local systems and providers under one brand name (Buhalis, 1994, 1997).

New wave of technological evolution

The International Federation on Information Technology and Tourism has identified the most significant technological developments forcing a new wave of technological evolution, as demonstrated in Fig. 5.1 (Werthner and Klein, 1999). The underlying trend of all this development is integration of hardware, software and intelligent applications through networking and advanced user interfaces. Interestingly, most of the technological tools required by the industry already exist. However, they may need improvement to enhance their speed, interoperability, reliability and adaptation to the

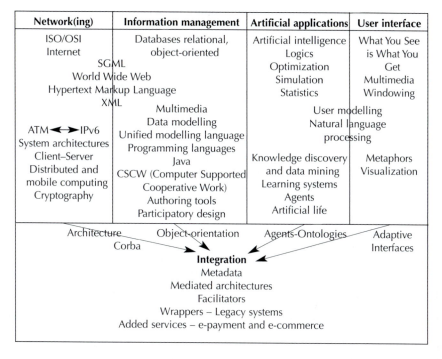

Network(ing)	Information management	Artificial applications	User interface
ISO/OSI	Databases relational,	Artificial intelligence	What You See
Internet	object-oriented	Logics	is What You
SGML		Optimization	Get
World Wide Web		Simulation	Multimedia
Hypertext Markup Language		Statistics	Windowing
XML	Multimedia	User modelling	
	Data modelling	Natural language	
ATM ←→ IPv6	Unified modelling language	processing	
System architectures	Programming languages		
Client–Server	Java	Knowledge discovery	Metaphors
Distributed and	CSCW (Computer Supported	and data mining	Visualization
mobile computing	Cooperative Work)	Learning systems	
Cryptography	Authoring tools	Agents	
	Participatory design	Artificial life	

Architecture　　　Object-orientation　　　Agents-Ontologies　　　Adaptive
　　　Corba　　　　　　　　　　　　　　　　　　　　　　　　Interfaces
Integration
Metadata
Mediated architectures
Facilitators
Wrappers – Legacy systems
Added services – e-payment and e-commerce

Fig. 5.1. Lines of technological evolution. (Adapted from Werthner and Klein, 1999, p. 132.)

industry and consumer needs. Fast and reliable networks are emerging to support media-rich applications and on-line video presentations required by both consumers and suppliers. Distributed and mobile communication as well as network architectures and protocols effectively support mobile computing and facilitate access to information from a wide range of media and geographical coverage. This will enable mobile users to access bases of information and purchase products and interact regardless of location. Development of client–server interfaces will empower end-users and will reduce the training required and the reluctance of new users. Advanced cryptography will improve on-line security and provide trusted and robust financial systems for electronic commerce. The development of electronic commerce, especially through the introduction of digital television, will force re-engineering of the tourism industry and propel new practices such as electronic ticketing, commission capping etc. Eventually, networking will

take advantage of a wide range of equipment such as on-line kiosks, in-flight or room entertainment systems, portable computers and palmtops, digital television as well as the Internet, Intranets and Extranets, in order to network all users and suppliers.

The above developments will support a more effective information management and will enable both organizations and consumers to take advantage of the information they gain. The development of object-oriented, relational databases will essentially enable interlinking between all information kept by organizations in order to generate synergies. Data modelling and knowledge management enhances the usage of operational data in the decision-making processes and will enable better informed operational and strategic choices. Automation of procedures by using smart cards and expert systems to reduce manual working procedures while Computer Supported Cooperative Work (CSCW) will facilitate the development of organizational knowledge management and enable employees to share experiences and solutions to established problems. Hence, intelligent applications incorporate knowledge from organizations to inform decision making at the level required. Finally, authoring tools will be used for facilitating information management end-user programming to support the customization of software to user requirements.

Software development is driven by the development of intelligent applications using artificial intelligence and complex algorithms to provide customized information and services. Office automation and full integration of front and back offices will enhance efficiency and effectiveness. In addition, the use of simulation and the processing of statistics will enhance the quality of the information used for decision making and will enable organizations to adopt more proactive approaches to management and marketing problems. Optimization and simulation applications will also enable organizations to develop alternative scenarios and to predict situations and potential outcomes based on previous experience. Knowledge discovery and data mining will support management and marketing functions by sharing experiences throughout organizations and by enabling proactive marketing based on personalized records of previous preferences. Learning systems and agents will increasingly accumulate and use knowledge productively to support employees and organizations.

Perhaps the most significant development during the last decade was the development of user-friendly interfaces which enabled nonspecialists to use computers without extensive training on each particular program or interface. The development of multimedia interfaces and particular interfaces based on the 'What You See Is What You Get' (WYSIWYG) and Windows protocols enabled most systems and applications to become accessible to most people in organizations and to consumers, saving time and enhancing efficiency. Adaptive interfaces and the visualization of computing functions simplify processes and empower users to take advantage of systems and applications. In addition, user-friendly

interfaces enabled partner organizations to share resources, empowered interaction and maximized the outcome of value chains. The most challenging task for technological development is the integration of all applications and systems to enhance the management and marketing functions of the industry. The applications of the new wave of IT developments in tourism should empower tourism organizations and destinations to revolutionize electronic commerce opportunities. This will enable them to develop and sustain competitive advantage and avoid competitive disadvantage.

Empowering Consumers and Suppliers through IT: Demand and Supply

The development of new IT, and particularly the Internet, facilitated the rise of the 'new' tourist who is becoming knowledgeable and is seeking exceptional value for money and time, and participation in special interest activities. Thus, the relative importance of package tours, which are often based on low quality–low prices, is expected to decline in favour of independently organized tourism. A relatively new movement towards environmental preservation and appreciation for the local society is also evident. Tourists tend to participate in the experience by being active and spending their time on their special interests. Leisure time will increasingly be used for 'edutainment' (i.e. the exploration of personal interests for both personal and professional development). Flexibility in both consumer choice and service delivery processes is becoming a key element. Every tourist is different, carrying a unique blend of experiences, motivations and desires. Tourists from the major generating regions of the world have become frequent travellers, are linguistically and technologically skilled, and can function in multicultural and demanding environments overseas.

The usage of IT in the industry is driven both by the development of the size and complexity of tourism demand, as well as by

---

Box 5.2. IT-empowered developments enhancing customer satisfaction.

- User-friendly and customized interfaces
- Consumers have more information and enjoy greater choice
- Better understanding of consumer needs based on research interaction and data mining
- Differentiated and customized services according to personal preferences and attitudes, rather than sociodemographic segmentation
- Consumers feel empowered to get information on products and services they are interested in
- Pricing becomes more flexible as organizations are willing to provide great discounts for last-minute, targeted offered and special promotions
- A reduction in bureaucracy and paperwork frees time for better customer service
- Customizing the product and establishing 'one-to-one' marketing by using intelligence collected by loyalty schemes (e.g. dietary requirements, product preferences)
- New value added services (e.g. in-flight or in-room entertainment and information channels)
- Automation of tedious operational tasks through IT (e.g. in-room TV checkout)
- Personalized services (e.g. a telephone operator acknowledges a guest by name or waiter knows dietary preferences or requirements)
- Better integration of departments and functions of organizations toward better service
- Language barriers are increasingly reduced through development of interfaces to serve all target markets and also through automatic translation
- Accurate and much richer marketing research by collecting data from all transactions and enquiries

---

the rapid expansion and sophistication of new tourism products, which address mini-market segments. Increasingly, new, experienced, sophisticated, demanding travellers seek information about more exotic destinations and authentic experiences, as well as requiring to interact with suppliers to satisfy their specific needs and wishes. The contemporary/connected consumer is far less willing to wait or to put up with delays, to the point where patience is a disappearing virtue. The World Tourism Organization argues that

> the key to success lies in the quick identification of consumer needs and in reaching potential clients with comprehensive, personalized and up-to-date information
>
> (WTO, 1988)

Customer satisfaction depends greatly on the accuracy and comprehensiveness of specific information on the accessibility, facilities, attractions and activities of each destination. Consumers not only require value for money, but also value for time for the entire range of their dealings with organizations. This reflects people's perceived shortage of time, which is evident in Western societies. Increasingly, IT enables travellers to access reliable and accurate information as well as to undertake reservations at a fraction of time, cost and inconvenience required by conventional methods. IT improves the service quality and contributes to higher guest/traveller satisfaction. A wide range of development empowers consumers, as indicated in Box 5.2.

There are several success stories on the Internet: Preview Travel (www.previewtravel.com) reached 6.4 million subscribers on 31 December, 1988, up 145% from the previous year. Expedia (expedia.com) (the Microsoft on-line travel agency) has emerged in the top 25 travel agencies in the US in less than 3 years. Some of the Expedia figures clearly illustrate the trends: US$8.5 million per week in travel-related sales; more than US$430 million in sales in October 1998; 1 million airline tickets sold already; 3 million visitors per month, and 3 million registered users. TravelWeb (www.travelweb.com) represents 18,000 hotels belonging to 90 chains. About 17,000 are bookable on-line and TravelWeb attracts 6.5 million page accesses per month. At the end of 1996 TravelWeb generated US$6.5 million, as annual net reservation revenue, while their predicted on-line travel sales by the year 2000 are expected to reach

Table 5.1. Global Internet Market in 1998.

Country or continent	Internet users	Population	Percentage of population
USA	164,081,940	264,648,291	62.00
Norway	900,000	4,348,410	20.70
Sweden	1,400,000	8,839,000	15.80
Finland	700,000	5,098,754	13.70
UK	4,100,000	58,394,600	7.00
Australia	1,100,000	17,657,400	6.20
Germany	4,300,000	81,338,093	5.30
Netherlands	800,000	15,385,000	5.20
Japan	5,200,000	125,200,000	4.20
Taiwan	800,000	21,125,792	3.80
France	1,200,000	57,903,000	2.10
Spain	700,000	39,188,194	1.80
Latin America	2,000,000	474,000,000	0.40
Africa	500,000	708,000,000	0.07

Source: Adapted from Rosen (1999).

US$4.7 billion. Marriott Hotels (marriott.com) already enjoys 13,000 visits per day and is now conducting well over US$1.5 million of business every month over the net.

It is increasingly evident that a large percentage of consumers have access to the Internet and are able to find information for their leisure and tourism interests. Although there is no accurate number of the people who are currently on-line, there are several indications (Table 5.1) illustrating that the number of on-line consumers is increasing rapidly, which justifies massive investments by organizations to develop their electronic presence. Most Internet users are well-educated professionals who travel frequently (KPMG, 1998; Smith and Jenner, 1998).

It is anticipated that the development of digital television will effectively bring the Internet to the living rooms of most families. User-friendly interfaces based on a television set and easily operated through a simplified keyboard will enable the vast majority of the population to have direct access to organizations electronically. This will revolutionize electronic commerce and enable the development of a mass digital market. Organizations which provide customized products and services and empower consumers to undertake their travel planning and arrangements in a fraction of the time required by conventional distribution channels through efficient interfaces will increase their market share and gain competitive advantages. Thus, destinations and principals need new methods to serve the new types of demand. It is becoming increasingly evident that in order to satisfy tourism demand and survive in the long term there is no choice but to incorporate new technology and enhance the interactivity with the marketplace (Buhalis, 1998a).

The Future: Developing Electronic Commerce for Tourism

The commercial viability of the Internet presence for tourism enterprises will depend on their success in receiving bookings through the Internet. A great number of hotels worldwide (51%) surveyed in 1998 already receive bookings through the Internet and the majority of the remaining properties are developing their facilities in order to be able to receive Internet bookings in the near future.

There are also several forecasts for the future of on-line tourism and travel shopping especially for the US where the

Table 5.2. Tourism electronic intermediaries emerging in the electronic marketplace.

	Expedia.com	ITN	Preview Travel	Travelocity
Registered users	2 million	4 million	3.4 million	2.5 million
Page views per month	n/a	15 million	n/a	40 million
Unique visitors per month	2,341,000	n/a	1,608,000	2,441,000
Visits per month	n/a	7.5 million	6.3 million	n/a
Estimated gross (bookings per month)	US$12 million	US$10 million	US$12 million	US$16 million

Source: Adapted from Sileo (1988).

penetration of the Internet is much higher than in other places. This is attributed not only to the high standard of living and the fairly low price for electronic equipment in the US, but also the fact that, unlike European countries, local telephone calls are effectively free of charge. Forrester Research predicted that travel and tourism would be second only to computer products as it anticipated the total on-line turnover on tourism and travel products to reach almost US$1.6 billion by the year 2000.

It is evident, therefore, that only tourism organizations and destinations that prepare their presence in the emerging electronic marketplace will be able to gain some of the projected benefits and achieve competitive advantages. In addition, several new electronic intermediaries are emerging to take advantage of the revolution occurring in the tourism marketplace (TIA, 1997; Wardell, 1998). They often use CRSs and GDSs and provide suitable interfaces to consumers who would like to book tourism products on-line. Table 5.2 illustrates the development of the major travel intermediaries' sites and their essential statistics. It is worth mentioning that only Travelocity emerged from the existing tourism industry (i.e. SABRE). All other intermediaries emerged and grew independently.

The structure of the on-line expenditure is also changing rapidly to include a much broader variety of tourism products. Airline tickets accounted for 90% of all on-line travel sales, generating US$243 million in revenue in 1996. However, the Travel Industry Association of America (TIA, 1997)

predicts that by the year 2002 the proportion of airline tickets purchased on-line is going to drop to 73% of all on-line travel sales, accounting for US$6.5 billion. Non-airline sales (hotel and car rental) will grow from US$31 million in 1996 to US$2.2 billion in 2002. On-line advertising on travel web sites will grow from US$2 million in 1996 to US$282 million in 2002, and will be the third highest source of revenue for travel-related web sites. A significant increase in direct bookings by on-line users for airlines, hotels and other travel business is also anticipated. Direct sales by suppliers are expected to grow from 22% in 1997 to 30% of on-line sales in 2002. The leading incentive for the direct sale transformation is to reduce commissions paid to travel intermediaries by establishing direct links with consumers. Although in 1996 less than 1% of all airline ticket revenue came from on-line sources, it is anticipated by that by the year 2002 this will increase to 8.2% and will be the leading travel purchase on the Internet (TIA, 1997).

Framework of Change and Implications for Tourism Management and Marketing

Information technology provides the tools to revolutionize the tourism industry, as illustrated in Box 5.3. However, the reliability and functionality of the tools, as well as their cost, needs to be improved while their use is advanced. This will enable the development of all the direct links required and

---

Box 5.3.   IT tools required to be developed further to be used by tourism organizations.

Web tools for e-commerce
- Object oriented
- Multimedia
- Modular construction tools
- Harmonization of existing systems
- Development of applications specific to tourism

Integration of distribution mechanism
- ATM-e-ticketing
- Computer Supported Cooperative Working (knowledge sharing/management, structured collaborative tools, control of contribution)
- Interaction between suppliers
- Virtual cooperation

Intelligent applications
- Learning environment → interface for customers
- Adaptive methods (user profile) → interface for customers
- Loyalty programme – customer tracking and marketing research

Quantitative tools and decision systems
- Geographical information systems for marketing and marketing research
- Navigation technology planning
- Marketing research tools collecting date on- and off-line

Interactive multimedia
- Stand-alone/CD-ROM
- Internet

---

the establishment of close partnerships between stakeholders in the industry, as illustrated in Fig. 5.2. The forecast developments will effectively bring a whole range of new benefits for the consumer as well as for tourism suppliers. These developments are expected to have major implications for the management and marketing of tourism enterprises.

Implications for the tourism consumer of the future

Consumer benefits will include more information/knowledge about products, services and destinations. This will enable consumers to have a greater involvement in planning their travel and building their own itineraries and, as a result, niche markets will grow rapidly. Consumers will seek personalized experiences and authenticity and they will be empowered through the new tools as well as their previous experiences. More information and competition will introduce cheaper prices and on-line bargaining which will enable suppliers to sell their distressed capacity and maximize their profit, while offering competitive pricing for the leisure/flexible traveller. Although the English language dominates both the Internet and international tourism, new tools are emerging to assist non-English speakers, such as automatic translation or regional sites in the local language.

Security of transactions and quality assurance of both services and information will be critical for the satisfaction of consumers. Although consumers are still concerned about giving their credit card details on the Internet, advanced encryption techniques pioneered by credit card companies will increase consumer confidence. However, it needs to be emphasized that transaction security over the Internet is also a perceptual issue. In most cases, consumers trust unknown waiters or shop assistants to disappear with their credit card while set-

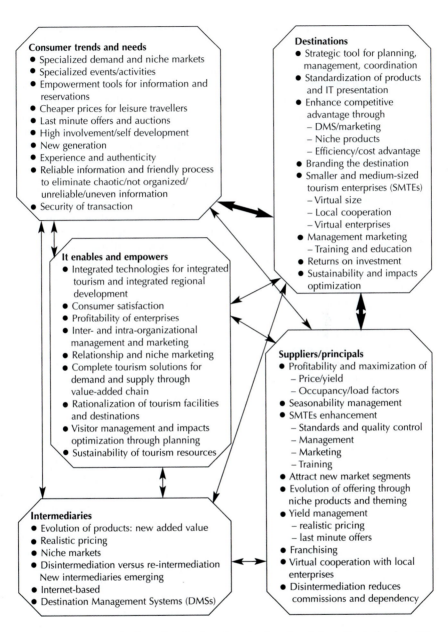

Fig. 5.2. User requirements for the rationalization of tourism based on information technology (IT).

tling their accounts or will happily give their credit card details to strangers over the phone or on a fax in order to purchase products and services. However, they are often reluctant to provide credit card details in a much more secure, encrypted electronic transaction which is often fully automated.

It is reported that electronic intermediaries such as Expedia and Travelocity had not experienced any security problems despite selling more than one million tickets online. To the degree that credit card companies improve the security of transactions and to the degree that consumers will start purchasing goods on the Internet, the security concerns will decrease rapidly.

Implications for tourism suppliers and small and medium-sized tourism enterprises

A wide range of opportunities and challenges emerge for smaller and medium-sized tourism enterprises (SMTEs) and destinations. Traditionally the vast majority of tourism suppliers are small, and hence can have enormous difficulties in marketing their products globally and competing with their larger counterparts (Buhalis, 1994; WTO, 1995d; Buhalis and Cooper, 1998; Buhalis and Main, 1998). The development of the Internet also empowers even tiny tourism organizations and destinations to be represented in the electronic marketplace and to network with consumers and partners alike. IT facilitates the amalgamation of independently produced products and enables the delivery of seamless tourism experiences. Hence, innovative entrepreneurs who appreciate the power of the new media and design and support a suitable presence in the electronic marketplace will be able to compete on an equal footing with some of their larger competitors. At the micro-level, tourism suppliers/principals will maximize their long-term profitability through yield management, networking and developing value-added chains and by enhancing virtual cooperations locally.

They may also be able to achieve competitive advantages if they manage to position niche products as unique and authentic. Enhancing the professionalism of SMTEs by marketing and management training will enable smaller companies to cooperate and compete by developing their knowledge as well as virtual size. Increasingly, the quality of service and the ability to differentiate tourism products depend on the level IT usage, as enterprises which take advantage of the emerging IT tools are able to interact closely with their consumers and adapt to new demands by constantly updating their tourism products. Using IT, the industry can create seamless experiences through developing ad hoc partnerships with local suppliers. Identifying niche markets through IT and packaging and distributing customized products also enable tourism organizations to differentiate their offerings and provide suitable products for niche markets at premium prices. IT tools are therefore instrumental in enabling tourism organizations to achieve competitive advantages. Failure to take advantage of the emerging technology may equally lead to competitive disadvantages, when organizations fail to adapt to change and to provide facilities and services offered by competitors. Only organizations which offer instantaneous, flexible and customized tourism products will be able to succeed in the global marketplace. Hence, IT changes the best operational practices in the industry rapidly and enables innovative operators to take advantage of the emerging tools.

Implications for tourism destinations and the public sector

Destinations emerge as umbrella brands, which will incorporate all local suppliers in the region (Buhalis, 2000). The public sector has traditionally played an instrumental role in planning, coordinating and marketing the destination and is expected to take advantage of the emerging IT tools and enhance the competitiveness of destinations as a whole. IT will also need to re-engineer the planning, management and marketing of destinations by operating a decision support mechanism which will focus on existing issues, legislation and markets and at the same time use complex forecasting mechanisms to assess future scenarios and demonstrate the best alternative decision for all stakeholders. IT should also provide essential 'info-structure' for the networking of all local enterprises and enhancing regional development. This can only be achieved by using IT to integrate regional economies in order to support the maximization of economic multipliers as well as the optimization of tourism impacts. Sustainability and redevelopment of resources will also need to be monitored and reinforced through IT applications. Destination marketing needs to focus on SMTEs and to ensure that they are well represented in the electronic marketplace (Buhalis, 1993, 1994).

One of the latest IT developments in the tourism industry is the proliferation of destination-oriented systems (Archdale *et al.*, 1992; Buhalis, 1993, 1997; Sheldon, 1993). Destinations are recognized as 'the raison d'être' for tourism and as amalgams of resources, products, facilities and services comprising the 'total tourism product' or the 'travel experience'. Destination Management Systems (DMSs) score heavily over CRSs for remote, insular and less developed destinations which attract a large number of independent tourists. In addition, DMSs can be suitable for destinations which cannot achieve adequate prices due to the domination of inclusive tour visitors and the purchasing power of tour operators.

The DMS concept can be taken a step forward to formulate an ideal and perhaps near utopian system, which could revolutionize all aspects of destination management as well as integrate all tourism actors at the local level. Destination Integrated Computerized Information Reservation Management Systems (DICIRMSs) address the entire range of needs and services required by both tourism enterprises and consumers for specific destinations. Although various elements proposed for these systems already exist in some DMSs, currently no operational DMS provides such a comprehensive and integrated service to its users. As far as economic benefits are concerned, DICIRMSs are instrumental in promoting diagonal integration at the destination level while they play a pivotal role to the disintermediation of the industry and the empowerment of principals in their intra-channel negotiations with intermediaries. Increasingly, however, it becomes evident that DICIRMSs will be unable to provide long-term competitive advantages for destinations unless constant innovation accompanies their development and operation, because most destinations will eventually utilize these systems. Instead DICIRMSs would be instrumental in assisting destinations and SMTEs to avoid competitive disadvantages by rival regions which utilize similar systems. In addition, DICIRMSs would enable destinations and SMTEs to bridge their distance with consumers enhancing their intrachannel power and their ability to negotiate with intermediaries. Being able to think strategically and take advantage of the opportunities emerging through the technological revolution is a prerequisite for achieving the described strategic benefits for both destinations and SMTEs. Education and training on strategic marketing and information technology in combination with development of vision for destinations will effectively determine the degree of benefits a destination will achieve. DICIRMSs emerge as a complementary distribution channel and as strategic tool to re-establish equity in the allocation of power and profit margins between distribution channel members. They also enable a host population to maximize positive tourism impacts (Buhalis, 1993, 1994, 1995, 1997).

Implications for travel intermediaries: travel agencies and tour operators

The Internet is also expected to change the role of tourism intermediaries; travel agencies and tour operators in particular (Kärcher, 1997; Wardell, 1998). Travel agencies have been the major brokers of tourism services and the interface of the industry with consumers. However, to the degree that the Internet empowers consumers to develop and purchase their own itineraries, the future of travel agencies becomes questionable, unless they take advantage of the new tools and re-engineer their processes. The recent commission capping by airlines around the world reinforces this statement and demonstrates clearly that unless intermediaries add value to the tourism product they will gradually lose market share as more consumers begin purchasing tourism products directly from suppliers.

Travel intermediaries will need to enhance their core competencies and concentrate on their travel advisers' role, providing expertise and saving time for consumers. In addition, they will be able to use sophisticated IT tools both to enhance the value of the tourism product and also to reduce the cost for their clientele. These trends are already evident in the business travel section, where the majority of agencies offer their counselling service for a fee rather than commissions on bookings. They should also concentrate on the human element, providing customized advice and assistance. For leisure tourism, travel agencies will also be able to enhance their competitiveness by offering cost reductions through vertical integration and buying in bulk from tour operators and suppliers.

Traditional travel agencies, therefore, will need to re-assess the situation and decide which market segment to concentrate on. Adequate equipment, training and service will be of paramount importance in order to maintain their competitiveness in the long term. Travel agencies will need to transform from booking offices to travel managers and advisers, as well as to add value to the travelling experience. Two strategic directions can therefore be followed: Travel agencies can either offer differentiation value, by designing high quality personalized travel arrangements which consumers will be willing to pay a premium for, or they can offer cost value by delivering less expensive products than their competitors, through standardization, high volume and consolidators. These two strategies will probably dominate travel agency offerings in the future. In addition, intermediaries can develop their Internet interfaces and enhance their presence in the electronic market. This is evident for a few companies such as Thomas Cook or TUI who are re-engineering their interfaces to enhance efficiency, maintain their clientele and enlarge their target markets internationally.

Different market segments will use different distribution channels for selecting and purchasing their tourism products. For example, people of an older generation and those who travel infrequently will probably continue purchasing tourism products from traditional travel agencies. However, business and frequent travellers may use on-line providers to arrange their itineraries and eventually purchase their tickets. This will depend on the security of Internet transactions; the reliability and quality of the information available on the Internet; and the convenience of the entire process. It is therefore critical for each travel intermediary to undertake a thorough analysis of their

strengths and weaknesses and develop their offerings to take advantage of the emerging IT opportunities.

Conclusions – IT Trends and Implications for Tourism

The above analysis clearly demonstrates that tourism marketing is constantly evolving, taking advantage of emerging IT tools to empower tourism marketing and management by providing cost effective tools for organizations and destinations to target appropriate market segments and to develop strategic tools. They also support the interactivity between tourism enterprises and consumers and as a result they re-engineer the entire process of developing, managing and marketing tourism products and destinations. It needs to be recognized that IT can contribute to both sides of the balance sheet as both opportunities and threats emerge from their use. Therefore, a thorough and realistic cost and benefit analysis is required by all tourism organizations in order to appreciate their position and the best action to take in order to enhance their competitiveness.

Several key trends drive the utilization of IT in tourism. The availability of new and more powerful IT tools empowers both suppliers and destinations to improve their efficiency and re-engineer their communication strategies. Increasingly IT will provide the 'info-structure' for the entire industry and will take over all the mechanistic aspects of tourism transactions. As a result, innovative tourism enterprises will have the ability to divert their resources and expertise into servicing their consumers and providing higher value added in the transactions. Consumers will be much more sophisticated and experienced and therefore they will be much more difficult to please. However, the emerging new technologies also pose threats for tourism enterprises. To the degree that location becomes much less important, global competition will expand rapidly and only innovative and flexible organizations will survive. In particular, SMTEs will need to enhance their understanding of IT in order to design and promote niche products, increase their virtual size and compete with large and powerful competitors and partners in the distribution channel. Travel intermediaries, and in particular travel agencies and tour operators, are already threatened by disintermediation as principals develop direct relationships with consumers and bypass them. This has led to commission capping and the introduction of special offers being available directly to the public only by electronic means. Intermediaries will increasingly need to refocus their operations on the added value offered to consumers rather than the mechanistic procedures of product searches and reservations.

Certain prerequisites are applicable for achieving success. Long-term planning and strategy as well as top management commitment will be needed to ensure that IT developments are dealt with at the strategic planning and management level of tourism enterprises. A rational management and marketing strategy needs to ensure that up to date IT tools are used, while investment in capable human resources should be a priority. Training throughout the business hierarchy will need to ensure not only that all employees are competent users of the emerging IT systems but that they can also develop commitment in using these innovative methods for communicating and interacting. IT applications will generate a paradigm shift in the tourism industry which will transform the best business practices and redefine the role and the competitiveness of all tourism enterprises and destinations. Hence, a thorough re-engineering of all business processes needs to ensure that tourism organizations do not simply automate, but that they redesign all interfaces and interactions with stakeholders. The emerging IT-based tools require constant innovation, investment in human resources and the development of a strategic vision and commitment. Intellect will be critical for the success of tourism enterprises and destinations and for their ability to develop their competitiveness using IT in the new millennium.

Acknowledgement

Several issues and ideas reported were discussed during the IFITT workshop: *Open issues and challenges in tourism and IT, Workshop toward a White Paper in Tourism and IT, Innsbruck, 21–22 September 1998* and during the ENTER conferences. For more information, access:
http://www.ifitt.org/ and
http://www.ifitt.org/enter/

6

Race and Ethnicity in Leisure Studies

Ray Hutchison

Introduction

The US population is more diverse now than at any time in its history. Almost everyone is aware of census projections suggesting that some time in the next two decades the number of people of African-American, Hispanic/Latino-American, Asian-American and Native American descent will surpass the white population in the US. Despite widespread public concern and often inflammatory political rhetoric, the Bush administration twice passed legislation increasing the number of people admitted as legal immigrants to the US each year – an important victory for the US Chamber of Commerce and other business interests. But it is important to note that changes in racial and ethnic composition are affected more by demographic forces such as family size and rate of natural population increases than by public policy. Even if immigration from Mexico were halted tomorrow, the Mexican-origin population in the US would still double in size over the next two decades, easily surpassing the African-American population as the largest minority group. Although numerically much smaller, the same demographic trends would result in a doubling of the Asian-American population as well.

This surely is one of the most profound demographic transitions in the nation's history. It is reasonable to ask, then, how is this trend reflected in research in leisure and recreation studies? There has been some recognition of the significance of this change, especially in studies commenting upon the changing demands for the management of leisure and recreation in public parks and recreation programmes and, to a lesser degree, in the management of other leisure and recreation programmes (museums, arboretums and the like). Just as managers of leisure and recreation facilities have focused on the potential impacts of a changing ethnic and racial composition of their client population, it is reasonable to expect scholarship in leisure studies to stay abreast of current important changes not only in the broader population groups that we study, but also with developments in complementary fields which study these groups.

In this chapter, we examine how the growing diversity of the US population is reflected in current research. But this poses another perhaps equally important question: How does research in leisure studies reflect changes which have taken place in the field of race and ethnicity? This field has seen substantial growth over the last decade, spurred by the development of new paradigms in response to the growing diversity of American society. Two trends are evident from even a cursory look at recent scholarship in the major journals: little attention has been given to changes in the ethnic composition of the population, and current research has overlooked emerging theoretical perspectives in race and ethnic relations (often described as a paradigm shift; see Omi and Winant, 1994).

Recent Trends in Leisure and Recreation Studies

Over the last decade there has been widespread acknowledgement of the important changes in the ethnic and racial composition of the US population, and of various programmes to incorporate diversity into academic programmes, scholarly research, the workplace and various public arenas (such as participation in public recreation activities). But these changes have found only modest reflection in published studies. A review of studies of race and ethnicity in leisure and recreation studies published in 1988 noted that: (i) there were few studies of the leisure and recreation activities of different groups; (ii) most studies focused on differences between blacks and whites and overlooked other (rapidly growing) ethnic groups in the US population; and (iii) published research did not reflect current scholarship in the field of race and ethnic relations. In that review, Hutchison (1988, p. 11) wrote that

> Problems of producing a coherent body of research are compounded by the lack of a unified theoretical framework for interpreting differences between whites, blacks, and other ethnic minority groups. Most published studies utilize the marginality and ethnicity perspectives developed by Washburne [1978] which questions whether differences in participation are due to the cultural characteristics of particular minority groups or to the social position they occupy in the dominant society.

What has changed over the last decade?

There continues to be little research on race and ethnicity within leisure studies

While the US population has become more diverse, this is not reflected in scholarship in the field. The tables of contents for four major journals in the field (*Journal of Leisure Research*, *Journal of Park and Recreation Administration*, *Leisure Science* and *Society and Natural Resources*) over the last 10 years include fewer than 30 studies with a specific focus on race and ethnicity. This presents us with an average of less than one study per year in each journal. In many of these studies, race and ethnicity is simply a residual category – an independent variable that appears on a survey instrument without specific definition or discussion (as discussed below, the ways in which ethnic and racial categories are created and the assignment of population groups to these categories is a major area of discussion in race and ethnic relations, but this topic is given little attention in our research studies). Even with these studies included in the total, research trends cannot be said to reflect the broader population changes taking place in society at large. This is not simply a matter of political correctness, as some might presuppose, nor is there a magic number to signify that the research has matched population totals. Indeed, these sorts of considerations serve only to trivialize the importance of race and ethnicity within a multiracial society such as the US. More than any other area of study in the social sciences, it is imperative that leisure and recreation studies recognize the meaning and significance of race and ethnicity in everyday life, and in the everyday activities of the many different ethnic and racial groups within our increasingly diverse society.

Most studies focus on differences between blacks and whites in the US population

The emphasis on difference among ethnic and racial groups may be traced back to the assimilationist theory of Robert Park and the Chicago School (Omi and Winant, 1994), which suggests that differences between ethnic groups and the dominant (white) culture will disappear as these groups are assimilated into mainstream culture. Although this perspective has been thoroughly dismissed in race and ethnic studies (as noted more than a decade ago; Hutchison, 1988), research studies continue to look for differences between the leisure and recreation activities and preferences of white and black groups. I recently reviewed a manuscript which examined the meanings given to and preferences for the natural environment, with multivariate analyses of variance among two sets of semantic differential measures for forest environment and environmental setting preferences – in other words, a typical study utilizing race as an independent variable to explain differences on various dependent measures. Across twelve different measures, there were statistically significant differences among white, black and Hispanic respondents on only two measures. Still, the original title of the manuscript was 'Ethnic/racial *differences* among meanings and preferences ... ' (my emphasis). I have reviewed many manuscripts which retain similar titles despite the authors' research findings that there are few differences in the activities of the groups they compared. It is striking that contemporary research continues to emphasize differences among ethnic and racial groups even when the research suggests how few differences exist among these groups (see Arnold and Shinew, 1998; Johnson and Bowker, 1999).

Some studies have sought to apply a race/class analysis of white–black behaviour, based upon the work of William J. Wilson. In *The Declining Significance of Race*, Wilson (1980) suggests that social class is a more important determinant of economic and social opportunity than is racial status *per se*. Because of common experiences in the educational system and work environment, middle-class blacks (or Hispanics) are more like middle-class whites (or Asians) than they are like lower-class blacks. There is an analogy to the statistical theory that underlies analysis of variance: the amount of variation within any particular ethnic/racial group is greater than the variance between groups. Race matters, but it is not the sole determinant of attitudes or behaviour. While there are important implications of this class-based theory for leisure and recreation studies, few studies look at the intersections of race, ethnicity and social class as these background variables might

influence individual experiences with and attitudes toward various leisure and recreation activities.

Studies continue to overlook other (rapidly growing) ethnic groups in the US

There is a small but growing body of research on Hispanic/Latino groups (see Irwin *et al.*, 1990; Carr and Williams, 1993), but these remain few, and by and large they suffer from many of the same problems identified with studies of African Americans: ethnicity is usually simply a categorical designation which may not be related to the outcomes being studied, and the basic parameters of the research follow an assimilationist model long discredited in race and ethnic relations. Research on other groups such as Asian Americans is, for all practical purposes, nonexistent. Ethnic differences may in fact be greatest between these new immigrant populations and other groups, and so we have missed an opportunity to examine important ethnic, racial and cultural influences on leisure and recreation activity.

Published research does not reflect current scholarship in race and ethnic relations

Class-based theories following the work of Wilson (1980) and others represent an important advance over earlier studies which seemed to assume that differences should exist among individuals occupying different ethnic or racial categories. As noted earlier, few leisure and recreation studies have adopted this approach; many continue to assume that whites and blacks (for example) occupy homogeneous social positions and any differences between groups can be explained by ethnic/racial/cultural differences among these groups. But even this class-based theory does not reflect current research in the field. As described in Omi and Winant's seminal work, *Racial Formation in the United States*, theories of race and ethnicity have gone through several paradigm shifts in the last century, including the assimilationist paradigm of Robert Park and the Chicago School and the class-based theory of W.J. Wilson (Omi and Winant, 1994). Omi and

Winant introduced a new theoretical paradigm based upon the process of racial formation, or the ways in which government policies and institutions serve to develop and then implement racial classifications.

More recent work has introduced other paradigms, the most important of which is variously labelled as ethnic identity, ethnic politics or ethnic representation. In this view, subordinated groups must resist their positioning as 'others' or 'minorities' and construct alternative identities as part of a politics of position or opposition (M. Cruz, personal communication, 1999). This requires a theoretical base which challenges the hegemonic world view of the dominant society based upon an understanding of shared social and cultural spaces and identities. The dominant culture, for example, may portray minority communities as disorganized, and minority families as unable to provide the appropriate cultural tools for their children. The ethnic or racial community needs to oppose these identities and forge new identities which recognize the role of local community structures and the importance of family and kinship structures within the community. Oboler's (1995) excellent study, *Ethnic Labels, Latino Lives: Identity and the Politics of (Re)Presentation in the United States*, presents these issues in her study of the construction of Hispanic ethnicity, including a discussion of the rise of the Chicano and Puerto Rican movements in the 1960s (an effort to establish an ethnic identity different from that given by mainstream society), ethnic and class differences within the Latino community, and the ways in which personal and social identities are affected by the myth of Hispanic homogeneity. The emergent racial theories form a significant challenge to scholars who wish to bring the importance of ethnic/racial differences into the study of everyday life.

An Overview of Recent Research Studies

While the basic trends found in recent studies have been noted above, looking at individual studies to see how these trends are represented within the scholarly journals is useful. Ironically, because of the paucity of attention given to this important topic, it is possible to note virtually all such studies in just a few short pages.

As noted above, most leisure studies of race and ethnicity include race simply as an independent variable, in conceptual terms no different from other variables such as class, gender or place of residence. Race or ethnicity is determined by the respondents' self-identification or reported category. There is no effort to discover an intervening causal variable which might link this background status with the preference or behaviour being studied and there is no discussion of how the preference or behaviour might serve to reinforce the beliefs or values of the ethnic subculture. Among the studies that offer this sort of comparison between blacks and whites are Johnson and Bowker (1999), Bowker and Leeworthy (1998) and Murdock *et al.* (1991). Other studies extend this comparison to include Hispanics, and in these studies there is at least some effort to provide a measure of 'cultural assimilation' which might be linked the behaviour or preference being studied. Carr and Williams (1993) and Shaull and Graham (1998) use a measure of English language familiarity to determine the level of cultural assimilation among their respondents. While this might appear to be the intervening causal variable missing from studies of other populations, it takes the basic assumptions from the now discredited assimilation model, which assumes that ethnic or racial minority populations will change their beliefs, preferences and behaviours as they become more like whites. Floyd *et al.* (1994, 1995) use both race and ethnicity to explore leisure preferences. While this is presented within the familiar 'ethnicity versus marginality' model, there is no measure of ethnic identification or discussion of how this would influence leisure preferences (in other words, if differences exist between whites and blacks that are not explained by social class or marginality, then these differences must be due to ethnicity or race).

A number of studies examine attitudinal and preference structures of various ethnic communities, such as Jones' (1998) discussion of African-American concern for the environment, Toth and Brown's (1997) study of racial differences in the meaning people give to recreational fishing, and Phillip's (1998b) study of race, gender and leisure benefits. Although these studies deal with a particular ethnic population and often provide contrasts with other (usually white) groups, they do little to explain how race or ethnicity may be related to specific attitudes or beliefs. There are no measures of ethnic or racial identity to link attitude or preference with ethnic background. One group of studies which has produced a consistent research finding involved environmental preferences for wilderness or developed recreation settings. Dwyer and Hutchison (1990) reported that African Americans prefer developed facilities while whites preferred wilderness settings. Phillip (1993) reported that whites ranked wilderness scenes as more attractive than blacks. Floyd et al. (1995) found that whites rated wildland activities higher than blacks. Irwin et al. (1990) and Bass et al. (1993) reported that Mexican Americans rated characteristics of developed recreation settings (such as parking spaces, picnic tables and toilets) more highly than did whites. While some logical theoretical explanations have been advanced for these differences (members of particular minority groups have not been socialized into wilderness activities in the same way as whites, for example), it is not at all clear that these research findings are related to specific ethnic or racial characteristics, as opposed to the consequence of urban residence, lower rates of participation in wilderness programmes as adolescents, or lack of opportunity due to work schedules, holiday benefits and lower levels of family income.

A limited number of studies have examined the cultural values and beliefs of specific minority populations, such as Hill et al.'s (1999) study of ecosystem management issues involving aboriginal groups in Queensland, and Langholz' (1998) study of rainforest use by Mayan Indians in Guatemala. In each instance, the studies deal with ethnic or racial minority populations within the respective country. While one could imagine a set of complementary studies here in the US (with studies of ecosystem management issues involving Native Americans), many researchers seem to think such issues are relevant only when they involve aboriginal groups. In reality, we need to expand our current research by recognizing the great diversity of ethnic and racial populations, and by identifying ethnic subcultures and values which are related to leisure and recreation preferences, activities, and the like.

Most studies published over the last decade have assumed that the ethnic and racial groups studied will have different behaviours (or preferences or beliefs) from the larger white population. It should be of some importance, then, to note that relatively few studies have discovered systematic differences among groups: Johnson et al. (1998) and Arnold and Shinew (1998) found no differences between their black and white respondents; Floyd et al. (1994) found no differences between middle-class white and black respondents; and Dargitz (1988) found no differences in fishing activity between whites and blacks. While Busser et al. (1996) report differences in outdoor activity participation for black and white adolescents, they do not discover differences for five other activity groupings, including personal growth, arts, nontraditional sports/games, community activities or sports activities. Phillip (1998b) does find differences in the peer group approval for 10 of 20 leisure activities by black and white adolescents, but, even in what appears to be an unambiguous research finding, for half the activities studied there were no differences.

Johnson and Bowker (1999) show no differences in black–white consumption activities (such as fishing and hunting), but do discover differences in nonconsumption activities such as camping and hiking. Apparently believing that all groups should be identical in their recreational pursuits, they conclude that managers need to attract more African Americans for forest-based outdoor recreation. Gobster (1998) provides a very different conclusion in his study of minority golfing. Indeed, this is one of the very few studies which breaks with the dominant assimilationist paradigm which views any differences between whites and blacks (or other groups), with the obvious policy implication that ethnic or racial minorities should behave the same as whites. Gobster's interviews with 35 focus groups in Chicago revealed that few African Americans had ever participated in golf (although the city has several black golf courses). He wisely suggests that the concept of equity be explored by managers: that is, it may not be necessary to expect that blacks (or Hispanics) will participate in the same activities at the same level as whites. Instead, managers should achieve an optimal mix of park and recreation programmes and services; these programmes and services will be likely to be different depending on the group served.

Implications

In an earlier review of leisure–recreation research on race, ethnicity and social class, Hutchison (1988, p. 10) presented three recommendations for future research: (i) definitions of basic concepts such as race and ethnicity must conform to their accepted meanings in race and ethnic relations; (ii) ethnic differences must be demonstrated by intervening measures of ethnic subculture; and (iii) future research must be expanded to consider the activities of other (white and nonwhite) ethnic subgroups. Given the increasing diversity of ethnic and racial populations within the US and the continuing paradigm shift in the study of race and ethnic relations, these seem reasonable and useful recommendations even with the hindsight of some 10 years. How can our continuing research on race and ethnicity meet these goals?

Definitions of basic concepts such as race and ethnicity must conform to their accepted meanings in race and ethnic relations

As described above, there has been an important paradigm shift in the study of race and ethnic relations. This shift has been away from the earlier assimilation approach which suggested that minority groups would, over time, take on the attitudes and behaviours of the dominant group. Wilson's (1978) work suggested that many of the differences between white and black groups may be due to social class rather than to race *per se*, and for much of the 1980s and 1990s this interpretive framework was used in leisure and recreation research (as in other areas of the social sciences). At the beginning of the 21st century, however, the field is confronted with another paradigm shift which challenges earlier notions of the basic definitions of race and ethnicity. Identity theory or identity politics argues that these are simply socially constructed categories which reflect the interests of various groups and dominant social institutions.

Although often presented as an oppositional approach to the study of race and ethnic relations, there is a great deal of overlap among competing theories. Anthropologists and sociologists have long argued that racial categories are not biologically determined, but instead are defined in specific ways by different cultures. Clearly, various ethnic or racial groups may accept or reject the definitions placed upon them by the dominant group. These actions establish the basis for furthering group identity, organizing political power and demanding recognition of group interests. It may make more sense to view theoretical developments in the field on a continuum which expands our understanding of the various meanings of race and ethnicity in contemporary society, rather than necessarily competing or oppositional theories.

Having said this, these theoretical developments clearly create a serious challenge for applied areas of study such as leisure and recreation research. How are we to define and operationalize race and ethnicity in our research if these are categories which are simply constructed by government agencies or utilized by the groups themselves for ethnic mobilization – neither of which necessarily reflects the way in which ethnic and racial identities and subcultural values and beliefs might actually influence behaviour? Our research cannot simply ignore these important theoretical developments; whether we use government data which has defined ethnic/racial categories in certain racialized ways (Omi and Winant, 1994) or use survey data where we have asked respondents to indicate their ethnic or racial background, we have placed ourselves in the midst of a fascinating and continuing debate. Leisure and recreation studies which use race or ethnic background as independent variables to explain differences among groups must include a discussion of this new paradigm. Studies which utilize census definitions and census data must acknowledge that the results are limited by racial formulations constructed by dominant social institutions (government agencies such as the census bureau, state and federal courts which are called upon to authenticate racial identities, schools which assign students to specific racial categories, and park managers who design programmes around the assumed preferences of different ethnic or racial groups). Most importantly, there is no reason to believe *prima facia* that these racial categories have any direct association with individual preferences or with leisure or recreation behaviour.

Ethnic differences must be demonstrated by intervening measures of ethnic subculture

The typical study compares the leisure and recreation activities of different ethnic and racial groups, and then controls for social class and other background variables before pronouncing whether the observed differences are due to marginality (social class), ethnicity (racial or ethnic background) or some combination of the two. We must recognize that, in most instances, this is a reductionist approach, and probably a dangerous one at that. If observed differences between groups cannot be explained by various background differences, we then assume the differences are due to the racial or ethnic backgrounds reflected in the categories to which groups have been assigned (these are the categories which have been constructed by the racial formulations of the dominant culture).

Research in race and ethnic relations, on the other hand, includes a variety of studies which look at the ethnic/racial identity of groups and individuals, asking the degree to which groups in fact have identifiable differences and whether individuals identify with the larger group identity. These studies would suggest that ethnic and racial identity exists more on a continuum than as a discrete category; some African Americans, for example, identify strongly with an African cultural heritage while others do not. (Although identification with a particular ethnic heritage may not in fact mean these individuals would behave any differently from someone who rejects this ethnic heritage.) In other words, observed differences among ethnic or racial groups should not be attributed to their ethnic background unless we have first identified an intervening measure of ethnic subculture.

While measures of assimilation have been used in several studies comparing the activity of Hispanic groups (Shaull and Gramann, 1998), even these are at odds with broader developments in race and ethnic relations, where references to 'assimilation' were replaced by 'acculturation' more than two decades ago. Once again, this is not simply a matter of meaningless semantics or political correctness. Assimilation privileges the position of the dominant group by assuming that other (minority) groups wish to and eventually will become indistinguishable from the white population, while acculturation assumes that ethnic populations may adapt and change some aspects of the dominant culture while rejecting others. It is important to note that these intervening measures of acculturation have been used in studies of Hispanics, but not for African Americans and other groups, where scholars still seem to assume that membership in a particular ethnic or racial group determines one's behaviour and values.

These examples also demonstrate the truncated understanding of race and difference in the US. As noted above, studies of leisure behaviour in Great Britain have looked at how leisure and recreation define and structure racial identities and racial interaction – a very different understanding of race from that found in studies in the US.

One of the few studies published in the US which makes use of this broader construction of the ways in which leisure activities interact with and reinforce ethnic and racial identity is Bialeschki and Walbert's (1998) historical study of Southern women textile workers in the pre-war years. There is considerable room for considering the ways that leisure and recreation activities may define or reinforce ethnic identities: urban parks in many cities include bocce ball courts, a common recreational activity among first and second generation Italian immigrants; soccer leagues are often organized around specific ethnic groups (such as the Central and South American [CASA] soccer league in Chicago); and participation in dance classes and competitions allows individuals to lay claim to and reinforce ethnic identities (whether Irish clogging and folk dancing or African dance and drumming).

Future research must be expanded to consider the activities of other (white and nonwhite) ethnic subgroups

Within the broad field of leisure and recreation studies, the attitudes and behaviours of various ethnic and race groups is barely a blip on the radar screen. As noted above, over the last decade there has been an average of one study each year published in the major journals – a very disappointing commentary on the field given the increased diversity of American society. This diversity suggests the need for studies of leisure and recreation activity among new ethnic communities – such as the 250,000 Filipinos living in the Chicago metropolitan community, the 300,000 Salvadorans living in the Los Angeles area and the 250,000 persons from the Dominican Republic living in the New York metropolitan area. Each of these groups have very different ethnic heritages and, one might believe, very different leisure and recreation activities. Perhaps these activities have comparable meanings and outcomes for each group – that in itself would be a major research finding – or it may be that these activities serve very different purposes within their local cultures. Again, expanding our research agenda to include new immigrant populations is not simply a matter of political correctness, but instead a powerful recognition of the diversity of American society. The current research agenda in leisure and recreation studies reinforces the mistaken idea that the US is a society of white and black, and that African Americans and other ethnic and racial minorities must identify with and participate in the same activities as whites to achieve cultural assimilation. Seen in this light, our research remains decades behind the paradigm shift and cultural understanding of the parent field.

A Concluding Note

The Kemer Commission Report highlighted the lack of recreational opportunities for young adults in central cities as a contributing factor in the race riots that swept across the urban landscape in 1964 and again in 1968. It is probably fortunate that our scholarly work does not have the same effect on individual or group behaviour, because the lack of research on this topic is just as glaring as the (continued) lack of opportunity for inner city youth. Just as in the broader society, our discipline requires a new commitment to better describe and understand the leisure worlds and recreation activities of the many different groups that now are part of the American mosaic.

For people interested in the broader meaning of race and ethnicity for leisure studies, one of the more fascinating areas of study within the burgeoning (or bursting) area of cultural studies is that of museum studies and tourism – particularly the critical analysis of how race and ethnicity may be used to market particular groups for consumption as museum or tourist oddities. This often requires the sanitization of the actual lived experiences of the ethnic or racial minority. In Hawaii, former sugar plantations – the site of labour exploitation of Japanese workers paralleling the slave plantations of the Old South – have been converted to luxury resort theme parks for Japanese tourists; and at Charleston, South Carolina, the old slave auction house has been restored and has become a focal point for both white and black tourists. Hollinshead (1998) notes that because tourism is based upon constructions of 'difference' and 'the other,' and is important for scholars to discover the ethnocentric views of people, places and historical pasts which are presented in everyday performative activities. Waitt (1999) studies how Australia's indigenous people have been marketed as 'hunter-gatherers' for the tourist industry, reinforcing the racial stereotypes of European as well as Asian tourists. A similar analysis could be carried out in the Twelve Pueblos area of New Mexico as well as other Indian reservations in the US. Such a study of tourism (a common leisure behaviour) is relevant to the study of race and ethnic relations in several respects, and here we can see how cultural analysis moves beyond the simple categorization of respondents within racial categories: in order to attract white tourists, who are used to thinking of Native Americans and American Indian culture in the past tense, 'traditional' arts and crafts are revived and marketed. Tourists are encouraged to participate and help fund this ethnic revival by purchasing objects to display in their homes. This process also acts to reinforce the ethnic culture (Native American artists and craftspeople can continue to produce these cultural objects) and may also help Indian tribes to preserve their culture (the proceeds may be used to fund tribal schools which teach the native language to younger members). In such ways leisure and recreation behaviours are influenced by, and reinforce, ethnic and racial difference. It is to this broader understanding of the interaction and influence of race and ethnicity in everyday life experience – not simply as categories for multivariate analysis – that leisure studies must aspire.

Part II

Resources: What Exists and How Did We Reach This Point

———————————————

7

Trends in Outdoor Recreation Supply on Public and Private Lands in the US

H. Ken Cordell and Carter J. Betz

The vast majority of the research pertaining to outdoor recreation trends in the US addresses the demand or use side of the picture. This makes it very difficult to track supply trends when planning for future programmes or investments. This chapter attempts to bring a little balance to this often one-sided picture of the outdoor recreation situation in the US. Provided here is an up-to-date national summary of the current status and recent trends in outdoor recreation supply. It is based primarily on the just released Renewable Resources Planning Act (RPA) Assessment in which the US Department of Agriculture (USDA) Forest Service provided a comprehensive national assessment of outdoor recreation demand and supply trends. This recent assessment was published under the title, *Outdoor Recreation in American Life* (Cordell, 1999). A number of other sources were also consulted to meet specific needs for information and these will be referenced where they are used in this chapter.

A Brief History of Recreation Supply in the US

The US has been blessed with abundant land and water, and generally a richness of natural resources. In the early years of this country, land and water were exploited for whatever profit or power they would yield. They were not viewed as aesthetic resources or recreation opportunities. They were viewed as commercial and industrial opportunities, as a direct means for subsistence, and sometimes even as obstacles to growth, development and progress. At the turn of the 20th century, however, this exploitive view of natural resources began to change. Those among the rising leisure class began to see natural land and water as amenities. Cities began to provide playgrounds, parks and limited leisure services. Train and automobile tours of 'wilderness' areas were privately provided for the wealthy (Douglass, 1999). Resorts and private summer or ski retreats for the very wealthy were being developed at a rapid pace. But in the first half of the 20th century, America was still mostly rural and agrarian. Many among its working class had little interest in recreating in the same out-of-doors where they had just been labouring.

Many early federal and state initiatives to establish systems of public lands were not motivated by causes or concerns about providing sufficient outdoor recreation opportunities for their citizenry. For example, the establishment of the National Park System was motivated mostly by a desire to protect the resources of these areas, not by a perception that people needed a place for hiking and taking photographs. National forests were established mostly to assure a future reserve of timber, not by a need for scenic drives and places to camp. And so it was with most public land initiatives in the first half of the century. It was at the local and state government levels that a movement emerged to establish a system of parks and recreation areas to meet people's needs for recreation space and facilities. It also took the post-World War II economic boom and a cadre of enlightened parks and recreation champions to move the country firmly into an era in which supplying outdoor recreation opportunities was seen as one of the legitimate and important uses for the country's natural resources, urban and rural.

The importance of outdoor recreation in the American lifestyle grew tremendously throughout the 1950s. Noting this rapid increase in importance and the growing strains on the nation's outdoor spaces and facilities, the 85th Congress established the Outdoor Recreation Resources Review Commission (ORRRC) in 1958 to assess the upsurge in interest in outdoor recreation and report back its observations and recommendations. This first national, landmark assessment of outdoor recreation triggered unparalleled expansions in both public and private recreation resources. Among the federal expansions that occurred throughout the 1960s and 1970s were the establishment of the National Wilderness Preservation System, the National Trails System, the National Wild and Scenic Rivers System, National Recreation Areas and other national systems. As well, a highly significant piece of legislation was passed to provide funding for outdoor recreation, the Land and Water Conservation Fund (LWCF). Most of the funds authorized under the LWCF were targeted to become matching grants to state and local governments. The effects of these grants were tremendous and can never be fully measured because the 'seed-funding' effect provided by the LWCF reached far beyond the direct recipients of grants.

Throughout the 1960s, 1970s and into the 1980s, legislation at the federal level and expansion of park and recreation systems at the state and local levels fed growth of the public outdoor recreation supply system of the US (see Siehl, Chapter 8 for more details). In addition to the establishment of systems of protected and multiple-use lands, new legislation covering the mandates of federal agencies, such as the USDA Forest Service and the Bureau of Land Management (BLM), included language explicitly adding to these agencies' mandates responsibilities for providing public recreation opportunities.

As all this was happening in the public sector, the private sector was undergoing an undreamed of expansion along a broad array of venues in response to the ever-expanding US economy. From an early emphasis on resorts and tours, private sector services, facilities and areas for outdoor recreation have expanded to include water parks, guiding and outfitting services, cruises into waters previously considered wilderness, scenic overflights and a vast array of outdoor equipment and clothing.

In the limited space afforded, this chapter will attempt to examine briefly recent trends in outdoor recreation supply, i.e. since the late 1980s, when the previous national RPA assessment was done. Federal, state, local and private sector trends will be covered. This examination will show that tremendous advances in the US supply of outdoor recreation have occurred. The momentum begun in the 1950s, and accelerated by the ORRRC in 1960, is shown to be continuing, although also changing.

Methods and Data

Describing the supply situation in the US, and doing justice to its vastness and diversity, requires large amounts of data from innumerable sources, public and private. To accomplish this description for the RPA Assessment demanded of the USDA Forest Service, the acquisition of data and information from identifiable private and public sources must be ongoing. We have developed such an ongoing data system called the

National Outdoor Recreation Supply Information System (NORSIS). NORSIS is primarily a secondary source data system that includes enumeration of more than 400 supply elements from a large number of secondary sources (Betz and Cordell, 1998). County-scale data were the target for NORSIS, but where county-scale data were not available, credible sources at any available level (e.g. state, regional or national) were used. NORSIS includes federal, state, local and private sector data.

All data were cross-referenced to other sources for validation wherever possible. Most errors in secondary sources are undetectable, however, and the data must be accepted as acquired. As well, some previously available sources covering specific supply elements are no longer maintained by the source organizations or governmental agencies. This will no doubt be an increasing problem in future supply assessments where funding typically limits the assessment effort to the use of secondary sources.

The one exception to relying on secondary supply data sources in the RPA assessment is the National Private Land Owners Survey (NPLOS). NPLOS is an original data source in that it is extracted from a mail survey conducted by the authors cooperatively with the University of Georgia of a national sample of private owners of land in tracts of 4 or more ha. These data describe owner and nonowner recreational access to private rural lands across the country (Teasley et al., 1999).

Supply Trends

In this section on current supply and supply trends, we include both rural and urban outdoor recreation supply and all three levels of government – federal, state and local. As well, up to the limits of secondary data availability, we also cover the private sector, with focused coverage of private rural lands in a separate subsection. The general approach is to first describe the overall current supply for each of the public and private sectors we cover, and then identify salient trends in these sectors. In the final

section to this chapter, we report the results of an analysis of trends in supply indices that represents a composite of both public and private supply measures. These composite supply indices were developed by running principal components factor analysis across the 400+ NORSIS variables to identify the individual NORSIS variables which loaded most heavily on each factor (Betz et al., 1999).

Federal land and water

First, we describe the supply situation in the federal sector. Historically, nearly all federal land and water have been open for public outdoor recreation. Accessibility, however, varies through the presence of roads or other access facilities, the permissibility of crossing adjacent private lands to get to the public properties, availability of information for the potential public user and proximity to population centres. As noted by ORRRC, there is a significant spatial disparity between the regional location of federal land and the regional residence of most of the US population (Fig. 7.1). Although the population in the West is projected to grow faster than in the East, most federal land will still be remote for most of the US population.

There are seven primary federal resource managing agencies that either directly provide outdoor recreation opportunities or indirectly offer them through lease arrangements with state, local or nongovernmental providers. Among these, the two with the largest total surface area are the USDA Forest Service (Department of Agriculture, 77.5 million ha) and the BLM (Department of the Interior, 108.3 million ha). Together these agencies manage more than two-thirds of the 263.9 million ha of federal land and water. Both agencies operate under a philosophy of multiple-use management and both have vast tracts of undeveloped land, some very remote from population or access. In addition, these agencies provide thousands of developed recreation sites, with the USDA Forest Service providing by far the most such sites. The next largest agencies are the National Park Service (NPS) (33.7 million ha) and Fish and Wildlife Service (FWS) (36.6 million ha, both in the Department of

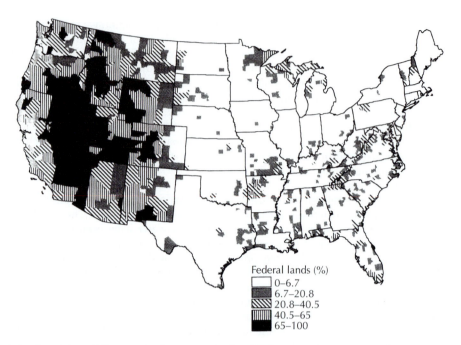

Fig. 7.1. Proportion of US county land area in Federal ownership. Source: 1992 National Resources Inventory, USDA-NRCS.

the Interior). These Interior agencies seek to balance resource protection with public recreation use. For both of them, resource protection is the overriding priority. Visitor 'enjoyment' is an explicit part of the NPS mission at the 375 managed units and affiliated areas. The FWS manages more than 500 National Wildlife Refuges, many of which are not open for public use. Public use at refuges must meet a standard of 'compatibility' with habitat and wildlife conservation management.

The US Army Corps of Engineers (Department of the Army, 4.7 million ha), Bureau of Reclamation (BoR) (Department of the Interior, 2.6 million ha), and Tennessee Valley Authority (TVA) (Independent, 476,835 ha) are commonly referred to as the big three federal water-resource agencies. Each primarily manages reservoirs and other water development projects (such as lock and dam systems) on which water-based recreation is allowed. For the most part, these projects are nearer population centres than many other federal properties. The projects of the BoR are in western states and TVA projects are

entirely in the South along the Tennessee River and its tributaries.

Two other federal recreation providers are the Department of Defense (with land area estimated at 10.1 million ha) and native Indian lands (estimated at about 22.3 million ha). Military base lands are managed for recreation by base residents for the most part, but numbers of them offer broader public access. Tribal lands are administered and managed for recreation and other uses with assistance from the Bureau of Indian Affairs (Department of the Interior). Public access and opportunities vary with each individual military installation and tribal reserve depending on the primary uses and governance of those areas.

A highly significant aspect of the federal supply of outdoor recreation is the systems of designated areas managed by several federal agencies. The Congress has constantly been adding hectares and kilometres to these systems of designated federal recreation areas. Below are shown the existing total hectares or kilometres in these systems and the percentage increases since 1987:

- National Wilderness System 41.9 million ha (+15.5%)
- National Recreation Areas 2.8 million ha (+10.7%)
- National Recreation Trails 16.1 thousand km (+14.0%)
- National Wild and Scenic Rivers 17.4 thousand km (+40.5%)

Two important new programmes that illustrate a trend towards improving the way the federal system provides opportunities for outdoor recreation are the Scenic Byways and Watchable Wildlife programmes. Undertaken as partnerships, these schemes involve a variety of federal, state, local and private collaborators and are essentially umbrella programmes that embrace numerous scenic driving and wildlife viewing opportunities. The genesis of both programmes was heavily influenced by recommendations from the President's Commission on Americans Outdoors in the mid-1980s. Since the late 1980s when the National Scenic Byway programme was started by the Federal Highway Administration, more than two dozen states have either begun or enhanced their scenic roads programmes. Federal agencies have designated many scenic byways involving roads passing at least partly through their lands.

A 1990 memorandum of understanding, coordinated by Defenders of Wildlife and involving 15 federal, state and nongovernmental groups, identified a coalition of organizations for engagement in the national watchable wildlife movement. The goal of watchable wildlife programmes is to increase public awareness, appreciation and support for wildlife. The principal elements for making the scheme work include establishment of: (i) a network of nature (wildlife, bird, fisheries and wildflower) viewing sites; (ii) a universal viewing site signing system (with the 'binocular' logo); and (iii) a series of watchable wildlife viewing guide books. Central to this programme is education through interpretive signing, guide books, festivals, walks, ranger talks and other approaches.

The Scenic Byway and Watchable Wildlife programmes are representative of the growing number and magnitude of federal, state, local and private coalitions as a new and refreshing way of addressing important outdoor recreation supply issues. Budget trends in federal agencies indicate clearly that appreciable growth in appropriated funds for agency-only management of the federal estate is highly unlikely. The recent implementation of fee programmes for administration to visitors at federal sites is never likely to produce enough revenue to address the ever rising number of issues and needs on the 263.8 million ha of federal land. In the authors' opinion, collaboration with each partner contributing whatever it can in the best way it can for the 'larger cause' will be one of the most effective strategies for continuing a sustainable supply of recreation opportunities on federal lands.

Overall, trends in the federal system of recreation supply have been mixed over the last 10–12 years. Most of the agencies have experienced constant to slightly decreasing current dollar budgets appropriated by Congress for recreation acquisition and management. Even for those experiencing increases, more funding has not turned around the shrinking amounts of funding ending up at the lowest-level administrative units where the actual resource and recreation-use management occurs. For the USDA Forest Service, for example, that would be at the ranger district level. These lower levels of 'on-the-ground' funding have been the result of higher costs and higher administrative assessments at the Washington and regional levels of most agencies.

Accompanying level-to-decreasing budgets have been reductions in professional staffing for recreation, some closures of field offices and an increase in the number of 'hats' worn by a reduced number of staff. To compensate, agencies are increasingly relying on volunteers to carry out day-to-day site maintenance and customer interface activities. As well, agencies are rapidly expanding the application of various fee structures in an attempt to generate greater revenues as one way of addressing rising management and maintenance costs. Currently, most of the federal land management agencies are piloting much expanded fee structures under special authorization from the Congress. This movement into expanded fees for federal recreation sites had been strongly resisted by the Congress for many years. And, as noted in the discussion above regarding the Scenic Byway and Watchable Wildlife programmes, federal agencies are increasingly seeking more partnerships with state and local governments and with private organizations and corporations in an attempt to share the costs and responsibilities associated with recreation and other resource management mandates. A look at budget actions on the parts of both the administration and the Congress show that unchanging or shrinking budgets are likely to continue for the federal recreation management agencies over the next few years. Coping strategies are emerging and some are very encouraging. However, the future without sound financial backing is an uncertain one.

Adjacent private land as a barrier to access to federal land

Increasingly, changing ownership and owner objectives for private land adjacent to federal lands is becoming an access issue (Peterson and Williams, 1999). More and more, landowners are closing historic access roads and sites at federal boundaries. Around the beginning of the 1990s, approximately 14% of the 186.2 million ha of forests, grasslands and deserts administered by the USDA Forest Service and the BLM lacked adequate public access as a direct result of adjacent private land access closures. Many previously maintained county roads and open private back roads have been gated or obliterated making them impassable. It appears that the percentage of federal land having inadequate access is likely to increase as land ownership goes from traditional ranching uses to private residence, resort or commercial uses. Recent data reported by the General Accounting Office confirm that this trend toward loss of access to federal properties across private lands is indeed continuing. Agency programmes to purchase or lease access rights across private properties are having only limited beneficial effects.

State government land and water

States provide important components of the overall supply of outdoor recreation opportunities in this country. States provide state parks, state forests, recreation areas, natural areas, scenic drives, historic areas and environmental education sites. Nationwide, state government ownership includes a total of about 4.8 million ha and includes 5543 areas, 90% of which are typically open for public recreation use at any one time.

Two-thirds of the overall area in state ownership is in state park systems (3.2 million ha). Although there are relatively large undeveloped areas within some of these state parks, most of them are no more than 40–80 ha in size and are much more developed than are federal lands. State parks are also typically much closer to populated areas than are the federal lands. The state parks are distributed much like the country's population, except for states in the Great Plains Region.

State forests are also significant contributors to the overall state recreation resource (around 20.2 million ha). State forests are usually managed by a state forest agency, typically a forestry commission, and have a politically appointed administrative head referred to as a state forester. State forests usually have more undeveloped area within their boundaries and by definition, the most prominent type of land cover is forest. The National Association of State Foresters report that only 23 of the 50 state forest systems nationwide are in states with an officially recognized recreation programme within the state forest agency. In these 23 states, the state forests are managed for recreation use as well as for other uses such as tree seed production and plantation forestry.

State fish and wildlife areas are a third major type of state-managed natural resources. Like state forests, these areas are usually managed by a separate fish and game agency, typically with a commission administrative structure. Fish and game areas provide mostly primitive facilities and dispersed forms of recreation, usually with an emphasis on hunting and fishing opportunities. A current national inventory of fish and game land does not exist, but the 1980 RPA Assessment estimated 3.6 million ha and the 1989 RPA Assessment estimated 5.7 million ha (Cordell *et al.*, 1990). This total area has no doubt increased since 1989. A recent article in the *Los Angeles Times* noted that fish and wildlife land in California had tripled since 1970, and the current amount in that state alone is around 334,000 ha. Thirty-two states also have river protection programmes, protecting a national total of about 21.7 thousand km of rivers from development or other exploitation.

The distribution of state recreation land and water much more closely matches the distribution of population than do federal recreation properties. In this way, the federal and state systems are highly complementary. Like the federal system, the trends for state recreation land and water have mostly shown growth. All categories of state recreation land and water have been growing in total area throughout the 1990s. There has been a 32% increase totalling 1267 new state areas available for recreation and adding almost 344,000 ha across the 50 states. With this expansion in areas, states generally are moving toward more year-round operation of their areas for day use, camping, cabin rentals and resort holidays. Lodges associated with the resorts and the revenue potential they offer have been expanding faster than most other components of state systems. Most of this expansion has occurred in state parks. In the 1990s there has been a 31% expansion in state lodges, bringing the number to more than 110 in 26 of the 50 states. A consequence of the movement of state systems to more year-round operating seasons and an elevation of the number and quality of facilities and services provided is likely to have a substantial impact on the make-up of state park clientele in the next few years.

Also like their federal cousins, state land and water systems are increasingly facing funding crises (Landrum, 1999). Unlike the federal systems, however, there was little reluctance on the part of legislative bodies to permit and even encourage greater self-sufficiency by charging more for a wider variety of services and access. From 1975 to 1995, for example, state park system revenues nationwide increased 364% and the proportion of their operating costs covered by on-site revenues increased from 35 to 43%. During this same period, legislatively appropriated funding for state parks has risen only 286%. A concern among professionals within the state systems is whether or not lower-income people are being priced out by rising fees and thus may stop using state parks and other state lands. In addition to a much expanded emphasis on increasing revenues, state systems are also looking at peripheral commercial opportunities external to the parks, partnerships for cost sharing and marketing to increase visits as ways to raise more revenue and reduce costs.

Local

Outdoor recreation sites and local parks are major components of the leisure opportunities provided by municipal, county and special district local governments. At the local level, outdoor opportunities tend to be much more developed and management more user oriented, as contrasted with federal or state lands which tend to be more undeveloped and nature oriented. Typical local outdoor sites include parks, trails, athletic fields, golf courses, tennis courts, exercise areas and playgrounds. Often, local sites and facilities are within the neighbourhoods whose citizens they serve, thus being far more accessible to a wider range of users than state or federal lands.

Many local parks are known for their passive areas and open space which provide opportunities for a variety of recreational activities. Local areas often focus on features such as lakes, jogging/cycling trails, hiking/equestrian trails, beach areas, cross country skiing/snowmobiling trails and sometimes amusement rides or athletic tracks. A 1993 study identified more than 4500 local government recreation agencies, about three-quarters of which were municipal departments, 19% of which were county agencies and about 7% were Special Recreation Districts (Beeler, 1999).

Greenways are a highly significant contribution that local government makes, especially in urban areas where green space is often scarce. Greenways are typically linear parks, often following stream courses, that provide a variety of recreation opportunities, while at the same time serving resource conservation purposes. Greenways are often the result of collaborative initiatives that have widespread grassroots support among citizens, local government and local organizations. A 1995 estimate showed more than 500 'current' developing greenway projects in the US and more than 5000 existing greenways (Searns, 1995).

Like federal and state systems, municipal and county systems are experiencing financial pressures. Finances for both capital improvements and operations are increasingly difficult to obtain. Many local systems are inadequately funded to acquire land, develop new facilities and renovate existing facilities. Many local systems face inadequate funding for administrative and programme staffing and for operating and maintaining areas and facilities, especially the newer ones. Often local governing bodies provide capital improvement funding for new projects without sufficient ongoing funding to care for these new projects. More immediately than the federal or state systems, local recreation systems directly experience the outcomes of changes of social conditions and behaviours. Crime and violence are among these changes and are increasingly a characteristic of urban life. Often, local parks are places where deviant acts are carried out, including vandalism and assault.

Generally, local government park and recreation system expansions have been favouring athletic fields, ball courts, passive recreation spaces and parks. Much less emphasis in this expansion has been put on recreation centres and water sites. The expansions in the parks 'half' of the local park and recreation systems have specifically emphasized the addition of trails, conservation areas, open space, playgrounds and more green space (Beeler, 1999).

Private sector

By all indications, the private sector is rapidly expanding in many ways its role as a supplier of outdoor recreation goods, services, travel and sites in the US. However, data describing the private sector are difficult to obtain, making this sector the one about which we know the least. Proprietary data, unkept data about small businesses and the absence of systematic database development are among the factors making it is so difficult to paint a comprehensive national picture of trends in private supply. From the variety of sources available, however, we have pieced together a reasonably sound description of some trends in private supply.

First, we examine trends in privately supplied camping grounds in the US. The source is Woodall's national campground directory. In 1987, there were 8062 private campgrounds in Woodall's listing. In 1996, this same directory with apparently no change in the criteria for listing showed only 6900 private campgrounds, a decrease of 15%. Individual campsites decreased from approximately 984,000 to 812,000 during this period. In contrast, downhill ski areas increased between 1987 and 1996. From 384 in 1987 there was a rise of 65 new areas with accompanying increases in lift capacity of 38%. Cross country skiing areas increased 51% from 421 to 636 in this same period.

Other trends are shown below and illustrate a mixed trend pattern:

- Marinas +15.2%
- Boat rentals −0.6%
- Bicycle rentals and retail outlets +69.3%
- Organized camps −22.1%
- Golf courses +39.2%
- Outfitters and guide services +48.0%

Another indication of activity and growth by the private sector is trends in sales. Based on Consumer Expenditure Surveys done by the Bureau of Labor Statistics, US consumer spending between 1985 and 1997 increased strongly (see below). The heaviest growth was in women's active wear, girl's active wear, fees for recreational lessons, out of town trips, athletic gear and camping equipment.

- 1985 US$27.4 billion
- 1987 US$28.2 billion
- 1990 US$34.1 billion
- 1993 US$36.3 billion
- 1997 US$48.4 billion

Based on the household survey conducted for the National Sporting Goods Association (NSGA, 1999), the following trends in spending for recreational equipment, footwear, clothing and transportation (bicycles, boats, recreational vehicles and snowmobiles) have occurred since 1989:

- 1989 US$50.9 billion
- 1991 US$49.8 billion
- 1993 US$51.9 billion
- 1995 US$59.8 billion
- 1997 US$67.3 billion
- 1999 US$71.3 billion (projected)

These estimates are larger than those reported above by the Bureau of Labor Statistics because they include all sports equipment, indoor and outdoor. The Bureau's trends show an average annual growth rate of +6.4% while the household survey for the NSGA shows an average rate of +4.0%. As the demand for outdoor recreation experiences rises, mostly on public lands and sites, so too do spending and revenues in the private sector. Particularly strong has been spending for recreational transport, which grew from US$16.4 billion in 1989 to US$25.5 billion in 1999 (projected). This is an average annual growth rate of 5.5%. Driving this growth in the last few years was sales of recreational vehicles. Other recent strong growth categories included snowboards (up 21% from 1997 to 1998), fishing clothing (+17%) and camping/backpacking clothing (+14%).

Trends in Access to Privately Owned Rural Lands

In 1995/96, a cooperative study between the Southern Research Station of the USDA For-

est Service and the Agricultural and Applied Economics Department of the University of Georgia was undertaken to assess outdoor recreation trends on private rural lands (Teasley et al., 1999). The focus of the NPLOS was on landowner preferences and attitudes related to permitting public access. The range of tract sizes studied in the NPLOS was from 4000 to over 16,000 ha.

Rural landowners use a variety of ways to earn income from their land, including grazing cattle, sharecropping and leasing to outside interests. Protecting their land is of great importance and one way of doing this is through posting (a legal statement printed on signs 'No Trespassing'). Approximately 40% of landowners post their property, and on tracts where posting occurs, the average area enclosed is 80.9 ha. Among the problems landowners have experienced and which may have led them to institute posting were destruction of property, littering, poaching and disruption of privacy. Landowners said they began posting so they would know who was on their property and when, to prevent damage to property and livestock, and to be safe. Close to 80% of the land leased to clubs or individuals for recreation was posted, either by the club or by the landowner. Ninety-eight percent of landowners said they would post the same or more of their land in the future.

One-third of rural landowners said that portions of their tract were completely closed to everyone outside their own household or family. More than 70% reported that they engage in recreational activities themselves on their land and almost 50% said they had allowed access to people they knew, but who are outside their family. However, only 15% of rural landowners said that some of their land is open without restrictions for recreation uses by outside people, whether they know them or not. On average, the total number of different people landowners reported as having used their land was 14 per year. The types of recreational activities pursued on private land are varied. Hunting, fishing, hiking and camping were the top activities listed by owners. Most landowners reported that they have not changed their attitude or approach much on the issue of access in the past 5 years. But there does seem to be a trend towards limiting public access even further in the future.

Comparing the 1996 NPLOS with the 1986 NPLOS we see several notable trends. Average reported tract size has decreased from about 74 ha in 1986 to nearly 56 ha in 1996. Hunting remains the most popular recreational activity pursued on private lands, although a number of other activities are gaining in popularity. The percentage of landowners who post at least some part of their land has risen from 33% in 1986 to 41% in 1996. The average number of ha that owners posted per tract has decreased slightly from 93.9 to 83.4 ha, perhaps reflecting in part the trend toward decreasing average tract size.

Results from NPLOS surveys in 1986 and 1996 indicate that the percentage of private lands on which access for recreation to individuals a landowner does not know is permitted decreased from 25 to 15% in the 10 years from 1986 to 1996. At the same time, access to private land by individuals known by the landowner has remained more or less stable (47% in 1986 and 50% in 1996). Leasing of land by owners for recreation has also remained fairly stable, with slightly more than 3% of landowners reporting they leased land in 1996 compared with slightly less than 4% in 1986.

Liability issues are of increasing concern to rural landowners, but a substantial proportion do nothing to limit liability. An exception is in the North, where the majority of landowners have insurance. However, given the prevalence of litigation in the US, the issue of granting access at the risk of a lawsuit if an injury occurs is likely to become a larger issue and influence on the availability of private land for public recreational use. This possibility is reinforced by landowner predictions that they will make less land available in the future.

Because most urban dwellers do not participate in the types of recreational activities typically occurring on rural private lands, the trend toward more limited access may not have very much of an effect on overall supply. Participation growth has been occurring mainly in activities focused on either special land features or conditions (e.g. caving, rock climbing, downhill skiing) or focused on developed facilities (e.g. visiting nature centres, team sports, camping) (Cordell, 1999). For the most part, these activities do not occur on private land. Recreation activities with the most potential on private lands seem to include hunting, fishing, wildlife observation, bird watching, primitive camping and hiking. Though trends show falling participation in hunting, it is expected that demand for quality lease hunting on private land will remain high. Trends also suggest there may be increased opportunities for the leasing of private land for fishing and nonconsumptive recreation.

Trends in Supply Indices

To examine regional changes over the last 10 years across all jurisdictions, public and private, indices were computed to show trends in per capita availability of outdoor recreation opportunities between 1987 and 1997. The 14 indices developed highlight areas in the country where the rate of growth of recreation resource availability is either keeping pace with, exceeding or falling behind the rate of population growth. Population has been growing in most counties in the US. Fourteen indices were computed. These were named Local Facilities, Open Space, Great Outdoors, Wildlife Land, State and Private Forests, Western Land, Camping Areas, Federal Water, Large Water Bodies, Whitewater, Flatwater, Lowland Rivers, Developed Winter Areas and Undeveloped Winter Areas (Betz et al., 1999).

In almost all regions of the country (North, South, Rocky Mountains/Great Plains and West Coast), there have been per capita increases in greenways and rail-trails (Open Space). Organizations promoting trail and greenway development have become much more numerous in the last 10 years. Increased government funding for projects to develop these types of resources has been partly responsible for these increases. There also has been increased availability of State and Private Forests and of Developed Winter resources. These trends reflect in part increases in state park land reported earlier and increases in capacity of downhill ski areas. More than two-thirds of the people in the North region live in counties that had stable or increased availability of land protected for wildlife habitat (Wildlife Land). In contrast, more than 90% of the population in the North region live in areas that had declining per capita availability for five of the resource types: (i) Great Outdoors, resources that include national forests, national parks and wilderness areas; (ii) campgrounds and campsites (Camping Areas); (iii) recreation opportunities on federal water projects (Federal Water); (iv) coastal resources and associated private businesses (Large Water Bodies); and (v) Flatwater and other wetland resources.

Despite relatively larger than national average population increases in the last 10 years, resource availability growth was more consistent in the South region than in any other region. More than 90% of the population lived in areas with stable or increasing recreation supply for three of the resource types, including both types of urban resources (Local Facilities and Open Space) and Lowland River opportunities. For all of the land resource types, at least 36% of the South region's population lived in areas that had stable or increasing per capita resource availability. The South region was the only region where more than half the population lived in areas with increases in the Great Outdoors resources – USDA Forest Service, NPS and Wilderness. The only resource factor for which a large percentage of the South region's population had declining per capita availability was Flatwater and wetland resources, reflecting increases in population near these resources and development and conversions of these to other uses.

Most of the population in the Rocky Mountain region live in areas with increasing or stable per capita resource availability for six of the 14 resource types. The six types are Open Space (greenways/trails), Wildlife Land (land set aside for habitat preservation), Large Water Bodies and associated boating opportunities, Whitewater and wild river resources, Lowland River resources, and Developed Winter skiing resources.

Because of relative stability in the federal resource base and increasing population, there was a decline in this region for three resource types: Great Outdoors, Western Land and Federal Water (federal water projects). In addition, more than 90% of residents experienced reduced per capita availability for Flatwater and wetland resources.

The West Coast region was the only region where most people lived in areas that had increases in per capita availability of Flatwater and wetland recreation opportunities. Other resource types for which a majority of the regional population had availability increases included Open Space (greenway and trail opportunities), Wildlife Land (habitat preservation land) and Lowland River resources. On the other hand, this region was the only one in which less than half the population had per capita increases in the availability of Developed Winter opportunities. Five resource types had declining availability in Local Facilities (developed urban resources), Western Land (BLM and agricultural land), Camping Areas (camping opportunities), Federal Water (BoR and Corps of Engineers) and Whitewater and wild river opportunities.

In general, developed recreation opportunities are increasing or at least keeping pace with population growth in most regions of the country. Developed camping opportunities are the lone exception. For this traditional overnight resource, population growth has exceeded camping capacity growth, especially in the Northeast and along the West Coast. Resources centred on land, water and river resources protected by conservation groups, state park systems, or the federal government also have shown stable or growing levels of availability for many Americans.

Per capita availability of several types of resources is declining. For some of these, reductions stem from a fixed resource base in areas where there is increasing population. Examples include beaches and coastal areas and opportunities provided by federal water management agencies, such as the BoR or the Corps of Engineers. For other resource types, the cause of decline is actual shrinkage in the resource base. Examples here include recreational access to private agricultural lands, fee areas for hunting and fishing, and wetlands.

Summary of the Dominant Trends and Their Implications

Beginning and continuing throughout the 1960s and 1970s, in part sparked by ORRRC, there was accelerated, large-scale growth of both the public and private sector systems of outdoor recreation supply in the US. Protected and multiple-use federal lands were added and legislation was revised to mandate management of most of the existing federal lands for outdoor recreation. States and local governments greatly expanded their parks, forests, playgrounds, sports fields and a host of other outdoor facilities and services. On the private sector side, growth in the provision of goods, services and facilities accelerated rapidly to respond to growing and changing demand. Overall, this was a bull market period for outdoor recreation in America. ORRRC did its work and did it well. The interest ignited by ORRRC, a truly landmark event in the history of outdoor recreation in this country, has had such impact that the impetus it created is obviously continuing into the 21st century. But, there are some clouds on the horizon of which we all need to be aware.

Since the early surges of the 1960s and 1970s, supply trends in the federal sector have been mostly up, but not across the board and at a decreasing rate. Facing flat to slightly declining real-dollar budgets during most of the 1980s and 1990s, most federal resource management agencies have had to curtail land acquisition and new development, although there has been rising demand. A backlog of site maintenance and facility upgrade needs of such large magnitude developed that much of it persists only partially addressed at this time. Even for those agencies which experienced increases in real funding there have been serious fiscal problems. Problems with 'making ends meet' are especially acute at the lowest-levels of administration where 'hands on'

resource and recreation use management occur. Higher costs and higher administrative assessments at the Washington and regional levels of administration without overall budget increases to account for increased costs have resulted in lower levels of funding reaching 'on-the-ground' management units.

Level-to-decreasing federal budgets have meant fewer professional staff to fill vital recreation management positions, closures of some field offices and the donning of more 'hats' by the professional staff left after the cuts. To compensate, federal agencies have increasingly had to rely on volunteers and a variety of human resource programmes (e.g. senior programmes) to carry out day-to-day site maintenance and customer service, use a wider variety and higher levels of fees in an attempt to generate greater revenues, and seek more cost-sharing partnerships with state and local governments and with private organizations and corporations.

A look at federal budget plans for the next 2–3 fiscal years offers little hope that the trend of shrinking to flat budgets will not continue as the norm for federal recreation management agencies. Even in the face of the huge projected federal budget surpluses, fed by the nation's remarkably strong economy, it looks like federal outdoor recreation funding will at best remain stable. This is not because the agencies fail to request increases; it is the erosion that occurs as agency budget requests make their way through the federal budgeting system. Inadequate funding makes the nature of future federal recreation supply an uncertain one at best. Reliance on human resource programmes and on volunteers is not a reliable, long-term solution to inadequate appropriated budgets. These schemes flutter high in the political winds of this country and can disappear as quickly as they appeared.

Clearly, a federal system will survive. Its survival in some form is not really a pressing concern. Its ranks are filled with managers and administrators who are innovative and dedicated to finding ways to keep things working. What is of concern is inadequate, and uncertain, public financial backing which is pushing agencies to focus on policies and programmes that will maximize revenues, spread the costs of operation and maintenance with other organizations, and rely more on 'free' labour. Such a shift in the way 'business' is conducted must surely have consequences.

One potentially serious consequence of a rising focus on revenues is the strong possibility that some segments of the American people, who traditionally had been among the 'served', may become the unserved or under-served. Without solid public sector investment in staffing, facility maintenance and land stewardship, will or can the federal system optimally meet the needs of a diversifying American society? Access to all Americans must be a primary goal in the management of public lands.

Access is affected in many ways and a good example of access issues that are likely to rise in significance is the increasing incidence of the closure of private land that is adjacent land to federal lands. Shutting off public access to cross private properties which traditionally had been available is likely to become a crisis unless solutions are fast in coming. Such closure effectively makes these private lands a barrier to public access to federal recreation lands. Have we adequately stepped back to examine and plan for the likely consequences of continuing to fund inadequately public access to federal lands?

At the state level of government, a niche not being filled by the federal government is being very effectively addressed. Like the federal system, states have continued to expand their parks and other recreation opportunities. Because the distribution of state recreation land and water much more closely matches the geographic distribution of population, needs for conveniently located, nature-based, outdoor recreation, close to where people live, are being filled by state parks, forests and other state properties. State systems are in this way highly complementary to the federal system. In the 1990s there was a greater than 30% expansion, more than 1267 new state areas, added to state park systems nationwide. This is a solid contribution to the nation's supply

from the state level of government. Along with more sites for recreation, states are also providing access to sites and services for longer periods throughout the year, including day use, camping, cabin rental and resort holiday areas. A potential downside consequence of the movement of state systems toward more year-round, higher-service levels of operation is the possibility that associated higher fees may also exclude some people who cannot afford the added costs, just as might be happening in the federal system.

Still, even after acknowledging the considerable progress states have made with their systems of parks, forests and recreation areas, dilemmas mirroring the federal system loom in their future. State land and water systems are increasingly facing funding crises that will contribute greatly to shaping their future. To combat funding shortfalls, states have moved rapidly toward greater self sufficiency through programmes aimed at dramatically increasing revenues. From 1975 to 1995, state park system revenues increased 364% while legislatively appropriated funding rose only 286%. Based on an assumed average annual increase of 1.4%, visits to state parks increased only 30–35%. Obviously, the level of fees per visitor has risen dramatically. Greater fees across a wider range of services raises the same question that is being raised about more fees at federal sites and about the movement toward higher priced resort and lodge facilities at state sites, 'Will lower-income people be priced out and thus stop using state parks?'.

Local municipal and county systems, by far the most conveniently located of public sites, are also experiencing financial pressures. Many local systems are inadequately funded to acquire land, develop new facilities and renovate existing facilities rapidly enough to answer rising demands. Generally, the expansion of local government outdoor recreation systems that has occurred has emphasized athletic fields, ball courts, passive recreation spaces and parks. Much less emphasis has been placed on new recreation centres and water sites. In local parks specifically, expansions of supply have emphasized new trails, conservation areas, open space, playgrounds and green space. Ironically, too many local system expansions are not sufficiently funded for adequate operation and maintenance after their development. This lack of funding puts local systems in exactly the same predicament as federal and state systems, making them more dependent on instituting and raising the levels of fees to make up deficits.

In highly complementary ways, but not as independently as some would have us think, the private sector has also greatly expanded its role as a supplier of outdoor recreation goods, services, travel, information, sites and virtuality in the US. The solvency of private sector recreation businesses is highly dependent on adequate federal, state and local budgets for outdoor recreation. Without the sites, facilities, scenery, and the many other natural and built features provided by and under the care of the public sector, the private sector would be hard pressed to make their outdoor businesses successful, except in virtuality. How long would the numerous and lucrative fixed-wing or helicopter scenic flight businesses in the Denali National Park area in Alaska survive without Mt McKinley and the National Park? On the private sector side, one particular issue needing to be addressed is public access to private rural lands. This access has been declining for more than 20 years and will ultimately leave an appreciable void in supply if this trend continues.

Conclusion

Federal, state, and local supply systems continue to function as highly complementary components of our larger national system to provide a wide range of recreation opportunities from natural settings in remote rural areas to highly humanized playgrounds in urban neighbourhoods. This complementarity across the three levels of government and gradual growth in their capacity to provide recreation services and experiences has been the sinew of the American outdoor recreation system. From the spectacular scenery of federal lands to protected old mill sites in state parks to the transformed vacant-lot urban playgrounds, this country's outdoor recreation resources over the past five decades have produced unparalleled opportunities for its citizens to recreate and for the private sector to profit. Complementarity across the three levels of government, enhanced by private sector-provided goods and services, has evolved over time into a very effective and seemingly resilient system that meets a variety of leisure tastes.

But we must ask the question, 'How resilient can our recreation supply system be if uncertainties about base funding persist?'. Much of the 1980s and all of the 1990s have been marked by substantial uncertainties about funding for outdoor recreation, and leisure services in general, at all levels of government. At this point, there is little evidence that this uncertainty will not continue well into the future. Collectively, we who have chosen professionally to devote our careers to the study and care of this country's outdoor recreation supply system must understand the implications of current and likely future budget trends and must envision strategies for ensuring the sustainability of our outdoor resources in light of those trends. In the words of one former president, there must be 'No net loss'. While he was referring to wetlands, these words apply equally well to outdoor recreation supply. We must not lose any of the capacity of this country's outdoor recreation legacy to development, harmful exploitation or neglect because of inadequate funds, staffing or authority. Where open spaces and favourite places are lost to the inevitability of urban sprawl, we must find ways to replace our losses. However, the ability to take care of what we have and make up losses will always depend on the availability of an ongoing, stable base of funding.

Our interpretation of the most salient trends in the US supply system leads us to conclude that its sustainability is stressed and in many ways threatened. Continuing but slowing growth in the land and water area managed by federal, state and local governments; flat budgets at all three levels to take care of existent and added land and water area and greater reliance on nonappropriated sources for funding and staffing the system's operation and maintenance are not characteristics of a vigorous and healthy system. In the face of continuing and, in some places, very rapid population expansion, these trends quickly translate into substantial decreases in the per capita capacity of the American outdoor recreation supply system.

Slowed growth in per capita capacity pushes the issue of access ever so steadily out in front of other outdoor recreation issues. Of all the many issues in outdoor recreation, access is clearly the most pivotal one when we ask the question, 'Access for whom?'. A key to sustaining the capacity of our supply system is to do all that is necessary to assure everyone has access to some outdoor spaces, facilities and service-access which is barrier and hassle-free. There are many ways access can be lost. We pointed out some of these in earlier sections of this paper. For example, access and capacity are lost when private ownerships adjacent to federal lands close their land to the public's crossing it to reach public land. But perhaps the most serious threat to access for some people in American society is the trend toward more and higher fees. We need to ask and seriously reflect on the question, 'Who will be affected and in what ways will they be affected by the trend toward much expanded and elevated fees for access to public lands?'. This is a trend driven by inadequate base funding.

In our opinion, the future of outdoor recreation in this or in any country will depend on the emergence of a new cadre of 21st century visionaries. High-energy, not-to-be-denied champions of the 'great out-of-doors'. Champions just as engaged as their predecessors of earlier decades who will work tirelessly to examine access and other issues and who will provide enlightened guidance as we move into and through the 21st century. Many among the earlier champions in the US worked with or served on the ORRRC. They recognized that without quality outdoor environments and access to those environments, there cannot be quality outdoor recreation experiences. Without quality outdoor experiences, the growth potential for private industry that has existed to date will be seriously dampened. This future cadre of visionary champions must come not only from the politico, monied altruists, and monied corporate leaders of this country, they must come also from local birdwatching groups, small commercial interests, local conservation leaders, local government, resource professional associations, retiree associations, and all other outdoor stakeholder interests. It seems outdoor recreation is again at a transition time and its champions are needed.

Our emerging champions and leaders need to collaborate in the most effective way possible and speak in unison for better federal, state, and local recreation budgets and for the protection and care of our priceless, irreplaceable outdoor resources, both local and national. We sense that it may be time again for those champions to assemble and take a close look at the trends and issues surrounding our nation's outdoor heritage. ORRRC 2000 has a good ring to it. Hopefully this and other chapters in this book will go a long way toward informing that next outdoor recreation commission.

8

US Recreation Policies Since World War II

George H. Siehl

Introduction

The dictionary defines policy as 'a definite course of action adopted for the sake of expediency', or 'a course of action adopted and pursued by a government'. Many institutions, public and private develop policies. Principally, this review addresses the development of federal policy affecting recreation and associated natural resources issues in the US since World War II.

One characteristic of policy is that it does not exist in a vacuum; action and reaction continue among and between public and private players. Another characteristic is competition, both within government and with outside interests. At the federal level, differences between legislative and executive branches offer obvious conflicts, particularly when opposing political parties control the two branches.

Legislation seems the most obvious expression of policy, but administrative and programmatic initiatives within a department can create significant policy shifts as well. Competition may occur between executive branch departments over policy, where the president may serve as final arbiter. Such competition may arise because the agencies operate under different missions and legislative authorities, and may be compounded by differences in the agencies' 'corporate cultures'.

The Post-war Context: 1945–1957

The middle third of the 20th century was an era that transformed the US: an economic depression, a globe-altering war, rapid economic recovery and an unprecedented population explosion between 1946 and 1964 contributed to the changes.

Outdoor recreation changed along with many other aspects of life. Personal mobility, children at home and disposable income – elements that research shows contribute to recreation participation – all grew in the post-war years and continued upwards until the present. The strength of these societal changes would cause the participation in and variety of recreation to virtually explode in the post-war years.

Among the activities to grow rapidly after the war was skiing. Returning ski troops were instrumental in opening new ski areas that grew into some of America's most popular resorts, including Vail, Colorado; Sugarbush, Vermont; and Crystal Mountain, Washington (Burton, 1971). Burton credits the growth of skiing (and mountain climbing) after the war to the men trained by the Army as part of the 10th Mountain Division and to the availability of surplus equipment.

The white water rafting industry of today also grew from World War II roots, tracing back to the use of surplus life rafts. Wandless (1943) anticipated the conversion of the inflatable rubber life raft to recreational uses after the war. He wrote,

> When small pleasure craft resume cruising the seas and lakes and rivers of the world, the rubber boat will undoubtedly become an indispensable part of necessary equipment.

Another wartime innovation, the jeep, helped to diversify recreation activities and set the stage for a wide range of off-road vehicles (and the recreation conflicts they engendered). Such technology transfers, then and now, are not policy innovations, but shape requirements for new policy decisions to integrate the technology into the spectrum of recreation activities.

Visitors streamed into federal recreation areas in ever increasing numbers during the late 1940s and early 1950s. Appropriations did not increase to cover the higher management costs; indeed, with the outbreak of the Korean War in 1950, agency budgets were cut and facilities fell into disrepair (Everhart, 1972). This condition, following increasing public criticism, caused the National Park Service to propose a policy initiative, 'Mission 66', a 10-year programme to rebuild and expand infrastructure within the parks. President Eisenhower agreed to the budget proposal and Congress accepted and supported the initiative over the following decade.

Congress made most major structural policy decisions impacting recreation – the allocation of federal land for conservation purposes and the establishment of the National Park Service and the USDA Forest Service – long before the post-war era. Congress continued this conservation policy with the establishment of the Bureau of Land Management in 1946, melding some functions of the Grazing Service with those of the General Land Office (Clawson, 1983).

Modern Congresses' greatest contribution to recreation policy stemmed from the 1958 establishment of the Outdoor Recreation Resources Review Commission (ORRRC). This was a bipartisan response to the growing pressures on the existing recreation infrastructure.

The ORRRC Era: 1958–1968

Public Law (PL) 85–470, signed on 28 June, 1958, authorized the Outdoor Recreation Resources Review Commission, to consist of seven members (including the chairman) appointed by President Eisenhower and eight members from Congress, equally divided between the parties and the two chambers. The ORRRC had slightly more than three years to complete its work and report to the President and Congress. Within this time, its duties included:

- ... to set in motion a nationwide inventory and evaluation of outdoor recreation resources and opportunities;
- ... compile such data and in the light of the data so compiled and of information available concerning trends in population, leisure, transportation, and other factors shall determine the amount, kind, quality and location of such outdoor recreation resources and opportunities as will be required by the year 1976 and the year 2000, and shall recommend what policies should best be adopted and what programmes be initiated, at each level of government and by private organizations and other citizen groups and interests, to meet such future requirements.

The comprehensiveness and foresight of the charge was met by the competence and diligence of the Commission. Central to the work – and ultimate legislative success – of the group was the active involvement of its congressional members.

ORRRC drew upon a 25-member advisory council, governors, cabinet members and agency heads for information and insights. It did not conduct public hearings, although it was authorized to do so by PL 85–470. The Commission contracted with federal agencies and nonprofit organizations for preparation of 27 studies of various recreation topics as supplements to the final report, *Outdoor Recreation for America* (Outdoor Recreation Resources Review Commission, 1962).

ORRRC clearly falls within the description of applied policy research given by Kash and Ballard (1987), as do the recreation policy assessments of the 1980s that are discussed later in this review. These studies 'focus on the substantive conditions that have created issues or problems', and they deal with government policies 'to influence, manipulate, or control substantive activities or circumstances' (p. 601). ORRRC and the later President's Commission on Americans Outdoors (PCAO) also meet the criteria of being requested by decision makers and by involving the 'clients' throughout the process.

The first implementation responses to the report and recommendations from ORRRC came from President Kennedy. In March 1962 he announced that a Bureau of Outdoor Recreation (BOR) would be established in the Department of the Interior. Interior Secretary Udall subsequently created the bureau by secretarial order. Congress, in PL 88–29, later provided tasks to the Secretary, which he delegated to the BOR. These included the responsibilities for nationwide recreation planning and assistance to the states, and a directive to 'encourage interdepartmental cooperation, and promote coordination of Federal plans and activities generally relating to outdoor recreation ... '

Although the BOR dealt effectively with the states, it missed the deadline for the first nationwide outdoor recreation plan. It never fully achieved the 'interdepartmental cooperation' or 'coordination of Federal plans and activities' set out in PL 88–29.

The Recreation Advisory Council (RAC) was established under Executive Order 11017 by President Kennedy in April 1962. RAC comprised the Secretaries of Agriculture, Interior, Defence, Health Education and Welfare and the Administrator of the Housing and Home Finance Agency. Its functions included providing broad policy advice to federal agencies on outdoor recreation matters, and facilitating coordinated efforts among these agencies. The Executive Order listed these areas of concentration for the Recreation Advisory Council:

- the protection and appropriate management of scenic areas, natural wonders,

primitive areas, historic sites and recreation areas of national significance;

- the management of federal lands for the broadest possible recreation benefit consistent with other essential uses;

- the management and improvement of fish and wildlife resources for recreational purposes;

- cooperation with and assistance to the states and local governments;

- interstate arrangements, including federal participation where authorized and necessary; and

- vigorous and cooperative leadership in a nationwide recreation effort.

Over 3 years, the RAC published seven circulars addressing such recreation topics as executive branch policy on national recreation areas, policy on water pollution and public health aspects of outdoor recreation, and scenic roads and parkways. It contributed to the overall coordination of recreation efforts among the agencies, but it was expanded and converted to other duties under Presidents Johnson and Nixon. Eventually, RAC evolved into the Council on Environmental Quality, where the recreation component disappeared from the office name.

The ORRRC recommendations adopted through legislation lasted longer than the administrative initiatives. Among the most important laws were those establishing the Land and Water Conservation Fund (PL 88–578, 1964) the National Trails System (PL 90–543, 1968), the Wild and Scenic Rivers System (PL 90–542, 1968) and the Wilderness Preservation System (PL 88–577, 1964).

Later, Congress also passed numerous bills designating individual areas as components of these systems, and authorized many new and expanded areas of the National Park System. Congress earlier made a policy innovation in this regard when it first purchased private property to add to the National Park System in 1958. Before then, all parklands had been withdrawn from the public domain or transferred from other federal ownership such as US Department of

Agriculture (USDA) Forest Service or War Department. The Land and Water Conservation Fund (LWCF) fuelled additional purchases of private lands for addition to the National Park System and to the other land managing agencies for recreation purposes. These additions included national seashores, lakeshores and national recreation areas.

The LWCF is arguably the most significant legislative enactment from the recommendations of the Outdoor Recreation Resources Review Commission. In making the recommendation, the Commission recognized the broad nature of recreation and its many public providers. The LWCF provided financial backing to governments to meet the growing demand for recreation.

The LWCF Act implicitly recognized the various kinds of recreation opportunities provided by different levels of government. Federal agencies could use LWCF funds only for land acquisition. States, however (and local governments where a state government shared its LWCF allocation), could use their share for planning, land acquisition or facility development. The distribution of money to the states was based on a formula in which population played a key role, and required state preparation of a satisfactory statewide outdoor recreation plan. All LWCF money required a dollar-for-dollar match by state government.

In the decade following its passage, Congress often amended the LWCF. The changes included increasing the annual funding from US$60 million to US$900 million; making federal agencies, not the states, the principal recipients of annual funding; and ensuring that state funds were not used for indoor recreation facilities.

Congress also changed the LWCF funding mechanism. Originally, federal recreation area entrance fees, motorboat fuel taxes and revenues from sale of surplus federal real property were to provide the needed monies. These soon proved inadequate, so Congress approved the use of outer continental shelf oil and gas leasing revenues to make up any shortfall between income from the three original sources and the amount authorized for appropriation.

Congress recognized recreation as a component of federal land management agencies' prime mission in 1960 when it passed the Multiple Use Sustained Yield Act, PL 86–517. It stated, 'It is the policy of the Congress that the National Forests are established and shall be administered for outdoor recreation, range, timber, watershed, and wildlife purposes'. As a result of that action, recreation assumed a more prominent role among federal resource providers and made it easier, due to Congressional action, to designate tracts of land, within the federal estate, for recreation priority uses.

Congress approved wilderness legislation in 1964 after resolving a number of issues. Congress, rather than the agencies, was given sole authority to designate new areas as wilderness, for instance. The Wilderness Act included all existing USDA Forest Service wild and wilderness areas, some 9.1 million acres, as legislatively designated wilderness. Over 10 years, the 5.4 million national forest acres being administered as primitive areas were to be reviewed to determine if they were suitable for wilderness designation by Congress. Also, the Interior Secretary was to review within 10 years all roadless areas more than 5000 acres in national parks and wildlife refuges to determine their suitability for wilderness classification by Congress.

Section 3(d) of the Wilderness Act opened the process of wilderness recommendations to the public. That clause requires the resource agencies to give public notice and hold public hearings on each wilderness proposal before recommendations are submitted to the President and the Congress. Allin (1982, p. 156) wrote:

> From the point of view of the administering agencies, the impact of the Wilderness act's public participation requirement was to turn loose a horde of amateur land managers with an interest in preservation.

This 'horde' would have a profound impact on federal (especially USDA Forest Service) land management decisions in the following years. The role of public participation in federal land management would expand under later enactments, as discussed below.

ORRRC recommended, and Congress enacted, programmes to establish national systems of wild and scenic rivers, and trails. Passage of the enabling laws, PL 90–542 for rivers, and PL 90–543 for trails, came in 1968.

The concept of wild and scenic rivers was to preserve selected river segments in their wild, free-flowing condition. As more dams were built upon rivers to provide energy and irrigation, there was concern that the natural qualities of rivers were being destroyed. The Wild and Scenic Rivers Act (WSRA) slowed the loss of natural stream corridors. It designated eight initial components of the national system. Twenty-seven more corridors were designated for study by the Secretaries of Agriculture and Interior to determine if these rivers should be recommended for designation by Congress. This paralleled the mechanism established in the Wilderness Act, and was applied in the Trails Act as well. Congress approved the addition of numerous stream corridors to the system and listed more rivers for study in later years.

River corridor protection saw a productive interplay between legislative and oversight activity in Congress and the ongoing work of the ORRRC. In 1961, the Senate Select Committee on National Water Resources recommended the protection of some rivers in their natural condition. ORRRC noted this action and, in turn, recommended preservation of certain rivers 'in their free flowing condition and in their natural setting' (ORRRC, 1962, p. 177).

This interplay illustrates the important role played by the congressional members of ORRRC; by their awareness of current events on the Hill, these members could inform and infuse the work of the commission. The culmination of this interaction, perhaps, came in 1965 when Congress passed the Federal Water Project Recreation Act, PL 89–72. This fulfilled the ORRRC recommendation that outdoor recreation and fish and wildlife conservation should be among the purposes

considered in the planning and operation of federal water projects.

The National Trails System Act (NTSA) engendered less opposition than the wild rivers bill, except in cases where private land was acquired to extend trails from federal lands. Then, local landowners often objected to the perceived loss of privacy and possible vandalism they thought would be associated with public trails.

The NTSA initially established two trail categories: recreation and scenic. Two scenic components, the Appalachian and Pacific Crest trails, were approved in the Act. Recreation trails could be established on federal or other government lands, but scenic trails were confined to lands administered by the Departments of Agriculture and Interior. Subsequent amendments established historic trails as a third category and continued the designation of additional system components and new candidates for study.

The decade from 1958 to 1968 probably stands as recreation's golden era. From the enactment of the ORRRC authorization until the passage of the rivers and trails bills, recreation was high on the national agenda. The following 10 years constituted a pleasant afterglow, continuing the expansion of the new systems established by legislation in the 1960s. The peak spending on the Land and Water Conservation Fund in 1978 marks the symbolic, if not the real, ending of the golden era of recreation.

The golden era expanded the recreation estate through more lands, more staff and more money. It also showed the policy process at work. Circumstances of the moment and the issue were singular, perhaps, as political frictions of the time were merely partisan, not poisonous, and a degree of comity prevailed in Washington. The involved interest groups operated with somewhat less sophistication and far less money than is the norm today. Also, the beneficiaries included a broad swath of the American people. Why did the model not survive? In large part, the answer is found in a new perception of the world and our relationship to it: the new perception produced an array of new public policy issues that continue to evolve – and stir debate – even today.

The Environmental Era: 1969–1979

The end of the 1960s introduced both more complicated issues and more specialized interests. President Johnson's wife, Lady Bird, catalysed one part of the change, that dealing with natural resources. She crusaded on behalf of natural beauty in America, in an effort that sensitized millions to the quality of the world around us. While her campaign initially focused upon eliminating billboards and junkyards, it grew to encompass polluted air and water. Within a few years this broadened concern evolved into today's environmental movement.

Natural beauty, however, was featured as the topic of a 1965 White House conference, a report by the then current reincarnation of the Recreation Advisory Council (President's Council 1968) and a presidential message. Darling (1967) noted the significance of this period, writing that the White House conference on Natural Beauty 'was perhaps a turning point, because it clarified an enlarged concept of public responsibility and administrative innovation … '. He quoted from President Johnson's message on natural beauty, as follows, to characterize the change:

> Our conservation must not be just the classic conservation of protection and development, but a creative conservation of restoration and innovation. Its concern is not with nature alone but with the total relation between man and the world around him.

President Johnson submitted and supported many bills to bring his vision of this 'total relation' to reality. His noted powers of persuasion among his former congressional colleagues, and the growing public support for these initiatives, resulted in an impressive legislative record for the protection of cultural and historic resources and reduction of air and water pollution.

The ORRRC report (1962, pp. 140–141) described how polluted water reduced recreation opportunities, and recommended state efforts to 'preserve present water recreation resources and to regain those lost to public recreation because of pollution'. Conservation groups supported the air and water pollution control bills of the 1960s. The link to recreation emerged in the theme of 'fishable, swimmable waters' as these groups supported clean water legislation.

What recreation gained in improved recreation settings, it would lose in dedicated support in Washington, DC. Conservation groups, which had initiated and supported much of the recreation and wildlife legislation of the past, took a new focus: environmental issues. Their new mission was part altruism and part financial pragmatism; citizens were concerned about highly publicized issues of environmental contamination. By developing an active environmental protection agenda, the conservation groups could increase membership and funding from the concerned public. Soon, these issues took precedence over recreation and conservation.

As the issues changed, so did the staffing of these organizations. Once drawn largely from natural resource disciplines such as forestry and wildlife, the staffs now included lawyers and specialists in pollution control, public relations and fund raising. Interactions between interest groups and the resource agencies quickly shifted from the agency head's office or the committee hearing room to the courtroom. This transition was hastened with passage of the National Environmental Policy Act (NEPA), PL 91–190. This process-oriented law requires agencies to examine the nature and magnitude of environmental impacts generated by federal projects or legislation they would initiate, and seek to minimize any adverse impacts.

Apart from the time and money that agencies would expend in complying with NEPA, they had to change the way they did business. NEPA required public involvement early in the agency decision-making process. This greatly broadened public participation beyond what had been required by the Wilderness Act in 1964. Later enactments in the 1970s would make public involvement even more explicit, thereby reducing the internal decision making authority of federal agency 'experts'.

Legislation during the decade of the 1970s brought considerable change to the way in which the multiple use agencies, BLM and the USDA Forest Service, managed their lands. Recreation would be affected by these changes.

The public domain lands were not considered part of a recreation estate until the BLM was created in 1946. Before this, outstanding natural, scenic and archaeological sites on the public domain were transferred to the National Park Service, and many forested areas were transferred to forest reserves around the turn of the century and eventually to the USDA Forest Service. Even after BLM was formed, recreation management held lower priority than mining and grazing uses.

ORRRC indirectly influenced this management regime. As Congress began implementing the legislative recommendations of ORRRC, it also established a second important bipartisan body, the Public Land Law Review Commission (PLLRC), to review comprehensively the laws, rules and regulations controlling the use and disposal of the public domain.

PLLRC was authorized in 1964 by PL 88–606, and extended in 1967 by PL 90–213. Its report, *One Third of the Nation's Land*, issued in June 1970, included chapters on recreation, fish and wildlife, and environmental concerns. The PLLRC report cited the work and recommendations of ORRRC, and recommended that several ideas, such as the system of recreation land classification, be applied to BLM lands as well.

Many PLLRC recommendations were enacted in the 1976 Federal Land Policy and Management Act (FLPMA), PL 94–579. The principal policy formulation in the law is that, in general, the public lands should be kept in federal ownership, not transferred away. FLPMA recognizes recreation, fisheries and wildlife, archaeological values and preservation of natural areas as authorized components of the multiple use regime on public domain lands. Production of miner-

als, food, fibre and timber are similarly included in management programmes. This authority parallels that contained in the USDA Forest Service's Multiple Use and Sustained Yield Act, incorporating service programmes along with commodity production.

Recreation is further recognized in Section 202(c)(9) which requires the Secretary of the Interior to

> coordinate the land use inventory, planning, and management activities of or for BLM lands with the land use planning and management programs of other federal departments and agencies and of the States and local governments ... including, but not limited to, the statewide outdoor recreation plans ...

Public involvement in the planning process is required by Section 202(f), allowing participation by citizens, and federal, state and local governments. FLPMA also required an inventory and assessment of potential wilderness areas of 5000 acres or more in BLM roadless areas over 15 years.

Two laws in the 1970s, stemming from concern over clearcutting on national forests, significantly affected USDA Forest Service planning and management. They were the Forest and Rangeland Renewable Planning Act of 1974, PL 93–378, now generally referred to as the Resources Planning Act (RPA) and the 1976 National Forest Management Act (NFMA). The RPA, later amended by the NFMA, called for the development of a detailed knowledge base of forest resources and services as well as trends affecting the resources and services. The information supports building a comprehensive plan for the operation of the USDA Forest Service and, ultimately, the plans for individual national forests. Public participation is mandated as part of this process.

The Endangered Species Act of 1973, PL 93–205, had wide ranging impacts. Its emphasis on habitat preservation for affected species can interfere with agency missions and private land use decisions, delay or halt actions, and impose additional costs to projects. The law also altered the role of the Fish and Wildlife Service (FWS) from refuge and hatchery managers to national wildlife police officer. The law also affected recreation, as it made Land and Water Conservation dollars available for acquiring endangered species habitat.

Implementation of some of the new legislative authorities could cause problems. Each special area designation, for instance, reduced the options for goods and services that federal land managers might provide other users. Allin (1982, p. 159) writes of one of these specialized uses, wilderness:

> The Forest Service is not uninterested in wilderness preservation, but it has a multitude of competing interests to balance, and every legislative enactment that restricts its management options increases the pressure under which it must operate ... It is no wonder then that supporters of the agency's policy worried about mortgaging the forests' multiple-use potential.

Controversy grew over what some saw as an exclusionary agenda by the environmental community throughout the 1970s, particularly in the West. One result was the rise of the 'sagebrush rebellion', a reaction by western commodity and property rights groups.

The Era of Reinventing Recreation: 1980–1992

The sagebrush rebellion helped the Republicans gain both the White House and control of the Senate in the 1980 elections. Federal land management policies and environmental regulations were high on the list for change in the new administration. Appointments to key policy positions in resource and environmental agencies worked toward those changes. Among the most controversial of these appointees was James Watt, Secretary of the Interior.

The new directions brought by the Reagan team engendered hostility in the House of Representatives where the Democrats remained in firm control. Watt, who enjoyed the political and ideological combat, struck

sparks throughout his tenure. He abolished the Bureau of Outdoor Recreation, which he had headed during the Nixon years, and moved to abolish stateside funding for the LWCF, which had peaked midway in President Carter's preceding administration.

The new administration philosophy provided an opportunity to review and analyse options for recreation and federal land management. Siehl (1988) details recreation policy initiatives at the time. These include the twisting path that led to creation of the President's Commission on Americans Outdoors (PCAO), and two workshops held by the Senate Committee on Energy and Natural Resources in 1981 and 1982. These committee efforts were key building blocks leading to the PCAO, as they brought together key individuals who later sold the administration on the idea of a new ORRRC.

Other key steps in obtaining a new national look at recreation were the recommendation of the National Conference on Renewable Natural Resources in 1980, and that of the seven-person 1982/83 Outdoor Recreation Policy Review Group organized by Laurance Rockefeller (Resources for the Future, 1983).

The conference recommendation called for the incoming administration and Congress to 'mandate and participate in' a review of recreation supply, demand and trends, to 'set priorities for the future'. The recommendation added, 'The structure of the body and the mission might be patterned after the Outdoor Recreation Resources Review Commission of the 1960s' (American Forestry Association, 1980).

Similarly, the Rockefeller group called for legislation to establish a new ORRRC embodying the principles of the first. The Rockefeller study group called for a broadened scope of the new commission, however, noting:

> It cannot ignore the interrelationships and overlaps of outdoor recreation with many indoor activities associated with physical fitness. A new study also must recognize that outdoor recreation is linked, in ways that have not been adequately researched, to such factors as job satisfaction and

productivity, and family and social cohesion. Urban recreation also requires further attention (p. 2).

The report added that the focus of the new commission should be 'on the inter-action of people and outdoor resources', but the above recognition of recreation's conceptual breadth is noteworthy.

Senator Wallop introduced S.1090 on 19 April, 1983 to establish a new ORRRC. After being considered in two Senate committees, the bill passed the Senate on a unanimous vote in November 1983.

The House Committee on Interior and Insular Affairs subcommittee handling the measure held 3 days of hearings in 1984, received considerable supporting testi-mony, but killed the bill by inaction. The subcommittee chairman later told a conser-vation gathering that he did not want to give President Reagan a chance to sign a con-servation bill in an election year, and that he was suspicious of the kind of people Reagan might name with his share of the appoint-ments under the bill.

President Reagan had the last laugh; he authorized a recreation commission and appointed all the members. On 25 January, 1985, by Executive Order 12503, he author-ized the Presidential Commission on Outdoor Recreation Resource Review. Com-missioner appointment was not completed until August 1985, when President Reagan named Tennessee Governor, Lamar Alex-ander, chairman and appointed a bipartisan congressional group of four members and ten private citizens.

The group, the PCAO, held public hear-ings and strategic planning sessions with extensive public input around the country. Unlike ORRRC, PCAO also drew upon the academic community and resource agency professionals for research and analysis, in particular a comprehensive literature sur-vey and trend data.

President Reagan's charge to his commis-sion was generally as broad as that given to ORRRC. The Executive Order (EO) noted that the commission's recommendations should be 'consistent with the need for fiscal economy at all levels of government', which

some might consider a limiting condition, but certainly not inconsistent with the over-all administration philosophy. The EO also gave recreation a more contemporary image, reflecting the language of the Rockefeller policy review group report.

Although the PCAO would touch on pieces of the broadened concept of recrea-tion, it decided early to concentrate on outdoor recreation, a decision that disap-pointed many, including community-oriented recreation providers.

The PCAO report (1987b) balanced fed-eral and nonfederal recommendations – and generated a position shift between suppor-ters and opponents. It reflected an 'outside the beltway' view in calling for a 'prairie fire' of local action to establish recreation goals and build partnerships to achieve them. But the report also recommended increasing the LWCF authorization level from US$900 mil-lion to US$1 billion per year and converting it to a 'true trust fund' with money shared among all government levels. The report also called for a nationwide system of green-ways created by all units of government; the vision was for a green lacework across America, never more than a few minutes away from any citizen.

PCAO had an energizing effect at the state and local levels as a number of states and many localities passed recreation bond issues and forged lasting partnerships to achieve recreation goals. Greenways sprang into being, and are still being created or expanded.

PCAO's key federal recommendation, for a billion-dollar trust fund, was considered by Congress, but never enacted. Congress did approve a 25-year extension of the LWCF, although support for state and local recreation programmes remained minimal in annual LWCF appropriations.

In the 1990s, Congress enacted a pro-gramme for scenic byways, increased entrance fees at national parks, and more recently established a fee demonstration programme on federal lands, all in line with PCAO recommendations. Republican loss of the Senate in 1986 limited chances for more accomplishments. Had they retained con-trol, they would have been in a position to advance the recommendations from their President's Commission. Also, congressional members were not as fully engaged in the work of PCAO as their predecessors had been in the work of ORRRC. This clearly contributed to the lack of follow-through to enact commission recommendations. The late 1990s offer a period of ferment, of new approaches to recreation as government, industry, and nongovernmental organizations reassess what they are to do, and how they are to do it. It is unclear just what the footings for recreation's Bridge to the 21st Century will look like. That vision will become clearer in retrospect.

Trends and Implications

Finding trends has been important to recreation policy at least since the creation of ORRRC in 1958. Section 6 (b) of PL 85–470, listing the duties of the commission, notes that 'information available concerning trends in population, leisure, transportation and other factors' should be incorporated in making recommendations concerning recreation requirements in the years 1976 and 2000.

Subsequent laws and executive documents have explicitly or implicitly called for the development and use of pertinent trend information. Follow through, however, was not always adequate. The Rockefeller policy review group report referenced ORRRC's recommendation for research. However, the report stated:

> Two decades later, the data base for
> outdoor recreation remains, at best,
> primitive. There are few consistent data on
> participation trends over time. We are not
> sure what people would really like to do
> during their free time (p. 28).

The continuing series of trends symposia, established in 1980, is an important source of trend information. Although the trends symposium itself has evolved with each iteration, it has remained an important tool in policy analysis and development (O'Leary and Siehl, 1992).

How do we define recreation, to which all this trend data applies? From a policy perspective, there is merit in considering a simple definition. In this light, recreation is a voluntary activity undertaken by an individual for pleasure or other nonmonetary reward. What the individual does, singly or with others, indoors or outdoors, on public site or in private, is a variation on the basic theme of an individual activity. Surveys list dozens of activities – from watching TV to sky diving – that fall under the umbrella, but probably miss many more.

Thus the individual is the building block of the recreation universe. Policy implications follow, for as the individual decisions, satisfactions and reactions aggregate, they become the concern of the elected official, the marketer, the recreation manager, the policy analyst and the researcher. We apply new conceptual labels to the aggregates and associated elements: leisure, travel and tourism, supply and demand, public and private providers, market share, indoor and outdoor, costs and benefits, health and fitness, and an array of individual motivations such as socialization, competition and self image.

In recreation, these aggregates generate the need for public and private decisions because they affect many people, involve many dollars, and require the apportionment of financial or other resources. There are policies to guide these decisions but, too often, there are competing policies, each established because of the interests and actions of different aggregates working through the congressional committee structure of closely guarded areas of jurisdiction. This is our policy-making process in a democratic system.

We lack a policy for policies. No one tries to make the pieces fit. Looking back at the history of legislative successes in recreation since World War II, it appears a most favourable trend. Less obvious are the conflicts brought about by the successes of other, sometimes related, interests: NEPA, the Endangered Species Act and the Americans with Disabilities Act, for instance. Such overarching laws increase the responsibilities of federal recreation providers without increasing funds or workforce to meet the new responsibilities.

In public policy, the challenge for recreation will be gaining a fair share of resources and just treatment against other interests on the national scene in an era of greater challenges. The private policy component, industry's role, may prove critically important in the next century by shaping trends in demand through new activities, equipment, and venues; public policy may be faced with the task of keeping up with these changes if a closer working relationship is not formed between all of recreation's players.

9

Trends and Implications of Tourism Policy in Developing Countries

Salah E.A. Wahab

Introduction

Rightly described as the economic giant of the 20th century (Wahab, 1974), tourism has achieved unprecedented growth in the aftermath of World War II: from 14.4 million tourist arrivals and total receipts from international tourism of US$1.4 billion in 1948, to 625 million tourist arrivals and tourist receipts estimated at US$444 billion in 1998. It is, therefore, understood that measured in terms of arrivals and receipts, tourism has grown almost 43-fold over the last 50 years. The annual rate of growth has, of course, varied over these years, but on average it grew annually by about 4.8%. It has now become the world's leading industry employing more than 225 million people around the globe.

Tourism is not a clear-cut sector, but an all-embracing and pervasive domain of service and industrial activities. It touches upon almost all spheres of national life within the country. That is especially the reason why a sound state policy of tourism development should be formulated before any significant tourism investment projects are launched (Edgell, 1990).

The manifold economic, sociocultural, political and environmental advantages that tourism brings to a developing country, underpins the growing concern of governments to develop tourism and enter the competitive world tourist market (Hall, 1994). Governments have started, in order to achieve such an aim, to ask for technical and financial assistance from international organizations, realizing that tourism cannot be developed as it once was by simply building hotels and other lodging facilities. A programme of serious studies and sound investments should be mounted, tailoring the country's tourist supply to meet the steadily expanding and constantly changing tourist demands. This has brought about corresponding expansion and changes in the type, range and structure of travel plans and facilities in almost all parts of the world. The right type of accommodation, taking into account the number of expected visitors and their spending patterns, must be provided at the right place, at the right time, and within a predetermined carrying capacity for the whole country and its potential tourist destinations.

Lack of Sufficient State Support to Tourism

The general lack of a comprehensive approach to the priority attached to tourism and its development limits in many developing countries, is perhaps the most striking factor that makes tourism still a trial and error sector in these countries. As a mainly service industry, tourism has generally taken third place in economic planning or in state priorities after productive sectors such as agriculture and manufacturing. Moreover, there has generally been little coordination between the various tourist components that provide goods and services to tourists and the actions of the public and private sectors (Elliot, 1997).

> Another aspect of the lack of public interest was the controlled use of natural resources within a general physical planning framework. The growth of tourism, when uncontrolled or insufficiently controlled, has resulted in harmful effects on the general physical environment. Through the pollution of beaches and the spoiling of many other natural assets, the future of tourism cannot be entirely left to the sole desires and interests of a private sector which is only governed by profit making dictates. It should, even in a clear-cut market economy orientation, be adequately and ably supervised by an impartial National Tourist Administration (NTA), otherwise tourism development would contain the seeds of its own destruction
> (United Nations, 1973)

Tourism is a Controversial Sector

However, tourism has been and still is subject to many controversial views about its role in economic development. First, tourism development, in the eyes of some writers, is not without a price. The price it exacts resides not only in its investment costs, but in the preservation costs of its cultural and natural heritage against wear and tear and misuse by tourists, the undermining of social standards and traditions, the pollution of the natural environment and undesirable changes in the natural landscape (Hamilton, 1972; Lea, 1988).

Secondly, tourism is viewed as an activity which is highly dependent on economic conditions prevailing in the niche markets as well as on the whims of the main tour operators and other technologically advanced transport and handling companies. Such criticism is answered by the fact that such dependency is not a characteristic confined to tourism, as it is a transcending concept in international trade (Jenkins, 1992). Thirdly, tourism is particularly criticized in that it involves many imports in developing countries which leads to narrow profit margins. Moreover, very limited tourist receipts generally remain at the developing destination in view of the wide array of foreign currency leakages.

Despite these critical views, tourism continues to attract increasing government attention across the globe, which would seem to necessitate greater emphasis on policy determinants.

Tourism in a Global Policy Context

Tourism policy can have various contexts according to what different countries wish it to be. However, by and large, it embraces the normative and strategic goals of tourism in a country. It may also include the main measures by which organized communities attempt to reach those goals, thus influencing socioeconomic development through tourism. The influence, whether aiming at growth or limitation, must be a conscious action on tourism development justified by the prevailing socioeconomic and political systems.

Government function in tourism: a redefinition

The multidimensional nature of the tourism industry gives rise to multiple variables acting jointly and/or separately to produce a wide range of areas for government policy making. Referring to the 'diversity of the activities which collectively constitute the tourism industry', Wheatcraft (1989) describes governments relationships with tourism in the following terms:

> All corporate planning must start from a precise definition of the purpose of the business or the mission role ... In a normal business organisation, this is something on which the board of directors and the

owners can and must agree. The basic purpose of the tourism industry is, however, something on which only governments can agree. And, if they do not, the tourist industry is likely to be left with some impossibly difficult decisions about its future course of development.

Fayos-Sola (1996) rightly stressed that with regard to the changing nature of the tourism industry, and especially in the context of the establishment of a new development paradigm, the so-called 'new tourism era', which is gradually replacing the old model of mass tourism:

> the governments of particular countries are forced to redefine the very essence of their respective tourism policies and seek new forms of cooperation with both the private sector and society as a whole.

Government policy making is the most important government function as it is the indispensable prerequisite for sound tourism development strategic planning. It embodies the government's general political, economic, social and environmental goals that are necessary landmarks at the national and regional levels. This would be true in developing countries as well as in developed countries (Richter, 1989).

National tourism policy in some developed countries are usually confined to embodying the most important tourism goals, which reflect overall national needs constrained by the existing market and resource factors. Typical examples would be the US Tourism Policy of 1981, embodying 17 goals, and the Canadian Federal Tourism Policy of 1990, which includes eight major goals. The constraints of market and resources are affected as a result of feedback resulting from the generated policy (Wahab, 1993).

It is essential that tourism goals are set in concert with the broader economic, sociocultural and environmental objectives of the destination (Mowforth and Munt, 1998). They must support broad national, regional and local interests (see OECD, 1992).

Main Trends in Tourism Policy

As indicated by Lickorich (1991), policy goals such as the actual or potential importance of tourism, economic growth, employment creation and balance of trade are the main parameters within which the state wants to see tourism develop, guiding the private sector by clearly indicating what types and volume of tourism are acceptable, and in which locations.

Governments have long exercised controls in some countries and areas, most particularly in respect of exchange rates and hotel service prices. Governments can influence the development of tourism in certain areas by setting the conditions and the scope of financial concessions, and regulating conditions of access to land, for example by allowing only long-term leases or rights of usufruct on land for foreign investors.

State involvement in the orientation, regulation and reasonable control of the tourism industry might be deemed necessary to attain a growth rate which is regarded by governments as desirable and sometimes necessary. Such a growth rate would be higher than the market-driven rate (Wahab and Pigram, 1997).

After stating the broad tourism goals with due consideration of external and internal constraints, more specific objectives should be articulated. Examples of these are sociocultural, environmental and organizational objectives that derive from the broad tourism goals such as those clearly set out in the recent Egyptian tourism policy statement laid down by the National Council on Productivity and Economic Affairs of the Presidency, which was prepared by its tourism committee chaired by the author (Egypt National Council on Productivity and Economic Affairs, 1997).

Determinants of national and regional tourism policies

Davidson and Maitland (1997) refer to Baum's (1994) research survey into the determinants of national tourism policies, where he categorized various National Tourism Organizations' (NTOs) replies to his survey by national economic criteria, dividing responses into three categories:

Group A   Countries with a per capita income of less than US$1000 (39% of total responses).

Group B   Countries with a per capita income between US$1000 and US$8000 (18% of total responses).

Group C   Countries with a per capita income greater than US$8000, which includes the UK (41% of total responses).

The survey resulted in average ratings for eight key objectives of national tourism policies in the following order: (i) to generate foreign revenue; (ii) to provide employment nationally; (iii) to improve regional/local economy; (iv) to create awareness; (v) to provide employment regionally/locally; (vi) to support the environment; (vii) to contribute to infrastructure development; and (viii) to create goodwill.

These determinants of tourism policy cannot be left entirely to the sole discretion and action of the National Tourism Administrations (NTAs) but should be the concern of a coherent state mechanism to be monitored by the NTAs. Pearce (1989) argues that 'while the activities of the NTAs may influence the path of tourist development directly, other more general or more indirect powers exercised by other central government agencies also may have a significant and perhaps greater impact'.

It is, therefore, necessary that the tourism policy, or perhaps its more detailed strategies, should indicate the various roles played by NTAs and other central and regional government departments and agencies and develop enough coherence between these roles. The most important factor, however, should be the binding effect of tourism policy and detailed tourism strategies upon all government agencies. This can only be achieved through legislation.

Diversity of the mandates of NTAs

While the main task of the state in tourism is to provide a suitable legal, regulatory and fiscal framework allowing the tourism industry to develop efficiently, NTAs in developing countries differ in their mandates and jurisdictions. Some would assume minimum functions such as assistance in facilitation, coordination, industry control and promotion, both domestically and overseas. Others would have much broader functions such as those in Egypt, Jordan, Tunisia and Turkey. These functions are investment incentives, dissemination of tourism information, ensuring the balanced and sustainable growth of tourism, offsetting market failures and seasonality, diversifying the tourist product, planning and supervising tourism education and training, and so on. Such diversity would derive in the main from differences in the socioeconomic and juridicopolitical systems prevailing, as well as from the priority attached to tourism and its historical development at the destination.

Shift to market mechanism policy trends

In many countries there is a gradual but marked shift to a market economy. This does not mean the state's withdrawal from policy making but a more subtle change from entrepreneurial action to positively paving the way for private enterprise to assume its role as the main tourism actor. This is usually done through the gradual privatization process of public sector concerns, business guidance through legal and regulatory control of the industry, planning, and leading but not monopolizing overseas promotion and marketing, coordinating and facilitating tourist development, assisting in ensuring quality services through several tools, including planning quality education and training. This has to be spelled out in the policy objectives, which are subject to change in time and space.

Globalization as a new mega-trend in state tourism policy

It is now accepted fact that the world is moving toward globalization as a fundamental mega-trend of world development. This should result in dramatic changes in the nature of the tourism industry and consequently in tourism policy in various countries, particularly in the developing world.

The global trends in the tourism industry should firmly focus on the consumers' preferences, which normally change rapidly due to technological advances and concomitant changes in economic and sociocultural variables. These variables cause diversification of lifestyles, the emergence of new market communication systems, new information and distribution systems, a thorough investigation and research into global tourist markets, the development and adjustment of corporate structures and the consolidation of competitive strategies and creation of competitive tourism advantages. The preservation of cultural identity within the global context where 'complete uniformity in cultural terms is remote and reflects interconnectedness rather than unity' (Robinson and Boniface, 1999) would require special attention in the tourism policy of developing countries.

Technical assistance in tourism policy making

As tourism policy formulation, implementation and management require a high level of expertise, this could present an obstacle in some developing countries particularly those newly emerging as tourist destinations. Such obstacles could be overcome or at least mitigated through World Tourism Organization (WTO) technical assistance programmes and/or bilateral aid that would require the creation of able government agencies that escape the onerous procedures and constraints often found in public administration.

To ensure success in tourism policy making, a developing country would need to apply flexible internal management methods and rules in addition to maintaining consistency with the national development policy as a whole.

Implications of Tourism Policy

Apart from the aforementioned main state functions in the tourism field, other supplementary activities are, conceptually or empirically, important commitments of the NTAs nationally and of authorities at the regional and local levels. Example of these are:

- General scientific and applied research and studies relating to tourism supply and demand including the collection and analysis of statistics indispensable both for research and for policy formulation.

- Conducting or sponsoring studies of tourism generating markets in view of establishing, where possible, specific models for each of those markets which should form part of marketing intelligence strategies.

- Surveying the country's tourist attractions and facilities with an objective assessment of their comparative advantages.

- Mounting a general tourism development strategy for the whole country in the light of the three points shown above, which should encompass important issues such as land use and general physical planning, determination of tourist priority developmental areas based on pre-established criteria including availability of resources, competition, and opportunity costs, and the provision of guidance as to the type of tourism which, based on economic, sociocultural, and environmental grounds, is deemed desirable. This would contribute to the creation of permanent new jobs.

- Suggesting plans of the required tourist supply components, including accommodation of various types, which the private sector could invest in, and providing guidelines for reducing the saturation of traditional destination regions and localities by redistributing the movement of visitors.

- Jointly planning marketing campaigns with the private sector and leading their implementation in various niche markets.

- Providing support for quality education and training programmes along WTOs TEDQUAL (manual on quality education and training in tourism) studies.

- Protection of the environment and national heritage.
- Providing the necessary guidelines for the tourism business sector to act in accordance with the prevailing and potential globalization trends to protect the national interests within the framework of the 1994 treaty on the free trade in services (General Agreement on Tariffs and Trade).

The Necessity of the Right Government Machinery

Thus, all the above activities should necessitate the existence of a suitable machinery that fits properly into the government hierarchy as previously mentioned.

An autonomous NTA would be either sufficient or insufficient depending upon the internal structure of the respective organizations apart from the NTA, whatever its status government. Normally, apart from the NTA, whatever its status is, there would be an inter-ministerial council or committee to ensure policy formulation, its amendment, implementation, and coordination at the highest level. The composition of this inter-ministerial body varies from one country to another, but in this author's view, it should be chaired by at least the Prime Minister if not the Head of State. Apart from ministers of the various departments involved, leading figures representing the tourism private sector and recognized scientific experts should also be members. This inter-ministerial body should have its own full-time professional secretariat to prepare the necessary working papers and studies, or cause them to be ready, to facilitate the work of this inter-ministerial body and to ensure the execution of its decisions.

In some countries, apart from such composite tourism machinery, a separate image building and tourist overseas promotion organization is also created. Examples of such organizations are found in France (Maison de France) and in Spain (Turispagna). In developing countries, fewer examples exist, such as the Egyptian Tourist Promotion Authority (ETA) and the newly

created Jordanian Tourist Board. Kenya, Chile, Columbia and Costa Rica are other examples of countries with a separate structure for tourism promotion and marketing (WTO, 1995b).

In other countries, in view of the changing patterns, structures and trends of tourism in the world, a new trend toward semi-public NTAs involving a partnership between the private sector and local authorities could be expected along the lines of Maison de France.

Conclusions

Formulating a national tourism policy in developing countries has become imperative. Governments in many developing countries have changed their roles due to the shift to the market economy system, fierce competition between tourist destinations, the emergence of what could rightly be called 'New Tourism', and the influence of globalization trends. The primary trends in tourism policy are manifested in the state priority attached to tourism, facilitating frontier formalities, promoting socioeconomic development, efficient utilization of resources, enhancing employment, creating a stable and effective business environment, and partnership between the public and private sectors (WTO, 1997).

Implications of the tourism policy would be various strategies aiming at achieving pre-established goals and objectives. Examples of these strategies are tourism overseas promotion strategy, the strategy for safeguarding quality standards, domestic tourism strategy, matching tourist supply and demand strategy, tourist education and training strategy and so on.

Within these various strategies, there should be some safeguards against mismanagement of tourism. These safeguards would lead to sustainability and avoidance or at least mitigation of various detriments to tourism (Wahab and Pigram, 1997).

The implementation of Agenda 21 by the United Nations, prepared after the Earth Summit at Rio de Janeiro in 1992, requires a major shift in priorities, involving a full integration of sustainable development considerations into economic and social policies and a major redeployment of human and financial resources both at national and international levels (WTO, 1995a). Furthermore:

> innovations brought about by the marriage of computers and telecommunications creating information superhighways makes possible, faster and better communication and information dissemination in developing countries at substantially lower cost through global computer networks and satellite-linked telephone and televised systems
>
> (United Nations, International Commission on Peace and Food, 1994)

Such recent developments should result in more pressing needs for tourism policy determinants to become more sophisticated and scientifically oriented in developing countries. Tourism's rapid changes require more flexible and responsive government organizations to deal with the consequences of development.

10

Trends in Recreation, Tourism and Protected Area Planning

Stephen F. McCool and Michael E. Patterson

Planning may be defined as 'linking knowledge to action' (Friedmann, 1987). In the times of turbulence and change that typify the late 20th and early 21st centuries, connecting knowledge to action not only becomes more important but more of a necessity. It is more important because the futures that we implicitly design with planning activities are more contentious, and thus greater interaction among affected publics to come to agreement on a desired future is needed. It is more of a necessity because the way to achieving the desired future is tied to identifying actions that will intervene in the ongoing social context. Planning is thus not only a way of identifying a desired future, but it is a process that helps us identify what road to take to this destination.

How we go about planning for recreation, tourism and protected areas is greatly affected by how we, as planners, perceive the planning situation[1]. Protected area, recreation and tourism planning has been guided by almost universal attention to the rational-comprehensive model, which focuses principally on identifying goals, searching for alternatives, evaluating them and choosing the technically most preferred alternative. This planning paradigm makes a number of implicit assumptions about the planning situation (such as the problem being well defined, unlimited time and resources, a single actor, decision-making power held by the actor) that are usually invalid in the real world. While this model's greatest strength is its apparent rationality, there is growing recognition that such rationality is bounded by a number of significant variables. And in the contentious and, as some would maintain, chaotic times of today, this model has been subject to increasing criticism (e.g. McCool and Stankey, 1986; Forester, 1989).

Planning for recreation, tourism and protected areas occurs within a context characterized by uncertainty, where goals of development and protection are frequently contested, and multiple interests compete not only for scarce resources but also for the political power influencing their disposition. Planning can no longer be viewed as simply a technical process where one follows a manual detailing a prescribed series of steps. Protected area, recreation and tourism planning is being influenced by a

---

[1] We recognize that a host of factors may influence the planning procedure, including legal mandates, the political context, budget and so on. Nevertheless, within this larger context, how planners perceive the situation will greatly affect how they go about implementing planning.

© CAB *International* 2000. *Trends in Outdoor Recreation, Leisure and Tourism* (eds W.C. Gartner and D.W. Lime)

variety of growing global changes in perceptions of democracy, preferences for more intimate public participation, concerns about distributional effects of management, and accelerating concerns about the sustainability of natural resource management actions.

In this chapter, we detail seven significant trends developing in the practice of recreation, tourism and protected area planning informed by the above changes. We hold that these trends form the foundation for planning in the 21st century.

Trend 1

The types of planning settings confronted by recreation, tourism and protected area planners have moved from tame problems to wicked problems and messes

As chaos and change have continued to buffet recreation, tourism and protected area planning, there has been increased conflict over the goals and objectives to be attained (see Trend 2). At the same time, there has been a trend, based in the ecosystem science and conservation biology disciplines, to consider human and natural processes occurring at larger spatial and longer temporal scales. The scientific knowledge available that deals with these larger scales is limited, thus increasing the degree of uncertainty and risk associated with planning decisions (Dovers and Handmer, 1993). The problems that occur where there is agreement on goals and scientific agreement on cause–effect relationships may be termed 'tame' ones. Technocracies, such as traditional recreation, park and tourism planning organizations, are ideally suited to solving tame problems because such solutions are generally well developed and are performed routinely through the use of rational-comprehensive planning models. Such models have as their greatest strength a systematic process for evaluating how well specific alternatives technically perform in achieving agreed-upon goals.

However, planners are increasingly confronted with situations characterized by disagreement on what goals a particular protected area should pursue, what recreation activities are appropriate in a park, or what social functions tourism development should serve. For example, the practice of recreation, tourism and protected area planning has moved from a site and facility orientation at small scales to larger scale policy and management issues, such as management of snowmobiles and bison in Yellowstone National Park. Tourism planners are confronted with growing public sentiment that tourism not only provides employment, but should also meet quality of life goals and help conserve scarce resources.

In these situations, scientific and technical information may play a role, but one which informs not dictates; problems are dealt with successfully only through negotiation because the problem is one of conflicting values, not necessarily lack of credible science. These types of problems are termed 'wicked' (Allen and Gould, 1986). Other planning settings are confronted not only with contested goals but a lack of scientific information as well. For example, the impact of snowmobiling on the mobility of the bison population in Yellowstone National Park is a subject of great conjecture, but limited scientific data. These situations may be termed 'messes' because they often entail a set of linked problems. In messy situations, problems are resolved (not solved) only temporarily because the context is continually changing (Ackoff, 1974). As Thompson and Tuden (1987) have argued, the planning process is significantly different in each situation. For wicked problems and messy situations, the legal power and responsibility to plan has been separated from the political power needed to marshal resources for implementation. Thus, planning processes must account for the pluralistic nature of the planning environment. In this environment, technical planning processes operating outside a public dialogue tend to create more in the way of disagreement than agreement.

Implications

Planning has been based on the rational-comprehensive model, but changes in society, a universal desire for effective plans, and new ways of looking at knowledge suggest significant, structural changes in planning processes in the future. Messy situations and wicked problems call for planning processes based on dialogue and social learning (Friedmann, 1987; Stankey *et al.*, 1999) that explicitly deal with politics. For recreation, protected area and tourism planning agencies, these trends suggest that new ways of approaching issues, emphasizing learning, collaborative action and consensus-building, take precedence over model building and scientific analysis in identifying potential futures and suggesting interventions to arrive at a desired condition.

Trend 2

There is a growing linkage between recreation, tourism and protected area planning and broader social policy goals

The reason for protected areas has changed dramatically since 1872 when Yellowstone National Park was legislatively established. Recreation areas have always provided settings that not only satisfy leisure time needs of citizens but also serve other socially significant functions, such as reducing vandalism, providing open space, protecting wildlife habitat, and so on. Tourism development traditionally has focused on increasing revenues and economic opportunity for businesses and their employees. These traditional functions of recreation, tourism and protected areas form the foundational rationale for engaging in these activities.

Yet, there is growing recognition that protecting natural areas, enhancing tourism opportunities or providing recreational settings are actions tightly entwined with quality of life goals that are distinct from, and often in conflict with, economic development goals. These quality of life objectives include preserving our cultural and natural heritage, enhancing economic opportunity (which contains more than jobs or labour income, such as opportunities for vertical advancement), and a host of other socially desirable values such as increased

family cohesiveness, reduced crime, greater educational opportunity. Tourism development is increasingly viewed as a means to generate funding for the management of protected areas, through fees, charges and revenue sharing, and as a way of helping communities cope with economic restructuring that has accompanied the declining economic importance of natural resource commodities. For example, tourism development in the Flathead Valley in Montana has helped the community deal with the significant decline in forest products processing that occurred there in the 1980s. To some extent, tourism development has provided alternative employment opportunities, and has encouraged the development of the community's social capital, thereby enhancing the area's ability to cope with economic and political change.

However, as goals for recreation, tourism and protected areas have expanded, so has the conflict over these goals. Goals represent a desired future, and with an increasingly pluralistic society, there are many desired and potentially conflicting desired futures. Planning therefore becomes a conflict resolution strategy, where planners help communities confront and resolve their competing visions. Recreation, tourism and protected areas can be viewed as some of the choices in resolving these conflicts.

Implications

Linking planning for recreation, protected areas, and tourism requires fundamental consideration of quality of life goals, the purposes of economic development, and functions of protected area preservation. For example, publically funded tourism promotion is conducted not to increase visitor attendance, but rather to achieve goals with respect to increasing labour income, enhancing educational opportunity and protecting the resident quality of life.

Trend 3

Planning is becoming more inclusive of the values incorporated into the planning process

Planning for recreation and protected areas increasingly recognizes that such reserves serve a multitude of important ecological functions other than providing opportunities for recreation. These include preserving biodiversity, protecting habitat for endangered species and allowing natural processes to operate with a minimum of human intrusion. Such planning has thus moved away from a functional to a more integrative orientation. For example, developing a winter recreational use management plan for Yellowstone National Park cannot be done without consideration of bison population dynamics, which in turn may affect grizzly bear populations. While these linkages and multiple values may appear to make planning more complex, the appearance is only an illusion: planning was always complex, it is just that reductionistic models failed to recognize this complexity and often led to surprises (Lee, 1993).

This more inclusive consideration of broader values has two distinctive dimensions. First, the types of values included in protected area, recreation and tourism planning have diversified. Yellowstone National Park serves as an outstanding example. Established in 1872 as a 'park or pleasuring ground', Yellowstone remains an attraction for the annual American pilgrimage to nature. Stephen T. Mather, the first director of the National Park Service, envisioned a park where the accoutrements of civilization in the form of fine villas and high art dotted the islands of Yellowstone Lake – one can almost envision young women with their parasols and young men with their beaver hats strolling on these islands. While conserving scenery and natural 'objects' was a focus of the first century of the park's management, much of the planning energy went into accommodating recreational uses and eliminating wildlife species, predators, that killed the 'good' nature.

In the 1960s, this attitude began to change, stimulated in part by the Leopold report that suggested that parks represent a 'vignette of primitive America' while providing the initial recognition of complex ecological dynamics. A series of controversies over wildlife, particularly elk and grizzly bears, forced a greater recognition not only of the complexities of planning, but

the realization that parks serve important functions in protecting habitats and populations of threatened and endangered species. The restoration of wolf populations in the mid-1990s further served to identify the value of parks as places for recovery. Recreation is now viewed not as the dominant use to be accommodated but as one of several overlapping, and frequently conflicting, values of national parks.

The second dimension of this change has occurred because of shifting ways in how we think about what is being managed. Instrumental and narrow definitions of protected area resources (for example, trees, animals, mountains, streams) are giving way to more holistic definitions. Margaret Shannon has argued:

> ... many of our resource conflicts hold us captive because of our myopic focus on things (a log, a tree, a deer, scenic beauty) as if they were 'resources', ... (we need) to move our focus away from tangible 'things' that are part of the resource relationship and toward the resource relationship itself
> (Shannon, 1991)

Nature itself is tightly associated with our spiritual dimension; it may be impossible to clearly, and in a quantitative way, specify what is nature and what is natural – obviously questions at the heart of protected area planning. Likewise, we may start asking 'whose nature do we protect?' and, more importantly, we should ask 'who gets to ask the questions and who gets to make the decisions'.

Implications

Clearly, more inclusive and more holistic thinking – what is the resource: soils or solitude? – challenge existing paradigms of protected area planning as they will in the tourism area. Tourism planning is dominated by 'happy talk' and building 'better brochures', with little discussion of the powerful and positive recreational experiences that can occur if we appropriately market a destination area, consider quality of life issues for residents of destination areas, and deal with frequent structural distortions of power in decision making. The narrow functional promotional emphasis in tourism planning has not been challenged yet on the same scale as the 'pleasuring ground' concept of national parks. But this is only a matter of time. Furthermore, planners will need to be increasingly more cognizant of the systemic linkages when planning. For example, recruiting a new minor league baseball team and providing it with a park in which to play, may significantly negatively impact the quality of life of a local neighbourhood as they pay the traffic congestion and noise costs.

Trend 4

There is more integration of tourism considerations in national park planning and vice versa

National parks exist within a context of communities economically dependent on them. Likewise, many state or regional level tourism industries have increasingly recognized that the sustainability of their industries is linked to the careful management of parks and other wildland areas. For example, 40–50% of Montana's tourism industry economic impact is directly associated with wildland recreation settings (Yuan and Moisey, 1992). Given the linkages developing between communities and protected areas, specific management actions within the protected area may bring significant economic impact to the community. For example, proposals to reconstruct the Going-to-the-Sun highway in Glacier National Park, Montana, will result in an estimated loss of between US$81 and US$161 million in gross expenditures from nonresidents in the state of Montana, because the road will be closed (Nickerson and Nickerson, 1998). While this points out the importance of economic linkages, there are others, including ecological, aesthetic and cultural ones as well. Actions which impact on these linkages will affect communities.

Thus, increasingly, there has been broader recognition of the effects of national park planning options on tourism, and conversely, the effects of investments in tourism promotion on protected areas. Tourism promotion activities tend to increase demand for the recreational opportunities and resources within protected areas. Promotion content may influence the image visitors will have of the area and assist in the development of on-site expectations. Park planners and managers will then need to have in place the management systems to deal with increased visitation and potentially unrealistic or inappropriate expectations.

Implications

This higher level of integration has not only enhanced the quality of the resulting plans, thus increasing the probability that the plan will be implemented, but it has also brought new challenges, such as how local and national stakeholders are integrated into the planning process. While many of the interests that local and national stakeholders retain may be shared, others will be competing. Integration of different values in planning requires the planner to actively seek out and involve different interests both early and continuously in the planning process. A planner, in an increasingly diverse American society, cannot hope to adequately represent all these interests, a responsibility implicitly assumed by planners.

Trend 5

Planning has moved away from simplistic, carrying-capacity-based paradigms to those more focused on management of desired social and biophysical conditions

Carrying-capacity-based planning processes tended to define protected area and tourism planning problems as those of too many people. While such processes spawned a great deal of useful research attempting to link the number of people or visitors with social and biophysical impacts, they did little to protect the social and biophysical conditions desired or determined appropriate for the area.

Approaches emphasizing establishing use limits carry the appearance of 'scientific objectivity' but in reality conceal a variety of value judgments (Krumpe and McCool, 1997). They fail to explicitly address the question of what conditions are appropriate/acceptable and the question of how to manage an area to achieve those conditions; instead they emphasize implementing limits on recreational use without consideration of other more effective, yet less intrusive, measures. Establishing a recreation carrying capacity requires that a number of conceptual and practical conditions be met (Shelby and Heberlein, 1986; Lindberg et al., 1997; Borrie et al., 1998). In most cases, these conditions (such as agreement on goals, a specifically identified relationship between use levels and impacts, control over access) cannot be met.

The fundamental rationale for establishing a carrying capacity is to balance a goal of allowing recreational use, while still protecting the pristine qualities of the protected area. Carrying capacity does not do a good job of addressing this goal because it fails to recognize that allowing recreational use inevitably leads to some degradation; therefore, the ultimate question is one of how much impact will be socially or politically acceptable. Resolving the conflict between goals of providing access and preserving pristine qualities requires that one be identified as ultimately constraining, but can be initially compromised (Cole and Stankey, 1997). This goal is compromised until further change is no longer acceptable. Then the other goal is compromised as much as necessary to prevent the changes in the initial goal from becoming unacceptable. In protected areas, pristine conditions generally represent the ultimately constraining goal, but are initially compromised until further change is socially unacceptable. From that point, recreational use is managed to prevent any further impacts.

Research has shown that the relationship between use levels and impacts is anything but simple and linear: a variety of variables affect this relationship. Research and planning have both advanced to the point that recognizes that carrying capacity is a reductionistic, naive and inappropriate paradigm upon which to base actions that protect rec-

reational settings or tourism-dependent communities. Systems that focus on understanding what conditions are desired, what impacts are acceptable and what is unacceptable, and what actions will lead to accepted goals, are increasingly used to find resolutions to planning problems. Several such systems exist, most notably the Limits of Acceptable change and the Visitor Experience and Resource Protection processes developed by the US Department of Agriculture (USDA) Forest Service and US Department of the Interior (USDI) National Park Service (Stankey et al., 1986; Denver Service Center, 1993; McCool and Cole, 1997). Others such as Visitor Impact Management developed to address visitor use issues in National Parks (Graefe et al., 1990) and the Tourism Optimisation Management Model (Manidis Roberts Consultants, 1997) developed in South Australia have also been initiated to respond to similar problems. When combined with a public involvement strategy that emphasizes dialogue and social learning, these processes make for a powerful tool in resolving conflict, developing management resolutions and protecting the qualities that make parks special places.

Implications

Managing for desired resource and social conditions, both in protected areas and as a goal of tourism development, will require not only additional research to understand linkages between use and conditions, but also increased interactive and deliberative public involvement processes (see Trend 6). These processes will help to identify and then integrate public desires for future conditions, suggest scientifically efficient ways of achieving those conditions and determine the social acceptability of actions and conditions.

Trend 6

Changes in philosophy and tactics of public involvement in recreation, tourism and protected area planning

One consequence of the move from tame to wicked problems and messes (Trend 1) has been a paradigm shift in philosophy and tactics of public involvement. Most resource agencies were founded under a Progressive Era philosophy in which the public was seen as the beneficiary and user of the resource, but was accorded little role in the decision making process (Hays, 1997). Within this model, the public interest was seen as something that could be discovered by neutral, scientific experts. And, in fact, only experts were thought to have both the technical qualifications necessary to understand the problems and the ability to transcend petty political squabbles of self-interested groups to serve the general public interest (Williams and Matheny, 1995). This philosophy was embodied by the rational-comprehensive planning process and during the period following World War II, planning increasingly became the domain of experts who claimed their knowledge about the future and how to get there was superior to the user/beneficiary.

The nature of public relations efforts under this model followed two routes. The first may be described as an intermediation model in which public input was seen as just another source of data or input which expert planners used to make the decision (Sirmon, 1993). The second emphasis of public relations efforts reflected a belief that interactions with the public should focus on education that increases public faith in science, and served primarily as a means to the end of letting experts make the decisions (Williams and Matheny, 1995).

Beginning in the 1970s, the public revolted both against the idea of being excluded from planning processes concerning the future, and being treated in a condescending way as implied by the above two routes. Ultimately this reaction by the pubic has forced planners to make fundamental shifts in how they view the public, the concept of public interest and the nature of public relations. Increasingly, the public is seen not just as the beneficiary and user of resources, but as the arbiters of the public interest. That is, the public interest is not seen as something that can be objectively discovered and defined once and for all through science but as something that is continually evolving

and must be repeatedly created through public dialogue (Williams and Matheny, 1995). Public relations efforts have moved away from the intermediation model and public education toward a focus on communication, building trust and establishing long-term relationships. These shifts have led agencies to experiment with more collaborative decision making processes in which members of the public are not just another source of input for decision makers, but active participants. Examples of recent collaborative efforts in recreation and protected area planning include development of a controversial wilderness management plan for the Charles C. Deam Wilderness in Indiana (Slover, 1995), resolution of a conflict between ORV use and an endangered shorebird on Cape Cod National Seashore (Barry, 1998), development of the recreation management direction for the Bob Marshall Wilderness (McCool and Ashor, 1984), and the Inimin Forest Management Plan (Duane, 1997).

Implications

In general, collaborative, learning, consensus-building models of recreation, tourism, and protected area planning have been resisted by planners. However, to move forward in ensuring that the public interest is represented in tourism promotion, for example, those potentially affected but not included will effectively 'veto' such plans if not involved. Tourism promotion agencies thus must shift their emphasis, narrowly defined as advertising and promotion, to a more inclusive notion of economic development. Such a shift means greater public involvement simply because development requires public consent about means and goals.

Trend 7

Planning is moving away from standards-based decisions and cookie cutter solutions to needs-based resolutions tailored to the needs of individual situations

How many recreation facilities of what type are needed to adequately serve a community? This apparently relatively straightforward (but exceedingly complex) question had formerly been answered by turning to national level handbooks that indicated that so many facilities were needed per unit population. This standards-based system failed for the same reason that it was popular: it was simple. It implicitly assumed that technically trained recreation planners adequately represented the public interest and needs. However, as someone once noted 'to every complex question there is a simple answer, and it is wrong'. The move away from generic standards-based solutions to needs-based resolutions is occurring as a response to trends noted previously. Of primary importance are the recognition of problems as wicked, of the importance of viewing problems at a different scale and that the public interest is continually evolving and created through public dialogue.

Recognizing problems as wicked in nature highlights the importance of paying careful attention to the particular context of the specific planning problem being addressed. For example, conflicts over plans can arise from a variety of sources including: (i) disagreements about the data or facts that serve as the basis for the plan; (ii) disputes about goals or values used to interpret the desirability or appropriateness of alternatives; (iii) concerns regarding equity or distributional issues; or (iv) issues related to what decision making processes communicate about relationships (e.g. how much a particular group is valued or who has power and how it is exercised) (Duane, 1997). In any given situation, opposition to plans may reflect any one or some combination of these sources of conflict. Standardized solutions are inadequate, in part due to their failure to recognize that as the context changes, the nature and source of the opposition may also change and therefore a solution acceptable in one place may fail to address issues relevant to a different time and place.

Another aspect of planning problems that makes standardized solutions inadequate is associated with the concept of scale. Often previous attempts to incorporate public input into planning processes have focused on an individual level analysis exploring attitudes and preferences or economic analysis of proposed benefits without attention to the characteristics of the specific community in which those benefits were to accrue or who would bear the costs. However, there is growing recognition that feasibility must be considered at a community level scale as well, which is not simply an aggregation of individual preference curves. Analysis at this scale deals with questions such as whether or not the community has the capacity to resolve conflicts, has the infrastructure to take advantage of the predicted potential benefits of a plan, and whether the anticipated changes are consistent with the existing community's goals (Enck, 1998). For example, Duane (1997) suggests that the ability of a community to resolve conflicts depends on the existing status of a community's 'social capital' (power relationships, norms of reciprocity, trust and networks for civic engagement). A planning process that works in one community may fail in another due to differences in context at the community scale. The uniform application of facility and recreation standards fails to account for these dimensions.

A final problem with standardized solutions is that they fail to recognize that the public interest is something that is continually evolving and created through public dialogue. In a sense, standards-based planning is anything but adaptive. This denies the local community voice, increasing the likelihood of conflict stemming from relationship/power issues even when the goals, values and interests might otherwise be palatable to the community.

Implications

Agencies need to move away from simplistic notions of solutions and answers. These are no longer adequate to address the growing complexity and diversity of demands on natural resources. New approaches to dealing with planning, such as transactive planning theory or soft systems methodology (Checkland and Scholes, 1990) may be more appropriate planning paradigms. Coordination, a chief goal of centralized, top-down planning that is often characterized by 'cookie-cutter' solutions can be achieved through incentives at lower scales.

Conclusion

We maintain that recreation, protected area and tourism planning is beginning a new era – one that increasingly involves the public in meaningful dialogue and roles, recognizes the pluralistic nature of American politics and society, understands the 'messiness' of problems, and is more inclusive not only of those for whom the planning is done, but of the values at stake as well. Much of this change has not been brought about by the planning profession, unfortunately, but has been forced upon it by a public resolutely dissatisfied with the results and process of rational-comprehensive planning. New paradigms of planning, where public participation may be indistinguishable from the planning process, are in the works, not only in urban situations, where the challenges of planning have spurned innovation, but also for protected areas, recreation and tourism agencies. We would expect that movement to new ways of doing business – towards Freidmann's 'non-Euclidean' approaches – to be challenged, not so much by the public, but by the planning profession itself, because such approaches threaten the 'culture of technical control' (Yankelovich, 1991) characterizing planning in natural resource and tourism settings.

Planning is not the sole domain of technocrats, nor do planners have exclusive claims to representing the public interest. While such assertions developed out of 'New Deal' models of public agencies, an increasingly diverse American public has grown suspicious of agency motivations and actions. Only through changes in planning paradigms will greater agreement on means and ends, rather than disagreement, occur.

11

Coming of Age: History and Trends in Outdoor Recreation Research

Robert E. Manning

Introduction: From Diversity to Direction

One of the most distinctive characteristics of outdoor recreation research is its inherent diversity (Manning, 1999). First and foremost, outdoor recreation itself is diverse by definition, as it addresses both people and the natural environment. Issues in outdoor recreation are conventionally dichotomized into environmental science concerns (e.g. ecological impacts) and social science concerns (e.g. crowding and conflicting uses). This paper deals only with social science research in outdoor recreation. But even within the social science domain, outdoor recreation research may be approached from a variety of disciplinary perspectives, including sociology, psychology, geography, political science and economics. Finding commonality and trends within these discipline-based studies can be complex. Indeed, simply finding the research in the variety of journals and other publication sources in which it is reported can be difficult.

Outdoor recreation research also tends to be isolated in space and time; studies are widely scattered geographically and are conducted over varying periods. At least on the surface, an early study of developed campgrounds in an Eastern park can be diffi-

cult to integrate with a more recent study of wilderness use in the West. Outdoor recreation has also been subject to wide methodological diversity. Even though the dominant research approach has been to survey on-site visitors, there has been substantial variation in sampling techniques, the scope of such studies, and the way in which important variables have been conceptualized and measured.

Finally, substantive findings from outdoor recreation are also diverse. Visitors to parks and related areas participate in a variety of outdoor recreation activities, represent a broad spectrum of socioeconomic and cultural characteristics, and often report varying attitudes and preferences regarding a host of recreation management issues.

However, within this broad diversity, several theoretical, methodological and substantive directions or trends can be observed. Dominant trends include: (i) evolution of recreation research from primarily empirically based studies of visitor characteristics and use patterns to more theoretically based studies of visitor behaviour; (ii) development of conceptual frameworks that allow integration of multiple studies; (iii) development of theoretical models of important recreation issues; and (iv) continuing evolution of recreation

research to address emerging societal problems and issues. These trends are briefly
described and illustrated in this chapter.
These trends have substantial implications
for both outdoor recreation research and
management.

A History of Outdoor Recreation Research: Epistemological and Methodological Evolution

Outdoor recreation is not a discipline in the
conventional academic sense. That is, it is
not a basic branch of knowledge like
biology, mathematics or sociology. It is an
applied field of study focused on an issue or
problem that has attracted the attention of a
broad segment of society. Though research
in outdoor recreation can be traced back 50
years or more (e.g. Meinecke, 1928; Bates,
1935), sufficient attention was not focused
on outdoor recreation for it to emerge as a
field of study until after World War II. During the 1950s, rapid gains in economic
prosperity, ease of transportation, increasing leisure time and other social forces
converged to produce dramatic and sustained increases in the use of outdoor
recreation areas. Problems in the form of
environmental impacts and crowding began
to attract the attention of both professionals
and the public as manifested in articles in
national magazines and professional journals (e.g. DeVoto, 1953; Clawson, 1959a).
Outdoor recreation as a field of study had its
genesis in this period.

The beginning of serious social scientific
study in this field in the US, and perhaps
worldwide, began with the Outdoor Recreation Resources Review Commission
(ORRRC) reports. ORRRC was a presidential
commission established in 1958 to assess
the status of outdoor recreation in America
(Siehl, Chapter 8). It published its widely
read summary report, *Outdoor Recreation
for America*, in 1962 along with 29 special
studies (ORRRC, 1962). The paucity of outdoor recreation research before that time is
evident in one of the special studies which
surveyed the outdoor recreation literature.
The introduction of the report stated:

> The outline prepared as a guide for the
> bibliographic search assumed the existence
> of a substantial body of material relating
> rather directly to outdoor recreation. As the
> actual hunt progressed, the true situation –
> that the field (if it is yet that) of outdoor
> recreation has been but sketchily treated –
> became more and more evident
>
> (Librarian of Congress, 1962, p. 2)

The bibliographical catalogue of the Library
of Congress had no subject heading, 'outdoor recreation'. Fewer than ten entries
were found in this study that referred to
outdoor recreation in their titles.

Most of the early research in outdoor
recreation was ecologically oriented. This
was, at least in part, because most outdoor
recreation managers were professionally
trained in the traditional biological disciplines or fields of study, including forestry
and wildlife biology (Lime, 1972; Hendee
and Stankey, 1973). An early observation
noted that social scientists traditionally
paid little attention to the broad issue of
leisure and recreation. The multidisciplinary nature of outdoor recreation, however,
gained recognition in the post-World War II
period. Social problems such as crowding
began to supplement traditional concerns
for environmental impacts, and participants
in outdoor recreation activities were recognized as having socioeconomic characteristics, attitudes and preferences that
might be of interest to park and outdoor
recreation managers. Emphasis on the social
aspects of outdoor recreation was furthered
in the 1960s and early 1970s by a series of
calls for research on outdoor recreation in
several major social science disciplines,
including sociology (Catton, 1971; Hendee,
1971), economics (Clawson and Knetsch,
1963), psychology (Driver, 1972), geography
(Mitchell, 1969), and a general multidisciplinary approach (Lucas, 1966).

Early social science research in outdoor
recreation and leisure in general was primarily descriptive, focusing on the activities
and social characteristics of the participants. The ORRRC studies noted earlier are
examples of this type of research. Early
observers criticized this work as 'little else
than a reporting of survey data' (Berger,

1962) and 'sheer empiricism' (Meyersohn, 1969). Absence of a strong theoretical foundation, along with an overemphasis on applied problem solving, has been a continuing criticism of outdoor recreation research (Moncrief, 1970; Hendricks and Burdge, 1972; Crandall and Lewko, 1976; Burdge *et al.*, 1981; Riddick *et al.*, 1984; Iso-Ahola, 1986a). For example, an analysis of papers published in the *Journal of Leisure Research* from 1978 to 1982 concluded that two-thirds 'lacked an explicit statement about the theoretical basis of the study' (Riddick *et al.*, 1984).

However, evidence suggests this has changed over time as outdoor recreation research has developed and matured. As early as 1970, it was noted that the field of outdoor recreation was beginning to move beyond the descriptive phase and into more explanatory studies (Moncrief, 1970). Moreover, synergistic effects of outdoor recreation and leisure research were beginning to materialize. A study of participation in water-based recreation published in 1974, for example, noted that 'in the investigation of any problem area there must be a systematic and rigorous effort by many so that studies are progressive and research findings are accumulative, if a critical mass of theoretical and substantive knowledge is to emerge' (Field and Cheek, 1974). The authors concluded that, 'In the study of leisure, we are coming of age'. The same year, an assessment of research published in the *Journal of Leisure Research* reached a similar conclusion: 'The study of leisure is approaching the threshold of real accomplishment' (Burdge, 1974).

Progress in recreation research is evident in more recent analyses. An examination of papers published in four recreation-related journals from 1981 to 1990 found that most included a theoretical or conceptual framework (Henderson, 1994b). Moreover, there is evidence that recreation research has proved effective and efficient. A study of the US Department of Agriculture (USDA) Forest Service found that most important innovations in outdoor recreation management were derived from research (Anderson and Schneider, 1993; Schneider *et al.*,

1993). The study concluded that 'recreation resource management research ... is considered important and successful by managers and researchers'. A second USDA Forest Service study assessed the value of social science more broadly and concluded that:

> social science research can help managers work more effectively with their clients and partners to increase 'customer satisfaction', increase support for resource management programs and policies, reduce controversy and conflict, reduce the need for restrictive rules, laws, and regulations relating to resource management and use, and reduce management costs
>
> (Jakes *et al.*, 1998)

The effectiveness of recreation research in the National Park Service also has been documented (Machlis and Harvey, 1993). Finally, an economic study suggests that, based on efficiency, we may be under-investing in outdoor recreation-related research (Bengston and Xu, 1993).

Evidence suggests that recreation research also has become multidisciplinary, even interdisciplinary. Early analyses of outdoor recreation noted its inherent multidisciplinary nature, and that research should span the traditional social science disciplines (National Academy of Sciences, 1969; Van Doren and Heit, 1973; Crandall and Lewko, 1976). A study of scholarly journals in recreation suggests that research is moving in this direction (Burdge, 1983). Authors and editors of these journals reveal a trend away from a disciplinary approach to outdoor recreation to a more multidisciplinary treatment. Contributions from the traditional social science disciplines of sociology, psychology and economics have declined relative to contributions from researchers in the broader park, recreation and related departments, whose studies are broader in nature and more appropriate to problem solving in an inherently interdisciplinary field.

If the quality of outdoor recreation research is debatable, the quantity is not. Just 11 years after the scant literature base uncovered by the ORRRC studies, a bibliography on outdoor recreation carrying capacity was developed, containing 208 citations (Stankey and Lime, 1973). A 1978 bibliography on the subject of river recreation contained 335 citations (Anderson *et al.*, 1978). One of the bibliographies included in this citation has nearly a thousand citations, while the others have more than a thousand (Echelberger *et al.*, 1983; Kuss *et al.*, 1990; Daigle, 1993). Despite this apparent increase in outdoor recreation research, basic information on use and users of parks and related areas remains patchy at best. A recent survey of areas managed by the National Park Service found that most parks lacked basic visitor-related information, including socioeconomic characteristics, residence and satisfaction (Manning and Wang, 1998).

Research in outdoor recreation has, then, evolved in the classic manner of most emerging fields of study. Most early studies were descriptive and exploratory, substituting data for theory, and were disciplinary-based. An expanding data base allowed more conceptual and analytical development, and ultimately a more multidisciplinary and interdisciplinary approach. These trends are evident in the scholarly journals in which recreation research is reported. The early studies of the 1950s and 1960s are found in journals of sociology, psychology, economics and forestry. As research activity expanded, the developing field of outdoor recreation created its own multidisciplinary scholarly publication outlets, including the *Journal of Leisure Research* in 1969, *Leisure Sciences* in 1977, and the *Journal of Park and Recreation Administration* in 1983.

Development of Conceptual Frameworks: Carrying Capacity and Other Paradigms

The preceding section suggests several trends in outdoor recreation research, all of which are methodological and epistemological. However, there have been a number of substantive advances as well, including the development of several conceptual frameworks that provide a more holistic or integrated structure from which to understand and ultimately manage outdoor recreation. A long-standing example of such a conceptual framework is carrying capacity.

Rapidly expanding recreation in the 1950s and 1960s gave rise to concerns over appropriate use levels of outdoor recreation areas. While interest in the impacts of recreation on the natural resource base predominated, attention was beginning to shift to the effects of increased use on the quality of the recreation experience. Early studies prompted theorists to search for a conceptual framework to help formulate outdoor recreation policy. A resulting paradigm was carrying capacity.

Carrying capacity has a rich history in the natural resource professions, substantially predating its serious adoption in the field of outdoor recreation. In particular, the term has received wide use in wildlife and range management, where it refers to the number of animals of any one species that can be accommodated over time in a given habitat. Perhaps the first suggestion for applying the concept of carrying capacity to outdoor recreation was recorded in the mid-1930s. A National Park Service report on policy recommendations for parks in the California Sierras posed the question, 'How large a crowd can be turned loose in a wilderness without destroying its essential qualities?' (Sumner, 1936). Later in the report, it was suggested that recreation use of wilderness be kept 'within the carrying capacity'. The concept of carrying capacity became a more formal part of the outdoor recreation field when it was listed as a major issue by Dana (1957) in his problem analysis of outdoor recreation, and as a result of its prominence in the deliberations and writings of the ORRRC (ORRRC, 1962).

The first rigorous application of carrying capacity to outdoor recreation came in the early 1960s with a conceptual monograph by Wagar (1964). Perhaps the major contribution of Wagar's conceptual analysis was the expansion of carrying capacity from its dominant emphasis on environmental effects to a dual focus including social or experiential considerations. Wagar's point was that as more people visit an outdoor recreation area, not only the environmental resources of the area are affected, but also the quality of the recreation experience. Thus, carrying capacity was expanded to include consideration of the social environment as well as the biophysical environment.

Wagar's original conceptual analysis hinted at a third element of carrying capacity, and this was described more explicitly in a subsequent paper (Wagar, 1968). Noting a number of misconceptions about carrying capacity, it was suggested that carrying capacity might vary according to the amount and type of management activity. For example, the durability of biophysical resources might be increased through practices such as fertilizing and irrigating vegetation, and periodic rest and rotation of impact sites. Similarly, the quality of the recreation experience might be maintained or even enhanced in the face of increasing use by means of a more even distribution of visitors, appropriate rules and regulations, provision of additional visitor facilities and educational programmes designed to encourage desirable user behaviour. Thus carrying capacity, as applied to outdoor recreation, was expanded to a three-dimensional concept: environmental, social and managerial considerations.

Carrying capacity has attracted intensive focus as a research and management concept or paradigm in outdoor recreation. Several bibliographies, books and review papers have been published on carrying capacity and related issues, and these publications contain hundreds of citations (e.g. Stankey and Lime, 1973; Graefe et al., 1984; Shelby and Heberlein, 1986; Stankey and Manning, 1986; Kuss et al., 1990). Yet despite this impressive literature base, efforts to apply carrying capacity to recreation areas has often resulted in frustration. The principal difficulty lies in determining how much impact or change should be allowed within each of the three components that make up the carrying capacity framework: the naturalness of environmental resources, the quality of the recreation experience, and the

extent and direction of management actions.

The growing research base on outdoor recreation indicates that increasing recreation use often causes impact or change to the environmental, experiential or managerial components of carrying capacity. However, despite increasing knowledge about recreation use and resulting impacts, the critical question remains: how much impact or change should be allowed? This issue is often referred to as the 'limits of acceptable change' (Frissell and Stankey, 1972). Some change in the recreation environment is inevitable, but sooner or later the amount, nature or type of change may become unacceptable. But what determines the limits of acceptable change?

Recent experience with carrying capacity suggests that answers to the above question can be found through formulation of management objectives and associated indicators and standards of quality (e.g. Lime and Stankey, 1971; Stankey et al., 1986; Stankey and Manning, 1986; Shelby et al., 1992; Manning and Lime, 1996; National Park Service, 1997b). This approach to carrying capacity focuses on defining the type of visitor experience to be provided. Management objectives are broad, narrative statements defining the type of visitor experience to be provided. Indicators of quality are more specific, measurable variables reflecting the essence or meaning of management objectives; they are quantifiable proxies or measures of management objectives. Indicators of quality may include elements of the biophysical, social and management environments that are important in determining the quality of the visitor experience. Standards of quality define the minimum acceptable condition of each indicator variable.

Research has given rise to several frameworks for determining and applying carrying capacity to outdoor recreation. These frameworks include Limits of Acceptable Change (LAC) (Stankey et al., 1986; McCool and Cole, 1997), Visitor Impact Management (VIM) (Graefe et al., 1990) and Visitor Experience and Resource Protection (VERP) (Manning et al., 1996a; Hof and

Lime, 1997; National Park Service, 1997b). All these frameworks incorporate the ideas about carrying capacity described above and provide a rational, structured process for making carrying capacity decisions.

Several applications and evaluations of carrying capacity frameworks and related processes have been developed and described in the literature (e.g. Ashor *et al.*, 1986; Shelby and Heberlein, 1986; Graefe *et al.*, 1990; Vaske *et al.*, 1992; Manning *et al.*, 1995a,b,c, 1996a,b; National Park Service, 1995b; Manning and Lime, 1996; Manning, 1997; McCool and Cole, 1997).

Other conceptual frameworks developed in the recreation literature include the Recreation Opportunity Spectrum (Brown *et al.*, 1978; Clark and Stankey, 1979; Driver *et al.*, 1987), indicators and standards of quality (Stankey *et al.*, 1985; Manning *et al.*, 1998) and several classification systems of recreation management practices and related management processes or handbooks (Lime, 1977; Manning, 1979; Cole *et al.*, 1987; Anderson *et al.*, 1998).

Development of Theoretical Models: Crowding and Other Issues

Substantive advances in outdoor recreation research have also focused on a growing number of issues or topical areas. These issues have been the subject of many studies whose findings can be synthesized into theoretical models that guide further research and management. Crowding is a prominent example of such an issue.

There is a relatively long history of concern over the effects of increasing use on the quality of the recreation experience, beginning even before the post-World War II boom in recreation participation (e.g. Adams, 1930; Leopold, 1934). Shortly after the beginning of the period of rapidly expanding outdoor recreation in the 1950s and 1960s, a number of popular articles began to generate widespread interest in this topic (e.g. DeVoto, 1953; Clawson, 1959a).

Adoption of the concept of carrying capacity, particularly the expansion of the concept to include a social carrying capacity

component, provided a convenient foundation on which to base theoretical and empirical crowding research. Wagar's (1964) conceptual analysis of carrying capacity is an appropriate place to begin discussion. This analysis suggested that, 'When too many people use the same area, some traditional wildland values are lost'. This was illustrated with a series of hypothetical relationships between crowding and a number of human motivations inherent in outdoor recreation participation.

Early empirical studies of crowding (e.g. Lucas, 1964; Stankey, 1973) were followed by theoretical development. Several theorists developed a quantitative model of the effects of increasing use on the recreation experience, based on the economic concept of marginal utility (Clawson and Knetch, 1966; Alldredge, 1973). Substituting recreation visits for input and satisfaction for output, the theoretical constructs of production economics suggest that as visitors are added to a recreation area, the marginal satisfaction of each individual visitor will progressively decline due to crowding, but total or aggregate satisfaction will increase. This process continues until the marginal satisfaction of the nth visitor no longer exceeds the drop in satisfaction of previous visitors. At this point, aggregate satisfaction begins to decline and social carrying capacity has been reached.

The driving force behind this model is an assumed inverse relationship between use level and satisfaction; for the individual, increased use causes decreased satisfaction. This approach to crowding has been called the 'satisfaction model' (Heberlein and Shelby, 1977). However, subsequent theoretical and empirical studies have suggested that crowding is considerably more complex. These studies have led to development of an expanded crowding model.

An expanded model of crowding incorporates findings from three broad areas of research: (i) normative definitions of crowding; (ii) coping behaviours; and (iii) methodological issues. The normative approach to crowding suggests that use level is not interpreted negatively as crowding until it is perceived to interfere with or disrupt one's objectives or values. This approach has proved fertile for theory building and testing in outdoor recreation (Gramann, 1982; Manning, 1985, 1986a; Stankey, 1989; Westover, 1989). A variety of factors have been found to influence normative interpretations of crowding. These factors can be grouped into three basic categories: (i) personal characteristics of visitors (e.g. motivations, preferences, expectations and experience); (ii) characteristics of other visitors encountered (e.g. type and size of group, behaviour and perceptions of alikeness); and (iii) situational variables (e.g. type of recreation area, location within an area, and environmental factors).

Coping behaviours also have been found to influence crowding in outdoor recreation. It has been hypothesized that outdoor recreationists utilize three primary forms of coping behaviour: displacement, rationalization and product shift. Displacement is a behavioural coping mechanism in that it involves spatial or temporal changes in use patterns. Rationalization and product shift are cognitive coping mechanisms involving changes in the ways visitors think about recreation experiences and opportunities. Empirical research has helped document the extent to which these coping behaviours are adopted by outdoor recreationists (Anderson and Brown, 1984; Hammitt and Patterson, 1991; Robertson and Regula, 1994).

Finally, a number of methodological issues have been identified that help explain the sometimes complex relationship between use level and crowding in outdoor recreation. These issues include a nonlinear relationship between use level and contacts or encounters among recreationists, alternative measures of contacts or encounters, and the multidimensional nature of visitor satisfaction.

Theoretical models have been developed in the literature for a variety of other outdoor recreation issues, including recreation conflict (Jacob and Schreyer, 1980; Manning, 1999), motivations and benefits in outdoor recreation (Haas et al., 1980; Driver, 1996; Anderson et al., Chapter 18), substitutability of recreation activities (Iso-Ahola, 1986b;

Brunson and Shelby, 1993), and recreation specialization (Bryan, 1977; Ditton et al., 1992; Kuentzel and McDonald, 1992).

Evolving Issues: Race, Ethnicity and Other Concerns

Research in outdoor recreation continues to evolve to meet societal interests and needs. An important example of expanding research interest is the relationship between race/ethnicity and outdoor recreation. Interest in effects of race and ethnicity on recreation have been evident since the very early stages of outdoor recreation research. Two of the ORRRC studies in the early 1960s, for example, reported significant differences in outdoor recreation participation between blacks and whites (Hauser, 1962; Mueller and Gurin, 1962). Interest in this issue expanded in the 1960s and early 1970s, in part as a function of the civil rights movement. Racial unrest in this period was attributed, at least in part, to poor quality and inequitable distribution of recreation opportunities (National Advisory Commission on Civil Disorders, 1970; Washburne, 1978). Contemporary concern over issues of equity and social and environmental justice has focused additional research attention on this issue. Interest in this subject area is likely to continue to grow in intensity and importance as minority populations of several types continue to expand relative to the traditional white, European-American majority. Research tends to fall into one of two basic categories: (i) studies that explore differences in recreation patterns between or among racial and ethnic groups; and (ii) studies that attempt to explain such differences.

Research on recreation patterns associated with subcultural groups has been conducted in a variety of contexts and has employed varying research methods. However, study findings have been nearly universal in their conclusion that whites participate more often than minority populations (particularly blacks and Hispanics) in traditional outdoor recreation activities (e.g. Washburne, 1978; Washburne and

Wall, 1980; Stamps and Stamps, 1985; West, 1989; Dwyer, 1993; Johnson *et al.*, 1997b). The ORRRC studies noted above were the first to document this pattern, and it has been found to persist over time. A national survey conducted in 1977, for example, found that blacks participated less than whites to a statistically significant degree in several outdoor recreation activities, including camping, boating, hiking/backpacking, hunting, skiing and sightseeing at historical sites or natural wonders (Washburne and Wall, 1980). Similarly, a more recent on-site survey conducted at a nationwide sample of federal and state parks and outdoor recreation areas found that blacks comprised only 2% of all visitors while representing 11.7% of the US population (Hartmann and Overdevest, 1990).

In addition to participation rates, studies have also found a variety of differences in recreation patterns and preferences among subcultural groups (e.g. Kelly, 1980; Washburne and Wall, 1980; Dwyer and Hutchison, 1990; Blahna, 1992; Gramann *et al.*, 1993; Pawelko *et al.*, 1997). Most of these studies have addressed differences between whites and minority subcultural groups, particularly blacks and Hispanics. Findings suggest that, compared to whites, minority subcultural groups tend to:

- Use and prefer 'urban-oriented' recreation facilities and services.
- Participate in larger groups that often include extended family and friends and consist of more diverse age groups.
- Use and prefer more highly developed facilities.
- Participate in activities that are more fitness and sports-oriented.
- Have a longer length of stay at recreation sites.
- Use areas that are closer to home.
- Use land-based rather than water-based areas.
- Make more intensive use of facilities and services.

A second basic area of research has focused on why there are differences in recreation behaviour among subcultural groups. Research in this area has been both theoretical and empirical. Three basic theories have been advanced to explain differences in recreation behaviour among subcultural groups. The first two theories were developed in a seminal study by Washburne (1978). This study suggested what were perceived to be the competing theories of marginality and ethnicity. The theory of marginality suggests that minority subcultural groups, particularly blacks, suffer from economic and related disadvantages as a result of historic discrimination. These disadvantages act to inhibit participation in outdoor recreation by means of cost, transportation, information, location and other barriers. The theory of ethnicity, on the other hand, suggests that differences in recreation behaviour are a function of subcultural values; subcultural groups such as blacks and ethnic minorities reflect cultural values different from the dominant white, European-American culture, and these values manifest themselves in recreation behaviour. A third basic theory has been developed more recently and focuses on racism or interracial relations (West, 1989). This theory suggests that minority subcultural groups may experience personal or institutional forms of discrimination that inhibit their participation in selected recreation activities.

A number of studies have addressed and tested these three basic theories (e.g. Washburne, 1978; Washburne and Wall, 1980; Klobus-Edwards, 1981; Stamps and Stamps, 1985; Floyd *et al.*, 1993, 1994; Shinew *et al.*, 1995; Johnson *et al.*, 1997a, 1998). Tests of the marginality and ethnicity theories are often addressed in the same studies. The most common research approach is to measure recreation behaviour across two or more subcultural groups while statistically controlling for a variety of socioeconomic variables such as income and education. This allows direct comparison of individuals of similar socioeconomic status. If differences in recreation behaviour are reduced or eliminated in such tests, then this suggests support for the theory of marginality. If differences persist, then this suggests support for the theory of ethnicity.

Several studies have also asked respondents more directly about barriers to participation in outdoor recreation as a means of testing the marginality and ethnicity theories. Tests of the interracial relations theory generally rely on surveys to determine the extent to which minority subcultural groups report having been subject to personal or institutional discrimination, and the degree to which this is a barrier to participation in outdoor recreation.

The research indicates some support for all of the three basic theories described above. This has led to a more contemporary view that the relationship between recreation behaviour and subcultural factors is complex and can be understood only through consideration of multiple and possibly interrelated influences (McDonald and Hutchison, 1986; West, 1989; Johnson et al., 1997b, 1998). For example, clearly there are strong interrelationships between subcultural groups and socioeconomic status: historic patterns of segregation and discrimination are reflected in lower socioeconomic status of blacks and other minority subcultural groups. It is reasonable to suggest, therefore, that subcultural values may be influenced by socioeconomic status and that both the marginality and ethnicity theories may influence recreation behaviour.

Research on race and ethnicity suggests several potential management implications. To the extent to which the marginality theory is valid, special efforts should be made to ensure equal access to outdoor recreation. Potential actions within the scope of individual managers include provision of public transportation, location of parks and outdoor recreation areas closer to minority populations, and development and marketing of recreation programmes more directly to minority subcultural groups. Management implications of the ethnicity theory are quite different. To the extent to which this theory is valid, recreation facilities and services should be designed to meet the recreation-related values of minority subcultural groups. The literature suggests such adaptations might include an emphasis on more developed facilities closer to home and facilities designed for larger groups and more active uses. Finally, the racism or interracial relations theory suggests that managers should re-examine their agencies and programmes for evidence of institutional discrimination (e.g. discriminatory pricing policies) and should be proactive in furthering programmes to promote racial harmony.

Along with race and ethnicity, a number of other contemporary issues are evolving in the outdoor recreation literature, including the relationship between gender and outdoor recreation (Henderson, 1990, 1997, Chapter 2; Shaw, 1994), the appropriate role of user fees in outdoor recreation management (Reiling et al., 1992; Lundgren, 1996) and the characteristics and impacts of new forms of outdoor recreation such as mountain biking (Watson et al., 1991; Chavez et al., 1993; Chavez 1996a,b).

Conclusions: Trends and their Implications

Outdoor recreation research has clearly evolved and matured over the past several decades. The beginning of serious social science research in outdoor recreation can be traced to the ORRRC in the early 1960s. Since then, the outdoor recreation research literature has expanded dramatically. Even though this literature is diverse in terms of theoretical approaches, research methodologies and issues addressed, several trends are evident.

First, recreation research has evolved from primarily empirically based studies of visitor characteristics and use patterns to more theoretically based studies of visitor behaviour and the underlying meanings of outdoor recreation. Thus, the literature has evolved from primarily descriptive studies to more analytical or explanatory studies. The theoretical basis of outdoor recreation research has evolved from more disciplinary-based studies derived from sociology, psychology and economics, to more interdisciplinary studies conducted by scientists educated and housed in park, outdoor recreation and related departments.

Second, the research-based literature in outdoor recreation has been synthesized to develop a number of conceptual frameworks that are useful for integrating multiple studies, and ultimately guiding further research and management. Examples include carrying capacity, the Outdoor Recreation Opportunity Spectrum, indicators and standards of quality, and several classification systems of recreation management practices and related management processes or handbooks. Third, the synergistic effects of an accumulating body of research have developed a strong theoretical understanding of a number of important issues in outdoor recreation, including crowding, conflict, motivations and benefits, substitutability and specialization. Fourth, issues addressed in outdoor recreation research continue to evolve to meet societal interests and needs. Examples of such issues include the relationship between outdoor recreation and race, ethnicity and gender, the appropriate role of fees in outdoor recreation management, and the characteristics and impacts of new forms of outdoor recreation such as mountain biking.

These trends have had substantial implications for both recreation research and management. The evolving, multidisciplinary, explanatory approach to outdoor recreation research has developed a stronger theoretical foundation for understanding outdoor recreation. Resulting theoretical models have provided an intellectual framework within which to integrate multiple studies, and helped guide additional research by isolating important variables and relationships as well as suggesting a series of hypotheses for further empirical testing. A stronger theoretical basis for understanding outdoor recreation has contributed, in turn, to recognition of outdoor recreation as an important, applied field of study with concomitant academic departments, scholarly journals and an established scientific literature.

Management of outdoor recreation has benefited directly from advances in the research base. As noted earlier in this chapter, a recent study of the USDA Forest Service found that most important innovations in outdoor recreation were derived from research (Anderson and Schneider, 1993; Schneider et al., 1993). Theoretical models of crowding, conflict, motivations and benefits in recreation, substitutability of recreation activities, and recreation specialization have allowed for management of these issues on a more informed basis. Moreover, conceptual frameworks developed from the recreation literature have resulted in a series of structured approaches designed to guide recreation management. Examples include Limits of Acceptable Change, Visitor Experience and Resource Protection, and the Recreation Opportunity Spectrum. Finally, outdoor recreation research can evolve to address emerging management issues such as the relationship between outdoor recreation and race, ethnicity and gender, the appropriate role of fees in outdoor recreation, and new forms of outdoor recreation such as mountain biking.

The evolution of outdoor recreation research has been instrumental in building a foundation for outdoor recreation as a professional field of study. Research has resulted in a strong, multidisciplinary, theoretical and empirical scientific literature. This body of knowledge can and should be used to guide future research, and to inform management action. Moreover, this scientific literature should be incorporated into professional education programmes aimed at both students and practitioners. In these ways, research can help the field of outdoor recreation continue its professional evolution and its 'coming of age'.

Part III

Participation: How We Are Using Resources

12

Trends in Americans' Outdoor Recreation

H. Ken Cordell and Gregory R. Super

Most of the participation trends we report in this chapter are from two recent sources. The first is the 1995 National Survey on Recreation and the Environment (NSRE 1995), a national participation survey led by H. Ken Cordell. The NSRE is the latest in the United States' continuing series of National Recreation Surveys, the first of which was done under the auspices of the Outdoor Recreation Resources Review Commission in 1960 (Cordell *et al.*, 1996). Design of the activity participation questions in the 1995 NSRE was kept consistent with previous National Recreation Surveys to enable us to describe trends in participation across a variety of outdoor recreation activities. The second source of participation trends is the just completed federal assessment of outdoor recreation and wilderness, done every 10 years by the US Department of Agriculture (USDA) Forest Service, as required by the 1974 Renewable Resources Planning Act (RPA) (Cordell, 1999). Other sources are included as appropriate and needed to describe that flourishing phenomenon in modern US society that we call outdoor recreation.

A Brief History of Outdoor Recreation in the US

Outdoor recreation has always been an important part of the American lifestyle.

However, until recent decades and except perhaps for the affluent, it probably was not highly significant for very many people. Before World War II, there was little public call for government provided recreation areas. Outdoor spaces were plentiful then, and because many people worked out of doors, they were not very inclined to seek fun and relaxation in the setting where they had just spent a number of hours toiling to earn a living (Douglass, 1999). Following World War II, however, vastly improved transportation, the institution of time off for holidaying, indeed the growing popularity of taking family holidays, dramatic changes in work venues, spreading affluence and a host of other social changes, altered forever the role and significance of outdoor recreation in Americans' lives.

The country's first comprehensive national assessment of outdoor recreation was done by the Outdoor Recreation Resources Review Commission (ORRRC) between 1958 and 1960 (ORRRC, 1962). Among the key findings of that assessment were:

- The simple activities are the most popular – driving for pleasure, walking, swimming ...
- Outdoor opportunities are most urgently needed near metropolitan areas ... where three-quarters of the people will live ... by the turn of the century ...

© CAB *International* 2000. *Trends in Outdoor Recreation, Leisure and Tourism*
(eds W.C. Gartner and D.W. Lime)

- ... Considerable land is now available for outdoor recreation, but it does not effectively meet the need.
- Outdoor recreation is a major leisure time activity, and it is growing in importance ... by the year 2000 there will be a threefold increase.

In 1960, the ORRRC found that about 90% of Americans participated in some form of outdoor recreation. They speculated that demand would rise dramatically from that time onwards. A flurry of activities at federal, state and other levels responded to the ORRRC report and its recommendations. Systems of designated federal recreation lands, newly available funding, enhanced state park systems, expanded roles beyond sports and programmed recreation at the local level, and an interest-sparked private sector marked the country's enormous push forward throughout the 1960s and 1970s to be responsive to the ORRRC recommendation that we expand the capacity and diversity of recreation opportunities in this country. Undaunted by Vietnam, the 1972 gasoline 'crisis', inflation, and a myriad of other social and economic events and trends which could have curbed appetites for outdoor recreation, Americans have availed themselves of the resulting expansion of capacity in ever increasing numbers and across a growing variety of participation venues.

In the mid-1980s, the President's Commission on Americans Outdoors (1986), followed by the Reagan Administration's Task Force on Outdoor Recreation (Domestic Policy Council, 1988) found demand continuing to grow as it had been both before and since ORRRC. Large percentages of the fast growing American public continued to engage in outdoor activities. By the 1980s, the population and the styles of outdoor recreation participation had begun to diversify well beyond the driving for pleasure, picnicking, walking and camping styles which were so highly popular in the 1950s and 1960s. In its national assessment of outdoor recreation and wilderness in the late 1980s, the USDA Forest Service summarized the following (Cordell *et al.*, 1990):

- ... the rate of increase in some outdoor recreation activities has slowed in recent years, ...
- ... New activities are appearing, however, and are being added ...
- ... long-distance holidays are being replaced by more frequent, close-to-home recreation trips ... near urban areas.
- ... wilderness (and other backcountry) recreation visits slowed in the early 1980s, but since 1986, reported wilderness recreation use has begun to increase again.
- Downhill skiing, cross-country skiing, swimming, backpacking, visiting prehistoric sites, running and jogging, and day hiking will grow faster than ... other activities (and most forms of outdoor recreation will continue to grow).

In this chapter, participation trends over the years, whether showing growth or not, are identified and discussed as they occurred at the close of the 20th century. In the final section, we attempt to identify the management and policy implications of these trends.

Long-term Participation Trends

The most recent USDA Forest Service national RPA assessment examined long-term trends by comparing participation estimates from the 1960, 1965, 1983 and 1995 National Recreation Surveys (Cordell, 1999). The trends reported in that assessment were based primarily on the 1995 National Survey on Recreation and the Environment, which was the latest of the continuing national recreation surveys. In Table 12.1, indexed growth is reported in numbers of people indicating they had participated in the nine outdoor activities tracked across all of the previous national recreation surveys relative to the population growth which occurred during that 35-year period.

Numbers of people participating in six of the nine activities shown in Table 1 grew

Table 12.1. Indexed growth since 1960 in millions of US persons 12 years or older participating in outdoor recreation by activity relative to population growth since 1960 (1960 index = 1.00).

Activity	Growth index by year			Millions of persons in 1995 (12 or older)
	1965	1983	1995	
Snow skiing	2.19	6.50	10.08	26.2
Canoeing/kayaking	1.65	5.77	6.73	17.5
Cycling	1.98	4.63	4.87	63.3
Camping	1.44	2.99	4.50	58.5
Sailing	1.46	2.90	2.72	10.6
Swimming	1.17	1.63	1.92	118.0
POPULATION	1.10	1.44	1.65	216.0
Fishing	1.13	1.48	1.47	63.3
Horse riding	1.47	1.44	1.38	16.2
Hunting	1.10	1.08	0.99	20.6

Sources: 1960, 1965, 1983, and 1995 Federal National Recreation Surveys (Cordell *et al.*, 1996).

faster than population in terms of percentage change from the base year, 1960. Fastest growth in participation was in snow skiing (which in 1995 included snowboarding), canoeing/kayaking (which is mostly whitewater), cycling (which now includes mountain and tour biking), and camping (both developed and primitive). All activities, except hunting, grew at rates faster than population growth between 1960 and 1965. Similarly, all activities but hunting and horseback riding grew faster than the population between 1960 and 1983. Fishing was added as an activity not growing as fast as the population by the time the 1995 NSRE survey was conducted. Clearly, long-term trends point to fast-paced growth in technology-driven, adventure activities (snow skiing, canoeing/kayaking and cycling being examples); moderate growth in the more traditional, family-oriented activities (e.g. camping and swimming); and slowing growth or declines in participation in consumptive activities (fishing and hunting). Numbers of participants in sailing and horseback riding decreased somewhat between 1983 and 1995, probably because of rising expense and greater difficulty in finding suitable places for these activities. From 1960 to 1995, the population of persons aged 12 and older grew 65%, reaching a total of 216 million.

Recent Participation Trends

Our recent studies have shown that 94.5% of Americans 16 years old or older participated in some form of outdoor recreation during the 1994/95 NSRE survey period. Among those activities included in both the 1983 and 1995 National Recreation Surveys, walking for pleasure, sightseeing, picnicking, swimming in natural waters, fishing, cycling and birdwatching were the most popular in 1995 (Table 12.2). Participation levels for these seven activities exceeded 25% of the population for 15 of the 21 activities listed in Table 12.2. Growth from 1983 to 1995 in percentages of the population participating exceeded the percentage growth of population. The growth index shown in column two of Table 12.2 shows that birdwatching, hiking, backpacking, downhill skiing and primitive camping were the five fastest growing activities in terms of percentage change in number of participants between 1983 and 1995.

In order of millions of people reporting participation, the eight most popular activities in 1983 were: walking for pleasure (number one), picnicking, sightseeing, fishing, cycling and swimming in natural waters (these two tied for fifth most popular), motor-boating, developed camping and day hiking. In 1995, the order of activities by

Table 12.2. Indexed participation growth between 1983 and 1995 and millions of persons participating in the US in 1995 who were 16 years or older by outdoor activity (1983 = 1.00).

Activity	Growth index 1983–1995	Millions in 1995
Birdwatching	2.55	54.1
Hiking	1.94	47.8
Backpacking	1.73	15.2
Downhill skiing	1.59	16.8
Primitive camping	1.58	28.0
Off-road driving	1.44	27.9
Walking for pleasure	1.43	133.7
Sightseeing	1.40	113.4
Motor-boating	1.40	47.0
Developed camping	1.38	41.5
Swimming in rivers, lakes, ocean	1.38	78.1
Snowmobiling	1.34	7.1
Cross-country skiing	1.23	6.5
Picnicking	1.16	98.3
Sledding	1.16	20.5
POPULATION	1.15	200.1
Water skiing	1.13	17.9
Cycling	1.02	57.4
Fishing	0.96	57.8
Horse riding	0.90	14.3
Sailing	0.90	9.6
Hunting	0.88	18.6

Sources: 1983 and 1995 Federal National Recreation Surveys (Cordell et al., 1996).

levels of population-wide participation showed the greatest number of people were walking for pleasure (remaining at number one as it had been in 1983), the next greatest number were sightseeing (moving up from third in 1983), next picnicking (falling from second in 1983), swimming in natural waters (moving up from fifth), fishing (falling from fourth in 1983), cycling (falling from fifth), birdwatching (not among the top eight in 1983), and day hiking (remaining at number eight). Millions participating in developed camping and motor-boating both dropped below the threshold which would have qualified them to be among the top eight activities in 1995.

Shifts in Annual Days of Participation

Trends in the number of days participants devote to specific recreational activities is another indicator of shifts in activity popularity. For most of the activities included in both the 1983 and 1995 surveys, there were only minor shifts in percentages of participants among the three levels of participation days per year (1–2, 3–10 and more than 10 days per year) (Table 12.3). The activities for which the percentages of participants across the different levels of participation days per year remained distributed about the same in 1983 and 1995 included cycling (where more than half the participants participated more than 10 days per year), horseback riding (where almost half the participants engaged only 1–2 days per year), canoeing or kayaking (where about half participated only 1–2 days per year) and developed camping (where more than half participated between 3 and 10 days per year). Other activities with minor shifts in participation days included motor-boating, swimming outdoors in pools, swimming in natural

Table 12.3. Shifts in percentage of people 16 years or older in the US participating by activity and number of days of participation per year, 1983–1995.

| Activity | Participation days per year | | | | | |
| | 1–2 | | 3–10 | | More than 10 | |
	1983	1995	1983	1995	1983	1995
Cycling	12	14	32	32	56	54
Horse riding	48	48	27	26	25	26
Canoeing or kayaking	50	50	39	41	11	9
Sailing	**56**	**49**	30	33	14	18
Motor-boating	33	29	38	39	29	32
Swimming in outdoor pool	14	13	38	38	48	49
Swimming in lakes, streams or ocean	19	18	42	46	39	36
Fishing	**21**	**8**	**43**	**30**	**36**	**62**
Hunting	**19**	**11**	**42**	**37**	**39**	**52**
Backpacking	39	41	**46**	**40**	15	19
Camping in developed campgrounds	26	24	51	52	23	24
Camping in primitive campgrounds	**36**	**30**	46	48	18	22
Day hiking	28	29	**46**	**40**	**26**	**31**
Nature study including birdwatching	15	17	29	30	56	53
Off-road vehicle driving (includes motorcycles but not snowmobiles)	23	23	39	40	38	37
Downhill skiing	34	33	**43**	**49**	**23**	**18**
Cross-country skiing or ski touring	**51**	**37**	**35**	**47**	14	16
Snowmobiling	**40**	**46**	36	32	24	22

Source: 1982/83 and 1994/95 National Recreation Surveys (Cordell *et al.*, 1996).

waters (lakes/streams/ocean), nature study (including birdwatching) and off-road vehicle driving.

Cells in Table 12.3 showing a 5% or more shift in percentage of participants are highlighted. Activities with cells thus highlighted include sailing (a shift toward more days per year), backpacking (more days per year), primitive camping (more days), day hiking (more days), downhill skiing (fewer days) and snowmobiling (fewer days). Also in Table 12.3 are the highlighted names of activities for which there were major shifts of 10% or more among participation levels. These highlighted activities included fishing, hunting and cross-country skiing. The nature of the shifts for all three of these activities was toward more days per year. This was particularly true for fishing and hunting for which the shifts were strongly toward participation of 10 or more

days per year. For cross-country skiing, the shift per participant was from 1–2 days to 3–10 days per year.

Shifts in the Demographic Make-up of Outdoor Participants

Many significant changes in the socioeconomic make-up of outdoor recreation participants have occurred since the 1983 national survey (Cordell, 1999). While some of these changes mirror shifts in the demographic make-up of the US population, some other changes do not.

The most notable of changes, which seem mostly to mirror population-wide demographic shifts, are the substantial increases in proportions of participants who are college educated, who are of nonwhite races, who live in households earning more than

US$50,000 per year, who live in one- or two-person households, and who are going to school or are retired. Also mirroring population demography trends are the substantial decreases in proportions of participants who have completed high school, but who have not completed more than high school; who earn below US$25,000 per year in family income; and who are from households with five or more members. Percentages of participants who are female, who have less than a high school education, whites, those in households with incomes between US$25,000 and US$49,999, persons from three- or four-person households, the employed, those temporarily unemployed, and those keeping house, either changed only slightly or remained the same in 1995 as in 1983.

There have been a number of changes in the demographic profiles of outdoor participants that have not kept pace with the changing profile of Americans in general. For example, increases in the proportion of participants who are college educated have been somewhat less than the increase in their proportion among the general population, and increases in the proportion of participants who are black have been less than the increase in their percentage of the general population. On the other hand, growth in proportions of participants from one- or two-person households exceeds generally the growth in their proportion of the population, and the growth of retired participants exceeds overall their growth as a proportion of the population. Likewise, increases in proportions of participants earning more than US$50,000 per year exceed their growth as a proportion of the population. Heath (1997) found that the 'well to do' are more likely to participate in more activities than those earning less income per year. Heath also found that greater proportions of those in very high income categories participate in 'prestigious' sports such as tennis, snow skiing and sailing, more so than in hiking and camping. Heath also pointed out that golf and motorboating are among the recreational pursuits favoured by the 'rich'.

Trends in Public Use at Federal and State Sites

Federal

In addition to participation trends in percentages among outdoor activities, trends in visitation at public outdoor recreation sites is a good indicator of overall demand shifts. Visitation at federal sites has typically been reported in units of measure called visitor-days and/or visits. A visitor day is a cumulative total of 12 h of recreation use by one or by several different people at the same or at different times. A visit is a count of single entry of one person into and their use of a recreation area for any amount of time. A visitor day is an appropriate measure of participation when the need is to estimate total site contact time and management impact by visitors. A visit is the more appropriate measure of participation when customer service is the primary management target, in that it measures a customer encounter. The ratio of visits to visitor days is roughly estimated to be around 2.1 : 1 at public sites.

Since the Federal Annual Fee Report was discontinued in 1993, only some of the federal agencies which manage or lease recreation sites or services have continued to report recreation visitation. The Tennessee Valley Authority (TVA) and the Bureau of Reclamation discontinued visitation reporting altogether due to shifting priorities. The other five federal agencies have continued to report visitation in some form. Using the former annual Federal Recreation Fee Report (USDI, 1974–1992) and any other available recent tabulations by individual agencies, the 10-year trends in visitor-days at recreation sites managed by the seven federal resource managing agencies (TVA, Fish and Wildlife Service, Bureau of Reclamation, Bureau of Land Management, National Park Service, Corps of Engineers and USDA Forest Service) are compared for the years 1986 and 1996 (Fig. 12.1).

For some agencies, like the Bureau of Land Management, TVA and USDA Forest Service, trends show significant annual

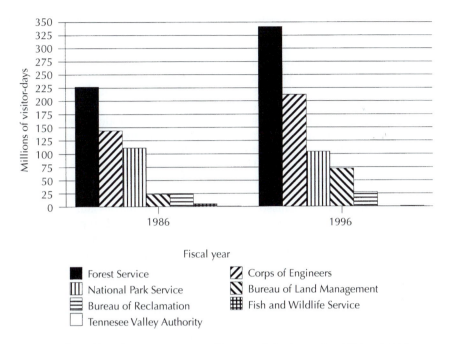

Fig. 12.1. Trends in visitor-days at areas managed by seven federal agencies, 1986 and 1996.
Source: Federal Recreation Fee Reports and the respective agencies (Cordell, forthcoming).

increases in visitor-days. For the National Park Service and the US Fish and Wildlife Service, there were declines in visitor days of use. Visitor days at Bureau of Reclamation reservoirs increased slightly. Overall, visitor-days of use at federal sites and areas increased by more than 40% between 1986 and 1996. The bulk of this increase (some 222 million visitor-days) occurred on USDA Forest Service, Corps of Engineers and Bureau of Land Management land and water areas.

Since the USDA Forest Service's last national assessment in 1987, the status of outdoor recreation on federal land has been uncertain. Limits on federal spending overall, shifting priorities for federal funding and reductions of agency staffing all are factors which have contributed to the difficulty of maintaining federal recreation use statistics. It appears, however, that recently there has been a resurgence of interest in and commitment to outdoor recreation and tracking recreation use on land and water managed in the public interest by the federal government. For example, the USDA Forest Service is currently completing a national pilot of sampling approaches for improving estimates of recreation visits (Kocis, forthcoming). Whether or not better statistics on federal recreation visitation are forthcoming, local managers are reporting that visitor pressures are continuing to rise and are manifesting themselves in a number of ways. At some well known destinations, use is rising more rapidly than services, capacity and budgets. At some of the more popular of these destinations, fees, mass transit and visitor load limits are being instituted to accommodate these rises in use. At most destinations, types of equipment, diversity of users, seasonality of use, kinds of activities sought, and in many other ways, the demands on recreation sites and management are changing.

State

State park visits, traditionally termed attendance, are usually reported separately for day use and overnight use, and by fee and nonfee area designation (McLean, 1999). Indications are that visits to state parks are increasing. Between 1992 and 1996 there was a modest increase nationally in the number of visits to state parks that averaged 1.4% and represented 10 million new visits annually. Only the Pacific region experienced a decline in attendance between 1992 and 1996. The annual mean attendance between 1992 and 1996 was 730 million visits, with the peak occurring in 1995. The long-term trend, however, has been steady growth in visits to state parks with occasional short-term fluctuations caused by unusually hot or wet summers.

Day use is much greater than overnight use in the state parks of the US. The majority of these day visits are by individuals, families, friends and groups on outings to parks reasonably close to their residence (McLean, 1999). Of all visits in 1996, only 7.9% were overnight. In 1992, the percentage of people staying overnight was 8%, suggesting a consistency over time in the share of the growing overall number of visitors to state parks who stay the night.

Growth in visits to state park fee areas was 8.2% between 1992 and 1996, while visits to nonfee areas grew just 6.1% (McLean, 1999). It appears that fee areas are gaining somewhat in share of use, although the reasons for these increases are elusive. One estimate which is somewhat revealing is that in 1996 there were a reported 1998 areas with some type of entrance fee within the overall total of 5091 areas operated by state park agencies. If accurate, these totals indicate that about 40% of state parks charge some type of fee. Day use at nonfee areas is approximately 32 times greater than overnight use in nonfee areas. Overall there was less than 1% growth in use of overnight facilities between 1992 and 1996.

Whether the trend in use is up modestly or up strongly, it is apparent that recreational use of state parks is highly important to Americans. The total number of visits to state parks is three times the level of visitation at national parks, even though the overall area in state parks is substantially less. The access to natural areas represented by most state parks with their wide variety of opportunities close to people's homes is obviously important and attractive to many Americans.

International Tourism in the US

In addition to domestic demand for outdoor recreation, millions of people from other countries take trips to the US for pleasure, to visit friends and/or family, or for business. For a large percentage of these international travellers, the vast network of forests, parks, protected areas, refuges and recreation areas in the US is an important part of their travel itinerary. Traveller choices of outdoor recreation destinations are typically influenced by the existence of public lands and natural resources. The more popular destinations are typically those with ample natural attributes, developed recreation areas, and accommodations and services nearby. The US Department of Commerce has identified tourism as the third largest industry in the US.

The International Pleasure Travel Market Studies, jointly sponsored by the Canadian Tourism Commission, the US International Trade Administration and tourism industries, have been conducted through personal interviews in 24 countries throughout the world since 1986. This research is designed to gather information on actual and planned long-distance travel, and includes questions that help reveal how travellers view forests, parks and recreation-related activities. Almost without regard to the origin of travellers, outdoor-related activities and visits to parks and forests are important motivations for visitors in planning their trips to the US (O'Leary and Lang, 1995). The ratings of importance of forests and parks in international travel decisions ranged from 91% for Venezuelans to 70% for the Japanese. This intense interest in natural environments and outdoor recreation activities has persisted during the 10 years that the International Pleasure Travel Market Studies have been conducted.

In the last 10 years, international visits to the US have grown about 66%, going from about 27.8 million visits in 1987 to an estimated 46.2 million in 1997 (O'Leary, 1999). Receipts from this travel also grew, expanding from US$30.5 billion in 1987 to an expected US$88.9 billion in 1997 (US Department of Commerce, International Trade Administration, 1996). Canadians led the 1996 arrivals to this country with 15.3 million visits. Mexico (8.5 million), Japan (5.0 million), the UK (3.1 million) and Germany (1.9 million) completed the 'top five' inbound visitors from other countries. Impacts from the economic downturn in Asia are yet to be fully understood, but they will surely change the distribution of arrivals among countries of origin. Arrivals are distributed unevenly among US states with the coastal and border states ranking highest in numbers of international visitors.

Discussion and Implications

Across communities and segments within American society, outdoor recreation has maintained its enormously popular status over the years. Although new forms of participation are appearing all the time, a persistent underlying basic motivation for outdoor recreation is to have the opportunity to experience nature by viewing it, travelling through it, and for brief periods at least, living in it.

Both long-term and short-term trends point to continued growth in outdoor recreation across all segments of the population, some more so than others. If these trends continue (and there is every reason to believe they will), pressures for places to recreate and for added recreation infrastructure to support growing numbers and diversity of recreation seekers will continue to build. The more salient of the growing pressures and challenges we anticipate include:

- The most popular beaches, forest sites, water sites, parks and special attractions are almost sure to face increasing use levels and more frequent periods of congestion, especially during peak recreation seasons of the year. These anticipated high levels of use and congestion will sometimes present demands and situations beyond the experience and training background of most outdoor recreation site and public land managers. Heavy pressures are especially likely to occur at popular water sites which have always been a major attraction for a wide variety of outdoor recreational activities. These pressures will take on added significance with advances in motorized technology which makes these water sites more easily accessible.

- There will undoubtedly be many more and many new types of conflicts between different recreation user interests arising from anticipated congestion and sometimes from incompatible modes of participation among a growing diversity of recreation interests. This growing number and diversity of interests must 'compete' for access rights to the limited number of areas and sites for a growing diversity of outdoor recreation activities. Particularly challenging will be accommodation of access needs for motorized and nonmotorized uses and for solitude and the more socially oriented forms of participation. Organized groups representing motorized, nonmotorized and other specific outdoor recreation interests will grow in number and in the size of the constituency they represent. As public agencies continue to open the planning and decision processes to public involvement, these organized groups will have an increasing voice in public land management. Increasingly, organized groups will be integrated as partners in helping to manage and protect public lands, access rights and unique resources.

- New technologies and better modes of accessing remote countryside will continue to shift the nature of the demand for outdoor recreation in the more isolated areas. Most affected by these shifts will be the more traditional, passive forms of rural outdoor recreation where quiet, natural settings for learning, reflection and nature appreciation are sought. Also impacted will be traditional forms of active participation where new technologies enable more and different kinds of use onto the resource; for example, whitewater canoeists experiencing personal watercraft use. The resource, and especially fragile sites and sensitive habitats for animals and plants, will feel the impact of increased wilderness recreation uses.

- Because of persistent rises in the popularity of outdoor recreation, public and private land management policies and practices which are not directly aimed at providing recreation opportunities, such as timber and wildlife management, will increasingly interact with and be of intense interest to larger numbers of people across a broader spectrum of society with increasingly diverse interests and cultural backgrounds. This will make resource management many times more challenging and will call for increasingly innovative, collaborative approaches backed by sound research. We have observed in the last few years that federal land management objectives have begun a major shift toward increasing recreation management relative to other resource uses.
- Public and private sector providers will need to continue to provide viewing and learning, social gathering, and swimming opportunities to meet rising demand by the majority of the American public. Many of these types of opportunities can be provided near the urban conurbations where most of those seeking such opportunities live. However, rapid near-city development and conversion of natural lands such as forests will make provision of near-city opportunities increasingly challenging.
- Equitable access to developed sites and dispersed areas across all segments and interests in our society will almost certainly be an increasingly important and hard-to-resolve issue. A particular challenge will be to assure universal accessibility, at least at most recreation areas. As access management tools,

such as charging fees and disseminating information on opportunities continue to evolve, the equity of access implications of such tools will increasingly be issues of contention among different social groups and different segments of recreation interests. Continued increases in visits to most federal and state forests and parks will put added pressures on public managers to adopt different management policies and styles. Fees and reservation systems will spread. Information dissemination programmes will and should expand. Greater attention must be paid to potentially unequal effects of these policies on lower income, less well-educated, and place-confined segments of our population.

- Scenic quality will increasingly be an issue that managers of recreation areas and of natural lands in general must address as growth and interest in sightseeing, viewing and learning activities, and other scenery-dependent activities drives the demand for aesthetically pleasing settings.
- Markets for outdoor activities are not only expanding, they are also changing as new forms of participation are discovered; as the backgrounds, perspectives and tastes of recreationists change; and as constraints and opportunities shift. In that these changes are in fact very much dependent on the spectrum of opportunities made available, public land management policies will be under increasing scrutiny to determine how well they are serving the demands and needs of Americans across all social strata, while at the same time providing private sector business opportunities.
- Rapid increases in the diversity of the population in race, culture, age, income and other factors will change the demand for outdoor recreation, especially in regions and states where immigration is occurring. The resulting increase in population diversity will result in different preferences, expectations, and ways of seeking and

participating in outdoor recreation. Management policies and solutions of the past will only partially fit these emerging shifts in demand and the new forms of recreation which will be pursued.

- Because most forms of outdoor recreation participation depend so heavily on natural settings, which differ between different regions of the country, and because most of these forms continue to grow in popularity, domestic tourism and associated recreation travel can be expected to continue their growth as long as transportation remains as affordable and as convenient as it is today. Outdoor recreation travel and tourism contributes substantially to the growth and diversity (and thus stability) of rural economies. This contribution is likely to grow not only in terms of local incomes and jobs, but also in the share of income and jobs among economic sectors at any economic scale.

- International travel to the US for outdoor recreation will increase pressure on the US supply of outdoor opportunities, particularly at the most popular national parks and other well known tourist destinations. International effects will be greater near border and coastal states. Increasing domestic and international travel and tourism in the US will create opportunities for large-scale private businesses to provide services, accommodation and information. As the interest in defining and managing for sustainable communities and natural systems grows, ecotourism is likely to become a popular and viable approach for simultaneously achieving both.

- Research will become increasingly important in helping us understand and better anticipate the many changes that will be occurring on many different fronts. Ongoing national participation surveys and on-site studies of various user groups and interests will help reveal the linkages between recreation behaviours, preferences and social changes and should give some 'feel' for

market shifts as or before they happen. Improved data, monitoring systems and better defined management objectives which are in touch with recreation demand shifts, which are constantly occurring both domestically and internationally, will be necessary to successfully manage outdoor recreation in the future. Over the past two decades, the loss of interest in recreation visitation, customer satisfaction and economic impact information has proved to be an obstacle to achieving highly effective and timely management and policy specification.

Conclusions

Outdoor recreation continues to be a basic aspect of the American lifestyle most of us have come to expect. The 1995 National Survey on Recreation and the Environment has shown that most people in American society participate at some level and in some way in outdoor recreation. Traditional land, water and snow/ice settings are very much in demand to satisfy our growing appetite both for traditional outdoor recreational activities, as well as for a growing list of new activities which are driven by better access and by rapidly evolving technology and information availability.

Over the years and still today, most in demand are places for casual activities such as walking, family gatherings and sightseeing, and for places to visit and learn, such as beaches, historic sites and other sites of interest. These activities and outdoor places appeal to a wide spectrum of people from inner cities, suburbs and the rural countrysides alike. Usually it is the combination of entertainment, fun, learning, and seeing which are basic motivations for pursuing these activities.

Recreation participation across all types of settings, especially on our federal and state lands are experiencing growth. Often this growth is across a number of different activities which occur at the same sites and in the same settings, sometimes resulting in conflicts and needs for carefully considered

management strategies which offer everyone opportunities. The increases in
participation which are occurring are not
just in the numbers of people participating
occasionally, they also represent growth in
the total number of days and trips annually
that people take for their preferred recreation. Total days and numbers of trips for
outdoor recreation by the US population
represent a huge market for the goods,
equipment and services which facilitate participation and for access to places with
quality settings for participation.

An opportunity exists for expanding the
scale and breadth of benefits from our natural lands and water. Realizing this
opportunity can only occur with close collaboration between providers in both the
public and private sectors. Each has a critical role to play. Let that collaboration
always proceed in an environmentally
responsible manner.

13

Trends in Hunting Participation and Implications for Management of Game Species

Tommy L. Brown, Daniel J. Decker, William F. Siemer and Jody W. Enck

Introduction

Of all the recreation activities social scientists have studied, hunting may be the most multifaceted in terms of its diverse implications to society and the related dilemmas managers face in regulating it. Hunting is enjoyed by millions of people continent wide; by people in every state and province in the US and Canada. Hunting is more than a form of recreation to many participants (and many nonparticipating acquaintances (Stedman and Decker, 1996)); it is a way of life and a part of the culture of many North Americans. This attribute of hunting – involvement by people who do not go afield but who are a part of the larger hunting culture, makes analysis of trends difficult but adds to the importance of understanding hunting trends.

The cultural significance of hunting extends not only to Native American groups and those who depend upon hunting for subsistence, but also to modern American and Canadian cultures that, despite hunters being predominantly male, otherwise encompass all demographic characteristics. In a 1993/94 survey, wildlife managers across the US and Canada identified more than 60 different types of hunting traditions they believed to be important for cultural reasons to some groups of residents within their state or province (Brown *et al.*, 1995).

People are motivated to hunt for a variety of reasons and hunters experience many satisfactions through their involvement. Studies across the US since 1968 have shown consistently that bagging game is not the strongest motivation for hunting (Duda, 1993). Being outdoors for relaxation, aesthetic aspects of the hunting experience, companionship and expression of skill have usually been of greater importance than expectations or desires for bagging game. Decker *et al.* (1987) identified achievement, affiliative and appreciative aspects as providing primary experience goals for New York hunters.

Hunting differs from other recreation activities in that it often involves the intentional killing of sentient wild animals, including popular, attractive mammals such as white-tailed deer anthropomorphized by the entertainment media. In recent decades major conflicts in values have been expressed between groups of people who believe animals have rights, including the right not to be harassed or killed (i.e. hunted) by humans, and other people who may accord wildlife tremendous respect and appreciation, but do not extend to these creatures the concept of rights. The vast majority of Americans still approve of hunting. In a 1993 national survey, 73% of Americans approved of hunting (22% disapproved) and 81% believed hunting should remain legal (Duda *et al.*, 1998). The animal rights movement has had some impacts on hunting, however, to the extent that at their instigation some states have experienced citizen-initiated ballot referenda in which specific types of hunting have been banned.

Hunting also has served as the primary method for controlling many game populations. When some game populations grow too large, vast numbers of the public may be adversely affected. Deer, elk or moose present real hazards to people from collisions with motor vehicles; deer and elk damage crops and nurseries and retard regeneration of forests; beavers flood cropland and roads; and ducks and geese foul lake shorelines, ponds, golf courses and public parklands. In addition, issues of public safety, pets and livestock become more pronounced as populations of large carnivores such as mountain lions increase. As many of these wildlife populations have increased in recent decades, the number of stakeholder groups with direct concerns about wildlife management has grown. Hunting has a direct bearing on these myriad human–wildlife interaction issues.

This chapter examines trends in hunting and the future of hunting as a recreation activity, consistent with the theme of this book of exploring leisure, recreation and tourism trends. However, the future of hunting has far broader implications than characteristics of most recreation activities. These considerations and implications are examined as part of the broader trends in human dimensions of wildlife management.

Hunting Participation Trends in the US

Three sources of information help us understand hunting trends in the US. First, the US Fish and Wildlife Service (FWS) has conducted a national survey of hunting (as well as fishing and nonconsumptive wildlife activities) approximately every 5 years since 1955. These data provide useful insights about trends but they are not conclusive, for two reasons. First, the survey methodology has changed over the years with respect to minimum age of hunters included in the survey and the recall period of individual surveys. In an effort to minimize recall bias, the 1991 and 1996 surveys have collected data from hunters periodically during the study year, whereas previous surveys were implemented early in the calendar year and requested recollection of participation data for the entire past calendar year. Second, hunting participation between any two adjacent 5-year periods has been relatively stable. Although these national surveys use large sample sizes, the combined standard errors between any two surveys have often been large enough that differences in participation indicated by any two temporally adjacent surveys could be attributable to sampling (as well as methodological differences noted above) rather than actual changes in participation.

The annual licence sales data collected and reported to the FWS by the individual states provide another measure of hunting participation. States sell a variety of types of hunting licences including resident and nonresident, big game and small game, and combination licences that may include all hunting or hunting and fishing combined. This makes accurate estimation of hunter numbers difficult (e.g. one hunter could buy big game and small game licences separately, whereas another might buy the combined licence). Despite the possibility of double counting, each state wildlife agency director is required to estimate the number of total paid hunting licence holders (people who are licenced to hunt, not licences sold) and to certify that number annually and report it to the FWS. This requires states to estimate proportions of people who are multiple licence holders in order to avoid inflation of hunter numbers.

These annual licence sales data also are not conclusive indicators of the number of participating hunters nationally or in a given state. Examples of limitations of licence holder data for trend analysis are: (i) some states have allowed hunters over a particular age to obtain a free senior licence (some states have initiated and subsequently revoked this practice or changed the applicable age); and (ii) some states do not require a landowner to purchase a licence to hunt exclusively on his own land. Nevertheless, licence sales data are useful in analysing hunting participation trends because, with the exceptions noted above, they have been carried out consistently over several decades and the total estimates of paid licence holders are derived from direct counts, not from sampling.

A third indicator of hunting participation that is useful in examining the direction of hunting trends is annual registration data from hunter education courses. Almost all (49) states require prospective hunters to complete a course of several hours dealing with hunting safety, ethics and other topics before they can purchase their first hunting licence. Registration data from hunter education courses provide a useful estimate of annual recruitment into the hunter population and provide valuable insights into likely hunting participation 15–30 years into the future. The age and other socio-demographic characteristics of hunter training recruits also offer insights through research into the sustainability of the hunting population by relating such characteristics to long-term involvement.

US Fish and Wildlife Service survey results

The FWS (US Fish and Wildlife Service, 1997) estimates that 14.0 million Americans 16 years of age and older hunted in 1996, compared to 14.1 million in 1991. Differences in the two estimates are not statistically significant, so we should infer that nationally, the number of participants remained essentially constant over this period. Regionally, participation rates in hunting also were very similar between 1991 and 1996, with two exceptions: (i) the number of hunters in the Pacific states increased by 9%; and (ii) the number of hunters in the Middle Atlantic states declined by nearly 17%. These differences are statistically significant at the 95% confidence level.

By major types of hunting, 11.3 million Americans hunted big game, 6.9 million hunted small game and 3.1 million hunted waterfowl. Estimates show an increase nationally in big game hunters from 10.7 million in 1991 to 11.3 million in 1996, although the difference is not statistically significant at the 95% confidence level. The number of small game hunters dropped from 7.6 million in 1991 to 6.9 million in 1996 (difference is statistically significant), while the number of migratory bird hunters remained relatively constant over the 5-year period at about 3 million. The number of days afield increased at least slightly for all types of hunting between 1991 and 1996 (8.9% overall); the largest increases occurred in big game hunting (20%) and in waterfowl hunting (19%).

Moderate to large increases in hunting-related expenditure occurred between 1991 and 1996 when compared in constant or inflation-adjusted dollars. Trip-related expenditure increased by 30.3%, and expenditure per day increased by 19.5%. Equipment-related expenditure increased by 46.2%. Items with particularly high percentage increases included purchase of: decoys and game calls (138.2%), muzzle-loaders and primitive weapons (77.3%), hunting dogs and associated costs (75.9%), telescopic sights (67.2%) and shotguns (58.9%). Other hunting-related purchases and expenses with large increases from 1991 to 1996 included magazines and books (127.6%), binoculars and telescopes (94.3%), processing and taxidermy costs (74.4%), special clothing (72.7%) and membership dues and contributions (55.3%).

Longer-term results from FWS surveys suggest that hunting participation increased nationwide through 1975, when a peak of 17.1 million hunters 12 years of age and over hunted at least 3 days. This figure dropped to 16.3 million in 1985. More recent FWS surveys do not have comparable data (Brown, 1995). The number of hunters 6 years of age and older (reported by an adult member of each household) remained essentially constant from 1980 to 1990 (US Fish and Wildlife Service, 1997).

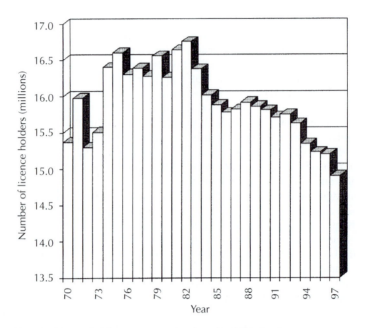

Fig. 13.1.   Paid hunting licence holders. Source: US Fish and Wildlife Service.

Paid hunting licence holders

Despite the possibility of some error in estimating total paid licence holders from the totals of all individual licences that permit hunting, these estimates are calculated consistently from year to year and have been required by the FWS for several decades. Thus, even if the totals contain some error in estimating individual licence holders, the error should be consistent over time and the estimated totals should reflect changes in hunting participation.

The estimated national total of paid hunting licence sales (Fig. 13.1) shows that licence sales peaked in 1983. Sales have generally declined since then. In 1997, the last year of record, sales were at their lowest point since 1970. While hunting licence sales in aggregate have been declining nationally, state trends vary considerably. In 1997, the states of South Carolina, North Dakota, Colorado and Alaska experienced record sales (in Colorado this is due primarily to a high demand for big game licences by nonresidents). Figure 13.2 shows the period in which peak sales were achieved by state. In addition to the states whose sales

peaked in 1997, the northern tier of states from Wisconsin to Montana, plus South Dakota, had very recent peak sales. On the other hand, 13 states, in several parts of the US, had licence sales peak in the 1970s and sales in another 20 states peaked in the 1980s. Sales in most of the Eastern and Midwestern states peaked by 1980.

Figure 13.3 illustrates the extent to which paid licence sales have declined from their peak across the US. The sharpest decline has occurred in California, which in 1997 was at only 43% of its peak licence sales. A total of 19 states, in many parts of the country, had sales in 1997 of less than 75% of their peak sales.

Hunter education graduates

All states have hunter education programmes for prospective hunters. These programmes have been in existence at least since the 1970s (state-managed hunter education started decades earlier in some states). Furthermore, completion of such a programme before one can obtain a hunting licence is now mandatory in all states except Alaska. This requirement gives those inter-

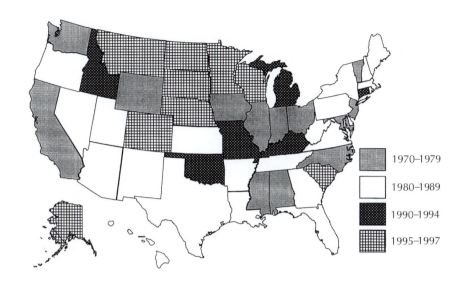

Fig. 13.2. Peak year, paid hunting licence sales. Source: US Fish and Wildlife Service.

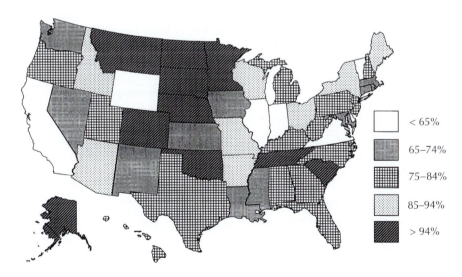

Fig. 13.3. 1997 licence sales as % of peak sales year. Source: US Fish and Wildlife Service.

ested in hunting trends an early data point not available for any other recreation activity – a recruitment indicator. Trend data in the recruitment of hunters over time provides a good indicator of what we can expect in the coming decades, with respect to hunting trends, if we can estimate attrition from the activity over the period. The individual states keep records of the number of hunter training graduates each year.

Nationally, the number of hunter education graduates remained steady from 1985 to 1997 (Table 13.1). Regional differences exist, however, with trends varying widely

Table 13.1. Hunter education graduates by region, 1985 and 1997, and percentage change.

Region	Number of graduates (Thousands)			Percentage change	
	1985	1991	1997	1985–1997	1991–1997
New England	19.4	22.8	20.4	5.2	−10.5
Middle Atlantic	121.9	95.5	87.4	−28.3	−8.5
South Atlantic	103.6	108.5	92.2	−11.0	−15.0
East North Central	94.7	100.3	106.8	12.8	6.5
East South Central	51.1	60.9	56.4	10.4	−7.4
West North Central	74.5	88.2	96.6	30.0	9.5
West South Central	73.5	75.2	81.0	10.2	7.7
Mountain	62.7	63.7	65.7	4.8	3.1
Pacific	49.1	46.9	49.6	0.1	5.8
Total (US)	650.5	662.0	663.1	1.9	0.2

from one region of the US to another. In the east, the number of hunter education graduates has declined about 10% since 1991, and graduates in the south Atlantic states (Bureau of the Census regions) declined by 15% since 1991. The trend in the middle Atlantic states has been declining over a longer period, with a drop of 28% since 1985 and 8% just since 1991.

The four central regions all experienced some growth in the number of graduates from 1985 to 1997, with strong growth of 30% in the west North Central states. However, more recently, the east South Central region experienced a drop of about 7% between 1991 and 1997. The Mountain states have experienced slight growth and the Pacific states have remained steady, with a growth of nearly 6% in the Pacific region between 1991 and 1997.

Factors Associated with Changes in Participation

Typical of most recreation activities, several factors appear to affect hunting participation over time. Some factors generally have had a positive influence on hunting, while others have had a dampening affect on hunting participation. These factors and their effects will be examined briefly. We suspect that a number of social trends not carefully monitored (i.e. for which periodic data are not available) affect hunting participation. We will indicate factors for which there are supportive data and those for which we must speculate.

Demographic factors

Most demographic factors that influence hunting have had a negative effect on participation for at least the past 20 years, and are projected to continue to affect hunting participation negatively for the foreseeable future. Even the general increase in the projected US population may not result in an increase in new recruits – hunting participation in the US, as a percentage of the population, has declined since 1980.

Perhaps the single greatest demographic trend correlating with constraining hunting participation has been the gradual urbanization of the population. Hunting has traditionally drawn participants most heavily from rural areas and villages. Previous research has shown that those who grew up in hunting families and went afield in their youth were most likely to continue the activity, while those who took up hunting later, having been introduced to the activity in other ways, were more likely to discontinue the activity (Purdy *et al.*, 1989). Heberlein and Thomson (1997), examining the possible effect of mandatory hunter education courses on participation, concluded that any effect was small, but that effects of urbanization and changes in hunting culture (for which a good measure was not available) are large.

A general negative correlation exists between the extent of urbanization of a state and the proportion of people in it who hunt. By 'extent of urbanization', the proportion of residents who live in urbanized areas appears to be a more critical variable than population density of the state. In California, America's most populated state, less than 2.5% of residents 16 years of age or older hunted in 1996 (US Fish and Wildlife Service, 1997). Also, less than 5% of the population 16 years of age and older hunt in Arizona, Connecticut, Florida, Hawaii, Illinois, Maryland, Massachusetts, Nevada, New Jersey, New York and Rhode Island. Some of these states have large expanses with low population density, but the vast majority of residents live in highly urbanized areas. At the other extreme, at least 20% of the population 16 years of age and older hunted in Idaho, Montana and South Dakota in 1996. It seems that many people who grew up in less populated areas have moved to urban and suburban areas to live and work, and many of these people do not continue to hunt or do not teach their children to hunt.

A second force related to urbanization involves not movement of people to the suburbs, but movement of the suburbs to them. As an example, 17 of New York's upstate counties were classified as metropolitan areas by the Bureau of the Census in 1970. By 1995, 30 upstate counties had received metropolitan designation. Brown and Connelly (1994) found that among demographic variables available annually, the variable most highly correlated with hunting (negatively) over a 30-year period was nonfarm employment. We believe this variable acts as an indicator of a much broader change from a rural or small town to an urban or suburban environment and associated lifestyle.

Kelly (1987) analysed National Recreation Surveys and commercial surveys (Nielsen, Simmons) during the 1970s and through the mid-1980s, finding declines of about 30% nationally in the proportions of younger age groups who were taking up hunting. In reference to the importance of fathers introducing their sons to hunting, Kelly noted that as these younger males mature to the time when they have children of appropriate age to start hunting (which will occur within the next 5–10 years), substantially fewer will introduce their children to hunting than was the case in the previous generation.

Other demographic variables also act as negative influences on future hunting participation. The highest rate of participation in hunting is among white males, but minority populations (African Americans, Hispanics) are increasing at a faster rate than the Caucasian population. Moreover, only 4% of the rapidly growing US population 55 years of age and older hunt, compared with 8% of younger adult age groups. It is noteworthy that the mean age of hunters has increased somewhat in the past decade, and that hunting participation among adults is relatively constant up to age 54. Between 7% and 9% of each age group from 16 up to 54 hunted in 1996 (US Fish and Wildlife Service, 1977).

Social factors

Hunting is deeply ingrained in the culture of several million North Americans, both indigenous and nonindigenous (primarily Anglos and a limited number of African Americans and other minorities). To many of these people, hunting is far more than a recreation activity; it is an integral part of their culture. Moreover, a variety of cultural traditions are expressed and are manifested through hunting. Lamar and Donnell (1987) and Marks (1991) indicate the cultural manifestations of hunting in the South and how they have evolved in unique ways. Miller (1992) documented some of the important rituals and traditions associated with hunting in deer camps in the Northeast. State wildlife directors identified regional types of hunting with strong cultural importance beyond variations in deer or elk hunting or rabbit and squirrel hunting that would be familiar to many lay people. Examples include wild hog hunting in the South, prairie chicken hunting in the Plains states, ptarmigan hunting in eastern Canada, and cougar hunting in the West (Brown *et al.*, 1995).

However, cultural norms change. Because hunting is primarily a nonmetropolitan activity passed down from fathers to sons (only 1% of American women hunted in 1996, compared to 13% of men), it is difficult to imagine hunting growing in popularity. For the vast majority of children of preteen and early teen years, most of their peers will not hunt. Junior high and high school athletic activities, computer and television activities (whether educational or strictly entertainment) and a host of other leisure activities compete for young people's time. Moreover, increasing work and other commitments compete for time and opportunities adults have in order to pass hunting and other outdoor activities on to young people. While good measures of these factors are elusive, it is highly likely that these sociocultural factors will on balance exert a negative influence on the future of hunting.

Supply factors

Supply factors include primarily game populations, access to land for hunting and hunting regulations. Populations of many big game and waterfowl species have increased substantially over the last quarter century. East of the Rockies, white-tailed deer populations reached all-time highs at some point in the 1990s for all areas except northern New England, Florida and Texas (state wildlife agency estimates as compiled by *Deer and Deer Hunting*, 1998). Deer are also plentiful in some areas of states where populations are now at record levels. With fewer hunters in most states, seasons have been extended, allowable harvests have been gradually increased, and special seasons for archery and muzzle-loader hunting have been implemented in many states. Populations of wild turkey also have increased in much of the East.

A recent study of access to private lands east of the Rockies found that roughly 40% of rural landowners posted (a legal statement printed on signs 'No Trespassing') their lands (Cordell *et al.*, 1998). About half these owners allowed others to use their lands for recreation. Nationwide, most hunting occurs on private lands, although 47% of hunters make some use of public lands (US Fish and Wildlife Service, 1997). Studies of posting and landowner attitudes have occurred in various states since the late 1950s. It appears that more landowners post their lands now, primarily as a means of actively controlling the use of their lands. However, no clear evidence exists of a shift in the number of owners who allow hunting on their lands.

Substantial acreage has been lost to hunting over the decades due to suburban development and the splitting up of rural areas into plots so small that the amount of open space where hunting can occur legally has declined. The amount of hunting that occurs on private lands where these obstacles are not present probably has not changed substantially. However, many landowners are managing their lands with tighter controls (e.g. posting). As a result, it is probably more difficult in recent years for new hunters or hunters who have recently moved into an area to find a place to hunt.

As white-tailed deer populations have grown, many states have extended the season for hunting deer, and offered special seasons for archery hunting and muzzleloader hunting. These longer seasons, plus the increased supply of deer in much of the country, no doubt accounts for the fact that the number of big game hunters has remained constant between 1991 and 1996 while other types of hunting have declined, and the average days afield per big game hunter have increased by more than 50% since 1980 (data from FWS 5-year surveys).

Implications for Management of Game Species

If the trend of stable to decreasing numbers of hunters continues, achieving effective wildlife management for some economically important wildlife species will be difficult in many places in North America. The high and growing numbers of problem-causing game species such as deer, elk and Canada geese managed primarily through hunting presents tremendous implications for wildlife managers. The traditional tool of management for such species – hunters – may not adequately meet population control needs in some situations. Worsening matters, the factors that seem to be influencing hunting recruitment and retention are resulting from social and economic megatrends. These are not forces that information and education (I&E) programmes, public informational meetings or press releases from a state wildlife agency can curb. Essentially, they are outside the wildlife manager's influence.

What does this outlook mean for the future of hunting and wildlife management? Basically, we believe two developments might lie on the horizon, neither with a positive outcome vis-à-vis the growth or even stability of hunting. First, managers will need to develop alternatives to recreational hunting to achieve wildlife management objectives – population control for some species – in many situations where hunting is not feasible, such as cities and suburbs. Research and development of alternatives are already under way. Predicting exactly where this activity will lead is difficult, but with both the wildlife management and humane treatment communities working on alternatives to hunting, though for very different reasons, it seems likely that extraordinary changes lie ahead. Recent breakthroughs in immunocontraception research and application, for example, support this speculation.

Second, urbanization trends will erode social support for hunting. Conditions that will reinforce if not accelerate this erosion include: (i) public repulsion with firearms; (ii) the physical, psychological and social distance of an increasingly greater proportion of citizens from rural traditions such as hunting; and (iii) the attractiveness of humane and animal rights arguments for a citizenry whose anthropomorphic images of

wildlife are created by entertainment media. These all point to greater social pressure to abate hunting and to deter recruitment of new hunters from the general population. With prospects mentioned earlier for developing alternatives to hunting that can mitigate wildlife problems faced by urban and suburban residents, arguments about the 'management tool' status of hunting will weaken.

Despite the limitations the above trends pose for hunting, the increases in hunting expenditures between 1991 and 1996 point to a large number of current hunters whose involvement seems to be increasing. While hunter numbers are not growing, current participants are spending more time afield than in previous years. Moreover, their expenditure patterns suggest that as a group they became more personally invested in hunting during this 5-year period. Increased expenditures for primitive weapons and bow-hunting may suggest a pattern of specialization for many hunters. More certainly, these expenses in combination with large increases in special gear, books and magazines about hunting, and membership dues and contributions point to a hunter population with an increased involvement and commitment to hunting.

A question facing the wildlife management profession is whether traditional hunting can remain a viable means of controlling populations of some wildlife populations in rural environments. For example, with deer populations increasing and hunter numbers remaining constant at best, deer constitute a serious threat to human welfare. We suggest that some fundamental changes in wildlife management philosophy, hunter education, and hunter attitudes and behaviours are needed for continued reliance on hunters to control overabundant game populations to be reasonable, even in rural areas.

We postulate that the time is at hand for two interrelated shifts to occur in the wildlife management paradigm. First, the normal paradigm of game management over the past century has been one of managing to protect wildlife and to distribute benefits from scarce wildlife resources fairly across users (i.e. hunters). We are now in a situation where many game species are locally over-abundant; they exceed people's tolerance of risk for problems such as economic loss, health threats and safety hazards. The summer 1997 issue of *The Wildlife Society Bulletin* was devoted to problems related to overpopulation of white-tailed deer. Wildlife management philosophy must shift to reflect this change.

Management of recreational hunting needs rethinking, too. Many studies of hunting satisfaction have been used to guide development of hunting regulations for the management and harvest of game species, but these have largely reflected the preferences of hunters who have approached hunting as a recreation not a management activity. For example, many hunters have little interest in shooting does, and as a group do not shoot as many does as they have the opportunity to take legally (Decker and Connelly, 1990; Enck, 1996). With the number of hunters dwindling and numbers of some game species growing out of control from a tolerance perspective, managers need to take some novel, perhaps extreme, actions to achieve management in expansive rural habitats. Generally, education about the role of hunting in game management and incentives that lead to management-effective behaviours by hunters are needed to help ensure that hunters play a larger part in wildlife management than they have in the past. Education programmes also need to highlight the community-service aspect of effective hunting/game management programmes. Hopefully the combination of actions will change the beliefs and attitudes of hunters, and of nonhunters in the communities where they live and hunt to help control problem species.

Summary

Hunting is many things: a recreation activity, an important sociocultural element in the lives of many people, a means of obtaining food for some people, and the primary means used by wildlife management agencies for controlling game populations. Change in the rate of hunting participation has occurred very slowly. Most measures indicate that hunting participation peaked between 1980 and 1985 and has gradually declined thereafter. Hunting has traditionally been most popular in rural areas with farming families and others who live 'close to the land'. Demographic projections indicate that these populations will continue to decline. We expect hunting participation to decline also, despite increases in many types of game populations throughout much of the US.

Thanks in part to increased game populations and lengthened hunting seasons, hunters' expenditures increased substantially between 1991 and 1996. Increases in archery related expenditure and primitive weapons suggests the occurrence of some increased specialization by hunters during this 5-year period. Regardless of specialization, the increased mean number of days spent afield combined with increases in many types of expenditures indicates that involvement in hunting and commitment to the activity increased over this period.

As we move into the 21st century, hunting opportunities appear to be good. Access to private lands, where most hunting occurs, has been something of an obstacle in the past. However, as game populations increase and landowners suffer increased damage to crops, landscape plantings and woodlands, they may be more willing to grant hunting access than in previous times. In fact, we predict that controlling game population will become a major problem for wildlife agencies, that hunting seasons will need to be further liberalized, and that other means such as immunocontraception will need to be perfected and used in conjunction with hunting to control game populations.

14

Trends in Casinos and Tourism for the 21st Century

William R. Eadington

Introduction

The most important trends regarding casinos in many countries over the past few decades have been their increased legal presence, substantial expansion in the size of typical casino operations and of legal gaming in aggregate, and the diversity of nongaming offerings put forward by casino enterprises. These trends have emerged during a period of rapid and fundamental change in casinos, in terms of ownership, management styles and strategy, and general public perceptions.

It is generally understood that a casino is a physical venue that offers table games (blackjack, roulette, craps, baccarat, poker, etc.) and/or slot machines (reel-type slot machines, electronic gaming devices, video poker machines, amusement with prize machines, 'pokies', fruit machines, etc.) Because of variations in laws from jurisdiction to jurisdiction that permit or prohibit certain types of gambling games or devices, there can be some ambiguity in what should be considered a 'casino'. For example, facilities that offer bingo along with paper pull-tabs (similar to instant lottery tickets, sometimes called 'paper slots') would not be considered casinos, whereas entertainment centres that include bingo and electronic gaming devices, but no table games, would

usually be classified as casinos.

Casinos can range in size from quite small (e.g. top end London casinos might have fewer than a dozen gaming tables and no slot machines; cruise ship casinos might have only one or two blackjack tables and a handful of slot machines) to enormous (e.g. Foxwood's Casino in Ledyard, Connecticut, has approximately 300 table games, 4000 slot machines, a poker room with 55 tables, and a bingo hall that accommodates more than 1500 patrons at a time.) A casino is a specific site (i.e. a building, a boat), whereas casino-style gaming can be offered in non-casino locations (i.e. slot machines or video poker machines in bars and taverns, poker offered in bars and taverns or card clubs).

In the middle of the 20th century, casinos were largely considered dens of iniquity, and could be found only in a few scattered venues in faraway places. By the end of the century, casino gaming had become a major presence in the leisure economies of countries all over the world. This transition has occurred for a variety of reasons, including:

- A growing acceptance of gambling as a recreational activity;
- increased legitimacy of casino gaming as a business;
- a shift from entrepreneurial and closely held gaming companies to corporate

ownership;
- the increased professional competence of gaming regulatory bodies; and
- a desire of governments to exploit the economic spinoffs from casinos for fiscal, tourism or economic development purposes.

These factors have contributed to legalization of casinos and casino-style gaming in a variety of forms in jurisdictions all over the world.

Historically, casinos have been closely associated with glamorous tourist destination resorts such as Monte Carlo, the French Riviera, Baden Baden, Lake Tahoe and Las Vegas. However, though there is a high correlation between casinos and tourism, not all casinos cater to tourists, or cause expansion of tourism markets. In recent years, many casino jurisdictions were authorized for the explicit purpose of revitalizing a declining tourism industry, or acting as a catalyst that would cause substantial tourism development. But the ability of a state, city, province or country to use casinos as a major stimulus for tourism development or expansion successfully is dependent on a wide range of characteristics and considerations.

The challenge for most governments pursuing a tourism strategy is – by definition – to develop a casino industry that brings in more outsiders than locals. If this can be done, considerable ancillary benefits for the local or regional economy can be captured. However, more and more frequently, newly authorized casino markets cater more to local residents than to tourists. This is particularly true when casino gambling is not prohibited elsewhere in the region. There have been many instances in recent years where tourism development expectations have not been met. In such cases, proponents of legal casinos have been disappointed, or at least surprised, by the actual impacts and development patterns related to casinos.

This analysis looks at trends in casino gaming in various parts of the world in the context of tourism, and makes some observations and projections on the importance of some of these trends. A general framework for understanding the linkages between casinos and tourism is presented.

A Brief Overview of the History and Status of Casinos and Casino-style Gambling in Selected Countries

Until the 1960s, casino gaming remained largely prohibited in most countries of the world (Cabot *et al.*, 1993) There were a few exceptions, such as the small elite casinos found in specific locales in Germany, France, Austria and Monaco. Large mass-market casinos were operating in Nevada and parts of the Caribbean by mid-century, but not in very many other locations. Because of a deserved reputation that linked casinos either to criminal activities or criminal elements, or to the damage that gambling inflicted on people's lives, they were prohibited in most societies.

Except for Nevada, access to legal casinos in these specific locations was typically quite limited. For the most part, casinos were in destination resort areas or spas, away from major population centres. Almost by definition, their major clientele was tourists. This geographic positioning was undoubtedly due to a widespread belief that casinos were inherently damaging to some proportion of the population, and especially to those of limited means. Thus, if casinos were to be tolerated, they should only be allowed if they were placed away from urban areas. Thus, only those who could afford to travel to casinos – or to linger in resort areas – would have the opportunity to gamble.

The legal presence of casinos began to change significantly after 1960. A number of countries, states and provinces authorized casinos in the 1960s and 1970s, including the UK, Spain, Australia, Holland, New Jersey (USA), and Malaysia. Each is briefly discussed below.

The UK accidentally legalized an unregulated casino industry in 1960, when Parliament tried to eliminate or modernize 19th century laws prohibiting social gambling. The original legislation (which had various unforeseen consequences) gave way to the Gaming Act 1968 that established a highly regulated casino industry made up of membership clubs that would cater only to 'unstimulated demand' for gambling. The law did so by de facto limitation of the number of casino licences, prohibition of marketing or promotion of the business in a variety of ways, and imposition of a variety of other social controls. Furthermore, because of a belief that slot machines posed the most serious threat of social impacts from casino gaming, their presence was severely limited in British casinos. Initially, casinos were permitted only two slot machines per facility. This has recently been increased to six, with the possibility of further moderate increases in the future (Kent-Lemon, 1984; Miers, 1996).

The Gaming Act 1968 did not anticipate tourist-based casino patronage; its concerns centred on the consequences of prohibition of gambling on the domestic population. Thus, casinos were permitted in urban centres, as well as in some seaside resorts. The London casinos did become important outlets for international patrons from the mid-1970s onward, but the provincial casinos have always catered to a local clientele. British casinos are physically quite small by American or Australian standards, and largely invisible to the general public because of the various constraints of the law.

The British casino industry is quite small by comparative standards. In 1997–1998, 115 casinos were operating in the UK, which is approximately the same number that existed in 1970, when the current legislation came into effect. Gross gaming winnings were about £490 million (US$800 million), of which about 65% came from London-based casinos (Gaming Board for Great Britain, 1998). Gross gaming revenues from British casinos made up only about 7% of the legal gaming revenues in the UK. In contrast, about 50% of all gaming revenues in the US (a total of US$25 million) were generated by casinos (Christiansen, 1998).

In Malaysia, the government granted one company an exclusive licence to operate a casino at Genting Sempah, in the mountains about an hour's drive from the capital city of Kuala Lumpur. The casino, commonly referred to as Genting Highlands, opened in 1971. Catering primarily to ethnic Chinese populations in Malaysia and southeast Asia, this facility over time has become an important centre of regional international tourism from Thailand, Singapore and other regional Far Eastern countries. Interestingly, the casino is not highlighted very much as a tourism asset by Malaysian tourism officials, and is given very little attention within Malaysia because of the majority Muslim population's fundamental opposition to gambling (Cabot et al., 1993, pp. 441–442).

Australia authorized casinos in a number of small cities in various parts of the country in the 1970s. A private sector monopoly casino opened in Hobart, Tasmania, in 1972, and another later opened in Launceston. Other casinos then opened in Alice Springs and Darwin, in the Northern Territories. These were small casinos that catered to a mix of local and tourist markets. Only Hobart, which attracted fly-in customers from Melbourne and Sydney, generated significant tourism business (McMillen and Eadington, 1986).

By the early 1980s, there was an increasing presence of casino gaming in various parts of the world. However, with few exceptions, urban casinos – especially American-style easily accessible casinos – were still prohibited. But, beginning in 1985, Australia led the way in introducing true urban casinos. The Australian cities of Perth and Adelaide, along with the smaller city of Townsville and the resort area of the Gold Coast, opened private sector monopoly casinos in 1985. These were subsequently followed by urban casinos in the 1990s in Canberra, Brisbane, Melbourne and Sydney, along with a resort casino in Cairns and another on Christmas Island. New Zealand followed Australia's lead by permitting exclusive franchise privately owned casinos in the cities of Christchurch and Auckland in the early 1990s (Cabot et al., 1993).

After the death of Franco, Spain legalized casinos in the late 1970s. Casinos were intended to serve as a catalyst for international tourism, so they were for the most part in destination resort areas along Spain's coastlines. However, instead of attracting international tourists, most customers to Spanish casinos were Spaniards. More importantly, however, the Spanish government in the late 1970s also authorized slot machines outside casinos, in arcades and in bars and taverns. As a result, by the late 1990s, more than 20 years after the establishment of permitted casino-style gaming in Spain, the Spanish casino industry generates gaming revenues of about 50 billion pesetas (US$300 million), which is less than one-tenth the revenues generated by Spanish slot machines found outside casinos.

Holland established a government company (Holland Casinos) to own and operate legal casinos in that country in 1972. Their motivation was twofold: to establish casinos in destination resort areas to attract domestic and international tourists, and to combat the illegal casinos that had emerged in many of Holland's cities, the so-called 'Golden Ten' casinos. Initially, Holland Casinos opened casinos only in destination resort areas. However, by the early 1980s, casinos were introduced into the major cities of Amsterdam and Rotterdam. By the late 1990s, there were ten operating casinos in Holland (Polders, 1988; Thompson, 1988).

In the US, the first legal casino jurisdiction outside Nevada was Atlantic City, New Jersey, which authorized casinos by an initiative process in 1976. This was a highly regulated tourist-based casino industry in a declining destination resort area. Atlantic City has subsequently become the second largest casino market in the world, after Las Vegas, with large casino–hotel complexes that cater to mass volume gaming and tourism. Gaming revenues from Atlantic City's 12 casino hotels were US$4 billion in 1998, compared to US$6 billion in gaming revenues generated by more than 100 casinos in Las Vegas.

Other countries have also introduced casinos, often with the hope or expectation of stimulating tourism. In the Philippines, a government-owned company, PAGCOR (the Philippine Amusement and Gaming Corporation), established casinos in cities and in resort areas in that country, but these casinos now cater predominantly to local residents. More recently, PAGCOR has established strategic partnerships with private companies to run casinos in the country aimed primarily at international premium players (Cabot et al., 1993).

Greece authorized exclusive franchise private sector casinos in the early 1990s, the first European country to embrace the American (easy access, mass market) model of casinos. However, difficulties arose both in the bid process to allocate the casino licences, and with regard to social impacts once the casinos were operating. The bid for a casino in Athens was cancelled in 1994 after it had been awarded because of a change in government and because of increased social concerns. In 1996, the Greek government imposed a 5000 drachma (US$16) entrance fee on casinos, purportedly to control excessive gambling by citizens of limited means. The view was expressed that casinos had led to a substantial increase in bankruptcies among residents who lived close to the casinos. None the less, in 1999, nine casinos were operating in Greece.

Canada did not begin serious casino development until the early 1990s. Before that, only limited 'charity' casinos (which would raise revenues for 'good causes', sponsored by nonprofit and charitable organizations) could be found in the country, especially in the western provinces of Alberta, Manitoba and British Columbia. However, beginning in 1990, government-owned monopoly urban casinos opened in Winnipeg, Halifax, Montreal, Windsor, Hull (near Ottawa) and Regina, as well as in destination resort areas at Niagara Falls (Ontario), Charlevoix (Québec) and Sydney (Nova Scotia).

Some Canadian casinos – such as Windsor and Niagara Falls – are clearly positioned to meet the demand for casino gaming from Americans across the border. However, most Canadian casinos cater primarily and predominantly to their immediate urban markets (Campbell, 1994).

The rapid spread of casinos in the US began in 1988 and continued for the next 5 years, with authorization of small stakes

Table 14.1. US legislatively authorized non-Indian casinos, 1998.

State (date of enabling legislation)	Number of casinos (maximum allowed)[a]	1998 Gaming revenues (US$million)	Permitted location
Nevada (1931)	230	8065	Local zoning
New Jersey (1976)	13	4045	Atlantic City only
Iowa (1989)	5	n/a	Navigable rivers
Iowa (1994)[b]	12	496	Navigable rivers
Illinois (1990)	10 (10)	1107	Navigable rivers
Mississippi (1990)	29	2177	Designated waterways, dockside
Louisiana (1991)	14 (15)	1323	Designated waterways
Riverboat casinos Louisiana (1992) New Orleans land-based casino	0 (1)	0	Site of former Convention Centre
Colorado (1990)	51	479	Three designated mining towns
South Dakota (1988)	53	44	City of Deadwood only
Missouri (1992)	12	853	Designated waterways
Indiana (1993)	11 (11)	1339	Designated waterways
Michigan (1996)	0 (3)	0	Detroit only

[a] As of 1998.
[b] Iowa relaxed restrictions on its riverboats in 1994.

mining town casinos in South Dakota and Colorado, and restricted riverboat casinos in Iowa, Illinois, Mississippi, Louisiana, Missouri and Indiana. The number of casinos, gross gaming revenues, and locational restrictions on US non-Indian casinos are given in Table 14.1.

Most of these 'new jurisdiction' casinos are different in character than the destination resort casinos of Nevada and Atlantic City. Most of their visitors come from within a 100-mile radius, and for the most part, they are 'day tripper' visitors rather than overnight tourists. Customers to these casinos are for the most part single-purpose visitors, and concentrate their efforts on gaming rather than on a variety of other tourist-style activities. Because of this, the economic impacts of casinos that cater to local markets are considerably different – and generally lower in magnitude – than true tourist-oriented destination resort casinos (Eadington, 1999).

In the US, there has been a move toward urban casinos as well. Though most of the 'new jurisdiction' casinos are in small communities or rural locations, some are in, or close to, major cities such as Kansas City, St. Louis, New Orleans, Cincinnati, Memphis and Minneapolis. The only state to authorize casinos between 1994 and 1998 was Michigan, which authorized three urban casinos in Detroit in 1996. The state's voters were largely motivated by the presence of a Canadian casino in Windsor, directly across the river from Detroit, that was generating about 80% of its business from Americans. Temporary casinos were scheduled to open in Detroit before the end of 1999, with the permanent casinos expected by 2003.

The urban casino experience in the US has so far been somewhat mixed. The monopoly land-based casino in New Orleans, which opened at a temporary site in 1995, closed within 5 months when the operating company declared bankruptcy. The company at the same time halted construction on its US$900 million permanent casino. Part of the reason for this situation resulted from the financial and political demands placed upon the private sector operator who had overestimated the size of the market. The conditions imposed by the legislation on the operator turned out to be so onerous that the casino was not economically viable (Rittvo, 1997). A reorganization plan was adopted in 1998, and the land-based casino re-opened in the fall of 1999. However, the financial difficulties continued into 2000.

Other states have also met with challenges regarding urban casinos. There have been financial difficulties with some casinos in Kansas City, Missouri, and one of the original companies, Boyd Gaming, closed their operation in 1998. Another operator, Hilton, gave up their casino licence and sold their riverboat casino facility in 1999 rather than go through a potentially embarrassing investigation involving questionable contributions to an official who was involved in the original bidding process. Also in Missouri, continuing political opposition to casinos forced elections in 1994 and 1998 to clarify constitutional issues dealing with permitted games and with the definition of navigable rivers and where riverboat casinos could be located. This kind of ongoing challenge has contributed to the instability of the Missouri casino industry's long-term outlook.

Indian tribal casinos operate in nearly 20 states as of 1999, and owe their legal status either to favourable court interpretations of the Indian Gaming Regulatory Act of 1988, or to negotiated compacts with states. Though some Indian casinos are near urban population concentrations, most Indian casinos are some distance from city centres on rural Indian reservation land (US General Accounting Office, 1997). By 1997, Indian gaming casinos in the US were generating revenues of nearly US$6 billion per year. This is particularly impressive in light of the fact that, before 1990, there were no legally sanctioned Indian casinos in operation in the US (Christiansen, 1998).

According to the National Gambling Impact Study Commission, as of 1996, there were approximately 109 Indian casinos in 14 states. Eight of these casino facilities accounted for more than 40% of the US$4.5 billion of gross gaming revenues in 1995 (National Gambling Impact Study Commission, 1999). Since that date, additional Indian gaming facilities have opened in California, Connecticut, New Mexico and elsewhere, and gaming revenues for Indian gaming in general have grown considerably.

In the last half of the 1990s, the proliferation of casinos slowed considerably in most parts of the world, with only a few jurisdictions authorizing casinos since the end of the American legalization boom in 1993. South Africa authorized 40 casinos, allocated among the nine provinces, in 1996, and was in the process of granting licences in 1998 and 1999. A casino opened in Jericho, in the Palestinian territory of Israel, in 1998. However, the government of Turkey shut down that country's casino industry in early 1998 because of religious opposition and participation in the industry by members of organized crime.

Other trends: the spread of casino-style gaming

In spite of the recent slowdown in new legalization of casinos, there has been a continuing expansion of other forms of casino-style gaming in various countries. Slot route operations (the placement of slot machines and other gaming devices in bars, taverns or arcades) has occurred in a number of jurisdictions, including the states of Montana, Oregon, South Dakota, Louisiana and South Carolina, as well as in various Canadian provinces, most Australian states, and New Zealand. Racetracks in some American states (Louisiana, Iowa, Delaware, Rhode Island and West Virginia) successfully lobbied for the right to have slot machines or other gaming devices at the tracks. The primary argument put forward in these cases is the need for economic relief. Businesses of various types, especially those who are adversely affected by competition from newly authorized casinos, argue that the 'playing field can be levelled' only if they are permitted slot machines.

An interesting insight into the effect of introducing such casino-style gaming in competition with casinos can be seen by the experience in Spain and in South Australia.

As mentioned earlier, more casino-style gaming takes place in Spain outside casinos – in bars and taverns – than in the 20 or so Spanish casinos. In South Australia, a single permitted casino, centrally located in the city of Adelaide, began operations in 1985. Slot machines outside casinos were first permitted in 1994 in hotels and bars. In 1993/94, the fiscal year before the introduction, the Adelaide Casino had gross gaming revenues of approximately A\$120 million (US\$80 million). Only 3 years later, with the competition of noncasino slot machines, the Adelaide Casino's revenues had fallen by approximately 40% to A\$70 million, whereas gaming revenues for slot machines outside casinos grew from nothing to A\$360 million.

From the Spanish and South Australian experience, two things seem clear. First, many customers prefer the convenience of slot machines and electronic gaming devices close to their place of residence over both destination resort casinos and urban casinos. Second, the introduction of slot machines outside casinos considerably grows the market for casino-style gaming, taking a portion of revenues from what otherwise would accrue to the casino industry. However, the placement of slot machines outside casinos, though more popular in terms of revenue generation, may trigger significant negative social impacts and more political backlash than site-specific casinos. This has been reflected in the late 1990s with controversies over the presence and rapid spread of such gaming machines in various jurisdictions, including South Carolina, Ontario, Victoria and Alberta.

The Evolution of Gambling as Entertainment

Clearly, the casino industry has been one of the most dynamic segments of the leisure industry and of tourist industries for the last quarter of the 20th century. However, it is not obvious where these trends are heading, especially with regard to tourism. Thus, it is useful to speculate on the implications of current trends in casinos and casino-style gaming into the 21st century.

The future direction of casinos can perhaps best be seen by examining those markets with the greatest degree of internal competition. In the late 1990s, the most competitive casino gaming markets are found in the US, in the jurisdictions of Nevada, Atlantic City and Mississippi. Each of these can be described as a private sector destination resort tourist-based market, and each has relatively limited legal restrictions on new entry, especially in comparison with standards adopted elsewhere in the world.

Las Vegas – the world's largest casino market – evolved in the 1990s with three waves of new mega-casino resorts offering a variety of amenities and attractions beyond traditional casino products. Beginning in 1989 with the opening of The Mirage (and continuing into the 2000s with such properties as Excalibur, Luxor, Treasure Island, MGM Grand, Stratosphere, New York New York, Monte Carlo, Bellagio, Mandalay Bay, The Venetian, Paris and the Aladdin) Las Vegas went through a major transformation. It began the period as a destination resort area centred on casino gaming. By the new millennium, it had become a multifaceted entertainment and convention venue, still with gambling as a major theme and casinos as major revenue generators, on a scale that put it beyond competing destinations virtually anywhere else in the world. The intensity of this transformation was reflected by the extent of corporate capital outlays in Las Vegas. Between 1998 and 2000, for example, six major investment projects (five new and one existing mega-casino resort) on the Las Vegas Strip cost nearly US\$8 billion.

With most of the new developments in Las Vegas in the 1990s, the dominant features were the Disneyesque character of the architecture, heavy theming, entertainment attractions and thrill-based recreational opportunities. This transformation was most dramatic for developments on the Las Vegas Strip. In that market, the proportion of revenues generated by nongaming activities in licenced casinos approached 50% of total revenues by 1998, as a result of a concerted diversification of offerings.

In the 1990s, Las Vegas Strip resorts – and

Las Vegas itself – became well known for spectacular entertainment productions, upscale retail shopping areas, substantial convention facilities, unique animal attractions (dolphins, white tigers, etc.), various simulation and thrill rides, museums and world class restaurants. Though gaming was still an important part of the Las Vegas experience for the majority of visitors, the major casino companies decided that the best way to compete against the widening proliferation of casinos and casino-style gaming in other jurisdictions was to make Las Vegas compelling for many other reasons (Christiansen and Brinkerhof-Jacobs, 1997). Thus, providing a variety of entertaining attractions, and identifying and targeting particular market niches, became the most observable strategies followed. With more than 120,000 hotel rooms by 2000, Las Vegas provided a variety of diversions for a clientele who were clearly there to be entertained (O'Brien, 1998).

Other competitive casino markets adopted less grandiose but similar strategies for their own growth and evolution. Atlantic City, which for much of its first two decades was the only casino centre in the northeastern US, catered mainly to a 'day tripper' market. Concerted efforts in the 1990s pushed Atlantic City more and more in the direction of becoming a true destination resort, with increased room capacity, improved convention facilities and heavier theming of its resorts. However, in spite of its role as the second largest gaming market in the US, it remained far behind Las Vegas in the extent of its offerings. In dramatic comparison to Las Vegas, approximately 80% of the 12 Atlantic City casinos' total revenues in 1998 came from gaming (O'Brien, 1998).

Smaller competitive casino markets, such as Reno/Tahoe in Nevada and Tunica County and the Gulf Coast in Mississippi, also tried to diversify their resort offerings in the 1990s in response to growing competition, and in order to strengthen customer loyalty and to broaden their customer base. Such efforts included construction of hotel towers, golf courses, entertainment venues and convention facilities. These jurisdictions were more vulnerable than Las Vegas to the risks of competition arising from newly authorized casino industries or legalization of slot machines in nearby jurisdictions. The strategic concern was to provide a broader base of attractions if casino-style gaming was going to be more readily available in their traditional feeder markets.

One of the difficult challenges for these areas was being able to attract substantial financial capital for new investment into the smaller casino markets. After the Las Vegas Strip, no other region in the US could attract the kind of financial capital, or expected return on investment, to justify billion dollar resort projects. Without billion dollar projects, no one besides Las Vegas could insulate themselves from the growing competition that proliferation of gaming in America had brought about. In many respects, this posed a 'catch-22' situation for US casino cities that will continue well into the 21st century.

Outside the US, competition within the casino industry is difficult to find. Most casino markets are franchised monopolies or have significant legal barriers to entry. For jurisdictions with such protected market status, and for monopoly or oligopoly urban casinos in particular, it is far more difficult to justify strategic investments that broaden the nongaming entertainment appeal of casino facilities. Protected market status often undermines the rationale for diversifying into nongaming areas. Thus, it is unlikely that such casinos will experience the kind of entertainment and facility diversification that is taking place in Nevada, Atlantic City and Mississippi.

Sometimes protected market status can create a dangerous complacency that leaves the casino industry vulnerable to legalization of casinos in nearby jurisdictions, or in an expanded presence of casino-style gaming. This certainly is the issue that confronts casino industries as diverse as riverboats in Illinois and Indiana, and urban casinos in Australia, New Zealand and Canada.

Conclusions and Implications

There is little doubt that casino gaming will continue to be a growth industry into the early part of the 21st century. The steady increase in positive public attitudes regarding casino gaming as a legitimate form of entertainment will bring that about. However, there is some question as to whether casinos will be able to establish themselves or remain as an important part of tourism industries in many countries, states and provinces.

In general, casino customers gravitate toward casinos or gaming venues close to their residences unless there are substantial nongaming attractions that can entice them to travel further to visit destination resort casino areas instead. Without such exciting alternatives, much of the demand for casino gaming will be captured in local or regional markets, rather than in destination resort casinos.

Las Vegas provides a useful model of a casino resort area that has effectively positioned itself to compete effectively against convenience casinos and casino-style gaming. Because of its leisure and entertainment diversification, it will continue to exhibit a strong tourist character regardless of external competition. However, it might turn out that Las Vegas is historically unique. It is quite possible that no other resort area will be able to amass the infrastructure, tourism amenities, and critical mass of private sector mega-casino properties to build a global destination resort around its casino industry.

This carries a strong message for jurisdictions with casinos, or those planning to develop casinos, with respect to their broader tourism strategies. Part of the message is to avoid overestimating what casinos might be able to accomplish. At best, casinos might complement existing tourism resources in attracting visitors to an area and therefore expand the tourist market. However, unless competing jurisdictions in the region prohibit casinos and other forms of casino-style gaming, casino industries that do not provide a wide array of nongaming attractions will be vulnerable to more convenient venues that can effectively offer the same gaming products. In markets with significant competition, casinos will take on more and more of a local character, attracting much of their patronage from within a fairly small radius of the casinos themselves.

In summary, the ability to replicate Las Vegas' success, or to experience the excess profitability that has characterized many new jurisdiction casino markets in the 1980s and 1990s, will diminish as competition for the gaming and leisure dollar increase and the supply of casinos and outlets for casino-style gaming expand. Policy makers who hope to use casinos as major catalysts for tourism development need to be realistic in assessing the likelihood that casinos will have a major impact on their overall tourism product. If not, they might end up sorely disappointed.

15

Health Tourism Trends: Closing the Gap between Health Care and Tourism

Anna Pollock and Peter Williams

Introduction

While tourism and the pursuit of health have long been connected, few North American organizations have specifically linked these two phenomena in a pragmatic sense. This is not the case in Europe where many segments of the tourism industry have had long-standing ties with health-related organizations and travellers. This chapter examines the emerging trend of health tourism in North America; characterizes the management responses to the trend; describes the policy and planning barriers to be overcome in building stronger linkages between tourism and traditional health care professionals; and recommends policy and planning shifts that are needed to create stronger synergistic connections among the tourism industry, health care and government agencies. It does so as a contribution to the growing but relatively undeveloped field of health tourism in North America.

Health tourism concepts

During its relatively short North American existence, the concept of health tourism has evolved from being primarily medical care focused (Goodrich and Goodrich, 1991; Goodrich, 1994) to placing heavy emphasis on health promotion. This chapter centres its discussion on the health promotion dimension of health tourism. In this context, health tourism is defined as:

> leisure, recreational and educational activities removed from the distractions of work and home that use tourism products and services that are designed to promote and enable customers to improve and maintain their health and well-being.

Health and wellness attitudes

Critical to an appreciation of the potential strategic linkages between health and tourism is an understanding of changing attitudes concerning health and wellness. The view of health as merely an absence of disease was challenged as early as 1946 by the World Health Organization (WHO). It defined health as a state of complete physical, mental and social wellbeing, not merely the absence of disease or infirmity (WHO, 1946). This larger, holistic vision of health gave root to the wellness movement of the 1970s in which individuals assumed a more participatory role in their health care. While the emphasis was initially placed on physical fitness and the body, there has been a subsequent recognition of the need to balance the needs of body, mind and spirit through activities and experiences in healthy environments (Lalonde, 1974; Edlin and Golanty, 1985).

As a consequence of this shift in perception, health promotion programmes which enable people to increase control over and improve their own health have developed. More than ever before, North Americans are now encouraged to participate in the maintenance of their health not only for their own benefit, but also as a means of controlling escalating health care costs. Over the past decade, North Americans have witnessed substantive increases in the number and quality of fitness centres associated with private gyms, public community centres and commercial hotels. Similarly, there has been a surge in the variety of tourism destinations offering health resort facilities and services (e.g. spas, retreat programmes and wellness centres) which focus on helping clients achieve higher levels of health, vitality and wellbeing (Burt, 1995). In this context, such health tourism destinations have among their underlying goals, the aim to have the guests go home 'better' than when they arrived – more fit, healthy, relaxed and enlightened (Monteson and Singer, 1992; Horgan, 1995).

Health and tourism: historical linkages

In many ways the relationship between health and travel is an ancient one. In fact, the roots of key words associated with tourism point to a strong relationship between the two concepts. Tourism is a generic term used to describe a range of primarily commercial aspects of recreation and holidays. All these terms have linkages to the concept of healing and integration of body, mind and spirit. For instance, the term recreation is associated with renewal, rejuvenation, replenishing, recharging and revitalizing the physical body. As well, the term holiday is derived from 'holy days' or special days of celebration. These holy days were typically linked to rituals and festivities associated with spiritual calendars, when people remembered a spiritual dimension of their wholeness and intrinsic holiness. Similarly, the term vacation comes from the Latin vacare – to empty, to let go, to stop, to still the mind and allow the subconscious mind and its creative processes a chance to work. Other descriptions of tourism's history also suggest that the current interest in health

tourism is deep rooted in the traditions of many cultures (Andestad, 1994). In this context, tourism as an enabler of physical, mental and spiritual health is returning to its original roots.

Contemporary Health Tourism Market Drivers

There are a number of important consumer trends that suggest the market for various forms of active, fitness or health-oriented holiday will grow substantially over the next few years.

Shifting consumer values

The 1990s have witnessed the beginning of a shift in North American consumer behaviour from the acquisition of things to experiences (Forbes, 1996). Research suggests that travellers are becoming more interested in improving themselves intellectually, emotionally and physically, than they are in goals such as 'making money, getting promoted at work, or acquiring clothes, houses and cars' (Cardozo, 1992).

Similarly, as real incomes have not increased substantially over the past decade, consumers have demonstrated a greater interest in attaining values such as meaning, self-fulfilment and self-autonomy (Redekop, 1997). Seeking a higher quality of life became a powerful motivator underlying most consumer behaviour at the close of the 20th century (Adams, 1997). Health tourism facilities like spas and wellness centres uniquely provide the 'space and place' that allow guests to seek harmony, balance and permanent lifestyle changes. They also offer some people a healing atmosphere – one in which they can 'take stock' and refocus in a supportive environment.

Increased stress

Over the past 15 years the leisure time of the average adult has shrunk, while the duration of the working week has grown significantly. For many working people, it now approaches the 50-h week once only associated with sweatshops (Burt, 1995). As a result there is a decreasing amount of nonwork time available for less stressful leisure and other informal off the job activities. Consequently, holiday time has become an asset of appreciating value at least from a stress reduction perspective. To help counteract the stresses associated with the increasing demands of the workplace, more and more employees are saying that holidays are 'vital to health and wellbeing' (Kooyman, 1990).

Coincidentally, the linkage between mini-holidays and stress reduction is also being recognized by some members of the health care profession. For instance, research suggests that mini-holidays provide people with breaks, without totally removing them from their routine. These shorter leisure periods tend to be even more relaxing than long holidays – especially for those in high pressure jobs. They require less planning, preparation, money and lead time and hence may be more spontaneous (Kooyman, 1990). Similarly, it seems reasonable to assume that those health tourism destinations that offer 'hassle-free' holiday experiences will probably have a competitive advantage in tomorrow's emerging marketplace.

Ageing boomers

Between 1996 and the year 2000, some 78 million American baby boomers turned 50. It is this generation that fuelled the fitness boom of the 1980s and sustained a US$30 billion industry including equipment, clothing, vitamins, sports gear and health club memberships (Russel, 1995). It is also this generation that is very aware of the advantages of pursuing more healthy lifestyles (Morris, 1996).

Businesses are already serving the wants and needs of baby boomers as they pass through difficult transitions. Sales of skin creams, suntan lotions, hair colouring, cosmetics, vitamins and nutritional supplements are surging as millions of boomers join the battle against ageing. Self-help books, dealing with everything from spirituality to home decorating, have become so popular that *The New York Times* publishes a bestseller list for them (Russel, 1995).

It is highly unlikely that baby boomers will act like the more traditional mature market which preceded them. More likely, they will create a 'mid-youth' market that indulges itself in a search for fun and self-fulfilment, despite the responsibilities associated with being mature (Smith *et al.*, 1997). This trend will probably be most pronounced among baby-boom women who, after years of managing the responsibilities of children and family, will finally be able to satisfy their personal pent-up demand for self fulfilment and betterment (Redekop, 1997).

Retirees

The estimated size, wealth, and travel preferences of the current and future 'seniors' market in North America is well documented (NTA, 1997; Redekop, 1997; Smith *et al.*, 1997). Tomorrow's senior market is likely to be attracted to travel destinations that offer active, healthy, sociable amenities, even though they may not regularly use them. The health and fitness patterns of these seniors offer useful insights into their probable future involvement in health tourism opportunities. However, programmes may need to be tailored toward an older, active but less physically demanding clientele (IHRA, 1997). Research suggests that they will demand a much richer range of social activities and learning opportunities than their less educated, less well-travelled senior predecessors (Lux and Migliaccio, 1994). Most of these emerging seniors consider themselves younger and more active than they actually are in chronological terms (Sheehy, 1995).

Rising health care costs and personal health care

Health care costs in North America are rapidly escalating (Griffin, 1995). Recognizing that these increases are unsustainable, many health and medical care providers are encouraging the public to take a more proactive role in pursuing preventative personal health care strategies. As a consequence, many North American consumers are slowly moving away from the 'quick fix' mentality and are attempting to make personal changes, which will help them to 'turn the clock back'. Health tourism facilities are potentially well positioned to assist these people in their efforts to make these changes in their lifestyles. Such destinations could play significant roles in providing the locations and facilities required to kick start and/or strengthen consumer resolve to undertake healthy living programmes without the distractions of daily life. They could also offer the professional staff needed to provoke, encourage and empathetically support health tourism visitors at critical times during their transition to healthier living activities (Griffin, 1995).

Mind and spirit attention

Attitudes toward health care are broadening. In 1992 more than one in three Americans used some type of alternative therapy and spent US$13.7 billion on alternative treatments – more than half the out-of-pocket expenditure for all conventional physicians services in the US during that time (Eisenberg *et al.*, 1993). Similar figures were estimated for other countries. In Canada, one in five Canadians were found to be using alternative therapies (Richmond, 1991).

Whereas a few years ago, activities such as yoga and meditation were considered 'new age', now they are mainstream (I-SPA, 1995). As an extension, many North Americans are looking for more meditative, creative and spiritual dimensions in their lives. While some customers want to use their stay at a health tourism destination 'to empty and still the mind' in order to reflect, others are seeking creative outlets, which help them to rejuvenate and replenish (Morgan, 1994). Those health tourism destinations that focus their investments on such specialized programming will be well positioned to contribute to the spiritual, psychological fulfilment and self worth needs of their clientele (Griffin, 1995).

Environmentalism

The past decade has witnessed the growing importance of products and services which are designed to improve or sustain the physical environment and enable participants to better understand their relationship with the natural world (Hawkes and Williams,

1993). More mainstream travellers than ever before are looking for destinations which provide a better balance between humans and nature. In recent years, a growing number of health tourism destinations in North America have been incorporating activities into their visitor programmes which focus on achieving health through integrating the body, mind and spirit, with experiencing healthy natural environments. They are doing this through strategic partnerships with members of the rapidly expanding nature and outdoor adventure travel industry.

Health Resort Market Characteristics in North America

The health tourism market can be subdivided into existing (current facility and programme users) and latent (high affinity nonusers) demand groups. Surveys suggest that about 33% of US travellers consider the presence of health facilities in a destination as important to them when planning their holiday trips (Burt, 1995).

Existing demand

It is generally assumed that the health tourism market is dominated (75%) by female travellers. This estimate is based on their heavy use (up to 90%) of day and destination spa facilities. However, current markets for health tourism destinations are believed to be more evenly distributed between women (60%) and men (40%) (Griffin, 1995). The current female market primarily consists of women working outside the home and retired homemakers.

Women working outside the home

Female baby boomers (35–55 years of age) have lifestyles characterized by the struggle to juggle professional, personal and family demands. Their primary motivation for involvement with health tourism is to relieve stress. They are concerned about their health and their appearance and are willing to experiment with new physical, psychological and spiritual therapeutic activities. They view health tourism experiences as a necessity rather than an indulgence because they understand how debilitating ill health might be for themselves and their family. They are affluent and frequent travellers and are willing to try new types of health tourism packages in varying travel destinations. However, they are constrained in their choice of destinations by limited amounts of leisure time. The more flexibility they have in their choice of health tourism products and services, the better. Generally, their health tourism experiences can be characterized as relatively short stays (e.g. an average of 2.5 nights) with a spouse, friend or female family member (Horgan, 1995).

As the baby boomer population ages, and the time and financial constraints associated with raising families diminish, it is expected that the female cohort of this group will remain the mainstay of the health tourism market for the next 20 years. This group is also most likely to encourage men to attend health tourism programmes. However, their success in this regard will be related to how well they are able to convince men that such pursuits are an investment in improved work performance, stress management and health (Orbeta-Heytens, 1995).

Homemaker/retired women

Comprising older females (55+ years of age), this group has more time and disposable income than their younger, professional, counterparts. They perceive a health tourism holiday as an indulgence. In this regard, they prefer beauty treatments to more physical (e.g. massage) and psychological (e.g. stress management) programmes. These females may resist attending a health tourism destination initially, but they tend to become loyal repeat visitors after experiencing such locations. In fact, they often become important health tourism 'ambassadors', passing on important testimonials to their friends.

Latent markets

Beyond existing markets, several national and international travel groups exhibit considerable development potential for health tourism destinations. These include corporate employees, leisure couples, senior citizens and families.

Corporate employees

Happy, healthy workers reduce turnover and increase productivity, leading to loyal customers and increased revenues for corporate organizations. As companies increasingly recognize the importance of their intellectual assets, health tourism destinations will have increasing opportunities to attract corporation employees for 'wellness' retreats, 'lifestyle enhancement' activities, and team building and leadership programmes.

Increasingly, the presence of health facilities and innovative wellness programming in tourism destinations are becoming important factors in the site selection criteria for many meeting and incentive planners. In many companies, health-related pampering is considered something that is better earned than purchased. While there is currently much more of a response to health tourism marketing in the corporate US, there is also considerable evidence that Canadian corporations are investing in their employees' health through a combination of programming and promotion activities (CFLI, 1994a,b). In this regard, companies are increasingly recognizing that health is a function of wholeness and balance as well as physical fitness, and are encouraging their employees to pursue health tourism opportunities.

Leisure couples

As females encourage health tourism trials, more couples will use such services. Time constrained couples are beginning to exchange the indulgent holidays in which they return more overweight and sometimes more stressed after the event than before, for stays at health tourism destinations. In such situations, it is quite likely that females will pursue spa-related activities, while their male counterparts might golf in the morning and then pursue a sports therapy treatment in the afternoon. Such couples might then dine out on gourmet health cuisine and attend seminars and workshops on lifestyle changes later in the day (Griffin, 1995).

Senior citizens

Health tourism destinations in North America have barely scratched the surface of the growing market of elderly, affluent consumers. This segment of the population is living longer and, depending on lifestyle choices, has the opportunity to enjoy their retirement years in good health. Through the introduction of appropriately priced educational programming combined with social programmes that offer single participants the chance for camaraderie, fun and learning, health tourism destinations could tap an expanding market of consumers with the time, money and motivation to maintain good health. At present, only a fraction of health tourism facilities offer medically based programmes designed for more mature travellers. These customized programmes might include diet and exercise to address specifically chronic diseases related to cardiovascular problems, cancer, diabetes, hypertension, arthritis and osteoporosis (Griffin, 1995).

Families

Past research suggests that many potential health tourism enthusiasts feel that their children would not be welcome at such destinations (Woods, 1992). In particular, these studies suggest that many females believe that the stereotyped reflective and tranquil atmosphere associated with health tourism facilities is likely to be incompatible with the presence of active youngsters. However, it should also be noted that family attendance has strongly increased at such destinations in recent years (Whitiam, 1993).

In this context, there may be an opportunity for health resort destinations that offer a much wider range of programmes designed to cater to families by offering activities for children that free the adults to participate in more health-related activities. In light of the lack of fitness among young people, the opportunity to introduce lifestyle changes to the entire family in a fun and playful setting might also have appeal to younger families.

However, care would have to be taken to segregate the children from conventional spa-goers in order to reduce potential areas of conflict.

International travellers

The long-haul pleasure travel market studies conducted in several of North America's leading international markets indicate that the level of interest in health tourism destinations varies considerably among geographical travel markets. In particular, the highest incidence levels are associated with Mexico. For instance, about 43% of all past long-haul pleasure travellers from this destination have actually visited a health spa on previous international trips (Williams et al., 1996). The lowest health tourism affinity levels for this type of international travel product are associated with market generating countries that already have elaborate health tourism industries. In particular, Japan, France, Germany and Italy all have had long histories of health tourism facilities and programmes available for their citizens. Indeed, in most of these countries, visits to such facilities are subsidized by the state. Consequently, it would seem unlikely for large numbers of travellers from these market origins to be seeking similar, non-subsidized opportunities abroad.

Management Implications

Many tourism destinations and businesses have opportunities to adopt the strategic position of being catalysts and partners in encouraging and supporting active, healthy lifestyles. However, such positioning carries with it many private sector and public institution policy, planning and marketing implications. From a private sector perspective, specific initiatives should be encouraged with respect to both product development and marketing.

Private sector product development implications

Companies and tourism destinations interested in building their health tourism potential should respond to the foregoing market forces by:

- positioning health tourism products and services within core health care themes related to wellness and health care as it relates to body (fitness, wellness, beauty), mind (relaxation, self-expression and learning) and soul (meditation, spiritual development);
- providing a broad and flexible range of programming which reflect the needs of different market niches for various forms of personal care, on-site amenities and facilities (e.g. providing à la carte services which respond to consumer time constraints and the need to 'multitask' while on holiday);
- developing nature-based, indigenous, environmentally 'pure' products, that place less emphasis on equipment, technology and facilities and more on natural experiences and materials derived from nature;
- creating health treatment programmes which are capable of withstanding the tests of consumer confidence with respect to their overall integrity and efficacy;
- building more 'low frill' health tourism products that require less capital investment and emphasize high levels of personal service and innovative programming;
- working collaboratively with health care professionals to build more holistic health tourism products for discerning consumers.

Private sector marketing implications

There is a need for integrated and collective approaches to communicating information about health tourism destinations and products. Such communication initiatives should be sponsored by a combination of interested tourism businesses and related health industries (cosmetics, equipment and health food suppliers, self-help health media producers). Ideally, the messages communicated should centre on creating greater awareness concerning tourism's potential role in creating opportunities for

health and balance through renewal, recharging, recreating, rest and relaxation (Burt, 1995).

Health tourism marketing efforts should be directed at consumers, the travel trade community, as well as the health care community (i.e. general practitioners, therapists, counsellors and practitioners of alternative or complementary medicine, personnel responsible for health promotion in government and business). It should utilize the combined integrity and knowledge of qualified and respected practitioners of complementary therapies as well as health promotion agencies to deliver the message.

Public sector policy implications

Ideally, health tourism should not be viewed in isolation, either from the issues affecting tourism in general, or more importantly the issues associated with health care, health promotion, and the delivery of ancillary leisure and recreation services. However, the synergistic linkages that could exist between health care and tourism in North America are barely recognizable. Indeed, few tourism enterprises have successfully connected their operations to the task of healing. This is a situation diametrically opposite to the European experience (Williams *et al.*, 1996). Before the health tourism industry can move ahead in a concerted fashion, there are a number of public policy issues that need to be addressed.

Curative rather than preventative treatment philosophies

The North American medical system has been characterized as a 'sickness system' focusing more on curing disease, as opposed to a health promotion system dealing with preventing illness. Many North American public health institutions operate in a system that attends to the infirm, with precious few moments offering holistic ways to improve their health (Granger, 1996). For the most part, doctors are currently paid to treat the sick, not to prevent patients from visiting their offices. Health tourism offers medical practitioners an attractive way to encourage improved patient health.

Health institution structures

Traditional western medical philosophies have also helped shape the ways in which North America has structured many of its health institutions. Typically, discrete institutional departments have their separate focus, budget and own sense of exclusivity regarding the delivery of their services. As a consequence, health care professionals, for example, have not considered that the tourism industry could convey a message about health, and tourism marketers rarely consider health care practitioners as possible channels of distribution to their consumers. While most medical health plans in North America do not cover the cost of health tourism programmes, this should not diminish the opportunity, for those who do have the funds to participate in such programmes, to learn about such options through the health care practitioners.

Health promotion focus

Evidence has been available for some time that shows that health status is powerfully associated with educational attainment and its corollary, economic status. A small rise in the educational or economic level of an individual or population often has a far greater health benefit than many other health programmes combined (Levin, 1987). Consequently, many health promotion strategies have tended to focus more on the socioeconomic determinants of health rather than on behavioural and other lifestyle-related determinants.

Since many leisure opportunities in North America are often regarded as not being distributed in a socially equitable fashion, health promotion professionals consider few leisure-based health interventions appropriate. Because tourist activities are typically associated with the more affluent members of society (those with the disposable income to afford a holiday), its support by public health promoters might be perceived as pandering to the middle and upper classes of the population and smacking of elitism. Unfortunately, the historical association of health tourism in the western world with a wealthy pampered upper class has tended to reinforce this view. However,

even consumers who are not economically disadvantaged can benefit from the support, sanction, and encouragement of the health care and business community. Taking time out for personal health care and investing in one's health is a goal suited to all members of society.

At the same time, decision makers within public tourism departments need to see health as a significant motivator for tourist trip decisions. Health-related benefits are increasingly being cited as one important factor in the holiday decisions of travellers (Williams *et al.*, 1996). As such, health tourism can represent an important element in strategies for community development and regional economic revitalization (Bywater, 1990).

Health versus sickness investment orientation

In many North American organizations, a greater focus on health investments is needed. Currently in many jurisdictions, legal statutes dictate that full time employees receive a minimum number of days 'paid leave for sickness'. In such cases they are actually paid to be sick. Ironically, there are no financial incentives for participating in programmes that prevent disease.

While many large companies may invest in some form of wellness programming, this is often beyond the resources of public institutions, small companies and self-employed individuals. However, the escalating costs of health care to the public purse are also well recognized. Indeed expectations that these expenditures will increase as baby boomers age are seen as a foregone conclusion. Given the importance of tourism to the economy of many North American regions, there is good reason for bridges to be built between the health care community and tourism providers (Gee *et al.*, 1994).

Certification and standards

Because of the wide range of therapies and treatments offered by the health tourism resorts and spas, there is a need for some form of standardization and quality control. An independent system of qualification and certification for health tourism businesses is needed. This applies to both the programming and personnel associated with health tourism operations.

Personnel working at health tourism facilities need a unique set of skills. In addition to being able to demonstrate above average levels of concern and interest in their client's welfare, they must adhere to the highest of ethical standards and practices. To gain credibility in the marketplace, they also need the support of the medical profession in acknowledging the efficacy of the types of treatments to be delivered. Public institutions should encourage health tourism operations to develop and publish such standards for their operations, so as to protect consumers and operator/employers.

Conclusions

Health tourism shows every sign of 'coming of age' in North America. Indeed, there are a number of market forces which are working together synergistically to ensure that the demand for health-related tourism (either directly or indirectly) is likely to grow substantially over the next decade. Opportunities exist to harness these market forces and make them work for the fledgling health tourism industry. However, to capitalize on this opportunity several initiatives must be undertaken that all evolve around a more integrated approach to health promotion. In this context, the strategic tasks require the support and commitment of tourism industry, health care, complementary therapy and corporate stakeholders. They are as follows:

- *The Tourism Industry*: There is a need to create an awareness of the importance of health as an underlying travel motivator with senior government and tourism industry decision makers. Health tourism is currently perceived as of small economic significance even though it can play an important role in helping government achieve specific development objectives and also contribute to a

fresh and powerful repositioning of some destination regions.

- *Health Care Practitioners*: Most health care practitioners are unaware of the variety of health tourism opportunities available and are unsure as to the integrity and quality of these programmes. The health tourism sector needs to inform doctors of their existence and invite feedback on the products and services available at health tourism destinations. Many patients may be more inclined to 'take a break' at their own expense if sanctioned by a medical practitioner. This does not require the doctor to make recommendations to patients concerning one destination over another but merely to pass on information about the options available. The key to success is to stress that health tourism operations exist to support and not undermine the medical profession in its treatment practices.

- *Complementary Therapy Practitioners*: The number of individuals offering a range of complementary therapies, treatments and opportunities for personal growth and learning has mushroomed in recent years. Most are in centres close to densely populated areas. Conversely, most health tourism destinations are away from these congested centres in order to offer their clients a clean, unspoiled tranquil environment. Health care practitioners need to be informed of the facilities and services available in such destinations, and be invited to offer their programmes periodically in such environments.

- *Corporate Community*: A focus on positioning health tourism destinations as desirable places for company meetings would enable managers and employees to achieve two goals at once: take care of their personal health needs while making a productive contribution to the company. By combining health-related programmes with meeting-related services, health tourism destinations can position themselves competitively for emerging corporate travel markets.

16

Festivals and Special Events: Life Cycle and Saturation Issues

Donald Getz

Introduction

The new millennium was accompanied by massive, unparalleled global celebrations that will be remembered long afterwards for their impact on the entire events sector. Even before this outpouring of creativity (and brash commercialism), growth in the number, size and diversity of festivals and special events has been staggering, so this trend will clearly continue well into the 21st century.

It is entirely appropriate that the turn of a century is marked by the renewal of old and creation of new events, as long as both hindsight and forethought accompany the revels. We look back over the past century so that we can more purposively move forward into the next. Indeed, rapid expansion of the events sector raise serious concerns for all stakeholders, encompassing culture, tourism, leisure, sport, the arts, and many corporations and agencies which sponsor and participate in events.

While this period of growth has been exciting and full of opportunities for an emerging profession, can it continue? What are the implications of having so many, potentially competing, events in existence? And as the majority of periodic events age – most of them are now relatively youthful – will they enter a period of decline or a golden age of permanent maturity?

In this chapter the major forces shaping growth and diversity in the events sector are briefly summarized. Then the product life cycle concept is explained and its potential implications for events are discussed. Inherent in the model are the notions of innovation and diffusion, of competition and market saturation. Implications are drawn for policy, planning and management of events and the events sector.

Forces Shaping Event Growth and Diversity

Trends, and major forces shaping the events field, have been discussed by several authors (Getz, 1991, 1997; Janiskee, 1994, 1996; Murray, 1995; Wicks and Schultz, 1995; Goldblatt, 1997; Ryan et al., 1998), and from their works it can be seen that no single causal factor explains the phenomenon of growth. Given that festive, competitive, entertaining, business, political, recreational, social and educational events are an integral part of culture, there is certainly good reason to conclude that recent trends are largely a consequence of global growth in population, disposable incomes, mobility, and increased leisure and travel. But more specific forces have also been identified.

Strategic event development

One major force is the strategic emphasis placed on events by numerous and diverse agencies with mandates to promote places, and tourism destinations in particular (Kotler *et al.*, 1993) and by those using events to further charitable or social causes (Graham *et al.*, 1995). On the corporate side, event marketing has emerged as an effective tool in fostering profitable relationships (Schreiber, 1994; Morrow, 1997). Indeed, there can be no doubt that without the substantial expansion of sponsorship in the last two decades, many events would not exist or would not have grown as they did (International Events Group, 1995; International Festivals Association, n.d.). While corporate sponsorship and public-sector grants cannot be taken for granted, there is no reason to believe that this form of strategic event development will wane.

The baby-boomer influence

The size and tastes of the 'baby boom' generation have impacted heavily on events, as the preferences and the family orientation of 'baby boomers' have fuelled many community festivals. This force will continue to influence entertainment and sports well into the 21st century, after which much greater attention will be focused on the needs and wants of 'generation X' (i.e. late boomers born 1955–1964), 'baby busters' (1965–1976) and the 'echo boom' (1977–1994) (see Dunn, 1993; Mitchell, 1995). Increased cultural diversity is also a major force (Rossman, 1994), leading to growth in both multicultural and ethnic events.

Leisure forces

Within the leisure sphere, events have performed an important and expanding role. They animate attractions and other social settings, as well as motivate travel – especially for short getaway breaks. Consumers, mostly urban based, enjoy events in rural communities and resorts. They have tended to crave more excitement and variety, but are also more demanding of quality and convenience. With the entertainment industry becoming a major force in modern society, events have become more entertainment oriented, sometimes to the detriment of celebration or educational values.

None of the major forces acting on the events sector shows signs of diminishing. What is worrying is that explosive growth has possibly generated too many events in some areas, or of certain types, or too many that are inadequately managed or financed. While the trend remains one of growth, it is perhaps easy to discount talk of saturation and decline. Nevertheless, policy makers and event managers engaging in strategic planning to ensure future survival and success will be examining these risks.

Product Life Cycle and Saturation Concepts

Just as people grow, mature then die, so too might individual product brands (i.e. specific events), classes of product (e.g. festivals based on a genre of music), or an entire category of product such as music festivals. The product life cycle is a widely referenced marketing concept that purports to explain these changes and provide appropriate strategic responses, although it is certainly not accepted as 'law'. Levitt (1965) first made the concept popular, but it is described in virtually all marketing texts and has been applied to recreation programmes, tourist destinations and events.

Four stages are included in the usual product life cycle model: introduction; growth; maturity and decline. The concept is usually applied to new product classes, such as a new event genre, but can also be applied to a new firm or organization. However, most new events are now entering a crowded field occupied by many similar events, and this fact can be very important – particularly in that competition for resources and consumers must be a major consideration.

There is an intuitive appeal to this model, largely because of our human experience with life and death, but also because everyone is likely to be familiar with products, including events, that have faded or failed. As events grow they can lose their community identity:

> Therefore, event organizers have to find ways to guide growth while still maintaining the features of the event which made it popular in the first place
>
> (Hall, 1992, p. 120)

> Many of the events and festivals that do not stay fresh and modernize are likely to go out of existence ... Competing for event audiences whose expectations continue to rise will require new management strategies and an emphasis on service quality
>
> (Wicks, 1995)

Janiskee (1994), based on his database of community festivals in the US, found there had been almost exponential growth in their numbers between 1930 and 1991. There had been annual increases averaging 4.6% and a doubling in number about every 15 years, although five distinct spurts had been detected. Almost 40% had been created in the 1980s alone. Janiskee believed that such growth cannot be continued indefinitely and that a glut already exists in some areas. There are time-tested festivals which ' ... are likely to survive and stabilize at some acceptable level' but also ' ... the day may soon arrive when non-viable community festivals are discontinued at a rate approaching or exceeding the rate of new festival establishment'.

Andersson (1987) believed that events able to plug into international information networks are more likely to succeed in attracting visitors and commercial sponsorship, while those events relying on subsidies are more likely to die out as public funding dries up. In this scenario, life cycle is related both to resources acquired and to possible overdependence on one source. In addition, innovative managers are seen to be better able to tap new resources and therefore to succeed and survive.

One long-standing event examined is the Calgary Exhibition and Stampede (Getz, 1993a, 1997). Many traditional events like this can be found internationally, as they have become icons or hallmarks for their communities. Residents support and attend them in part because they are cultural traditions, but their success must also be attributed to constant adaptation. The Stampede, however, was found to have reached a plateau in attendance, attributed by management to lack of space for physical expansion, and so efforts were being concentrated on increasing the yield from prime tourist segments.

Walle (1994), in examining the event genre (i.e. product class) called cowboy poetry gatherings, argued that a shakeout would likely occur as supply (the number of events) began to exceed demand. But this would have a beneficial outcome in that premier events would remain to better serve the market. Referring to the Elko Cowboy Poetry Gathering, Walle observed that its organizers had found a distinct strategy to differentiate itself from the others in its class.

The life cycle is also linked to the concept of innovation diffusion, as put forward by Rogers (1962). When the product is new, it requires effort to get people to try it and become repeat customers. Some people will attend an event, for example, only after other, more adventuresome event-goers have reported on its attractiveness. Five types of consumers have been identified in this context, namely: innovator, early adopter, early and late majority, and laggards. There is also likely to be a group who will never try a genre of event, let alone specific events.

Competition and saturation

Can there be too many events? Jones (1993, p. 24) reported that there were an estimated 900 festivals each year in the UK, and noted: ' ... there is a danger that we may be reaching saturation point.' She observed that a report by the Policy Studies Institute in 1992 discovered that more than half the festivals were running a loss and concluded that organizers would find increasing difficulty in competing for audiences. Further, many lacked basic marketing skills and could not generate sponsorship revenue. Britton (1991) observed that the multiplication of events places growing emphasis on novelty and spectacle as the basic motivator.

Based on analysis of his large database on American festivals, Janiskee argued:

> The recreational day-tripper zones of many cities are already glutted with festivals during the most popular weekends and holidays, and with at least 1,000 new festivals added to the national inventory each year, the problem is sure to grow
> (Janiskee, 1996, p. 129)

Richards (1996b), commenting on the situation in Europe, observed that there had been considerable growth in the number of cultural events, in part owing to their popularity within tourism development strategies. But as he noted:

> There are some indicators, however, that many festivals and special events may be losing their novelty value as far as many visitors are concerned
> (Richards, 1996b, p. 323)

He also suggested that in the long run ' ... events can suffer from a "waning effect", whereby increasing levels of investment are required to generate similar visitor numbers'.

Life cycle and organizational culture

While the popularity of event themes and programmes might be expected to rise and fall, depending on factors such as fad, fashion, publicity and competition, so too might the fortunes of the event organization. Indeed, the organizations running festivals (Getz and Frisby, 1988; Frisby and Getz, 1989) have been revealed to face multiple challenges for their very survival. As discussed by Getz (1993b) the concept of corporate or organizational culture can help explain why some events grow and others do not, and why some go through crises that threaten their survival, quite apart from their position in the marketplace. And because 'learning organizations' (Senge, 1990) are more likely to be adaptable, the absence of strategic planning and research

functions within event organizations helps explain why some will decline or fail (Getz, 1998).

Destination life cycles

In the tourism literature a debate has raged for many years over the applicability of the life cycle concept to destinations. Postulated by Butler (1980), the notion is that resorts, communities and areas experience an evolution in their appeal to visitors, in part related to emerging capacity constraints which act as limits to growth. Some, like Atlantic City, have been observed to rise and fall, then be rejuvenated. Many single case studies and a smaller number of comparative studies have raised many questions about the model's applicability to destinations. For example, through research on Niagara Falls, Getz (1992) concluded that the destination was in a permanent state of maturity in which examples of product introduction, growth, maturity and even decline occurred simultaneously. Events were being used to attract new and repeat visitors and to encourage longer stays.

If a destination declines in popularity, so too will some of its attractions and events. If it is the events and attractions which weaken first, the destination might suffer in turn. However, many events are not tourist attractions in the first place (most events being dependent on local and regional demand) so a destination's evolution will not necessarily vary directly with that of its events or events sector.

Critique of the Life Cycle Concept

Lambkin and Day (1989) suggested that a population ecology model might be more appropriate and useful than the life cycle concept. Drawing on nature, this model suggests exponential growth can occur when firms enter a new 'resource space', but eventually a carrying capacity is reached and an equilibrium is achieved, possibly through organizational deaths. Over time, the inevitable scarcity of resources implies more intense competition, so organizations must adapt strategically. In this context ' … performance is a consequence of the effects of the prevailing competitive conditions in combination with the structures and strategies of different firms'.

But however appealing, it might be a mistake to apply an organic analogy to social organizations (Lambkin and Day, 1989). After all, do cities and institutions normally fade away and die? Most do not, because people invest heavily in them, and depend on them for continuity. In addition, weak and even failed events can be rejuvenated or reborn if their backers want it to happen. The less an event is tied to purely commercial success factors, specifically profit, the less likely it is to succumb to competition or old age.

Unlike permanent attractions, events can be moved spatially and temporally in response to environmental or internal problems, can be shut down for a year or more, and even reincarnated under a new name and management, without necessarily suffering permanent harm. The case of the Canadian Tulip Festival (noted in Getz, 1991) is instructive, as this event was deliberately renamed Festival of Spring, went bankrupt, then re-emerged as the Canadian Tulip Festival under new management. Civic authorities played a pivotal role in this evolution through funding decisions.

A case can certainly be made for deliberately terminating events that do not meet their objectives, fail on tests of efficiency or can easily be substituted. From the perspective of a destination, community or policy field (such as arts, culture or sport), the life cycle of an individual event is not necessarily the major concern. It is the overall range or portfolio of events that is important.

In a commercial context, which applies to private events, the life cycle is measured in terms of both sales and profits, with sales first growing quicker than profits, then profits declining as price competition intensifies. Hart et al. (1984) said the life cycle model was, in fact, a sales curve. Its value was in helping to assess market potential and market share, but it is definitely not a predictive model. Nor is it useful for

selecting competitive strategies, they argued, because everyone in business knows and uses the model!

Because many events are of the non-profit nature, other measures of value or success will be required. Usually attendance is taken as the best measure of demand, but it could be more meaningful to specify paid versus free attendance, total expenditure of visitors, the proportion of tourists versus residents attracted, length of tourists' stay, or the ratio of repeat to first-time visitors. For many events a measure of service value will be most appropriate (e.g. target segments reached, charitable revenue generated) or of communications effectiveness (e.g. publicity generated, changes caused in awareness and attitude).

If intangible measures are to be used (e.g. not demand, revenue, profits, attendance), monitoring evolution of an event through the life cycle will be more difficult. How will a manager know, for example, when a service-oriented event begins to decline if the primary objective is to provide the community with a wholesome, family social experience or the goal is to foster a sense of community pride? Special research will obviously be required, measuring, for example, public attitudes and preferences.

In fact, events are different from most consumer products in a number of important ways (see Box 16.1). But while these differences suggest events can exist independent of the forces affecting commercial products, this is true only to a degree. Events can fail for many reasons (see Box 16.2), regardless of attendance or any other measure of success being used. Market forces or competition might or might not figure prominently in event decline or failure, but these factors should always be a concern to managers.

A further complication with applying this model to events is the attitude of managers and organizers toward the issue of competition. Many event organizers do not believe they have direct competitors (Getz, 1998), but it is obvious that competition exists at any of several levels:

● for the total leisure/entertainment

Box 16.1. How events are different from other consumer products.

Intangibility	Events must be experienced and are inherently different every time owing to the blend of programme, management, environment and visitor interactions. Production and consumption of events are simultaneous, leaving no room for pre-inspection or recall (managers have only one chance to get it right).
Flexibility and adaptability	Despite their innate uniqueness, managers can change elements of events even as they are produced (i.e. flexibility) and can certainly modify them over time in response to environmental forces (i.e. adaptability).
Nonprofit status	Success or value of these events must be evaluated differently; economic demand or revenues are not necessarily appropriate.
Multiple stakeholders	Event value varies among organizers, the community at large, sponsors, supporting agencies and participants. Success or failure might mean different things to each party.
Tradition	Many events have the status of institutions or are traditions within cultural groups, making them less sensitive to market forces (and perhaps to change).
Noncompetitive environment	Many event managers do not believe they have direct competitors for consumers, either because of their timing (none others offered) or genre (appeal to different segments). However, all events compete at a general level for consumer awareness, interest and commitment, and for resources.

Box 16.2. Possible reasons why events fail.

Supply factors
- Direct competition (numbers, types, locations, aggressiveness of other events)
- Indirect competition (consumers have too much choice for leisure and entertainment budget)

Demand factors
- Population decline in market area
- Demographic shifts in population which reduce target segments (e.g. older population, fewer families)
- Decline in disposable income among target segments
- Shift in leisure time (lower demand for events) and preferences (e.g. away from events)

Management factors
- Unattractive product, poor service
- No strategic planning (i.e. inability to learn and adapt)
- Ineffective marketing
- Incompetence or corruption

Other external forces
- Political and regulatory changes which prejudice the event
- Lack of community support; negative attitudes toward event because of impacts
- Absence or decline in vital resources (human, monetary, venues)

---

budget of consumers (e.g. events versus cinema or travel);
- for other forms of the same or similar genre (e.g. perceived substitutability between touring musicals and music festivals);

- with all other events in the same locality (i.e. consumers will not go to them all);
- with all other events held simultaneously (time conflicts).

If events are free, the nature of competition changes. Price is not the issue, but rather a combination of the total time budget, interest levels, and knowledge of consumers about available choices that will affect demand. Even if competition for consumers is weak, events must still compete for venues, volunteers, monetary resources and political support. In smaller communities it might be the competition for volunteers that leads to decline.

Very little research has been conducted on event failure and life cycles, so there is no body of evidence to support or challenge the concepts. A systematic examination of event failures is required, as well as comparisons with long-lived events.

Implications

For event managers and organizers

Even if there is no certainty involved with the life cycle concept, nor with the population ecology model, there are enough related issues to force organizers, managers and other stakeholders to give serious thought to how decline and failure can be prevented, or how success (however defined) can be sustained over time.

The most basic advice to be offered (Lambkin and Day, 1989) is that event organizers must avoid complacency in relation to their resource base and competitive position, and avoid the self-fulfilling prophecy of believing that decline or death is inevitable. Adaptation strategies are required, and these should be based on continuous research and evaluation to achieve a 'learning organization'.

Table 16.1 depicts the four hypothetical life cycle stages with strategic implications for a new event in a new class of events, in column A (drawing from Berkowitz *et al.*, 1991), and for the new event in a crowded field, in column B (adapted from Lambkin

and Day, 1989). In this way the diagram also reflects the population ecology model in which resource limits and competition are critical factors.

The strategies shown in Table 16.1 are not exclusive to side A or B, and the most appropriate strategies cannot be prescribed. They must emerge from the event's own research, needs and goals. In general, new events entering a resource-rich environment (i.e. little direct competition and sufficient resources for all events to grow for some time) should aim to become more efficient in their use of resources and more secure in their resource base, because competition will surely mount. For the majority of new events entering a crowded marketplace, a choice of strategies is available: either develop a large-scale event that has the efficiencies of scale to weather most obstacles it will have to face, or find a small competitive niche to exploit. Organizations entering a crowded field will have to be more innovative and adaptive from the onset, which forces established events to react or lose market share.

Rigorous feasibility studies are needed at the onset to examine the competitive environment, potential demand and market share, and available resources. For all periodic events it is worth considering the merits of constant innovation in programme elements, combined with maintenance of traditional elements that have broad appeal. In this approach, constancy and change are mutually beneficial.

Finally, Box 16.3 lists a set of critical success factors derived from the previous discussion, including points made by Walle (1994). These factors can be used as a checklist for performing a 'survival audit' on any event and its organization.

Implications for policy makers (leisure, social and cultural)

Festivals and events play an important role in the life of most communities and cultural groups. This is recognized through funding programmes and direct production of events by many agencies. Consequently, these providers and partners can legitimately adopt policies and programmes to ensure the sur-

Table 16.1. Life cycle stages and implications for event management.

Stage	New event, new genre	New event, crowded field
Introduction	• No direct competition, abundant resources, risks exist because of unknown markets • Stress awareness and sell the new genre first • Foster trials by innovators • Pricing may be high (skimming profits) or low (penetration of markets)	• Many existing competitors, no guarantee that growth or profitability can be achieved, markets are established for the genre (i.e. there is less market uncertainty) • Must do feasibility study • Develop large scale and cost efficiencies or niche markets
Growth	• Should experience rapid sales growth (or attendance) and achieve maximum profitability (or perceived value) • Must differentiate from growing number of competitors or diversify • Must increase repeat visits (loyalty) while still attracting first-timers	• Constant innovation and differentiation • Attempt to grow total event demand through cooperative marketing and expansion of market (e.g. tourism) • Be a learning organization
Maturity	• Demand will increase, but growth rate slows for the total genre • Profits decline if competition leads to price wars • Laggards are the last to try the genre • High costs to attract new customers, so focus on loyalty • Reduce overall marketing costs	• Price competition might be essential • Constant attention to cost efficiencies is required • Sustain traditional elements but regularly add new programme elements
Decline	• Demand and profits decline, possibly due completely to environmental forces • Strategic options: delete the event, keep it going as long as possible with reduced costs, contract out to more efficient operators, change the product, reposition it, influence the market	• A shorter life cycle can be expected in a crowded field, shakeouts occur as resources are fully consumed and competition intensifies • Plan rejuvenation or termination strategies right from the introductory stage

vival of important events, but perhaps more importantly should ensure their goals are being realized through the entire portfolio of events in the community. Because many events are substitutable, potentially yielding the same social or cultural benefits to the population, the failure or decline of individual events is not necessarily a problem.

Implications for policy makers (economic development, place marketing and tourism)

From a tourism destination perspective, it will be increasingly difficult to establish or elevate events to the level of prominent international touristic appeal. Realistically, destinations can expect to contain a large number of events with primarily local to regional appeal, and only a few periodic or one-time events that generate substantial tourist numbers. This 'pyramid' principle applies to all sizes of community and destination, as each must concentrate resources and marketing effort to achieve one or a few major events. As competition increases, it becomes harder for a given event to reach the pinnacle of touristic appeal, and harder

Box 16.3. Critical success factors for sustaining events.

- Purpose: know your core mandate or mission
- Vision: develop a clear vision to a desired future state
- Focus: on uniqueness and strengths; do not imitate others
- Strategic planning: anticipate the need for change and develop appropriate strategies, be a learning organization
- Strong community support: become an institution based on authenticity and cultural value
- Tradition: people can count on popular elements year after year
- Innovation: foster learning and creativity, be adaptable and flexible
- Adequate resources: generate a surplus for re-investment
- Professionalism: strong, professional organizations and managers
- Quality: in programme and service
- Loyalty: foster loyal market segments, sustain loyal volunteers
- Image: become Hallmark events, giving identity to the host community, the image of event and destination are inseparable or mutually reinforcing in the minds of outsiders and residents alike
- Marketing: responsive to consumer needs and preferences but not driven solely by market forces, sustain the vision!

or more expensive for communities and destinations to host events successfully at that level.

Rather than overemphasize one or a few events, it makes more sense to cultivate a diverse portfolio of events (see Getz, 1997) in which occasional mega-events, permanent, and one-time regional and local events provide a hedge against organizational failures or turmoil in the environment. Forging partnerships with other policy fields will also ensure that events with tourism value are sustained, as events meeting multiple goals will have broader support.

Greater seasonal and geographic spread of events should be a priority for place marketers, economic development officers and destination planners, as research in several countries reveals that events tend to concentrate in peak tourist seasons and in major population centres. This limits their tourism and promotional value and exposes the portfolio to higher risks. For similar reasons, thematic differences should be cultivated and marketed.

Implications for event marketing (sponsorship)

Sponsorship of events will often be based on corporate decision making which considers first and foremost the expected life cycle of the pertinent marketing strategy, then the life cycle of the event itself. Indeed, a sponsorship pull-out could be the trigger for event failure, in the case of overdependence on one revenue source. This fact argues for a partnership arrangement between event organizers and sponsors so that long-term planning can take both perspectives into account. Sponsors can help event managers monitor trends and stay ahead of the competition. Stable, successful events will appeal more to sponsors.

The monitoring and evaluation of trends

All strategic planning and management depends on research, not the least of which is continuous monitoring and evaluation of trends. This chapter has attempted to demonstrate how essential the process is, and it also reveals many of the difficulties: finding the most pertinent and current sources of information; sorting out conflicting indicators; evaluating the quality and utility of information; applying the analysis to planning and management decisions.

Event management and event tourism is a very broad subject area, involving data and analysis from many sources on demographics, economic conditions, societal values, leisure preferences, marketing initiatives and so on. No single source continuously brings these together and draws implications for the events sector, but membership in professional organizations (e.g. International Festivals and Events Association, International Special Events Society) will prove valuable. Many professionals go to association conferences and seminars for the explicit reasons of learning from others' experiences and about trends.

As each planning and management situation is somewhat unique, the establishment of a targeted set of indicators will be useful. The planner or manager must determine what forces and trends are most important (and these shift over time), and how the information will be collected and used. Ideally, the indicators will cover economic, social, technological, cultural and political factors – some of which will be found to be more important than others.

Indicators must be valid in that they truly impact on event planning and management, reliably measurable (i.e. consistently accurate) and the data must be in a form that can be analysed and evaluated by the user. Internal indicators of trends will consist of those measures made by the organization including actual attendance, visitor characteristics, quality of product and service, and quantitative performance measures such as indicators of effectiveness (i.e. degree to which goals are attained) and efficiency (at what cost).

The main types of environmental indicators (i.e. external to the organization) will be:

Demand Indicators
- population levels and demographics (especially for target market segments)
- awareness and perception of the event leading to desire to attend
- competition (direct and indirect)
- impediments (such as disposable income, accessibility, time pressures)

Political Indicators
- grants and other support received
- attitudes toward the event and its impacts

Technological Indicators
- technological developments affecting demand (such as marketing channels) and operations (such as reservations and ticketing systems)

Social and Cultural Indicators
- measurable impacts of the event on the community
- fads and more permanent value shifts

How are indicators of forces and trends employed? Simple trend extrapolation can be useful over the short term, as in predicting next year's attendance, but is fraught with perils in that underlying causal forces are unknown. If research and analysis can demonstrate that, for example, known population, demographic and economic changes are causing demand to rise, than much more certainty can be made in forecasting the future. This in turn leads to better planning decisions.

Another strategic use of trend data is scenario making. Scenarios can be written in the form of descriptions of possible or desired future states, enabling strategic planners to plot the actions necessary to stave off or achieve the future state. A hypothetical 'decline' state is one such scenario. How can it be avoided? Under what circumstances might it occur? Do we have trend data suggesting that a decline is likely, and by when? (For more detailed discussion of research, trend analysis, indicators, forecasting, and management information systems, see Ritchie and Goeldner, 1994.)

Conclusion

It is tempting to think that competent managers should be able to understand forces, monitor trends, anticipate the need for adaptation, and implement effective change strategies, thereby ensuring permanent success for the event, organization or destination. But some environmental trends are imperceptible, while others are abrupt and potentially catastrophic. The most that can be expected is that planning will, to a degree, protect one from known and unanticipated problems.

Consequently, strategic thinking and planning, based on knowledge of the life cycle and related concepts, will prove valuable. But it will not immunize events, organizations and destinations from the sometimes damaging effects of external forces such as intense competition. Nor will it necessarily protect against internal failures due to organizational culture or incompetence. Sometimes events will fail, and others will have to be drastically altered to avoid extinction. In other cases, managers might want to anticipate ultimate decline and plan their own, timely demise.

17

Cultural Tourism: Challenges for Management and Marketing

Greg Richards

Introduction

Cultural tourism is one of the largest and fastest growing segments of global tourism. According to the World Tourism Organization, some 37% of international trips are connected with culture. In the US, 45% of pleasure trips planned in 1996 included visits to historic sites. This broad market indicates that cultural tourism is moving away from its former association with a narrow cultural elite toward becoming a significant global phenomenon. As the cultural tourism market grows, the focus of cultural tourism is also rapidly changing from a preoccupation with sites and monuments into a much wider phenomenon, covering all aspects of 'high' and 'popular' culture. Cultural tourism consumption is no longer restricted to 'serious' and purposeful visits to revered cultural sites, but has also become part of the 'atmosphere' of places, to be soaked up by tourists and residents alike.

The expanding cultural product is also becoming increasingly popular with policy makers and marketeers in all corners of the globe. As the White House Conference on Tourism in the US (1995, p. 2) notes 'every place in America – rural area, small town, Native American reservation, big city – can develop cultural tourism'. Cultural tourism is perceived as a growth market which can deliver tourism's holy grail of high quality, high spending visitors. In the rush to jump on the cultural tourism bandwagon, however, the potential negative consequences of this type of tourism are often overlooked, and the needs of the cultural tourists themselves are often ignored. The rapid development of this market means that relatively little is known about 'cultural tourists' or the phenomenon of 'cultural tourism'. This chapter presents a review of recent market research conducted on cultural tourism in Europe and identifies trends which will be significant in the development of cultural tourism in the coming century.

What is Cultural Tourism?

Defining cultural tourism has proved extremely difficult, particularly because of the definitional problems associated with the concept of culture. According to Littrell (1997), culture can be viewed as comprising what people think (attitudes, beliefs, ideas and values), what people do (normative behaviour patterns or way of life) and what people make. Culture is therefore composed of processes (the ideas and way of life of people) and the products of those processes (buildings, artefacts, art, customs, atmosphere). Looking at culture in this way, cultural tourism is not just about visiting sites and monuments, which has tended to be the traditional view of cultural tourism (Bonink, 1992), but also involves experiencing the way of life of the areas visited. Both activities involve the collection of new knowledge and information. Cultural tourism can therefore be defined as:

> The movement of persons to cultural attractions away from their normal place of residence, with the intention to gather new information and experiences to satisfy their cultural needs.
>
> (Richards, 1996a, p. 24)

According to this conceptual definition, cultural tourism covers not just the consumption of the cultural products of the past, but also of contemporary culture or the way of life of a people or region. Cultural tourism can therefore be seen as covering both 'heritage tourism' and 'arts tourism'.

The Development of the Cultural Tourism Market

The development of cultural tourism as a major market has paralleled the democratization of both culture and tourism during the 20th century. In the past, tourism was the preserve of a cultured elite, for whom travel was a means of accessing the classical culture essential to a well-rounded education (Towner, 1985). During the 20th century, however, cultural tourism began to emerge as a market segment thanks to the growing number of people who could travel, and the increasing education levels of those travelling. Culture became a part of the tourism product, and cultural tourism became an established market segment, served by specialist tour operators and fuelled by local cultural development policies. In the 21st century, however, the distinctions between culture and tourism are likely to become increasingly indistinct, as we find ourselves enveloped in what Urry (1990) has termed the 'culture of tourism'. Culture will cease to be a product packaged for tourist consumption – tourism will be culture.

An increasing cultural content of tourism products has been one of the defining characteristics of tourism consumption in the 20th century. As MacCannell (1976) and other authors have pointed out, tourism has become a collection of signs or commodities. This has created a culture of sign creation, as well as a culture of sign consumption. Whereas modern forms of tourism consumption were dominated by well-defined divisions between cultural tourism and other market segments, such as beach tourism or winter sports, the dedifferentiation associated with postmodernity and the proliferation of cultural signs are dissolving these clear-cut distinctions (Rojek and Urry, 1997).

Research by ATLAS among cultural visitors to Amsterdam has indicated that the products that are today associated with cultural tourism have a much broader scope than the traditional 'sites and monuments' definition often found in the literature (Bonink, 1992). Consumers see not only major museums and monuments, such as the Rijksmuseum and Anne Frank's House as elements of the cultural tourism product, but also such diverse elements of popular culture as boat trips along the canals or walking tours through the Red Light District. Only the Sex Museum was excluded by a majority of respondents from the cultural tourism product (Goedhart, 1997).

Within this overall shift from modern to postmodern forms of cultural tourism a number of important trends can be identified:

Continued growth in demand, stimulated by higher levels of education and a thirst for knowledge

The basic motivation for cultural tourism is the search for new knowledge and experiences. This type of consumption is closely related to the increase in higher education participation in the developed world in recent decades. Cultural tourists generally have a high level of cultural capital, usually developed through formal education. The democratization of higher education has, for example, expanded the proportion of Europe's population with a higher education to 21%, but this source of growth in the cultural tourism market may wane in time due to lessening government support for higher education in developed countries.

An explosion of supply of cultural attractions, which is rapidly outpacing the growth in demand

Each place considers that it has a unique culture to market to tourists, and sees cultural attractions as the primary means of capturing the economic benefits which this can bring. In addition, a growing number of events and festivals are being developed as a means of adding cultural content to public spaces and adding to the attractiveness of cities and sites, particularly out of season (see Getz, Chapter 16).

A blurring of the distinction between 'high' and 'popular' culture, and between culture and economy, which have been fuelling the growing supply of attractions and events

The original heritage focus of many cultural tourism developments is now broadening to include all aspects of culture, including popular music, gastronomy and even whole landscapes. In the 1980s there was a spectacular expansion in industrial heritage attractions, and the 1990s are seeing a marked growth of popular culture attractions, such as the childhood home of former Beatle, Paul McCartney. This is also causing a spatial diffusion of cultural tourism development beyond the traditional centres of high culture, such as the cultural capitals of Europe, to areas with less prominent historical resources. The cultural capital idea, which has increasingly been seen as a way of promoting less popular cultural destinations, is now being taken up in the US as well (White House Conference on Tourism, 1995).

An extension of the cultural tourism market toward mass tourism through the opening of new popularized cultural attractions

The number of visitors with a general interest in culture seems to be growing faster than visitors with a specific cultural motive in terms of the number of visitors to attractions

(Richards, 1996a). This is causing the market of some attractions to shift away from the specialist visitor with a high level of cultural competence, towards the mass market. This is also generating an increased demand for more sophisticated and easily accessible modes of interpretation.

Divergence between large and small scale attractions

The rapid increase in cultural attractions which has taken place since the 1980s has been marked by the emergence of a new postmodern style of attraction (Richards, 1996c; Velazquez Cortes, 1996). These new attractions are generally characterized by smaller-scale facilities, a focus on specialist markets rather than universal values, links with postmodern subjects such as architecture, design and heritage, more emphasis on the appearance of the building and displays rather than their content, and increasing links with commercial forms of culture. Examples include heritage centres (such as Jorvik, the Viking Centre in York) and museums such as the Coca Cola Museum in Atlanta and the Design Museum in London. At the other end of the scale there is a tendency to try to cluster cultural attractions into mega-projects or cultural districts, such as the Cultural Quarter in Sheffield, Bunker Hill in Los Angeles or the Dallas Arts District (Zuzanek, 1992).

Globalization and localization of cultural tourism demand and supply

Cultural forms are becoming increasingly globalized through improved communications, the increased integration of the global economy and the influence of tourism. Cultural institutions which used to be inherently place-bound are now becoming increasingly footloose. Internationally famous museums are beginning to develop subsidiaries in other regions or even on other continents. For example, one can now visit the Guggenheim Museum in its original location on what has become Museum Mile opposite Central Park in New York, or in the downtown Soho branch, or in Venice, and most recently in Bilbao, Spain. Such developments are beginning to take on aspects of a 'Macdonaldized' franchise system (Ritzer, 1993), as demonstrated by the US$25 million paid by Bilbao for the right to use the Guggenheim name and to fill the museum with borrowed artworks. At the same time, however, there is a relocalization of global culture through the appropriation of globalized cultural themes by specific places. Specific artists and writers whose output was formerly considered part of a universal cultural heritage are now being grounded in particular locations by using their work to identify places, regions or even whole countries. Rojek (1993) provides numerous examples of the creation of 'literary landscapes' in the UK, such as Shakespeare's County, Hardy Country and Catherine Cookson Country.

A growing commercialization of cultural tourism, through the creation of commercial cultural tourism products and the provision, distribution and sale of information on cultural products

Commercial cultural tourism products are increasingly being offered through specialist and generalized tour operators, and by individual cities or regions, or by consortia. The world's leading cultural tourism operator, the German company Studiosus, for example, has seen business grow from 27,000 clients in 1985 to 96,000 clients in 1997. In the future, more individualized or modularized cultural tourism products will be offered through new media, and particularly on the Internet. This should help to solve the considerable distribution problems which are experienced with cultural tourism products, particularly in the case of cultural events. TUI, the leading German tour operator, currently has a special cultural events brochure and is now developing products for sale via the Internet.

The emergence of a group of 'new producers' from the cultural field who have discovered tourism as a means of capitalizing their knowledge of culture to create new forms of employment

This group is beginning to exert increasing influence over the products which are brought onto the market (Goedhart, 1997),

particularly in major urban centres (see below). Cultural tourism has become part of a general cultural production system, where space is being developed for cultural production and consumption. The role of the new producers as cultural intermediaries is therefore becoming crucial in expanding and shaping the supply of cultural tourism products.

These trends are illustrated by recent studies of cultural tourism undertaken by the European Association for Tourism and Leisure Education (ATLAS) in 15 European countries in 1992 and 1997. This analysis looks at the basic features of the cultural tourism market revealed by the research, which covered more than 12,000 cultural visitors. The basic questions addressed by the research are the visitor profile, visitor motivations and activities at the destination.

A Profile of Cultural Tourists in Europe

The ATLAS survey covered not just tourists, but all visitors to a range of cultural attractions and events in Europe. More details of the research programme and methodology are contained in Richards (1996a,c). The surveys indicated that tourists accounted for about 60% of the visitor sample and local residents made up the balance of 40%. Most of the tourists interviewed were domestic tourists (58%). Of the foreign tourists, 11% came from outside Europe, with the overseas visitors being dominated by North Americans and Australasian visitors.

Education

Most of the cultural visitors had a high level of education. More than 40% of respondents had a higher education, and 11% were still studying in further or higher education. The proportion of visitors with a higher education was therefore much greater than the general level in the European Union (EU). Cultural tourists were in general even better educated, but this is partly related to the higher average age of the cultural tourists.

Occupation

A majority of the respondents were either employed (50%) or self-employed (11%). Students formed an important element of the cultural visitors (11%), as did retired people (11%). Of those currently working, many respondents had a professional occupation, and managers and directors (12%) were also well represented. This indicates that cultural visitors are mainly employed in high status positions, which matches their high education level.

Income

The high occupational status also relates to relatively high average incomes. Almost 45% of the 1997 respondents came from households with a gross annual income of 30,000 Euro or more. The average income lay around 22,000 Euro, more than 25% higher than the EU average.

Age

The cultural tourist often has a high degree of cultural capital in respect of the sights that they visit, but this does not always mean that cultural tourists are old. Recent increases in higher education participation has produced a large group of younger cultural consumers: up to 40% of the visitors to some attractions in the ATLAS research were under 30 years of age. Cultural tourists were in general older than the local residents interviewed, with 44% of the tourists being aged between 40 and 60 years old.

Motivations

Research on cultural tourism in different countries has consistently indicated that not all visitors to cultural attractions are culturally motivated. Bywater (1993), for example, makes a distinction between culturally motivated, culturally inspired and culturally attracted tourists, with the highest level of cultural motivation being accorded to the culturally motivated visitors. In the ATLAS research, it emerged that 13% of cultural visitors were culturally motivated, 30% were culturally inspired and 57% were culturally attracted. The culturally attracted tourists, who only have a secondary interest in culture, therefore make up the majority of cultural visitors. These general cultural tourists, for whom a visit to a cultural attraction is an incidental part of their holiday, appear to have become a more significant part of the market in recent years. In the UK, for example, national surveys of inbound tourism show that the proportion of tourists with a specific cultural motive declined from 10% in 1989 to 6% in 1993, while the share of general cultural tourists grew from 26 to 28% over the same period (Foley, 1996).

When the cultural visitors were asked to evaluate a range of potential motivations for their visit, it became clear that the desire to experience new things and learning were very important motivations for the majority of visitors. The 1997 research indicates, however, that the concept of learning is interpreted fairly broadly. The drive to experience new things is particularly important (de Cauter, 1995). The research confirms that the distinction between culture and leisure is becoming more vague – cultural tourism need not be taken seriously any more, but can also be seen as a form of relaxation. There is also evidence that for many cultural tourism has become habitual – 60% of the respondents agreed with the statement 'When I go on holiday, I always visit a museum'. Social motivations were considered less important, although the influence of friends was more evident for respondents with a cultural occupation, because their social network is likely to revolve around culture. The split between 'specific' and 'general' cultural tourists is even clearer in the responses to the statement 'I am visiting this attraction for my work'. A high proportion of respondents with a cultural occupation indicated that their visit was connected with work.

The cultural tourist in Europe is first and foremost a skilled consumer, for whom the pursuit of culture is a form of personal development (Richards, 1996c). There is an increasing desire for novelty in contemporary society, and culture provides an excellent source of novelty, allowing people to discover new cultures and also providing opportunities for people to learn for them-

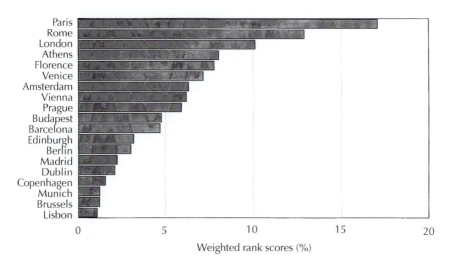

Fig. 17.1. Ranking of European cities as cultural destinations. Source: ATLAS Survey (1997).

selves. The skilled consumer can create their own novelty as a cultural tourist, through painting, languages, crafts, gastronomy and other activities. As qualitative research among cultural tourists in different European countries shows, the search for novelty and the desire to learn are at the top of the agenda for most cultural tourists. One should not interpret the desire for 'learning' as we might understand it in the narrow traditional sense of receiving and storing information, but in the more active sense of self-development.

For many tourists, culture is very often a general, rather than a specific, experience. You no longer have to visit museums to find culture. Culture is also to be found in the bars, restaurants and streets of European cities. As the distinctions between traditional high culture and popular culture begin to disappear, elements of high culture are also increasingly being mixed with popular culture to produce new cultural forms. The new cultural tourist might visit a museum during the day, but the evening is more likely to be spent at a musical or a disco than at the opera.

Different types of tourists require different marketing approaches. Not only do motivations differ, but the role of holiday experience is increasingly important. First time visitors are far more likely to accept the traditional sites and monuments approach. Second and third time visitors are more likely to seek out the living culture, as they have already done the 'must-see sights' on the first visit.

Museums are undoubtedly the most popular form of cultural attraction for cultural tourists. In 1997 more than 50% of the tourists visited a museum during their stay in the research location. Monuments (40%) and galleries (30%) were also very popular, but the performing arts (23%) and festivals were less frequently visited. This supports the distinction made in the 1992 research between 'heritage' attractions, which have a low visit threshold and 'arts' attractions, which are often less accessible, because of the limited time of performances, the difficulty of obtaining information and tickets and the language barriers which are often involved.

In 1997 a new question was posed about the popularity of a number of major cultural tourism destinations with cultural visitors. The results show that Paris, Rome and London are by far the favourite cultural tourism destinations in Europe (Fig. 17.1). This is related to the high concentration of real cultural capital in these cities (Richards, 1996c). A second group of cities, which includes Athens, Venice, Florence and Amsterdam also scores relatively well, particularly with visitors with a cultural occupation. These cities tend to be smaller, and in addition to a rich historical past have a wide range of museums, monuments and also a great deal of 'living culture'. Cities which fall outside the top ten usually have less attractions, or are perceived as offering less atmosphere. The combination of a rich supply of real cultural capital and living culture or atmosphere was often decisive in the destination choice of specific cultural tourists (Goedhart, 1997).

The Supply of Cultural Attractions

An increasingly important aspect of cultural tourism is the role of cultural producers in assembling the cultural tourism product. The demand for cultural tourism to a particular city can be closely linked to the amount and quality of real cultural capital (Britton, 1991; Zukin, 1991, 1996) that it has. This real cultural capital provides the basic raw material for the 'new producers' or 'new cultural intermediaries' to develop products for cultural consumption (Richards, 1996c).

The new producers occupy a key position in the cultural tourism system, determining which products are fashionable, and which products will be offered on the market. The new producers are predominantly from a cultural background and have a cultural education, and therefore possess a great store of personal cultural capital, which they convert into economic capital by designing products with a high symbolic value for consumption by the new bourgeoisie. These relationships tend to strengthen existing hierarchies of cultural consumption in Europe, which are reflected in the ranking of European cities by new producers and consumers alike. This makes it very difficult for 'new' cultural destinations to break through and capture a significant share of the European cultural tourism market.

The importance of real cultural capital in generating markers in the cultural tourism market is also becoming evident in the trend toward 'mega-events' and 'blockbuster exhibitions'. Because of the increasing globalization of cultural tourism demand, the cultural distance between host regions and their visitors is often increasing. This means that markets associated with the highlights of a globalized culture are likely to attract larger numbers of tourists than those associated with local or national culture. Mega-events aimed at a global audience have therefore become an important part of the tourism marketing strategies of many countries (e.g. Bos, 1994). The evidence is that events associated with cultural figures with a global profile are much more successful in attracting international tourists than those attached to more localized culture. In The Netherlands, for example, the numbers of tourists visiting major exhibitions on artists such as Rembrandt, Vermeer and Van Gogh have been increasing steadily since the 1960s. Not only are the numbers of tourists increasing, but the proportion of tourists from outside Europe has also grown, indicating that these events are appealing to a truly global audience. In contrast, a major exhibition of the works of Mondriaan, a leading Dutch member of the 'Stijl' movement had disappointing visitor numbers. Mondriaan is an abstract artist whose work is well known in The Netherlands, but the complexity of his work has prevented him from becoming an international cultural megastar.

Implications of Trends

Public policy

For public policy makers, the blurring of the distinctions between high and popular culture, and cultural and economic elements of policy make the formation of cultural tourism policy increasingly challenging. Efforts must be made to break down the often entrenched barriers between the different cultures within government bodies and cultural organizations themselves. Landry and Bianchini (1995) have recently suggested that this is one of the keys to creating the 'creative city' for the new millennium.

Another important point which will need to be addressed by policy makers is the need to create great public spaces for the next century. As commercialization moves in to translate the cultural needs of tourists into consumption opportunities, there will be a growing need to create and preserve spaces which facilitate the meeting of cultures, and therefore create opportunities for cultural innovation. The 'Cathedrals of Consumption' referred to by Ritzer (1998) will need to stimulate the same kind of public interaction as their religious counterparts did in the past.

Management

Attention must be paid to the visitor experience, particularly as the cultural sector becomes more professional and the cultural tourist expects a better quality product. Increasing attention must be paid to the needs of different groups of visitors, particularly through better interpretation. In interpreting culture to visitors, most authors are agreed that authenticity and truthfulness in presentation are crucial (Zuzanek, 1992). As authenticity and truth are relative concepts, however, the fact that perceptions of authenticity and truth vary among visitors, and that authenticity can emerge over time (Cohen, 1988) means that considerable skill will be needed in managing these messages. It is also becoming clear that in a postmodern landscape of relative truths, the product which lays claim to the best story will usually be most successful. The stories created in the future will probably need to be more sophisticated than the fairly standard 'heritage tales' which have been created over the past two decades.

Planning

Because of the increased competition in the cultural tourism market, more account must be taken of competing events and attractions, and direct competition minimized through efficient planning and cooperation. Even if direct competition from other cultural events can be minimized, planners will still need to be aware of growing indirect competition from other events. As the boundaries between cultural events and other types of events blurs, cultural planners will need to avoid losing market share to other events and fixed attractions.

In order to develop cultural tourism effectively, it is also vital to increase the level of dialogue between the tourism and cultural sectors. In Los Angeles moves are being made in this direction by the recently created Cultural Tourism Department of the city's Visitor and Convention Bureau. The aim of the department is 'to build lines of communication between cultural and travel industry professionals through educational and social programmes as well as to create a computerized resource for information about Los Angeles' cultural community' (Real 1997, p. 182).

Marketing

Effective marketing of cultural tourism requires a better understanding of motives and increased targeting of specific cultural interests. One of the major problems in cultural tourism development in the recent past has been the tendency toward supply-driven demand. As museums and heritage centres have opened at an increasing rate, so the initial surge in pent-up demand for cultural products has turned into a dilution of the market, with visitors being increasingly thinly spread over a burgeoning number of attractions. Falls in the average number of visitors per attraction have been evident in most European countries in recent years.

If cultural tourism is going to grow in the 21st century, therefore, a more market-oriented approach to cultural tourism development is required. Although every location by definition has unique cultural products to offer, visitors will only come if they are sufficiently motivated.

Conclusions

In the future, cultural tourism will have to be approached in a far more systematic and professional manner than in the past, particularly if the rapid market growth in recent years is to be exploited and controlled effectively. One of the major tools which will become increasingly important in this process will be the development of new media, and particularly distribution of the cultural tourism product via new media. A current weakness of the cultural tourism product is the fragmented nature of the product and the lack of efficient distribution systems. With the use of the Internet, for example, it will become much easier to give easy access to a much wider range of cultural tourism products. This applies particularly to cultural events, which at present have much higher accessibility barriers than fixed attractions. To make such systems work effectively, however, communications between the tourism sector and the cultural sector will need to be improved, so that the tourist industry better understands the cultural product, and the cultural sector better understands the needs of tourists.

18

Planning to Provide Community and Visitor Benefits from Public Lands

Dorothy H. Anderson, Ron Nickerson, Taylor V. Stein and Martha E. Lee

Introduction

This chapter explores the trend toward the benefits-based management (BBM) framework of leisure and amenity goods and services for wildland recreation management. This chapter also suggests future research and application needs to continue BBM's conceptual evolution and enhance implementation efforts. The BBM framework has evolved over a 25- to 30-year period as researchers' understanding of visitor activities, desires and motivations has grown. Recreation researchers have sought to identify the types of experiences and benefits realized by visitors who recreate in wildland recreation areas. More recently, researchers have begun to examine the range of benefits which recreation opportunities in natural areas provide to nearby communities (Stein and Anderson, 1998; Stein et al., 1999). At the same time, recreation managers have moved towards more collaborative planning models, sought greater public participation in decision making, built more partnerships with other providers and interest groups, and better recognized the need to understand visitor expectations.

One cumulative effect of these recreation research efforts and the evolving management climate is the way in which researchers, public recreation policy makers and administrators think about, plan and manage wildland recreation areas. A complementary increase in the understanding of effective recreation planning and management strategies has allowed BBM researchers to develop a strong emphasis on direct application of research results to management planning, policy development and actions. In recent years, BBM's emphasis on identifying desired outcomes and managing toward those outcomes has attracted a growing number of recreation researchers and managers throughout the US and Canada. As researchers and managers look forward to the future, BBM provides a rich framework for providing the types of recreation opportunities that will satisfy visitor and community needs, protect the critical resources found within wildland recreation areas and ensure that quality experiences and benefits are attained within the current management environment of structural change and limited financial resources.

Moving From Activity-based Management to Benefits-based Management

BBM emerges from the belief that the kinds of outdoor recreation-related experiences and benefits visitors desire are extremely diverse, and from a belief that managers should provide recreation opportunities that target the realization of the experiences and benefits desired by the public. Although Wagar (1966) argued 30 years ago that understanding the nature of recreation experiences and benefits was important to effective recreation management actions, recreation management is still evolving into a BBM framework. Researchers and managers began the evolutionary process by realizing that recreation resource management is partly activity oriented, with visitors having a set of favourite activities they engage in and managers having some responsibility to provide opportunities for those activities (Bruns *et al.*, 1994). Some people like to hike, others like to cycle, others wish to camp, while others simply enjoy picnicking or participating in an interpretive programme. Early recreation research produced evidence to support the conclusion that individuals who participate in different activities seek different sets of experience outcomes (Manfredo *et al.*, 1983).

Activities-based management

Supported by research results linking recreation activities and visitor satisfaction, recreation managers sought to provide a variety of activities for visitors to enjoy. This early approach to meeting recreation demand is known as activity-based management (ABM). ABM views the provision of multiple activity opportunities as the principal end product of management actions (Wagar, 1966; Brown and Haas, 1980; Stein and Lee, 1995). The result is a strong emphasis on facilities (Brown and Haas, 1980; Stein and Lee, 1995). ABM was designed to provide quality recreation attractions (e.g. resources, facilities or both), information and interpretation, controls against crowding and visitor services (e.g. rest room maintenance, rubbish collection and rule enforcement) (Bruns *et al.*, 1994). This one-dimensional approach assumes that the setting is essentially unimportant to the quality of a visitor's experience. Consequently, ABM believes the visitor will have satisfying experiences in virtually any setting the manager provides as long as opportunities for desired activities exist (Bruns *et al.*, 1994). Many agencies adopted ABM early on to guide their development, planning and daily management activities.

Even though early research testing of ABM showed relationships between activities and experience outcomes, it also revealed that protecting the resource and providing activity opportunities did not automatically result in satisfying recreational experiences for visitors (Manfredo *et al.*, 1983). This research effectively demonstrated that visitor behaviour and experience outcomes were a function of several psychological dimensions that are a reaction to the setting in which an activity takes place (Driver and Brown, 1975; Driver and Tocher, 1983; Manfredo *et al.*, 1983; Driver *et al.*, 1991c). In addition, researchers and managers began to realize attempts to offer recreation opportunities without consideration of the setting severely limited their efforts to conduct recreation resource inventories and to identify effective management alternatives for a particular site (Driver *et al.*, 1991c).

Experience-based management

Experience-based management (EBM) emerged to explain the psychological and setting relationships associated with participation in recreation activities. EBM extends ABM by describing a recreation opportunity as the opportunity to engage in certain desired activities within preferred settings to achieve satisfying experiences (Driver and Brown, 1978; Manfredo *et al.*, 1983; Lee and Driver, 1995; Bruns *et al.*, 1994; Stein and Lee, 1995). EBM entails both a shift in research direction and management focus. Research direction shifts from a focus on what people do when they recreate to understanding the relationships among how, why and where they recreate. Management focus in EBM shifts from providing activity opportunities as the primary output of recreation engagement to providing a mix of recreation opportunities that target realization of desired visitor experiences. These research and management shifts entail a corresponding effort to understand the psychological outcomes of recreation participation (Manfredo et al., 1983; Stein and Lee, 1995). These outcomes are conceptualized as desired experiences in EBM (Driver and Brown, 1978; Bruns et al., 1994).

At the federal level, National Park Service, US Department of Agriculture (USDA) Forest Service, and Bureau of Land Management recreation planners and managers have adopted the EBM framework. Many state agencies charged with providing wildland recreation opportunities operate at least implicitly in the EBM framework. Even though they may not be developing EBM objectives, some managers strive to control visitor activity and setting features in ways that lead to production of satisfying visitor experiences (Bruns et al., 1994). EBM researchers and managers realize that not all activities produce similar experiences in all settings. Natural resources, visitor expectations, activity opportunities and facilities differ between sites. The result of these differences is that elements in the set of desired beneficial experiences from particular activities change somewhat according to the setting (Manfredo et al., 1983; Virden and Knopf, 1989; Yuan and McEwen, 1989). For example, campers in a primitive setting have been found to have less desire for sharing and leading experiences than campers in more developed areas (Virden and Knopf, 1989).

At the same time, some beneficial experiences may be common across sites (Knopf et al., 1983; Schreyer et al., 1984; Nickerson, 1998). For example, river floaters on 11 different rivers representing a range of settings all reported similar desires for friendship, escape and exercise (Knopf et al., 1983); visitors to six different Minnesota state parks representing a range of settings, reported similar desires for learning about nature, being with friends and family, and exercise

(Nickerson et al., 1997a,b,c, 1998a,b,c; Nickerson, 1998). Managers need to be sensitive to these differences and similarities when determining the appropriate mix of activities, recreation opportunities, and settings for a given site. If they are not, some visitors may have negative experiences (Bruns et al., 1994).

Although EBM's recognition of the importance of considering desired visitor experiences in recreation planning and management is an improvement on ABM, EBM limits the descriptions of recreation outcomes to on-site experiences. It does not address the role that desired visitor experiences play in attaining a broader set of benefits that might be associated with a particular recreational site (Bruns et al., 1994; Stein and Lee, 1995; Driver and Bruns, 1999). In addition, EBM focuses primarily on the individual visitor and does not address the value of recreational sites beyond personal visitor satisfaction (Bruns et al., 1994; Stein and Lee, 1995). Yet, recreation managers', as well as researchers', intuition tells them that the value added to people's lives extends beyond the individual on-site recreational experiences (President's Commission on Americans Outdoors, 1987a; Driver et al., 1991b; Jordan, 1991; Parks and Recreation Federation of Ontario, 1992). For example, visitors may see improved work performance as a result of participation in recreational activities. Similarly, the value of recreation areas to communities is much broader than on-site visitor experiences. Recreation sites are viewed by residents of nearby cities and towns as valuable amenities that strengthen the economy and increase their sense of community pride and overall quality of life (Stein and Anderson, 1998; Stein et al., 1999).

Benefits-based management

Recognizing EBM's limitations and building on the ABM and EBM frameworks, researchers in the mid-1980s began to develop the BBM framework of leisure and amenity services to explain the relationship between desired experiences and broader benefits. BBM seeks to understand not only individual on-site beneficial experiences, but also the off-site benefits, which accrue to individuals, society, the economy and the environment from the provision of public recreation opportunities (Brown, 1984; Driver *et al.*, 1991b; Lee and Driver, 1995; Bruns *et al.*, 1994; Schleicher *et al.*, 1994; Stein and Lee, 1995; Nickerson, 1998). BBM, which incorporates and expands upon both ABM and EBM, has opened a new field of recreation management research and a new management paradigm for recreation resource managers (Lee and Driver, 1995; Bruns *et al.*, 1994).

Fundamental to BBM is the concept that a benefit extends beyond the on-site experiences that are EBM's focus. A benefit may be defined as 'a change that is viewed to be advantageous – an improvement in condition or gain to an individual, to a group, to society (community), or to another entity' (Driver *et al.*, 1991b, p. 4). A benefit, therefore, can be viewed as the value-added portion of an individual's recreation experience (Bruns *et al.*, 1994; Driver and Bruns, 1999). This definition includes prevention of a worse condition or maintenance of a desired condition (Driver, 1997). For example, continued exercise contributes to maintenance of good cardiovascular health. Similarly, a benefit can be looked at as the value-added portion of a community's role as tourism provider for persons recreating on nearby wildland areas. In this case, the value added might include such things as increased tourism dollars and enhanced community pride. In a recreation management context, benefits can also be realized by the natural environment, plant or animal species, or cultural resources through a sense of stewardship (Rolston, 1991). For example, a recreation area might improve a region's environmental quality by protecting important species and ecosystems. In this case, a value added to the environment might be protection of a region's biodiversity or improved water quality because nonpoint source pollution to a particular river is reduced by the protected recreation area.

Unlike experiences, which are short-term and on-site, benefits are both short- and long-term and can be attained both on-site and off-site (Driver *et al.*, 1991b; Lee and Driver, 1995; Bruns *et al.*, 1994; Lime *et al.*, 1994; Stein and Lee, 1995). The recognition that off-site and long-term benefits are important outcomes of recreation is a major advancement over EBM's focus on on-site and short-term outcomes.

According to BBM, benefits can be associated with one of four general categories: personal, societal, economic and environmental. Personal benefits are those that accrue to individual recreationists as a result of their participation in some activity. Among the personal benefits are health and wellbeing, self-image and self-satisfaction (Driver *et al.*, 1991c; Parks and Recreation Federation of Ontario, 1992; Bruns *et al.*, 1994; Schleicher *et al.*, 1994; Nickerson, 1998). Social benefits are often aggregated personal benefits and include social bonding, community satisfaction and cultural identity (Allen, 1991; Parks and Recreation Federation of Ontario, 1992; Bruns *et al.*, 1994; Bruns, 1995). Economic benefits are tied to individual and societal productivity and include the products of employment, tourism, and recreational goods bought and sold (Brown, 1984; Parks and Recreation Federation of Ontario, 1992; Bruns *et al.*, 1994; Stein and Anderson, 1998; Stein *et al.*, 1999). Environmental benefits result from environmental health and protection, increased awareness of environmental impacts of human actions, and investment in wildland recreation areas (Rolston, 1991; Bruns *et al.*, 1994).

It is important to recognize that the visitor's on-site beneficial experiences remain an important component of BBM. BBM suggests experiences and benefits are related to one another in a 'chain of causality' (Lee and Driver, 1992; Bruns *et al.*, 1994; Driver, 1994; Driver and Bruns, 1999). The causality chain describes the temporal nature of benefit accrual and helps explain the relationships between short- and long-term benefits and the corresponding connection between on-site beneficial experiences and off-site benefits. In its most fundamental form, the causality chain explains how beneficial experiences lead to the realization of benefits. On-site beneficial experiences are the initial outputs from the recreation engagement and the initial inputs into the benefit attainment process. For example, a relaxing experience might lead to decreased job stress. It is also believed that one benefit can lead to a second benefit, which can lead to a third, and so on. For example, an individual who benefits from decreased job stress might have improved work performance, which could lead to a higher salary and so on.

Although the majority of recreation resource management research has focused on the individual, BBM extends wildland recreation's impact outside park boundaries.

> Adoption of BBM has significant ramifications ... (M)anagers focus on their customers to facilitate customer realization of sought benefits, including value added to households, local communities, and the environment. This means that managerial attention shifts from concentrating mostly on on-site customers to concentrating equally on both on- and off-site customers
> (Driver and Bruns, 1999, pp. 38–39)

Incorporating all four types of benefits into recreation resource management corresponds well with the holistic approach described within the ecosystem management literature (Grumbine, 1994). Similar to ecosystem management, BBM argues that recreation management impacts society both temporally and spatially and managers must not confine their planning and management to just the people or resources within their managerial units. Also, BBM places noneconomic values on an equal footing with economic values. It does not stress a particular type of benefit, but acknowledges that different benefits are related to the land and to each other.

Trends in Benefits-based Management Research

Understanding the wide range of benefits and their relationship to each other and to beneficial experiences through empirical research is difficult. However, such knowledge improves understanding of human interactions with the natural environment; increases the number of management options available to managers; and improves the quality of management actions. Most of the early BBM research focused on economic benefits (Driver et al., 1991b; Parks and Recreation Federation of Ontario, 1992). In recent years, researchers have sought to refine the conceptual framework and shift research attention to documentation of noneconomic benefits (Lime et al., 1994; Stein and Lee, 1995; Stein and Anderson, 1998; Stein et al., 1999). Previous EBM and motivation research work and the development of conceptual models to explain the production of benefits has aided in crystallizing the BBM framework and establishing a foundation for this new research direction. At the same time, an effort has been made to connect research documenting specific benefits with recreation management on public lands (MN DNR, 1997, 1998; USDI BLM, 1998).

Beginning in the early 1970s, recreation researchers began developing motivation scales to explain why recreationists choose to participate in various recreation activities (Driver, 1977; Driver et al., 1991c). A great deal of this work builds on research conducted to test three critical social psychology theories; reasoned action, planned behaviour and expectancy (Brown and Haas, 1980; Ajzen and Driver, 1991; Driver et al., 1991c). Central to all three of these theories is the belief that human behaviour has a strong volitional component guided by an underlying set of beliefs and attitudes (Ajzen and Fishbein, 1972; Ajzen and Madden, 1986; Ajzen, 1988, 1991).

Research applying the theories of reasoned action and planned behaviour to recreational settings has provided promising evidence that the theorized relationship between attitudes, beliefs, motivation and behaviour is present (Young and Kent, 1985; Ajzen and Driver, 1991). These findings support continued research into the relationship between visitor motives (desires) and recreation behaviour and ultimately the outcomes from participation in recreation opportunities. This research has also aided in the development of measurement scales that are being used to assess visitor experience preferences. Driver's (1977) initial experience preference scales have evolved to produce a set of individual desired psychological outcomes for recreation participation (Driver *et al.*, 1985, 1991c; Knopf *et al.*, 1983). Much of the EBM research used and tested these scales to assess visitor motivations, document desired experiences, and improve upon the measurement scales (Brown and Haas, 1980; McLaughlin and Paradice, 1980; Manfredo *et al.*, 1983; Schreyer *et al.*, 1984; Virden and Knopf, 1989; Yuan and McEwen, 1989).

BBM researchers have sought to extend the applicability of these scales to analyses of the beneficial experiences accruing to individuals from recreation engagements (Driver *et al.*, 1985, 1991b,c; Lee and Driver, 1992; Bruns *et al.*, 1994). Although results are encouraging that the theorized relationships exist, little research has been conducted to date, and most of the research has been confined to wilderness areas (Brown, 1984; Driver *et al.*, 1985, 1991c; Lee and Driver, 1992). Pilot tests are currently under way in several locations nationwide in cooperation with the USDA Forest Service to extend recreation research from wilderness areas to other settings. Among these are urban parks, heavily used Bureau of Land Management lands, national forests and state and local parks (Bruns *et al.*, 1994).

Beyond the development of motivational scales to test the critical relationships between recreation behaviour and desired outcomes, a second major contribution to the conceptual advancement of BBM is the development of conceptual models to explain the relationships among the major factors influencing the production of benefits. Brown (1984) developed a benefits production model that sought to explain how benefits are produced, what factors influence their production, and how benefits can be seen as an outcome of recreation management. He suggests that five interrelated processes occur which result in production of benefits: (i) production of

recreation opportunities by management; (ii) production of recreation experiences by visitors; (iii) production of societal benefits from management actions to provide recreation opportunities; (iv) production of individual and societal benefits from an individual's recreational experiences; and (v) production of societal benefits from use of recreation resources.

This model was one of the first models which identified the key variables involved in producing both individual and societal benefits and the relationships among those variables. It also better identified the role of managers, recreation visitors, and communities in the creation and attainment of benefits. Brown's (1984) production model has been adapted as a framework for much of BBM's conceptual and research work.

The production model clearly depicts the value-added component of BBM and conceptualizes the importance of feedback from visitors and society to managers to ensure that the process continues to produce the desired results. Brown (1984) also identifies the need for continued research to test the relationships depicted in the model, and to understand the nature of the actual benefits attained from the process better. Although this model made an important contribution to the BBM framework, it focuses primarily on the production of personal and societal benefits. Economic benefits are viewed as a subset of societal benefits and environmental benefits are not directly articulated in the model.

Bruns (1993) presented a modification to Brown's (1984) model for community (societal) and personal (individual) benefits that enhances the benefit production process by incorporating the type and quality of off-site services and attractions that can influence the quality of experiences and benefits attained. He also introduced the visitor's characteristics (i.e. the amount of awareness they have for the attractions in the area and visitor demographics) and travel characteristics (i.e. the market segment that the visitor represents, the type of trip planning the visitor conducted, and a general profile of how the visit to the recreation site relates to the overall trip). These adaptations highlight what occurs on-site as only one of several factors influencing the visitor's complete mix of desired and accrued experiences and benefits. Despite this advancement toward a broader representation of benefit production, the Bruns (1993) model essentially focused on the production of personal benefits. It did not clearly depict the value-added relationship between experiences and benefits nor did it clearly illustrate that both on-site and off-site benefits are attained as a result of the recreation engagement.

Figure 18.1 adapts Bruns' (1993) model to incorporate an even broader perspective on the process used to realize personal and community benefits. In this model, off-site attractions and preferences, visitor characteristics, and travel characteristics are included and on-site beneficial experiences are shown as an antecedent component of the realization of both short- and long-term personal and social (community) benefits. The model also shows that realization of social benefits are directly influenced by on-site beneficial experiences and attainment of personal benefits. The adapted model also displays links between personal and community benefit attainment and service quality preferences expressed by visitors and society.

The development of motive scales to measure psychological outcomes from recreation and the creation of conceptual models to explain the relationship of the factors influencing benefit attainment have been major contributions to the evolution of the research agenda and BBM. At the same time, BBM's evolution has included the development of a strong applied component. BBM enhances EBM's encouragement for managers to develop management objectives that target specific outcomes. One of BBM's intended results is that managers will develop BBM objectives that allow them to target management actions toward realization of a specific mix of experiences and benefits most suited to a specific site. Since managers use management objectives and actions to control many of the setting attributes important to the recreation experience, BBM assumes that recreation providers influence the quality of life for individuals and society, thereby improving economic and environmental health.

In recent years, several pilot tests have been conducted in the US and other countries to research and implement the BBM framework. Personal benefits research has been conducted on Bureau of Land Management lands in Colorado, on the Coconino National Forest in Arizona, on the Jefferson National Forest in Virginia and in six Minnesota State Parks (Itasca, Tettegouche, St Croix, Interstate, George Crosby Manitou and Forestville/Mystery Cave). Oregon's Bureau of Parks and Recreation and neighbouring communities to two of Minnesota's state parks (Itasca and Tettegouche) have also participated in pilot tests to assess the community benefits of wildland recreation. Other national, state, and local recreation management agencies have also expressed an interest in moving toward a BBM approach. In addition, recreation researchers and managers from several countries (Australia, Canada, Denmark, Finland, New Zealand and Norway) have begun to conduct benefits-based research, education and implementation.

Among the personal benefits identified by the pilot tests which visitors desire and attain is a range of benefits from recreation engagements which include enjoyment of the natural scenery, getting away from the usual demands of life, learning more about nature, keeping physically fit and experiencing solitude (Stein, 1994; Stein and Lee, 1995; Nickerson, 1998). Among the community benefits identified in the pilot tests are an increased sense of community pride, increased identity for the area surrounding the recreation site, employment, increased community sensitivity to environmental issues, and places to preserve/conserve various natural and unique ecosystems in larger natural areas (Stein, 1997; Stein and Anderson, 1998; Stein et al., 1999). Increased family satisfaction, interactions, and stability; enhanced leadership skills among young people; and a sense of attachment or belonging to the community have been identified as some of the community benefits in the Portland, Oregon, project (Borrie and Roggenbuck, 1995).

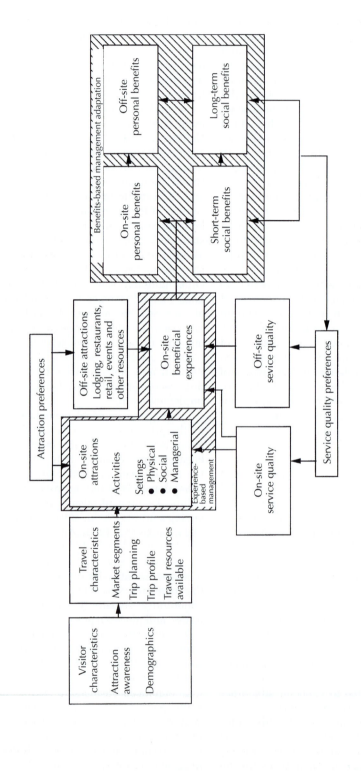

Fig. 18.1. Proposed benefits-based management framework displaying factors influencing realization of personal and social outdoor recreation experiences and benefits. Adapted from: Bruns (1993). Using social information for park and recreation management. In D.H. Anderson, D.W. Lime and W. Morrissey (Coordinators). *Outdoor Recreation Management in the 90s*. Continuing education course conducted at the University of Minnesota, St. Paul, Minnesota.

Trends in Implementing Benefits-based Management

An important component of the BBM pilot tests conducted in the US has been application of research results to management actions. Results of the pilot studies are being used at the federal level by the USDA Forest Service to develop new approaches to recreation resource management which respond to people's and the nation's needs for the year 2000 and beyond. Other federal and state agencies involved in these studies are also adopting a benefits-based approach to recreation resource management as a result of this research. The Bureau of Land Management has developed a management plan based on the results of their pilot tests. In Minnesota, direct linkages between the pilot test research and management planning has occurred at Itasca and Tettegouche state parks (MN DNR, 1997, 1998). At Itasca and Tettegouche, management goals, management zoning and park vision statements have been heavily influenced by the research. At Itasca State Park, specific target benefits have been established that the park will attempt to provide opportunities to attain. Work is also under way to develop guides for applying the BBM framework to management decisions (Anderson and Stein, 1997).

Several Canadian Provinces (particularly Alberta and Ontario) have also taken a leadership role in implementing what is referred to in Canada as a benefits-driven approach to management of their provincial parks. Although the Canadian experience has focused more on use of the benefits-driven approach as a budgeting and marketing tool based on research conducted elsewhere and less on conducting original research than is perhaps the case with the pilot tests in the US, Canadian researchers have organized several tools that assist managers with implementation of the benefits-driven approach. Among these are slide shows and video tapes, 'how to' manuals and speakers guides. The Canadian Parks and Recreation Association (1997), in cooperation with several provincial park associations has also published *The Benefits Catalogue* that lists some of the specific benefits identified by BBM research conducted to date.

Other national, state and local park agencies and professional organizations are expressing a growing interest in movement toward BBM research and implementation. For example, Portland, Oregon's, Department of Parks and Recreation is designing recreation programmes in selected city parks to deliver specific benefit opportunities. Moreover, the National Recreation and Park Association has published several articles in their monthly journal regarding BBM (Allen, 1996; Driver, 1997; Dustin and Goodale, 1997), conducted training institutes at their annual conferences, and developed implementation guides for managers. Managers who have taken an interest in the BBM framework see it as a way to understand their clientele better, identify and manage recreation areas for specific outcomes, enhance management accountability, and aid in budget preparation and distribution. In addition, an awareness of how a community benefits from a particular recreation area can increase managers' understanding of the role wildland recreation areas play in the larger landscape. This recognition aids in regional planning and natural resource management. It also aids in efforts to increase community support and efforts to increase citizen involvement in decision making (Stein et al., 1999).

Implications for Benefits-based Management

Study of the relationships between visitors' beneficial experiences, activities and desired settings within the BBM framework is relatively recent. Component parts of this framework have been researched, but the recent pilot tests were the first efforts to examine relationships between multiple components of the framework. Examination of whether visitors actually attain the beneficial experiences they consider most important to their visits has also just begun. Perhaps the most important implications are related to the observation that visitors come to recreation areas with a set of experience, activity and setting preferences, and that they report an ability to attain the experiences and benefits they seek. Equally important is that residents of nearby cities and towns report they attain benefits from local recreation areas. If managers and planners are to develop management objectives and recreational opportunities effectively which promote benefit attainment at a given recreation area, it is important to remain cognizant of which benefits the visitors to the site and local residents attain and do not attain.

Implications for agency managers

Visitors to several different BBM pilot test recreation areas have reported that many of the same experiences and benefits were important to their decisions to visit the different areas. For example, visitors to the various sites indicated that opportunities to find solitude and escape, to enjoy nature and to learn from their visits were important. Visitors to the pilot test sites also consistently reported an ability to attain those experiences and benefits they considered most important to their visits. This result supports the observation that there is probably a core set of experiences and benefits associated with particular types of wildland recreation areas (e.g. national forests, national parks or state parks). Although additional research is necessary to document the specific core experiences and benefits better, results for the pilot tests reveal finding opportunities for solitude, escape from the pressures of home, learning about nature, enjoying nature and improving family relations are likely to be among this core set of desired experiences and benefits.

Visitors to the pilot test sites also identified several activities as most satisfying. One implication of this is that visitors are able to attain their important experiences and benefits from one of several activities that they identify as most satisfying. Management planning should incorporate the concept that many of the same experiences and benefits are attainable from a variety of activities and settings. A likely outcome of such a planning perspective is that some of the

same recreational opportunities will be provided at several locations – giving managers more information to market recreation opportunities for appropriate users (Knopf, 1990).

Equally important to considering the similarities between recreation areas as management objectives are written as the need to recognize that differences do exist between recreation areas in terms of the desired and attained experiences and benefits. The pilot test results provide insight into how the experience and benefit attainment processes relate to particular setting preferences. Management planning to accommodate different setting preferences needs to do so within the context of the desired beneficial outcomes.

The need to select carefully the recreational opportunities that will be offered at a given recreation area in relation to the desired beneficial outcomes involves writing clear and measurable management objectives and target benefits for each recreation area. Since the attainment of experiences and benefits is more complicated than a bivariate relationship between an activity and a beneficial experience, management objectives which consider multiple variables become an important tool that planners and managers can use to identify which recreational opportunities might have the greatest likelihood of aiding visitors in attaining their desired beneficial outcomes.

Implications for agency planners

The emerging evidence, supporting the observation that a core set of important experiences and benefits might exist for similar types of recreation areas, supports the conclusion that regional recreation planning might consider a core set of recreational opportunities in multiple locations. Among these might be opportunities for solitude, family bonding, enjoying nature and learning. Recognition of a core set of important experiences and benefits might translate into ensuring that the natural and cultural resources found within each recreation area are protected, remote trail opportunities are offered, picnic areas and campgrounds that offer opportunities for family togetherness and other core experiences are provided, and interpretive programming is made available.

At the same time, it is important for regional planning efforts to recognize that visitors come to specific recreation areas seeking particular experiences and benefits. Planning also needs to consider the unique characteristics of each recreation area and its associated visitors when determining the types of recreational opportunities that should be provided. This consideration might translate into offering a variety of camping, picnicking and hiking opportunities regionally. For example, some recreation areas within a given region might focus on providing remote backpack camping, challenging hiking trails and small picnic areas, while others might focus on providing more developed drive-in camping, paved trail and large group picnicking opportunities. Ongoing research and monitoring at multiple locations will be necessary to aid managers in identifying the particular mix of benefit opportunities appropriate for particular recreation areas. In addition, continued publication of accurate visitor information brochures that describe the different opportunities available in a region can aid visitors in selecting those locations most likely able to provide opportunities for them to attain the experiences and benefits they find most important.

In addition, recreation planning for a given site needs to consider those opportunities provided by other public and private recreation providers within the region. For example, private recreation providers near a public recreation area might provide ample horse riding, drive-in camping or snowmobiling opportunities to serve the area's needs. In these cases, a management plan for the particular public recreation area might suggest those types of opportunities should not be duplicated within the public recreation area. However, the public recreation area might be in a better position to offer other opportunities not adequately provided by private providers.

Implications for collaborative planning and management

Recreation planners and managers must understand the diversity of complex and important benefits recreation areas provide to local residents. They must develop plans to sustain natural recreation areas that recognize the natural characteristics, which distinguish these areas, are essential to maintaining opportunities to attain desired benefits associated with these areas. Community residents, who live close to natural areas managed for recreation, see enormous benefits derived from the natural characteristics protected in these recreation areas. The pilot test results indicate that both personal and community benefits are attained by local residents from nearby recreation areas. The personal benefits studies indicate that local community residents use nearby recreation areas for some of their outdoor recreation endeavours and attain personal benefits from those endeavours. Local residents also report that these recreation areas are part of their community identity, pride and health. People live in those communities because they enjoy the stress relief, aesthetics and quality of life provided by recreation areas.

Economic benefits derived through nature-based tourism are also important to local communities and cannot be ignored in public recreation area planning. Nature-based tourism has become important to the economic growth of many communities. At the same time, it is important to consider the environmental benefits associated with protection of natural areas when planning nature-based tourism opportunities. Planners and managers must understand their role in working with communities to provide sustainable regional tourism opportunities that allow access to recreation areas without causing irreparable damage to the natural resources. They must work collaboratively with communities to develop management plans that balance increased tourism with natural area protection.

Active engagement of community members in planning and management processes increases the likelihood that benefits are accurately articulated and incorporated into management plans for wildland recreation areas. Since the passage of the National Environmental Protection Act in 1969, which mandated public involvement in public land use decision making, the trend toward increased citizen participation has continued to grow. Increased citizen participation in natural resource decision making and increased inter-agency cooperation are also outcomes of the trend in a growing number of agencies toward adoption of ecosystem based management (Grumbine, 1997). Identifying and considering benefits most important to neighbouring communities in wildland planning and management decisions is consistent with these trends. Public participation is the most efficient means in which to improve the production of community benefits. It is also something local communities demand from their public land managers. By using appropriate methods and focusing communication on how people and communities benefit from recreation, planners and managers are more likely to create management plans which local communities, as well as visitors to those communities, support.

Articulating the community benefits of recreation areas is becoming increasingly important for public agencies faced with increasing competition for funding, demands for accountability and demands to be more responsive to public needs. Public meetings, community questionnaires, focus groups, and increased interaction with managing agencies through citizen advisory boards, friends' groups, and volunteer opportunities gives community residents the opportunity to tell planners and managers how they want to benefit from wildland recreation areas. In turn, this knowledge greatly aids planners and managers in providing appropriate opportunities for visitors and local communities. Also, understanding community benefits wildland recreation areas provide, aids in establishing common regional planning goals that effectively incorporate recreational needs into planning efforts.

Future Research

To investigate visitor and community benefits derived from wildland recreation areas more fully, researchers should consider using a mix of qualitative and quantitative research methods. The many variables to consider when examining visitor and community benefits are impossible to capture using only one of these methods. Qualitative research methods which seek to describe and understand rather than predict seem to be the most efficient methods to understand the complex relationships among communities, wildland recreation areas and benefit opportunities. Therefore, a greater focus on describing the culture of the community in terms of its relationship to a wildland recreation area would avoid getting bogged down in the multitude of variables inherent in understanding community benefit opportunities. Qualitative methods that are promising in this area include focus groups, nominal group process and in-depth interviews with individuals.

Quantitative methods must not be forgotten, however. According to Driver *et al.* (1987, p. 296), 'It is impossible to state accurately the magnitude of any benefits inferred from this "perceived benefits" research that used introspective reports'. Quantitative methods, which include both one-time and longitudinal studies using paper and pencil survey methods, are proven methods for gathering data on desired and realized benefits from randomly selected visitors and community residents to infer to large populations.

Personal benefits research

Several BBM research topics need to be examined more thoroughly and others are yet to be explored. Additional research is necessary to explore relationships between experiences and benefits considered important by visitors and their ability to attain those experiences and benefits in other locations. Similarly, research in other locations is necessary to examine the relationship between benefits identified as important by visitors and visitor setting preferences. This research might seek to identify similarities and differences between multiple sites and aid in development of core management objectives that might be applicable to a variety of locations.

Future research should also be conducted at the pilot test sites as part of an effective long-term monitoring and evaluation system. For example, the relationship between important beneficial experiences and visitors' ability to attain those experiences should be periodically examined at these locations to monitor changes in the nature of these relationships over time. Additional follow-up research should also be conducted periodically to identify changes in setting preferences and those beneficial experiences visitors consider important. Management objectives and actions might require adjustment if such research identifies a change in this relationship.

A series of future research topics also emerge from the fact that most of the existing BBM research has focused on personal on-site experiences and benefits. The BBM framework is much broader than on-site experiences and benefits and includes off-site long-term personal benefits, economic benefits, community benefits and environmental benefits associated with particular recreation sites. Research on community benefits has only recently begun and little research has been conducted on the nature of environmental benefits.

Additional personal benefits research is needed to articulate better the differences between an experience and a benefit, differences between on-site and off-site benefits, and linkages that might exist between short- and long-term benefits. Additional personal benefit research is also needed to understand how settings, customer satisfaction, demographics and general trip profiles influence the benefit attainment process. Furthermore, researchers are just beginning to understand how to apply research results to management actions. Research is needed to understand how to transfer knowledge to managers better, develop BBM influenced management objectives, and alter planning models to accommodate knowledge gained from BBM research work.

Community benefits research

Research on community benefits is relatively new. To strengthen the understanding of community benefits, future research should continue to identify specifically how communities benefit from wildland areas. Recreation researchers have devoted a great deal of effort to inventory an extensive list of individual experiences and benefits that result from recreation experiences (i.e. stress relief, environmental learning). A comparable list of community benefits should also be created. Initial identification of these community benefits has been conducted as part of the Ruby Canyon–Black Ridge and Minnesota State Park Benefits-based Management Pilot Studies (Borrie and Roggenbuck, 1995; Stein and Lee, 1995; Stein, 1997; Stein and Anderson, 1998; Stein et al., 1999), but more research needs to be done.

Also, community benefits research should incorporate wider samples of community residents. The pilot tests focused on key stakeholders within communities. These pilot tests did not include random samples of community residents. Future research should focus on eliciting desired community benefits from randomly selected groups of community residents. These people might have different perceptions and beliefs regarding how their community can and should benefit from wildland recreation areas. Random samples will also allow researchers to test relationships identified in the BBM models (Brown, 1984; Bruns, 1993) using multivariate statistical techniques (i.e. factor and cluster analysis).

As wildland recreation areas are diverse, it is reasonable to assume that the community benefits they provide are also diverse. To date, very few pilot tests have been conducted in very few places across the country. Other areas of the country need to become involved in community benefits research. For example, heavily used parks such as the Great Smoky Mountains and Yellowstone might yield different sets of benefits from each other, as well as from those found in state parks in Minnesota or BLM lands in Colorado.

A more intensive look at the communities themselves is also needed. For example, community benefit research should examine whether different demographic groups within a community attain different sets of benefits from a recreation area. In addition, community characteristics probably influence the kinds of benefits a community might attain. For example, a town that lies just outside a wildland recreation area's boundary will probably receive a different set of benefits than a community 20 miles from the area. Characteristics such as distance, size, primary occupation, average age of residents and community function would all be useful indicators in defining appropriate and sustainable community benefits.

Environmental benefits research

The type of benefit which has received the least empirical attention among BBM researchers is the environmental benefit. The Canadian Parks and Recreation Federation (1997) has identified several perceived environmental benefits associated with recreation areas. Among these is that provision of parks, open spaces, and protected natural environments contribute to environmental health, environmental protection and an increased possibility of a healthy environmental future (Canadian Parks and Recreation Federation, 1997). Support continues to remain strong around the country for natural areas that protect water quality, species diversity, air quality and other important environmental features. Driver (1992) reminds us that one of the reasons for creation of federal wilderness areas listed in the 1964 Wilderness Act was to preserve areas that offered primitive types of recreation opportunities. Authors of this legislation saw the important link between recreation areas and protection of natural environments. The 1992 United Nations Conference on Environment and Development in Rio de Janeiro recognized a link between environmental quality and economic development (Callicott and Mumford, 1997). Economic development in some parts of the world is driven, at least partially, by a growing nature-based tourism industry. Recent ecosystem management lit-

erature has explored the relationships between human desires and needs, community economic needs and ecosystem health as essential components of implementing sustainable management regimes in natural areas (Jensen *et al.*, 1996; Callicott and Mumford, 1997; Grumbine, 1997).

Although these conceptual presentations of relationships between natural areas and environmental benefits are extremely important, empirical evidence to document the specific environmental benefits of given recreation areas is lacking in many cases. It is as important for researchers and managers to understand how a recreation area benefits the environment as it is to understand the personal, economic and community benefits. Furthermore, it is important to understand how the environmental benefits derived from a particular natural area are related to the production of personal, community and economic benefits. For example, does a wilderness area produce different personal and community benefits because it provides a series of environmental benefits that are different from other areas or does the wilderness area produce different personal and community benefits simply because it is more remote and rugged than a state park adjacent to an interstate highway? Research understanding these relationships is important to the development of sustainable management objectives and monitoring approaches to measure the ecological health of natural areas managed for recreation. Additional research on the environmental benefits associated with recreation areas can also be used by policy makers as they consider establishment of new recreation areas and preservation of existing recreation areas.

Concluding Remarks

Research efforts in BBM continue to yield positive results. Planners and managers are enthusiastic about implementing, monitoring and evaluating BBM plans. Wildland recreation visitors and residents of communities near wildland recreation areas are eager to participate in efforts to identify desired benefit opportunities, as well as work with planners and managers to provide those opportunities. Researchers, planners, and managers should continue their efforts to work with visitors and communities in the identification and production of benefit opportunities in wildland recreation areas. They should especially look for ways to improve public participation in BBM decision making. Improving methods of gathering public input and analysing public input will result in a better understanding of the relationship between visitors and communities and the resource. It will also result in a better knowledge base for managing public lands.

Part IV

Evaluation and Valuation: Determining How Valuable the Resources Are and What is Happening to Them

---

19

Trends in Leisure Value and Valuation

George L. Peterson and John B. Loomis

Introduction

This chapter explores trends in the eco-nomic value of outdoor recreation, with emphasis on public land-based recreation not traded in markets. We first establish a background of value concepts to avoid mis-understanding about what monetary value does and does not measure. Confusion about such concepts frequently causes needless debate about economics. The chapter then investigates trends in recreation value issues, trends in the development of meth-ods for estimating the economic value of recreation, and trends in empirical esti-mates. The concluding section summarizes the main points of the chapter and then discusses where the trends in recreation value and valuation methodology are likely to go in the future.

Background Concepts and Definitions

Value as preference and appreciation

As far as public land management policy is concerned, 'value' is an expression of human preference and appreciation. One might argue that natural resources have functional value to nonhuman species or relative to abstract philosophical maxims, but only values justified by sovereign human preference as expressed through

legitimate political, economic, and legal institutions are relevant to public land man-agement policy. As stated by Santayana (1896):

> We may therefore at once assert this axiom, important for all moral philosophy and fatal to certain stubborn incoherences of thought, that there is no value apart from some appreciation of it, and no good apart from some preference of it before its absence or opposite ... Or, as Spinoza clearly expresses it, we desire nothing because it is good, but it is good only because we desire it.

Aristotle (320 BC) complicates the question, however, when he observes,

> As every knowledge and moral purpose aspires to some good, what is in our view the good at which the political science aims, and what is the highest of all practical goods? As to its name there is, I may say, a general agreement. The masses and the cultured classes agree in calling it happiness, and conceive that 'to live well' or 'to do well' is the same thing as 'to be happy'. But as to the nature of happiness they do not agree.

Preference and the value it creates are in the eye of the beholder. Some might argue that value is absolute as defined, for example, by the preferences of god or by virtue of some absolute framework of morality or truth.

One that holds such a view is but one among many, however, who may not agree.

Individual versus collective preference

Human preferences express values both individually and collectively. Individual preferences create the 'short run' or everyday framework of personal values, such as find expression in recreational choices, market transactions and voting booths. The short-run values operate within the enablements and constraints created by the institutionalized 'long-run' value structure of society, as produced by expression of collective preference through law, politics and cultural tradition. Short-run preferences thus generate economic values within the boundaries established by the social contract created by collective preference.

The several facets of individual value

Individual values take many different forms, not all of which can be captured in an economic framework. Failure to differentiate among these concepts often confuses discussion of economic value.

Aesthetic and moral value

Santayana (1896) distinguishes between aesthetic and moral value. *Aesthetic* value is intrinsic in the experience as an end in itself, whereas *moral* value is something instrumental to avoidance of evil or attainment of a higher or future good that may require sacrifice of present pleasure. Economic values may be aesthetic or moral. Also, economic values created by final demand and aesthetic values are similar in that they are an end in themselves. Values generated by intermediate demand and moral values are similar in that they are a means to an end other than self. Moral value is also of direct relevance to recreation as it pertains to the trade-off between work and leisure. Is outdoor recreation a pure consumption of pleasure without productive return, or does it lead to personal and social benefits that make it a productive investment?

Operative, conceived and object value

Morris (1956) classifies values as operative, conceived and object. *Operative* value is the domain of the preferred as implied and justified by the actual choices people make. *Conceived* value concerns what one believes is preferable, despite whether it actually is preferred by operative choice. *Object* value is 'concerned with what is preferable (or 'desirable') regardless of whether it is in fact preferred or conceived as preferable'. For example, a person whose highest priority is long and healthy life may choose to consume too much red meat high in cholesterol (operative value) as a matter of taste and/or obsessive-compulsive behaviour while believing that other dietary choices are preferable (conceived value). They may be misinformed, however, about what dietary choices actually promote long and healthy life. The choices that are, in fact, preferable, given the persons' highest priority, are object values. Economic values as expressed in markets or market-like situations are strictly operative, being justified by consumer sovereignty as the outcome of consumer choice. If the context in which one expresses preference or makes a choice places the person in the role of citizen or agent of another's interests rather than a consumer, the result may be conceived value (Blamey, 1995; Sen, 1977).

De jure and de facto value

Preferences based on legally defined sovereign rights justify *de jure* value. The rights and powers that justify such values vary from society to society, depending on the governing institutions. People also may have preferences that are not based on sovereign rights or effective powers, however. Such preferences yield *de facto* values that are important to people, but policy generally ignores them until they find expression by effective legal or political means. Economic values may be either de jure or de facto. If the question is one of legal rights, only de jure value is relevant. If, however, the question is about actual economic welfare, de facto values also are relevant.

Direct and derived value

Human preference assigns *direct* value to the preferred object. The direct preference also assigns *derived* value to objects or conditions on which the preferred object depends by functional relationship, even when the person expressing the preference is not aware of that relationship. For example, good health depends, among other things, on a sufficient intake of vitamin C. Vitamin C therefore derives value from preference for good health regardless of whether vitamin C is an object of direct preference. Because sailors in ancient times were not aware of the functional dependence of good health on vitamin C, they often contracted scurvy.

Derived value is the focus of much uncertainty in natural resource management because of the extreme and poorly understood complexity of the ecosystems in which we participate. In recognition of this uncertainty, the precautionary principle (Taylor, 1991; Haigh, 1993) is finding application in policy around the world. For example, the Endangered Species Act (1973) assigns direct value to endangered species in the US as an expression of collective preference, while also assigning derived value to the environmental conditions and processes on which they depend. Operative, conceived and object values all generate derived values, which coincide only in the presence of perfect information and rational preference. Derived value will be external to economic accounts when the individuals having the preferences that create the derived value are not aware of the functional relationship.

Intrinsic value

Biologists and ethical philosophers sometimes refer to *intrinsic* value as independent of human appreciation. They may mean thereby their own conceived values, or they may have posited a philosophical criterion of value other than human preference, such as a philosophical maxim, or what they believe to be the preference of God, nature or nonhuman species. For example, one argument is that genetic information produced by millennia of genetic experimentation has intrinsic value because we cannot replace it if lost. Another is that nonhuman species have rights that validate nonanthropocen-

tric values. A third argument is that the power humans have to save or destroy other species creates an ethical duty to exercise that power in benevolent ways (Rolston, 1981, 1985, 1994). Such values are preference-based for those who hold them, but as with any personal preference, there may be no legally defined rights to support them and they may lack collective justification at the level of sovereign public policy. They are nevertheless part of the broader tapestry of human values. Economists sometimes refer to existence value or, more broadly, non-use or passive use value, as 'intrinsic'. This economic concept of intrinsic value is, however, strictly operative and based on human preference.

Normative value

A value advocated by one agent as a standard or norm by which to judge the desirability of something to a second agent is a *normative* value. For example, philosophers, theologians, educators or scientists might advocate certain criteria as values by which to judge the goodness or badness of human behaviour. Such values are normative with respect to public policy until adopted and validated by the sovereign authority of the society in question. They are also normative with respect to any individual whose preferences do not agree with those values. Even when lacking sovereign justification, however, normative value may be an important value component. It may be the product of specialized knowledge not shared by the people or their governing powers and therefore not yet incorporated in personal preference or canonized by political sovereignty. Keeping and advocating this value account is the domain of scientific, educational, philosophical and ecclesiastical institutions. It is an information system worth scrutinizing by those whose rights and lives may be affected, but it generally is external to economic accounts.

Marginal and total value

Marginal value is the value of one more or less unit of the thing in question. *Total* value is the value with versus without all units taken as a whole. A related concept is the value with versus without the function or service performed. If the thing in question is the only way to obtain the function, that is, if it has no substitutes, total value is the value of the function or service performed. The 'diamonds and water paradox' illustrates these concepts. Under normal conditions a single ornamental diamond is worth far more than a single drink of water. The total value of all ornamental diamonds is worth far less, however, than the total value of water. Life can continue very well without ornamental diamonds, but without water it ceases to exist. Failure to differentiate among marginal value, total value, and the value of the function or service performed is a common cause of confusion in economic debate.

Outdoor recreation benefit as a household production process

It is important to differentiate among the values of the outdoor recreation opportunities (sites, resources, facilities), the value of management of the opportunities, and the value of the recreation itself. Recreationists combine the opportunities and related management with time, travel, skills, personal equipment, and on-site activity in a household production process to obtain the benefits they seek, whether simple feelings of pleasure or productive outcomes such as physical fitness or skill development (Becker, 1965; Bockstael and McConnell, 1981, 1983). The value of recreation opportunity and management derive from the role opportunity plays in the process by which the recreationist produces the desired outcome.

The special case of economic value

Definition

Economic value is the amount of money one is willing to exchange for a good or service. As expressed through markets or market-like situations, it is strictly operative and justified by consumer sovereignty, that is, by human preference as the outcome of choice. It may be direct or indirect, but if the individuals or collectives assigning economic value by their preferences and choices are not aware of the dependency relationship,

the derived value will be external. Equilibrium between supply and demand (relative scarcity) determines marginal prices in a market economy. Personal values determine whether to accept the price and make a transaction.

Priced and nonpriced value

Markets establish marginal prices for things that have the characteristics of private goods, that is, are rival and excludable in consumption. A good is nonrival in consumption if consumption by one person does not diminish the amount of the good available for consumption by another person (e.g. a sunset). It is nonexcludable if the owner cannot prevent consumption by a person who refuses to pay. Markets fail to establish prices for things that are nonrival and/or nonexcludable in consumption, are exchanged in markets that are imperfect because of external or monopolistic diseconomy, or are nonpriced by policy choice. The market price also fails to measure changes in wellbeing brought about by a nonmarginal change in supply. Absence of efficient prices for things people value causes inefficiency and inequity in the allocation of resources, a condition economists call market failure (Randall, 1983).

The difference between financial and economic analysis

Financial analysis includes only direct monetary transactions. The purpose is to measure the financial efficiency of the agency, as with profit and loss statements and balance sheets in the private sector. Financial analysis accepts existing prices on face value and considers only the priced components of the transactions in question. *Economic* analysis is broader, however. It endeavours to include all nonpriced values as well as priced values in the analysis. The objective of economic analysis is to evaluate overall social well being, whereas the objective of financial analysis is to evaluate only the financial return to the agency or firm in question.

Economic analysis addresses two objectives, economic efficiency and economic equity. The economic efficiency objective asks whether the aggregate economic gain at the scale in question exceeds the aggregate economic loss, including nonpriced gains and losses, and without regard for who gains and who loses. The equity objective asks whether the distribution of gains and losses across society and over time is fair. Political conflict resolution decides the equity question, based on exposure of the distribution of economic gains and losses by economic analysis.

Nonpriced recreation value

Many outdoor recreation sites have unique natural features that make them attractive. They also tend to lack nearby substitutes. Such sites are locationally monopolistic with downward-sloping demand functions, as opposed to the horizontal demand functions that face firms in competitive markets. Left to the private sector and unregulated, such sites might be managed monopolistically for maximum profit, resulting in inefficient and inequitable allocation of economic costs and benefits. Government often steps into such situations to preserve the unique resources and correct the monopolistic diseconomy. The additional nonpriced economic benefits thus produced when the government charges an efficient price lower than the monopolistic price needs to be accounted in economic analysis. If the policy context is with versus without access to the site in question, additional nonpriced benefits accrue because closing the site would be a nonmarginal supply change and would impose a higher price in the form of additional travel cost for access to a substitute and/or lower quality and less satisfaction with what the substitute has to offer. Although access to public land is often excludable in theory, the managing agency might decide to provide recreation opportunity below the efficient (marginal cost) price or free of charge for social merit purposes, as with city parks.[1] Alternatively, access control and fee collection may cost more than the revenue obtained thereby.

Economic analysis should include as nonpriced value any money people would have been willing to pay if otherwise excluded. Nonpriced value increases economic wellbeing, because it is money people would have spent on recreation but can spend on other things while still enjoying the benefit of recreation access. This benefit is known in economics as consumer surplus or net willingness to pay (WTP). The analysis also should include any distributional or equity impacts of pricing policy (Walsh et al., 1989).

Trends in issues of management philosophy and policy

Increasing recognition of nonpriced value

A discussion of trends in valuation of outdoor recreation must include two components: (i) changes in issues of management philosophy and policy regarding the kinds of value to include and the process for including them, and (ii) trends in the values themselves and methods for measuring them. One of the most important trends in the first camp is increasing recognition that while monetary value is an important piece of the puzzle, it does not present the full picture. People often choose to participate in outdoor recreation because it attracts them or simply feels good. Why it feels good is often a mystery, even to the participants. They may give reasons for participation when queried in order to justify their choices, but the root causes of the attraction may be buried deeply in the psyche or even in the genome.

Development of benefit-based management

There are often many beneficial consequences that flow from participation in outdoor recreation (Driver et al., 1991a; 1996). Those benefits, which accrue either to the individual participants or to society as a whole or both, may not be the direct causes of the preferences that motivate choice. The participants may not even be aware of some benefits actually produced by their activity. If not, economic value as derived from their

---

[1] For a discussion of pricing policy for public outdoor recreation areas, see Rosenthal et al. (1984) and Walsh et al. (1989).

choices or expressed preferences will not measure the full or correct value of the activity. For example and metaphorically speaking, an economist will tell you that the 'value' of a given meal is the sum of money consumers are willing to pay for it, say US$15. A nutritionist, however, will dissect the meal into its nutritional consequences and explain the effects of those components on personal health. If the consumer's highest priority is good health while operative choice is based on taste in ignorance of the nutritionist's information, there will be dissonance between economic value and the value derived by functional relationship with the consumer's overriding preferences. Management of recreation resources to produce or facilitate production of beneficial outcomes is called 'Benefit-based Management' (Lee and Driver, 1996; Driver and Bruns, 1999). Recreation resource management theory is moving away from management of inputs and outputs toward management for beneficial outcomes.

Identification and measurement of recreation benefits

The nonpriced component of the economic value of outdoor recreation is difficult to measure. Available methods, including travel cost analysis and contingent valuation are not without controversy, even when done well, and doing them well can be expensive. In many situations, especially small-scale project-level decisions, the cost may not be justified. Other emerging philosophical and policy trends likely to continue into the future are: (i) scientific explanation of the benefits of leisure in the 'nutritionist' sense and (ii) development of noneconomic meaningful measures of the beneficial outcomes of public investment in outdoor recreation opportunity.

Trends in Economic Value and Valuation

Trends in recreation issues to be valued
Broadening measurement of economic value of recreation
During the infancy of recreation valuation, the first steps taken were simply to value

recreation currently taking place at existing recreation sites. These included reservoirs and national parks. Both the travel cost method and contingent valuation method were employed during this time. Quickly following this was application to the pressing recreation problems of the late 1960s and 1970s, evaluation of the benefits of proposed sites. This was a more challenging effort and the initial solution to this was the forerunner of benefit-transfer approaches: transferring of existing travel cost method demand curves from similar sites.

While these were relevant first steps, the retrenchment of the Federal government during the Republican era of the 1980s brought greater emphasis to improving the benefits of managing existing sites, rather than opening new sites. The 1980s saw the full development of multisite travel cost models. By pooling data across sites of varying quality, a coefficient on site quality could be estimated. Improved site management could then be visualized as shifting the demand curve for the recreation site outward. The area between the original site demand curve and the improved site demand curve, was the increase in visitors' net WTP for the improved site. Key quality parameters modelled were water quality (Smith and Desvousges, 1986) and fishing quality (Vaughan and Russell, 1982).

Increasing demand for recreation coupled with little or no increase in supply during the 1980s also brought the economic benefits of reducing congestion to the forefront of the research agenda. Unfortunately, the travel cost method is not well suited for valuing reductions in congestion. In part this is due to visitation being both the dependent variable and an indicator of congestion. However, the contingent valuation method was well suited to this task. Two approaches were used to value reductions in congestion: (i) estimating the value of existing recreation during peak and off-peak periods to isolate the higher benefits of reduced congestion (McConnell, 1977) and (ii) asking existing visitors how much they would pay for hypothetical reductions in congestion (Walsh and Gilliam, 1982).

Trends in economic valuation methods

Revealed preference or actual behaviour methods

The travel cost method was the first valid recreation valuation method developed. The formalization of this model is often credited to Clawson (1959b). Economists quickly embraced this method since it is essentially estimating a demand curve using cross-sectional observations of prices (travel costs) and quantities (trips). The first models used the available secondary data: grouping of trips taken by distance zones, hence the name zonal travel cost model. There were dozens of applications of this model from 1959 to 1973 for national parks (Clawson and Knetsch, 1966), reservoirs (Grubb and Goodwin, 1968; Cesario and Knetsch, 1976) and sport-fishing (Brown et al., 1964).

The concern over refining the price variable to include the opportunity cost of travel time, led to the development of the individual level travel cost method (Brown and Nawas, 1973; Martin et al., 1974). The focus on the individual level continues today in travel cost demand modelling. One reason for this is the closer tie of individual demand models to the consumer demand theory which describes individual behaviour. Unfortunately, applying simple regression techniques to individual data may result in biased coefficients that will overstate the consumer surplus or net WTP. As a result, some of the early individual observation studies produced some very large estimates of WTP (Martin et al., 1974). Individual observation models have survived because of the development of improved econometric models to better capture the subtleties of individual behaviour such as recreation participation and trip frequency.

The most elaborate of the individual level travel cost models are models of site choice. Borrowed from transportation planning, these multisite models account for site quality as well as quality and location of substitute sites (Morey, 1994). Because of the explicit accounting of substitute sites, these models often produce some of the lowest estimates of net WTP.

Contingent valuation

The other primary approach to valuation of recreation and recreation quality is the contingent valuation method (CVM). Davis (1963) is generally credited with the development of this method. Due to its reliance on stated WTP, rather than actual behaviour, CVM was slower to gain acceptance among economists. Early CVM analyses utilized an open-ended question format, asking visitors the maximum they would pay. This 'state your value' question format further engendered scepticism among economists. With the development of the dichotomous choice or 'take it or leave it' format (Bishop and Heberlein, 1979) and its formalization by Hanemann (1984), application of CVM studies mushroomed during the 1980s. The more market-like, price-taking behaviour coupled with the availability of qualitative choice statistical models such as logit and probit, helped to bring greater acceptance of CVM for measuring recreation use values.

Contingent behaviour

In the 1980s, a hybrid approach was first used by Walsh and Olyienk (1981) and Ward (1987) that involved asking visitors how they would change the number of trips they would make if site quality changed. The premise was that it was easier for visitors to state accurately how their number of trips would change in response to quality, than to express such a change in monetary terms.

Combining revealed and stated preference methods

Until the early 1990s, contingent valuation and travel cost methods were seen as competing approaches to measuring WTP. Studies looked at the convergent validity of the two methods (Bishop and Heberlein, 1979; Mitchell and Carson, 1989). Cameron (1992) suggested that contingent valuation and travel cost data could be used in a complementary way as each provided information on different aspects of the same preference mapping of visitors. That is, information about the vertical intercept of

Table 19.1. Comparison of economic value (US$1996) of selected outdoor recreation activities from three literature reviews.

Activity	Sorg and Loomis, 1984 (1965–1982)	Walsh et al., 1992 (1968–1988)	Loomis and Shrestha, 1998 (1977–1998)
Camping	22.83	25.82	51.65
Picnicking	26.53	22.95	48.06
Motor-boats	27.98	41.80	48.76
Float boats	53.05	64.47	39.21
Hiking	30.09	38.51	44.63
Skiing	47.23	37.74	21.25
Hunting	57.58	49.41	61.55

the demand curve might be more easily discovered using contingent valuation, while information about the horizontal intercept might be easily revealed with travel cost data. Today, there is a blossoming research programme in combining stated and revealed preference data (Adamowicz et al., 1994).

Trends in empirical estimates of the economic value of recreation: 1970–1997

Interest in summarizing the empirical literature dates back to Dwyer et al. (1977). However, the US Department of Agriculture (USDA) Forest Service has been one of the prime supporters of systematic summarization of the literature so as to provide economic values of recreation for the Resources Planning Act. One of the first published comprehensive summaries of the valuation literature was performed by Sorg and Loomis (1984). The next major update was by Walsh et al. (1992) and Smith and Kaoru (1990). This latter study only included travel cost method derived values so will not be used here.

In Table 19.1, we illustrate the moving average of inflation adjusted values for hunting (big game, small game and waterfowl), camping, picnicking, hiking and boating taken from the three main literature reviews performed to date. The first study is from Sorg and Loomis (1984) and the second from Walsh et al. (1992). The third literature review is an update of recent studies (largely since 1988) conducted by Loomis and Shres-

tha (1998). This data contains a few earlier studies obtained from previous unpublished literature reviews of McNair (1993).

Our results show that the value of camping, picnicking, motor-boating and hiking have increased over time. However, this is not a perfectly controlled comparison, because there have been methodological changes in the valuation techniques over this period and the composition of the recreation areas studied have changed. For example, in the case of hiking the more recent data of Loomis and Shrestha (1998) includes a study for a wilderness area in the southeast US. The scarcity of wilderness opportunities in the southeastern US makes wilderness hiking quite valuable. Skiing appears to have decreased in value since the more recent studies focused on cross-country rather than downhill (which the earlier studies concentrated on).

One of the innovations of the Walsh et al. (1992) and the Smith and Kaoru (1990) work was to summarize systematically the values in the literature using a statistical technique called META analysis that can control for the valuation methodology, and to a lesser extent the quality of the recreation site. This approach uses the value per day or trip recorded from the study as the dependent variable and characteristics of the study method and site as the independent variables.

This technique can provide us some insights regarding the trend in the economic value of recreation over time. For example, even after adjusting different years' study values for inflation, Walsh *et al.* (1992) found the values from the more recent period (1980–1988) were on average US$7.97 lower than those from the earlier period (1965–1979). Smith and Kaoru (1990) also found a negative time trend of US$2.50 in their study of travel cost method estimates over time.

These decreasing trends are in contrast to a META analysis on the Loomis and Shrestha (1998) data (Loomis *et al.*, 1998). This more recent effort which more fully accounts for recreation activity differences as well as for methodological differences and site composition effects found a small, but statistically significant positive time trend in value of recreation ($P = 0.003$). In particular they found the value increased by about US$1 a year (0.92 to be exact). There is nearly a 30-year time span in this data (10 years more than previous studies) and the sample is heavily weighted toward more recent studies of the last 10 years.

Implications for Management

The philosophy and policy of recreation resource management are moving away from focus on inputs and outputs to emphasis on beneficial outcomes. Important trends include: (i) recognition of nonpriced and derived values that are external to market mechanisms and traditional management methods; (ii) derived values that are often hidden from management and recreation participants behind a veil of complexity and ignorance; (iii) development of meaningful measures of recreation benefit by which to evaluate achievement of management objectives and customer satisfaction; and (iv) development of benefit-based management. These trends will both facilitate and require closer collaboration between research and management as we move into the future. They also will require more intense continuing education of managers and a greater willingness to reach out for new concepts and improved techniques. One of the most important and challenging opportunities will be to implement adaptive management

framed in the scientific method and executed through effective collaboration with research. As emerging trends in management philosophy and policy unfold, management increasingly will be an adventure in exploration of new territory. If properly documented and guided by the scientific method, innovative management actions can be a series of experiments by which to accumulate and apply new knowledge.

For example, recreation valuation has moved from simply providing the economic value of the current quality of recreation to being able to value changes in the quality of recreation experiences. Examples include increasing fishing catch rates and reducing congestion. Thus, managers have tools to evaluate the economic benefits of their management programmes aimed at improving the quality of recreation experiences. This same research provides empirical guidance on the benefits of limiting recreation use to within social carrying capacity of the recreation area.

Conclusion

Meaningful discussion of trends in the economic value of outdoor recreation requires clear understanding of the meaning of economic value. In this chapter we dissect the word 'value' into several components to identify the concepts that economic value does and does not include. As determined in markets and market-like situations, such as with market prices or measurement by travel cost analysis or contingent valuation, economic value is strictly operative, that is, the result of actual choices, and therefore may fail to capture conceived and object values, or philosophically based intrinsic or normative values. Because of imperfect information, it may also fail to capture important derived values created by hidden functional dependence of what people choose or prefer on other things.

An important philosophical trend in outdoor recreation value that digs into and beyond the foundation of economic value is what we have called the 'nutritional' approach. It is an approach that aims at better understanding of the deeper social, spiritual and experiential benefits. This approach is based on growing recognition of a need to manage recreation and recreation opportunity for production of beneficial outcomes, including but not limited to economic outcomes. It requires research to expose derived values that result from recreation choice and the production processes by which management actions affect outcomes. It also includes emphasis on education that helps customers and managers better understand the consequences of their choices.

The actual trend in the dollar value of recreation is often difficult to discern due to changes in the measurement methodology and the composition of recreation sites studied over time. Much as ecologists have begun to establish and monitor long-term ecological research sites, recreation analysis would benefit from establishing similar benchmark sites. By monitoring visitor use, visitor experiences and economic value at the same site with standard measurement methods, we may be better able to detect changes in the real economic value, as well as the deeper social, spiritual, and experiential benefits, of outdoor recreation.

20

New Developments in Measuring Tourism as an Area of Economic Activity

Stephen L.J. Smith

Introduction

Tourism has become a significant economic activity in a majority of the world's nations and is likely to continue to grow in the long term. The World Tourism Organization (WTO) (1998b, p. 4) suggests several reasons for this growth:

- Increasingly rapid, safe, and affordable transportation;
- Growing interest in learning more about other nations and cultures plus greater information on destinations; and
- Long-term increases in disposable incomes and discretionary time in some parts of the world.

Tourism induces social, environmental and economic change in the places frequented by visitors. While all types of change draw attention from policy analysts, economic impacts are arguably of greatest interest to most governments. The reason for this is that tourism has the potential to be a significant export commodity for a destination and thus a contributor to the Gross Domestic Product. Tourism is also a source of job creation, especially for individuals entering the labour force with limited skills.

Governments thus seek methods to monitor the economic magnitude and evolution of tourism. However, for the reasons described below, the measurement of tourism as an economic activity has been difficult. Most economic impact measures of tourism are ad hoc indicators based only on visitor survey data covering variables such as the number of trips and expenditures. These are sometimes supplemented with attempts to measure indirect and induced effects through so-called tourism multipliers. While such measures have been useful, they have certain weaknesses. In particular, they are usually developed independently of other, more general, systems of macroeconomic indicators, particularly Systems of National Accounts, the international convention for describing and measuring the magnitude and interrelationship of the industries that comprise national economies. Lacking any connection with Systems of National Accounts, it is not possible to make valid comparisons between the magnitude of tourism and traditional industries. Further, the lack of international consistency in the definition, collection and reporting of tourism economic indicators means international comparisons are not always reliable.

This chapter describes the evolution of a method that allows the measurement of tourism as an economic activity in a way that permits valid comparison with traditional industries. We begin with a brief description of the evolution of 'tourism' as a statistical concept. The reasons why tourism has defied measurement in Systems of National Accounts are then examined. Subsequent sections introduce the concept of a Tourism Satellite Account and describe extensions of Satellite Accounts into new tools for policy analysts and planners to make more informed decisions about the tourism industry. In brief, the trend in defining and measuring tourism has been toward: (i) international consensus in terminology; (ii) closer ties with standard measures of traditional industries; and (iii) growing precision and sophistication in measurement and analysis.

History of the Definition of Tourism and Related Terms

The English terms, 'tourism' and 'tourist', date from the late 18th or early 19th centuries. The second edition of the *Oxford English Dictionary* (1994) quotes a 1780 advertisement, *Ode to Genius of Lakes in North of England*: 'He throws the piece only into the way of actual tourists'. It also cites *Sporting Magazine* with the use of the word 'tourism' in an 1811 article: 'Sublime Cockney Tourism' to describe the new phenomenon of working class pleasure trips.

Tourism and tourist lacked any particular technical meaning until 1937 when the Committee of Statistical Experts of the League of Nations (OECD, 1973) proposed the first operational definition of 'international tourist': anyone visiting a country other that which is their usual residence for more than 24 h. The Committee explicitly excluded workers, migrants, commuters, students, and travellers who did not stop en route through a country on their way to another country.

Over the next few decades, a series of international statistical commissions refined the definition of tourist and related terms as well as introduced some new terms

to deal with various classes of visitors. In 1991, the International Conference on Travel and Tourism Statistics, held in Ottawa, reached a consensus on concepts and terminology that would: (i) offer worldwide practical application in both developing and developed nations; (ii) be as simple and clear as possible, and as consistent as possible in the world's major languages; (iii) provide the basis for consistency in international statistics; and (iv) permit integration with statistics drawn from Systems of National Accounts. Among the important advances at this conference was agreement on the very concept of tourism itself.

Tourism, the Conference delegates agreed, is the activities of persons travelling to and staying in places outside their usual environment for not more than one consecutive year for leisure, business and other purposes (WTO, 1994b). There are several important aspects of this definition. First, tourism is a demand-side concept; that is, the activity of the consumer is central to the concept, not the nature of commodities produced.

Second, tourism is more than just pleasure travel; it includes travel for many purposes as long as the primary purpose of travel is other than the pursuit of remuneration from within the place visited. Thus, business travel in the form of travel to conventions, installation and maintenance of equipment, corporate meetings, and sales calls in situations where the sales representative is paid by their company back home (rather than directly by remuneration from the person making the purchase) are tourism. Travel for medical reasons, pilgrimages, visiting friends and relatives, and many other personal purposes also are tourism. Not all forms of travel, though, are tourism. Travel for the purpose of commuting, to change residence, as well as travel by diplomats or members of the armed forces while on duty, refugees, nomads, and border workers are explicitly excluded from the definition of tourism.

The Problem of the Tourism Industry

For a group of businesses to be considered an 'industry', they must meet three criteria: (i) they must produce a relatively homogeneous product; (ii) they must use essentially the same technology; and (iii) the number of businesses and the financial value of their output must be substantial enough to merit statistical attention as a discrete sector.

These criteria imply the need for judgement as well as for the possible appearance and disappearance of industries as society, technology and economies evolve. Fifty years ago, there was no computer manufacturing industry. It is now a substantial one. A century ago, horse-drawn cart manufacturing was a significant employer and source of income. It is no longer recognized as a distinct industry.

While the number of businesses and the magnitude of their output is important, the matters of 'homogeneous product' and 'the same technology' are central to determining whether a group of businesses can be considered an industry. Variations in product or technology can be accommodated to a degree using a hierarchical model of 'industry'. One such hierarchical model is the North American Industrial Classification System (NAICS). This system consists of five levels for most industries, ranging from the highly general single-digit level (e.g. 1 = 'primary' industry, or the composite of agriculture, forestry, fishing and mining) through more precise five-digit industries.

For example, the growing of wheat is a five-digit industry (NAICS 11111). It is also part of a more general four-digit industry, 'grain and oilseed farming' (NAICS 1111). This, in turn, is part of a still more general three-digit industry, 'crop production' (NAICS 111). Crop production, combined with some other three-digit industries, constitute the comprehensive two-digit 'agriculture, fishing and forestry' industry (NAICS 11).

Given this malleable notion of industry, can one speak of a general tourism industry? To answer that, consider two familiar components of tourism: accommodation and transportation. While there is some variation in the range of accommodation service and technology – hotels and motels provide beds inside a permanent building, campgrounds provide space for sleeping out of doors or in a temporary shelter – all provide space for rest and sleeping, a more or less homogeneous product.

Transportation firms also offer, at a general level, a homogeneous product: movement of people. One can specify variations in product depending on the mode of travel – ground, air, water – but all involve moving people. So, can one combine accommodation, transportation, and other sectors into a comprehensive concept called the 'tourism industry?' The answer is, 'No, not in the conventional sense of industry'.

Although one often hears the phrase, 'tourism industry', in the context of policy analysis, lobbying and advocacy efforts, education, and destination marketing organizations, tourism is not an industry for two basic reasons. First, the differences in the product of accommodation firms (keeping people in one place) and that of transportation firms (moving people around) are too great to qualify as a homogeneous product. Second, tourism is fundamentally a demand-side concept, characterized by the activities of certain consumers. Industries are defined in terms of their products, not their customers. While the marketing literature (Medlik and Middleton, 1973; Jefferson and Lickorish, 1988; Smith, 1994) argues that, from the customer's perspective, a tourism experience should be viewed as a single, integrative experiential product involving the services of many businesses from the time the visitor leaves home to the time the visitor returns; traditional measures and definitions of industries do not accommodate this perspective. Tourism is something people do, not something an industry produces.

Interest in the economic importance of tourism has not disappeared in the absence of traditional macroeconomic measures related to tourism. So, as noted previously, tourism analysts developed ad hoc measures to estimate direct expenditures on accommodation, food and beverages, transportation, recreation and entertainment, and retail. Occasionally, attempts were also made to estimate the indirect and induced effects of tourism through the calculation of tourism multipliers. While some of these models have been widely accepted, the accuracy of the results were sometimes suspect, particularly with respect to multipliers. In no case could the results be meaningfully and reliably compared to data for conventional industries. This did not, however, stop some special interest and lobby organizations, such as the World Travel and Tourism Council (1995), from making unscientific claims that tourism is 'the world's largest industry'. None the less, the idiosyncratic methods such as those used by the World Travel and Tourism Council do not permit any valid comparisons between tourism and traditional industries or the magnitude of tourism among nations.

Given both the problems posed by the nature of tourism as a form of economic activity and the continuing need for credible and comparable measures of tourism as an area of economic activity, many groups and governments continued to press for new measures of tourism. In the middle of the 1980s, a new approach that could provide such information was being outlined by economists and statisticians in several nations – the Tourism Satellite Account.

The next section discusses the emergence of Satellite Accounts as an important trend in measuring tourism. However, before introducing the method, some key definitions and concepts need to be introduced.

Core Concepts and Definitions

Consumers engaged in tourism are *visitors*; visitors consist of *tourists*, who stay overnight, and *same-day visitors*, who do not. Although tourism is not defined in terms of the production of commodities, one can still speak of tourism commodities. In the context of measuring the economic magnitude of tourism, *tourism commodities* are goods and services for which a significant portion of demand comes from visitors. In the con-

text of Canada, 24 tourism commodities have been identified. These belong to the broad classes of transportation, accommodation, food and beverages, recreation and entertainment, and travel trade.

Tourism commodities are purchased not only by visitors but by local residents and others whose activities do not meet the definition of tourism. For example, individuals in the process of changing residences may stay at a hotel; diplomatic officials may travel by air. Visitors also purchase non-tourism commodities such as groceries, clothing, newspapers and books, and suntan lotion during their tourism activity. The bulk of the demand for these commodities, however, comes from people who are not involved in tourism at the time of the purchase.

Although there is no tourism industry in the conventional sense of the term, one can still speak of *tourism industries* as those industries that produce tourism commodities. In Canada, 16 tourism industries have been identified in the sectors of transportation, accommodation, food and beverages, recreation and entertainment, and travel trade. Although these appear to be the same categories as for commodities, the distinction between commodity and industry must be kept separate: industries produce commodities.

While industries are also defined by the primary commodity they produce, some tourism industries also produce nontourism commodities. Hotels sell, for example, clothing, dry-cleaning services, and telecommunication services. Some airlines sell duty-free gifts or rent electronic entertainment equipment (headphones for movies and recorded music). Conversely, some nontourism industries produce tourism commodities. Certain department stores sell meals and a few rent cars. Governments operate museums and attractions. This complex pattern of tourism industries producing tourism and nontourism commodities, as well as nontourism industries producing tourism and nontourism commodities has been a major hurdle to the measurement of the magnitude of tourism economic activity in a way that permits comparison to the output of traditional industries. Tourism Satellite Accounts provide a way over this hurdle.

A Brief History of Tourism Satellite Accounts

French statisticians, in the early 1980s, were the first to propose the concept that would become known as a Satellite Account. Their ideas were in response to the need to measure aspects of national economic activity that are inadequately identified in the System of National Accounts, such as tourism, transportation, education and health, or are completely ignored, such as the environment and household work. The WTO, too, called for the development of a new system to provide a 'uniform and comprehensive means of measurement [of tourism] and comparison with other sectors of the economy' (Secretary General, WTO, 1983). The goal of such a system was not just to permit interindustry comparisons within one nation, but to allow for greater harmonization and comparability of tourism statistics among nations. Recognizing their potential importance, the Organization for Economic Cooperation and Development (OECD) also called for the development of Tourism Satellite Accounts and developed recommendations for their construction (OECD, 1991, 1998b).

In North America, the National Task Force on Tourism Data (1987) considered the idea of a Satellite Account and asked Statistics Canada to develop the concept further. A proposal was developed by Lapierre (1991) and presented to the 1991 Ottawa Conference. This proposal provided the basis for work within Statistics Canada that eventually resulted in the first phase of a working Satellite Account (Lapierre and Hayes, 1994). Also in 1994, the WTO presented a set of recommendations regarding tourism statistics, initially worked out at the 1991 Ottawa Conference, to the United Nations for acceptance.

Over the next few years the WTO released increasingly refined drafts of *A Satellite Account for Tourism* that describes the features of Satellite Accounts, the concepts and definitions needed for these accounts, principles for recording data, the basic structure of Satellite Accounts and possible extensions of these accounts (WTO, 1998b). These drafts incorporate the basic principles and design features of the Canadian Satellite Account as the recommended model for Accounts in other nations. In addition to Canada; Australia, the Dominican Republic, France, New Zealand, Norway, Poland, Spain, Sweden and the US have or are actively developing their own Satellite Accounts.

What is a Tourism Satellite Account?

At a simplistic level, a Tourism Satellite Account is a method for creating a synthetic tourism industry by combining the bits and pieces of conventional industries that produce tourism commodities. The term, 'satellite', indicates this method is an extension of the System of National Accounts. More technically, a Satellite Account is a comprehensive, multilayered information system that collects, orders and interrelates statistics describing all significant quantitative aspects of tourism.

The Satellite Account creates a tourism dimension in the input–output framework of the System of National Accounts. The input–output framework is, in effect, a series of matrices in which the inputs consumed by every industry from the outputs of all industries are identified and measured. The Satellite Account provides a method whereby a synthetic industry known as 'tourism' can be extracted from the System of National Accounts.

The linkage of a Satellite Account with the System of National Accounts provides two essential qualities. First, it means that estimates of the size (outputs) of tourism can, for the first time, be reliably and consistently compared to the size of traditional industries. No other approach to measuring the size of the tourism industry provides tourism data that can be consistently and accurately compared to data from other industries.

Secondly, input–output matrices balance. The total output of any industry is equal to the total inputs from that industry by all consumers of that output. The System of National Accounts thus provides a discipline that prevents under- or overestimation of the size of any industry.

A key element in the interpolation of this synthetic tourism industry is the estimation of tourism ratios. *Tourism ratios* are the percentage of each tourism commodity consumed by individuals (visitors) engaged in tourism. These ratios are estimated based on detailed household and consumer surveys of family expenditures as well as travel expenditures; these are supplemented by business surveys collecting operating costs for various types of businesses.

It should be emphasized that tourism ratios and the Satellite Account itself focus on expenditures by individuals, businesses and governments made directly in support of individual trips. Capital expenditures for items like roads, airports, aircraft and motor coaches are not considered. Such expenditures support the development of the tourism industry and make tourism possible, but they are not considered part of the tourism industry, *per se*. Recall the definition of tourism: the activities of persons temporarily away from their usual environment. Again, this is a demand-side concept; capital expenditures are associated with production or the supply side. Expenditures by governments on the operations of tourism services such as travel information centres or campgrounds are also not part of the Satellite Account. As Meis and Lapierre (1995) explain:

> this is an important point. Canada's TSA [Tourism Satellite Account] currently measures tourism's economic importance relative to 'business sector GDP [Gross Domestic Product]'. This is ... 'all transactions who produce goods and services for sale at a price that is intended to cover the cost of production. These include corporations, unincorporated business enterprises, independent professional practitioners, and government business enterprises ... This means that the measure of GDP used in the TSA is not

the same as the broader measure more usually used in national accounting, and that includes capital investment and the government sector.

An Overview of Tourism Satellite Account Methodology

The Satellite Account starts with expenditures and receipts for tourism industries. These are then classified as exports, imports or as personal expenditures. Expenditure and receipt data are derived from various household and business surveys, the Consumer Price Index and the National Accounts themselves. The data are then allocated by appropriate commodity and industry categories. Finally, the complex flows of tourism commodities among various producers and consumers are captured through the use of the input–output matrices. Finally, the Gross Domestic Product contribution of tourism activity is estimated.

Issues and Limitations in the Current Satellite Account

Timeliness

Satellite Accounts are data and labour intensive. They not only require extensive amounts of precise and reliable data related to production and consumption of certain commodities, they are developed as an extension of a nation's economic input–output matrices, which are even more data and labour intensive. As a result, there is an inevitable lag between the collection of data and the development of a Satellite Account. Because the Canadian input–output matrices are updated only every 4 years, the Satellite Account is also updated only every 4 years. From an analytical perspective, this lag is not likely to be as serious as one might assume. The critical aspects of input–output matrices are the fundamental relationships among industries in terms of production and consumption. These basic relationships usually do not change dramatically over a few years. However, in terms of providing information for decision makers to use in policy analysis, planning and assessing the performance of tourism industries, much more current data are required. New tools (the National Tourism Indicators, described below) combining the structural insights of the Satellite Account with more current data, have been developed to assist decision makers.

Pre- and post-trip expenditures

Currently the Satellite Account focuses on expenditures made only during a trip. However, trip-related expenditures are often made immediately before or after a trip, such as the purchase of photographic film and film developing. While many of these purchases are not tourism commodities, ideally estimates of such expenditures should be included in a Tourism Satellite Account. The challenge is one of developing reliable sources to obtain these estimates.

Consumer durables

The handling of personal capital or durable expenditures has been a matter of some debate. For example, the purchase of a boat is often clearly associated with tourism activity, but was not included in the original Satellite Account because the purchase of such items is not normally associated with a single trip. However, it is recognized that expenditures on consumer durables conceptually represent trip-related purchases and could be incorporated into a Satellite Account in some fashion, assuming the existence of accurate and reliable data sources. The following summarizes current proposals for the handling of two major categories of consumer durables.

Purchases of single-purpose vehicles

Purchases of items such as recreation vehicles, boats and snowmobiles will be prorated according to some tourism ratio reflecting the percentage of use of these items that meets the definition of tourism. This ratio is assumed to be in the 96–100% range for recreation vehicles; similar estimates will be made for other types of vehicles. Unlike purchases of airline tickets

or hotel rooms, though, estimates of the volume of expenditures on single-purpose vehicles will not be made at the level of the individual or household. Rather, some estimate will be developed reflecting total consumer spending on a single-purpose vehicle in any given year; the tourism ratio will then be applied to this aggregate figure.

Purchases of second homes or cottages

Unlike the purchase of vehicles, which is a form of personal consumption, the purchase of homes is considered a capital purchase. That is, the purchase of real estate is production, not consumption. This means that, to ensure that Satellite Account results remain comparable with the other outputs from the System of National Accounts, the purchase of second homes cannot be included as a consumer expense. However, the use of second homes and cottages do represent a form of consumption even if the value is only implicit because the owner does not pay rent to himself. Some estimate of the imputed rent for the use of private second homes and cottages outside the usual environment could be incorporated into a Satellite Account.

Beyond the Tourism Satellite Account

With the basic Satellite Account operational, several initiatives are under way that will extend its usefulness. Two of these are refinements to the Satellite Account itself: (i) an expanded labour market module, and (ii) creation of Provincial Accounts. Two other initiatives represent new analytical tools based on the Satellite Account: (i) the National Tourism Indicators, and (ii) the Tourism Economic Impact Model.

Employment estimates generated by the Satellite Account are derived based on total labour costs and average compensation rates paid in each sector. The results provide an estimate of the number of full-time equivalent positions in each tourism industry. The number of full-time equivalent positions is then prorated by the tourism ratio for each industry to provide an estimate of the number of jobs directly attributable to tourism. While this information is useful for certain policy purposes, industry and labour associations prefer to have an estimate of the total number of people employed, regardless of the number of hours worked per week or the number of weeks worked per year. Further, they are usually interested in the total number of people employed in each sector, unadjusted by the tourism ratio. The reason for this is, as some human resource leaders have, in effect, argued, 'We don't train full-time equivalents; full-time equivalents don't pay union dues. We deal with real people'. As a result, work is now proceeding on developing a *labour market module* within the framework of the Satellite Account that will provide data on part-time, full-time, seasonal and year-round employment, hours and wages. The module will allow an analyst to specify the level of aggregation or detail with respect to counting either jobs or employees.

Another request from provincial governments and industry leaders has been to create *Provincial Satellite Accounts*. There are substantial regional and provincial variations in the size, structure, and performance of tourism industries, so having data at only the national level fail to provide adequate insights into what is happening in different parts of the country. An unpublished feasibility study by the Income and Expenditure Accounts Division, Statistics Canada (1998) confirms that the creation of Provincial Accounts is technically possible, although restrictions on the availability of data and confidentiality concerns in some smaller provinces will mean that some industries, such as those in transportation, may be reported at only a highly general level (e.g. reported as 'transportation' rather than as specific forms of transportation).

As noted previously, there is a significant time lag in the release of new Satellite Account information. This means that Satellite Accounts are not useful for monitoring the performance of the tourism industries or tracking current changes in domestic and international volumes of travel. To provide this type of timely information, a new tool,

the *National Tourism Indicators*, was developed. The Indicators are based on the ratios and relationships identified in the Account, and combine these with data drawn from the visitor surveys to provide quarterly data within 75 days after the end of the reference quarter. The data cover more than 300 aspects of tourism demand, supply and employment.

The National Tourism Indicators have been extrapolated back to 1986, so it is now possible to examine a time series of data related to cycles in tourism supply and demand (Wilton, 1998). For example, the time series reveals that total tourism expenditures (seasonally adjusted, constant 1986 dollars) increased by 26%, two percentage points higher than the increase in the Gross Domestic Product. This supported a 22% increase in person-years of tourism employment, nearly twice the 12% increase in the overall business sector. An econometric analysis of the trend data also reveals that fluctuations in domestic tourism supply and demand closely follow the overall business cycle, but the amplitude of the tourism cycle is about 50% greater than the business cycle. In other words, domestic tourism replicates business cycle change, but with an amplified pattern (Wilton, 1998).

Finally, a national *Tourism Economic Impact Model* is under preparation. As described previously, the Satellite Account looks only at direct spending associated with tourism. The full impacts of tourism in a nation's economy, however, extend beyond direct spending. These impacts include indirect impacts, resulting from the purchase of goods and services by businesses that meet the needs of visitors, as well as induced impacts, resulting from wages and salaries paid to employees of tourism businesses. The impact model looks at direct and indirect, but not induced, effects.

One critical issue in the impact model is the matter of leakages. The purchase of imported items represent a loss of income – a leakage – from the business sector. Government revenues from, for example, admission charges for national parks, withdrawals from inventory, and sales taxes are other types of leakages. The impact model is designed to account for the impact of leakages on the overall economy as well as on tourism sectors.

The model makes a distinction between gross production and value added. Gross production is measured by the total revenue generated by an industry; it includes the purchase cost of goods produced by other industries as well as value added through processing. Looking only at gross production across several industries can result in double counting, because the output of one industry used as an input in a second industry will also appear in the value of the output of the second industry. The impact model separates gross production and value added to avoid this problem.

The model produces three types of multiplier: gross production, Gross Domestic Product and total impact. The *gross production multiplier* estimates the impact of a given increase in tourism expenditures on total output of the economy, including leakages associated with sales taxes. The *Gross Domestic Product multiplier* describes the impact on total value added from the same expenditure. This multiplier is normally less than one because of the existence of leakages (theoretically it could exceed one because subsidies are considered the opposite of taxes; thus a heavily subsidized industry, such as passenger rail travel, could have a Gross Domestic Product multiplier more than one). The *total impact multiplier* is the sum of direct and indirect effects, divided by the initial expenditure. This multiplier is always greater than one because it includes the value of the initial expenditure plus all the direct and indirect impacts.

The new impact model will allow users to specify alternative scenarios such as increased domestic demand or increased air travel to explore the impacts of such changes on specific sectors – say, accommodation, or recreation and entertainment. However, there also are some important limitations in the impact model. As noted, the model does not look at induced effects, nor is it able to estimate the impacts of non-economic events such as unusual weather, labour disruptions or currency exchange rates. The model does not address visitor motivations, demographics or predict or track the effectiveness of advertising.

The relationships among inputs and outputs across all sectors are assumed to be fixed. A given change in demand for some commodity, say a 5% increase, will be reflected in both a 5% increase in inputs into the production of that commodity and a 5% increase in the output of that commodity apportioned across all industries producing that commodity. In other words, the model assumes there are no: (i) limitations in supply; (ii) changes in prices resulting from changes in demand; (iii) changes in consumption patterns; and (iv) changes in productivity resulting from new technology or packaging. Finally, the model does not address the impacts on government spending or employment resulting from increased tourism revenues. On the other hand, impacts resulting from government activity, such as advertising, that result in an increase in tourism demand can be modelled.

Conclusion

For the first time, through development of Tourism Satellite Accounts, businesses and governments will have defensible, reliable measures of the true impact of tourism on an economy. The method has become the internationally accepted model for measuring the role of tourism in national economies. Satellite Accounts not only provide a deep, quantitative understanding of the nature and structure of tourism, they also provide the basis for tracking the performance of the various sectors of tourism as well as their very evolution. The full impact on governmental policies has yet to be realized, but Tourism Satellite Accounts represent a revolution in how governments measure, and thus perceive, tourism.

Despite recent success in creating these Accounts, much work remains to be done. Satellite Accounts and supporting statistical systems still have to be developed in the majority of nations. Those nations that have operating Accounts need to improve further the reliability and accuracy of the data that feed their Accounts. Work still needs to be done to implement, update, refine and expand the basic definitions and classifications of tourism supply and demand included in the *Recommendations on Tourism Statistics* (WTO, 1994b). The development of tools to extend the results of Satellite Accounts to industry, such as the development and publication of industry productivity and performance benchmarks, also are needed to ensure the development and maintenance of political support for Satellite Accounts.

With respect to the issue of maintenance, it must be emphasized that Satellite Accounts are not one-time studies. They should become a fundamental managerial and policy tool for governments and industry. They thus require regular updating and a reliable, credible, and stable statistical system. Tourism has become an economic activity of strategic importance in many nations; it is timely that tools are now being developed to provide tourism analysts and policy makers with information to ensure its continued contribution to economic growth. It is not possible to provide general estimates of the cost of creating a Satellite Account. Cost is, in part, a function of the extent and quality of existing data sources as well as a variety of technical decisions related to the scope of the Satellite Account a nation chooses to develop. These matters are beyond the scope of this brief chapter; however, Satellite Accounts are expensive. In the long run, though, the cost of ignorance and misinformation about the true value of tourism in an economy is likely to be even greater.

21

Trends in Tourism Economic Impact Estimation Methods

Daniel L. Erkkila

Introduction

Many approaches exist for quantifying tourism and travel impacts on regional economies of all sizes. Demand for economic impact information seems to have increased in the 1990s at the same pace as industry growth itself and consumers of impact information can be found everywhere, from public sector agencies at all levels of government (and nongovernmental organizations) to private sector clients. Suppliers of tourism economic impact information are growing in numbers as well and their make-up is nearly as diverse as the consumers. Today, regardless of whether you are a consumer or supplier of tourism economic impact information, you probably will not be severely limited by method, data or tools. That may not have been true 15–20 years ago.

This treatment touches on the main tools used and reported by analysts and summarizes research findings, paying close attention to the most often cited advantages and limitations of various estimation methods. References are made for the reader who would like to follow up on details or examples. Most of the principal methods emerged outside tourism, accounting for the number of nontourism sources reported.

Historical Issues

For a variety of reasons, information from tourism economic impact studies is often criticized and dismissed by decision makers as lacking credibility. This is probably less the case today than in years past and to some degree may be closely tied to tourism's increasing visibility on Main Street in general. Regardless, as tourism's image and stock among economic development officials grew, thereby diffusing some economic impact credibility concerns, problems still arose because of the highly technical nature of the models used. Also, the use of national data as a proxy for local survey data, and the significantly different answers produced when different models were used to solve similar questions, often combined to confuse policy makers being 'educated' about tourism as an economic engine. Ongoing structural differences between models used, databases and applications also contributed to planning confusion.

Probably the most significant and longest standing issue facing planners is the fact that estimation of the economic impacts of tourism is difficult because tourism and travel as an industry does not cluster for quantitative analysis as neatly as nearly all other industrial sectors of an economy. Industry is categorized into similar types by

© CAB International 2000. *Trends in Outdoor Recreation, Leisure and Tourism*
(eds W.C. Gartner and D.W. Lime)

the North American Industry Classification System (NAICS), currently replacing the US Standard Industrial Classification system. These categories are used for economic estimation analyses. Tourism, however, is not classified as a unique industry. Tourists spend their money, for example, at gas stations, local restaurants and motels. The codes used to classify these activities aggregate them into broad categories. For example, gas stations are classed with gross sales for all wholesale and retail petroleum products, restaurants are classed with all restaurants and bars, and motels are classed with all types of lodging. Determining what percentage of these expenditures is the result of tourism and separating out consumption by tourists, local residents and business travellers has been a significant analytical problem. Current national data collection methods do not adequately account for most of the activities collectively attributed to the tourism and travel industry.

Defining what is to be measured within an economic impact study is another factor that influences the results. Just what defines a 'tourist' varies widely. Definitions which impose minimum distances travelled or overnight stays will lead to different impact estimates than definitions which define a tourist as 'anyone travelling anywhere for any length of time' (Fleming and Toepper, 1990). Some even question whether tourism is an industry to be analysed as such, or rather as a market (Wilson, 1998).

Estimation Methods[1]

Visitor spending generates immediate, *direct* or primary benefits to the firms and communities where the visitors are staying, in the form of travel-related payroll income, jobs and taxes. Their spending also generates secondary benefits to the community's economy, the summation of indirect and induced benefits. Firms generate *indirect* benefits to the community as buyers and sellers of goods and services

from suppliers within the economic area to support their businesses. These purchases generate additional output. Those suppliers purchase goods and services from additional suppliers and the chain of purchasing and selling continues until the initial tourist purchase completely leaks out. Leakage describes economic benefits accruing to industries outside the target area due to importation of goods. Finally, payroll income received by all employees in the economic chain represent *induced* benefits that fuel household spending. In simplistic terms, then, a community's economic well being is enhanced by generating high levels of primary (direct) and secondary (indirect and induced) benefits while minimizing leakages. Additional background and reference may be found in Frechtling (1994a,b).

This chapter focuses on trends in methods for estimating the full range of economic benefits (primary and secondary) that flow from tourism activity. First, however, it is worth commenting on the methods aimed at measuring primary benefits.

Primary benefit measurement methods

Probably the most well known model for tracking statewide traveller spending has been the Travel Economic Impact Model (TEIM) devised by the US Travel Data Center (Frechtling, 1994b). Described as a cost factor approach, individual state estimates of employment, payroll and tax revenues generated by travel spending were reported. TEIM estimates were derived from national survey data on travel activity. TEIM direct impact estimates frequently became the data source for subsequent secondary benefit analyses.

Other methods covered by Frechtling (1994b) include direct observation, bank return, residual receipts, seasonal differences, supply-side judgemental (i.e. tourism satellite accounts, discussed by Smith, Chapter 20), expenditure ratio and surveys. Each carries its own utility and limitations. Mail survey nonresponse bias and recall bias, for example, may limit data obtained through sample surveys of travellers for

---

[1] This discussion is taken from an earlier review by Erkkila and Penney (1994).

expenditure information. Researchers have discussed and devised a variety of approaches to avoid or overcome data collection issues, such as traveller diaries to overcome recall bias as suggested by Gartner and Hunt (1988) and Faulkner and Raybould (1995).

Multipliers

Economic impact estimation methods serve to produce multipliers which measure the relationship between an injection of (tourist) dollars into an economy and the amount of economic activity that results. Multipliers are used to measure changes in business transactions and output, income levels, government revenue, foreign exchange and employment (Archer, 1977, 1978; Archer and Fletcher, 1988). The magnitude of the multiplier will depend upon the pattern of the initial round of tourist spending and the extent of the region's economic base and linkages. The larger the region's economic base, the smaller the tendency to import and the larger the regional value added, the greater will be the multiplier (Var and Quayson, 1985).

Multipliers have been categorized according to what they measure. *Type I* multipliers are the sum of the direct and indirect effects divided by the direct effects. *Type II* multipliers are the result of the sum of the direct, indirect and induced effects divided by the direct effects. These multipliers are calculated for models that consider households as an industry. *Type III* multipliers are the result of the sum of the direct, indirect and induced effects divided by the direct effects generated by a change in final demand. Type III multipliers estimate induced effects based on the changes in employment and population.

Advantages

Multipliers are advantageous to planners and policy makers seeking to explain or make decisions concerning the economic wellbeing of their region. A multiplier is a single number by which tourism impacts may be traced through the myriad interactions of an economy. Chappelle (1985) has suggested that this number could be used to evaluate public and private projects and

investments. As it may be enlightening to know how much income, employment and taxes may be generated by tourism development, multipliers provide a straightforward approach to quantifying such development.

Limitations

Archer and Fletcher (1988) list four major weaknesses in multiplier analysis. First, the available data are inadequate to compile a detailed model of the economy, a limitation that applies to all estimation methods. Second, tourism expenditure data may be inaccurate or too aggregated for use in a detailed model. Third, many models assume, inaccurately, that additional expenditures generate exactly the same impact as previous expenditures, i.e. there is production linearity. Finally, most multiplier models assume incorrectly that sufficient spare capacity exists to meet the demands of additional tourist expenditure, which implies additional income, taxes, and so on. This results in an overestimate of the impact of additional expenditure. Chappelle (1985) cites concerns expressed by others that multipliers cannot be extrapolated to other situations or regions. He also points out that multipliers apply only to the next incremental change in the region's economic structure and must be recalculated after the changes have been introduced into the transaction or coefficients table. Also, multipliers derived from different units of measure (e.g. output, income or jobs) may rank prospective investments or projects differently, causing problems in planning.

Input–output analysis

In the past decade, input–output (I–O) analysis has arguably become the most prevalent approach to estimating tourism economic impacts. It has been used to analyse everything from coastal tourism (Pomeroy et al., 1988) to big city conventions (Braun, 1992) to birding (bird watching) festivals (Kim et al., 1998). In I–O analysis, the economy is disaggregated into industries and the flow of goods and services among them is examined. It measures the input required by an industry to produce a given output. A tourism I–O analysis, for example, would describe the quantitative relationships between tourism and different aspects of the economy, such as the number of jobs created, the wages paid, and the gross receipts produced by businesses. The I–O model can be used to estimate the income, employment and production required to satisfy a given level of tourism demand. In addition, the model can be used to generate multiplier estimates, which enables consideration of secondary benefits (Archer, 1977; Kottke, 1988; Frechtling, 1994b).

Survey-based I–O Models

Regional I–O models can be based upon survey-based data collection methods to detail industry transactions. While most researchers cited here believe survey-based I–O models to be the most accurate estimation procedure available, they admit they are expensive to construct and have been described as insufficiently detailed for use in tourism studies (Chappelle, 1985; Stevens and Rose, 1985). The costs and efforts required in compiling the data are usually more than a small area can afford (Bushnell and Hyle, 1985; Miller et al., 1989). Their high cost of construction probably explains their limited use.

Nonsurvey-based and hybrid I–O models

In response to primary data collection issues, analysts have worked to develop models based on nonsurvey methods or a combination of survey and nonsurvey data. Szyrmer (1989) views nonsurvey methods as one of the few alternatives to costly and time-consuming full-survey data collection methods. Nonsurvey regional I–O models are based upon national I–O tables adapted to derive I–O accounts for individual states or counties (Mak, 1989). At the national level, the Bureau of Economic Analysis (BEA), Department of Commerce, establishes the classifications and flows of payments that make up the national I–O model. Small area I–O models have been constructed and used at the state and local level. Some examples of regional models include Regional Input–Output Modeling System (RIMS II) by the US Department of Commerce, Automated Input–Output Mul-

tiplier System (AIMS), and Economic Impact Forecast System (EIFS) used by the Army Corps of Engineers (Bushnell and Hyle, 1985).

Models that combine survey with non-survey data, commonly called 'hybrids', may now be living up to what some researchers once predicted would be the most promising option for the future (Round, 1983; Richardson, 1985). Hybrid models employ primary data where it is critical to define or enhance the description of global tourism economic activity with existing secondary, structural data of other industry sectors. The analyst may be able to strike a reasonable compromise between the high cost of primary data collection and the issues associated with models built on secondary data. Archer and Fletcher (1996), for example, found that their hybrid model not only described foreign visitor impacts to a national economy but also produced data that showed that some markets produced higher returns from tourism expenditures than others – helpful information for marketers.

IMPLAN

Originally developed for and by the US Department of Agriculture (USDA) Forest Service, IMPLAN may be one of the most widely used I–O impact models in the US today, possibly because it has evolved from a mainframe application into a PC-based system. It is made up of software and 'reasonably priced' databases that allow users to craft regional I–O models for any county (or contiguous combination) in the US. Users can develop their own multipliers, create a hybrid model by changing system components such as production functions or trade flows, and generate custom reports as needed. Ease of desktop use, coupled with annual database updates to the national I–O table and state/county data sets probably explain expanded use of I–O analysis. A trend increasingly showing up in discussions of impacts, methods and analytical issues suggests that analysts are taking advantage of IMPLAN's availability. Johnson and Sullivan (1993) and Kim et al. (1998) show examples where IMPLAN provides a description of tourism economic impacts, as does Johnson and Moore (1993). Its use is increasing and its flaws are being reported along with mitigation measures that enhance analysis, as Leones *et al.* (1998) did regarding the Type III multiplier problems reported earlier (Charney and Leones, 1997).

Social accounting matrices (SAM)

The social accounting matrix, or SAM, is a special case of I–O model formulation that has emerged on the tourism impact scene. Traditional I–O models focus only on production activities, or industry gross outputs, in contribution to a set of final goods demanded. The SAM brings in information that allows welfare significance to be attached to the volume or value of gross output, including impacts on income distribution and factors of production (Bulmer-Thomas, 1982). Because a SAM will include more information than an I–O model, I–O models are actually a subset of the SAM. Wagner (1997) describes a regional SAM that provides tourism linkages among regional production and consumption of goods and services, in addition to the distribution and composition of income. His analysis brought out interrelationships between household spending and tourism investment. A different spin on hybrid models was created by West (1993) when he combined a SAM framework with an econometric model to look at tourism impacts in Australia. SAM capabilities are now a part of the IMPLAN system.

Advantages

Early on, practitioners have reported many advantages of I–O analysis as a realistic method of tourism assessment. Archer (1978) and Fleming and Toepper (1990) saw the ability of I–O to examine the leakages, the links between sectors, and the effects of change to be of great value to policy makers and planners. Fletcher (1989) saw the attention focused on sectoral interdependencies that exist in an economy and the flexibility of the structure as benefits. He also cited the capability of studying all levels of impact (i.e. direct, indirect and induced) as a

strength. Stevens and Rose (1985), Chappelle (1985) and Johnson *et al.* (1989) point out that the nonsurvey-based models are relatively inexpensive and highly detailed, which has made state or regional models devoted to tourism feasible. Chappelle (1985), Archer and Fletcher (1988) and Briassoulis (1991) cite I–O comprehensiveness and flexibility as advantages.

Limitations

The most common issue, documented by Stevens and Rose (1985), Chappelle (1985), Frechtling (1994b), and others has been the lack of a tourism sector. The lack of data forcing the use of national coefficients and the unreliability of available data are reported to be the major constraints (Archer, 1978; Bendavid-Val, 1983; Tyrrell, 1985; Szyrmer, 1989). Fletcher (1989) believes that most secondary data are unsuitable because they are rarely accurate at the level of detail needed. As a snapshot of a regional economy at one point in time, this static nature of the model limits impact analysis and forecasting (Weber, 1986), as lags between expenditures and multiplier effects are not measured. The assumption of linearity inherent in most models, where output increases the inputs of materials, services and factors of production in the same proportions and from the same sources, is a questionable assumption. This assumption ignores the possible existence of economies of scale within sectors or the transfer to different suppliers (Bendavid-Val, 1983; Frechtling, 1994b). Kottke (1988) sees the I–O approach with aggregates of entire industries rather than a set of firms as a drawback, which also makes the feasibility of municipal level analysis questionable. He also finds that results are not easily translated into applied recommendations. Trends in research continue to uncover ways to overcome many of the deficiencies of I–O modelling (Maki, 1997) and will help to improve impact estimates derived from this method.

Econometric methods

A regional econometric model is a set of equations describing the economic structure of a regional economy such as a state, province or metropolitan area. The parameters of the equations are estimated by regression equations, as distinct from an I–O model in which parameters are based on single point observations. The equations are grouped in categories which reflect the economic theory as applied to, for example, product markets, labour markets, firm behaviour, government behaviour and migration (Bolton, 1991). Econometric models are often multiple-equation systems that describe a regional economy's structure and they can be used to forecast income, employment, and other economic indicators. They employ time–series data (Leitch and Leistritz, 1985) and many econometric models incorporate I–O subsectors (Weber, 1986).

Computable general equilibrium (CGE) models are one type of econometric tool that has been around for some time but has not appeared to find wide acceptance or use outside academic circles. Zhou *et al.* (1997) constructed a CGE model and compared tourism impacts against a similarly framed I–O model to evaluate differences. State agency clients and others have applied the REMI (Regional Economic Models, Inc.) model to tourism policy, investment and impact issues. REMI incorporates both dynamic, econometric components with an imbedded I–O interindustry structure (Treyz *et al.*, 1992; Treyz, 1995).

Advantages

Because making I–O model technical coefficients dynamic is difficult, their usefulness as a forecasting tool is limited (Briassoulis, 1991). The advantage here goes to econometric models, which are much more attuned to forecasting long-term changes in an economy (Perryman and Schmidt, 1986). Leitch and Leistritz (1985) state that econometric approaches to multiplier estimation can accommodate a vast array of factors that include local and nonlocal data. Their use in estimating regional multipliers is rigorous, sophisticated, and their ability to establish confidence limits imparts credibility. Econometric study has also resulted in evaluating the relationship between an independent variable, such as price or income, and dependent variables (i.e. elasticities). Eadington and Redman (1991) have demonstrated several tourism applications, showing, for example, that tourist expenditures are income elastic and thus sensitive to income change. They also applied an expenditure allocation model, a type of econometric model that creates a system of demand equations, to traveller-spending decision making, showing how a consumer will distribute expenditures among goods, given the prices of those goods.

Limitations

Econometric models suffer the same fate as other forms of analysis – lack of data. In most developed nations, there is abundant data for national model building, but data for regional models are limited or scarce and, when available, are rarely from a unified source. Time series and cross-sectional data exist for national levels, but are scarce for regional areas (Leitch and Leistritz, 1985; Perryman and Schmidt, 1986). The lack of investment and export and import data is normally an obstacle to estimation of these components in regional models. Regional output data are weak or missing outside manufacturing, so analysts must resort to controversial methods to predict total gross regional product. Leitch and Leistritz (1985) point out that econometric approaches are not manageable by the lay public and require advanced technical knowledge for interpretation.

Economic base analysis

Economic base analysis is the simplest model of economic theory. The approach divides the local economy into two segments. The first unit, the basic, consists of firms that sell goods and services (exports) outside the region. The second, the nonbasic, consists of firms that supply goods and services to customers within the region. According to economic base theory, exports are assumed to be the prime mover of the local economy and consumer spending is considered to be related entirely to the level of regional activity (Leitch and Leistritz, 1985; Frechtling, 1994b).

Economic base theory holds that all economic activity can be classified as basic or nonbasic. Both sectors are related to exogenous demand, the basic sector directly and the nonbasic sector indirectly by supporting the basic sector. When exogenous demand for the exports of the regions increases, the basic sector expands. This generates an expansion in the supporting activities of the nonbasic sector. The level of nonbasic activity in a region is determined through a functional relationship with basic activity, known as the multiplier effect. It is expressed as the ratio of basic to total regional employment, population or income (Milon *et al.*, 1982; Bendavid-Val, 1983; Leitch and Leistritz, 1985). A variety of sources, like the US Census Bureau, provide the data for allocation of sales, employment and payroll figures among basic and nonbasic markets (Frechtling, 1994b). The location quotient is the most widely used method for measuring the economic base, followed closely by the minimum requirements technique. Location quotients delineate between basic and nonbasic components by summing the individual industry estimates of employment exports for each industry using a national frame of reference. The minimum requirements technique compares a region's employment structure with samples from similarly sized areas rather than a national frame of reference (Richardson, 1985). Economic base studies with a focus on tourism economies are not widely reported.

Advantages

Frechtling (1994b) and Leitch and Leistritz (1985) suggest several positive attributes about economic base analysis. Economic base models are the simplest and most inexpensive methods available. Analysis can be accomplished with a minimum of resources and within a very short period. If output, earnings and income data are consistent with one another, economic base models can produce consistent estimates. The model is easy to apply across varied areas and the input data needed are usually available on a timely basis. In addition, the model is efficient in using the available data. The size of the multiplier indicates the extent of

secondary employment generated by tourism, important in areas with extensive unemployment or in regions with a shortage of labour (Archer, 1978).

Limitations

Archer (1978) feels that economic base analysis has very little relevance to policy making and planning. He states 'the approach is theoretically unsound' because it depends on two unrealistic assumptions. First, all economic growth is treated as originating in the exogenous sectors, assuming growth is not possible in a closed economy. Second, all outside injections of money are considered to have the same multiplier effect upon the regional economy, whether the money comes from private, government or tourist activity. These assumptions have been shown to be incorrect by other forms of economic analysis. Frechtling (1994b) adds that other important variables to regional growth are not recognized in economic base studies, including interregional capital flows and technological changes. Leitch and Leistritz (1985) list model shortcomings as the following: oversimplified, assumes fixed relationships, neglects imports, savings and the balance of payments, fails to explain exports or inadequately estimates them, and neglects excess capacity.

Ad hoc models

Adaptation of the Keynesian income multiplier to estimating the income multiplier for travel expenditures was termed the 'ad hoc' multiplier by Archer (1978). Ad hoc models are concerned with, and developed for, a particular region or event. Ad hoc multipliers are relatively inexpensive in their data requirements and can be operated based on a sample survey of consumers and industry. The model can produce consistent results as long as the surveys are conducted uniformly. The ad hoc model must be constructed from the ground up for each area studied and requires technical and economic expertise (Frechtling, 1994b). Var and Quayson (1985) applied Archer's approach for tourist multipliers. Milne (1987) modified the ad hoc multiplier to derive differential multipliers and found them to be a suitable alternative to I–O models for regions or countries without the means to build I–O tables. The main weakness of ad hoc multipliers is their inadequate treatment of the induced effects.

Implications for Planning and Public Policy

While most data collection and modelling methods relating to economic impact estimation have been around for some time, their application to tourism economics have not. The focus of this review has been on methods and models. Observed trends in methods and their implications for tourism planning and public policy can be considered from the perspective of data, models and use.

Implications from data trends
Clearly the work on tourism satellite accounts has the greatest potential to affect planning and public policy issues. The ability to better explain tourism economic activity for subsequent modelling and analysis will improve development and investment alternative assessment and enhance policy maker choices. Process and data standardization will also help international assessments and reporting. The US Bureau of Economic Analysis' development of satellite accounts for benchmark I–O accounts of the US are based on recommendations by the Organization for Economic Cooperation and Development and the World Tourism Organization, which are also being adopted by other countries. Tourism satellite accounts linked with a SAM model will greatly strengthen tourism investment assessments, especially where welfare considerations are important. Study of the causal link between economic growth and employment and income distribution will add a rich dimension to economic evaluation of projects and programmes.

Overcoming definitional issues and research on data collection issues will also improve model impact assessments. Better traveller expenditure estimates and visitor counts, for example, will provide better front-end data for analyses where investment options are being assessed or public policy decisions are weighed in the balance.

Implications from model trends
Early tourism impact assessments were straightforward applications of a particular model applied to tourism economies. Two trends are observed: greater sophistication of models and more access to (and use of) proven approaches. Where hybrid models usually referred to I–O models that mixed survey and nonsurvey data structures, 'hybrid' could now apply to new approaches that 'conjoin' or link static I–O models to dynamic econometric tools. Applications of this technique are being reported in nontourism sectors (West, 1995; Rey, 1997) and tourism applications will no doubt follow. More sophisticated modelling, with the data enhancements predicted, could see models being tested for applications in tourism planning and public policy decision making.

More use of traditional methods, particularly I–O, have stemmed from technological advancements, like desktop computing. The IMPLAN model is an example where personal computers have not only made solving the matrix mathematics of I–O accounting simple, they have nearly made the analysis of regional economies a drag-and-drop exercise. On the plus side it brings powerful tools to more planning analyses and policy questions. On the negative side, not all users fully understand the tool they are wielding or the results they are reviewing.

Implications from use trends
Better data, more use, and greater model sophistication will certainly lead to broader application and consideration of tourism economic impact results in decision making. Tourism project evaluation methods such as benefit/cost analysis (Dwyer and Forsyth, 1998) and contingent valuation for nonmarket output valuation (Lundberg and Johnson, 1997) could be coupled with

improved economic impact assessments to portray broader and different economic perspectives of a specified regional touristic enterprise. For example, the USDA Forest Service was under attack by environmentalists for 'below cost' timber sales in the early 1980s. An argument was made that the programme in some regions had a negative cash flow only in a classic, financial sense. The agency responded by developing a reporting system that portrayed timber programme financial costs and revenues in an accounting framework, along with the economic benefits and costs (market and nonmarket) in an economic evaluation context and aggregate economic impacts from an I–O model. A similar approach may prove itself useful in providing different perspectives to the sustainability of tourism projects in regions around the country and world as public policy issues heat up in the years ahead.

Finally, a trend toward more serious questioning of the use of models and their results suggests maturation in the field that will also have implications on the kind and quality of analysis done for planning and policy making. Frechtling (1994a) sets out useful criteria for evaluating economic impact methods and determining their use. Further, Crompton and McKay (1994) and Crompton (1995) raise significant ethical questions about the use and misuse of tourism impact data that must be considered. Following these guidelines will greatly improve the quality of assessments and make them more credible to policy makers.

Conclusion

Many tourism economic impact estimation methods are available to an ever-increasing number of consumers desiring impact assessments. The most widely employed techniques appear to be those developed and tested to measure impacts from nontourism sectors of regional economies. The credible application of these and other approaches to tourism has been stymied primarily due to a lack of a data classification and collection system for tourism as a unique industry. The existing system in the US delineates and codifies economic activities and products by aggregating tourism as a service-based industry. This makes identifying expenditures and consumption by tourists and business travellers, separately from local residents, a significant analytical problem. Also, the lack of standard definitions for a tourist, visitor, or tourism's products and services, for example, has always further confused impact assessment.

Some impact estimation assessments focus only on the primary benefits from tourism, or the immediate, direct impacts that accrue to firms and communities in the form of travel-related expenditures. The Travel Economic Impact Model devised by the US Travel Data Center has been a visible example of a primary benefit estimation approach.

Most economic impact assessment methods expand the view, however, to include also the secondary benefits to the community's economy generated by tourist spending. Secondary benefits include the summation of indirect (interindustry transactions) and induced benefits (household payroll income). Multiplier analysis, I–O models and econometric methods are the most widely used techniques to describe the impacts of tourism development on regional economies. All have strengths and limitations in their application, which have been described earlier.

Implications from trends in data suggest that the development of tourism satellite accounts have the greatest potential to affect planning and policy issues relating to economic impact assessment. Standards for process and data definition will greatly enhance impact assessment because tourism will have its own set of product and activity codes for compilation into national data sets for further analysis. Two trends observed relating to impact estimation models include greater sophistication of models and more access to (and use of) proven approaches. Linking I–O models with econometric methods serves as an example of the direction tourism assessments may take. Trends in technological advancements, such as desktop computing, have made access to I–O models like IMPLAN easier. This brings a powerful tool to more planning analyses and policy questions but can lead to erroneous results if put in the hands of the untrained.

Finally, better data, more use and greater model sophistication will probably lead to broader application and consideration of tourism economic impact results in decision making. Furthermore, there has been a trend toward more serious questioning of the use of models and their results in the field; analysts have also suggested criteria for selecting models. Tourism economic impact estimation has matured from mere model demonstration exercises to introspective discussions of the ethical use of models and application results. This can only serve to greatly improve the quality of assessments and make them more credible to policy makers.

22

Holiday Styles and Tourist Types: Emerging New Concepts and Methodology

Sara Dolnicar and Josef A. Mazanec

Introduction

This chapter examines two trends regarding: (i) the way tourism managers are considering tourist typologies and (ii) the methods employed for constructing these typologies. The trends are briefly explained and evaluated in terms of scientific progress criteria. A case example is then presented to demonstrate the implications for tourism management.

Trends in Constructing and Using Tourist Typologies

During the last two decades, tourism researchers have modified their conceptual and methodological approaches towards constructing tourist typologies. Originally, it was the ambitious purpose of the psychologists, sociologists and anthropologists who studied tourist behaviour to construct a fundamental classification of tourists according to their basic motives. Famous examples are Eric Cohen's seminal publication on a sociological classification of tourist types (1972) which was not empirically tested until 1993 (Mo *et al.*, 1993). Equally prominent are Stanley Plog's (1974) distinction between 'allocentric' and 'psychocentric' travellers

(see also Plog, 1990; Smith, 1990a,b) and John Crompton's (1979) elaboration of push-and-pull factors. These terms are still popular today and have become household words in the contemporary study of tourism. Twenty years ago the providers of tourist services were still operating in a seller's market. They felt little need to adopt new concepts such as market segmentation based on lifestyle and psychographic research which had its first peak in the early 1970s (Wells, 1974). The situation changed when competitive pressure increased and marketing scientists entered the field, and tried to benefit from their experience in consumer markets and branded products. Marketing and, in its wake, tourism research gradually abandoned the idea of finding the all-purpose or the definitive only consumer/tourist typology. This development has favoured the refining of tourist typologies to make them instrumental for effective market operation. Even the theoretical underpinnings for constructing tourist typologies have evolved accordingly. Formerly, the tourist types were based on motives or on attitudes or on the activities pursued during their holiday. Nowadays, the type-defining (active) variables are collected from various sources of lifestyle (see the review of six typologies by Lowyck *et al.*, 1992). The concept of holiday style has emerged and offers a more complete framework for tailor-made tourist profiling. Researchers and practitioners have learned that there are numerous, or actually an infinity of, tourist typologies to serve specific marketing objectives. This is the first and conceptual trend.

At first glance, one may suspect that this trend is in contrast with the objective of scientific discovery. It is the common understanding that behavioural (and marketing) science aims at producing systems of explanatory hypotheses with the highest possible scope for generalizability. Thus, an accumulation of singularities – a special typology for each managerial decision situation – may fail to contribute to this long-term goal. But the crucial point is how to organize the process of generalization. This can be extremely cumbersome even in the most advanced and respected fields of science. The long-standing struggle of physicists to arrive at a Grand Unified Theory by integrating relativity and gravitational theory with quantum physics is a striking example (Hawking, 1980). In principle, tourism marketing research, despite being still in its infancy, suffers from the same problems. However, if it is true that the social sciences are condemned to be satisfied with only 'quasi-nomological' theories (Albert, 1957), there is no alternative to a two-step procedure: (i) first elaborate tailored models (small theories of limited empirical scope) for well-structured situations with precise antecedent conditions; (ii) then build a 'meta-theory' which points to the most promising explanatory models given the antecedents of a particular application situation. This is exactly what the search for situation-specific typologies aims to accomplish.

When the concepts evolve, the data-processing tools have to follow suit. More and more tourism managers expect their market research specialists to provide new segmentation (typology) results at short intervals. Therefore, a reasonable balance between the degree of sophistication and the ease of application is required for segmentation methods. In particular, the range for subjective judgement in the traditional clustering methods must be reduced. There are two directions where methodology improvements are sought. One is parametric and relies heavily on the development of general linear mixture models. The current state-of-the-art is perfectly covered by Wedel and Kamakura (1998). In addition to this mainstream segmentation methodology, it is tempting to foster a radically different line of research which is non-parametric and completely disposes of the rigorous distributional assumptions required for mixture models. These methods build on adaptive (data-driven) partitioning and exact (permutation) tests. Comprehensive documentation is under way.[1] Preliminary results are presented in Dolnicar et al. (1998). (Readers interested in a more rigorous treatment of the adaptivity issue are referred to the Appendix.) The contemporary improvement in methodology is the second major trend in segmentation and typology construction.

Understanding the New Marketing View of Consumer/Tourist Typologies

From the marketing point of view, a tourist typology represents a way of segmenting a travel market. The concept of 'types' implies a number of integrated personal and behavioural characteristics. As the structure of these segments is not known until some fairly sophisticated analysis has been performed, the exercise is called 'a-posteriori segmentation' in marketing jargon. The crucial point is that producing typologies is part of regular strategic planning. It depends on the marketing objectives and creates a strategic advantage for the company or destination operating a segmentation scheme more cleverly designed than those of its competitors. The rule of the game is simple: you are expected to invent your own

---

[1] See the web site of the Joint Research Programme on Adaptive Systems for applications in other areas of management science (http://www.wu-wien.ac.at/am/).

segments and be the first one to offer them a customized product! A-posteriori segmentation rests on the assumption that subgroups in a consumer population are homogeneous in terms of motives, attitudes and/or activities. This mental and behavioural homogeneity is likely to make them react to product offerings and promotional efforts in a similar way. The earliest approach to mastering such a market situation was known as 'benefit segmentation', introduced by Haley (1968). He argued that consumer groups seeking markedly different patterns of benefits should be considered to be natural segments in the market. From a behavioural science point of view, the notion of 'benefit' relates to the more general concept of 'attitude'. Benefits desired or expected are attitudes toward particular consumption goals – a well-known conceptualization since the Rosenberg (1967) perceived-instrumentality/value-importance-based model of attitude measurement.

Trends in the Foundation of Market Segments: From Types to Styles

Tourist types may be derived from survey data on travel motives, attitudes toward a destination (attraction), benefits sought or activities. Holiday styles are travel-related counterparts of ordinary lifestyles (Wells and Tigert, 1971; Wells, 1974; Darden and Darden, 1976; Cathelat, 1985; Bernard, 1987; Veal, 1989; Kramer, 1991; Kreutzer, 1991; Mazanec and Zins, 1992, 1993). Therefore, a more comprehensive set of variables is required to portray a temporary away-from-home lifestyle either in contrast or more or less in harmony with everyday behavioural patterns. Given a number of correlates to make the psychographically defined groups accessible to selective market operation, the types or styles become eligible as market segments.

A holiday style is a temporary life into which a tourist escapes from their usual surroundings. It includes observable and unobservable characteristics of the tourist. A holiday style represents a cognitive and

emotional state of mind as well as the concomitant behaviour. A-posteriori segmentation by means of holiday styles considers more than just one type of behavioural variables. It aims at uncovering the underlying motives and also seeks their observable consequences. This is not easy to handle in a standard mass survey. Motives are conceived as a state of arousal with no distinct directional effect toward a particular means of satisfaction (take questionnaire items such as 'to change pace' or 'to realize one's creativity' as examples). In the commercial travel surveys, many of the questions purporting to measure motives actually ask for the evaluation of some attributes of a tourist product. This, however, is the purpose of attitudinal rather than motivational items. While the motives are responsible for the arousal of behaviour, attitudes govern its direction and orientation (Kroeber-Riel, 1992). Consumers navigate through the world of products and services by constantly adjusting their personal hierarchy of attitudes. Satisfaction is an example of a transitory state of an attitude following a particular consumption experience. Another example of a more abstract and slowly changing level of attitudes is represented by value systems (Kamakura and Novak, 1992), which have attracted attention in travel segmentation theory and practice more recently. Motivational and attitudinal variables related to various domains of everyday life are combined to yield lifestyle types. If 'everyday life' is replaced by 'leisure travel', the output is called holiday styles.

Travel and holiday activities are another type of raw material for constructing a-posteriori segments (Hsieh et al., 1992). Questions about the tourist's activities are customary in travel or guest surveys. The concept of 'tourist roles' as suggested by Yiannakis and Gibson (1992) is closely linked with travel activities. Tourist activities easily lend themselves to segmentation purposes. The analyst, however, must take care to avoid the trivial single-item classification (sightseeing tourist, culture-seeker, museum-visitor) and to replace it with a multivariate activity pattern. In contemporary activity segmentation it is the 'activity bundle' which characterizes an activity segment. In a holiday style the activities are also expected to come up in symptomatic combinations.

The concept of a-posteriori segmentation via holiday styles is intriguing to tourism managers. It draws a more realistic picture of their customers who are more than just examples of a certain age in a particular income bracket and with more or less travel experience. The holiday type becomes a more complete entity by exhibiting more real-life contours. Holiday styles, like lifestyles, are more stimulating to the creative designers of trip packages or media advertisements. Elaborating segmentation schemes is a continuing mission for today's marketing strategists. They never aim at detecting the true segment structure in the market: instead, they launch a new typology which inspires a new specialization strategy and then operate – at least temporarily – in a quasi-monopoly.

The following application example utilizes the guest database of leisure travellers to Austria during the winter season 1997/98. City travellers are excluded, as it does not make sense to mix them with resort tourists. (The reader interested in a brief technical outline of the analytical procedures used is referred to the Appendix.)

Sample Application

The case example outlines a combination of typologies for an Alpine, central European country trying to understand the push-and-pull factors driving its visitors during the winter season. Prior experience with the explanatory constructs; location, season, sampling or time of measurement, are the typical antecedent conditions mentioned in the introduction.

A motivational typology

A tourist has certain expectations concerning their holiday. Within the entire universe of tourists such expectations may differ widely. The expectations are based on travel motives and it is very likely there are groups of tourists that share a common set of motives. The goal is to identify these specific subgroups and profile them in order to support strategically oriented decision making. In a first step, profiles of classification variables for each segment have to be compared with the average and the profiles of other segments. This informs about the segment-specific benefits. Next a second descriptive step focusing on other than the active segmentation variables is necessary to help marketing managers target these segments.

The database of the Austrian National Guest Survey (winter 1997/98) contains a sufficiently large number of approximately 3000 resort tourists, who are neither city travellers nor necessarily keen on skiing (Zins, 1998). The regular guest survey measures the travel motives with a slightly modified instrument developed by the *Europäisches Tourismus Institut GmbH* at the University of Trier, Germany. The motives are operationalized by means of four-point scale ratings for personal statements on travel-related desires, preferences and consumption goals. The respondents gave their opinions about the importance of 21 different holiday aspects (e.g. relaxation, comfort, sports), which were aggregated from the four-point scale to binary values denoting the 'important' and 'unimportant' category. Some of these statements are too specific, but the majority may be considered as indicative of abstract travel motives. It is hypothesized that the winter tourists, although being on holiday in the same region, are still heterogeneous in terms of travel motivation. The resulting 0–1 data were analysed using the senior author's TRN32 vector quantization program (see Appendix and web page http://leisure.wu-wien.ac.at/software/). The solution featuring ten motive types was superior in terms of statistical criteria and with regard to the contextual interpretation.

The motive types are named according to the most conspicuous motive items (Table 22.1). Their size varies between 4% (Type M5) and 18% (M3). The types within the groups separated by double bars share some commonality in their motive patterns. They

Table 22.1. Motive types.

Number	Motive types	Size (%)
M1	Snow and ski	11
M3	Modest and isolated	18
M2	Rest, romanticism, nature	10
M4	Ease and comfort at any price	12
M5	Hard to motivate	4
M6	Rest-seeking health tourist	7
M10	No sports but culture	5
M7	Physical fitness	16
M8	Live your creativity	6
M9	The restless	10

Table 22.2. Activity types.

Number	Activity types	Size (%)
A1	Dining out and evening entertainment	27
A2	Excursions and sightseeing	18
A3	Skiers-only	35
A4	Never go out	20

could be merged if larger segments are required. Taking a closer look at these types, it turns out that the dominant motives of type M1 are their serious concern for sufficient snow cover and the guarantee of staying in an attractive skiing region. Type M4 is characterized by a strong desire for excellent service quality in a highly comfortable environment, being (in conjunction with M8), the least concerned about prices. Physical training, pleasure, fun, social events and entertainment are the motivational highlights for type M7, with rest and relaxation being rather unimportant. Type M10 does not value physical activity and challenge; also 'health and wellness' are rather meaningless. Given the fact that city travellers had been excluded from the analysis, type M10 exhibits a remarkable desire for cultural offerings (attaining seven times the average frequency in this motive element).

An activity-centred typology

For designing trip packages it is also important to learn how tourists spend their time during their stay. The manager needs to know about the activity mixture typical of a group of tourists. Twenty-seven activities were listed in the guest survey questionnaire. The respondents ticked the activities they performed at least 'sometimes', producing a binary data set. The activities data were subject to the typology representing network method, leading to a four types' solution

(Table 22.2). The four activity types share some commonalties; alpine skiing, for example, is important for three out of the four types. On the other hand there are marked differences. Type A3, for instance, never engages in walking or hiking, while type A4 never goes out for dining or night entertainment. Type A3 concentrates on alpine skiing, with snowboarding, or sometimes cross-country skiing, being part of this pattern; while activity type A4 is a skier of average frequency but, in contrast to A3, is enthusiastic about walking and hiking.

Judging the marketing value of the motive and activity types

Types are not particularly attractive as market segments unless they differ significantly in terms of market response. Two indicators available from the guest survey come close to sales and revenue information: daily expenditure and length of stay. The differences between motive types are significant, but are smaller between the activity types (Table 22.3). Segments A4 and A1 appear to be equally attractive. The 'skiers-only' are the largest segment; but with a length of stay of only seven nights, however, they activate less purchasing power than the 'excursions-and-sightseeing' type.

It is hypothesized that combining the motives and activities classification into holiday styles will generate more distinct and pronounced segments, where motivation statements coincide with travel activity patterns.

Generating and profiling holiday styles

Market segmentation aims at identifying tourist subgroups that are homogeneous in

Table 22.3. Marketing value of motive and activity types.

Motive/activity type number	Daily expenditure (US$)	Rank	Length of stay (nights)	Rank	Size (%)
M8: Live your creativity	126	1	8.9	2	6
M7: Physical fitness	117	2	7.1	9	16
M4: Ease and comfort at any price	112	3	7.7	6	12
M2: Rest, romanticism, nature	103	4	8.5	3	10
M1: Snow and ski	103	5	7.6	7	11
M6: Rest-seeking health tourist	102	6	9.2	1	7
M9: The restless	100	7	7.5	8	10
M5: Hard to motivate	95	8	8.1	4	4
M3: Modest and isolated	92	9	8.0	5	18
M10: No sports but culture	84	10	6.3	10	5
A4: Never go out	110	1	8.1	3	20
A1: Dining out and evening entertainment	108	2	8.2	7	27
A3: Skiers-only	103	3	7.0	1	35
A2: Excursions and sightseeing	93	4	8.6	5	18

Table 22.4. Three holiday styles.

Number	Holiday style	Size (%)	Motive type	% of motive type	Activity type	% of activity type
M10–A2	Culture-focused nonskier	3	M10	67	A2	19
M7–A3	Sports- and excitement-oriented skiers	9	M7	57	A3	26
M6–A2	Rest- and health-oriented travellers	4	M6	57	A2	22

as many aspects as possible. So far, the reader has been confronted with two different segmentation solutions. It is tempting to examine a segmentation scheme including both activities and motivations. Instead of searching for clusters within a monstrous data set with 27 activity and 21 motive items (paving the way for all sorts of uncontrolled inter-variable trade-off effects) a safer solution was chosen to build holiday styles from activity and motive types. Supposing that the motive and activity patterns are not independent of each other, one should expect partial overlap and partial incompatibility. Given the concept of abstract motives, the same motive drive may lead tourists to different activity patterns. Combining both aspects thus establishes a more realistic picture of a holiday style. The two cluster solutions are cross-tabulated and holiday styles become visible as intersections with a large percentage of overlap. Where respondents are evenly distributed over the cross-tabulation cells, no systematic relationship, and thus no holiday styles, can be postulated.

Cross-tabulation indicates the existence of a few holiday styles in the sense explained above. Three such styles are worth mentioning (Table 22.4) as likely to

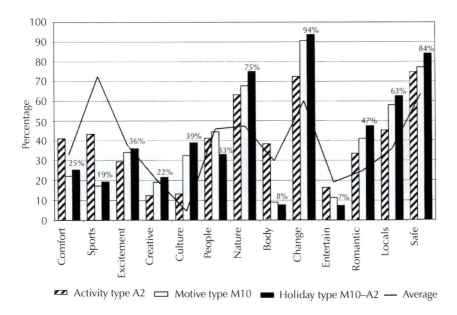

Fig. 22.1. Selected motives compared.

capture the destination manager's attention. These holiday styles turn out to be more distinct and pronounced than the original activity and motive types. The culture-focused nonskiers are described in detail to demonstrate the differences occurring in the interpretation and their consequences for targeted marketing action.

The motives of this holiday style exhibit even more interest in culture than the 'excursions and sightseeing' activity type and the 'no sports but culture' motive type (Fig. 22.1). Culture-focused nonskiers also care more about nature and experiencing change in their environment. Furthermore, safety and a romantic/nostalgic atmosphere play a more prominent role during their holiday and the lifestyle of the locals receives more attention. It becomes apparent from Fig. 22.2 that all members of activity type A2 spending time on sports are excluded from the holiday style M10–A2, resulting in an activity profile without any sports at all. On the other hand, cultural activities still retain their importance: theatres, musicals, operas and museums are visited by a larger percentage of 'culture-focused nonskiers', whereas relaxation

seems less important. In summary, there is a clear shift toward a more specific winter-culture-tourist than was found for the A2 and M10 types separately.

The 'culture-focused nonskiers' are a very homogeneous group of travellers with clear preferences and activity patterns. However, they do not reach a spectacular position when judged and ranked in terms of performance variables such as daily expenditure and length of stay. The rest-and health-oriented travellers and the sports- and excitement-oriented skiers, on the other hand, exceed the activity segments regarding these criteria.

Judging culture tourists by daily expenditure and length of stay uses nonspecific market response criteria and does not seem appropriate for this group. Other aspects are superior in assessing their market value. If the interpretation of this holiday style as 'culture-focused nonskiers' is correct, one would expect these tourists to differ in variables indicative of culture-orientedness, comprising expenditure on cultural attractions, satisfaction with cultural offers, and indirect indicators such as the percentage of repeat visitors known to be lower among

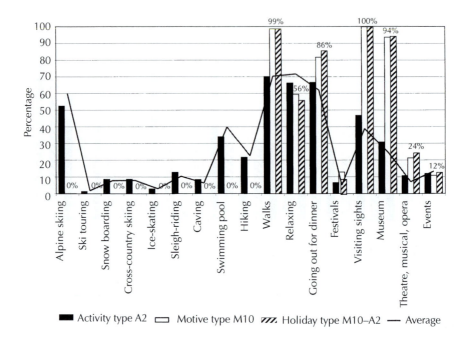

Fig. 22.2. Selected activities compared.

culture-seeking travellers, or length of stay typically being shorter for these guests.

When analysing these descriptive variables for activity type A2, motive type M10 and holiday style M10–A2, these expectations are met to a large extent. First, the expenditure for entrance fees for cultural attractions is higher[2] (US$12) than among both the 'no sports but culture' (US$8) and the 'excursions and sightseeing' (US$5) groups. Second, more members of this group report positive experiences with cultural offerings (17%), with more members complaining about cultural offerings as well (34%). Also the level of entrance fees for cultural attractions was judged in a much more subtle and discriminating way, with far more guests expressing positive surprise (20%). Furthermore, the percentage of tourists being on a short trip was significantly higher (32%) than in any of the component groups the holiday style originated from; there was very little prior holiday experience in Austria (21%), the intention to

revisit the destination was lower (42%), as were the average total expenditures per capita (US$524) and the expenditures for sports and ski-lifts per capita (US$3 and US$12, respectively). Further differences in demographic and travel behaviour variables are omitted due to lack of space.

Obviously, the 'culture-focused nonskiers' represent a more distinct and pronounced group of travellers than the original culturally interested activity and motive types. The holiday style may not seem particularly attractive for target marketing when judged by daily expenditures and length of stay. However, with expenses for cultural activities and attractions ten times as high as the average, the 'culture-focused nonskiers' remain the segment of choice for the managers of cultural attractions or regions focusing an cultural tourism.

[2] All differences reported between holiday styles and activity/motive types are significant at the 95% level.

Implications for Tourism Management

Once the number of segments is fixed and each submarket has been analysed and valued in detail the newly established segmentation scheme forms the basis for strategic market planning. It starts with the decision on which segments to target and eventually leads to the implementation of marketing action specifically tailored to holiday styles.

Holiday styles stimulate the product/ service design of travel packages and imaginative communication strategies. They tell the manager about the commonalties and the diversities of some 'real-life' traveller segments. Condensing multivariable classifications into styles also reduces the danger of misinterpretation. Motive items like 'fun' and activity items like 'going out at night' convey a different meaning once they become either strongly or weakly associated with 'excitement,' or when they relate to different age groups.

In the case example, choosing the activity type 'excursions and sightseeing' when aiming at the culturally interested would have caused such a misinterpretation. The culture tourists defined this way would engage in sports, while the expenditure on cultural attractions would not even have reached half the amount spent by the 'culture-focused nonskiers'. Choosing the motive type 'no sports but culture' would have been less misleading. Here, the tourists would not have cared much about sports and the expenditures indicated a greater interest in cultural attractions. Still numerous expenditure figures would have been overestimated and the relative preponderance of students would have been neglected. By the same token one would have missed the fact that the vast majority travel with their partners and have very little experience of Austria and a low intention of revisiting it.

Summary: How Does the Case Example Fit into the Big Picture of Tourist Market Trends?

The case study lends face validity to the claim that there is no unique and ultimate solution for tourist market segmentation. Depending on the idiosyncrasies of the destination or attraction the managers have a range of opportunities. If they are willing to follow the trend of creating styles or of merging types into styles they get a reward. The holiday styles promise to engender more pronounced segments that are homogeneous in terms of motives and activities simultaneously. It is not the purpose to segment on psychographic variables such as personal values first and to predict activities afterwards (Madrigal and Kahle, 1994). Instead, holiday styles depend on combined patterns of motivational or attitudinal tourist attributes and tourist activities. A traveller merely stating he is adventurous is one thing, the same traveller actually taking a risk is a different matter. Styles provide a greater variety of matching tourist products and promotional messages with corresponding segment properties. The overall trend is in favour of differentiation and specialization in the marketplace. For the mass markets it is unlikely that any subtle strategy of micromarketing will ever be able to cater to the individual tourist. A holiday style approach, however, may succeed in uniting the economies of scale and scope with the illusion of individuality.

Appendix
'Type-producing' Methodology

Constructing typologies and a-posteriori segmentation has been a domain of cluster analysis and its associated tools for significance testing for quite some time (Formann et al., 1979; Mazanec, 1980, 1984). More recently, tourism research has discovered that adaptive methods from the neuro- and biocomputing toolbox offer some promising alternatives. For instance, the method of Self-Organizing Maps (SOMs) assists in solving clustering problems while preserving topological properties of the data (Kohonen, 1982, 1984, 1990, 1997 for a review; Mazanec and Zins, 1993, 1995, 1998; Dolnicar, 1997 for marketing research applications).

The SOM is mainly criticized for two reasons: (i) The SOM update rule (for continuous variables) is not a gradient descent process and thus hinders the mathematical analysis of the asymptotic behaviour of an explicit objective (energy) function; (ii) SOMs impose a rigid framework (a predetermined grid) of neighbourhood relations that the update algorithm has to respect during the training. It may be desirable not to impose rigorous neighbourhood connections but to have them learned and unlearned during the training. A novel procedure is employed in this study: the TRN model was introduced under the name Topology Representing Network (Martinetz and Schulten, 1994). This employs the neural-gas algorithm by Martinetz et al., (1993) to perform a topology-sensitive vector quantization. As in the SOM, competitive learning is the underlying principle. In simple words this means that a set of prototypes (archetypical cases or segment centres) are competing to approximate the frequency distribution training rule adjusts not only the winning prototype but all prototypes according to the rank order of distances between a data point and the first winner, second winner, etc. Thus, the neural gas method exploits a higher amount of information stored in a system of prototypes. As in SOMs, the similarity between data points and their prototypes (cluster centres) is measured by the Euclidean distance d between the ith prototype's coordinates (or weights) vector $\mathbf{w}_i$ **and a data vector $\mathbf{x}$** with values $x_1, \ldots ,_m$ arriving as input:

$$d_i = \|\mathbf{x}\| - \mathbf{w}_i\| = \left(\sum_{k=1,\ldots,m} (x_k = w_{ik})^2 \right)^{1/2}$$

$$\text{with } \mathbf{x} = (x_1, \ldots , x_m)$$
$$\text{and } \mathbf{w}_i = (w_{il}, \ldots , w_{im})$$

During the training the system of prototypes is repeatedly exposed to input vectors randomly selected from the data set. Starting from an initial weight distribution of small random coordinates it learns to adapt its weight structure according to the distribution pattern of the input data. Each prototype learns to take responsibility for a homogeneous subset of data vectors. The weight update follows the learning rule (Martinetz et al., 1993):

$$\Delta w_i = \epsilon \cdot h_\lambda (k_i (x, w_i)) \cdot (x - w_i) \quad i = 1, \ldots , N$$

$0 < \epsilon < 1$ is a learning constant. $k = 0, 1, \ldots , N - 1$ and $k_i(\mathbf{x}, \mathbf{w}_i)$ indicates the rank number k associated with each prototype. Thus rank 0 denotes the winning prototype, 1 the second-closest node (the co-winner), etc. As in the SOM the prototypes compete with each other and only the winner i' with $\|\mathbf{x} - \mathbf{w}_{i'}\| < \|\mathbf{x} - \mathbf{w}_i\|$, $\forall i$, gets full update. The units in its neighbourhood are allowed to improve their fit by a weight update with

$$h_\lambda (k_i (x, w_i)) = \exp (- k_i (x, - w_i)/\lambda)$$

where λ is a decay constant that decreases during the training. For $\lambda = 0$ the process is equivalent to the online version of the popular K-means algorithm. The update rules outlined above have been shown to optimize an explicit cost function where the co-updating of adjacent prototypes resemble a fuzzy assignment of data points to the best, second-best, third-best prototype. The neural gas algorithm was shown to excel K-means as well as the SOM and the maximum-entropy clustering procedure (Martinetz et al., 1993).

Up to this point the training process does not enforce a topographic mapping of the data points into a set of prototypes subject to a learned adjacency structure. This step was added by Martinetz and Schulten (1994). Adjacency is conceived as a dichotomous concept in the TRN. Two prototypes are neighbours or not. The adjacency learning and unlearning process is based on the similarity of the winning prototype and its closest competitor. Each data point arouses a winner/co-winner pair for which it either confirms or establishes the adjacency relation. Adjacency connections for pairs that do not get confirmed for a number of successive updates die out but may emerge again later on. The age and lifetime parameters in this learning process are subject to exponential decay during training. In a simulation experiment, the authors demonstrate that the TRN is capable of preserving rather complicated topological structures. It seems to render a perfect topological mapping as long as the grid of prototypes is dense enough to approximate a manifold of lower dimensionality embedded in the high-dimensional data space.

Any partitioning (non-hierarchic) method requires that the analyst sets the number of clusters. As the dispersion-based criteria use to be of little help an interpretation-based heuristic called the Simple Structure Index (SSI) was applied (Dolnicar et al., 1998). The SSI honours an increase in the number of clusters if a large difference of two cluster centres is at least found for one variable; it penalizes this increase if the size of these clusters is small and the variables involved carry little information (i.e. do not vary much). In case that more than one cluster solution attains a high SSI value, the best solution in terms of identically classified pairs of data points in repeated runs is selected.

Acknowledgements

The exploration of the vector quantization method used in this study was part of the Joint Research Programme SFB010 on 'Adaptive Systems and Modelling in Economics and Management Science' sponsored by the Austrian National Research Foundation (FWF).

23

Biophysical Impacts of Wildland Recreation Use

David N. Cole

Introduction

The biophysical impacts caused by recreation and tourism are often a serious problem that must be addressed through planning and management. This is particularly the case in wildlands, less developed recreational settings, and locations where the emphasis is on ecotourism or wilderness experiences. Immersion in 'natural' settings, whether to study and observe nature or to experience peace and tranquillity, is a powerful motivation for many recreationists and tourists. Natural environments draw people to them and, in turn, are degraded by people if the number of recreationists is too high, if people act in inappropriate ways or if the settings are inappropriately managed.

In developed recreational settings, biophysical impacts have been intensively managed for many years. Sites are often hardened, traffic is confined, behaviour is restricted and, if need be, amount of use is limited. Where applied appropriately and rigorously followed, such developed recreation programmes have been successful in providing opportunities for recreational use while keeping impacts to acceptable levels.

Only in recent years, however, has it become widely recognized that impact management is equally important in wildlands. Although wildlands are less intensively

used, the importance of maintaining natural, largely undisturbed conditions makes recreation management extremely challenging (Hammitt and Cole, 1998). This challenge is further attenuated by the extensive nature of wildlands, the lack of resources available given relatively low recreation use, and the desire to avoid restriction and regulation in these wild settings.

Trends in Biophysical Impacts and Their Management

Many of the obvious biophysical impacts of recreation use have been well documented (Liddle, 1997; Hammitt and Cole, 1998). For example, trampling by recreationists – whether on trails, campgrounds, picnic sites or in areas of dispersed activity – affects vegetation and soil. As plants are trampled, their height and vigour declines and ultimately they may die. If enough plants die, vegetation cover declines, leaving areas of bare ground. Since some plants are better able to tolerate trampling disturbance than others, durable plants increase in relative abundance and species composition changes. Soil organic horizons, when exposed to trampling, can be abraded and eroded away, exposing mineral soil. Exposed mineral soil is compacted by trampling, which causes additional changes such as reduced water infiltration, increased runoff, and accelerated erosion. These changes, once initiated, have synergistic effects that are not self-limiting even if the source of disturbance is removed. Increased runoff and erosion accelerate the exposure of mineral soil which leads to further increases in runoff, erosion and so on.

Some of the most serious impacts of recreation are not readily obvious to the casual observer. Vegetation removal, loss of organic horizons and soil compaction alter soil biotic communities, organic matter decomposition rates and nutrient cycling, changes that can severely reduce the resilience of these sites. Disturbance of animal populations, both through alteration of habitat and unintentional harassment, can have long-term and widespread effects (Knight and Gutzwiller, 1995). Because disturbed animals can move, impacts to animals can have more far-reaching effects than impacts to plants and soil. Moreover, because animals are capable of teaching their offspring, effects of disturbance can be passed from generation to generation. Finally, impacts to water and aquatic systems – from contamination with wastes to increased nutrient inputs – are poorly understood but potentially serious, particularly given the recreational attraction of water and riparian systems.

Magnitude of biophysical impact

Although there is some anecdotal evidence to the contrary – that some locations are in better condition than they were several decades ago – the impacts of recreation use appear to be increasing over time in most places. More places have more affected trees, damaged vegetation and bare ground, exposed and compacted soils, disturbed wildlife and contaminated waters than in the past. These trends can be illustrated by reference to a series of long-term campsite impact studies conducted in wilderness areas and national parks in the US. Wilderness and national park campsites provide good case studies because campsite impacts are severe and yet often not tightly controlled by management.

The total impact of recreational use on campsites is a function of both the severity of impact on individual campsites and the total number of affected campsites. Impact levels are highest when there are a large number of campsites and individual campsites are highly impacted. Therefore, to evaluate trends, it is necessary to assess both change in the condition of individual campsites and change in the number and distribution of campsites. The first of these components of change was evaluated using a sample of established campsites in the Eagle Cap Wilderness, Oregon (for 11 years), in the Bob Marshall Wilderness, Montana (for 9 years) and in Grand Canyon National Park (for 5 years). Change in the number and distribution of campsites was evaluated by listing all the campsites in portions of the Lee Metcalf Wilderness, Montana (for 16 years), the Eagle Cap Wilderness (for 15 years) and the Selway-Bitterroot Wilderness, Montana (for 12 years).

The assessment of conditions on individual campsites found tremendous variation in amount of change, both among and within campsites (Cole and Hall, 1992). Certain campsites improved, while others deteriorated, and others remained relatively unchanged. In many cases, one type of impact increased on an individual site, while another type of impact decreased on the same site. In the Eagle Cap Wilderness and Grand Canyon National Park, the number of sites that generally deteriorated exceeded the number that generally improved. In the Bob Marshall Wilderness, the number of sites that improved exceeded the number that deteriorated. However, in all three study areas, most changes were small and conditions on most campsites were relatively stable.

Anecdotal evidence suggests that some of the most aesthetically displeasing types of impact and a few of the most severely impacted wilderness destinations have improved over time. Most wilderness visitors report, for example, that litter and rubbish are a much less serious problem than they were a decade or two ago (Lucas, 1985; Cole et al., 1995). 'Pack-it-in, pack-it-out' messages asking recreationists not to leave their trash and litter have been quite successful (Roggenbuck, 1992). There also are a number of popular wilderness destinations that were heavily impacted more than 50 years ago by particularly destructive styles of use (very large groups, numerous horses and mules, frequent large campfires and elaborate facility constructions at campsites) that are much less common today. Conditions in some of these locations have improved greatly, reflecting the success of intensive management programmes (see for example, Parsons, 1979, 1983; Marion and Sober, 1987).

These examples of substantially improved condition are more the exception than the rule. There is little reason to be overly optimistic or pessimistic about the future condition of long-established sites. Continued use of these sites may cause some additional impact, but the amount of additional deterioration is likely to be low in comparison to the deterioration that has already occurred. On the other hand – with the exception of less litter and improvements in a few of the most severely damaged places – there is little evidence that management attempts to mitigate site impacts have been very effective. The severely damaged sites of today are not likely to look all that different a decade or two into the future.

Changes in the number and distribution of campsites have been much more pronounced than changes in the condition of long-established campsites (Cole, 1993). In three wilderness areas, the number of campsites has increased markedly over periods of 12–16 years: 53% in the Selway-Bitterroot Wilderness, 84% in the Lee Metcalf Wilderness and 123% in the Eagle Cap Wilderness. In each of these areas, visitors are allowed to camp virtually anywhere. The primary exception is a prohibition on camping within a short distance of lake shores. They can also choose to camp either in an existing campsite or on a previously undisturbed site. The substantial proliferation of affected campsites that has occurred in each of these wildernesses suggests that existing sites get used frequently enough to be maintained in a disturbed state, while numerous new campsites are being sought out, used and left in a disturbed state. The result is a dramatic increase in total impact over time, with most of the increase occurring as a result of the creation of new sites.

Campsite proliferation has been less of a problem along trail corridors than in destination areas. Visitors may be more content to camp wherever they end up while en route to their final destination. Visitors appear more inclined to seek out and use an undisturbed site when they reach their destination. Proliferation also appears to be most pronounced in regularly used but only moderately popular destinations. In places that are not used regularly, there are likely to be few sites used frequently enough to be highly impacted. In very popular areas, most of the potential campsites have already been affected; consequently, there is little risk of further impact proliferation.

The tendency for impacts to proliferate no doubt results from both visitor behaviour and management programmes. Anecdotal evidence suggests that more visitors are using the more remote portions of wildlands than in the past. Many formerly pristine lake basins, for example, now have evident trails and evidence of camping. Guidebooks have been a prominent source of information enabling visitors to more confidently venture off-trail. In the Sierra Nevada of California, for example, guidebooks were written during the 1970s that described virtually every reasonable off-trail walking route in the mountain range. Unplanned trails developed along virtually all these routes. Moreover, once visitors arrive at a destination, they appear more inclined than in the past to pioneer a new site rather than use an existing one. This pioneering trend is likely to continue as interest increases in ecotourism and adventure and risk recreation.

These tendencies are often aggravated by management actions. Educational campaigns, with the intention of reducing impact problems, frequently ask visitors to avoid popular places and seek out more remote locations. Low-impact brochures often illustrate how to select and use a low-impact campsite – usually a site with little evidence of previous use. Improper, careless, or even frequent use of such sites will leave them substantially damaged. In many places camping is prohibited on many traditional campsites close to lake shores. Consequently, new campsites further from lake shores develop and the traditional lake shore campsites seldom recover rapidly. They are not very resilient and they continue to be used for picnicking and occasionally camping. The net effect is an increase in campsite density.

In some wildlands, however, management has been effective in limiting campsite proliferation by prohibiting or discouraging the use of undisturbed sites. Usually this involves either designating campsites or simply asking visitors to use well-established sites. The aim of this management strategy is to concentrate and confine use and impacts. Since conditions on long-established campsites are relatively stable, regardless of use frequency, the frequent use of a small number of sites results in less aggregate impact than less frequent use of a large number of sites (Cole, 1994). Marion (1995) reports, for example, that an impact concentration programme at Delaware Water Gap National Recreation Area reduced the impacted area on campsites by 50% over 5 years. Such a management programme can counter the general trend of increasing impact observed in most places where the location of use is uncontrolled.

Biophysical impact monitoring

A decade or two ago, most wildland managers were aware of and concerned about biophysical impacts but had little objective information about impact levels or trends over time. Consequently, impact management programmes were commonly whimsical and inconsistent, determined largely by the values, biases and perspectives of the individual managers in charge. Moreover, in many places, managers tended to stay in one place for only a few years. This meant that the shortcomings of relying on subjective impressions of impact problems were further aggravated by the short-term perspective available to most managers.

More recently, as natural resource management issues have become increasingly controversial, public acceptance of whimsical and inconsistent management has waned. In the recreation management field,

there has been considerable interest in goal-attainment planning systems, such as the Limits of Acceptable Change (LAC) and Visitor Experience and Resource Protection (VERP) frameworks (Stankey et al., 1986; McCool and Cole, 1997; USDI National Park Service, 1997). With these frameworks, management decisions rely on systematic and objective monitoring data. As a result, many wildland recreation areas have recently developed impact monitoring programmes.

The earliest attempts to monitor recreation impacts probably involved use of repeat photography and casual observation. Neil Bayfield, one of the pioneers of recreation ecology (the scientific discipline concerned with recreation impacts), was perhaps the first to publish a method for rapidly monitoring the condition of trail systems (Bayfield and Lloyd, 1973). His approach involved taking quick measurements of a number of impact parameters at a large number of systematically located, temporary stations along the trail system. This approach has been revised and extended in attempts to increase accuracy and precision, as well as to provide more useful types of data (Cole, 1983a; Lance et al., 1989; Marion, 1994). Coleman (1977) developed an alternative approach – taking a small number of detailed measurements of trail cross-sectional area at permanent sampling stations – as a means of monitoring trail erosion.

Campsite monitoring evolved similarly, beginning with repeat photography. The first published descriptions of how to monitor campsite impact were Frissell's (1978) proposed condition class method and Schreiner and Moorhead's (1979) radial transect technique. From these initial suggestions, more elaborate and precise protocols were developed (Parsons and MacLeod, 1980; Cole, 1983b, 1989a; Marion, 1991). Systems vary in their use of qualitative versus quantitative descriptors, temporary versus permanent sampling sites, and single versus multiple impact parameters.

As is the case with trail monitoring, managers typically must choose either a technique that provides a large number of rather imprecise measures or a technique that provides a small number of more precise measures. The appropriateness of any technique is determined more by the nature of the information managers' need than the relative precision of the technique. Intensive, precise techniques are more useful for assessing change on established recreation sites and in places that are heavily used and impacted. Extensive, less precise techniques are more useful for assessing site proliferation and for surveying lightly used and impacted areas. Combining techniques is another useful option. For example, a few rapid assessments can be made on all sites, with more detailed measures being taken on a sample of sites.

The trend toward increased use of improved monitoring frameworks and protocols is a positive one. Nevertheless, progress has been slow and further progress is not guaranteed. Only 39% of National Park Service wilderness areas monitor campsite impacts and fewer than 10% monitor trail, wildlife or water quality impacts (Marion *et al.*, 1993). Monitoring programmes have often been proposed, developed and initiated, but then slowly wither away. This often occurs when there is a shift in management or when the personnel who developed the programme move away. Data is often collected but never used. Techniques are often selected based on familiarity rather than a thoughtful assessment of the most appropriate technique for the situation at hand. The root cause of most of these problems is inadequate institutional support for monitoring. In many cases, nobody accepts responsibility for monitoring. Should it be undertaken by planners, managers or researchers? Many managers feel their job is to 'take action' rather than to conduct studies – a common view of what monitoring is.

As the world's population grows, biophysical impact problems resulting from recreation and tourism will increase concomitantly. The primary hope for avoiding this future is to raise the level of management professionalism. The collection, storage and analysis of objective monitoring data are critical to professional management. Unless managers make monitoring a higher priority than it is today they will not be able to thwart effectively the trend toward increased impact described above.

Low-impact visitor education

Visitor education has been widely touted as the most appropriate approach for managing recreation in primitive wildland settings (McCool and Lucas, 1990). Many impact problems are more a result of inappropriate behaviour than of too many people (Cole *et al.*, 1987) and inappropriate behaviour can be changed through visitor education (Roggenbuck, 1992). Although some researchers caution against expecting too much from education (McAvoy and Dustin, 1983; Cole, 1995), everyone agrees that visitor education must be a fundamental part of any programme that attempts to control the biophysical impacts of recreation. Visitor education programmes have increased in quantity and quality around the world. One useful example is the development of low-impact education programmes for wilderness lands in the US.

The early historical development of low-impact educational programmes in wilderness is difficult to trace. Clearly, informal education must have a long history but the identity of the earliest educators has been lost. When early rangers observed visitors doing things that damaged wild places, they informed them of alternative practices that were less damaging. During the 1960s, public land management agencies began promoting the 'pack-it-in, pack-it-out' slogan to reduce litter in wildlands. About this time, the National Outdoor Leadership School included low-impact education in the curriculum of their courses (Petzoldt, 1974). These efforts evolved over the years so that, by the late 1970s, the need for visitor education was widely accepted, at least in theory.

Until the mid-1980s, however, the effectiveness of these efforts was limited by two factors. First, the information available on low-impact techniques was limited to the idiosyncratic personal experience of the educator. Little scientific information on recreation impacts was available and there were no networks for sharing ideas about low-impact techniques. As a result of differences in personal experience and opinion, many low-impact recommendations were in direct conflict with each other (Cole, 1989b). Secondly, educational efforts were uncoordinated and almost entirely opportunistic. Meaningful educational opportunities were largely confined to chance encounters with rangers and educational campaigns consisted primarily of a few general slogans, like 'pack-it-in, pack-it-out' or 'accept the challenge'. In a few places, recreationists might be given brochures with low-impact messages or they might read low-impact messages on bulletin boards. However, other potential educational media were poorly developed.

Since the mid-1980s, substantial progress has been made in overcoming these limitations. The US Department of Agriculture (USDA) Forest Service in collaboration with the National Outdoor Leadership School (NOLS) compiled both existing research on recreation impacts and low-impact educational materials from wildernesses and parks around the US. Recommendations were reviewed for internal consistency and congruence with scientific theory and research findings. This work culminated in the publication of the first comprehensive report on low-impact practices (Cole, 1989b) and the first popular book devoted to the subject, *Soft Paths* (Hampton and Cole, 1988). Both products have had substantial influence throughout the US and abroad. For example, the report has been translated into Spanish for dissemination in South America. *Soft Paths* provided the basis for a *Soft Paths* video, it has been revised and expanded (in 1995), and it has spurred the writing of half a dozen other books on low-impact techniques.

Of equal importance, an ambitious national programme to disseminate consistent low-impact educational messages in a coordinated manner has been developed. In the early 1990s, the four federal land management agencies with responsibility for wilderness management (USDA Forest Service, National Park Service, US Fish and Wildlife Service and Bureau of Land Man-

agement) joined with NOLS to develop and distribute 'Leave-No-Trace' (LNT) educational materials. This partnership formally adopted a set of six low-impact principles based on those in the *Soft Paths* video. They developed booklets (about 20 pages each) on LNT practices specifically adapted for each of more than a dozen different regional environments and user groups. Finally, they developed and taught a series of 'train-the-trainer' courses on LNT practices. Through these courses, land managers, educational organizations and other public groups are given the tools to educate others in LNT techniques. By 1996, more than 300 people had graduated from these courses (Swain, 1996), most of whom have gone on to train many others. Moreover, a consistent set of educational materials, based on the best available information, can be requested over the phone by anyone.

Given the initial success of these efforts, the outdoor recreation industry and a more diverse group of other private interest groups were brought into the partnership in 1995, with the formation of LNT, Inc. This more diverse group of partners is better able to promote the LNT message and to raise the funds needed to develop new and improved messages and educational materials.

Along with progress in the development of more educational materials delivered in a more consistent and comprehensive fashion, the content of low-impact messages has also become more sophisticated. For example, a common early low-impact recommendation was to avoid visiting popular places in the wilderness. The basis of this recommendation was that impacts and crowding could be reduced if visitors were more widely dispersed. Use dispersal can be an effective management strategy in some places. Research has shown, however, that dispersing use can also increase both resource impacts and crowding because dispersal increases use levels in places that are relatively pristine and uncrowded (and therefore highly vulnerable) and decreases use levels in places that are already so impacted and crowded that they are not highly vulnerable (Cole, 1997).

Our improved understanding of these

relationships suggests that spreading people and their impacts widely is an effective strategy in low-use places, while the exact opposite – concentrating people and their impacts – is the most effective strategy in popular locations. The simple, often counterproductive, past recommendation to disperse use has been replaced with today's more sophisticated set of three recommendations: (i) in popular places, concentrate use; (ii) in pristine places, disperse use; and (iii) avoid places that are lightly worn or just beginning to show signs of use. While the message has become more complicated for the visitor, the visitor now has the tools to choose the most appropriate course of action in any given situation.

Implications of Trends in Biophysical Impact and Management

Despite increased attention to impact monitoring and the increased quality and quantity of low-impact visitor education programmes – both positive trends – the biophysical impacts resulting from recreation use are increasing. Increased biophysical impact threatens to diminish the attributes that attract recreationists and tourists to wildlands. Changes in public policy, planning and management are needed to reverse this trend or even to keep the rate of deterioration from accelerating. Increased biophysical impact is largely the result of population growth and increased participation in recreation and tourism. Each year, more and more people are using wildlands and leaving their imprint on the land. Three primary strategies for dealing with this situation are: (i) to add to the lands available for recreation and tourism; (ii) to limit recreation and tourism use; and (iii) to reduce per capita impacts.

Increased biophysical impact also results because impacts occur rapidly but are long lasting (Cole, 1994). Studies have shown, for example, that camping can substantially alter a previously undisturbed site in just a few months of use (Marion and Cole, 1996). In contrast, impacted sites closed to further camping can show relatively little recovery even in a decade (Cole and Hall, 1992). Con-

sequently, recreation impacts tend to accumulate over time. Even with a constant level of use, impacts will increase if use distributions are allowed to shift around. With shifting use, new impacts are constantly being created while old sites that are no longer used remain affected for a substantial period. The contribution of shifting use patterns to the trend toward increased impact can be reduced by controlling the distribution of recreation use, by adopting a management strategy of confining, containing and concentrating use.

Public policy implications

Assuming there is little that can, should or will be done about population growth or increased participation in recreation and tourism, the other potential broad societal response to the trend of increased impact would be the allocation of more land to wildland recreation and ecotourism. Decisions about the appropriateness of alternative land allocations should be based on careful consideration of many factors that are beyond the scope of this chapter. The allocation of more land to recreation and tourism would certainly benefit recreation users but, because it would mean that less land was allocated to other competing uses, such a decision would conflict with the interests of others.

A more focused response to the trend of ever-increasing impact is to press for more professional management of recreation and tourism. Through increased professionalism, decreasing the per capita impact of recreationists should be possible. Increased professionalism would require the allocation of additional resources to management. Even more important, however, is the need for a new perspective in which recreation management is recognized as complex, difficult and extremely important.

Managers naturally tend to spend most of their time and resources on responsibilities for which either the rewards of success or the costs of failure are high. Few managers are rewarded for doing a good job managing recreation and few are held accountable for doing a poor job. Consequently, management of recreation tends to receive less priority than programmes considered more important – programmes for which managers are held accountable. Management of the biophysical impacts of recreation is unlikely to improve until more resources are allocated to their management. In times of fiscal restraint, this is unlikely to occur unless recreation management is defined as a critical responsibility reflected in the evaluation and reward system of line officers.

With more resources, research programmes could be expanded. We need to learn more about the nature and significance of recreation impacts, the factors that determine their distribution and severity, how they might best be monitored, and how they can be effectively controlled. The resultant increase in knowledge would provide one of the necessary supports for an improved management programme. Another necessary support is careful planning and monitoring. Management programmes need to be based on specific objective statements of the conditions a recreation area is to provide, as well as monitoring data capable of identifying situations where objectives are not being met. Finally, managers need sufficient training, as well as the political will to make difficult management decisions.

Another important policy decision involves the allocation of resources between popular, heavily used and already severely impacted recreation areas, and areas that are more remote, less popular and less damaged by recreation use. Typically, virtually all available resources have been allocated to popular areas, the places where most people go and where biophysical impacts are most evident. Cole (1997) argues, however, that this allocational decision is short-sighted. Remote, lightly used places deserve a higher proportion of available resources than they currently receive. Remote, wild places are unusually precious, because they offer the greatest contrast to commonly available recreation landscapes. Their near-pristine state also makes then unusually vulnerable to degradation. Finally, because they are relatively vulnerable, they are more likely to respond positively to good management and negatively to bad management than more heavily used places.

Planning and management implications

Financial and institutional support for monitoring needs to be improved. Although increased attention to monitoring is one of the positive trends noted in this chapter, substantial further progress is needed. The importance of monitoring needs to be institutionalized, as do personnel and funding requirements. Monitoring is an ongoing task that is fundamental to making wise decisions about where management is needed, which actions should be taken, and how existing programmes need to be adjusted. Short-term, one-shot and poorly funded monitoring programmes will simply not be adequate. There also are substantial challenges to developing efficient monitoring techniques, but these technical challenges pale beside the problems of inadequate institutional support.

Low-impact education programmes – while clearly improving – also need further attention. One particular need is a better understanding about how to educate recreationists and tourists effectively. Currently, most educational programmes are predicated on the belief that lack of knowledge is the primary factor keeping recreationists from complying with low-impact recommendations. Educational messages are churned out; in booklets, brochures, on signs and videos; on the assumption that recreationists will attend to, comprehend, accept, access, recall and comply with them. Decades of research in persuasive communication suggests this is an unlikely outcome (Eagly and Chaiken, 1993); that persuasive communication programmes are not likely to succeed unless careful attention is devoted to all stages of the communication process.

Finally, management programmes need to be more concerned with the proliferation of impacts, since proliferation is more commonly the source of increased impact than the intensification of impact on individual sites. This suggests increased reliance on use and impact containment strategies, the most proven means of minimizing the per capita impacts of recreation and tourism.

24

Assessing Social Impacts of Resource-based Recreation and Tourism

Patricia A. Stokowski

Introduction

Attention to the social impacts of resource-based recreation and tourism has grown over the past 30 years, partly as a result of legislation mandating impact assessment in federally funded development projects, but also as a result of more general public interest in and concern for environmental issues and the consequences of development policies and actions. The US National Environmental Policy Act (NEPA), signed into law on 1 January, 1970, created the formal legislative requirements for assessing and documenting social impacts. Section 102 of that Act calls for the 'integrated use of the natural and social sciences and the environmental design arts in planning and in decision making which may have an impact on man's (sic) environment' (Erickson, 1994, p. 7). Subsequent to the 1970 Act, state and local legislation incorporating environmental and social assessments into forest, park and resource area planning has emerged, and guidelines for analysing social and environmental impacts have been adopted by various governmental and nongovernmental agencies, in the US and internationally.

The term social impact assessment (SIA) refers to a process of anticipatory social science research focused on analysing the direct, indirect and cumulative effects of technological and social change in a system with the stated purpose of providing technical information and analysis to decision makers engaged in public policy formation and planning (Bowles, 1981; Leistritz and Murdock, 1981; Finsterbusch et al., 1983; Branch et al., 1984; Freudenburg, 1986; Dietz, 1987). SIAs are required for projects that occur on public lands, affect public resources, or receive federal funding; these include, for example, plans to develop an oil shale industry in a mountain community (Gulliford, 1989), construct a dam or hydroelectric project (Taylor and Bryan, 1987), or open a federal nuclear storage facility (Scott et al., 1987).

SIA occurs as part of the environmental impact assessment process, and social data and impacts documentation are published in environmental assessments (EA) or environmental impact statements (EIS) that disclose information related to current conditions of a site, expected changes to the affected environment under a variety of alternative decision choices, and potential mitigation strategies for identified negative impacts. Under NEPA guidelines, assessment of the affected environment requires (in addition to analysis of physical and biological effects) analysis of a range of potential social impacts (at individual, group and institutional levels), their magnitude under different conditions, the distribution of impacts, and the interrelationships among impacts. The specific types of impacts to be studied in a given project are usually identified in assessment processes prior to the initiation of research.

Beyond formally mandated EISs and SIAs, public interest in social impacts is evident in contexts where SIAs may not be required. Research literature in recreation and tourism provides many examples of general studies of social impacts – research projects undertaken for purposes of furthering basic or applied research goals, even when there is no legal mandate to conduct the research or involve the public, and no expectation of directly or immediately influencing public policy. Particularly in tourism contexts, researchers undertake and encourage social impact studies to better understand the effects of public or corporate decisions and actions, to aid planning, and to reduce potential negative impacts of development. Compared to SIA procedures, policy applications from general social impact studies are not always direct or immediate; results are typically published in agency technical reports or in scholarly journals, rather than in EA or EIS documents that are open to public scrutiny.

In both social impact assessments and social impact studies, the range of potential impacts studied is diverse, and includes psychological, social, economic, cultural and political outcomes that arise from policy revisions, actions or decisions of resource managers, plans for or adoption of community development programmes, and other actions leading to social change. A rich tradition of social impact studies related to the effects of large-scale energy exploration and extraction projects on small, rural communities can be found in the rural sociology literature (some studies also describe impacts of rapid community growth on recreation and tourism; see Cortese and Jones, 1977). Many community studies in sociology, anthropology and recreation and tourism may also be read and interpreted as studies of social impacts.

Social impact studies and assessments

have been usefully applied in natural resource settings, and new approaches to social impacts analysis are continually evolving. The broad focus of topics and issues in resource-based recreation and tourism, however, produces not one, but several, significant trends:

- Analysis of quantitative impacts (e.g. economic outcomes) tends to take precedence over analysis of qualitative impacts (e.g. social, cultural, or political outcomes).

- Since measurement and analysis of social impacts is complex, case studies predominate and theory development has been slow to emerge.

- Research about social impacts tends to be conducted only at single moments in time, and longitudinal research is rare.

- Social impact research tends to focus on internal aspects of a system under study, and often ignores the boundary-spanning nature of impacts.

- Social impact studies tend to adopt a reductionist and linear model, ignoring complex interactions among entities involved in a development project.

These trends are elaborated in the following section, which details the current status of impacts research in resource-based recreation and tourism. Later, each trend is addressed separately, and their implications are summarized at the end of the chapter.

Current Status of Impacts Research in Recreation and Tourism

The term resource-based recreation and tourism is used here to refer to experiences related to natural areas/amenities that serve as activity sites or attractions for recreation or tourism. These include formal, designated places (such as parks, forests, wildlife areas, scenic byways and others), as well as informal or vast areas (such as scenic landscapes, water resource areas, settings with unique spiritual qualities, resource-dependent communities and others), and

Table 24.1. Common social impacts studied in resource-based recreation and tourism.

Outdoor recreation	Impacts type	Tourism
Regional socioeconomic effects (expenditures, jobs, sales)	Economic	Regional socioeconomic effects (expenditures, jobs, sales)
Per capita income		Per capita income
Agency revenues		Local government revenues
Infrastructure improvement		Entrepreneurial activity
		Opportunity costs
		Leakage
Social/physical carrying capacity	Social	Social/physical carrying capacity
Benefit achievement		Tourist–guest interactions
Development of competencies		Demonstration effect
Social cohesion on-site		Crime, delinquency, social welfare costs
Recreational conflicts		Local community cohesion
Maintenance of historic artefacts	Cultural	Maintenance of historic artefacts
Maintenance of cultural values		Maintenance of cultural values
Preservation of scenic values		Change in traditions and customs
		Intercultural communication
		Changes in material culture
Partnership benefits	Political	Institutional capacity
		Growth machine politics
		Community conflict/cohesion
Environmental concerns (pollution, traffic, noise)	Other	Environmental concerns (pollution, traffic, noise)

include places of obvious significance, as well as places that may be physically unremarkable, but are perceived to have special meaning for subsets of recreationists or tourists.

Social impacts research in recreation and tourism extends across a diverse array of case studies, resource settings, and variety of impact types, but most research assumes a simplified model of impacts creation where the initial stimulus for change is provided by a public or private entity initiating action. In recreation, land management agencies at federal and state levels tend to be the source of changes leading to impacts; in tourism, the sources stimulating change may be resource agencies, government or nongovernmental organizations, or private corporations or businesses. Three broad actions typically lead to impacts analysis: (i) regular agency planning processes, such as preparation of general management plans; (ii) changes in management or policy, such as decisions to apply new use regulations,

fees, permits, area closures or other on-site changes; and (iii) growth processes in the form of new development, construction, or business expansion. The first two categories are most common in resource-based recreation, while the last category is more likely to occur in the context of resource-based tourism. Table 24.1 lists some of the more common impacts that have been studied in research about resource-based recreation and tourism (see also: Mathieson and Wall, 1982; Pearce, 1989; Pearce *et al.*, 1996).

Social impact assessment in resource-based recreation

A review of impact analysis sections from several EIS documents prepared for federal agency management planning allows three generalizations about the current state of social impact assessment (SIA) in resource-based recreation. First, the definition and boundaries of the 'affected environment' (usually including natural, cultural and social environments) tends to be remarkably similar across federal agencies, regardless of the specific goals of the planning effort. This is because EA and EIS documents must demonstrate compliance with an array of state and federal legal statutes related to clean water, endangered species, historic and wilderness preservation and other issues; the assessment process thus becomes circumscribed by legal requirements.

Secondly, recreation resource agencies typically subdivide the social environment into categories that include visitor activities and experiences, scenic values, area operations, transportation and traffic, health and safety features, concessionaire activities and regional economic effects. Aside from the last, most categories refer to objective impacts that are internal to the forest, park or resource area system. For example, in the National Park Service's (1995) Grand Canyon EIS, the 'impacts on operations' section briefly considered negative interactions between park visitors and park employees – but there was no discussion of interactions fostering community cohesion among tourist groups, residents of communities outside the park and Native American communities in the region. Elements of the social environment seem to be limited primarily to those that can be measured easily, those that are within the boundaries of a resource place, and those that ignore social processes.

Thirdly, data included in the EIS documents are primarily quantitative in nature (see NPS, 1997a, for an example). Considerable effort is devoted to estimating labour force needs, tourist and employee expenditure patterns, population effects and impacts on services, relative to proposed alternatives, but little attention is given to quality of life values, place attachment, social interaction possibilities, cultural resiliency, gender issues, meanings of recreation experience and other qualitative indicators. An EIS for a wilderness area (BLM, 1987), for example, provided only very limited data describing social environment issues. It contained no information about people beyond descriptions about numbers of visitor-days, miles of trails and roads available for human use, and lists of potential on-site recreational activities.

These three generalizations suggest that environmental and social impact assessments offer only limited utility in understanding impacts generation in resource-based recreation. The documents provide extensive information often without corresponding theoretical focus; they support a primary goal of documenting the occurrence of impacts. Moreover, since SIAs are published in individual management plans, it is rare to find comparative impacts research across park or forest jurisdictions. Additional research evaluating whether predicted impacts actually occurred, and what forms they took, is needed. Currently, comparisons across EIS documents can only reveal trends in what managers think might happen, not assessments of what really did or did not happen – though, presumably, implementation of a management plan would provide opportunities for research and evaluation of actual outcomes.

Finally, these documents generally do not explain the rationale for including specific publics in the assessment process. Agencies involved in preparing EIS documents are required to involve relevant publics throughout the process, from identifying goals, scoping and preparing alternatives, to evaluating data and making final decisions. Input is usually solicited from citizens and interested parties (other agencies, organizations and interest groups) in a variety of public and private settings, from working groups to public meetings. Letters mailed to an agency expressing the views of interested parties are also obtained and are sometimes included in the EIS document. Throughout, the intent is to provide opportunities for relevant publics to provide and review information, and discuss, debate and challenge conclusions drawn from the data. While public inputs to the process may be substantial, it is not always clear how those inputs are analysed or used in planning or decision making. If public participation is only a standardized process 'allowed' by a recreation agency, the potential for various publics to be real partners in decision making seems limited. Views of some affected publics may never be expressed; access and competence remain problematic, as do equity and social justice (Shannon, 1987).

Impact studies in resource-based recreation

An extensive literature exists to detail the values of recreation participation and the benefits that might accrue to agencies and communities providing outdoor recreation opportunities. Beyond early studies of site demand and individual user benefits (Hughes and Lloyd, 1977), recent work has focused on amenity resource valuation (Peterson *et al.*, 1988) and analysis of regional economic impacts of recreation (Bergstrom and Cordell, 1991; Stynes and Stewart, 1991). The IMPLAN input–output model used in national forest planning also formalizes a methodology for assessing the impacts of multiple use policy choices on regional economies (Loomis, 1993).

Despite Clawson and Knetsch's (1966) early model of the recreation experience, much of the research about social and social-psychological aspects of recreation has focused on the on-site segment of the continuum. No theoretical approach has had more influence on recreation management than that of social carrying capacity (see, for example, Hendee *et al.*, 1978). If increasing levels of visitor use on-site produce changes in the recreation experience, then how might managers determine the amount of change that is acceptable, the magnitude of effects created by differing amounts of change, and the strategies for maintaining high-quality recreation experiences? An extensive body of research derived from this model investigates relationships among crowding, density, privacy, tolerance, conflict, participation norms and satisfaction with the recreation experience (see Manning, 1986b, 1999). Practical solutions (zoning systems, use rationing, pricing strategies) for managing recreation experiences have been proposed (Hammitt and Patterson, 1991; Shelby and Vaske, 1991; Kuentzel and Heberlein, 1992; Loomis, 1993). Comparative research evaluating variation in impacts under different levels of management would also be useful to extend carrying capacity theorizing.

A relatively underdeveloped area of research into resource-based recreation impacts is centred around community/ agency interactions. Interest in partnership formation, conflict resolution and collaborative management of recreation resources has stimulated studies that focus on community-level interactions among resource agencies, governments and residents of nearby cities and towns, and organizations and interest groups (Colfer and Colfer, 1978; Carroll, 1988). The potential for research that considers the impacts of policy changes on social systems is unlimited, particularly given the complex nature of many resource-related planning problems.

It is clear that the general study of social impacts in resource-based recreation is not very well advanced. Individual level outcomes of on-site activities are fairly well documented in the carrying capacity literature, but beyond a limited number of community studies, there has been little interpretive research and only minimal focus on entities larger than social groups. Research remains context-dependent, studies do not present a cumulative or integrated set of findings about the types and qualities of impacts that might arise from different kinds of social change, and analyses of policy-related consequences are limited.

Impact studies in resource-based tourism

The emergence of impacts research in tourism can be traced to the differing agendas of public/private resource provision. Governments invest in natural resource attractions and services to improve public welfare, while private tourism entrepreneurs create attractions and services to fill business niches, respond to market conditions, and optimize individual profits. Tourism developers do not face the same bureaucratic and legislative mandates as governmental entities, and their planning timelines are usually shorter. Private tourism development also usually occurs in community settings rather than on resource lands that are set aside from private development. In combination, these factors raise a host of social impact issues that are not usually central in public recreation settings.

Yet, even though the tourism engine may be primarily driven by private interests, there is substantial public agency linkage with the tourism industry. One way this occurs is through reliance of private tourism businesses on public natural resources as the basis for the tourist attraction. Ski resorts, for example, are often situated on public lands leased from the Forest Service or other agencies, so must comply with federal and state conservation laws. Whenever a resort corporation wishes to expand operations, they must work with the relevant agency to prepare an environmental impact assessment (see, for instance, the EIS for the Sugarbush, Vermont, ski area; USDA Forest Service, 1998). Beyond EIS and SIA preparation, tourism developments may also be subject to federal or state legislation related to endangered species habitat, water flow and quality, wetlands maintenance, historic preservation or hazardous waste site clean-up.

Cohen (1984) divided the sociology of tourism into four areas of interest: studies about tourists themselves; studies about tourism systems; studies about interactions between tourists and local residents; and tourism impact studies. Of these, studies of tourism systems provide often-cited examples of formal models that attempt to explain how tourist destinations change over time. Miossec's 1976 evolutionary model of regional tourism (as described in Pearce, 1989) links resort growth to transportation networks, changes in tourist behaviour, and planning controls. Butler's (1980) model of tourist destination life cycle, based on the number of tourists visiting a destination, applies the notion of carrying capacity to tourist areas. Doxey's 1975 'irritation index' (as described in Pearce, 1989) suggests that residents progress in mood from euphoria to antagonism as tourism grows or expands in their community. These and other models (Getz, 1986) provide useful frameworks for asking questions about the impacts of tourism development.

Another area of emphasis in tourism impacts research focuses on interactions between tourists and residents of communities experiencing tourism growth. Smith's (1989) classic book presenting sociological and anthropological case studies about tourist (guest) and resident (host) encounters was one of the first to evaluate the positive and negative impacts of tourists on receiving societies. Studies of the cultural consequences of such interactions have been well represented in the tourism impacts literature (see MacCannell, 1976, 1989; van den Berghe, 1993). A quantitative approach to host/guest interactions is seen in the numerous studies of residents' perceptions of tourism development, demonstrating that different groups of local people often have very different views about tourism's impacts (for example, business owners and tourism industry workers tend to be more supportive of growth activities than other citizens).

Studies documenting economic, social and institutional impacts arising from community tourism development are numerous (see e.g. de Kadt, 1979; Preister, 1989), and among these, analyses of the regional economic impacts of tourism are especially common. Since developers and promoters acclaim the potential of tourism to provide new jobs, raise personal incomes, stimulate regional business development, create tax revenues, and in general, 'grow economies', it is natural that researchers have focused on the economic benefits of tourism (Eadington and Redman, 1991). Other studies of social and institutional effects of tourism development, however, challenge the perceived notion of widespread economic value. Researchers have shown that tourism transforms host communities and societies, but it is not clear how tourism compares with other forms of modernization as an agent of social change. Studies documenting the effects of tourism development on specific types of resource-based communities, including islands, seashores, mountains and other resource places are readily available in the tourism literature (see e.g. Stansfield, 1969; Price, 1992; Gill and Williams, 1994; Stokowski, 1996; Towner, 1996). Many of these also incorporate some assessment of environmental impacts, since the quality of the resource base is intimately linked to the success of the development.

Research about ecotourism and adventure travel (see e.g. Boo, 1990) has also documented the consequences of tourism's growth on resource places and remote native cultures. While economic effects are often expressed as gains (although leakage remains problematic), the social, political, and cultural consequences for local societies are often viewed as negative.

Discussion

The theoretical basis for social impact studies can be found in classical theories of individual benefit maximization, and social and political organization and modernization. The ultimate goal of impacts research is to predict the future and control unwanted outcomes of social change. To do so, relevant impacts data, measurement practices, and criteria for evaluating alternatives, are needed. Evaluation of the current status of impacts research in resource-based recreation and tourism provides documentation for elaborating the five trends identified earlier.

First, analyses of economic benefits of resource-based recreation and tourism are common in impacts studies. Well-developed quantitative techniques exist to measure these impacts, and their analysis seems to be given high priority in policy applications. Economic values are seen to be more 'defensible' than other types of social impacts, and so are useful in justification of agency decisions. Over-emphasis on economic impacts, though, can minimize attention to other types of social impacts that may be equally relevant in planning, management and policy making. As Wondolleck (1996, pp. 258–259) noted, 'The conventional systematic, technical analysis conducted by resource managers is essential to making informed decisions, yet ... hard-to-define values do not fit within the traditional paradigms of professional land management'.

Second, while many types of negative as well as positive social, cultural and political impacts are evident in recreation and tourism projects, measurement is complex and case studies prevail. There is no single set of indicators or methods that must be included in all social impact studies, and focus differs according to agency goals, theoretical approach and complexity of the system. Many unanswered questions remain about the form, magnitude, potency, durability or resiliency of impacts over time in resource-based recreation and tourism settings.

Third, impacts research in resource-based recreation and tourism is often conducted only at one point in time, either when a new proposal is introduced, or after a development has opened. Longitudinal research is needed to extend research beyond mere documentation of the presence/absence of social impacts, and to determine how impacts are interconnected and linked across social systems more generally. Social impacts research should be extended to consider the individual and cumulative effects of impacts across the entire spectrum of planning or development – from initial announcement, to discussion, decision making and operation – and by strengthening measures of perceived and actual impacts outcomes (Stokowski, 1996).

Fourth, differences in approaches to the study of impacts in recreation and tourism result both from legislative requirements mandating research needs, as well as the nature of the system under study. Public recreation resources tend to be bound geographically (a 'park' has specific acreage and is managed by a specific agency), while tourism systems often include an array of public and private participants and resources. When impact studies are conducted in either context, the focus tends to be internal, ignoring the boundary-spanning nature of impacts. A park may be required to conduct impact assessments relative to management decisions implemented on those resource lands, but the consequences of those decisions may extend beyond park borders into adjacent communities or regions. Likewise, tourism developments in a community adjacent to a protected resource area often have no mandate for preparing impact assessments, yet their outcomes may impinge on the quality of experiences obtained, or the management options available, within the adjacent resource place.

Fifth, contemporary social impact studies in resource-based recreation and tourism tend to be reductionist, tracing actions or decisions made by a corporate entity (a governmental agency, a nongovernmental organization, a private business) in causing or inflicting impacts upon a host community, a regional economy, or visitors to a resource place or attraction. This model ignores the historical context of decisions and actions in which individuals and agencies operate. A more realistic, complex model, however, suggests that resource agencies, tourism developers, residents of communities, and even visitors and tourists themselves, might generate impacts. Impacts may also accrue to all of these entities, each of whom has different goals, status, requirements for public accountability, and ability to cause, absorb or deflect impacts.

Implications

There is widespread agreement about the benefits of conducting social impacts research, but problems remain in understanding how to identify relevant impacts, measure them, and incorporate results into planning and policy making for resource-based recreation and tourism. Regardless of whether research is conducted for a formal impact assessment or a general study of social impacts, implications for future research can be drawn from each trend identified above.

Trend 1: quantitative/qualitative analyses

Both impact assessments and studies require defensible methods and measurement, and a specific concern noted in the literature relates to analysis of non-quantitative aspects of social impacts. Issues such as human values, morals and ideals; community quality of life; sense of place; and societal well-being, are integral to human experience, yet may not be amenable to quantitative accounting. Qualitative or

interpretive research is needed, but unlike quantitative tools (such as cost–benefit analysis in economics), these approaches remain poorly developed in impacts research and in social science more generally. There are obvious reasons why agencies might want to rely on primarily quantitative data in making and defending decisions, but methods for incorporating meaningful qualitative indicators in data collection procedures and evaluation processes must also be developed.

Trend 2: complex analyses

The choice of impacts to consider in any given study is generally a function of the types and number of issues raised in the scoping process preparatory to SIA work, or the theoretical/practical interests of a social impacts research team. Setting the boundaries of the research task too strictly, though, may narrow the scope and scale of research to topics that are managerially relevant but not complete enough to reflect changes in the surrounding social and physical environment. For example, defining a community only by geographic borders may exclude social relationships and interactions beyond those borders that are affected by or affect impacts dispersion or mitigation. Disregarding difficult-to-measure variables or ignoring variables that affect only a small segment of a population is also problematic. Without comparative studies to determine whether policies, plans or developments have similar outcomes regardless of setting, theoretical development will be impossible.

Trend 3: longitudinal research

The use of SIAs is mandated in planning when federal properties or funds are involved. Agencies routinely prepare EA documentation while developing their general management plans, and the results of assessments are used to evaluate agency goals or alternatives for action. Incorporation of results from nonmandated, general social impacts studies in policy making processes, however, is less clear. Research is often carried out for theoretical exploration, or is proprietary to the funding source and not subject to community, government, or interest group review. The preponderance of case studies in social impacts research makes it difficult to generalize across studies that use widely divergent methodologies, approaches, settings, or theories. In addition, the inability of researchers to predict with certainty the types, quantities and magnitude of many kinds of social impacts leaves such studies vulnerable to disregard by policy makers and publics.

The solution is to extend the focus of both social impact studies and SIAs to include a longitudinal focus as well as broader contextual details surrounding proposed alternatives. Additionally, there is a need to understand secondary or indirect and cumulative effects of social change over time, and effects that are dispersed across space (tourism impacts, for example, occur not only in destination regions but also in regions that generate tourism demand and transit regions through which tourists pass; see Pearce, 1989). Criteria are also needed for making comparisons among proposed alternatives of SIAs so that relevant political consequences are made apparent (K. Branch, Seattle, 1999, personal communication).

Trend 4: boundary-spanning

An emerging international focus on regionalism and globalization requires new effort towards visionary planning. Future studies of social impacts will need to factor into analyses an understanding of localism (local history, culture, society, economy and politics) as well as a sensitivity to broad, external organizational and power influences (at regional, national or international levels) that are interwoven within the local context. An example is provided by the emergence of ideals such as ecosystem management, which – particularly in those forms that require extensive coordination and integration across public and private landowners as well as across resource types (Loomis, 1993) – will require a broad vision considering how to maximize positive and reduce negative impacts across administrative boundaries.

Trend 5: complex interactions

Traditional models of impacts production and mitigation will, in the future, be inadequate for understanding the complex interactions among resource agencies, publics and communities, and impact assessments and studies cannot rely on simple causal models that limit analyses to linear relationships. All components of a revised impacts model must be called into question. Research is needed not only about impacts themselves, but about the types of agency decisions that produce changes in the social environment, the form of the changes themselves, and the eventual creation and mitigation of social impacts. A circular, contextualized, and historical model of impact creation, rather than a linear causal model, is required. Such a revised conceptualization raises a host of nontraditional questions for social impact studies and assessments. How do participants construct realities about resources and resource places, and can those separate realities ever merge? How and why do some visions of reality come to the forefront, while others languish? What impacts are most meaningful to each interacting party (and how would a researcher analyse impacts if these were also fluctuating in meaning)? Who is responsible for mitigation if the parties are engaged in a process of mutual reality construction? Clearly, the 'cookbook approach' to defining and analysing impacts, and the particularistic forms of many current social impact case studies, are inadequate for more critical theorizing.

Summary

The benefits of social impacts research in resource-based recreation and tourism are generally accepted. Based on the historical development of this research area, five trends – related to analysis of quantitative impacts, use of case study methods, lack of longitudinal research, focus on internal aspects of systems, and applications of linear models – were identified. The implications of these trends are seen primarily in planning, management and policy making for resource-based recreation and tourism. Implications include the need for more interpretive, comparative and longitudinal research, and more complex approaches to theorizing about impacts across local, regional and global scales. The consideration of social impacts in resource-based recreation or tourism can be expected to produce more equitable, value-centred, communal and civic approaches to amenity planning and management, and contribute to the preservation of valued community qualities and desired landscape settings. Ultimately, attempting to predict social impacts and incorporating their evaluation into resource-based recreation and tourism planning, management and policy should bring us closer to desired goals of community and environmental sustainability.

Part V

Development: How Resources Are Organized For Use

25

Development Economics

John Fletcher and Stephen Wanhill

Introduction

The undoubted growth in the economic prosperity of the major industrial countries together with the travel revolution brought about through holidays with pay, lower international transport costs in real terms and information technology, has seen world tourism grow to a truly global business. One billion international arrivals are predicted for 2010, reaching 1.6 billion by 2020. Past growth has not been without fluctuations caused by shocks and cycles in the world economy, but what is remarkable is the resiliency of the industry through troubled times.

Discovery grows exponentially, thus the expansion of technology has made instant reservation and confirmation possible, to the point where the customer expects an immediate response and, if not, chooses another product. Technology will lead to increasing integration between the different sectors of the industry to allow the customer to put together 'bespoke' packages all on the same system, making the world an electronic marketplace. It has also brought down the real cost of travel, and in so doing has brought countries closer together. Thus long haul has come nearer to short haul, which in turn has permitted the former to grow faster than the latter.

Technological improvements and the accumulation of capital have enabled societies to move from agriculture, through production industries, to the service economy. In doing so, these processes have radically changed economic thinking about development, as this chapter will show. Many smaller states have jumped the intermediate stage by moving from primary industries to the tertiary service sectors, using tourism as the development vehicle. By this means they have generated substantial increases in their living standards, something that would never have been contemplated in the classical theories of development worked out in the early part of the 19th century.

Theories of Development

The progress of economic thought in respect to development has been coloured by the historical circumstances in which economists found themselves. Much of the thinking is reflective of observations of the world in which the writers lived and the prognosis for the future was derived from extrapolating perceived relationships to some limit point. With hindsight, it is possible to look back and wonder how development theorists missed the obvious and promulgated the obscure, yet this is to take their reasoning out of context. As will be shown in what is to follow, despite many wrongheaded notions, some of the ideas of earlier writers still have meaning in the modern world.

Classical economics

The classical thinkers at the turn of the 19th century immersed themselves in the world of agricultural production. Because they could not foresee technological development, nor the possibilities of voluntary birth control, they came up with the gloomy prediction that population growth would outstrip agricultural output, thereby leading to stagnation and periodic outbreaks of famine. The mechanism for this was the law of diminishing returns, which comes about from applying more and more labour to a fixed supply of land and so lowers productivity. The 'doom' scenario is where the population eats its 'seed corn' so there is nothing left to plant. Such scenarios are observed in less developed countries (LDCs) today and form headline news stories, but the circumstances which have brought them about are more political than economic.

What the classical economists did realize was the importance of capital accumulation for economic growth. It was their fear that population growth would diminish the surplus or profits available for investment. Investment is the engine of growth and development, as may be seen in the following simple model:

- From the demand side, Gross Domestic Product (GDP) may be expressed as

$$\Delta GDP = Consumption + Investment \qquad (25.1)$$

$$Consumption = c(GDP) \qquad (25.2)$$

    where c = the propensity to consume.
    Substitution of Equation (25.2) into Equation (25.1) and collecting terms, gives
    GDP = Investment / $(1 - c)$
- From the supply side, the potential increase in GDP is

$$\Delta GDP = k(Investment) \qquad (25.3)$$

    where k = the incremental output-capital ratio.

Dividing Equation (25.3) by Equation (25.2) and noting that $(1 - c)$ is the propensity to save, s, results in the fundamental growth relationship

$$\Delta GDP / GDP = sk \qquad (25.4)$$

The left-hand side of Equation (25.4) is the rate of growth of GDP, which is determined by the savings rate (s) in the economy (the means for investment) multiplied by the productivity of that investment, as given by k. For GDP per capita not to fall, the value of sk must match the growth rate of the population. This has been defined as the steady state or natural rate of growth.

Marxism

It is somewhat of an enigma that the classical thinkers were writing at a time when tremendous innovations were being made that would reshape the economies of Western Europe, usher in the factory system of industrial production, and would see the growth of major cities as centres of industrial output. The rise of the business class (capitalists) controlling the means of production was seen by Karl Marx in terms of social conflict, through the exploitation of the value of labour provided by the working classes (the proletariat). Profit in Marx's terms was the 'labour surplus value' appropriated by capitalists from the workers and, within this, capital contained the seeds of its own destruction. The expansion of capital would be accompanied by a falling rate of profit and, in attempting to maintain their position, capitalists would invest in labour-saving technologies, thus creating a reserve army of unemployed. Furthermore, the growth of monopoly power from capital accumulation would encourage the demise of small businesses to the ranks of the proletariat, as capitalists competed for market share.

Marx's prediction was that eventually the proletariat would revolt and seize control of the means of production, which would then be invested in common ownership to bring in an era of socialism. In time, socialism is displaced by communism and the state, with its power to compel, withers away. The irony is that Marx's revolution took place in the least capitalistic country in Europe, Russia. Nevertheless, his views are still influential as a creed for populations discontented with their governments or concerned about the globalization of capital and its ability to act independently of democratically elected governments.

Marx's insight into the capitalist system can be found in the dilemma facing many of today's governments, when contemplating the microelectronic and IT revolutions, which have displaced old 'Fordist' labour-using production processes. On the one hand it is hard to accept the political consequences of rising unemployment, while on the other, countries cannot afford not to invest in new technologies if they are to remain internationally competitive. The solution lies in the new jobs that technologies create in their wake and an appropriate welfare safety net to ease the transition process.

Stages of development

In the post-war period, a historical comparison between industrialized countries and LDCs led Rostow (1971) to expound a theory of development which asserts that the transition of an economy from a traditional society to an age of mass consumption is possible through a series of economic stages. The most important stage is the 'takeoff' when resistance to change in traditional ways is finally overcome and modern industries begin to expand. It is characterized by:

- A sharp increase in investment;
- Rapid growth in at least one substantial manufacturing sector; and
- Institutional reform to support the expanding modern sectors of the economy.

Rostow's analysis is more a generalized interpretation of economic history than a theory, but it found favour with multinational aid agencies because it promised a takeoff for LDCs once a sufficient infusion of capital was made. When a country lacks sufficient domestic savings, there is nothing wrong with borrowing from outside, provided the money is invested wisely. Too often it has been the case that the money has been spent on prestige projects or has simply disappeared, with corresponding limited effects on economic growth.

As was consistent with the economic thinking of the time, the takeoff stage would be achieved through a planned package of industrial developments with infrastructure support. This spurred the construction of a range of deterministic planning models to set targets for investment and production. Emphasis was given to rapid capital accumulation and investment in basic industries, with the state being given a strong planning role. Furthermore, pessimism about export opportunities contributed to import substitution strategies as yielding the best returns. In this context, the service economy would develop to meet the needs of local industry, rather than as an export industry in its own right.

Unfortunately, despite the availability of foreign aid, many LDCs do not have the business environment to take on such massive investments as implied by Rostow's takeoff stage. Hirschman (1958), noting that many developing countries already have a mixture of investments and are not starting from scratch, recommended a strategy of supporting those sectors of the economy that initiate further investment decisions. Specifically, planners should consider the interdependence of one investment project with another and encourage investment in sectors that have the greatest complementary effect, as identified by their backward (purchases) and forward (sales) linkages with the rest of the economy. In this respect, tourism has strong backward linkages to different enterprises because of the broad range of goods and services demanded by visitors.

Modern development policy

The modern view envisages the broad objective of a development strategy to be one of raising living standards. This cannot only be seen through increasing levels of per capita GDP; it includes welfare, the environment

and enhancing the opportunities for all citizens to participate in and benefit from the
activities of society. This must include the
eradication of absolute poverty, provision of
employment opportunities, and the reduction of huge disparities in inequality,
because of the political tensions they generate and because egalitarian policies result
in more citizens realizing their potential,
thus enhancing social and economic efficiency. In a democracy, the difficult task of
government is to build a consensus on these
issues, drawn from shared values, traditions, cultures and a sense of belonging.

The instruments for achieving the above
aims are carefully selected development
projects, which link this modern view to the
work of Hirschman (1958). Deterministic
planning models were helpful in setting
goals, but the reality is one of uncertainty in
which the information is defective and the
various economic agents are not under the
planner's control. So what is needed are
robust development strategies and flexible
institutions that operate well under a wide
set of relevant environments. The current
consensus, based on theory and experience,
is that markets should be given primacy in
the production and allocation of goods and
services, but to obtain socially desirable outcomes it is the task of government to provide
an institutional infrastructure in which markets can function.

Thus, traditional demand management
policies and state planning have been abandoned in favour of macrostabilization
policies to ensure sound money and micro-
policies to make markets work better. This is
less so in LDCs due to their political structure and the lack of private institutions to
take on development. Concern is for action
to remove the structural rigidities that have
given rise to the dualistic nature of many
LDCs, where the traditional and modern are
found alongside each other. Bitter experience has shown that market-oriented
projects in LDCs with inappropriate macroeconomic policies have struggled to survive.
This acknowledgement heralded in an era of
structural adjustment, dating from the
1980s, to build onto the characteristics of
dualism already accounted for in the eco-

nomic appraisal process (Wanhill, 1994).
The purpose is to ensure a better economic
climate, so new projects could function
more efficiently, thus improving returns.
However, governments are not alone in their
task. The problems of poverty, unemployment and income inequality are perceived
in an international setting, so there is a range
of multinational agencies to assist countries
in their development objectives.

Development in a Market Economy

The modern view of development has come
about for reasons that are both theoretical
and empirical. The economic theory of markets as an efficient means for allocating
resources is well documented. The prices
set in the marketplace serve as the adjustment mechanism by:

- Rewarding sellers;
- Rationing available supplies among
  buyers;
- Relaying information forward from sellers, showing relative costs of
  production or scarcity value, and back-
  wards from customers, showing their
  relative preferences by what they are
  prepared to pay.

By this means, markets are able to deal with
some of the fundamental issues in economics, namely, what should be produced, the
method of production, and for whom the
product is produced.

However, it has been the continuing globalization of competition and the classic
failure of state planning (as has been witnessed in the appalling productivity record
of the Eastern European countries), leading
to the collapse of the communist system,
that has given confirmation to the market-
oriented view. Globalization and reduced
transport costs have facilitated export-
oriented strategies and the transfer of
technology between countries in which
there is little role for the state. This is in
marked contrast to some of the propositions
arising from Rostow's analysis.

Since the mid-1990s, world trade has

been growing at about 6% per annum, just over twice the rate of world GDP, making economies more open and increasing the internationalization of activities and inter-dependency between countries. This opening of trade and the export success of the South East Asian countries (despite internal troubles caused by poor economic management and the impact on global stock markets) have shown that the promotion of exports can be an effective strategy for the transfer of technology and enhancing the competitiveness of domestic industries.

Key trends

The most significant trends to note from the global changes are:

- Increasing financial openness giving rise to mobility of capital: the capital controls that existed in the post-war period until the 1970s are being dismantled. The IT revolution is accelerating this process;
- Accordingly, enterprises are becoming increasingly footloose and relocating in their major export markets;
- The impact of technology in speeding up the innovation process from invention to placing new products in the marketplace, which, in turn, accelerates obsolescence;
- Despite restrictive immigration policies there has been increasing international labour mobility. Better education and falling transport costs have seen a rising flow of young workers to the industrial countries;
- International mobility of ideas, know-how and culture; in an increasingly computer literate population, no government striving for technological development will be able to stop its citizens from surfing the web.

Role of government

With the rise in market power and the globalization of competition, it is becoming more difficult for the governments in the industrial democracies to meet their traditional obligations in terms of education, social security, health and pensions,

because of resistance to high taxes by the electorate. This has led to cutbacks in public expenditure, privatization of infrastructure, and the demand that some public merit goods such as museums, galleries and parks, which also form part of the tourist product, should charge for their services. The view is forming that in an economy that has the appropriate institutional structure to ensure that markets perform as they are supposed to, then there should be no reason to have more than a small state enterprise sector.

Regional Development

The issue of state intervention at the regional level has waxed and waned with the political complexion of governments. While regional disparities are obvious, there were no clear guidelines for intervention other than market failure, and the spatial direction of industry has run counter to the current policy view that the location decision is part of the market adjustment process. For some time, the theoretical underpinnings of regional growth analysis could not support the pragmatic interventionist approach.

Regional growth theory

The development of the fundamental growth relationship (Equation 25.4), which dominated the economic literature until the late 1980s was based on the neoclassical models of Solow (1956) and Swan (1956). The neoclassical economic tradition of growth, whether applied at a national or regional level, stresses the influence of basic supply factors such as labour force growth, the growth in capital stock, and some exogenous technical change, on the level of output. This approach draws heavily on the assumption that the market allocates resources efficiently so that at any one time regional disparities are a transitory phenomenon as resources are reallocated between regions to achieve convergence toward some steady-state rate of growth. Moreover, Barro and Sala-i-Martin (1995) have shown that this convergence process is relatively quick, halving regional disparities every 12 years. The prescription for policy is clear; allow market forces to act and wait. In practice, the flexibility in factor movements and prices that this requires are rarely, if ever, achieved and so the neoclassical perfect competition adjustment mechanism fails to operate. Furthermore, the idea that technical progress 'rains down from heaven' to make labour steadily more productive contradicts common-sense policy notions of encouraging savings/investment and efficiency to boost economic growth. These criticisms are underlined in newer growth theories, which take account of market power and knowledge accumulation as generating competitive advantage through increasing returns to scale. In these circumstances, private returns are no longer the same as social returns and so there is no longer any reason why market allocation should be efficient.

The lack of realism and the failure of the neoclassical paradigm to recognize the importance of demand has led post-Keynesian economists to place particular emphasis on the role of regional exports as the main generator of output growth. Growth is seen as demand determined for the simple reason that no region's development could be constrained by supply, when factors of production are mobile. A significant aspect of this export-base explanation of development has been the way in which the principle of cumulative causation through knowledge accumulation has been built into models of regional development (Kaldor, 1970; Dixon and Thirlwall, 1975). Thus, once regional disparities occur, they tend to become cumulative and self-perpetuating as regions exploit the benefits of economies of scale and greater specialization. This is known as Verdoorn's Law (1949), which is, in essence, 'learning by doing' that raises productivity and feeds into the competitiveness of the region's exports, in turn raising output growth, which stimulates the continuation of the cumulative process.

The concepts implicit in the Verdoorn relationship may also be found in the 'growth pole' ideas of Perroux (1955) and Myrdal (1957): the efficiency of growth

poles make them magnets for movements of economic resources, including the labour force from other regions. The underlying adjustment processes can be identified in the backward and forward linkages. With backward linkages, as enterprises move to the core, they increase demand, making it more attractive for other firms to locate at the core. In the case of forward linkages, the more firms move to the core, the easier they make it for existing firms to buy the same product diversity at lower prices, due to greater specialization and lower transport costs.

Implications for Tourism

Tourism development

With tourism set to be one of the main international economic drivers in the 21st century, together with increasing demands from the domestic population for leisure and recreation, the industry is a development option that few governments can afford to ignore. Yet the increasing withdrawal of the state from matters to do with industrial development makes it necessary to query whether the public sector has any role in tourism.

Public Sector Role

The case for government involvement in tourism can be made along traditional lines in terms of the:

- Complexity of the tourist product;
- Institutional structure;
- Guardianship of the resource base;
- Market failure.

The complexity of the product is indicated by the characteristics of a tourist's journey, where it will be appreciated that the trip is not a single product, but rather it is made up of components supplied by a variety of organizations with different objectives and different economic structures. Furthermore, each offering may be considered unique, as visitors add their own preferences to the total experience. In this manner, the tourist becomes part of the production process.

Market success is the delivering of the right mix of components to satisfy the demands of the visitor, but this delivery requires coordination and cooperation. A critical difference between tourism and many other agents of development is that of inseparability, in that tourism is consumed at the place of production, thus involving itself with the host community, and requiring some commodification and sharing of traditions, value systems and culture (Cohen, 1988). Since the tourist industry does not control all those factors which make up the attractiveness of a destination and the impact on the host population can be considerable, then the essence of successful tourism development is the creation of a 'partnership' that is incentive compatible for the various stakeholders in the activity of tourism; central and local government, quasi-public bodies such as tourist boards, voluntary organizations and charitable trusts, the private commercial sector, the local community and the visitors themselves.

As a rule, it may be observed that the greater the importance of tourism to a country's economy the greater is the involvement of the public sector, to the point of having a government ministry with sole responsibility for tourism. In this manner, the options concerning the development of tourism can be considered at the highest level of government. The ideal institutional structure is one that is compatible with the global marketplace in which the tourist industry finds itself, but offers the incentives for the 'partnership' to engage in socially and economically constructive activities, thus avoiding or resolving conflict and preventing actions which enrich one partner at the expense of another. Typically the emphasis is placed on trust, but this is commonly surrounded by a legal framework that gives powers of compulsion, something that is necessary for long term agreements. What makes the public sector unique is that the state has a monopoly on the legitimate use of force to ensure compliance.

The concept of sustainable development (Brundtland, 1987) is infiltrating the policy framework of many government organiza-tions and agencies, primarily through concern expressed for the natural environment. However, in tourism there is the broader relationship of visitors to the physical and social environment, and so sustainability may be summarized as development which meets the needs of present tourists and host regions while protecting and enhancing opportunities for the future (WTO, 1993a). The public is evidently becoming more aware of the perceived adverse effects of tourism on the environment and it has become fashionable to 'go green': Muller's (1997) 'green viruses' appear to be spreading. Some operators have consciously taken the decision to reduce their consumption of natural resources to the benefit of the organization and staff alike. Others have used the concept that green tourism is equated with 'soft' tourism, which has low impact and is therefore acceptable, as little more than a marketing tactic. But, in general, there has been a rise in the 'green' lobby, which the industry must take account of from the standpoint of both its markets and the increasing volume of legislation. However, green tourism, ecotourism or alternative tourism (the words are often used synonymously) are in essence small scale solutions to what is a large scale problem, namely the mass movements of people travelling for leisure purposes. Thus, there is still a requirement to continue to create large 'resortscapes' capable of managing high-density flows.

If the institutional framework is to function in a way that is socially compatible, then there is a prerequisite for local involvement in the development process to encourage discussion about future directions. This has generated interest in models of community tourism development (Murphy, 1985; Inskeep, 1991). Cultural conflicts need to be resolved through, say, staging development and using marketing communication channels to prepare guests better for their holiday experience. As a rule, the greater the difference in lifestyles between hosts and guests and the less the former have been exposed to visitors, then the longer should be the period of adaptation.

The market failure argument follows on

from what has said above, namely that environmental protection and community ownership of the development process are not guaranteed by the free market. Those who argue for the market mechanism as the sole arbiter in the allocation of resources for tourism are ignoring the lessons of history and are grossly oversimplifying the heterogeneous nature of the product. The early growth of the seaside resorts during the latter half of the 19th century, as, for example, in the UK, was the result of a partnership between the public and private sectors (Cooper and Jackson, 1989; Cooper, 1992). The local authorities invested in the promenades, piers, gardens and so on, while the private sector developed the revenue-earning activities, which enhanced the income of the area and in turn increased property tax receipts for the authorities. Thus, embodied in the tourist product are common goods and services, which are either unlikely to be provided in sufficient quantity if left to the market mechanism, or available without cost, as is the case with natural resources. The principal concern for the environment is that indiscriminate consumption, without market regulation, will cause irreversible damage that cannot be compensated by increasing the stock of other capital.

The upshot is that the single-minded pursuit of private profit opportunities within tourism may be self-defeating, as many older resorts have found to their cost (Plog, 1973). The outcome may not be the integrated tourism development which distills the essence of the country in its design, but a rather crowded, overbuilt and placeless location with polluted beaches; one that is totally out of keeping with the original objectives set by the country's tourism policy. For example, the major hotel developments that took place in the resorts of southern Spain during the 1960s and early 1970s were completed under laissez-faire expansionism with little consideration given to planning or control.

Tourism policy

The precise nature of a country's stance on tourism investment is determined by the kind of development the government is looking for and what role it envisages for the private entrepreneur. In most cases, economics forms the basis of tourism development plans. Within this framework three objectives tend to be given the central position, subject to the proviso that it is no longer considered acceptable in political terms that these objectives should be achieved at a cost to the environment or by adversely affecting the host community:

- Employment creation through spreading the benefits of tourism, both direct and indirect, to as many of the host population as possible;
- Foreign exchange earnings to ensure a sound Balance of Payments;
- Regional development, notably in peripheral areas, which, by their very nature, are attractive to tourists and often have few alternative developments.

It is important that governments should not set objectives that may seriously conflict with each other. Too often governments talk of tourism quality yet measure performance in terms of numbers. Yet, the question of the environment is a difficult one to maintain when it threatens to be a drag on the economy in matters of employment creation. The implementation of policy therefore becomes a process of maintaining the balance between the various objectives as opposed to trying to maximize any single one. Legislation and investment support given by governments for tourism developments are the instruments used to realize the balance of objectives set by the country's tourism policy.

Regional tourism strategy

Much of regional tourism development planning is underpinned by the growth pole principle, with the aim of raising regional export values through tourism. The focus is the creation of a destination through an investment strategy that provides a balanced range of facilities to meet visitor requirements and at a level which gives the area 'tourism presence' in the marketplace. As an illustration, within the European Union, upon the adoption of the Single European Act in 1987, there was a commitment by the Union to promote economic and social cohesion through actions to reduce regional disparities. In response, the 1992 Maastricht Treaty acknowledged, for the first time, the role of tourism in these actions (Wanhill, 1997).

To achieve the desired level and type of tourism development in Europe, member states may invoke a variety of policy instruments or levers on the demand and supply side as part of their partnership role. But, since the late 1980s, greater emphasis has been given to stimulating small tourism firms and indigenous development for long-run sustainability, as opposed to attracting large scale inward investment projects. However, it would be naïve to suppose that tourism development could be effective in every region or locality. Increasing market segmentation will generate niche markets for some areas, but the cost of supplying these markets could be prohibitive.

Conclusions

With tourism marked out as one of the key economic sectors for the 21st century, it has raised development and employment opportunities that few governments can afford to dismiss. Modern development economics assigns a greater role to market power to determine the allocation of resources, with government being given the task of providing the institutional structure for markets to function. However, the complexity of the tourist product and the current emphasis on sustainable tourism, indicates that, based on past experience, uncontrolled commercial development is likely to create more problems than it solves. It is right and proper that the private sector should concentrate on commercial criteria for their investment projects, but successful development requires that there should be a partnership between the various stakeholders in the activity of tourism.

The role of coordinating such a partnership, to achieve the desired level of tourism development, falls on the public sector. The economic theory suggests that targeting specific projects and concentration to ensure 'tourism visibility' is the most appropriate strategy. Given that tourist movements will increase both nationally and internationally, there will be a need for more regulation and improved management of tourism resources to prevent environmental degradation. The current approach cannot be one that tries to reverse the market changes that have taken place. Such a policy would now be difficult to implement, as the increasing globalization of economic activity has reduced the power of national governments to control their destinies. Rather, the move should be toward a more pragmatic approach to intervention and regulation that should place an increasing emphasis on international collaboration.

It would be convenient if there were a few instruments or levers, which could be considered optimal for the implementation of tourism policy. Certainly, the tourist industry responds strongly to legislation and the availability of finance, but the tourist product varies so much around the globe that it is customary for states to adopt a bundle of instruments and adjust them over time, in response to feedback information on their workings.

26

Globalization and Tourism

Peter F. Keller

Introduction

Globalization is a trend that requires some clarification. What in fact does the term mean? And what are the driving forces behind this controversial process? As with other trend-setting developments, globalization too has its countercurrent. Is the increasing internationalization of the world irreversible, or is the local level regaining importance?

Such questions are of particular interest in relation to tourism-dependent sectors of the economy, which are strongly affected by this mega-trend of globalization. The rapidly growing demand for ever more distant travel destinations is helping to reinforce and accelerate the process of globalization. The clearest evidence of this would surely be provided by an analysis of the structures of the world market. Other questions that arise in this context are as follows: Does the internationalization of demand not lead to the destruction of mature supply structures in the traditional destinations? Can small-to-medium-sized enterprises (SMEs) cope with the additional competition and the changes associated with this process (Fig. 26.1)?

The latter question can only be answered by means of careful analysis of the development prospects under conditions of globalization. This analysis must focus particularly on the tourism markets, production

conditions, company structures and the local factors. The main question here is whether there is a need for action in the area of tourism policy, and if so who should be taking such action?

Mega-trend at the Turn of the Century

The term 'globalization' is a typical buzzword of the 1990s. It refers to the ever increasing networking or integration of players in the world economy. It is not, however, a purely economic phenomenon, but rather a mega-trend which is resulting in the internationalization of all social, cultural and political relations (Keller, 1996).

The march of civilization toward a global condition is manifest, dynamic and heterogeneous. This process is indeed nothing more than the adaptation of the parts of a system to the system itself. It is a process that is making the world smaller, doing justice to the image of our planet as a closed circle – a sphere, a 'globe' or put another way, a 'global village'.

As a matter of fact, there is nothing new about globalization. Adam Smith, the father of the modern science of economics, has already described the phenomenon. Economic historians indeed have come to the conclusion that the world economy was even more open before the World War I than

© CAB International 2000. Trends in Outdoor Recreation, Leisure and Tourism (eds W.C. Gartner and D.W. Lime)

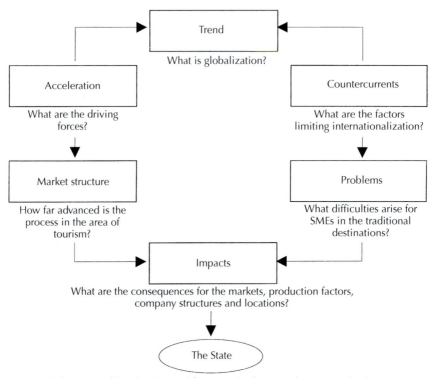

Fig. 26.1.   The globalization process – the important questions from the tourism policy point of view.

it is today. What is new is the extent to which the process has been gathering speed. It began with the transition from fixed to flexible exchange rates and the liberalization of capital transfers and financial transactions. Another new aspect is the intensification of networking that has come with technological advances in the areas of transport and telecommunications. And the extent to which globalization now extends to all corners of the globe is also new. Internationalization is no longer a phenomenon that affects only the trade triangle of America, Europe and Japan. Today's global market includes a growing number of emerging economies.

Variables of Acceleration

The forward-going process of globalization is driven by the coincidence of fundamental economic, political and technological changes occurring in the same time frame. Among such variables of acceleration we may number the triumphal advance of the market economy with the corresponding retreat of the planned economy; the establishment of worldwide competition as the ethic of free trade and the global norm; the improvement of living standards, and the lowering of transport and communication costs. Tourism has played a part in accelerating these changes which, in turn, are having a considerable impact on the tourism market itself.

The introduction of market economy organization in countries that were formerly run as planned economies under communist regimes, and the gradual transition to the same open market economy in the developing and emerging nations has resulted in a much larger total market. The phenomenon known variously as 'Reaganomics' and

'Thatcherism' was used to describe the process of internal deregulation adopted by the leading western industrial nations. At the international level it went hand in hand with liberalization across national boundaries. In contrast to the General Agreement on Tariffs and Trade (GATT), the new World Trade Organization also regulates trade in services and the protection of intellectual property. The capital and currency markets have been extensively liberalized. The worldwide trend toward liberalization is accompanied by another phenomenon, that of regional integration. Meanwhile the European Union, which is planning a major extension of its sphere by moving its frontiers eastwards, is in the process of creating an almost completely deregulated economic and monetary union with the introduction of the Euro.

In a world economy that has been extensively liberalized, competition helps to ensure innovation, increased productivity and growth. In conditions of global competition, the winners are the countries with the most open economies. The globalization process confirms the theory of comparative costs of David Riccardo. Each nation benefits from free trade in making use of its relative cost advantages and competitive advantages. Protectionism acts as a brake on growth and improvements in the standard of living. In the wake of the so-called 'Asian crisis', which has brought the banking system to its knees in some emerging nations, a great many economists have called into question the worldwide liberalization of capital transactions and have at the same time called for the introduction of controls (Baghwati, 1998). They are forgetting the fact that it is not free trade so much as the structural weaknesses of the banking systems of the countries in question, with the lack of international fair play and rules governing competition, that are at the root of the current economic difficulties.

Competition also creates the conditions for technological progress which in turn helps to speed up the process of global integration. I am referring in particular to innovations in the areas of transport and communication. The speed of travel in this jet age has increased dramatically. In the heyday of the Wild West, as in Europe's *belle époque*, a mail coach could cover up to 160 km in a day. A modern jet covers up to 1000 km in just an hour. Information, including images, travels at the speed of light today.

It is beyond a doubt that tourism benefits greatly from the variables of acceleration that are part of the globalization process. The spatial growth of the world market has brought a number of brand-new destinations into the limelight. The new international destinations arriving on the market are overtaking the traditional tourism countries. The general improvement in living standards thanks to competition has opened new regions of the world to tourism. The East Asia–Pacific region has thus become an important area for tourism in just one decade. As for intercontinental tourism, this sector owes its above average rate of growth to technology's conquest of time and space, and to the fact that transport costs have been greatly reduced. A great many of the new tourism countries depend almost entirely on the availability of inexpensive flight connections.

International tourism not only benefits from favourable exogenous developments, but has the effect of a motor that speeds up the development of worldwide integration. In the emerging and developing nations, the net currency effect contributes greatly to the creation of modern economies. Globalization is not a zero sum game. It also brings considerable growth potential to the traditional tourism countries, potential which indeed has not been fully exploited in all places!

Internationalization and Localization

There are, however, economists who consider globalization as no more than a myth. They like to point out that industry has been shrinking due to international competition in terms of productivity, while maintaining its share of global output in real terms (Baumol, 1991). The services sector, on the other hand, which to some extent at least is tied to a specific location, continues to gain ground.

The internationalization of industry thus contrasts with the localization of services (Krugman and Obstfeld, 1991). We may safely conclude, therefore, that global competition factors are not alone in determining wages, prices or the general development of the economy. Future economic development will depend much more on the independent (endogenous) growth of service economies with strong ties to specific locations.

Tourism in particular is affected by these contradictory trends of internationalization and localization, and the tradeoff between them. Contrary to the opinion of many politicians, tourism-dependent sectors of the economy are much more internationalized than other sectors. In all the most developed nations, tourism is involved in intensive import–export competition. The spending of foreign visitors in the host country constitutes the export portion, and the spending of residents of the host country on foreign travel constitutes the import share. The degree of internationalization of a given branch can be measured with the help of the Index of Revealed Competitive Advantages (RCA), which identifies the export surplus by relating the export and import totals.

The degree of internationalization depends on the development of tourism demand. As the key magnitude of the tourism phenomenon, this is strongly influenced by the ever greater distances covered by those who travel to ever more remote locations. But tourism demand benefits the local economy through tourist spending. Which sectors of the economy are tourism-dependent can be determined by tracing these expenditures. A characteristic of these 'incoming' branches in developed economies is that the largest share of value added is in the home market. In contrast with the less developed countries, there is scarcely any need to import intermediate goods from other countries (Keller and Koch, 1995).

As an internationalized sector of the economy with high value added for the home market, tourism acts as a strong multiplier in developed countries. It is, however, exposed to competition on a worldwide basis. The potential client is free to choose from products that range from skiing in the Rocky Mountains to swimming in Bali at the other end of the globe. Global competition for clients with considerable purchasing power means that there are no guarantees of success even for suppliers offering unique services of the highest quality. Increasingly important are the price and the general economic conditions in the production location. In this context the question that must be asked is whether the emerging and developing countries enjoy more favourable local growth potential than do the highly developed nations, with their hard currencies and relatively high levels of cost.

Structure and Development of the World Market

The international demand in tourism has been more or less developed to the same extent as air travel, and to a slightly greater extent than world trade and the world economy as a whole. Indeed a country must have reached a certain level of development before it can enjoy real tourism growth. The tourism world market is virtually a closed shop, open almost exclusively to the most developed countries, which share similar demand preferences and supply structures.

International tourism is a matter of 'competition between equals'. As recently as the 1950s, international tourism was limited to just a handful of Organization for Economic Cooperation and Development (OECD) countries specializing in the business of tourism. But whereas in 1950 the overnights amounted to just 25 million in the area of international tourism, by 1997 their number had increased to 612 million, a figure which above all reflects the increase in international tourism made possible by the interdependency of the OECD countries and a general improvement in the standards of living in this area. A good two-thirds of the total remains concentrated in the western industrial nations.

What is new is the arrival of the increasingly market-oriented developing and emerging nations among the group of countries that count most in tourism on a quantitative basis. This is in fact a relatively small group, which in the past few years has managed to attract more than 90% of the flow of private capital. The growth of tourism has been greatest in 12 emerging economies of Eastern Asia, Latin America, China and India (World Bank, 1998). With the exception of the island states, the poorer developing countries participate relatively little in the globalization process. In these countries, the most pressing problem is the need to alleviate poverty, in an effort to improve the chances of these countries one day being able to integrate the world market in tourism.

The geographical distribution of tourism flows and revenues is not homogeneous in the wider tourism world market that includes both developed and emerging nations. Despite the internationalization of demand, the home markets and the markets of the closest neighbours in each continent remain by far the most important regions of tourism in each of the respective continents intraregional tourism. The globalization process is far from being at an end, even in tourism. Some 82% of cross-border tourism takes place within these continental regions, for example Europe or East Asia–Pacific. Thus the people of central and northern Europe take their holidays in the Mediterranean region or in the Alps, while Australians prefer to visit nearby Bali and the Japanese go to New Zealand.

It is also a fact that intraregional tourism is only part of a country's income from all tourism activities, the extent of which depends on the size and state of development of the country concerned. Domestic tourism (i.e. the contribution to tourism revenues which the residents of a country make through internal tourism activities) is far more important than cross-border tourism in the most touristic countries like the US and France. There are, however, no coherent international statistics in this area. Even so, in the US we know that less than 10% of the population goes abroad for holidays. In France, domestic tourism accounts for some 70% of all overnight stays.

One of the most important indicators of globalization is intercontinental or 'long-

haul' tourism. Today this sector accounts for 18% of international tourism. The World Tourism Organization (WTO), revising upwards its earlier forecast, predicts this proportion will increase to about 24% in the year 2020. It is likely indeed that intercontinental tourism will increase substantially in terms of absolute figures, but more steadily in percentage terms. A glance at the flow of intercontinental travel in Fig. 26.2 indicates clearly that the frequency is the greatest by far on the North Atlantic route between North America and Europe, as well as between the East Asian–Pacific region and North America, and Europe (WTO, 1998a).

Structural Impacts

The internationalization of demand has not been without consequences. The traditional tourism countries have lost market share. This is a logical enough development, in view of the fact that the new competitors are growing at a faster and greater rate. Moreover, the lion's share of the new growth concerns intraregional travel in the East Asia–Pacific region. Finally, one must point out in this context that the traditional destinations are not taking enough advantage of the intercontinental growth opportunities.

Despite the fact that demand is growing everywhere, competitive pressure has continued to increase on the supply side. This phenomenon is being aggravated by the overcapacity that exists in the air travel and accommodation sectors. The extension of the world market has greatly increased the supply worldwide. From 1985 to 1994, in a period of 9 years, more than a million new hotel rooms have been created in North and South America, with an equivalent amount in Europe and an additional 740,000 in the East Asia–Pacific region. Based on these amazing figures, it is safe to conclude that globalization has led to competition on both price and quality between the various destinations, despite the extra growth. It is above all the SMEs that bear the brunt of this extra competition.

The extensive internationalization of tourism demand has resulted in the creation

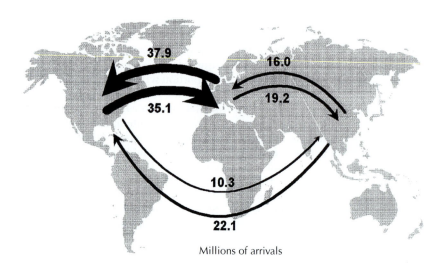

Millions of arrivals

Fig. 26.2. The globalization of international tourism – forecasts with regard to the most important intercontinental travel flow lines, 2010. Source: WTO, Madrid (1996).

of large corporations, which are in a position to take advantage of the ever spreading globalization of the economy. Airline companies, tour operators, hotel empires, resort developers and car rental firms operate according to global strategies, and make use of local competitive advantages in a worldwide market. Production is in their case industrial and highly professional. They are constantly expanding, making adroit use of their financial might and considerable influence in the marketplace. They are able to leapfrog any barriers to the mobility of production factors that might remain.

The globalization process is unsettling for all those enterprises, organizations and countries which, for whatever reason, have not managed to remain competitive. First and foremost among these are the traditional tourism countries. In most cases, these are plagued by unfavourable general conditions, often have to rely on out-of-date and unattractive infrastructures, are hampered by their lack of size or 'critical mass', and fail to make good use of the general advantages of the destination.

The basic question that needs to be asked today is whether or not the general economic conditions in highly developed economies are in fact favourable to tourism.

New competitors indeed benefit from soft currencies and low-cost production factors, or at least they will in the short- and medium-term. They are thus in a position to offer attractive prices, which means they are better able to compete on price.

State-of-the-art tourism infrastructure, equipment and installations are often lacking at every level in the traditional tourism countries. New attractions in particular are often lacking. The supply of accommodation may have fallen so far behind in some sectors that it falls well short of the level international hotel chains set as a minimum requirement. This is far from being the case in the new competitor countries. Most of these offer new attractions and installations designed to please modern tastes.

A problem common to all traditional tourism countries is the predominance of SMEs which suffer from low productivity and from what is sometimes called 'cost sickness'. Despite the difference between their productivity and that of the economy as a whole, their prices have to reflect the general level of prices in the national economy. Their services are expensive as a result. Major efforts may be made to counter this price disadvantage by providing exceptional quality. But this approach is rarely

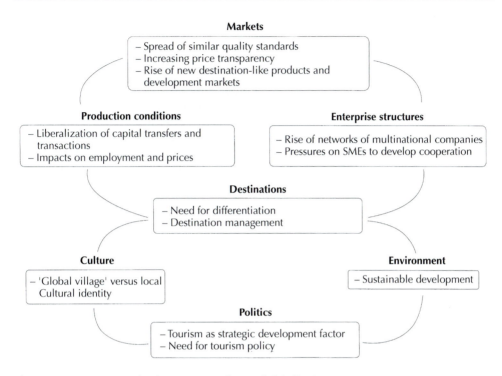

Markets
- Spread of similar quality standards
- Increasing price transparency
- Rise of new destination-like products and development markets

Production conditions
- Liberalization of capital transfers and transactions
- Impacts on employment and prices

Enterprise structures
- Rise of networks of multinational companies
- Pressures on SMEs to develop cooperation

Destinations
- Need for differentiation
- Destination management

Culture
- 'Global village' versus local Cultural identity

Environment
- Sustainable development

Politics
- Tourism as strategic development factor
- Need for tourism policy

Fig. 26.3. Future tourism development in conditions of globalization.

cost-effective. The new competitor countries, on the other hand, tend to operate through companies and organizations which are larger and more profitable.

At the destination level, traditional tourism countries tend to have extremely fragmented supply organization. The providers of various services are often reluctant to work as partners to create a common product. There is a lack of cooperation both horizontally and vertically. The situation is very different in the new tourism countries, where resorts have sprung up out of thin air, ready to operate as a cohesive system.

Implications for Development

The globalization process will have a considerable influence on future development. Here too, the main trend runs counter to a number of lesser trends. Based on our current knowledge we can safely reach several empirical conclusions regarding the devel-

opment of tourism in the conditions of globalization (Fig. 26.3).

Marketing
Markets

The question which currently concerns the markets is what preferences clients are likely to develop in the future. It appears that the world as a whole is developing similar expectations regarding the comfort of installations and the quality of services in tourism. On the other hand when it comes to choosing where to go, cultural differences and the uniqueness of destinations play an ever greater role, as do certain destination-like products such as leisure parks and cruise ships.

Global information and reservation systems are already having a major influence, and altering the typical tourist's behaviour. Today's tourist finds it increasingly easy to obtain information, with the help of multimedia technology, and to discover the most advantageous travel arrangements, the most attractive destinations and the best prices. This is having the effect of increasing price transparency worldwide, allowing the customer to make comparisons across the board.

Destinations

The arrival on the market of new destinations and destination-like products has resulted in a kind of touristic 'hypercompetition'. This forces individual destinations to differentiate themselves, to develop unique products and to reposition themselves with the help of new strategies. Destinations need to be built up and promoted in the same way as brands. Only then can one ensure that a location or region will never 'go out of fashion' (Keller, 1998).

To be consistent, an international brand policy must be able to rely on quality assurance at the destination level. Success in the positioning of a destination brand is not possible without attractive products. These new developments influence the organization of cooperation in the area of marketing at the local and national levels. In this age of globalization, destinations will only be able to take full advantage of their intrinsic advantages if they are managed in the same way as a corporation.

The marketing management of destinations is a good way of overcoming the fragmented structure of tourism-dependent sectors. It also puts the multiple supply options of a location to good use. Mature destinations, compared to resort corporations, have advantages as well as disadvantages. For indeed they are unique, inimitable systems, with much more to offer than destinations created out of thin air (Porter, 1990). Their attraction lies in the variety of the associated product range. They help tourism to integrate with society at large. Other effective long-term advantages of the traditional tourism countries include a high state of development, many years of specialization in the field of tourism, competitive awareness and a critical international clientele.

Management
Production conditions

The liberalization of transactions and capital transfers has increased the amount being invested in new destinations considerably. But while the production factor of capital has been extensively liberalized, labour remains as immobile as ever. In the case of less qualified labour, the low wages to be found in the developing and emerging economies have increasingly become the standard for industrial production. This has effectively meant the transfer of less productive jobs and sectors from the developed world to the developing world. At the same time the 'innovation explosion' in the developed countries has resulted in ever greater employment and income disparities between skilled and unskilled jobs.

It is not possible to transfer abroad the relatively less productive and personalized services of tourism, as is happening in industry, due to the location-specific nature of tourism. In conditions of globalization this fact puts the developed countries at a disadvantage in terms of wage costs and the recruitment of workers, jobs in tourism not being competitive on the local labour market. An important consideration here is whether or not a country has a policy of encouraging low wages or prefers to concentrate on highly qualified jobs. Clearly the extremely flexible US labour market with its policy of low wages is better suited to the needs of tourism-dependent sectors than are the countries of the European Union, with their more rigid labour markets that demand high qualifications and offer attractive working conditions and good wages.

Corporate structures

Basic factors like the labour market have a substantial influence on production conditions and organization. In future the important thing will be to increase tourism productivity, while trying to find a middle way between a 'service economy' and a 'self-service economy'. In terms of international competition it will be a matter of deciding which services are truly indispensable for the total touristic experience.

With the arrival of telematics it has become possible to develop new network-type corporate structures. We can expect to see a great deal more of these in tourism. A great many of the new networking types of companies already exist in all areas of tourism, many of them transnationals. For the most part these are institutionalized forms of cooperation. Among such transnationals one finds hotel chains, which allow the local SME members to maintain their operational independence, while at group level the concentration is on cooperative marketing efforts. This not only makes it possible to achieve economies of scale and scope in the area of marketing and brand management, but also in controlling transaction costs. This enables the smaller enterprises to, at least partly, overcome the disadvantages that go with small size.

Planning

Culture

The population is now aware of increasing worldwide integration (Robertson, 1992). A new world culture is being created, greatly influenced by mega-events including the Olympic Games and international exhibitions. This phenomenon is directly influencing the development of tourism, for such mega-events require travel by large numbers of people. 'Postmodern' society will increasingly be devoted to leisure and travel. The global village being created offers its own attractions, as alternatives to the traditional products based on natural and culture resources which until now have served as one of the main attractions for tourism.

The question we must ask is what role will authentic landscapes and monuments of culture have to play in this new global village. For a long time such resources as the Matterhorn in the Alps and the Pyramids of Giza acted as main magnets for tourism. In view of the uniqueness and inimitability of such attractions, competition was never total. The new competition, leisure parks and destination-like products, not only manages to imitate the originality of these traditional products, it is bringing demand

back from the periphery to the agglomerations.

Environment

This development is at least interesting from the viewpoint of ecological sustainability. There are, however, countercurrents, including the growth of tourism to the most remote regions of the world, a number of them relatively unexplored. This 'adventure and wilderness tourism' is often incorrectly referred to as 'ecological tourism'. The question that needs to be asked in this context is, can the lifestyle that goes with tourism originating in the developed world be extended to the entire planet and all peoples. If the peoples of India and China were to begin travelling as frequently as the West Europeans and North Americans, then the world's known reserves of oil could be expected to last no longer than another 8 years. To have some idea of just how much the process of globalization in tourism is already affecting the environment, one has only to think of the effect that kerosene, which for the most part is duty-free, has at 10,000 m, where its ozone-destroying toxicity is ten times greater than it is on the ground.

Government

Competition between places

The process of globalization has both friends and enemies at the political level. The pessimists speak of economic terrorism, the dictatorship of the financial markets, an alleged trend toward monopolistic practices, growing unemployment and what they see as 'social dumping'. The debate on globalization for the most part involves concepts derived from the liberal market economy. In the real world, the worst fears of the pessimists are unjustified.

In actual fact the effect of the financial markets is to discipline governments and their economic policies. Technological progress stands in the way of all attempts by the big multinationals to take over the market completely. An ever greater number of 'global players' concentrate their activities on their core business and systematically resort to outsourcing and spinoffs supported by downsizing. And finally, it has been proven that the process of globalization is not a 'destroyer of jobs', since the downsizing of industry in the developed countries has resulted in an increase in labour-intensive jobs in the services sector.

There is no doubt, on the other hand, that the globalization process does aggravate competition between places. This competition will ultimately decide which economic and social systems are to be counted among the winners, and which the losers. And finally it determines the touristic development of a country or group of countries. Thus for example in the western industrial nations the implementation of values such as 'the freedom of the citizen', 'economic wellbeing', and 'individual self-fulfilment' requires a highly developed economy and an efficient state that limits its activities to the essential. The question we must ask at this point is, what significance does this trend have for the tourism policy of these countries. There is no denying the fact that up-and-coming destinations in the emerging economies have had the benefit of state funds in developing and marketing new products. The traditional tourism countries thus find themselves caught up in a so-called 'prisoner's dilemma'. If they do nothing, they will simply continue to lose market share (Keller and Smeral, 1997).

Tourism as a strategic sector of the economy

For a number of reasons in conditions of globalization, a carefully planned tourism policy is essential for the creation of competitive advantages. As in the past, the best way to ensure optimum development of tourism potential at the local or regional level is with the help of coordinated, market-oriented planning. Moreover, it is in the interest of the competent state authority to constantly upgrade the infrastructure necessary for tourism. In tourism the state has an irrevocable duty as a co-producer of public goods such as security, means of transport and landscape protection. To the extent that tourism is a strategically important sector of the economy, a specific,

interdepartmental tourism policy needs to be developed at the level of the national or Federal government, to ensure the most tourism-friendly framework conditions possible.

France, Australia and Switzerland provide successful examples showing that active state promotion of innovation and cooperation on the supply side and the development and marketing of products at destination level is necessary to overcome market distortion in the fragmented small-business structure of the 'incoming' area and to use untapped competitive potential.

Conclusions

Globalization is an irreversible mega-trend which can be expected to have an ever greater impact on the economy and on society in future. It implies the increasing networking of human activities. The process will lead to a new global condition: it is making the world smaller, and bringing us daily closer to the global village about which we have all heard. The combined impact of fundamental political, economic and technological changes, all occurring more or less at the same time, tends to accelerate, intensify and spread further the process of globalization. The most important variables of acceleration are liberalization of cross-border economic exchanges, and deregulation within national boundaries, leading to ever greater competition, technological innovation and prosperity.

As in the case of all mega-trends, globalization unleashes conflicting forces. The internationalization of new areas of industry and services contrasts with the growth of place-specific services. Tourism is particularly subject to the opposing trends of internationalization and localization. As a buyers' market, tourism has been extensively internationalized. In contrast, the greatest share of tourism-dependent value added is place-specific. It follows that the overall economic conditions of a given place are destined to play an ever greater role as the competition for prospective visitors increases.

The focus of competition in the area of international tourism today is between countries that have already reached a high level of development. However, this select group now includes a growing number of emerging countries, which has led to an extension of the total market. The considerable growth in tourism worldwide is above all based on increasing exchanges between the more developed regions of the world. Intercontinental tourism is an increasingly important indicator of globalization. However, compared to domestic tourism and interregional tourism between countries of the world's leading tourism regions, it is not yet considered as important.

Although globalization in the field of tourism is as yet in the early stages, the first structural consequences can already be discerned. The traditional tourism countries are losing market share as their new competitors grow more and faster. As a result of overcapacity there is increasing competition on price, which puts SMEs at a disadvantage.

In the years ahead, the globalization process will lead to the standardization of comfort and quality worldwide. The increasing reliance on new information technologies will improve price transparency. The new multinational networks of large tourism enterprises will be in a better position to take advantage of the conditions of globalization than will the SMEs of the traditional tourism countries. Destinations with fragmented and multi-optional products and services will be under greater pressure to differentiate themselves from the competition than has been the case up until now. The disadvantages of small operators in the production and marketing of products and services in conditions of partnership can be overcome with the help of carefully planned destination management.

Tourism is today a strategic part of the economies of developed countries. The services it offers are life-enhancing 'experiences', based as much on unique and authentic cultural differences as on man-made attractions. In contrast to industry and the conventional services sector, the state is a co-producer in the creation of the 'world of experiences' behind each tourism product or service. For it is the state that makes available publicly owned property including unspoiled landscapes and the infrastructure on which tourism relies. Moreover, cooperation between service providers in tourism is often made possible by incentives from the state. This raises the question whether, in conditions of global competition, countries with an explicit tourism policy turn in a better economic performance than countries that do without such a policy.

27

Rural Tourism Development

Patrick Long and Bernard Lane

Introduction

In the early 1980s, Charles Kuralt, a Columbia Broadcasting Station television correspondent, travelled extensively through the back roads of the US recording and reporting his experiences to the eager American public. In his words, he tried to 'go slow, stick to the back roads, take time to meet people, listen to yarns, notice the countryside go by, and feel the seasons change' (Kuralt, 1985, p. xvi).

Kuralt documented his travels in a book titled, *On the Road With Charles Kuralt*. He describes his conversation with the editor of the local newspaper in Shelton, Nebraska, Douglas Duncan. Kuralt asked Duncan how one knows if one is in a small town. Mr. Duncan replied:

> You know you are in a small town when Third Street is on the edge of town;

> You know you are in a small town if you're born on June 13th and your family receives gifts from the local merchants because you're the first baby of the year;

> You know you're in a small town if you speak to each dog you pass, by name, and he wags his tail at you;

> You know you're in a small town if you

> dial a wrong number and talk for fifteen minutes anyway;

> You know you're in a small town if you can't walk for exercise because every car that passes you offers you a ride;

> You know you're in a small town when the biggest business in town sells farm machinery;

> You know you're in a small town if you write a check on the wrong bank and it covers it for you anyway; and

> You know you are in a small town if someone asks you how you feel and spends the time to listen to what you have to say
> (Kuralt, 1985, pp. 170–171)

The Kuralt–Duncan discourse touches on some of the key demand factors for rural tourism, factors which have helped propel tourism to the top of many rural agendas. Personal contact, authenticity, heritage, individualism – all are qualities sought by the visitor to rural areas, all are rural strengths. Twenty years ago the small town was seen as a dreary backwater. Now, small town values and destinations have become fashionable again. The media have become interested in all things rural and fashion is dictated to a great extent by the media. Tourism can be claimed to be a fashion-driven industry: rural tourism has become part of a global shift in fashionable leisure patterns.

The Rural World Today

Today, for the most part, rural communities across the US and throughout the world are not quite as idyllic as Kuralt describes them. It is not news that traditional rural economies are experiencing economic restructuring. It is also no surprise that any and all economic alternatives are being considered by elected officials, community leaders and residents of rural areas. In fact, some rural communities are actively seeking nontraditional industries such as prisons, nuclear waste sites and gambling, in an effort to stimulate their economy. The word heard today in the rural world is 'revitalization' – a term which generally means to

> resist the direction of deterioration and to move actively, even aggressively, in the opposite direction – to begin anew. This life that is to begin anew is one of energized, determined existence, resisting that which whittles away at being fully alive
>
> (T. Michael Smith, 1994, personal communication)

A whole series of problems besets the developed rural world; in Asia, in Europe, and in the Americas. Farm produce prices have fallen. Land prices have fallen. Service centres are retreating and centralizing, be they banks or hospitals or shopping facilities. Youth is moving out. These are not new processes: in the UK they are an extension of a 150-year-long process of rural retreat. Many parts of Europe have experienced a century of rural decline. And as Wallace Stegner graphically describes in his fictional history, *Wolf Willow*, many parts of rural America have been in decline since the 1920s (Stegner, 1962).

The paradox is, however, that in the midst of the latest stage of the retreat from the countryside, new forces are at hand which are bringing positive possibilities to the rural world. They are connected to changing transport and communication technologies, to fear of city crime and pollution, to early retirement to rural retreats. Tourism is just one of a whole new series of opportunities that rural communities can consider. But, like all new opportunities, understanding and exploiting tourism is a difficult process for most rural communities (Perry *et al.*, 1986; OECD, 1992, 1994).

Why can Tourism be Developed in the Rural Environments of the World?

The basic background to rural tourism's development lies in our changing mental perceptions of country life. In *Why Save Rural America?* Daryl Hobbs (1987) pointed out that an idealized rural US 'is a product of images, some based on experience, some created, and some based on selective perception and nostalgia', including 'images of bedrock values, virtue and general well-being. It is always in an outdoor setting that one popular commercial concludes, "Times don't get any better than this" '. With the growing size, homogenization, and complexity of metropolitan areas, rural authenticity, uniqueness and manageability is becoming an increasingly sought-after alternative. In other words, if we cannot sustain or recapture the ideal sense of place in our own workaday urban communities, we are likely to seek it out in our leisure time and on our own travels.

These mental constructs are not peculiar to Americans. They are affecting most affluent, educated urban peoples throughout the world. Today, rural communities are able to capitalize on the imagined rural world by promoting tourism. It is important to recognize that this behaviour does not necessarily constitute an exploitation of city folks' romantic illusions by greedy small-town sharpsters. But, for many rural communities, tourism development is now one of the few opportunities to enhance the local economy. It has been estimated by various sources that tourism is the US's third largest retail sales industry (Travel Industry Association of America 1997). In all US states, tourism is a significant industry, helping to create jobs, increase tax bases, generate direct revenue for both private and public entities and heighten civic pride. In the UK, following national surveys, the Rural Development Commission claimed in 1992 that tourism and recreation in rural Great Britain generated a gross income of £8 billion per annum and supported 400,000 jobs (Rural Development Commission, 1992). On a worldwide basis, the World Tourism Organization (WTO) predicts that tourism and travel could become the world's largest single industry early in the 21st century (WTO, 1996). No community – rural or urban – can totally ignore tourism's opportunities for wealth transfer and employment.

But What is Rural?

The problem of defining exactly what is a rural area is an international issue. Even within the US, there are a number of possibilities. Flora *et al.* (1992) in *Rural Communities: Legacy and Change*, have summarized several classification systems currently used for rural communities. The Economic Research Service (ERS) has placed all nonmetropolitan counties into three broad categories: urbanized (population of at least 20,000), less urbanized (urban population of 2555 to 19,999), and rural (those with no places of 2500 or more population). This definition also groups nonmetropolitan counties by those both adjacent to, and not adjacent to, a metropolitan county. The ERS also places nonmetropolitan counties into seven social and economic categories: farming, manufacturing, mining, specialized government, persistent poverty, federal lands and retirement destination.

The US Office of Management and Budget defines nonmetropolitan counties as those lacking a city of at least 50,000 or a commuting connection with a city of that size. Of the 3097 counties in the US, 2388 (or 77%) are designated nonmetropolitan. The US Census Bureau defines rural areas as all nonurban areas: an urban area is defined as cities of 50,000 or more population along with adjacent jurisdictions having a density of 1000 persons per square mile and other urban places with 2000 or more residents. Other federal agencies have different definitions of rural areas.

There is not, therefore, a universally accepted definition in the US of rural, and that creates problems when determining policy whether local, state or federal. But 'rural' can also be a self-assigned label that reflects a lifestyle, values and an environment desirable for its relative isolation and pace of living. Rural can be perceived as a place of safety, with solid values, surrounded by open space and natural beauty, where one is treated respectfully and friendly (Long, 1998). It is this perception that can be used very effectively in marketing the recreational experiences that drive the rural tourism industry.

What can be Considered Rural Tourism?

Lane (1994b) argued that, in its purest forms, rural tourism should be:

- By definition, in rural or remote areas;
- Functionally rural, meaning that it should be based upon the countryside's unique selling points of small-scale enterprise, open space, contact with or closeness to nature, and heritage – a heritage based on 'traditional' societies and working practices;
- Rural in scale – in terms of buildings, settlements and organization – and, therefore, usually small scale;
- Slow growing, connected with family enterprises, and long-term in nature; and
- Of many different kinds, reflecting the world's complex patterns of environment, economy, history and location.

Getz and Page (1997) modify the definition slightly, noting that on occasion large-scale operations do occur in rural tourism, that occasionally even locally owned enterprises grow rapidly and that the definition is likely to continue widening as the product palette which the rural entrepreneur offers broadens in scope.

Trends in Rural Tourism Development

Beyond a general shift in perceptions, four primary trends can be recognized as important in the expansion of rural tourism. These are factors that seem likely to spread through the population and across the world in the future.

The trend away from traditional resort destinations

The development of modern tourism began as a resort-based activity. Some resorts were purpose built – such as Coney Beach, Spain's Benidorm or the modern Disney Worlds. Others were major centres of cultural pilgrimage – London, New York, Paris, Prague, Rome or Sydney – which became resorts in a new 'City Tourism' trend. Plog (1991) describes the beginning of a shift away from resorts back in the 1980s, the shift toward what he termed the 'allocentric' traveller. His classic chapter entitled, *Where in the World Are People Going Now That There Is No Place to Go?* sums up this new wave (Plog 1991). Backed by demand for mild adventure and for special interest holidays, the rise of the 'Free and Independent Traveller' became the opportunity for many rural regions to enter the tourism business. Other factors back up the trend, not least being the health fears associated with sun, sea and sand holidays in a world of shrinking ozone layers. There also appears to be a growing perception, and unfortunately in some cases, reality, that urban venues are no longer safe.

New rural tourism market opportunities

The market factors causing a swing away from resort destinations were and are the opening opportunities for rural entrepreneurship in tourism. The Organization for Economic Cooperation and Development (OECD) (1994) report on rural tourism lists a series of other positive key factors, current or emerging, including:

- Increasing levels of education, encouraging exploration and outdoor learning activities;
- Growing interest in heritage, tradition, authenticity and rural life;
- The search for personal contact in a world of mass travel, anonymous hotels, shopping malls and video entertainment;
- A trend of taking multiple holidays per year, with opportunities to take a second short break in a rural location;
- Increasing health consciousness, giving a positive appeal to rural lifestyle and values such as fresh air, activity opportunities and stress-free situations;
- Market interest in high performance outdoor equipment from clothing to all-terrain bikes and high-tech climbing equipment;
- Growing interest in specialty foods and traditional country cooking techniques;
- The search for solitude and relaxation in quiet natural places; and
- An ageing but active population retiring earlier but living and travelling far into old age.

Enabling technology

It is hard to remember at the beginning of the 21st century just how remote rural areas were only a couple of decades ago. Now email, web sites, fax and telephone, airline services, highway improvements, and widespread car ownership have together transformed accessibility. In Europe and Japan, for example, high-speed train services running at 125–175 mph also have been key factors. Remote areas still exist, but they are fewer and only relatively remote. Indeed, speakers at a recent OECD conference proffered the view that rural remoteness was now so rare that it had become a positive unique selling point for tourism rather than a problem (Albarracin, Spain; OECD Territorial Development Service). Technological advances have also enabled product development for rural tourism to proceed, be it in cycling, walking, climbing or canoeing equipment. The electronic transmission of money and the plastic charge or credit card enables rural areas to take and bank tourism cash flows easily.

Mass media communication has had a dramatic effect on enterprise and political thinking within the rural communities of the world. No longer cut off from the mainstream, ideas about socioeconomic development and change permeate rural communities as never before. From general issues transmitted via television, to groups of country people travelling the world to see specific new practices, to email networks nurturing and spreading ideas and confidence through their users – technology has transformed so many country peoples' outlook on the world.

Acceptance of tourism in rural change

The changes outlined above have come just in time for many rural regions throughout the world. The ongoing loss of farm-based employment has reached the stage where basic service provision is becoming difficult and community viability is often threatened. Equally, the global farm produce market and its price fluctuations make it imperative to diversify rural economies to give stability and security.

Tourism is not a panacea for all rural problems, but it has a number of positive attractions. It can provide organic, low capital economic growth in locally owned businesses. It can provide 'pluri-activity', a situation where individuals and family units live from several jobs rather than just one, giving variety and reducing risk (see Bollman and Bryden, 1997). Tourism, if properly managed, can help justify and fund conservation of the natural and human heritage. The US national parks are a classic example of the power of rural tourism to help secure natural heritage areas. Some of the US's most visited public lands – Yellowstone, Yosemite and the Grand Canyon, among others – are in rural areas. On the human heritage side, Heritage Canada's work with its Heritage Regions Program has provided an object lesson in how rural tourism can help conserve human heritage for future generations (Brown, 1996).

Evolution of Rural Tourism

The development of rural tourism has now been through what could be called 'Phase One' of its evolution. Across the world, communities and enterprises have begun to practice the art of tourism in the countryside. Practitioners are learning its secrets of success – and the problems of failure. Academics are tracking its progress, and debating its concepts.

Farm-based tourism was an activity long practiced in some parts of Europe – with organizations such as France's Gîtes Rurales, Austria's Urlaub auf den Bauernhof and Britain's Farm Holiday Bureau enjoying success for more than 20 years. In the 1980s, such farm-based activity began to spread geographically and thematically, with a wide range of businesses and communities becoming involved in the process (Getz and Page, 1997). America's National Rural Tourism Development project, based at the University of Minnesota from 1988 to 1991, Canada's various provincial level Community Tourism Development programmes, and Britain's Rural Tourism Development Project at the University of Bristol have all been part of that first phase. These efforts have emphasized group and community working, especially in marketing and promotion. Internationally, the trend to rural tourism was recognized when, in 1994, the OECD's Rural Development programme worked with OECD's Tourism Committee to produce a substantial position paper on the subject (OECD, 1994).

An important part of the Phase One process has been the acceptance at the national political level that tourism was an important possibility for the future of the countryside. US President, George Bush's statement in October 1991, at a briefing before travel and tourism executives, typifies that recognition:

> This solid record of the [economic] growth of tourism has not gone unnoticed by small communities and by rural areas facing the challenge to diversify their economies. More and more rural communities are making tourism a part of their economic diversification options for the nineties. And

the U.S. Travel and Tourism Administration, along with other governmental agencies, are working to put small town America on the tourist map

(*Travel Industry Association of America Newsletter*, 1991)

Implications of Future Rural Tourism Development

The next phase for rural tourism development will be a much more complex one. It will be a phase of expansion, differentiation, consolidation and understanding. The following ten implications are likely to occur.

Competition will increase – provision will grow

As governments, communities and entrepreneurs hear of the concept of rural tourism, more are seeking to exploit it. At the local level that means more farmers offering accommodation, more heritage centres, more 'themed' restaurants, more opportunities to bike or ski or ride. Nationally it means more regions putting their offers together to market their wares collectively. Internationally, as long-haul travel grows, it means that we can expect increased competition globally. Already within Europe, the former countries of the Soviet Bloc and its satellites are working hard to exploit their rural heritage and low-cost labour supply. Latin America and Africa are increasingly active in the field. Visits to rural China or Korea are more of a possibility (Sofield and Li, 1997; Choi, 1998; Hall and O'Hanlon, 1998). Not all destinations will be successful. Nevertheless, the supply side will grow: possible oversupply will demand increasing skill and sophistication if businesses are to succeed.

More national and provincial/regional rural tourism policies

Rural tourism policies will increase but the manner in which those tourism policies are conceived and implemented will vary across the world. A battle of the political styles on policy will be enacted, probably with no final consensus about success.

In the US, for example, despite strong grassroots efforts, elected officials at the federal level will continue their 'hands-off' policy toward tourism generally. Select federal agencies (e.g. Department of Transportation, the National Park Service, the USDA Forest Service, Bureau of Land Management) will continue to provide, where staff and funding are available and political will prevails, support for special tourism initiatives and training. No formal policy for rural tourism is likely. In varying degrees, individual states will further or establish select programmes to expand their rural tourism product, thus increasing both visitation and travel expenditures. Such programmes will be based primarily upon cultural, historic and environmental themes.

In other western countries more state intervention will take place through a variety of methods. In Australia, a published national rural tourism policy is backed at the state level by a variety of more or less detailed policies and measures. In turn, local administrations in some parts of Australia are deeply involved in tourism development and promotion (Commonwealth Department of Tourism, 1994). In the UK, national strategies for rural tourism are more advisory than formal. The key to public sector intervention in the UK lies at the local district level, where salaried tourism development officers frequently work closely with the private sector. Public sector provision covers the costs of tourism marketing, tourist information, training, coordination, project planning and the provision of infrastructure such as signposting, heritage product development, trail and path creation and maintenance. The majority of UK local districts have their own tourism strategies, closely linked to the marketing function and to physical planning policies.

Two other types of European state-sector intervention should be mentioned. The former command economies of central Europe are attempting to develop rural tourism at a rapid pace through the wholesale importation of western experts and expertise. Operating at national and regional levels, they hope to convert public and private sector representatives, small town officials, and small farmers to pursue a new tourism enterprise culture for domestic and international markets. The process is a difficult one – but all economic and social change in emerging economies is fraught with problems. Capacity building and restructuring of rural economies are long-term issues: for many rural people in central Europe the experience of being a tourist is a novelty, let alone its professional practice (Augustyn, 1998; Hall and O'Hanlon, 1998).

In western Europe, the European Union's (EU) concept of the semi-autonomous regional enterprise company – referred to as the 794 LEADER local action groups – have been trying to implement broad rural development programmes since 1991. More than 80% of these programmes focus on the tourism sector. Overlaid across existing public sector organizations (and sometimes competing with them), these EU funded and professionally staffed groupings support a range of innovative projects undertaken by local action groups, regularly exchanging information and working together on a transnational basis (Nitsch and Van der Straaten, 1995). Total public funding over the period 1994–1999 is around 1755 million ECU; in addition private sector match funding is levered in by negotiation.

Despite a range of styles and approaches to public policy, all grapple with similar fundamental truths. Tourism is a fiercely competitive market where the private sector must be effective to ensure success of a tourism economy in the marketplace. The public sector rarely succeeds directly in the tourism business. But there is considerable scope for indirect participation. Just how far that scope should go, and what is best practice, remains to be seen.

Partnership building

The hallmark of most rural tourism enterprises is their small size. Small scale can be a competitive advantage; it gives guests personal contact, and it is a unique selling point for travellers from sprawling anonymous urban centres. But it can be a major problem for organization, marketing and product development.

Building partnerships among tourism businesses is an effective way of linking enterprises – and also linking enterprises to public sector assistance. Interest and skills in this area are likely to grow with partnerships taking many forms. At the local level, the now common tourism development committees and local business forums will continue their work. Their regional level counterparts have proved more difficult to develop because of local rivalries, but as communications and lifestyles make regional working easier, they are likely to grow. The US Scenic Byway Program has made great strides in regional cooperation partly due to its required corridor management plan developed by its respective regional partners. Such planning could be public-sector based (such as the Scenic Byway Program in the US or the South Pembrokeshire Action with Rural Communities (SPARC) in South Wales), or private-sector based, (such as Red Andaluza de Alojamientos de Casas Rurales (RAAR)) in Andalusia, Spain. It could be linear, based on trails or rail lines, such as the UK's rail partnership schemes, linking local marketing initiatives with rail companies. Or it may be of a type to exchange information nationally, including partnerships with groups such as the US's Outdoor Recreation Coalition of America or Sporting Goods Manufacturer's, to access vital and timely travel-related trends and information.

The market will grow

On the demand side, an increasing number of visitors seem to be avoiding more urban venues either because they have already visited these sites and are familiar with their offerings or these venues are no longer economically accessible. And the trends to individual active travel outlined earlier are likely to continue. They will be encouraged by new products and marketing factors discussed below.

Marketing will become more effective and sophisticated

Access to the market, market information, and marketing skills have always been problem areas for many rural tourism businesses.

But the trends are set to make these activities much more effective. Information about domestic and international travel trends, outdoor recreation patterns and product purchase information is becoming much more widely available due to expanded research and its publication. New Zealand Tourist Board's (NZTB) specialist publications on overseas markets for rural tourism are object lessons in good practice here (NZTB, 1995). Training will allow both individual businesses and partnerships to develop specialized marketing skills. The case for niche marketing of rural products has been thoroughly investigated and is increasingly well understood (OECD, 1995a,b).

A series of technical developments are becoming available to assist the rural niche market developer. At its simplest level, the widespread use of personal computers has allowed database development and direct mail operations to become the norm. But the biggest breakthrough is taking place from Internet marketing and promotion. Ever more sophisticated and user-friendly web sites, with linking facilities and on-line booking, are becoming commonplace, overcoming the tyranny of distance faced by many rural areas. Technology improvements in accounting, reservation systems and 'virtual reality' will enhance the competitiveness of rural tourism destinations across a truly global market.

Product development

Early rural tourism products were largely simple: sightseeing, walking and unsophisticated appreciation of rural life. Moving to the future, product development programmes are already ushering in an almost bewildering range of niche activities. Some are products of an increasingly aware and demanding market. Others stem from successful rural initiatives. Two examples illustrate this range of opportunities – cycle tourism and gambling.

Cycle tourism has transformed the attractiveness of areas without high scenic merit, or which are relatively flat, because dedicated cycle tracks or networks of quiet back roads can provide very valuable infrastruc-ture. The product has evolved from simple cycle hire to cycle holidays. Within cycle holidays there is a wide range of offers. At the top end of the market, luxury accommodation with back-up vans and masseurs are typified by international tour operators such as the US's Backroads and the UK's Country Lanes. Many other operators provide simpler accommodation, but offer luggage transfer arrangements. Mountain Bike holidays are also available – one enterprising UK rural operator offers short breaks under the title *Dirty Weekends* – washing and drying facilities included!

The golden age of expansion of gambling as a tourism development tool in rural areas, particularly in the US, has passed, although this niche activity will see some expansion among select communities and geographic regions. Native American Indian tribes will slowly expand their gaming offerings as markets are identified or expanded. There will continue to be pressure by the gaming industry, some politicians, and select real estate/land developers to expand resort, large city and riverboat gaming. In addition, gaming will continue to be suggested as one of the few alternatives to reviving dying racetracks.

The profits are simply too large for this tourism niche to disappear. What will result is the expansion of the limited or single licence system, ensuring that a community or area is not overwhelmed by a gaming economy and that a range of expected and necessary community services continues. The few examples available of rural community gaming provide an understanding of the importance of planning and how a gambling tourism economy is driven by scale, competition and a determination of who benefits (Long et al., 1994).

Training

To enable the diversification of rural economies into tourism, training opportunities are a vital prerequisite, as noted by the OECD's (1994) report and many other commentators. Indeed research into small tourism business failures highlights the lack of training and business planning as a major problem (McKercher and Robbins, 1998).

Small businesses, the economic backbone of rural tourism, are a special challenge to the training provider. Limited time, finances and personnel frequently make attendance at formal training sessions prohibitive. But technology advances, most specifically the Internet and World Wide Web, ensure that training and technical support will be easily available through distance learning, addressing some of these limitations. Increasingly, emphasis will be placed on training local trainers to a high and recognized standard.

Real estate issues

A major proportion of rural tourism activity is driven by real estate development. The ownership and development of land for second homes, holiday/timeshare apartments, factory shopping outlets, golf courses and other recreation venues will continue to grow. There is a range of contentious issues here, connected with outside investment, land and property prices, and the unbalancing of communities through retirement settlement. But the trend to build new locations and facilities and the trend to retire to safe, low-cost communities, will grow (Reid, 1995).

Development around heritage

Heritage, as an anchor for a rural community's tourism economy, will grow in controversy and be more fiercely debated at the local level. The role of the countryside as a repository of natural, built and cultural heritage is a vital one. Tourism can strengthen and revitalize heritage conservation. But there is a tradeoff when heritage is transformed into a marketable tourism product. Such tradeoffs can involve native peoples, historic artefacts and ways of life. Infused into the debate about the exploitation of heritage will be a range of new ideas from better heritage interpretation techniques using guides and trails and the ecomuseum concept, through to attempts to develop high technology, virtual reality operations. More appropriate and sensitive heritage tourism development, through heritage strategy development and heritage management techniques, should become better known (Herbert, 1995).

More sustainable tourism policy

The demand for tourism development policies – sustainable in all senses – will become universal. Although the concept of sustainable tourism dates back to the Europe of the 1970s, its full development and acceptance is relatively new, owing much to the deliberations of the United Nations Rio Earth Summit in 1992 on the Environment and Development. Sustainable tourism aims to create a balance between exploitation and conservation, to conserve the industry's vital seed corn as well as the natural and human world's heritage. The concept has been discussed at length in many places (Inskeep, 1991; Lane, 1994a), but the trend is already pointing to a widespread market and legislative requirement for sustainable development policies. In the UK, for example, government guidelines now require all local councils to prepare sustainable tourism development policies (Department for Culture, Media and Sport, 1999). Elsewhere in the developed world, environmental impact assessments are required for most developments of any magnitude.

Three themes are central here. First, more information and experience are now available about sustainable tourism planning. Second, there are more private sector companies and government agencies available to provide technical assistance. And third, pressure exists at all levels to make tourism 'fit' with a community's cultural, social, historic and environmental resources. With more than 16,000 rural communities in the US alone potentially adding to the rural tourism product, there is increasing competition for the traveller's money. The manner in which new destinations are developed, the attractions and services they provide, and the integrity by which they address social, cultural and environmental issues, will determine to a great extent, their success.

The charge is to assist rural areas in taking advantage of their tourism potential by identifying effective ways to assess and manage tourism through a strategic sustainable development plan. Such a plan must focus on building local and regional capacities for attracting visitors and on accurately assessing the impacts of tourism upon local communities and regional economies. And, importantly, tourism development must be guided by a vision that recognizes the economic value while maintaining the authenticity and integrity of the attractions and service that contribute to long-term success.

Conclusion

Like every human enterprise, rural tourism offers a mixture of opportunities and dilemmas. Rural residents have the power to steer rural tourism away from the pitfalls and toward its promise. Charles Wilkinson, University of Colorado natural resource law professor, effectively captures the qualities that most rural communities seem to be striving for today in this statement:

> We need to develop what I call an ethic of place. It is premised on a sense of place, the recognition that our species thrives on the subtle, intangible, but soul-deep mix of landscape, smells, sounds, history, neighbors, and friends that constitute a place, a homeland. An ethic of place respects equally the people of a region and the land, animals, vegetation, water, and air. It recognizes that [westerners] revere their physical surroundings and that they need and deserve a stable, productive economy that is accessible to those with modest incomes. An ethic of place ought to be a shared community value and ought to manifest itself in a dogged determination to treat the environment and its people as equals, to recognize both as sacred, and to insure that all members of the community not only search for, but insist upon, solutions that fulfill that ethic
>
> (Udall, 1990)

Rural tourism can be, and should be, not the exploitation of an illusion, but the celebration of an ideal. Indeed, to be sustainable over the long haul, tourism development must catalyse the development of the host community toward its own ideal. This does not mean that there is no place in rural tourism development for outsiders. Indeed, since rural decision makers are, by definition, relatively isolated and have limited resources, in order to use tourism as a community development tool they need help from state and Federal government and from other entities that can provide the necessary resources and vision.

Rural tourism has expanded beyond what we had come to know as the traditional major resort destinations. This is coupled with a substantial increase in consumer interest in the offerings and benefits of the rural tourism experience and a significant influence of technology that has narrowed the gap between urban and rural tourism marketing and promotion. In addition, tourism as a catalyst in rural change, has increased in acceptance by both policy makers and residents.

Although there has been a great deal of speculative hope that tourism can 'save' rural communities, much discussion, and some accomplishments, there are yet few standards by which to measure success. There are examples of well-established and profitable attractions, activities, and community tourism systems. What we lack most are accepted indicators by which to track over time the positive and negative impacts made by a tourism economy on community life. Such indicators will lead to better policies and better planning, ensuring that the greatest benefits are derived for all parties from a rural tourism economy.

28

Community Tourism Development

Gail A. Van der Stoep

In July of 1998, a sperm whale carcass washed up on the beach of western Newfoundland, just south of Port au Choix. The first reaction by many community residents was something like 'Get that stinky, rotting carcass out of here! It will turn away the tourists'. However, another resident – a local business owner and artisan – viewed the carcass differently: as a potential tourism treasure, washed in from the sea that for centuries has been a dominant influence on the lives and lifeways of residents of the area.

Trash or Treasure?

Was this small town, traditionally an outport fishing community, involved in community tourism development? Did its residents and businesses have a common vision? Were they basing their tourism product and image development on 'things authentic' within the community? Were they engaged in collaborative efforts? Was tourism integrated with other aspects of Port au Choix's community and economic development?

As have many of Newfoundland's communities, Port au Choix has been trying to redefine itself, at least partially, as a tourism community. In fact, with the decline of the Atlantic fishery, all of Newfoundland has been working to diversify its economy. Tourism is a major component of that effort; individual communities want to reap economic benefits from this diversification. To do so, however, each must be actively involved in tourism development.

Port au Choix is at the tip of a small finger of land jutting into the Gulf of St Lawrence,

about halfway between Gros Morne National Park and the tip of Newfoundland's northern peninsula. Currently it is reached from the south by a spur road off the main roadway that follows the western shoreline. The main road, first paved in the 1960s, was routed away from the jagged coastline to speed north–south traffic. It now bypasses the small community, thus removing Port au Choix from the main tourism corridor. To counter this displacement, the community must have attractions intriguing enough to coax people off the main thoroughfare and into town. The town council certainly did not want the stench of decay and an unsightly rotting lump of blubber to repel tourists, sending them back to Highway 430 before they ever reached town.

However, Ben Ploughman – a singer, writer, storyteller and owner of a craft shop – believed the carcass could become the cornerstone of the community's tourism efforts and image. At the same time, it could become a catalyst for building local pride and honouring the town's history. The sperm whale carcass could, he believed, be

flensed (the blubber cut away in the traditional manner of whalers), and the bones
cleaned and reassembled for an exhibit in
the local museum. The museum, recently
transferred to the community by Parks Canada when it moved to its new facility, could
feature an exhibit based on the sperm whale.
Stories could include the relationship
between the sperm whale and the giant
squid, the life cycle and migration of
whales, and the history of commercial whal-
ing in the Gulf of St Lawrence, begun in the
1500s by Basque whalers. These stories
could form a backdrop for telling the
centuries-old history of Port au Choix Indian
and non-Indian relationships with the sea.
Additionally, the actual flensing event
could be used as a special event for tourists,
and to draw them into other parts of the
community; and serve as a catalyst to bring
together community members to learn and
participate in a 'lost skill' once critical to the
area's early whalers.

Purpose of Community Tourism Development

While the tourism development ideas
described previously were the ideas of a
single Port au Choix resident rather than the
result of a community-wide, collaborative
tourism development planning process,
characteristics of Ploughman's ideas reflect
the purpose and ideals of community tourism development: basing tourism
development on an area's authentic natural,
historic and cultural resources; involving
numerous stakeholders within the community; and integrating tourism with other
aspects of community and economic development.[1]

Trend: Growth in Community Tourism Development

While research studies that either indicate
trends in implementation of community

tourism development approaches, or evaluate the effectiveness of such approaches,
were not found, publication and use of
numerous applied materials in the past 10
years indicate growing interest. Published
materials, which have developed from varied sources and applications, include
workbooks and manuals, textbook chapters,
and articles in conference and workshop
proceedings. Many of the approaches
applied to community tourism development
have evolved through more general community development, often implemented in
rural areas. Such approaches form a strong
foundation for the development of tourism
within a more comprehensive context. In
such approaches, the unifying goal is to
strengthen the social and economic fabric of
communities; tourism is simply one of the
threads in that fabric. Used appropriately,
evaluating tourism development options
can become a tool to bring together community members, adjacent communities and
even former adversaries. Many of the principles and experiences identified through
partnership efforts, primarily in the natural
resource management arena, are applicable.
These efforts have received more research
attention.

To provide some historical perspective,
in the late 1970s the University of Missouri
(1978) developed and published the first
edition of *Tourism USA: Guidelines for
Tourism Development*. While not specified
in the title, the purpose of this publication
was to aid communities interested in initiating or further developing tourism as one
component of their economic development
programmes. This volume was updated and
expanded in 1986 to include international
marketing and visitor services for special
populations. During the mid to late 1980s,
there appeared a series of articles and other
publications focused on community tourism development. Among them were
Blank's (1989) *The Community Tourism
Industry Imperative*; Murphy's (1985, 1988)

---

[1] Several concepts and programmes associated with community-based tourism development are mentioned
throughout this chapter. However, most are not discussed in great detail. For supplementary information,
see the chapters within this book on partnerships, public/private partnerships, social impacts of tourism,
sustainable development and best practices, conflict management, cultural tourism and place meanings and
attachments.

Tourism: A Community Approach and *Community Driven Tourism Planning*; and Sem's (1994) *Tourism Development Decision Models*. A chapter on community tourism development is included in Gartner's (1996a) *Tourism Development: Principles, Processes, and Policies*. Other authors have included tourism development within a broader approach to community and economic development. Examples are Matulef's (1988) *Community Development: A National Perspective*; Kretzmann and McKnight's (1993) *Building Communities from the Inside Out*; Bergstrom *et al.*'s (1995) *Collaboration Framework: Addressing Community Capacity*; and the Entergy Corporation's (1992) *Community Development Handbook*. Still others have proposed similar approaches in working with rural communities, especially those wanting to diversity economies beyond traditional agriculture: Fessenmaier and Fessenmaier's (1993) *Helping Rural Communities Prepare for Economic Development: Assessing and Developing Tourism Resources*; Brass's (1995) *Community Tourism Assessment Handbook*; Butler *et al.*'s (1998) *Tourism and Recreation in Rural Areas*. Despite the lack of specific community tourism trend data, increasing attention is being given to more coordinated and collaborative tourism planning, development and promotion in general, as well as to tourism planning integrated within a community or regional planning process. Reasons, often interrelated with other social, political and economic trends, are several.

Externally funded and imposed tourism development

Tourism has simply evolved in many areas, with no integrated plan or local policy control; often tourism development has been imposed on communities from external sources. Such is the case when outsiders, often 'corporate moguls', invest in an area that they believe can be exploited for their own purposes, often in ways incompatible with local priorities and ways of life. Impacts, often perceived as negative by locals, include traffic congestion, higher tax rates, stress on community infrastructure and emergency services, displacement of local residents from 'special places', outside cultural and social influences, and deterioration of natural and historic resources. Residents may feel they have lost control of their own communities. Community tourism facilitates regaining control over the type and level of tourism development.

Negative reaction to haphazard tourism development

While many communities are becoming more sophisticated in analysing development proposals, granting building permits and approving zoning variances, other communities have been caught off guard, not realizing the long term impacts of new development until changes have occurred. Tourism often develops haphazardly, based on opportunity to individuals (or individual businesses), rather than as a result of an integrated planning process. A recent flurry of development of tourism bureaus, convention and visitor bureaus and regional tourism associations, particularly in rural areas and small communities, indicates an interest in more sensible, integrated approaches to community tourism development.

> Tourism must be community driven. Not every community is suited for tourism development, nor is tourism suitable for every community ... [Tourism development] is not free, and it requires both resources and commitment that might be directed elsewhere
>
> (Calcote *et al.*, 1994, p. 7)

Need for economic diversification

Traditional industries (e.g. logging, mining, manufacturing) and agriculture (e.g. small family farms) have been undergoing major changes in recent years. Regional economies, community structures, personal lifestyles and land-use patterns have all been impacted, often in ways perceived as negative. Thus, many communities, regions, even countries, are seeking ways to diversify their economies and maintain or increase the quality of life for residents. Tourism provides one possible 'solution'. Those involved in tourism development often tout it as a panacea for economic development – an industry that is 'clean' and brings lots of external dollars into a community, region or state. However, costs and negative impacts have received increasing attention by researchers and, specifically within the framework of community tourism development, have been considered as communities make deliberate decisions about if they want to initiate (or expand) tourism involvement and, if so, to what extent and in what ways.

Increasing local participation in government actions

Another impetus for approaching tourism planning within the broader context of community development has been increasing action by organized citizen groups to: (i) thwart certain types of development (e.g. large chain discount stores, malls, fast food outlets); (ii) preserve and promote community town centres, main streets and landmark historic structures; (iii) stop development of industry, the building of prisons and raising of 'unsightly' communications towers; and (iv) prevent other changes perceived as threatening to their community and personal lifestyles, health and safety, sense of place and cost of living. Integrated community planning, to include tourism as a potential component, focuses on giving residents and stakeholder groups a voice and some degree of control in the management of change and development within their communities. This process involves residents in a deliberate process of 'social exchange' based on what they value, as individuals and as a community (Jurowski et al., 1997).

While these external factors have influenced a more coordinated community-based approach to tourism development, 'community tourism' is not a 'thing' that can be succinctly defined or easily recognized from external observation. Rather, it is a process based on a philosophy and guided by supporting principles. The concept has been used in a variety of ways, with different emphases and starting points in various communities. For this chapter, community tourism development is described as a community-level collaborative planning

and development process, focused on strengthening communities and within which tourism is considered one possible component. The tourism component is based on visitor access to authentic resources and experiences (natural, historic, cultural). The benefits of such an approach are discussed below.

Benefits of Community Tourism Development

The need for economic development or diversification is often the initial impetus for tourism development. However, other benefits accrue from community involvement in tourism planning, decisions and implementation. While some of the trends and triggers to community tourism development are described in the previous section, these other benefits may provide the sustaining force for long term community involvement.

Community buy-in and empowerment

When community residents are actively involved in debate about their future, and are allowed an influential voice in final decisions, they are more likely to support the actions, accept the impacts, and understand the social, economic and environmental takeoffs made with their development decisions. And they are less likely to use legal strategies to block development because the decisions are theirs, not imposed by others.

Reduced potential of lawsuits used to block specific development projects

See above.

Improved chance of long term success

When community members are involved in community planning and the associated development decisions, particularly those believed to benefit the entire community, they are more likely to support and participate in implementation for the long term. For example, imagine a community in which high school students are involved in a process to identify all of its natural, cultural and historic resources. This list is then presented in a community forum for resident assessment of importance and contribution to community identity. Results are used by the students to develop interpretive tourism brochures about the community's sites and themes. Community members – adults and youth – are involved, invested, and likely to support sharing their community with tourists (example from Marquette, Michigan).

Better understanding by residents of the community's history, culture and natural resources

Residents are often not aware of what resources exist within their communities, or which may be of interest to tourists. In some cases, potential tourist attractions may be the very things that remind local residents of 'bad times'. An example is a small Great Lakes community suffering economic hardship because the transportation systems (railways connecting with Great Lakes car ferries) and the freight they once hauled (e.g. lumber), once the lifeblood and economic base of the community, became obsolete. The historic complex of a railroad turntable, car ferry dock, lifesaving station and car ferry – potentially a strong tourism attraction – was perceived as an eyesore and an unwelcome reminder of the 'sellout' of the community by the industries that once supported it. Community tourism planning can help a community recognize resources and view some resources from different perspectives.

Increased sense of community identity and pride

Through involvement in identifying and assessing a community's resources, the spotlight is turned on sites, characteristics, people, history and other elements that may have simply been taken for granted by residents. What is familiar is often unrecognized for its value. In another example, this time in Jasper, Alberta, elementary and secondary students were invited to draw pictures and write short stories about the area's history and natural resources. The drawings and stories, in the children's handwriting, were used to produce wayside exhibits for visitors. The process of researching, drawing and writing made the students, their parents, and other residents aware and proud of their history and the mountainous natural environment they call 'home'.

Protection of 'sacred places' and sensitive resources

When residents identify the range of resources within their community, then have a voice in the tourism development plan based on those resources, they can choose to share some with visitors and not share others. Thus they can keep their 'sacred places' and stories – whether a secret fishing hole, sacred burial ground, private ceremonial event, or a 'shady' part of history – protected from prying eyes, potentially insensitive visitors, overcrowding and resident displacement, and accidental or intentional damage to the resources. When outsiders decide what should be included in the 'tourist package', residents have little or no control.

Implementation of strategies to minimize or mitigate potential negative impacts

When community members are proactive in making decisions about tourism, and are realistic about potential negative effects, they can design and implement strategies to minimize those impacts. For example, they may route tourists away from a particularly sensitive natural resource area.

Development and enhancement of community amenities for residents

Community amenities that serve tourists can and should also (perhaps primarily) serve residents. For example, in Leamington, Ontario, a small coastal community on Lake Erie, a community collaborative called *ErieQuest* became the entity through which government organizations, local divers and small businesses worked together to redevelop the waterfront. The impetus was enhancement of dive and other marina-based tourism, but the park, boardwalk,

memorials and other waterfront enhancements also provide residents with a
wonderful recreational facility year-round.

Opportunities to share resources

Working together for common tourism goals
– such as presentation of a unified community story and identity, efficiency of
information distribution to tourists and
funding of promotional efforts – individuals, businesses, government agencies, and
nonprofit organizations can share staff,
funding, ideas, information centres and
other resources to facilitate effective and
efficient use of these resources.

Keeping profits within the community

When community organizations and businesses are involved with local government
in tourism development planning, they can
develop policy and deed restrictions, provide grants and other incentives, and
otherwise develop an environment that
encourages local investment and involvement in provision of tourism facilities and
services, thus keeping profits within the
local community. This is an alternative to
relying on external corporate investment
and development that ultimately lead to
major leakage of money out of the community.

Principles of Community Tourism Development

Interwoven in the previous discussion of
community tourism benefits are allusions to
some of the steps used in community building (asset identification, strategic
community visioning, SWOT analysis
[identification and assessment of strengths/
weaknesses, opportunities/threats], impact
analysis, community theming and 'brand-
ing', leveraging of external resources,
development of action strategies and monitoring of impacts). Detailed explanations,
accompanied by worksheets, examples and
suggestions, are available in a variety of
other sources and, therefore, not included
here. Rather, the principles and philosophy

behind the trend of increased use of community tourism development approaches, as
synthesized from numerous sources, are
presented.

The definition of 'community' is left to the
group of people within a geographic area
who may specify community based on political structures (e.g. village, town, township,
city, village, county), geophysical structures
(e.g. watershed, valley, river corridor), cultural identity (e.g. ethnic community,
neighbourhood, agricultural community) or
other characteristic(s) that makes sense to
both the tourism providers and the tourists.

'Planning process' implies that planning is
ongoing, and involves monitoring and
evaluation of implemented tourism programmes, to include monitoring of
economic impacts, visitation patterns,
employment trends, social indicators, traffic
counts, environmental impacts, etc.

'Collaboration' means that all stakeholders are involved in the process of decision
making and management. Stakeholders,
depending on the community structure, can
include: elected government officials, government agency employees, planning
commission, economic development
authority, nonprofit entities (e.g. museums
and historical societies), land management
agencies (local, state, federal), business
owners (tourism-based as well as
nontourism-based), schools, landowners
and residents, and organizations such as
convention and visitor bureaus, chambers of
commerce, and tourism associations.

'Authenticity' means developing tourism
attractions, theme, and image (or 'brand')
based on natural, cultural, and historic
resources that are authentic and unique to
the community.

Several underlying principles of community tourism development are less obvious
in the description, but are nonetheless critical to the overall process and philosophy.
These include community empowerment
and control, sustainability (McCool and

Watson, 1995; Lipman *et al.*, 1996), linkages, and tourism attractions as community resources.

'Community empowerment and control' means that community members, together, make deliberate decisions about the future characteristics of their community. Issues may revolve around type and level of acceptable development; amenities desired; physical character of the community (both natural and built environments); and the community's sacred places and values. If a community decides it wants to share its resources with tourists in exchange for economic returns, then it must make a series of specific decisions to establish parameters for tourism development. With this must come a clear understanding that tourism development will create change; it is the community's responsibility to manage that change in a way that is acceptable and appropriate to the community.

'Sustainability' is a concept used widely in the last decade as applied to management of natural resources, economies, individual industries, and social/cultural entities. While a succinct definition – reaping benefits from resources while not destroying the resources themselves – is simple enough, it is applied to systems that, by their nature, are extremely complex and contain many interrelated components. Opinions often vary widely as to what type and level of resource degradation or change is deemed acceptable. Thus, 'sustainability' is most useful as a tool for making development and/or management decisions and for monitoring the impacts of subsequent actions.

The concept of 'linkages' is broad and, in the case of community tourism development, refers to a variety of connections important to the success of tourism. It includes human linkages (e.g. collaborative planning and management), communication linkages (e.g. sharing of information among tourism stakeholders and between tourism providers and clients), physical linkages (e.g. transportation system linkages, pedestrian corridors, visual access through design of physical space), experien-

tial linkages (e.g. tourism packages, tourism theme identification and use, multi-site discount tickets), promotional linkages (e.g. joint advertising, themed brochures) and others.

'Tourism attractions as community assets' is a concept fundamental to community tourism development. Most obvious, perhaps, is that attractions (museums, parks, harbours) must be acceptable, desirable and accessible to residents. Amenities (e.g. waterfront parks and boardwalks, public art, restaurants) also should be accessible and acceptable to residents. Less obvious, but just as critical, is that the community tourism development process – especially activities such as community inventory and assessment, community visioning, and identification of sacred places – can serve as a catalyst for building community identity, pride, vision, unity and social bonds.

Challenges of Community Tourism Development

Despite this attractive list of benefits associated with community tourism development, challenges do exist, just as they have been identified in the literature on partnerships (Selin and Chavez, 1995a,b; Selin and Myers, 1995; Selin *et al.*, 1997; Selin, 1998). First, it is often difficult for individuals and groups, especially businesses and tourism bureaus nurtured within a competitive capitalistic market, to work collaboratively. Often the assumption is that each community must compete for a slice of the tourist dollar pie.

Communities new to the tourism business sometimes make the false assumption that 'getting into the tourism market' is as simple as putting up a few promotional signs and distributing some brochures. They fail to recognize that tourism development means creating and nurturing a complex system, to include: commitment of financial and human resources to conduct an assessment of potential tourist attractions and experiences; enhancement of attractions; provision of support services and amenities (e.g. travel corridors, directional signs, parking, lodging, restaurants, shopping opportunities); expression of hospitality by all residents and businesses; provision and staffing of an integrated, consistent information system to assist tourists before and during their visits; creation and operation of an organizational structure through which tourism stakeholders share information and ideas; development of policies, regulatory instruments, financial incentives and other policy instruments to facilitate and guide tourism development in directions decided upon by the community (specific suggestions can be found in Butler et al., 1998); creation of a financial support structure for the tourism system (e.g. bed tax, tourism association membership fees); creation of a means for gathering or accessing existing tourism market data; and implementation of a process to monitor effectiveness and impacts (economic, social, environmental) of tourism development. In fact, a community should develop a strategic tourism development plan that either clearly shows integration with a community development plan or is embedded within the community's comprehensive and/or economic development plan.

Another challenge of community tourism development is that such an approach, as with all partnerships (Selin, 1998), takes a substantial commitment of time by stakeholders. While a goal of collaborative efforts is to seek common ground, the reality is that stakeholders often come to the table with baggage that is full of opinions, perceptions (often misperceptions) and judgments about other stakeholder groups. These barriers must be overcome before trust and open communication can be established.

In some communities, elected officials may have a strong influence on community priorities. If elected officials, possibly under term limit constraints, are the ones who spearhead tourism development efforts, then are replaced by officials not having the same priorities, efforts may not be sustained.

Many people become involved with issues only when they perceive a direct (often negative) impact on themselves.

Thus, a major challenge to community-wide collaboration is finding effective ways to interest and involve residents who perceive community development as peripheral to personal priorities, not their responsibility, or beyond their knowledge and ability.

Turnover in tourism enterprise owners, tourism organization staff, and tourism business employees occurs frequently. This creates challenges to consistency and longevity of coordinated tourism development efforts.

Some businesses may not operate in ways supportive of tourism. For example, efforts in North Carolina to develop heritage tourism based on handmade crafts were hampered initially by inconsistent and unpublicized hours of operation by craftspeople and lack of directional signs to artisan homes or workshops, often well off the 'beaten tourist path'.

Partnerships and collaborative planning and management require not only attitudes inconsistent with traditional hierarchical organizations, but a set of skills not typically taught in academic or training institutions, nor traditionally used in certain sectors. Problem solving, public involvement strategies, effective personal and nonpersonal communication, diverse computer skills, lifelong learning strategies, and critical thinking are all important. Nonprofit and public sector employees must be proficient in traditionally private sector skills: marketing, business plan development, strategic visioning and management, and research.

Stakeholders are often not familiar with the 'languages', operations approaches, missions and priorities of their partnering organizations. Thus, even communication is difficult.

Implications of Trends and Challenges of Community Tourism

Community tourism planning and development are growing, as is citizen demand for government accountability and for personal input into decisions affecting them and their communities. Thus, it seems prudent, both for increased efficiencies of tourism service delivery and for providing satisfactory experiences for tourists, that collaborative efforts in tourism continue. However, numerous factors, including pre-existing conditions and attitudes, challenge prolonged implementation. Tourism businesses, tuned into incentives of 'heads in beds' and profit margins, may develop partnerships with other tourism businesses. However, integrating tourism development within a broader community building context requires focused effort, including community desire, long-term commitment, strong leadership based on community capacity and willingness to involve the public actively and regularly in the planning *and* decision making.

This is not an easy shift to make. To some, it may seem as if smaller communities are more able to engage their citizens – because logistics are easier when resident numbers and geographic range are small, because residents may more easily perceive direct personal impacts of community development decisions, and because there may be fewer competing interests to meld. However, residents of small communities may be more likely to carry perceptual and emotional 'baggage' due to lifelong interactions with other residents. Also, their communities may be attractive to outsiders who move to these communities and who may have different ideas, values and priorities. Lifelong residents may be resistant to their ideas and values. Therefore, the actual nature of community involvement and collaborative planning is affected by the characteristics and history of individual communities. Nevertheless, some general implications related to public policy, management, planning and marketing can be identified. Suggestions discussed below are intended to facilitate application of community tourism development principles.

Public policy

Implications for public policy within individual communities will derive from the decisions made by a community about if, how much, and the type of tourism it chooses to develop. Butler *et al.* (1998) present five categories of policy tools that might be used: regulatory instruments (laws, licences, permits, quid pro quo exchanges), voluntary instruments (information and education, support for volunteer and non-governmental organizations, technical assistance), direct expenditures (funding specific development or rehabilitation projects, funding development of relevant businesses, entering into public/private partnerships, funding marketing and other research, funding promotional efforts), financial incentives (offering tax incentives; developing competitive pricing of public services; providing grants, loans, rebates or rewards for tourism-supportive activity), and simply choosing not to become involved in activities unsupportive of community and tourism development goals. Policy issues apply primarily to principles of community control, collaboration and process facilitation to develop authentic resources.

In some cases, facilitating community control may involve simply educating tourism and community development partners about how to access and use existing programmes to achieve specific goals. For example, a community that decides to enhance its authentic historic character by redeveloping its historic town centre, to both serve as a tourism attraction and provide community services, may need technical assistance in researching and applying for national or state historic register designation. If a community chooses to preserve and enhance its natural environment, it may need assistance in applying for heritage area or corridor designation. For example, in Michigan, a heritage routes programme allows communities to apply to have a stretch of road designated as a scenic, historic or recreation corridor. Specific criteria and management policies, with which the communities must comply, are associated with this programme.

In other cases, specific policies or policy instruments must be developed to facilitate or encourage certain kinds of tourism-related activity. To preserve an area's historic character, a community might develop deed restrictions, façade or other design controls, and sign design and placement guidelines. It might implement tax incentives or a grant programme to encourage historic façade or building restoration. It might provide technical assistance, using historic preservation guidelines, to restore, renovate or rehabilitate historic structures.

In yet other cases, a community may encourage construction of a replica. An example is the privately funded construction of a replica of *Friendship*, a 1797 three-masted square-rigger, to be docked at Salem Maritime National Historic Site in Massachusetts (Hierta, 1996). While public funds may not be available to support such efforts, other in-kind actions (e.g. providing free dockage for a historic vessel, extending sewer and power lines to a historic attraction, or restricting commercial development around a historic community) may provide critical assistance. To protect natural resources, a community planning commission may use environmental regulations to support decisions. For example, mitigation strategies that require protection of X acres of land or reconstruction of wetlands in exchange for development rights in a less sensitive area might be used. Developers may be required to provide a certain amount of green space, wildlife corridors or other natural resource area. Government might become actively involved in acquisition of waterway buffer strips, or purchase of development rights or easements along such corridors.

Planning

Planning is integral to the entire process of community tourism development. Yet it is perhaps the most difficult process to sustain, particularly to maintain involvement and buy-in by residents and organized stakeholder groups. The planning process is fundamentally different from simply hiring a firm, or having a team of consultants develop a plan behind closed doors. It means committing to involving stakeholders and allowing them to participate in decision making. It means making changes in attitude and approach toward building a community for the future based on human, natural, historic and other resource assets, and using collaboration rather than com-

petition (Flora, 1997). It includes shifts from:

- being involved in community development to community building;
- conducting needs assessment to asset mapping;
- focusing on clients and their needs to citizens and what they can contribute to the community;
- depending on individual leadership to a team of community contributors, and nurturing skills and contributions of community members; and
- using strategic planning (based on meeting identified needs) to strategic visioning (the agreed upon target community condition toward which a variety of actions could contribute).

In this approach, the vision becomes the community's 'bottom line' and serves as the fundamental criterion against which to assess the contribution of specific development ideas.

This planning approach, however, must struggle against attitudinal and organizational momentum, which tends to reinforce adversarial approaches to decision making and often involves negotiation, mediation and power plays. Some of the institutionalized processes are partisan political jousting and blatant use of 'pork barrel' politics and budget decisions; adversarial legal posturing that uses injunctions, lawsuits and legal negotiation to resolve controversies; the capitalistic economic system that relies on competition, buyouts and mergers to exert economic pressures and power; special interest lobbying that is based heavily on self-interest of the group(s) being represented. These 'business as usual' approaches do not automatically preclude successful community involvement and community-based tourism development; rather, they must be modified to fulfil different roles.

An example of a successful community planning process that integrates community building, economic development, environmental protection, and tourism opportunities is a process, initiated by a project called the Les Cheneaux Economic Forum, engaged in by a small community in Michigan's Upper Peninsula. Basing its discussions on scientific environmental impact and development trend data, the process involved residents (via public forums with adults and youth, volunteer task forces, and continuous communication through print and electronic media formats) in identifying its assets, developing a community vision (based on principles of long-term economic prosperity, natural resource protection, and local public participation), developing action plans, identifying stakeholder partners for individual projects, considering issues of sustainability, maintaining communication, implementing action plans, and monitoring impacts (Hudson *et al.*, 1998).

Following the Les Cheneaux example, and using principles identified earlier in this chapter to address challenges of community tourism development, other planning needs based on changing 'ways of doing business' include:

- identifying stakeholders and finding ways to clarify relevance of the process, facilitating their involvement, and ensuring their involvement in the decision making process;
- facilitating education of stakeholder organizations and residents about each other – their priorities and missions, operational procedures and constraints – to help build trust and create an environment in which they can talk and plan with mutual understanding, find common ground, and develop strategies that consider all perspectives and impacts. For example, Michigan's current efforts to develop cultural tourism are focused on bringing together members of the cultural community (e.g. museum directors) and tourism industry (e.g. hoteliers, CVB staff, tourism associations) to speak face to face, to learn each others' language and bottom line criteria, and to seek common ground. Museum professionals, who have difficulty perceiving themselves as 'businesses', must recognize needs of

tourists, such as having adequate rest rooms, parking space, and interesting stories and engaging exhibits; tourism professionals must recognize museums' concerns about protecting the natural and cultural resources for which they are responsible. To aid communities with such efforts, a national collaborative recently published a guidebook called *Partners in Tourism: Culture and Commerce* (Garfield, 1997);

- involving the community's youth in the process;
- finding ways to maintain stakeholder involvement over the long term; and
- developing effective processes to minimize and/or address conflicts among stakeholders (including reduction of litigation-based determinations) and to negotiate decisions that fairly balance community-wide social benefits with individual rights.

Management

Management, as used here, is defined as a way to implement, monitor and modify actions based on the community 'planning process' discussed above. As an extension of the planning process, it must incorporate strategies that continue to involve residents and stakeholder groups. This includes finding ways for organizations to share management responsibilities (and accountability) as well as the benefits of tourism and community development. This means basing 'success' on criteria in addition to personal, organizational, and business profits. It also means that monitoring and evaluation procedures must be built into implementation and management systems so that community members can assess effectiveness and make changes, as necessary. Some of the implications specific to managing the tourism component of community building include:

- assuring that attractions and amenities first serve residents effectively, and that tourist visitation does not displace or inhibit local access; this involves maintaining easy access (physical, economic and cognitive) to historic and cultural attractions, natural resource sites, and other attractions by residents as well as managing tourist transportation congestion that might discourage resident use;

- presenting the interpretive stories, identified as important by the community and which it chooses to share, in ways that both 'bring life' to the stories (for both tourists and community residents) and are linked with each other throughout the community; this means that attractions that focus on telling stories (e.g. museums, nature centres, theatres, tour organizations) should coordinate their interpretive efforts with those of tourism support services (e.g. restaurants, lodging establishments, gift shops, marinas, libraries); for example, placemats, menus, mini-exhibits and historic photos with interpretive placards, can be used in such facilities to tell parts of the community's story, and are particularly appropriate for use in adaptively reused historic structures;
- tourism organizations and community designers should consider, in the physical layout of facilities and the provision of services and attractions, ways to link tourism opportunities, experiences, and sites throughout a community in ways that are easily usable and understandable by tourists (see the discussion of linkages);
- implementing training and/or other programmes to help make all community residents and businesses part of the tourism system so they all work as hosts and information providers; this can be achieved only if the community has input into and accepts changes resulting from tourism; residents must understand that personal attitudes as well as service quality are critical to effective tourism delivery, especially if they desire long-term tourism involvement; and
- identifying and implementing controls to sustain the natural and historic environment, economy, and quality of life of the community; this effort requires continual monitoring and evaluation of tourism (and other development) impacts as well as of community attitudes, values and preferences.

Marketing

Marketing, which involves several components, is interwoven with planning and management elements of the community tourism development process. Marketing efforts are approached somewhat differently than with a traditional focus on market needs and preferences. Of course, initial market analysis, community asset identification, and continuous tourism monitoring are all parts of the process. This includes identifying the needs, preferences, spending and travel patterns of tourists. However, decisions about community tourism development actions are based not solely on those results, but on those results in conjunction with community priorities, preferences, values and vision. Implied specific actions include:

- developing a monitoring system to evaluate tourist satisfaction, to identify changes in tourist perceptions and preferences, to identify tourism impacts, and to monitor community attitudes toward tourism;
- educating communities about how to promote themselves, how to integrate their promotional efforts with regional and/or state promotional efforts (and themes);
- developing effective target marketing efforts consistent with community priorities;
- developing pricing strategies appropriate for target markets; and
- developing tourism packages (not only traditional hotel/restaurant/attraction packages, but joint attraction and/or experience packages that help tell the community story).

Conclusions and Challenge for the Future

Facilitating community tourism development involves a fundamental shift in attitudes about roles of 'specialists' and 'professionals' as they relate to citizens; a shift from competitive priorities to collaborative win–win priorities; and a willingness for stakeholders to look for common ground and areas of negotiation leading to win–win outcomes. Without this attitude shift, changes in approaches will be unsuccessful, at least for the long term. Among communities and certain stakeholder groups, and among professionals – land managers, tourism professionals, community planners, etc. – are people holding traditional values, perceptions of the roles of professionals, and a belief in traditional planning and governmental processes. Others are strict capitalists, for whom economic competition is sacred. Stakeholder involvement is considered to be too much trouble, to take too long, and not be worth the effort. However, the support for decisions arrived at jointly, rather than those imposed upon a community, are likely to be much better received, have increased community-wide and personal benefits, and be less likely to trigger legal challenge. Changes this fundamental are not easy or swift. Clear successes, based on relevant issues, must be showcased. Communities might experiment with small scale collaborative projects before embarking on community-wide tourism development. Additionally, education and training must present and nurture different attitudes; teach skills relevant to collaborative, team and community-building efforts; and provide opportunities for students/trainees to work in teams to solve problems, develop effective community building plans, and hone effective interpersonal communication skills. Educational requirements should allow more diversification in curricula rather than exclusively move individuals toward specialization. This may mean developing more integrative, problem-solving courses and experiences, and encouraging students to take courses within a variety of related areas. Without exposure to people, issues, and basic knowledge of other professions or stakeholder groups, it is difficult to learn the languages.

Perhaps this can lead people to consider the possibility at least that a tourism treasure is wrapped in a rotting carcass. Perhaps Port au Choix is on the right track in involving stakeholders to develop tourism and other community amenities to meet the needs of its citizens in a rapidly changing natural and economic environment.

Part VI

Management and Operations: Tools to Get the Job Done

29

The Role of Tour Operators in the Travel Distribution System

Nevenka Čavlek

Introduction

From the moment tour operators appeared on the market, the individual form of tourism has been complemented by package holiday tourism that has revolutionized travel and enabled a large number of people to join international tourism flows. The tremendous development in international air-passenger traffic and the favourable package holidays offered to tourism consumers by tour operators have clearly caused a rapid development in international tourism. Nevertheless, modern tourism has shown that its most distinctive characteristic is the mass participation of tourists. According to the World Tourism Organization (WTO), tour operators contribute annually around 25% of all world tourism travel. This means that in 1998 about 160 million international tourism journeys were created by tour operators (WTO, 1999). For their part, European tour operators account for around 50% of all package tours in the world (Čavlek, 1998). The concentration of demand in the tourism market has led to the concentration of tourism supply that is changing faster than ever and adapting to the new requirements of the market. Tour operators will continue to play a decisive role in meeting the requirements of this market.

Main Development Trend

The main trend that can be identified in the travel distribution system is the consolidation of tour operators in the tourism market. This is the result of global processes of development in the world economy that have had an inevitable influence on tourism travel and, with it, on the development strategies of the leading European tour operators. The business environment within which travel companies operate has become increasingly uncertain. Organizations have become bigger and more complex over the last two decades. To survive in the very competitive tourism market, it has become essential for the organizers and distributors of tourism to merge with or to purchase companies that deliver different components of the whole product that they supply on the market. On the other hand, practice in the tour operators' business has shown that the tour operators work with many risks and at the same time with very low net profit margins (Mundt, 1993; Youell, 1994). Therefore, it is important for tour operators to share in the profit of as large a number of different components of the whole product that they supply on the market as possible.

Dominance of tour operators in outbound tourism

The business of tour operators was created and has developed mostly in Europe. Although the US has been the driving force of the world economy, where the largest airlines in the world, the most extensive reservation systems, the biggest hotel chains and the largest travel agency chains have together paved the way for the development of tourism; in the field of the tour operating business the US lags behind Europe. Apart from the Europeans, only the Japanese (although with a shorter tradition) have a similarly strong habit of travelling abroad on package holidays. Unlike the tour operating business in Europe, the tour operating business in the US is mostly directed towards domestic destinations (approximately 70%). This is natural, considering the geographic vastness and attractive tourism destinations within this market, for instance Florida, California and Hawaii. Although there are about 2000 tour operators in the US, only 350 of them sell package holidays abroad, and 50 of the largest realize 80% of the total sales.

Although the largest tour operator concerns have developed in the most powerful European tourism generating markets (i.e. Germany and Great Britain), it should be emphasized that the number of inhabitants of a particular country is not the only, or the most significant, factor in the emergence of large tour operating companies (*FVW International*, 1998b). Indeed, the very fact that there are limits to the number of potential clients on the domestic market pushes tour operators to become active in other markets. An example is the case of tour operators in the Swiss tourism market.

By 1970, tour operators had already been recognized as an essential part of the modern tourism system (Mill and Morrison, 1985), only to become, in the later stages of their development, a dominant landmark in all the significant tourism-generating markets of the world.

The British market

The mass nature of travelling abroad on air-packages can be considered as the main feature of the British tourism market from the 1970s until now (Lavery, 1993). Although the share of package holidays in the total number of holidays abroad has gradually declined (from 73% in 1970, to 56% in 1990, and 52% in 1998), this type of travelling is still dominant on the market. From the moment when the British tour operators entered the initial stages of the package holiday business, the main characteristic of this market has been the incessant battle to win as large a market share as possible, which is usually done through a fierce price war and through the increasing concentration of business in the hands of a limited number of powerful tour operators. In the British package holiday market, more than 1000 tour operators have been registered. However, just 19 of them account for approximately 90% of total sales, while the four leading tour operators – Thomson, Airtours, Thomas Cook Holdings and First Choice – control 75% of the market (Holmes, 1999). These data reveal an exceptionally high concentration of business in the hands of just a few of the most powerful tour operators which strongly influence the domestic market of demand and have a strong negotiating position with business partners in the main tourism receiving markets.

In 1997, the size of the British air-package market, according to data from the British Civil Aviation Authority, amounted to 17.9 million tourists. The leading five tour operators in the British market achieved approximately 80% of the total turnover. Such a concentration of business has a positive effect for consumers, because in the battle to win a larger market share, the leading tour operators are constantly forced to reduce their prices. While consumers benefit from this, tour operators fall victim to their own business decisions. However, when a critical point is reached, tour operators are forced to reduce supply on the market, the average selling price of a package per passenger then starts to increase and the tour operators which have survived on the market enter the phase of recovery.

In 1992, more than 60% of all British tourists travelling to Spain (a total of 3.08

million) went on package holidays (Bray, 1996). Such a share of organized travel in relation to individual travel was even more evident in the case of Greece where, in the same year, nearly 90% of British people travelled on package holidays (a total of 1.58 million package holidays sold). In 1996, of the British package holiday market, Greece had a 12% share. At the same time, Turkey climbed from tenth place on the list in 1992 to third place in 1996 (from 220,000 tourists to 750,000), reaching an 8% share of the British package holiday market (Table 29.1).

Table 29.1. The top-ten list of the best selling destinations for summer holidays on the British market in 1996. The figures in parentheses refer to positions in 1992.

Position	Destination	Market share of package holidays (%)
1 (1)	Spain	39
2 (3)	Greece	12
3 (10)	Turkey	8
4 (6)	USA	6
5 (2)	France	5
6 (5)	Portugal	4
7 (7)	Italy	4
8 (4)	Cyprus	4
9 (-)	Caribbean	3
10 (-)	Malta	2

Source: *Observer* (8 December, 1996).

The German market

In Germany, which in the early stages of the development of tour operators was the second largest tourism-generating market in the world, the number of holiday departures outside the place of permanent residence has constantly grown. In 1970, the number of holiday trips outside the place of permanent residence for longer than 4 days amounted to 18.5 million, whereas in 1998 this number more than tripled to 63.4 million (Reiseanalyse, 1999, tourism market research in Germany). By analysing the development of the package holiday market

in Germany, we can conclude that with the increasing influence of tour operators and with the strengthening of their role in creating package holidays, the share of organized travel in the total number of holiday trips longer than 4 days has recorded constant growth. While the number of individual trips has decreased, the number of package holidays has grown. At the very beginning of the takeoff stage (1970) in the German tourism market, the ratio of organized trips to individual holiday trips amounted to 17 : 83. In 1982, this ratio was 26 : 74, and in 1998, the relationship between organized and individual trips amounted to 45 : 55. However, if we observe just the travel that German tourists took abroad, then we can notice a significant increase in organized travel compared to individual trips which amounted to 59 : 41 in 1989 and in 1998 jumped to 80 : 20.

The use of air travel by German tourists started to grow rapidly around the mid-1970s, when air-charter transport became increasingly significant. In the period 1976–1989, the share of holiday travel by air almost doubled. In the 1990s, this trend became even more pronounced, with a sharp growth in interest by German tourists in travelling on packages to long-haul destinations which, due to reductions in air fares, became very competitive in relation to traditional destinations.

The German package holiday market still has room for expansion. Although there are no precise data on the size of the German package holiday market, since these specific items of data have not been measured, some research has been carried out which can at least approximately depict the size and strength of this market (Freyer, 1998). In 1998, the size of this largest European package holiday market was estimated to comprise more than 30 million organized trips. This figure is based on the fact that 56 of the most significant German tour operators in that year realized a total of almost 24 million organized trips, producing a total turnover of about 24 billion DM from selling packages. Clearly, these operators represented about 70% of the total German market of organized trips. Therefore, compared with the financial year 1996/97, this market grew by 5.5% in the number of package holiday trips, or 6.9% in realized turnover (*FVW International*, 1998a).

The five leading German tour operators (Touristic Union International (TUI), Neckermann und Reisen (NUR), Luftfahrt Unternehmen GmbH & co. KG (LTU), Deutsches Reiseburo GmbH (DER), Frosch Touristic International (FTI)) represent more than 50% of the total tour operating business on this market, whereas the remaining 800–1200 tour operators share slightly less than half the business.

Through the examples of the British and the German markets, it can be concluded that tour operators, thanks to air-charter transport, opened new horizons in tourism, particularly by introducing new tourism destinations that were far enough away from the main tourism-generating markets to make travel by any other mode difficult to accomplish.

Phases of development

In order to understand the whole issue of the involvement of tour operators in the world market, it is necessary to observe their development within the framework of specific phases. In particular, it is necessary to analyse the history of organized travel after World War II, because, as pointed out by Van Doren and Lollar (1985), social, political, economic, technological and environmental changes after the war resulted in the 'consequences' that now shape the present travel industry. The conclusion can be drawn that we cannot apply one-sided criteria, valid only for one area of human activity, to examine the development of any phenomenon, let alone that of tourism and tour operators. A holistic perspective can be achieved only by combining criteria that include all the elements relevant to such a process of development. By applying the above principles and criteria, it is possible to establish the following stages in the development of tour operators: the introduction of tour operators into the tourism system, the take-off stage, the maturity stage, and the future stage of mass consumption, which are schematically summarized in Table 29.2.

Integration Processes on the European Market

Within the last few years, on the European as well as on the world tourism market, many important changes have occurred in the sphere of the vertical and horizontal integration of tour operators and tourism concerns. A present tendency is for tour operators to buy existing operators and retail travel agency chains in a particular market rather than to create new tour operators or their own travel agency chains. The logic of such a business approach is easy to understand. The investment necessary to buy an already well-established company is much lower than that needed to introduce a new company name on to the market (Goold and Sommers Luchs, 1996). The processes of integration within the German tourism market are numerous and significant. In the fight for a larger share of the market, large companies are taking over smaller ones almost daily. However, unlike the situation on the British market, where a large share of the market is usually achieved by using price as a weapon, so that tour operators, travel agencies and charter companies engage in exhausting price wars; on the German market, prices, at least until now, do not carry as much importance as they do in Britain. The German tourism market has mainly used diversification of the tourism product, rather than price, as the main weapon in market competition.

Until the beginning of 1998, unlike British tour operators, the leading German tour operators, with the exception of LTU, were not vertically connected with airline companies. However, in recent years, the involvement of German tour operators in long-haul markets has increased (i.e. the participation of long-haul destinations in the total programme of these tour operators has grown) and, consequently, the use of significantly larger airline transport capacities has encouraged tour operators to change their most recent business practices. On the other hand, the influx of British tour operators on to the European markets, and recently also on to the German market, has

Table 29.2. The main characteristics of the stages of development of tour operators.

Stage of development	Main characteristics	Environment	Leading tour operators
Introductory Stage 1950–1970	*Typical sales-oriented market* (limited number of tour operators on the market). Flourishing of charter air-companies. Beginnings of integration of tourism concerns.	*Fast socioeconomic transformation of society* (high GNP growth, increase in the number of days of paid holiday). Post-war modernization and motorization.	Horizon Clarksons Cosmos Touropa Scharnow Dr Tigges Club Méditerrané
Takeoff Stage 1970–end of 1980s	*Transfer from a sales-oriented to a consumer-oriented market* Increase of supply faster that that of demand. First tour operator bankruptcies. A large number of new names among tour operators. 'Apex' tariffs. Continuation of the process of integration. Sudden growth of the tour operators' offer of new tourism destinations.	*New era of air transport* (introduction of jumbo jets). Two energy crises. Deregulation of air-traffic.	Thomson Intasun, ILG Horizon Touristic Union International (TUI) Neckermann Kuoni Club Méditerrané American Express Owners Abroad
Stage of Maturity From the beginning of the 1990s	*Restrained consumption Package holidays take on the characteristics of consumer goods* Consumer sensitivity to prices. Very prominent trend in last-minute bookings. Change in the structure of supply with tour operators. Substitution of 'standard packages' for 'individualized packages'. Diversification of the market of demand. Increasing number of specialist tour operators. Large investments in CRSs. Tour operators outgrowing their own markets.	*Huge political and economic changes* (transformation of socialist economies into market economies; opening of borders of countries behind the Iron Curtain; free flow of goods and services). World recession. War in the Gulf. Creation of a single European market. Signing of the GATTS Agreement. Changes in the system of values of the population on the leading tourism-generating markets.	TUI Neckermann LTU Amexco Thomson Airtours Club Méditerrané Nouvelles Frontières Kuoni DER First Choice
Future Stage of mass consumption	*Globalization of the tourism product* Very prominent segmentation of tourism supply and demand. Several tour operators dictate the tourism market throughout the world.	*A significant growth in living standards in the so-called Third World countries Changes in the system of values of the population living in those countries* Further shortening of the working week (increase of free time). Two dominant orientations of values: one orientation towards material opulence and hedonism and the second orientation towards nonmaterial, alternative values and quality of life.	Hapag-Touristik Union (HTU) C & N Touristik Airtours Thomson Amexco

brought German tour operators into direct confrontation with competition from the strongest market of air-package holidays in Europe, which has prompted them to form mergers. The aims of these mergers are clear: through them, tour operators tighten their links with airline companies in order to: (i) increase their power on the market; (ii) weaken or eliminate some of their competitors; (iii) correct any mistakes made by buying smaller tour operators; and (iv) strengthen their low-profit business with the synergetic effects that come from cooperating with airline companies and from participating in their profits.

Germany is, according to the number of trips abroad, the strongest tourism-generating country in the world. Therefore, it is not strange that the largest tour operator in Europe – TUI – operates in this market. In 1998 TUI sold more than 5 million package holidays on the German market alone (*FVW International*, 1998b). Although the German anti-monopolies commission has for many years opposed the mergers of tourism concerns and the creation of oligopolies, the processes of vertical integration have been difficult to prevent. In the German travel market, there are two large 'blocks': The Reds, led by TUI, and The Yellows, presided over by NUR. At the end of 1997, the second largest tour operator group in this market, NUR, merged with the charter company, Condor, and a new holding, C&N Touristik, was created. In response to the creation of this holding, swift preparations followed to create a new holding on the side of the Reds. The German market has changed significantly since Preusag, whose basic activity lies in the fields of energy, raw materials and technology, entered the tourism business. In response to the creation of this holding, Preusag, which succeeded in obtaining a majority ownership of the largest tour operator in Germany and in Europe, TUI, which is almost the sole owner of the tourism concern Hapag Lloyd (which has an in-house charter company under the same name), decided to merge TUI and Hapag Lloyd and formed a new holding under the name Hapag-Touristik Union (HTU) by the end of 1998.

In a way, the German travel concerns are following the British model of vertical integration in the market; that is, integration with retail travel agency chains. This is seen in HTU's purchase of the biggest travel agency chain in Germany, First (with a stake of around 80%, the remainder being in the hands of Westdeutsche Landesbank – WLB), and has now in its hands the biggest distribution chain in Germany. However, the owner of HTU, Preusag, sought to expand further. Soon afterwards, Preusag acquired 25.1% of Thomas Cook, a British travel agency company that has lately been involved in tour operating as well as in the travel agency business (with the intention of becoming the major shareholder of Thomas Cook by the end of 1999). These have been very important strategic steps taken by German tourism concerns in the direction of distribution channels outside their domestic market.

The mergers of the mentioned tourism enterprises have not led to the creation of a monopoly. On the contrary, competition in the market has become stronger. Some market analysts predicted that this kind of vertical integration would reduce the package holiday offered on the market, but it actually widens it. The prices have also not gone up, as was predicted. Actually, they have been reduced. This situation is very much in favour of the customers who travel in even better conditions than before. One of the main reasons lies in the fact that the British tour operator, Airtours, entered the German tourism market in May 1998 by acquiring a 29.1% stake in the German tour operating group, FTI, and is intending to create a new tour operating force in this market. On the other hand, the fourth German tour operator, LTU, succeeded in linking itself with the mother company of Swissair, the SAir group, which bought 49.9% of LTU from WLB. This has given LTU extra strength on the German market, better chances of staying as a real competitor to the newly created holdings on the German market, and has opened the way to forming the first European charter alliance.

In contrast to the practice of concentration on the German tourism market (except for LTU), the integration of tour operators with airline companies and chains of travel agencies on the British market is well established, whereas mergers with hotel companies are generally avoided (except for Airtours). Without presenting a deeper analysis of this situation, it is believed that the basic reasons lie primarily in the geographic location of Great Britain, its distance from the main tourism receiving markets, as well as in its previous negative experiences with other forms of concentration on the tourism market. Thomson Travel Group owns the biggest charter airline company in the world, Britannia Airways, the travel agency chain Lunn Poly, with more than 800 branch offices and several tour operators. Airtours has a similar structure. It owns the charter airline company, Airtours International, and Premiair (Scandinavia), the travel agency chain Going Places (with around 700 outlets), several tour operators in Great Britain and abroad, four cruise ships and some hotels in receiving tourism destinations.

Capital Flows of European Travel Concerns

When the tour operators in the most powerful European tourism generating markets were no longer able to expand their business significantly on their domestic markets, and under the influence of global economic development, they started to internationalize. This was accomplished in part, by the strategic power, brought by international capital market businesses. In this pyramid, business can only be done and the battle can only be fought by the biggest, for example, the German travel concerns which, in most cases, are directly or indirectly supported by powerful banking capital. With the financial growth of these concerns, their influence on world tourism flows and global relationships will continue to increase. The conditions regarding inclusive tours are already dictated by tourism concerns which, as already stated, besides tour operators, most often own chains of travel agencies and/or airline companies, ships, hotels etc.

The motives for the expansion of British

and German tour operators outside their domestic markets have not always been the same. Whereas British tour operators enter foreign markets because they cannot expand further within their own market and because they need to exploit their airline-company capacities more fully, German tour operators can still achieve significant increases in their turnover on their own domestic markets. The main aim of German operators, it seems, is to become global European tour operators.

The leading European tour operators have polarized their spheres of interest so that they are moving towards markets which are structured in a similar way to their home markets. The German tour operators, for example, have turned toward The Netherlands, Belgium and Austria, and are increasingly interested in penetrating the markets of the neighbouring east European countries, since those markets are structured in a way similar to their domestic market. None of the mentioned markets was a typical market for air-package tours, neither were the companies bought by the German concerns vertically integrated with airline companies. As a result of the actions by the leading German tour operators, the Dutch and Belgian markets are almost completely in German hands. TUI bought two of the largest tour operators on the Dutch market (Holland International and Arke Reisen), and NUR conquered the Belgian market through its daughter company, NUR Reisen, by buying All Air and by purchasing the tour operator Sunsnacks.

The situation on the British tourism market until 1997 differed greatly from the situation on the Continent, where the largest and most powerful tour operators attempted, within the possibilities offered to them by a single European market, to reap the best possible rewards from their efforts. Unlike the entrepreneurial German tourism concerns, the British tourism companies had for a long time been observing with some suspicion the newly formed European tourism structure and could not decide whether to enter other European tourism markets. However, as much as it was convenient for the British companies to stay in their 'splendid isolation', with the arrival of other European companies on their market, they started to realize that the European Union (EU) brought with it different rules of behaviour and that long-term isolation could mean extinction from the market. For this reason, British tour operators have turned toward markets that have structural similarities to their own market. The most similar European markets are, of course, the Scandinavian and the Irish ones. Scandinavia and Ireland are typical air-package holiday markets, tour operators are vertically integrated with airline companies, the markets are particularly sensitive to price, and in all their features they reflect the business conditions of the British market. So it is not at all surprising that British tour operators have been practically ruling the Scandinavian market. Airtours was among the first British tour operators that ventured out of the domestic market, first by buying the SAS Leisure Group in 1994, and then Spies Holding at the beginning of 1996. It was precisely this expansion into foreign markets that enabled Airtours to exceed Thomson's results on the international market. Thomson Travel, still the leading tour operator in Britain, started to involve itself more in the Irish market in 1997, and somewhat later also in the Scandinavian tourism market and, in this way, the British tour operators' principle of isolation from overseas tourism markets conclusively ended.

However, as business conditions in the market of Continental Europe change under the influence of EU regulations on the creation of a single European tourism market, so opportunities for the access of British tour operators to this market are widening. For the first time, Airtours was able, by the end of 1997, to enter the market of Continental Europe, dominated by the leading German tour operators, with the purchase of Sun International which, apart from the domestic Belgian market, also operates in The Netherlands, France and Great Britain. In May 1998, Airtours made a decisive step in the German market by buying 29% of the shares of the very promising tour operator, FTI.

The analyses of the tour operators' ownership structure show that non-European capital is not involved in any significant way in the ownership of European tour operators (Bywater, 1998). The exceptions had been the Thomson Travel Group (owned until May 1998 by the Thomson Corporation of Canada and since then quoted on the London Stock Exchange) and the very small share of Japanese capital in Club Méditerranée and American capital in Airtours. Therefore, it seems more likely, as is already happening in practice, that the European tourism industry will move toward the global market rather than for foreign capital to significantly penetrate the European tourism-generating market. For example, Airtours is operating on the North American market, and the Swiss tour operator Kuoni has subsidiaries in India and Hong Kong. Due to the increasing interest shown by tourists in travelling to long-haul destinations, it can be expected that the largest tour operators, which generate a mass of tourists for long-haul destinations, will further try to exploit synergies in dealing with these markets in the sense of widening their activities in them. They will try, within the limits of legal possibilities, to direct the tourism-generating potentials from these markets toward other destinations in their programmes. They will ensure in this way a constant expansion of their activity and will strengthen their influence on the global tourism market, which means that the development of the tour operating business in the future will move from being an international and multinational business to being a global one. Therefore, it could be predicted that the largest tour operators in Europe will start directing their influence toward these markets by investing their capital in relevant tour operators or by buying them out completely.

Regardless of the different motives for the expansion of European tourism concerns, the new EU system evidently facilitates their growth, that tourism is becoming increasingly based on partnerships, that the ownership structure in European tourism today is all the more difficult to disentangle, and that the further 'Europeanization' and globalization processes of the tourism market greatly influence the establishment of new business relationships. It seems that European travel concerns are consistently moving toward further consolidation. All big tourism concerns are looking for further acquisitions to power their growth. The top targets will be regional companies and specialists on the domestic market and abroad, but even bigger mergers cannot be excluded.

Implications

With the strengthening of the process of horizontal and vertical integration, access to the market for new tour operators is becoming more difficult. First, concentration processes on the tourism markets have created powerful tour operators with an expanding network of travel agencies. An increasing number of small, independent tour operators and travel agencies have been swallowed up by these large organizations that have consequently become even bigger and more powerful. This situation puts the medium-sized and particularly the small tour operators at a disadvantage, because it limits their access to channels of distribution (the tour operator is a wholesaler, and usually does not sell its package holidays directly to clients, but does so using the services of intermediaries, mainly travel agencies) and to the leasing of charter seats. The small operators also have a less favourable negotiating position when contracting accommodation capacities at tourism destinations. As a result of the power which large mass-market tour operators have on particular tourism markets, small- and medium-sized tour operators can ensure their existence among the giants only if they become recognizable by offering to the market a specific and first-rate product.

Since the tourism concerns are usually owners or major shareholders of accommodation facilities in the main receiving tourism destinations, they can easily control or dictate the prices of these services, and make other requests or bend some rules in their favour. This implies that the competition created in tourism-generating markets is now also moving to the tourism receiving markets.

Many tourism receiving countries depend today on foreign tour operators. But, some of the receiving destinations, by allowing foreign tour operators to become extensively involved, have lost control of their own tourism development. One reason for this is that turnover based on foreign tourism depends on the will and readiness of tour operators to include or keep a particular destination in their programme. Since tour operators have full control of their product, they choose or abandon a particular market (the tourism receiving destination) depending on the prices of accommodation at those destinations, on the quality of the services, on the attractiveness of the destination, on its image, on the extent of their own investment and on many other factors. Their business interests and those of their business partners at the receiving destinations do not always match. Therefore, the risk of placing this receiving destination on the generating market in such a situation is particularly high, because changes, either in the market of demand or in the market of supply, which have negative effects on the demand for a particular destination, leave the tour operators without the means to directly or adequately intervene on the foreign tourism market. Moreover, since tour operators have caused structural changes in international tourism demand, directing it toward a lower economic category of consumers, the tourism supply of tourism receiving destinations adapted itself to receive this category of tourists, becoming at the same time less attractive to the higher economic stratum of consumers.

For tourism receiving destinations, whose placing on the generating markets mainly depends on tour operators, the situation is particularly unfavourable when they are mostly oriented towards only two or three markets. The situation becomes even more difficult when, in addition, most capacities have been leased to only a few tour operators from these markets. These risky situations for the receiving destinations can be lessened by their orientation toward a larger number of foreign markets of demand, and by the accommodation sector not leasing their capacities to only one tour operator from a particular foreign market, or by the formation of strong hotel associations which would have better bargaining power with tour operators.

The current trend in the development of the tour operating business puts greater pressure on the marketing strategy of the tour operator, due to the strong competition at all levels and to the increasing individualization of tourism travel. Simply stated, tour operators and tourism destinations will, in future, not only have to develop their products and services according to the wishes of their customers and according to new trends, but their success on the tourism market will increasingly depend on the more intensive marketing of their supply which will have to be directed more precisely toward appropriate demand segments. In conditions of increased competition, the product brand will gain more significance, and the battle for customers will be won by those travel organizers that have a stronger brand (which, needless to say, does not exclude the role of price in the battle!). How-

ever, the product brand cannot be built on an image of price alone. The consequence of all this will be a disproportionate increase in marketing, particularly with regard to promotional budgets, in comparison with the growth of tourism traffic. But whatever the marketing strategy in the future, it will be fully client-oriented. Today, there has already been a change in the marketing strategy of the leading world tour operators in their relationship toward the customer who is always put first, and care is taken to provide adequate personal service. A large number of tour operators have already become aware that a high quality service is the key to winning new customers and to keeping old ones. Some studies commissioned by tour operators have already confirmed that the cost of keeping regular, loyal customers represents only about 20% of the promotional budget needed for winning new customers. Therefore, it would be reasonable to expect that in future tour operators will put stronger emphasis on the need to have high quality staff; in other words, high quality staff will become their main advantage over the competition.

30

National Tourist Offices and the Language of Differentiation

Graham M.S. Dann

Introduction

As we stand on the brink of the 21st century there appear to be two opposing trends operating in international tourism. Both claim to be increasing at the expense of the other. Both have quite extensive traditions and may be respectively termed 'modernist' and 'postmodernist'. Each attracts its own band of academic followers and each constitutes a research trend in its own right.

The modernist trend derives from the scientific thinking of the Enlightenment and the rationalism associated with the maximization of profit in an era of industrialization and capitalism. This lengthy period was permeated by the ideologies of laissez-faire imperialism, nationalism and orientalism (Said, 1991), an age intolerant of nonconformity at home, and one which externalized differences abroad in order to subjugate them (Wang, 2000). National identity and self-confidence could thus be fostered by placing differences beyond the territorial boundaries of the centre and by subsequently claiming dominion over the periphery. Seen in this light, differences attributed to alien places and their peoples connoted weakness, simplicity, guile, danger and risk (Crick, 1994).

Into such an environment tourism was born. Under its protagonist, Thomas Cook,

and his successors, differences became safe and controllable. The appeal to the British working class was successful to the extent that it democratized travel. It reduced domestic differences predicated on social stratification and sought to regulate those differences overseas which had become the object of popular curiosity (Wang, 2000). The effects of exterior strangeness could be minimized by injecting large amounts of familiarity into foreign settings. Tour group guides would look after their protégés by offering well-ordered home-from-home experiences with occasional supervised doses of alterity. Their charges, in turn, would benefit educationally from mild and mediated exposure to otherness and morally from the solidarity provided by that in-group camaraderie nurtured in opposition to an out-group comprising destination people beyond the pale.

As time wore on, with guidebooks such as *Baedeker* reinforcing the norms and sanctions relating to limited contact with natives abroad, and domestic holiday camps providing the necessary regimentation at home, mass tourism, as part of mass production in general, gradually assumed the more contemporary form of the overseas package tour, made possible by the advent of modern transportation, especially the jet aircraft. By now the effects of difference associated with

© CAB International 2000. *Trends in Outdoor Recreation, Leisure and Tourism*
(eds W.C. Gartner and D.W. Lime)

distance had become even more reduced and tourists could be placed in the environmental bubbles (Cohen, 1972) of hotels belonging to airlines and tour operators. These homogenized enclaves of home, boosted by multinational chain operations and universal fast food outlets, were accompanied by a growth in placeless theme parks, shopping malls and cruise ships. Holidays had become efficient, calculable and controlled. McDonaldization and McDisneyization reigned supreme. The only remaining differences were those of a McLaks in Norway, a McQuesos and McHuevos in Uruguay, a groenteburger in The Netherlands, and Chicken Tatsuta in Japan (Ritzer and Liska, 1997, p. 100). Spain was simply home plus sunshine and India had become home plus servants (Theroux, 1985, p. 133).

Those who study the majority trend of the modern popularity of mass tourism are themselves currently in the minority, since an analysis of the mundane hedonism of the proletariat is apparently considered too uninteresting by most middle-class academics (Wheeller, 1993). Even so, there are researchers, such as Selanniemi (1996) and Hanefors and Larsson (1993), who prefer to examine charter tourists. For the people they investigate, destinational differences are far less important than the undeniable pleasures that placeless holidays bring. Indeed, such standardized locales as the playgrounds of Gran Canaria, Rhodes and Bodrum are simply referred to as the 'South'. Although their beaches and resorts have few distinguishing characteristics, at least they guarantee a good time with the well-proven formula of sea, sun, sand and sex (Chalmers, 1987, p. 45). Only those who spend their time elsewhere trekking around heritage sites appear unhappy. The accentuation of host cultural differences, it would seem, constitutes a recipe for holiday misery.

The second trend has its roots in the Romantic movement. Here otherness and difference were positively accentuated through accounts of faraway paradises inhabited by beautiful and noble savages (Wang, 2000). Travellers, encouraged no doubt by the art and literature of the period, went in search of exotic, unfamiliar, unpredictable and sometimes perilous situations, in order to return complete with their own publishable tales of alterity and difference, the oral and written means by which they could impress their more sedentary peers. The emphasis was on the extraordinary and unique of there, a counterpoint to the ordinariness and sameness of here.

In its later manifestations, the romantic exploits of the traveller were placed in opposition to the contrived modernistic experiences manufactured by the tourist industry, by emphasizing the former's authenticity which the latter tried to thwart (MacCannell, 1989). In contrast to the totalizing control of the package tour, the accent was placed instead on independence and freedom; above all a liberty to choose from a plurality of alternative offerings. There was special interest tourism catering to particular needs: ecotourism, soft tourism, responsible tourism, cultural tourism, dark tourism, and reality tourism – all indeed carrying the appendage tourism, but each nevertheless accompanied by a suitable epithet so as to clearly distinguish and dissociate it from a uniform mass tourism (Hall and Weiler, 1992).

The eclecticism on offer in this second trend responded very well to the condition of postmodernity, an ethos said to pervade the western world from the 1960s onwards, and even spilling over into some developing countries (Dann and Potter, 1994). Postmodern societies, it is claimed, are characterized by an overriding quality of dedifferentiation, a dissolution of group and grid, the weakening of traditional differences based on class, race and gender (Lash, 1990). The reasons for this post-Fordist (Urry, 1990) situation are many, ranging from globalization (i.e. the erosion of national boundaries by transnational interests) to the two-way migration of peoples and the consequent emergence of exprimitives (MacCannell, 1992). However, more germane to the current argument is the realization that sameness at home is conducive to the search for difference elsewhere. Whether this difference is real, out there and true is more debatable, since the mediatization of culture (another important feature of postmodernity) can provide an endless series of images and simulacra, along with a multitude of computer generated post-tourist (Urry, 1990) virtual reality displays that may in fact be replacing objective reality with something better – the playful pastiche of hyperreality (Eco, 1986). Yet, whatever the outcome of such a debate, one point is incontrovertible – difference, whether real or imaginary, is the very foundation on which all postmodern forms of tourism are constructed.

This second trend, although a minority situation, has nevertheless attracted a much larger group of tourism researchers today. Beginning with Boorstin (1987) who emphasizes the pseudo events of the tourism industry, the pursuit of difference is accentuated by MacCannell (1989) under the quest for the authentic, a line adopted by Graburn (1989) in his distinction between everyday and extraordinary (liminal or sacred) touristic experiences. Subsequently, Urry (1990) pinpoints the tourist gaze – that ocularcentrism which seeks difference in ludic attractions and distractions.

Since there are two clearly opposed trends in contemporary tourism and its researchers, such a dichotomy may pose a dilemma for many a destination seeking to promote itself. On the one hand, if it decides to cater to the majority mass market, it will have to be very careful in managing its rhetoric of difference. Too much emphasis may scare away potential customers and too little could mean the simple surrender of its national identity to suppliers with scant interest in the distinctiveness of a place. On the other hand, if a destination wishes to appeal to the specific needs of a presumed postmodern clientele it may end up only attracting a minority with very little likelihood of repeaters (as this type of tourist, by

definition, desires continually newer and more novel experiences). In practice, the problem is tackled by a division of labour. While tour operators predominantly address the modern mass consumer, most national tourist offices (NTOs) direct their attention to a postmodern target audience.[1]

However, given that there have been several studies of brochures of the former (e.g. Uzzell, 1984; Dann, 1988; Selwyn, 1993), the following account outlines how the latter attempt is managed linguistically by investigating the promotional literature recently disseminated by an adequate and representative sample of a number of NTOs. By content analysing the latest catalogues[2] of 30 typical and relatively small countries exhibiting at the November 1998 *World Travel Market*, and by adopting the general working hypothesis that the smaller the territory the greater the perceived need to emphasize the diversity of a limited number of unique attractions, this study seeks to explore three issues related to the second of the identified trends:

- the degree to which NTOs employ an explicit discourse of differentiation;
- the way in which a more indirect rhetoric of differentiation is employed; and
- the implications of promotional differentiation.

The Degree to which NTOs Employ an Explicit Discourse of Differentiation

Destinations, particularly those offering similar fare, are, above all, competitors. Hence, in their promotional campaigns, many sense the necessity to stress the manner and the degree to which they differ from

---

[1] A third, or middle, way between these two positions is quite rare, although it is evident in a few advertisements of some mass market beach destinations which wish to show that they also have green interiors for alternative experiences. Spain is a good example of this trend in its publicity surrounding Mallorca.

[2] Here reference is made to published material in a multi-page magazine type format. Unlike the tour operator's brochure, it concentrates on the wider offerings of the country rather than on the specifics of resorts, hotels and prices. The catalogue also provides a much fuller treatment than an advertisement.

their rivals. Here four basic options are available:

Option 1: in-difference: differences are contained within the host society but are not proclaimed to outsiders.
Option 2: out-difference, by *explicit* referencing to differentiation: the direct promulgation of difference to outsiders by use of associated expressions.
Option 3: out-difference, by *implicit* referencing to differentiation: the indirect promulgation of difference to outsiders through the use of comparison.
Option 4: out-difference, by *explicit and implicit* referencing to differentiation.

Of the 30 NTO catalogues examined, only one country (Luxembourg) chooses Option 1, thereby highlighting an overriding trend for the remaining 96.7% to select one of the three varieties of out-difference. Of these 29 NTOs: 18 select Option 2, 26 use Option 3, and 14 Option 4. This section looks at Option 2. The next explores Option 3.

Of the 18 explicit references to difference: eight are contained in the headline, 16 in the body copy and six in both headline and body copy. Alternatively stated, since only two countries (Bulgaria and Nigeria) employ explicit difference solely in their headlines and ten others solely in their body copy, the evident promotional trend is the tendency to be less ostentatious in differentiating themselves as destinations.

Turning to a more qualitative treatment, Table 30.1 provides the linguistic expressions and various contexts through which the 18 NTOs explicitly differentiate themselves.

From Table 30.1 it is possible to divide the explicit expressions into two more or less equally distributed major categories of differentiation: difference and uniqueness. The former (with frequencies in parentheses) comprises the words: 'different' (13), 'diversity' (4), 'difference' (3), 'distinct' (2), 'diversified' (1), 'distinguishes' (1) and 'variety' (1), constituting four of the headlines and 21 of the body copy expressions. Thus classified, three ancillary trends are discernible.

First, difference and uniqueness (along with their respective variants) are more than four times more evident in the body copy than in the headline. While this finding is to be expected, given the far greater length of the body copy in a catalogue, and hence the opportunity to feature, it does not necessarily follow that the probability of a given outcome results in its realization. Rather it suggests that there may be a reluctance among tourism promoters to display all their wares conspicuously.

Second, adjectives and adverbs are overall much more frequently employed than are nouns and verbs. These descriptors comprise 62.5% of the headlines, 86.1% of the body copy and 82.3% of both headlines and body copy. By contrast, the respective percentages for nouns are only 37.5, 11.6 and 15.7%, while those for the lone verb are merely 0.0, 2.3 and 2.0%. Thus descriptors in destination publicity appear to have greater salience for promoters than active or instrumental words, a situation which could indicate the targeting of a predominantly female audience – the decision makers in destination choice (see Craik, 1997).

Third, when the referents of the descriptors are classified, the breakdown shown in Table 30.2 occurs. Here the destination itself becomes the prime referent, while its attributes (pull factors – Dann, 1977) assume less importance in terms of their cultural and natural attractiveness. Interestingly, about one-fifth of the focus is on the tourist and those experiences and activities which correspond with motivational push (Dann, 1977; Uzzell, 1984).

The Way in which a More Indirect Rhetoric of Differentiation is Employed

Apart from destinations making direct references to their uniqueness and how different they are, there is another indirect way of managing diversity – by means of comparison. Just as tourists themselves when on holiday often compare features of the place they are currently patronizing with those of destinations they have visited in the past

Table 30.1. Explicit differentiation in 18 out of 30 National Tourist Office (NTO) catalogues.

Country	Headline	Body copy
Andorra		These pages show us pictures and words – *different*, possible and *peculiar* – and what and how Andorra is (1)
Bhutan		A four day Bumthang trek will reveal hidden treasures of life that many visitors have *never seen before* (14)
Bulgaria	Culture Bulgaria. Just *Unique*.	
Corfu	Corfu. Discover the *Difference*	There is so much to see in Corfu that even the regular visitor always finds *something new* (9) The visitor will always return to these sights, while finding *new* attractions to please the eye (9)
Estonia	Estonia. The Baltic Country with a *Difference*	The influences of many *different* invaders upon Estonia's ancient culture and what makes this Baltic country so *unique* (3) Centuries old folk art tradition gives local leather-work, ceramics and glass a *uniquely* Estonian look (5) Estonian handicrafts are *unique* (10)
Gambia		An environment of total peace and tranquillity typical *only* of the Gambia (2) The Gambia is a decision to learn and experience *different* things: a *different* lifestyle, a *different* culture and, of course, meeting *different* people (2) Visitors have come for a *different* holiday (2)
Haiti	Haiti *unique*	From the beginning Haiti dared to be *different* (1) We are eager to share our world with you and the magic that makes Haiti so *unique* . . . *uniquely* unforgettable (4)
Ireland	Ireland. Live a *different* life	History, myth and legend are interwoven to produce a *unique* cultural tapestry that is at once Ireland's past and present (4) (lunar landscape of the Burren, Co.Clare) A truly *different* world of legend, romance and traditional music (14)
Jordan		Jordan is a *unique* and blessed land of the old and new Testaments and the early years of Islam (13)
Nepal	Nepal. A world *of its own*	Because of the country's topographical *diversity*, wide *varieties* of outdoor thrills are available only minutes from one another (3)
Nigeria	Nigeria. A land of cultural *diversity*	
Poland		Poland continues to offer more and more interesting and *diversified* forms of rest to everyone (12)
Scotland		Scotland is such a *distinctive* destination. *Nowhere else* in Britain can you enjoy so many *special* experiences, all of them *uniquely* Scottish (2) Scotland – somewhere *different* (6) Many *differences* between the countries (England and Scotland) remain. Scotland's history, traced in its castles, battlefields, ancient trading links with France, Flanders and Scandinavia is *distinct* (7) Gretna Green visitor centre right at the border is a reminder that Scotland is *different* (8)
Syria		The wide *diversity* of its culture (1) A strange and *singular* world with its *special* beauties (8)
Trinidad and Tobago		Learn about Trinidad and Tobago. The two and *only* (1) A *different* kind of Caribbean calendar (4)
Tunisia	*Unique* Tunisia	Tunisia combines all the traditional qualities of a popular holiday destination, but then adds a few *unique* attractions of *its own* (1) Other Mediterranean countries have their street markets, but souks are a *unique* experience (2)
Turkey		After all, *diversity* is the most prized feature of favourite destinations (1)
Wales		There is something *more* to Wales. Something *unique* that *distinguishes* Wales and her people from all other countries in Britain (1)

Sources: respective countries' NTOs in references. Body copy page references in parentheses. Italicized emphases all added.

Table 30.2. Differentiation according to textual position and classified referents.

| Classified referent | Textual position | | | | |
| | Headline | | Body copy | | |
	Different	Unique	Different	Unique	Totals
Place/country	2	3	7	8	20
Culture/lifestyle/people/artefacts	2	1	6	5	14
Experiences/activities	–	–	6	4	10
Sights/attractions/scenery	–	–	2	5	7
Totals	4	4	21	22	51

('reminds me of X', 'just like Y'), NTOs also employ a language of contrast when seeking to outdo their potential rivals. However, if instead of simply stating that they are better than a single competitor in a certain respect (the use of comparatives), NTOs claim that their destination or one of its attributes is the best (the use of superlatives), several rivals can be eliminated at a stroke. In such a manner, appeals can be made to the sort of tourist who relishes the thought of visiting the most excellent on offer and, on return, relating the experience to other less fortunate acquaintances. A century ago, Veblen (1899) described this type of person as being driven by conspicuous consumption. More recently it has been referred to in the motivational terms of ego-enhancement (Dann, 1977) and the 'quest for the best' (Chalmers, 1987, p. 6).

Turning again to the 30 NTO catalogues, it can be seen that only one uses a superlative in its headline (Lithuania: Baltic Hospitality at its Best), reflecting no doubt the previously noted tendency of reticence towards placing destinational offerings up front. In the body copy, however, all but three of the countries (Haiti, Luxembourg, Trinidad and Tobago) unashamedly employ superlatives. As a matter of fact, there are 145 instances[3] present among the remaining

27 catalogues, an average of 5.6 per catalogue. Eight countries are in excess of this mean. Scotland, in top place, employs superlatives on as many as 28 separate occasions (some 19.3% of the total number of cases, and 16% more than could be expected by chance). The other destinations above the mean, along with their frequencies and percentages of the total, are: Tanzania 13 (9.0%), Wales 12 (8.3%), Slovenia 9 (6.9%), Poland 8 (5.5%), Uganda and Malaysia 7 (4.8% each) and Syria 6 (4.1%). Taken together, these eight countries (27.6% of those selecting Option 3) claim 62.7% of all superlatives. One can only speculate as to why these eight particular destinations are so much more in favour of superlatives than the remaining 19. Perhaps in the cases of Scotland and Wales it is that they regard themselves as being in an extremely competitive situation within the UK context, thereby seeking to establish a separate identity from that assigned to them in their overall joint marketing by the British Tourist Authority.

However, before entertaining that or any other suggestion, it is important to contextualize the 145 superlatives. Here, three content analytical criteria inductively emerge. First, it can be noted that while most (84.1%) claims to fame are stated unambigu-

[3] There are actually six more instances in the publicity of Nepal, Nigeria, Poland, Serbia, Slovenia and Uganda, which have to be deleted on account of their lack of meaningful referents. Thus, in the National Tourism Organization of Serbia's (1998, p. 19) claim that 'Sokobanja boasts of the waters with the highest radioactivity', it is not clear whether the referent is the world, region, country or local area.

ously, a minority (15.9%) come with qualifiers attached. For example, whereas the Tanzania Tourist Board (n.d., p. 19) describes Lake Tanganyika as the longest lake in the world, it concedes in the same breath that it is only 'the *second* deepest' and contains only '*one of* the richest concentrations of fish found anywhere' (emphases added). Similarly, the Jordan Tourism Board (1998, p. 9) states that 'Jerash *is considered* the best preserved and most complete city of the Decapolis', and the Wales Tourist Board (1998, p. 24) feels obliged to admit that Merthyr Tydfil was '*once* the iron capital of the world' (emphases added). Other qualifiers, such as 'arguably', 'reputedly', 'perhaps', 'amongst', 'some of the', 'believed to be' and 'practically' are in evidence too. Among these is discovered the following hypothetical assertion: 'If there had been an Academy Award for the best location, it would undoubtedly have gone to Scotland' (Scottish Tourist Board, 1998, p. 64).

Secondly, the nature of a claim is clearly heightened as the context ascends from the particular to the universal. Here readers are drawn from the level of a specific town or village, e.g. the Olevista Church – 'its green spire is the tallest in Tallinn' (Estonian Tourist Board, n.d., p. 13), to that of a country, e.g. 'Along Primorska's Wine Roads you will find the largest barrel in Slovenia, which holds more than fifty thousand litres of wine' (Slovenian Tourist Board, n.d., p. 15), of a region, e.g. 'Plordiv. The biggest and most beautiful of all towns in Thrace' (Bulgaria, Ministry of Trade and Tourism, n.d., p. 5), of a continent, e.g. 'Hamilton Mausoleum noted for Europe's longest echo – 15 seconds!' (Scottish Tourist Board, 1998, p. 19), and eventually to the entire globe, e.g. (Abuko Nature Reserve) containing 'the largest and smallest kingfisher in the world' (The Gambia, Ministry of Tourism and Culture, 1995, p. 11).

Taking into account the various marginal totals and collapsing the above levels, the following distribution of the 145 cases is yielded: world 67 (46.2%), continent/subcontinent/region 47 (32.4%) and country/city/town/village 31 (21.4%). Interestingly, when this new classification is cross-tabulated with the use/non-use of qualifiers, it emerges that qualifiers are attached in 19.4% of world superlatives and in 19.2% of continent/subcontinent/region superlatives, but in only 3.2% of country/city/town village cases (the overall mean being 15.9%). Thus, although claims are enhanced by increasing their levels, there is clearly an accompanying note of caution that many destinations introduce into their accounts for fear, perhaps, of outrageous allegations losing all credibility. Another danger, of course, is that in the individualistic, statistically driven societies in which millions of potential tourists exist, it is becoming easier for destinations to be found out in the act of touristic discovery. With *The Guinness Book of Records* (GBR) possibly becoming the secular equivalent of The Bible, many postmodern consumers now turn to the former's pages for the moral authority they so lack in their dedifferentiated lives. Indeed, one tourist authority (unfortunately excluded from this collection due to its regional nature), has even introduced the GBR[4] as an arbiter to substantiate its claim that Seville's Santa Maria del Sede is the second largest Christian church after the Basilica in the Vatican (Turismo Andaluz 1998, p. 21).[5]

With this important document to hand it is thus possible to look again at various destinational assertions in order to see whether perhaps even more qualifiers than had actually been used should have been employed. Although many of their claims are simply not featured in the good book, one can nevertheless bring a bit more precision to some of the others. In this regard, the Korea National Tourism Organization's (n.d., p. 2) claim that Korea has the oldest typeset book in the world is doubly sub-

---

[4] Interestingly, 'Guinness' is a registered trademark of 'Guinness Superlatives Ltd'.
[5] Unfortunately for Turismo Andaluz, *The Guinness Book of Records* explicitly rejects the Guinness inclusion of items with qualifiers attached (McFarlan, 1989, p. 3).

Table 30.3. Distribution of superlatives in body copy of National Tourist Office (NTO) catalogues.

| | Level | | | | | | |
| | World | | Continent/region | | Country/town | | |
Referent	Unqual	Qual	Unqual	Qual	Unqual	Qual	Totals
Natural attractions	12	4	20	1	10	–	47
Architecture/buildings	8	1	5	5	7	–	26
Flora and fauna	7	5	5	2	1	–	20
Language/literature/culture	8	1	2	–	5	1	17
People/health/sport	8	–	4	1	1	–	14
Art/artefacts	6	–	1	–	2	–	9
Food and drink	3	–	–	–	4	–	7
Technology and transport	2	2	1	–	–	–	5
Totals	54	13	38	9	30	1	145

stantiated by the GBR (the Dharani scroll produced from wooden printed blocks in AD 704 and discovered at Kyongju, as well as the circa AD 1160 28-page book of Tang Dynasty poems held by Yonsei University) (McFarlan, 1989, p. 150), but its claim to have the first ironclad warship is denied (that honour after all belonging to the HMS Warrior of Portsmouth, 1860) (McFarlan, 1989, p. 104). The Syria Ministry of Tourism (n.d., p. 4), too, is found to be correct in stating that it has the oldest alphabet (discovered at Ugarit in 1450 BC according to McFarlan, 1989, p. 147), but not so accurate in saying that Damascus is the world's most ancient city. Even the omitted epithet 'capital' (which would take it back to 2500 BC (McFarlan, 1989, p. 196)) may not suffice, as Sama'a in Yemen believes that it is the longest continuously inhabited city on earth (see Hack, 1998). The claims and counterclaims are endless and offer numerous opportunities for research into tourism promotion as a form of *Trivial Pursuit*.

Recognizing that such hyperbole can sometimes have a boomerang effect, one tourism authority (Bord Failte, 1998, p. 56) even tries to turn the situation to its advantage by introducing humour. Speaking of co-promoted Northern Ireland, it maintains: 'There are so many golf clubs that you can traverse the country by driving a golf ball

from one course to another', before adding parenthetically: 'This, like golfing yarns the world over, may turn out to be a slight exaggeration'.

Finally, the 145 superlatives can be classified according to their referent. In this regard, a perusal of the data quickly reveals the categories of natural attractions (47 instances), architecture/buildings (26), flora and fauna (20), language, literature and culture (17), people, health, sport (14), art and artefacts (9), food and drink (7), technology and transport (5). Thus, the lowest point on earth, the tallest mountain and the longest cave seem to have greater promotional pull than the first-ever passenger railway (not incidentally in Swansea as alleged, but in Whitstable). One reason why natural assets are favoured over manufactured attractions is that they may have greater appeal to the romantic in the postmodern client.

Bringing the three sets of information together, Table 30.3 is yielded, from which two other trends can be extracted. First, an easily calculable comparison of column percentages with total percentages shows that at the world level there is above average emphasis on flora and fauna, language/ literature/culture, people/health/sport, art/artefacts and technology/transport; at the continent/region levels on natural attractions, architecture/buildings, flora and fauna; and at the country/town level on architecture/buildings, language/literature/ culture, art/artefacts and food/drink.

Second, the tendency to qualify statements does not simply vary by level (as already noted), but also according to referent. Whereas the overall figure comes to 15.9%, in two contexts (art/artefacts and food/drink) there are no qualifiers at all (i.e. there is a greater tendency to exaggerate). By contrast, in the cases of architecture/ buildings (23.1%), flora/fauna (35.0%), and technology/transport (40.0%), the mean percentage is exceeded and the language becomes much more cautious. In these last three domains it can be further calculated at which level the use of qualifiers is at a maximum. For architecture/buildings it reaches a peak at the continent/subcontinent level (50%) and for flora/fauna and technology/ transport at the world level (41.7 and 50%, respectively).

The Implications of Promotional Differentiation

From the foregoing analysis it can be seen from the two general trends that there is a current tendency for small countries to assert their touristic identities through a language of differentiation in the publicity material of their NTOs and, in so doing, an associated attempt to appeal to the dedifferentiated condition of their predominantly postmodern customers. Yet, it is not a simple act of evocation. It is one that is moderated according to degree of directness, contextual level, textual positioning and type of referent. It is also an appeal whose continuation carries a number of implications.

First, although some experts (e.g. Hall and Weiler, 1992; Urry, 1995) maintain that niche marketing will expand to meet the increased demands of special interest/ special destination tourism, equally there are others (e.g. Chalmers, 1987; Craik, 1997) who believe that mass tourism will continue to grow for many years to come, particularly as a result of the merging of leading tour operators, airlines and hotel companies. Just

who will be right is difficult to say (Burns and Holden, 1995, p. 35). What is clear, however, is that NTOs have made their choice in backing one forecast in favour of the other.

Second, and perhaps by way of justification for their choice, the stressing of destinational uniqueness may be considered as an idiosyncratic reaction against an overall trend of destinational blurring associated with top-down globalization. As Brown (1998, p. 19) so admirably puts it: 'where states have reacted to the spread of interdependence by making efforts to reassert their differences ... tourism has the potential to show people that the world is not as undifferentiated as they thought'. Seen in this light, a counter-trend of indigenization may be viewed as providing the necessary local component to an otherwise unidirectional dismantling of national boundaries by transnational interests.

Third, and as a corollary to the above, the discourse of difference, through which NTOs promote the countries they represent, may be thought of as a reaction against the far greater tendency of external tour operators to delocalize place for their mass markets. Hence, the NTO rhetoric of differentiation can be understood as an act of disidentification or counteridentification against Western ethnocentrism (Hollinshead, 1993).

Fourth, the promotion of difference is something of a two-edged sword and may not always produce the intended result of attracting an affluent clientele in search of novelty. One of the characteristics of a postmodern target market is that the quest for difference cannot be adequately fulfilled by visiting the same destination more than once. Instead, and as previously noted, there is a tendency towards travel for its own sake, for merely ticking off different places as items on a check list as a means to acquiring more and more novel experiences (Rojek, 1997).

Fifth, once the language of difference begins to approximate the language of advertising, it will tend to lose credibility. Although qualifiers are in evidence in the material surveyed, they nevertheless constitute a textual minority. Even if their presence continues, NTOs may be attempted to abandon them with the realization that such conditionalities may well reduce the appeal of their attractions. However, if the verbal reservations are removed, there could be a consequent lapse into unsubstantiated claims and hyperbole, the very discourse that NTOs wish to avoid. Cliché, after all, pervades the rhetoric of their rivals, the tour operators and their brochures (Krippendorf, 1987).

Finally, there may be a growing awareness among destination people that NTO literature, in spite of its alleged indigenous authorship, may not in fact be representing their true interests, or indeed their real life situations. The tallest tower, the oldest department store, etc., may not be the best way that their differences as inhabitants of a unique place are optimally portrayed. One may therefore expect to hear a greater number of calls for more local participation in the preparation of NTO material. However, should that eventuality come to pass, it would not in itself guarantee an appeal to the market for the simple reason that their disadvantaged lives may not constitute a tourist attraction. Moreover, even if they did, there would still be the uncomfortable realization that they may never become capable of matching such ephemeral drawing power to equally volatile tourist motivation.

Conclusions

This brief account has identified two contrary trends in contemporary tourism, each of which has its counterpart in promotional strategy. One stresses the need for sameness or familiarity, the other difference or strangeness in its potential clientele. The criterion for the marketing of destinations is thus none other than that employed by Cohen (1972, 1979) in devising his typologies of tourists, a commentator who, in turn, derives his insights from the writings of Schutz (1944) and Simmel (1950) on strangerhood. Just as there are recreational and diversionary tourists corresponding to the

institutionalized mass variety – those who seek an upgraded extension of home in a foreign resort – so too are there experimental, experiential and existential tourists who, more independently, look for novelty through an ever-growing quest for otherness.

It is precisely this alterity which forms the theoretical framework for so-called 'alternative tourism', or alternative forms of tourism, whose essential characteristic is that they present another option to conventional mass tourism based on the hedonism of the four S's. The novelty that the former attempt to portray resides at three levels:

- It offers experiences which are seemingly different from those of day-to-day living in the tourism generating environment;
- It provides activities that are supposedly different from those of the controlled ambience of the hotel, beach and swimming pool; and
- It supplies apparent difference through exposure to the lives of destination people.

Why, then, all the hesitation – the use of moderated expressions, such as 'seemingly different', 'supposedly different', and 'apparent difference'? The answer to this question is to be found in the consequences of highlighting such difference. As we have seen, MacCannell (1989) argues that the authentic differences which tourists seek are, in fact, denied them by the tourism industry. What is promoted in reality becomes demoted through the staging of difference at the destination. Relatedly, Wheeler (1993) maintains that the actual quest for difference by more and more 'alternative' tourists in search of seclusion and nature has quite the opposite effect since, by virtue of paving the way for increasing numbers, it tends to degenerate into the mass tourism from which it had wished to escape. Ecotourism and its many variants are hence just egotourism in another guise.

By corollary, and in relation to the current focus of attention, what these two observers are surely querying is the genuineness of the rhetoric of difference. Are destinations truly as unique as claimed? Do they have the friendliest people, the most exotic customs, the finest cuisine and so on? Do the differences that they verbally and pictorially parade actually make a difference? In response to this crucial dilemma, the optimist will reply that, since difference is infinite, it can be multiplied indefinitely. The pessimist (and perhaps the realist) will respond that, because difference is finite, tourists will have to come to terms with the well-known situational paradox 'the more things change, the more they remain the same'.

31

Recreation Conflict Management

William E. Hammitt and Ingrid E. Schneider

Introduction

Outdoor recreation is an important component of leisure estimated to constitute one-third of our daily time and lifespan. The outdoor activities that many people pursue during their leisure are often valued more highly than their work activities. Because recreation activities are such critical life elements, it is no wonder that recreation conflicts occur. Conflict in outdoor recreation, whether it is between the Wilderness Society and a Federal agency, between recreation manager and visitor, or between different user groups, may be particularly prevalent given its unique setting and value. In fact, recreation conflict is inevitable and will increase as recreation importance and demands increase.

Conflict in outdoor recreation is one of the most common and difficult problems with which recreation managers must contend (Hammitt, 1988). In the next century, conflict among users will continue to be one of the most important issues among forest managers (Jakes *et al.*, 1990). Subsequently, the need for managers to acquire the vocabulary of and expertise in conflict resolution is omnipresent (Lan, 1997).

Before one can approach recreation conflict management and resolution, ascertaining exactly what denotes conflict is critical. Multiple recreation conflict definitions exist and include these components:

goal interference attributed to another (Jacob and Schreyer, 1980); a threat to a person or their belongings (Keller, 1990); a strain on the visitor's coping resources (Schneider and Hammitt, 1995) and a cumulative process rather than an immediate reaction (Owens, 1985). Other concepts similar to conflict and included as conflict by some authors are disgust, nuisance and annoyance associated with on-site recreation. There are also various levels and sources of recreational conflict that must be understood before one can approach recreation conflict management and resolution. Conflict types will be discussed in more detail later in this chapter.

Although recreation conflict appears the antithesis of both recreation managerial and visitor goals, we must also realize its potential positive influence. Recreation conflict can indicate when something within the current system needs attention and, thus, conflict forces one to test the management situation. In addition, recreation conflict can lead to ideas and solutions of superior quality because of the multiple parties and perspectives involved. Conflict also keeps the organization at a higher level of stimulation and, at the very least, prevents stagnation. A greater awareness of the possible impacts of conflict, both positive and negative, assists managers in changing destructive conflicts to constructive efforts (Lan, 1997). Fortunately, conflict resolution potential among recreation groups is high compared to other entities (Floyd *et al.*, 1996).

The history of recreation conflict management has evolved during four management eras since 1950; moving from the early period of conflict identification/conditions, to determining behavioural/perceptual factors of conflict, to the era of institutional/public involvement and ending with the current coping/resolution era. Following the eras of conflict management, we speculate on the future need for and means to developing enhanced ways to cope with and resolve recreation conflicts. The future trend in conflict management involves a shift from the stimulus to the response side of the conflict equation, meaning more emphasis on coping with and resolving conflict.

In summary, the focus of this chapter is: (i) the evolution of definitions and levels of recreation conflict; (ii) recreation conflict management eras, possible causes and management's response; (iii) conflicts and implications that focus on the need to understand better how people and institutions cope with and resolve conflicts; and (iv) conclusions concerning recreation conflict management trends.

Trend Overview

Management eras

Since the 1950s, four eras in recreation conflict management can be identified: use activity–space allocation, perception–cause, institution–public involvement; and coping–resolution. These are not mutually exclusive but represent an evolution of different strategies to understand and manage recreation conflict. A brief discussion of each era is offered, with a focus on the prominent management situations, causes, and responses to conflict during each.

User activity–space allocation era

Much of the 1950s and 1960s were dominated by conflicts resulting from rapidly increasing multi-activity use and competition for recreation space, particularly in

camping, hiking, and a bit later, water activities. Simply stated, recreationists were seen as competing for physical and social space during the same periods. The focus of recreation conflict management during this era was on identifying conflict occurrence, situational conditions of conflict occurrence, as well as activity incompatibility. The major causes of conflict were seen as over-use, activity and space incompatibility, and lack of resource-facility allocation. Little was known about user behaviour and preferences, leading to management solutions being expert or manager driven. Management's response was to separate conflicting uses and to allocate resources and activities in both space and time. For example, separate tent and recreational vehicle campground loops, zoning of lake and river uses, development of separate trails for ORVs, horses and hikers, and area use permits, were common management responses.

Research and management experience during this era led to the realization that recreation conflict was more than an activity incompatibility or space allocation problem. Reported conflict occurrence among respondents was not high (about 30%), yet capable of being quite important to certain user segments. Space, or a lack thereof, was not the cause of conflict, for separated incompatible users were still in conflict. Environmental–situational conditions were often less important than psychological perceptions as recreation conflict factors. These findings ushered in the perception–cause era of recreation conflict management.

Perception–cause era

If different activities and lack of ample space were the cause of conflict, then why did hikers hate horseback riders but not vice versa? Also, why did separated users still find conflict with each other's activity? Psychological perceptions, individual differences and human behaviour in general were at play in recreation conflict.

The 1970s included an emphasis on understanding the behavioural aspects of recreation conflict with a focus on motivations, user perceptions, preferences and social carrying capacity. The causes of conflict were seen as motivational differences among and within different recreation users (Stankey, 1973; Driver and Brown, 1978) and lifestyle diversity and recreation experience demands of users (Jacob, 1977; Jacob and Schreyer, 1980). Management's response to conflict was the development of recreation opportunity spectrum (ROS) strategies, social carrying capacity models and management techniques, and user education programmes to mitigate potential conflict by modifying user behaviour.

The work of Jacob and Schreyer (1980) provided the 'goal interference attributed to another's behaviour' definition to recreation conflict, as well as four factors and ten propositions that identified its potential. The four factors are defined below, while the reader is referred to Jacob and Schreyer's (1980) article for the ten propositions.

- *Activity style* = the personal meanings attached to the set of behaviours constituting a recreational activity (e.g. intensity of participation, status, definition of quality experience).
- *Resource specificity* = the significance attached to using a specific recreation resource for a given recreation experience.
- *Mode of experience* = the varying expectations of how the environment will be perceived.
- *Tolerance for lifestyle diversity* = the tendency to accept or reject lifestyles different from one's own.

These factors have been used extensively by researchers to understand conflict perception in recreation.

> In failing to recognize the basic psychological causes of conflict, *inappropriate* resolution techniques and management strategies are likely to be adopted
>
> (Jacob and Schreyer, 1980, p. 378)

For example, if lifestyle differences are to be recognized as a part of recreation behaviour,

> then conflicts arising from perceptions of incompatibility cannot be eliminated from recreation areas. At best they can be

incorporated into management's decision-making process in such a way as to minimize the intensity and dysfunctions of conflict

> (Jacob, 1977, p. 5)

Institutional–public involvement era

Additional and formal incorporation of the public's perceptions in natural resource decisions was mandated in the 1970s and, by the 1980s, conflict management that included public involvement was the norm. Institutionalized public involvement processes practically required interested recreation groups to organize and be involved in general management decisions, including recreation conflict. The management focus was not on individual perceptions of goal interference, but rather on recreation resource values and organized interest groups. These value differences were, and continue to be, the basis of many management conflicts in natural resources. The importance of public values as an input to resource management is emphasized by Creighton (1983), who also identifies value conflicts as the root of environmental disputes. Understanding value conflicts requires communication and, in recreation conflict management, communication occurs most frequently through public involvement.

Management's initial response to mandatory public involvement was obligatory and limited attempts were made to involve the public. Conflict during the institutional–public involvement era was exacerbated by a lack of government trust; part of a larger societal movement in which the public was challenging 'expert opinion' and even asking for second opinions among long established 'expert' professions, such as medicine and law.

> Conflict over the role of government stems from a combination of political value, personal experience and understanding of reality
>
> (Lan, 1997, p. 5)

Unfortunately, due to limited positive and inclusive involvement during this time, public understanding of resource management decision making reality may be skewed.

Involvement studies suggest that the public has been treated as an informant rather than an active partner (Blahna and Yonts-Shepard, 1989). According to results from a survey on planning and conflict, US Department of Agriculture (USDA) Forest Service managers have not adopted public interaction techniques commensurate with the reality of today's 'shared power world' (Cheng *et al.*, 1993, p. 35). Blahna and Yonts-Shepard suggest that

> despite the increased awareness of the value of public participation, there is still a lack of understanding of how to integrate public involvement in the planning process (Blahna and Yonts-Shepard, 1989, p. 210)

Citizen intervention in management is occurring with increasing frequency, subsequently requiring increased attention and efforts toward resolution (McMullin and Nielsen, 1991).

Coping–resolution era

Currently, recreation conflict is recognized as an inevitable part of outdoor recreation, partitioned into several types, and the result of varying perceptions and values among those involved. Increased fragmentation of publics has accelerated the frequency of confrontations and conflicts in natural resource management (McMullin and Nielsen, 1991). In response, research efforts are currently interested in the public's response to conflict and the processes involved in responding. Public responses to environmental decisions are complex because they involve conflicts among scarce resources and evoke strong emotions (Vining and Schroeder, 1989). Subsequently, understanding responses and resolving diverging responses are increasingly critical components to conflict management.

At the individual level, recreation conflict management has responded to this call by attempting to understand how visitors cope with conflict. Efforts have focused on identifying set responses to conflict (Hammitt and Patterson, 1991; Robertson and Regula, 1994) and moved toward developing a hierarchy of responses (Kuentzel and Heberlein, 1992). To gauge group responses

to conflict, managers still rely heavily on public involvement. Fortunately, public involvement is evolving toward collaborative planning procedures, where management's role is more of a coordinator among groups, rather than an authority, and the focus is on resolution. The dominant Forest Service resource management paradigm is decision making by experts but the emerging paradigm is consultative and participatory (Brown and Harris, 1992).

Evolving Concepts in Recreation Conflict Management

Broadening definitional complexity

An obvious trend in recreation conflict management is the broadening complexity of the conflict concept itself. The early conceptualization of outdoor recreation conflict as 'competition between two different activity groups for the same resource' has been recognized as too simplistic, for it ignored many social and behavioural aspects of recreational experiences. Later, outdoor recreation conflict was defined as 'any physical, social, or psychological obstruction arising within or between participants and their recreation goals' (Lindsay, 1980). The obstruction with recreational goals idea evolved into the most commonly accepted and traditional definition of recreation conflict: 'goal interference attributed to the behaviour of another' (Jacob and Schreyer, 1980; Schreyer, 1990).

Definitions of conflict as goal interference place great emphasis on the behaviour of others and stress that recreation goal interference not attributed to others does not necessarily equate with conflict. For goal interference to result in conflict, the interference must be attributed to another's behaviour. For example, bad weather, the fish not biting, or forgetting to pack appropriate equipment, may interfere with the fulfilment of planned recreational goals, but is not considered conflict by the traditional definition since it cannot be attributed to another's behaviour – only your own (Jacob and Schreyer, 1980). However, we contend that outdoor recreation situations exist

'Source' of impact \ 'Recipient' of impact	Visitors	Park management	Community
Visitors	1 Visitor–Visitor	2 Visitor–Park	3 Visitor–Community
Park management	4 Park–Visitor	5 Park–Park	6 Park–Community
Community	7 Community–Visitor	8 Community–Park	9 Community–Community

Fig. 31.1. Interaction model for various levels of recreation conflict. Source: Little and Noe (1984).

where no one else is directly or even indirectly responsible for goal interference, yet feelings of frustration, failure, nuisance, annoyance and even dissatisfaction are still just as prevalent as when the behaviour of another is responsible. Thus, perhaps it is time to expand the conflict phenomenon to include related emotional and behavioural aspects of disgust, nuisance and annoyance, whether attributed to another's behaviour or not.

If the ultimate purpose of recreation management is to provide quality and satisfying experiences, then perhaps the goal interference/behaviour of others conflict model is too restrictive. Perhaps the traditional definition of outdoor recreation conflict has been driven too much by management's desire to solve the problem; where conflict only occurs when attributed to another's behaviour; behaviour which managers can influence. As Jacob (1977) suggests, management's need to resolve all conflict, and even the concept of conflict resolution, may be a misconception. First, many conflicts confronting recreation resource managers have little to do with recreation itself. Second, in many cases resource managers can only hope to minimize the negative impacts of conflict, not resolve them. Third, many conflicts that occur within outdoor recreation experiences are capable of being handled by individual and group coping strategies, without the need for management's resolution. This latter relationship of coping to recreation conflict is developed later in this chapter.

Varying levels and sources of conflict

A second major trend in recreation conflict management has been the recognition that conflict involves many sources, far beyond the user to user activity–space problem. At least four sources of recreation conflict are typically recognized; including visitors, managers, local officials and residents, and government (Little and Noe, 1984; Schreyer, 1990). These sources interact in multidimensional ways, leading to an interactive framework with nine levels of conflict and opportunities for conflict management (Fig. 31.1). A brief example of the type of conflict that may occur at each of the nine levels is offered.

Visitor to Visitor

Little explanation is needed here, for this is the typical hiker versus ORV, canoe versus powerboat, skier versus snowmobile conflict. However, power equipment does not have to be the source of this type of conflict.

Trout fishers may be at odds with swimmers over the proper use of a resource. In all cases, the two groups do not share the same values regarding the 'proper' use of the recreation resource, and this value conflict has been known to develop into more overt forms of conflict.

Visitor to Management

Visitors often cause impact and conflict upon both management and the resource. An obvious example is that of resource degradation, such as camp site impacts, littering and inappropriate use of scarce resources (endangered species). Visitors often do not have the resource knowledge and ethics to use resources wisely, and are therefore in conflict with management.

Visitor to Community

Recreation, particularly in the form of tourism, can become an 'attractive nuisance' for nearby communities. The very attractiveness of the Great Smoky Mountains National Park and the birth of gateway cities such as Gatlinburg, Tennessee, means that nearby towns will suffer periodic problems with traffic flow, parking availability, littering and other functions of crowds. In more rural areas, the influx of 'foreigners' is in conflict with the traditional lifestyles of the 'locals'.

Management to Visitor

Visitors are not always the source of conflict; management is often the originating source. Restrictions on use are a common example here. Users may feel they have the right to use wilderness without obtaining a permit, or even if a given number of visitors are already using the resource. Management is charged with resource protection and regulations, yet recreationists want 'freedom of choice' when recreating and therefore may balk at the idea of not being allowed to use all areas of a park or forest.

Management to Management

Just as different visitor groups may have different sets of values regarding the proper use of the resource, so may management personnel from different agencies or even within the same agency have different values and beliefs regarding the management of resources. Management of fire and insects in wilderness is an example, where some resource managers feel strongly that both fire and insects need to be managed on an ecosystem basis, even in wilderness zones.

Management to Community

Management of recreation resources and use often conflicts with how local people from surrounding communities have traditionally used these areas. Newly formed parks that prohibit hunting, collection of ginseng, picnicking on the roadside and the use of shortcut roads are resented because local community residents have long considered these 'territorial' rights. In these situations, management is interfering with the recreational goals of local residents as they have traditionally learned to use resource areas.

Community to Visitor

Many national parks, such as Great Smoky Mountains and Rocky Mountain, have gateway cities that detract from the wildland recreation experience of some visitors. The highly developed tourist economies and gaudy visual displays of these areas are in conflict with the nonurban experience that many visitors are seeking. Tourism operated helicopter and plane flights over wildland areas are increasing conflicts for both visitors and management.

Community to Management

Special interest groups, community officials and even influential community citizens can place pressures upon management of nearby resource areas that result in conflict. Community interests may force management of nearby recreation areas to allow community events considered inappropriate by management. Conflict resolution is often necessary to arrive at an agreeable solution concerning these demands upon recreation management agencies.

Community to Community

Business interests within communities and among adjacent communities may be at odds in receiving concession contracts for recreational services. Competition among outfitters can be fierce and lead to recreational conflict, particularly when it comes to allocation allotment.

Each of these sources and levels of conflict have implications for recreation conflict management. However, in this chapter we are focusing primarily on visitor to visitor and visitor to park conflicts.

Implications

Recreation conflict, conceptually and managerially evolved substantially in the 20th century. From simplistic approaches to complex and dynamic understandings, conflict and conflict management are coming of age in recreation. Much of the emphasis in the past has been on the front end of the recreation conflict equation; dealing with the situational and perceptual causes of conflict. While this is essential to understanding conflict, it tells us little about the other end of the recreation conflict equation; how to cope with and resolve conflict. We suggest that understanding mechanisms of coping and conflict resolution are vital to the future of conflict management and detail them below, along with management implications.

Visitor coping with conflict situations

Visitor responses to conflict have been associated with crowding, the inception of conflict (Owens, 1985) and extended to responses to stress (Schneider, 1995; Schneider and Hammitt, 1995). Response to stress has been suggested as particularly applicable in outdoor recreation conflict since conflict and stress are intimately related, although not equated (Schneider and Hammitt, 1995). The traditional definition of conflict in outdoor recreation conflict research implies obstruction or interference, therefore leading to tension and/or stress. Previous conceptual efforts suggest response to recreation conflict be framed within an adapted stress-coping response model (Schneider and Hammitt, 1995) and empirical efforts suggest the framework is suitable

for outdoor recreation research (Schneider and Hammitt, 1995; Miller and McCool, 1998).

Focused on the individual's subjective interpretation of a transaction, the adapted model is based on Lazarus and Folkman's (1984) model, which has five major components: (i) person and situation factors; (ii) appraisals; (iii) stress; (iv) coping response; and (v) short- and long-term adaptational outcomes (Fig. 31.2). The person and situation factors work in conjunction to influence the cognitive appraisals. Cognitive appraisals determine if, why, and to what extent, a particular transaction is stressful. Situations appraised as stressful require coping and reappraisals that lead to adaptational outcomes. Coping manages both the stressful encounter and the emotions it generates.

Coping processes emerge if the primary appraisal determines a situation is stressful and the secondary appraisal identifies acceptable coping mechanisms and processes. Two basic coping processes are recognized in coping research: problem focused and emotion focused (Pearlin and Schooler, 1978; Lazarus and Folkman, 1984). Problem-focused coping processes improve the troubled person–environment relationship by managing the problem while emotion-focused processes relieve the emotional impact of the stress. Problem-focused processes are either directed at the environment or toward the self. Emotion-focused processes encompass a diversity of options such as distancing, selective attention or avoidance to draw attention either away from the stress or change its meaning. Rarely is one strategy used exclusively, but rather a combination of strategies is employed (Pearlin and Schooler, 1978; Pruitt and Rubin, 1986). Current research suggests recreationists avoid and distance themselves from the conflict and utilize social support mechanisms as available.

Both short- and long-term outcomes result from the coping process. Short-term effects may include positive or negative feelings, physiological effects or, in the case of outdoor recreation, diminished experiences. Long-term effects might include social functioning or morale. Long-term effects in

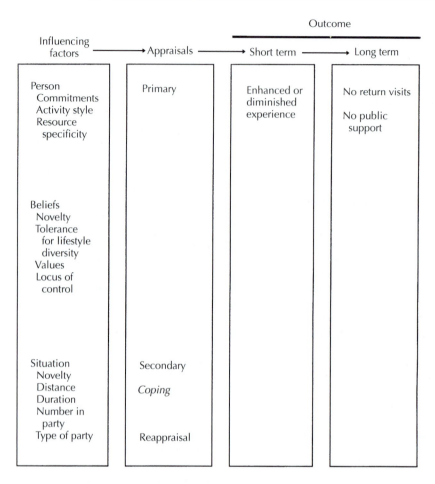

Fig. 31.2. Model of recreation conflict appraisal and response. Source: based on Lazarus and Folkman (1984).

outdoor recreation might include opposition to management decisions, negative publicity of an area, lack of public support and discontinued use of an area. While these effects may seem extreme, the emotion generated in confrontations is much more intense than choices in outdoor activities suggest (Knopp and Tyger, 1973).

A conceptual foundation based upon the stress response coping literature paradigm of Lazarus and Folkman (1984) reveals many similarities between an individual's coping response to stress and likely response to outdoor recreation conflict. Integrating research from the outdoor recreation and stress literature, outdoor recreation conflict is defined as a disruptive, stressful occurrence in the visitors' recreation experience involving a person–environment relationship which taxes a person's psychological resources. How visitors cope with recreation conflict is of primary interest in future conflict management. Research aimed at determining the relationships between situational, psychological and managerial conflict conditions and outdoor recreation visitor stress-coping responses is essential to conflict management. Once these relationships are understood, management strategies and techniques can be developed to better assist recreation visitors and managers at coping with and resolving conflict.

However, research and management pro-grammes in the area of conflict stress-coping responses are currently scarce. The full implications of coping mechanisms and res-ponses to conflict situations as a management tool will not be realized until research and management programmes are developed.

Conflict resolution

If conflict among individuals is not ade-quately coped with and diminished, it frequently accelerates to group level con-flict. At the group level, coping with conflict may be framed as conflict resolution. Con-flict resolution demands public involve-ment and therefore makes involvement a key component of conflict resolution. Con-flict resolution involves three steps: (i) analysis; (ii) confrontation; and (iii) resolu-tion. An important differentiation at this point is between conflict resolution and set-tlement. Although frequently used inter-changeably, resolution and settlement are dramatically different. Settlement implies suppressing differences through a power-bargaining context (Burton, 1990). In contrast, resolution is an outcome that develops from complete analysis and meets the needs of all concerned parties (Fisher, 1994). Inherent in the conflict resolution process is clear and open communication, mutual respect, shared exploration, an ori-entation to collaborative problem solving and a commitment to resolution. Active problem solving and high stakes ensure that although conflict exists, agreement is possi-ble, rather than compromise or 'smoothing it over' (Blake et al., 1964). These character-istics exemplify cooperative, rather than competitive, processes. Conflict resolution is characteristic of the emerging paradigm in resource management (Brown and Harris, 1992).

The first stage of conflict resolution is analysis. During this stage, the conflict's his-tory is explored and group positions on major issues identified. In the analysis phase, identifying the issues is the primary goal, which provides the base of discussion for the second phase, confrontation. Con-frontation involves further engaging the

parties with direct and face-to-face inter-action to focus on the most contentious issues. Within the confrontation phase, major conflicts are defined, alternatives gen-erated and solutions evaluated. The emphasis in these situations is creating a superordinate or overarching common goal among the groups (Sherif, 1958). Finally, actual conflict resolution is possible. Reso-lution transforms the conflict toward self-supporting, self-correcting and sustain-able relationships. As the resolution prevents further escalation, it works toward building sustainable relationships and structures that allow for equal identity among user groups.

Group level conflict management in out-door recreation, as indicated previously, has been approached through separation of users. Only recently have the values and attitudes of these groups come to the atten-tion of researchers. However, the primary issues of the conflicts still remain largely unknown or the best guesses of experts. Party confrontation and consultation is the next step toward group conflict resolution. Current management practices indicate that decision makers adopt a satisfying manage-ment approach and settle for compromise rather than resolution (Dennis, 1988). Familiarization with and incorporation of conflict resolution practices in recreation conflict management will enable managers to address challenges with greater success.

Conclusions

Conflict in outdoor recreation is inevitable, is an ongoing component common to many recreational experiences; thus a need exists to better understand and manage it. The complexity of recreation conflict manage-ment will also continue to broaden and expand beyond the concept of goal inter-ference attributed to the behaviour of another. Conflict often involves values and preference norms of individuals, and can occur far removed from the recreation place and the behaviour of individuals. One important point to realize is that stress, at some intensity level, is usually associated with conflict. The challenge is to recognize recreation conflict as a situational-response process that involves both an understanding of disruptive situations during recreation experiences and visitor responses to them. We imply a greater need to emphasize the response side of the conflict process, where individual coping and group resolution strategies are better understood.

New sources and levels of conflict will continue to evolve, and to challenge the past training of field managers and the decision making of government agency policy makers. Recreation managers must accept new sources and levels of conflict as part of the recreation management profession, realize that they are part of the conflict resolution equation, and seek appropriate training. This training must go beyond the resolution of user to user conflicts, for there is a shift toward more community to agency, and interest group to agency conflicts. Collaborative planning and nominal group resolution processes are essential future conflict management tools. Managers will need to 'learn to anticipate the shape of the future ... and build the institutional capacity to respond to' recreation conflict (Shannon, 1992, p. 2).

While recreation conflict may be inevitable, and management must continually increase its ability to respond to conflict, it must be realized that management can only hope to minimize the negative impacts of conflict, not completely resolve them in most situations. Indeed, conflict resolution management is a misconception if it simply refers to management and government agencies intervening in conflict behaviour, while ignoring the coping behaviour components of conflict mediation. This chapter's focus on process is critical as 'the process is at least as important as result: i.e. one cannot judge the value of a decision by looking at the outcome alone' (Knopp and Caldbeck, 1990, p. 18).

In summary, this chapter concludes that: (i) recreation conflict management is a broadening and complex phenomenon that will require new and innovative techniques; (ii) new sources and levels of conflict will continue to evolve and require new training of conflict resolution personnel; (iii) total conflict resolution is not realistic, for most conflict situations cannot be completely solved, but rather, only minimized to an acceptable level; and (iv) many recreation experience conflicts are capable of being handled by individual and group coping strategies, without the need for direct management intervention. Emphasis in the future must be on understanding the coping mechanisms of recreationists while under stress in conflict situations.

32

Service Quality in Resort Settings: Trends in the Application of Information Technology

Richard R. Perdue

Introduction

Quality is the most critical resort management challenge of the new millennium due to four separate, but converging trends. First and most important, our society is experiencing a major transfer of wealth. As their parents die, the 'baby boomers' are inheriting vast amounts of money. The parental generation, which lived through the depression, had always been fiscally conservative, preferring savings and low-risk investments. By contrast, the baby boomers have always been a spending generation, inclined to 'live for the present' and 'conspicuous consumption'. Many of these inheritances are being spent on resort real estate, fuelling the ongoing boom in resort condominium and time-share construction. As these resort 'guests' become 'owners', service expectations and demands for quality are rising to ever higher levels.

Second, there is an increasing emphasis on repeat visitation and relationship marketing throughout the tourism industry (Oppermann, 1998). Service quality and customer satisfaction are recognized as the primary factors affecting both repeat visits and word of mouth recommendations from previous guests (Rust and Oliver, 1994).

Third, resort guests expect higher and higher levels of quality, not only in resort design, but also in the quality and personalization of service they receive from resort employees (Kotler et al., 1999).

Fourth, for a variety of reasons, resorts are finding it increasingly difficult to attract and retain quality employees (Ledgerwood et al., 1998). Yet, quality employees have historically been considered the raison d'être of service quality in resort settings (Spiselman, 1995).

Facing these challenges, it is essential that resorts identify ways of increasing employee productivity, defined as increasing the quality of service provided to resort guests while, at the same time, reducing the number of employees per guest room (Quinn, 1995; Gee, 1996). Further, to be competitive for employees, resorts must identify ways of improving the quality of resort jobs; making resort jobs easier and more enjoyable (Ross, 1997).

Advances in the application of information technology (IT) are viewed as the key means by which these divergent goals may be attained (Poon, 1988, 1993; Van Hoff et al., 1995; Sheldon, 1997b). Between 1990 and 1994, IT investment per employee by the hotel and lodging sector grew from US$367 to US$1058, a cumulative growth of 188% over just 4 years (Margherio, 1997). Most projections view this trend as continuing and, potentially, accelerating over the

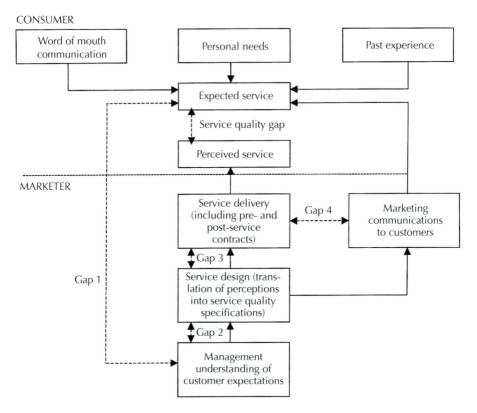

Fig. 32.1. The Gaps Model of Service Quality. Source: Parasuraman *et al.* (1985).

next decade. There is a great deal of uncertainty, however, in determining the appropriate forms and level of information technology. As stated:

> No single factor looms with less certainty or greater complexity for hospitality investors than how the industry can best invest in technology to gain competitive advantage
> (Cline, 1997)

The purpose of this chapter is to explore trends and applications of IT to service quality in resort settings.

Resort Service Quality: the Gaps Model

The Gaps Model of Service Quality (Parasuraman *et al.*, 1985) will be used to organize the following discussion of IT

trends in the resort industry (Fig. 32.1). Consistent with the service quality literature, the Gaps Model conceptualizes quality as the congruence between a customer's service expectations and the perceived quality of service received (the service quality gap in Fig. 32.1). Four potential gaps or problem sources are identified. First (gap 1), in order to design and provide quality services, management must understand customer expectations. Resorts serve an increasingly diverse customer base. Resort managers must understand customer expectations both overall and by a variety of market segments. Second, (gap 2) even if customer expectations are well understood, management must still design the products and services, which will satisfy those expectations. Third (gap 3), even if expectations are well understood and appropriate products and services have been designed, providing those services effectively is still critical.

Fourth (gap 4), customer expectations are a function not only of the customer's background and experience, but also of the marketing communications provided by the resort. Marketing communications must promise those services and products which the resort can effectively deliver. Over the past few years, new information technologies have been developed to address each of these gaps. In the following sections, IT developments and trends relative to each gap are presented.

Gap 1: Measuring and understanding customer expectations

Over the past decade, much of the research in the services marketing area has focused on developing measures of service quality (Martin, 1986; Oliver, 1997; Taylor, 1997). While the debate certainly continues (Brown et al., 1993), SERVQUAL has evolved as the predominant measurement tool (Parasuraman et al., 1993). Essentially, SERVQUAL measures and compares customer service expectations and perceived service. Several authors have adapted this instrument to the tourism industry (Knutson et al., 1990; Fick and Ritchie, 1991; Martin, 1995; Stevens et al., 1995).

The challenge of the next decade is not to develop these measures further. Rather, it is to develop service quality information systems that integrate various quality measures and make the results easily and quickly available to resort managers (Martin, 1986; Berry and Parasuraman, 1997). Specifically, the evidence strongly supports the need to monitor continuously both customer expectations and perceived quality. If expectations change or quality problems occur, it is extremely important for the resort to identify these changes quickly and respond with quality improvements or corrections. Two factors further complicate this process. First, presuming weekly or biweekly measures of consumer expectations and perceived quality, changes are defined relative both to the previous measurement period and, because of the cyclical nature of resort demand, to the same measurement period in the previous year. Consequently, the data need to be effectively

merged with these existing databases. Second, resorts tend to be very complicated organizations spread over a relatively large geographical area. Getting the right data to the right managers requires a sophisticated communication system. Key trends in this area include:

Trend 1: Development of electronic quality measurement tools

Increasingly, data are being collected using hand-held, battery-driven computers. Either respondents or survey administrators enter the data into the computers. The data can then be directly downloaded into a workstation where it is merged with the existing databases, and automatically analysed for important changes and problems.

Trend 2: Email distribution of service quality survey results

Once the data are analysed, customized reports are automatically prepared for each area of the resort. These reports are distributed by email communication systems. The combination of the above two trends makes it possible to collect data for a weekly Monday to Sunday period with the reports in managers' offices by Monday afternoon of the following week.

Gap 2: Service product design

Presuming that service managers understand customer expectations, the next potential problem is effectively designing service innovations which fulfil those expectations (Tax and Stuart, 1997). IT is being used in three distinct ways: (i) it is increasingly a means of monitoring and benchmarking the competition; (ii) it is being used to blueprint and improve service processes; and (iii) it is the basis of new product and service offerings. The following paragraphs further explore each of these applications.

In additional to traditional market research methods such as focus groups and conjoint analysis, monitoring and copying the competition has historically been an important means of new product development by individual companies in the service industries, including resorts. The general strategy has been to recognize a problem, research how other companies cope with that problem and copy what seems to work best (Lovelock, 1996). Advances in technology have made this process much easier. Over the past 5 years, virtually all major resorts in the US have developed Internet sites for marketing purposes. Many of these Internet sites include a form to sign up for an email list which is then used to provide periodic product and marketing information. By monitoring Internet sites and signing up for email lists, resorts can very effectively monitor their direct competition and benchmark themselves relative to any variety of existing resorts and service companies. 'Shopping the competition' has always been a key resort service quality process; now it is dramatically easier because of the shared information technologies created by the marketing communications function.

Importantly, however, this process of copying service innovations from other resorts ultimately may lead to a commodification of the resort product. Beyond their unique natural resource endowments, virtually all resorts will provide a very similar 'product portfolio', making it increasingly difficult for a resort to differentiate itself competitively based on product offerings. As this happens, ever greater quality pressure will be put on the process of service delivery.

Process improvement teams are commonly used to examine specific internal and consumer service processes. These teams consist of a cross-section of resort employees who, conceptually, bring different perspectives to examine and improve resort processes. However, influence-cost behaviour, wherein employees focus more on improving their own jobs rather than improving resort productivity and profitability (McAfee and McMillian, 1997), is a major problem with these teams. Quantitative tools are needed to focus on service process improvements that truly benefit the customers. Process blueprinting and fishbone charts are the primary tools used by these teams (Kingman-Brundage, 1989; Rust

et al., 1996). Essentially, a process blueprint maps a consumer's service experience from beginning to end and then develops corresponding maps of front-stage, backstage, and management employee actions. The output of a process blueprint is identification of failure points in the service delivery process. Qualitative critical incident research is then frequently used to assess these failure points further (Bitner et al., 1996). Fishbone charts are frequently the output of these critical incident analyses. Essentially, a fishbone chart looks like a fish with six ribs. The process problem is the head of the fish. The tail identifies customer and 'other' uncontrollable factors which contribute to the problem. The ribs identify internal causes of the problem as related to (i) facilities, (ii) materials, (iii) processes, (iv) front-stage employees, (v) backstage employees and (vi) equipment. Increasingly, IT software packages are being used to blueprint resort services, to develop fishbone charts, and to simulate and assess alternative processes improvements.

Finally, resorts are increasingly using IT as the basis for new service products (Dabholkar, 1994). Three interesting examples from Colorado resorts reflect this trend. For an additional fee, golfers at several resorts can rent carts with built-in GIS technology. Throughout the course, a monitor on the cart displays the exact distance to the next hole. Similarly, at some Colorado ski resorts this year, skiers can pay a fee, be given an electronic sensor to wear throughout the day as they ski, and at the end of the day be given a high-quality image of the mountain displaying all the ski runs which the individual skied that day. Finally, parents leaving children in resort daycare centres are given pagers. In the event of any problems, parents can be quickly found and notified.

Trend 3: Electronic monitoring of the competition

The use of the Internet and e-mail to monitor the service products offered by other resorts will continue to grow. As it grows, however, it will put even greater pressure on service quality process support systems and technologies.

Trend 4: Service process software applications

Resorts are increasingly using IT software to blueprint service processes, to create fish-bone charts of service problems, and to simulate service improvements. These soft-ware applications both enhance the quality of process improvements and dramatically reduce the necessary time and effort.

Trend 5: Information technology is increasingly the basis for new resort products and services

Resorts are constantly seeking supplemental products and services to offer to guests. Technological innovations frequently form the basis of these new products.

Gap 3: Service delivery

The primary goal of 'service delivery' tech-nology investments is to improve, facilitate, and speed up the actual delivery of services. Tourists, virtually by definition, tend to be very difficult and demanding customers for a variety of reasons. They are unfamiliar with the resort environment. They generally do not know where, how, or even when to participate in various resort activities. They tend to have invested a large amount of money in a relatively short resort holiday. They want/attempt to participate in a large number of different experiences over just a few days. And they are very impatient with service delivery delays and errors. Provid-ing guest service is, consequently, both physically and emotionally difficult. Employee burnout is a serious problem impacting service quality both directly through discourteous employees and indi-rectly through employee turnover (Loveman, 1998). Given the extreme diffi-culty of recruiting and retaining a quality workforce in many rural resort locations, employee satisfaction is virtually as impor-tant as guest satisfaction (Ledgerwood et al., 1998).

Three major applications of technology exist in this area. First, and by far most important, many resorts are significantly investing in technology to improve both resort processes and the ability of resort employees to answer guest questions. As examples, guest history and marketing/membership club databases are increasingly being used to reduce the amount of effort needed to check customers into resorts. Sim-ilarly, technology is being used to reduce checkout problems; guests can review their folios the night before checkout, notify the front desk of problems, have those problems corrected, and check out of the resort with-out ever going to the front desk. Information technology has also greatly reduced the complexity of night auditing of guest folios. Finally, networked computers are increas-ingly being used to provide question/answer databases to both employees and customers. These and a variety of other IT investments both improve process accuracy and reduce customer waiting time. At the same time, these IT investments also greatly reduce customer–employee conflict, making the employees' jobs dramatically less stressful and more enjoyable.

Second, information technology can also reduce number-of-employee needs, partic-ularly for services which have highly cyclical demand. For example, the guest checkout process, discussed above, has greatly reduced guest waiting time. It has also allowed the resort to level out the num-ber of employees needed at the front desk. Further, IT along with customer member-ship cards is being used in some cases to greatly reduce customer needs for some ser-vices. As an example, ski resorts are increasingly using membership cards to replace traditional lift tickets. Customers go directly to the lift, have their cards scanned, and are directly charged to their credit cards for that day's skiing. Skiers benefit with quicker access to lifts. The resort benefits by needing fewer lift ticket sales personnel. Importantly, both the customer and the resort should benefit from these IT invest-ments. The customer benefits through reduced processing time and process accu-racy improvements. The resort benefits through reducing the number of employees needed to support service processes.

Third, information technology is also being used to enhance the integration of resort services across different vendors (Tax and Stuart, 1997). Most resort holidays are actually purchased from a variety of vendors and intermediaries, including travel agency, transportation, lodging, food and beverage, recreation and entertainment, and shopping businesses. Much of the service quality movement focuses on the concept of 'seamless' experiences, wherein the customer is treated with an integrated system of services to fulfil their needs regardless of service ownership (Zeithaml and Bitner, 1996). As resorts increasingly form partnerships with air and ground transportation firms and concessionaire agreements with shopping, food and beverage, and entertainment vendors, information technology is being used to simplify both the purchase and on-site experience of customers. For example, IT is being used to support 'one-stop shopping' for resort holidays either by phone or Internet and to allow customers to charge products and services from a variety of vendors to their room folios.

Trend 6: Resort process improvement through information technology

IT is being used to: (i) reduce customer waiting time; (ii) improve process accuracy; and (iii) reduce customer information needs. Beyond guest satisfaction, enhanced employee satisfaction is a key benefit of these technologies.

Trend 7: Information technology may reduce the number of employees required

In selected applications, IT may reduce the number of employees required, but must, at the same time, enhance service quality and customer satisfaction. Generally, technology investments have been successful in levelling out the cyclical demand for employees. Efforts to actually reduce the number of employees are successful to the extent that the process also enhances guest satisfaction.

Trend 8: Information technology is being used to integrate customer experiences with multiple vendors

Information technology can both reduce the need for guests to provide the same information to multiple vendors and allow the resort to achieve a 'seamless experience' for its guests.

Gap 4: Marketing communications

Much of the excitement surrounding information technology in resort settings focuses on e-commerce using the Internet, and with good reason. In 1996, Internet users booked US$276 million worth of travel on-line. For 1997, on-line travel sales are estimated at US$816 million. By the year 2000, these sales could reach US$5 billion. Among US adults, 38% said they would use the Internet for their travel plans in 1998 (Margherio, 1997). Resorts are very rapidly adopting the Internet as a marketing communications tool. Five distinct levels of Internet technology are being adopted. First, the Internet is increasingly being used as an advertising fulfilment mechanism to which potential guests are directed by including web addresses in traditional advertising media. Additionally, many resort web sites have fulfilment requests forms through which customers can request traditional holiday information packages. Second, many resort web sites now include an email club enrolment form, including a short interests and demographic questionnaire. These e-mail addresses are increasingly being used along with sophisticated data-based marketing for direct email promotional campaigns, particularly for sales promotions and yield management purposes. The resort can decide on Wednesday evening to offer special products and discounts for the weekend and effectively promote them by email the next morning. Third, as security strengthens, many resorts are including on-line sales and reservations services. Fourth, many resorts are creating e-commerce catalogue sites where consumers can purchase resort clothing, equipment and souvenirs. Fifth, some resorts are creating on-line chat rooms where past guests can describe their resort experiences, including both positive and negative qualities.

As with any marketing communication, the key service quality issue is effectively delivering on the promotional promises (Zeithaml and Bitner, 1996). IT can be used to manage service promises effectively, including not only making realistic promises, but also keeping customers and travel agents informed of service availability and changes in schedules and offerings. For example, Colorado ski resorts include information not only on service offerings, but also on such issues as weather, travel and snow conditions.

Trend 9: Resorts are increasingly using Internet and email technology as key marketing communications tools

Initially, most resort Internet sites were essentially 'on-line brochures'. Increasingly resorts are improving their web sites to become more interactive and more enjoyable to potential guests.

Information technology is also being used to educate guests. Many times, a quality resort holiday is a function not only of what happens on the resort site, but also of guest preparation and equipment. Resort Internet sites frequently include 'what to bring' lists, equipment recommendations and special preparations. For example, high altitude sickness is a common and potentially fatal problem at Colorado resorts. Most resort web sites, consequently, try to educate the guest both on how to avoid becoming sick and on identifying and treating the illness.

Trend 10: Resort Internet sites are increasingly being used to provide guest education

Many of the problems which guests experience at resorts are avoidable through proper equipment and preparation. Information technology can greatly improve guest education efforts resulting in less problems both for the guest and for the resort.

Implications and Conclusions

As noted earlier, IT investments by lodging businesses grew by 188% between 1990 and 1994. Unfortunately, the correlation between these investments and lodging sector profitability is unclear, leading many experts to proclaim a productivity paradox

(Quinn, 1995). Technology investments do not necessarily result in improved short-term financial performance. Hence, the concept of a 'balanced scorecard' in assessing the impacts of technology on resort service quality (Kaplan and Norton, 1992). IT investments enhance resort performance in at least three ways, beyond financial return. First, IT investments may be necessary to remain competitive and maintain market share. Failure to keep up with the competition may result in significant losses. Second, IT is necessary to support an increasingly complex service environment. Resorts need to be adaptable and flexible to an increasingly diverse customer base. Third, and perhaps most importantly, IT can be used to improve the resort work environment. Consequently, a balanced scorecard needs to include: (i) both long- and short-term financial performance data; (ii) consumer data including resort occupancy, yield, cycle times and customer perceptions/satisfaction; (iii) employee data such as recruitment, training, retention and job satisfaction; and (iv) measures of innovation including both improvements in performance of traditional processes and the development and implementation of new processes. In each of these areas, most resorts have multiple technologies and corresponding databases. The challenge of the future is integration of these various databases. Being able to understand effectively the performance implications of improvements in service quality is critical. As experienced by the Ritz Carlton Hotel group, it is possible to win a Malcolm Baldrige National Quality Award for service quality and, at the same time, suffer significant performance losses (Hirsch, 1994), particularly in the short-term.

As noted earlier, resort service quality programmes focused initially on developing quality measures. Over the past few years, the emphasis has shifted to addressing specific quality problems and process improvement. Technology has primarily been used to tackle individual problems. The trends reported in the preceding sections highlight this approach. Very often different technologies are used by different parts of the resort. Significant coordination and integration problems are the norm. Over the next few years, more and more resorts will create information technology departments with the goal of better management of their technology investments.

33

Partnerships and the Changing World of Park Management

Will F. LaPage

We serve best through partnership, rather than patriarchy ...
Autocratic governance withers the spirit

(Peter Block)

Foreword

In the autumn of 1991, after a quarter century of no growth throughout its state parks, the State of New Hampshire acquired a large tract of undeveloped land within a 90-minute drive of hundreds of thousands of potential visitors. With no prospect of meeting the costs of developing and operating new parks for at least another decade, several hundred acres of badly needed recreation opportunities seemed to be headed for a dismal future of locked gates, illegal use and vandalism.

Yet, less than 4 years later, the park was open, contributing to the local economy and producing satisfied visitors. This miracle of bureaucratic efficiency happened as a result of a creative partnership with the Telephone Pioneers of America, the nation's largest corporate-based volunteer group. Just 30 miles down the road, at Odiorne Point State Park on New Hampshire's coast, a new friends' group was successfully completing a fund-raising effort of more than US$1 million to build an educational centre for their park, after having challenged the state legis-

lature to provide matching funds! 'Northwoods Meadows–Pioneer State Park' and the Friends of Odiorne Point are just two of the thousands of similar park partnership success stories from all across America that have helped to restore our tired public park systems, stretch scarce tax dollars and build community pride.

A 1994 survey of America's state park systems (LaPage, 1994a) found all states to be experiencing similar waves of volunteering and partnering. In 1996, the Northeast Region of the National Park Service reported having more than 5000 partnering organizations supporting its programmes across the 13-state region (US National Park Service, Northeast Field Area, 1996). The park partnership movement is international as well: Canadian Park Partnerships, in 1974, reported 44 member associations representing every province and 40 national parks, more than 10,000 individual members, more than 54,000 h of volunteer service, and financial assistance of more than US$6 million. As reported at the fourth International Outdoor Recreation Trends Symposium (Selin and Darrow, 1995), the definition of park part-

© CAB *International* 2000. *Trends in Outdoor Recreation, Leisure and Tourism*
(eds W.C. Gartner and D.W. Lime)

nerships is growing to include a rich array of formal and informal organizational arrangements – designer partnerships for every situation.

Where Did All the Partners Come From, and Why Now?

The widespread incidence of late 20th century volunteerism in America's public parks did not just happen. Although countless acts of individual and corporate generosity are the heritage of every public park system, it is only in recent years that volunteerism has emerged as an organized force. From Yellowstone to Central Park, advocates are no longer simply speaking out for bigger budgets, but are pitching in to fill the staffing voids. The President's Commission on Americans Outdoors (PCAO) recognized this emerging trend and recommended a partnering ethic to guarantee the future of diverse and satisfying recreation experiences for visitors to our public lands (PCAO, 1987a). Undoubtedly contributing to what appears to be a spontaneous emergence of park helpers are the successful models that have resulted from years of park professionals' frustration with the paradox of short-term budgets and the need for long-term resource protection (LaPage, 1995). As Uhlik (1995) points out in his step-by-step model of partnership development, those frustrations are echoed by the public's tactical shift from park advocacy to park activism.

Volunteerism is a form of activism and, like other expressions of social and environmental activism, it is triggered by a combination of dissatisfaction with the status quo and a citizenry that is willing and able to get involved. When the source of dissatisfaction is a highly publicized decline in the condition of public lands, trails and historic sites, and when there is a legacy of pride in those public assets, the ingredients for volunteer activism are nearly in place. All that is needed is the spark to ignite the prairie fire and coalesce the concerned citizens. That spark may be struck in many ways: a park closure, drastically reduced hours of operation, an invitation from park officials to get involved (or sometimes a rebuff from the same source), a media exposé of park conditions, or a socially conscious corporate adoption of parklands. Park closures for lack of an operating budget or just the threat of a closure, have resulted in the birth of many friends' groups. The visible effect of years of deferred maintenance in nearly all park systems helps to highlight the need for action. When the badly deteriorated, Civilian Conservation Corps vintage, facilities at Cardigan State Park in northwestern New Hampshire were removed in the early 1990s, a friends' group materialized overnight to design, donate and build replacement facilities.

The phenomenon of volunteer armies of activists coming to the rescue has been linked by many observers to a declining ability of government to address park needs and a concurrent rise in citizens' abilities to fill the void (Selin and Darrow, 1995). The Government's impending failure to preserve its parks adequately has been foreseen for decades, and responded to by many blue-ribbon commissions at every level of government. That failure is the inevitable result of:

- the expansion of public lands without commensurate increases in operating budgets;
- the unabated growth in demand for access to those lands, often in the face of sharply declining real budgets and staffing; and
- a widespread obsolescence of park infrastructure at a time when public parklands have fallen to the bottom of government priorities.

The extent of this failure to fund public park systems adequately can be appreciated by realizing that volunteering and partnering are but two of several management strategies now being used to close the budget gap. Other strategies include closures, sharply reduced services, increased user fees, privatizing, leasing, management contracts and the appointment of more blue-ribbon study commissions (who are volunteers themselves and, hopefully, park advocates). Necessity has clearly spawned a growing collection of new ways to conduct the business of park management. Many new ways are proving superior to those that they have displaced, and are probably permanent, despite future funding levels. Partnerships, particularly those based on volunteerism, are in that category because they are a proactive and democratic solution.

Despite their enormous successes, the viability of partnerships as a new management paradigm is likely to remain heavily dependent upon a continuation of those economic and social forces that dominated its gestation period. Most obvious among these are limited public funding combined with low rates of inflation, increased discretionary time, a desire for meaningful involvement, early retirements, flexibility in workplaces and hours, relative residential stability and strong local pride. Until the idea becomes widely adopted by park professionals and fully integrated within the parks bureaucracy, showing up in the budgeting process, in development planning, in annual reporting, and the performance evaluations of managers, the possibility of reverting to old styles will slow the process of building partnerships. However, it cannot derail the partnership movement, because the probability for full funding to protect, manage, maintain and interpret America's vast public parks estate without partnerships is zero! The demands being placed on our public lands have vastly outgrown the capabilities of traditional management models.

So, Where Will the Trend End?

Just as the financial crisis in parks did not happen in a vacuum, the new look in park organization charts will largely be shaped by broader trends in government and new ways of conducting the public's business. However, parks have a unique opportunity to become leaders in that movement because public lands in general, and parks in partic-

ular, represent Americans' most intimate relationship with their government. Most of these lands were set aside because they embody pride in heritage, while offering opportunities for inspiration, renewal and refreshment. We insist that these values and these opportunities must continue to be available to our children. The recent trends in volunteering and partnering provide clear evidence that when these resources and these opportunities are threatened, Americans will take direct action. That action is not simply an expression of a wider cynicism about government in general, it is personal, focused and insistent.

Parks have the opportunity for becoming more than a nursery for reinventing government, they are an adventure in rediscovering democracy. The realization that stewardship of our public lands is ultimately a societal, not a professional, responsibility drastically changes organizational strategies, from delegation to collaboration, and from regulation to education. The notion that an organization's mission can be achieved faster, more effectively, and with more permanence by expanding the army and giving it a sense of ownership, makes the idea of daily repetitive maintenance obsolete. Park agencies can pick up visitors' rubbish, or visitors can become partners in maintaining the beauty of their own lands. Agencies can spend astronomical sums trying to protect their borders from development by buying up buffer zones or they can partner with local communities to create limited development zones. Parks can become police states in an attempt to protect their assets and artefacts from theft and destruction, or they can achieve full protection by alerting and empowering their publics. Parks can fund their own limited programmes of promotion, education and information about parks, or they can allow corporations to underwrite these programmes. And, agencies can plan in a vacuum, operate independently – and die; or they can become full-fledged members of the community – and survive. The obstacles to achieving these higher levels of performance are almost entirely imaginary. There may be an occasional legal constraint, but more often the resistance is rooted in the insecurity of 'turf!'.

The essential ingredient for change is a shift in focus away from the organization and its almost sanctified procedures and toward its clients and results. Partnering for parks may have begun as a shadow trend, an expedient for coping with inescapable social and governmental forces, but its successes are rapidly moving it toward a mega-trend status of its own. And, in doing so, it spins off new styles of management, new emphases on constituency building and consensus building, new approaches to stewardship of park resources through stewardship of human resources, and real measures of performance and accountability. In short, the trend is unlikely to end until the mandate for park protection is fulfilled and real accountability is in place.

New management styles

Administrative resistance to partnerships is often rooted in concerns for authority and ethics, or, 'where is my authorization to work with partners, and under what conditions is it appropriate to solicit help?' In a representative democracy, the people delegate authority to elected representatives who, in turn, delegate the functions of government to professional administrators. While there is no provision for a further delegation of responsibility back to the electorate or to some portion thereof, there is also no direct prohibition against expanding the management team as long as it does not exceed the budget. When that expansion improves the team, while reducing the budget, it epitomizes public administration's principle of efficiency. To be partners in the enterprise of government does not mean an equal sharing of accountability, it is simply a sharing in getting the job done. That sharing is accomplished by opening wide the doors of government and identifying the roles of each partner. Those doors have already been legislatively opened by many mandates for the public's involvement in park planning and impact assessment. It is an obvious step to share the implementation of those plans. Yet, it can be a big step in terms of legal liability and potential conflicts of interest.

The major difference in style is that of the open door – the constant invitation to volunteer, to be a part of the team, to share in the work and the rewards of healthy parks. Opening the door is relatively easy. Jointly defining roles is much more difficult. Leasing, concessions and cooperative agreements have been used by park agencies for generations to define public–private relationships in parks. In nearly all park agencies, these tools have experienced variable success, sometimes becoming political footballs because of a failure to insist on shared visions and to work as partners to achieve those visions. But, park partnering for the 21st century means something other than legally binding agreements and supervising performance contracts.

Many of today's partners are not interested in formal agreements, or in being supervised. Corporations, friend's groups, nonprofits, individual volunteers, schools and other agencies are seeing parks as a vehicle for building a sense of community, of pride, of belonging and of giving something back. Volunteering is a movement that often does not lend itself to traditional styles of coordination, organization and regimentation. If parks are going to capitalize on this potential fully, they will need to look beyond the handbook, the policy manual and the chain of command for guidance. As Selin and Darrow (1995) summarized the problems of partnerships, the red tape, the lack of communication, professional fears, and the heavy-handed approach of many bureaucracies, result in a less than ideal partnership nursery. Nurturing friends' groups and sustaining volunteerism are more like tending a garden than they are like steering a ship.

Consensus and constituency

The goal of partnering is to achieve the parks' missions of protection and public service fully. However, an inevitable spin-off of any partnership is an expanded constituency for parks. Expanding the traditional constituency to include, for example, corporate America, brings not just large donations to the cause, it brings talent, labour, advocacy, image and awareness. The corporation obviously benefits from the park's image, but the park likewise benefits from the corporation's recognition of it as worthy of support. That recognition translates to a message that is both direct and indirect. Indirectly, the message encourages others, such as corporate employees, business associates, politicians and opinion leaders, to increase their levels of support for park goals. The indirect kinds of benefits, like advocacy, that result from most corporate partnerships can vastly exceed the direct assistance provided. For other kinds of partnerships, the direct benefits are likely to be more of a bonus, for example, partnerships with universities (for research), with other agencies (for shared staffing and programmes), with other tourism enterprises (for joint promotion), and with friend's groups (for management assistance). In every case, the partnership helps to assure success, and the success helps to assure continuation and expansion of the partnership base. In fact, growth of the partnership base alone may be a better indicator of a park's success in achieving its goals than are some of the more traditional measures such as park visits and cost : income ratios.

Growth of the partnership base carries with it a geometrical increase in the difficulty of achieving a consensus. Partners do not appreciate being surprised by unilateral policy changes in such matters as user fees, capital development, information programmes, seasons, hours and emergency closures. They do expect to be consulted (after all, their image is now at stake too), and they do assume that their advice will be used. Having two partners more than doubles the concerns because there is now a three-way network. Adding just one more partner potentially results in a ten-way communication network and a commensurate increase in the opportunities for miscommunication and conflicting desires among partners. Many park organizations today are working with dozens of park partners. Achieving a consensus now becomes the manager's full-time occupation, and requires a considerably different set of skills than was necessary in the traditional hierar-

chical organization. Two solutions become immediately obvious: limit the number of park partners or expand the number of administrators working with the partners; for example, the addition of a deputy administrator to manage the traditional organization, thereby freeing up the administrator to work exclusively with partners. The latter effectively creates two organizations and even greater complexity. Arbitrarily reducing the number of partnerships for purely administrative convenience is impossible to defend. The answer is to recognize and celebrate the diversity of the partnership resource through organizational stewardship. Just as the problems increase, so do the successes. Park partners may be more effective than park professionals in communicating a new land ethic (Roggenbuck *et al.*, 1992).

Stewardship

Partnerships, like dollars, staff, infrastructure, land and water, are park assets. Maintaining partnerships is not what most park managers were trained in: it is not currently an available course of study in undergraduate training for park professionals. And yet, it is probably the most important resource management skill for park professionals to acquire. Fortunately, training for stewardship of human resources is available in many other ways, but it must be sought.

As Peter Block reminds us, choosing stewardship as an alternative to leadership is a conscious decision (Block, 1993). It requires the enlightened view that care taking is the antithesis of stewardship. The 'care and feeding' approach to partnerships is a guaranteed formula for failure. Equals do not need to provide incentives and rewards to each other for doing their jobs. Being treated as an equal and valued partner is sufficient. Stewardship of park partnerships means: (i) providing opportunities, an open door, for collaboration on a meaningful level; (ii) creating the conditions to make that collaboration successful; and (iii) sharing the rewards.

Opportunities for partnership should include an array of responsible and rewarding roles that span all park operations. There cannot be a division of responsibilities that is based on 'appropriate' roles for nonprofessionals: 'you sell the hot dogs, we do the nature programmes'. Some of the most challenging roles for park partners are those professional tasks not presently being done because of inadequate budgets and staffing. Monitoring of biological diversity, of visitor satisfaction, and of the effectiveness of interpretive programmes are essential to the business of park management and are the kinds of real contributions for which many prospective volunteers and sponsors are looking. All parks have urgent needs, but the open door to partnerships is more than sharing the list; it requires listening and developing a role that will be mutually rewarding.

In addition to challenging tasks, the conditions for successful partnering include such obvious concerns as legal liability coverage, workers' compensation, training, and the informational tools to do the job. The single most important condition is an organizational ethic toward partnering; a welcoming attitude by all that partners and volunteers are an affirmation of the importance of their own jobs, not a threat to them. In mature public agencies, with employees jaded by a history of budget and personnel cutbacks, such an attitude may be slow in developing.

Sharing the rewards of the partnership seems obvious, and yet the risk of taking partners for granted is a very real one. Partnering results in an extended family that has all the attributes of any extended family with very busy members. The credits for a job well done need to be enthusiastically, not perfunctorily, extended to all. And finally, stewardship, to be successful, must step out of the straightjacket that has historically bound accountability to control. Control of a far-flung, multiplayer team, made up of independent entities and creative thinkers, is a dream at best. A paradigm of monitoring and mid-course corrections may be more appropriate for 21st century park management.

Accountability

While legal accountability for park assets must remain with park administration, the level of that accountability, under a partnership model, can only be enhanced. True accountability for park assets is more than fiscal detail; it requires an aggressive response to the mandate to 'preserve and protect for future generations'. With sponsorships and partnerships, many parks will find it possible for the first time in their history to begin to monitor conditions photographically, to take counts of species composition and density systematically, and to sample the social and experiential impacts of park programmes representatively. Over time, it will become possible to measure trends and establish an early warning system for management to address changing conditions before the crisis stage. Partners can be responsible for programmes without being accountable for them, but partners will want to see better accountability measures emerge as a result of their efforts. Partnerships provide both the impetus, and the means to make realities of today's euphemisms about 'park stewardship', and 'park accountability'. Concepts of continuous inventory of park conditions and performance, candid assessments of the trends, published reports to the 'stockholders', and full accountability for results, are essential principles for viable partnerships. Without these principles, partnerships become just another screen to obscure failure and to diffuse responsibility and accountability.

Those park organizations that have already moved into the 21st century style of stewardship through partnership, such as national parks of the northeast, are finding that 'steering more and rowing less' is providing substance for accountability reports (US National Park Service, 1994). Conversely, those park administrations that see partnering as just another programme for the bureaucracy to cope with, with layers of formal approvals, sanctions and signatures, have the form of accountability but are really delaying the remarkable benefits of conservation by participation.

The Future – A New Wave of Conservation Action for Parks?

The performance of park partnerships, during the closing years of the 20th century, combined with their promise of guaranteeing the future flow of park benefits and protection of park assets, means that partnering is not a fad, it is a movement. It might more accurately be called a new wave of conservation – conservation by participation, a logical, and necessary, evolution from the earlier waves of conservation through designation of public lands, through acquisition, and through professional management.

The very practical two-step planning process, of recognizing the inevitable and then finding a way to take advantage of it, suggests that park organizations should consider restructuring, and rethinking their strategies in ways that will facilitate the growing demand for participation and partnering. An accountability report to the public, showing where gaps exist between their mandate and their current performance levels, might be a useful – if painful – first step in pinpointing where change – and help – is needed.

Recognizing that form follows function, partnerships can provide the spark for a meaningful reorganization of the bureaucracy's chairs. The misnamed 'business management office' might emerge as the 'accountability office' and be staffed with programme auditors rather than purely fiscal watchdogs. The obsession for tracking dollars without equal attention to goal attainment has, all too often, created internal adversarial settings where natural partnerships could have flourished. The regulations-bound personnel office, in recognizing that the employees are the organizations' 'first partners', might reconstitute itself as the 'professional development' office, a place where cooperation and collaboration are taught and practiced. The maintenance office might better be viewed as the 'stewardship office', thereby encouraging partnerships and providing a show window on the state of our parks. What a change in pride and morale

that would herald! Operations and management, once they have rejected the control model, might logically become the 'partnership office' and focus on guiding complex institutions rather than trying to run a hierarchy. The information office might add to its public contact function the essential networking between and among partners, while also assuming the role of organizational conscience and commitment builder, by becoming the park 'development' office. 'This is political reform within the organization' (Block, 1993), and it is infinitely more desirable than arbitrarily imposed change from the outside.

Partnerships can be a less comfortable world in which to work, taking enormous time and energy (Selin and Darrow, 1995). The complexities are great, but the rewards are greater. Partnerships can make the difference between success and failure (LaPage, 1994b). The partnership world is a lot less lonely because it is an affirmation of the importance of the mission and a helping hand to restore stewardship to its rightful place in the profession. It is the profession's best chance to avoid the legacy of a multibillion dollar deferred maintenance bill on these irreplaceable national assets.

> Partnerships are not necessarily easy; they require thick skins, forgiveness, clear communications, trust, shared visions, and back-up systems in case of failure ... they may seem much messier than traditional, clear-cut, boundary-driven, land management. But, when they succeed, the sense of public ownership, inclusion, cost-effectiveness, and community empowerment are well worth it
> (US National Park Service, 1994)

The park's office deserves to be a place where the vision that created our diverse systems of public parklands, historic sites, trails and natural areas, is matched by a similarly dynamic organizational culture. Any new definition of parkland protection has to include the lands outside the boundaries. The ultimate protection within those boundaries requires an appreciation of the fact that people deserve to live and work in park-like settings. That is a goal requiring endless partnering, and one that frees the parks professional from park boundaries and from traditional definitions of park protection.

The late 20th century emergence of partnerships all across the landscape of America's public parks, combined with the phenomenal successes of many of those ventures, can be viewed as a harbinger of both a rejuvenated public park ethic and a new management paradigm. The implications for achieving park goals and the potential impacts on park management, and on the park profession, are likely to be extensive. Partnerships are not just the newest buzzword for doing the public's business. They are not a creative blowout patch for systems that have outgrown their management capa-bility, a temporary fix until the money supply catches up. They are a powerful constituency that will challenge the way we define and achieve the goals of parks in the 21st century. They contain the seeds of a new wave of environmental conservation that can match all those earlier waves, a wave of protection through popular participation. And, as the social equivalent of the symbiotic relationships in nature that parks seek to preserve, they enhance our ability to deal with complexity. Partnerships have already altered park management styles at every level of government. Their potential for improved stewardship, accountability, consensus building and organizational structure of public parks is just beginning to be realized.

34

Tourism and Sustainability: a Positive Trend

John J. Pigram

Sustainability and Change

Few terms have been subject to such close scrutiny and dissection of meaning as sustainability and sustainable development. In simple terms, the concept of sustainability expresses the notion that people must live within the capacity of their environment to support them. A sustainable world is an environmentally bounded one (Jacobs, 1995), developing within sustainability constraints of maintenance of human resource-creating potential, waste management capabilities, environmental services, and compatible sociocultural values and structures.

In the context of human existence, sustainability implies a fresh approach to planning for the future and a renewed commitment to use resources in a way that sustains such use. Yet, some would argue that sustainability has little to do with planning, and equate the concept with radical conservatism and an argument against change. Such a perspective confuses sustainability with change avoidance and resistance to change.

Others see sustainability as a question of the maintenance of balance or equilibrium over time (Dahl, 1996), with the focus more on nonsustainability and the forces tending to disturb equilibrium. Thus 'sustainability can only be achieved when all forces upsetting the balance are removed' (Dahl, 1996, p.

29). Taken to the extreme, this viewpoint could be seen to seek the retention of existing social, economic and political structures and the continuation of present conditions and life systems. However, Dahl acknowledges the certainty of change and the need to incorporate the dynamic elements of productive systems and social structures into a new, higher, and, presumably, preferred condition of sustainable equilibrium.

For such a state of 'ultimate balance' to be achieved and sustained, the processes contributing to renewal must compensate for the failures, losses and sources of disequilibrium. On this basis, Dahl (1996) warns that some supposedly 'developed' economies are operating in a demonstrably unsustainable mode, founded on unrealistic projections and assumptions concerning industrial potential, technology and social transitions.

Sustainability is multifaceted and any tendency to view sustainability as an unidimensional state ignores the several dimensions of the concept as it applies to human activity and development. Possibly, most concern has been expressed over ecological sustainability and the pressure of population growth and resource consumption on life support processes. These concerns are of particular relevance to tourism, where sustainability of environmental attributes under threat from the intrusion of masses of visitors may foolishly be traded off against the prospect of more immediate economic returns. However, the multidimensional nature of sustainability demands that it also be demonstrated with reference to social and cultural considerations, legal structures, societal values, and economic and financial concerns. Economic realities cannot be ignored in favour of ecological sustainability. Putting it bluntly, maintenance of a pristine environment to avoid resource degradation or social disharmony is of little relevance to the sustainability of a tourist enterprise if the loss of revenue, or the increase in operating costs as a consequence, is such as to threaten the long-term economic viability of the operation.

The Trend Toward Sustainable Development

The search for a more compatible relationship between humans and their environment is not new. The potential consequences of unrestrained expansion of resource exploitation coupled with population growth were highlighted in the report, *Limits to Growth* (Meadows and Meadows, 1972). Subsequently, the publication in 1980 of the *World Conservation Strategy* by the International Union for the Conservation of Nature prompted many countries to formulate their own national strategies. Increasingly, sustainable management of resources became accepted as the preferred way to match the needs of conservation and development. This view, formalized in *Our Common Future*, the report of the World Commission on Environment and Development (1987, p. 4), defined sustainable development as ' . . . development that meets the needs of the present without compromising the ability of future generations to meet their own needs'. Since then, the trend toward sustainable development has gathered strength and been applied in a wide range of human contexts including the tourism sector, in an attempt to address simultaneously both developmental and environmental imperatives.

It is difficult to argue on conceptual grounds against such a desirable, if somewhat fuzzy, objective. However, the concept takes on more meaning and practical relevance when supplemented by specific guiding principles. In the context of tourism, these have been articulated by any number of national and international agencies and organizations, and typically embrace components of:

- conservation and enhancement of ecological processes contributing to biological diversity and the maintenance of ecological integrity;
- intergenerational and intragenerational equity;
- anticipatory environmental policy incorporating the precautionary principle;
- community participation and endorsement; and
- legislative support.

If all of this sounds familiar, it should not be surprising. Indeed, the concept of sustainable development has been challenged as merely a reworking of long-standing philosophies about conservation and stewardship of resources for the future. What is new are its widespread endorsement and the incorporation of a proactive environmental dimension into corporate strategic planning and business management. In Canada, Murphy (1994, p. 276) referring to the tourism industry, reports that:

> The majority of corporations have established systems and programmes to comply with the new (environmental) regulations, but a further minority has moved 'beyond compliance' into a proactive mode of management. In Australia, the precautionary principal, intergenerational equity, conservation of biodiversity and ecological integrity, and improved valuation and pricing of environmental resources, are embodied in federal and state legislation. At the same time, considerable advances are being made in the implementation of best practice environmental management, especially by the larger scale industrial, commercial and tourism enterprises.

Despite the endorsement of sustainable development as the catch-phrase of the 1990s, the concept has been questioned as a contradiction of terms. The suggestion is one of conflict between 'sustainable', implying ' ... a state which can be maintained, is ongoing, perhaps even unchanging' (Wall, 1997, p. 43), and 'development', which implies change. This view can be challenged. Given that development is concerned with the manipulation of the environment to achieve desired goals, sustainability demands interference in the process in the interests of sustainable growth and development.

Sustainability is not about maintenance of the status quo, be that the capitalist system of much of the western industrialized world, or the continued suppression of the aspirations of the developing world. Moreover, sustainability does not exclude change or elevation to a preferred state of development in terms of human betterment and enhanced life opportunities. To see this as a contradiction is to confuse product and process, outcomes with pathways, ends and means. The focus is on process, and the identification of sustainable processes of development, not on any fixed, predictable product of that process. The emphasis is on getting the process right (sustainable) as each level of development leads to (changes) the next. Shortcomings in the process will either make the preferred stage of development unattainable, or mean that it is distinctly short-lived. Thus, sustainability and development are not opposites but complementary. If the process underpinning development is not sustainable, development will be compromised and will ultimately stall.

From Sustainable Development to Sustainable Tourism – a Logical Trend

Although the publication of the report, *Our Common Future*, makes no reference to tourism, it did help usher in a new era of environmental concern of immediate relevance to the tourism sector. Sustainability

is, or should be, a fundamental consideration for tourism since its viability is dependent upon the maintenance of the environmental qualities which underpin its development and growth. Tourism is, to a large degree, a resource-based activity. Sustainable development of these resources demands that they be managed in keeping with ecological imperatives, but in a way that meets the economic needs of the industry and satisfies the experiential aspirations of tourists, while maintaining the social and cultural integrity of hosts and guests.

Global concern for the environment was given renewed impetus following the United Nations Conference on Environment and Development in Rio de Janeiro in 1992. The Earth Summit as it was called, and Agenda 21 that followed, led to a commitment to make travel and tourism a model industry for environmental improvement. Since then, government agencies and tourism organizations in several countries have undertaken a number of policy initiatives to promote the sustainability message.

Yet, imprecision and confusion continue to bedevil the concept of sustainable development as it applies to tourism. Butler (1993) stresses the importance of identifying those aspects of tourism that it may be appropriate to encourage, based on the principles of sustainable development. He makes a distinction between 'sustainable tourism' and 'sustainable development in the context of tourism'. According to Butler (1993, p. 29), sustainable tourism is ' ... tourism which is a form which can maintain its viability in an area for an indefinite period of time'.

The limitations of such a definition are immediately obvious when the conditions which might have to be met in maintaining that viability, and the costs which might be entailed by other claimants to the common resource base, are considered. No activity can be sustained in a vacuum without reference to broader interests and other resource uses. Butler offers an alternative definition of sustainable tourism that places it within this broader context:

 ... tourism which is developed and

maintained in an area (community, environment) in such a manner and at such a scale that it remains viable over an indefinite period and does not degrade or alter the environment (human and physical) in which it exists to such a degree that it prohibits the successful development and wellbeing of other activities and processes

(Butler, 1993, p. 29)

Issue might still be taken with some of the terms used in this definition (e.g. the vagueness of 'viable', 'successful', and 'wellbeing', and the specificity of 'prohibits'). However, it acknowledges that tourism must compete with other activities and resource users and the achievement of sustainability cannot be at the expense of those competing interests. In other words, sustainability at all costs, is not an option, nor is it realistic. Tradeoffs between sectors may be necessary and must be anticipated in the interests of the greater good (Wall, 1997).

Wall goes on to pose a number of 'intractable questions' about the goals, objectives and time horizons of sustainable development in the context of tourism. However, these can be addressed in a multidimensional construct of sustainability, comprising ecological, economic and sociocultural concerns. A holistic appreciation of sustainability acknowledges the interrelatedness of these components, and the process of sustainable tourism development must simultaneously accommodate the nexus between them (Wahab and Pigram, 1997).

Unsustainable Tourism Development – Against the Trend

Given the differences in perception of sustainable tourism and the multidimensional nature of the concept, it is perhaps easier to identify forms of tourism which are unsustainable than to specify those which satisfy preferred characteristics of sustainability. Whereas tourism can have beneficial consequences for the environment, most prominence appears to be given to negative impacts. It is these undesirable effects on the natural and built environment and on host communities that lend credence to the view

that tourism is an inherently unsustainable human activity. Some observers remain convinced that ' . . . in the long run tourism, like any other industry, contributes to environmental destruction' (Cohen, 1978, p. 220), or conserves only the things that are of potential or actual tourist interest.

It is not difficult to substantiate claims of resource degradation arising from the predatory effects of seasonal migrations of visitors and resulting disturbance to, or destruction of, natural features. Erosion of the resource base is a serious consequence for the environment. This can range from incidental wear and tear of vegetation and soil, to vandalism and deliberate destruction or removal of attributes that contribute toward the appeal of a setting. Incremental deterioration is accelerated on occasion by the adoption of ill-advised remedies or compensatory actions intended to mitigate the depredations of tourism, e.g. the introduction of the invasive bitou bush to stabilize dune erosion along the Australian coast. Pollution, both direct and indirect, is another conspicuous manifestation of the detrimental effects of tourism.

The built environment in urbanized tourist zones may also be impaired by using incongruous technological innovations or inferior design and inappropriate architectural style of tourist facilities. The social fabric of resident communities, in turn, can be disrupted by conflict and dissention with visitors, and by congestion and overtaxing of the infrastructure and basic services. This can be a particular problem in developing countries where the contrast between the lifestyle and living standards of tourists and that of host communities is more marked.

Indeed, the pursuit of the elusive goal of 'development' through the introduction of tourism holds particular dangers for countries of the Third World. Whereas the biophysical environment might show the most immediate and obvious effects, it is the traditional culture and way of life that are most under threat.

The important point, however, is that it does not have to be like that. The environment of the Cook Islands in the mid-Pacific Ocean offers a useful illustration. The emphasis in the island tourism structures is on native materials and style with the height 'no higher than the coconut palms'. Government policy on indigenous tourism in the Cook Islands goes on to state that:

> Tourism should not be the means for us to change our way of life but an incentive to make us more aware of what we are in terms of our culture, customs and traditions. This should not be interpreted negatively to mean that all changes that affect our way of life must be avoided. Change is inevitable. Instead, a positive rate and direction of change and how we manage that change and its conflicts are more important ... The guiding principle should be: preserve that which is good, modify or destroy the bad, and adopt the new to strike a balance
>
> (Okotai, 1980, p. 173)

Some 20 years later, the Cook Islands remain a quiet haven offering a special kind of tourist experience in a delightful, authentic island environment and cultural atmosphere. Development has taken place, but compatibly with that environment. The emphasis is on the process by which tourism evolves to a different, but still sustainable, level and mode of development.

Toward Sustainable Tourism Development

The Cook Islands experience demonstrates how satisfying and sustainable tourism settings grow out of complementary natural features and compatible social processes. There is growing evidence that large sections of the tourism industry are committed to the principles of sustainable development and see merit in the adoption of sustainable practices in the interests of maintenance of environmental quality and commercial viability (Pigram and Wahab, 1997).

Unfortunately, the tourism–environment relationship is very often expressed in terms of opposing alternatives – either protecting the environment for tourism or protecting the environment from tourism. However,

these perspectives should not be seen as mutually exclusive. Current trends suggest that it should be possible to ensure that tourism-related development contributes coincidentally to environmental enhancement.

As noted earlier, tourism is primarily a resource-based activity: tourism and nature conservation are not merely interrelated, they are interdependent. Thus, tourism should stimulate measures to protect and conserve nature, thereby leading to the maintenance, or even substantial enhancement of natural areas, with subsequent increases in visitor satisfaction. Sustainable tourism development must be environmentally sensitive and consistent with long-term nature conservation. It can also contribute to a wider appreciation of nature by promoting, and making more accessible, interesting sites and aspects of the natural world.

In the built environment, the design of contemporary tourist complexes also appears to be benefiting from the demands of a more discerning tourist population. Whereas there remain many examples of unfortunate additions to the tourist landscape, modification of the environment for today's tourist is marked increasingly by quality architecture, design and engineering. Higher standards of safety, sanitation and maintenance, and upgrading of infrastructure and services, represent a significant improvement to the environment of the host community, as well as helping to ensure that tourism development proceeds sustainably. Increased awareness of the existence value of historic sites and antiquities, too, has been stimulated through cultural tourism which, in turn, has prompted the need for sensitive planning and management of heritage resources in the interests of sustainability.

The implications for closer government–industry linkages are clear. The key to achieving environmentally compatible forms of tourism and, ultimately, a sustainable tourist industry rests on recognition by the public sector of the need for environmentally sensitive policies and planning, and a positive response by private sector interests to the sustainability imperative.

Increasing environmental awareness glob-ally has contributed to progress toward environmentally compatible tourism. At different levels the tourism industry has reacted by entering into partnership with environmental groups, and has consulted effectively with host communities and resource management agencies to support conservation objectives. Strategies and activities range in size, as do the mecha-nisms utilized.

In some instances, sustainable tourism objectives are being integrated into develop-ment plans and proposals and promoted by national and international tourism organiza-tions. One example, at the international scale, is the Green Globe Scheme sponsored by the World Travel and Tourism Council as a vehicle to convince tourist firms to 'green' their operations (Turner, 1995). The scheme emphasizes the link between good environ-mental practice and good business and offers advice on tailoring corporate practice to environmental considerations.

A comparable undertaking at the global level is the International Hotels Environ-mental Initiative. Launched in 1992, the aim is to increase environmental awareness and to encourage greater environmental sensi-tivity among hotel management and staff. The group comprises leading world hotel chains and has produced a joint operations manual, *Environmental Management for Hotels: The Industry Guide to Best Practice* (International Hotels Environmental Initia-tive, 1992). The manual is intended as a voluntary code of conduct and offers a use-ful reference and guide for upgrading environmental procedures in areas such as waste management, energy consumption, noise and congestion, purchasing policy and staff training. Large hotel corporations in Asia and the Pacific have endorsed the initiative and several have produced in-house Codes of Practice. Elsewhere, other tourism companies and groups such as Brit-ish Airways and Canadian Pacific Hotels and Resorts have undertaken the develop-ment of comparable environmental programmes.

These moves reflect the beginnings of a global trend toward the 'greening' of tourism reported to the Globe 92 International Con-ference on Business and the environment (Hawkes and Williams, 1993). The tourism industry appears to be accepting that future prosperity relies heavily on the mainte-nance of the environmental qualities on which it depends. Moreover, in a more environmentally aware world, green tour-ism not only offers new experiences and opportunities, but makes good economic sense in terms of reduced waste and lower operating costs (Pigram, 1996). At the same time, the trend toward more sustainable modes of operation has serious implications for those elements in the tourism industry, which are slow to respond to the expecta-tions of a 'greener' clientele or to satisfy a more demanding regulatory regime.

The Greening of Australian Tourism

In common with other parts of the indus-trialized world, concern has been expressed about environmental problems associated with tourism in Australia, and pressure is growing to ensure sustainable forms of tour-ism development (Ding and Pigram, 1995). Australian tourism developers and opera-tors are demonstrating increased understanding of environmental concerns and the Tourism Council of Australia has drawn up an Environmental Code of Prac-tice in consultation with conservation groups, industry bodies and planning authorities (Tourism Council of Australia, 1998). The Code represents strong endorse-ment of sustainable forms of development by the Australian tourism industry.

Further evidence of the trend toward sup-port for sustainable tourism development in the Australian coastal zone is given by the Federal Government publication, *Coastal Tourism: A Manual for Sustainable Devel-opment* (Department of Industry, Science and Tourism, 1997). The manual reiterates the interdependent dimensions of sustain-ability – economic, environmental and social – and the relevance to sustainable tourism development (noted earlier) of the linkages between them.

The manual offers a useful checklist for

sustainable tourism identifying the following features:

- Use of nonrenewable resources at a rate in keeping with the availability of renewable substitutes;
- Use of renewable resources in keeping with replenishment rates;
- Minimization of energy, water and other inputs;
- Release of pollutants at a rate in keeping with the capacity of the biosphere to process them;
- Avoidance of irreversible impact on biodiversity and ecosystems and ecological processes;
- Maintenance of a diverse range of recreational and cultural opportunities for present and future generations;
- Ensuring benefit to local and regional communities socially and economically;
- Demonstration of economic viability without affecting the capacity of other sectors of the economy to achieve sustainability.
(Adapted from Department of Industry, Science and Tourism, 1997, p. 4.)

The switch to sustainable modes of operation in tourism in Australia and elsewhere appears to be gaining momentum, especially at the larger scale corporate levels of the tourism industry, and with it, increased preparedness to apply the principles of best practice environmental management to tourism development.

Best Practice Environmental Management and Tourism – An Emerging Trend

There is no clearly established pathway to sustainable tourism but the concept of best practice environmental management offers a meaningful framework within which to achieve environmental excellence in the industry. Put simply, best practice denotes the preferred approach to managing an organization or business relative to accepted levels of achievement in comparable enterprises. When linked to environmental performance, best practice environmental management represents the most effective means of achieving sustainable growth in a competitive world (Pigram, 1996).

Among the perceived benefits to be gained from the application of best practice to environmental management are:

- Cost savings through greater reliance on recycled materials, elimination of wasteful procedures, and avoidance or minimization of legal liabilities for breaches of regulations.
- Enhancement of the public image resulting from improved environmental performance and demonstrated sound corporate citizenship.
- Increased environmental awareness within and beyond the workplace.
- Introduction of innovations and continuous improvement in operational standards and environmental management.
(Adapted from Cornwall and Burns, 1992.)

The implication is that progress toward sustainability is mutually beneficial – both for the tourist enterprise and the tourist. Overall, environmental excellence, fostered by enlightened management practices marked by new, cleaner, technologies and an emphasis on resource conservation, recycling and reuse, presents a cleaner, greener image, to a more discerning market, with clear potential for enhanced economic viability.

Key elements in a successful move toward best practice environmental management are a proactive strategy or action plan which recognizes the link between environmental excellence and competitiveness, and adoption of an environmentally inclusive system of organization incorporating environmental indicators and audit processes.

Public sector measures representing essential steps toward achieving this objective include:

- Survey of the tourism industry at varying scales of operation to establish present levels of awareness of the roles of environmental management, and to document measures currently in place.

- Consultation with the tourism sector – operators, agency professionals and tourists – to identify recognized features of best practice environmental management, the most promising areas of opportunity, and the benefits to be derived from their adoption.
- Agreement on effective courses of action most likely to contribute to increasing environmental awareness, and to preparedness to apply enhanced environmental management in tourist operations.
- Identification of barriers and constraints to adoption of best practice environmental management in the tourism sector, including personal, sociocultural, economic and structural impediments.
- Identification of change agents important in facilitating the adoption process, including peer pressure, supplier pressure, industry organizations, incentives and awards, regulations and sanctions, education and communication, and market forces emerging through guest preference for superior environmental performance.
- Nomination of benchmark tourist enterprises and practices and benchmarking mechanisms to compare environmental performance.
- Establishment of targets in space and time and priorities for implementation of best practice environmental management.
- Development of monitoring and feedback mechanisms and the application of performance indicators to audit progress toward achievement of targets.

The expectation that tourism establishments will be developed and managed at the highest standards of environmental excellence needs to be tempered by knowledge that significant impediments stand in the way of rapid and widespread enhancement of environmental standards. The expertise,

expense and long-term commitment of resources involved in lifting environmental performance inevitably mean that the adoption of best practice environmental management can be ' . . . a minority activity, confined, in the main, to a few large firms' (Goodall, 1995, p. 34). The implication is that the nature and structure of the industry act as barriers to the adoption of best management practices.

Foremost among these barriers is the wide diversity in the scale of operations and the prevalence of small independent components. Goodall describes the tourism industry as: 'a fragmented, competitive, high-risk industry, dominated in tourist destinations by many, small, family-operated firms' (Goodall, 1995, p. 35). The challenge is to offset these impediments and achieve something of a 'trickle down' effect in the spread of environmental best practice to all levels of tourism activity (Pigram, 1996).

Collaboration between the various sectors of the tourism industry in a more relaxed regulatory regime is the preferred option in pursuing higher environmental standards. Under such a regime, a more feasible, practical, and effective alternative to best practice environmental management, is an approach which seeks to eliminate worst practice (Pigram, 1996). Removing management practices that are not environmentally acceptable would make an immediate contribution to improved industry performance. In the short term, such a move would be likely to receive more ready acceptance and endorsement as the 'best practicable environmental option' (Goodall, 1995, p. 36). By implication, tourist developers and operators not prepared to adopt a more enlightened approach to tourism–environment interaction are likely to be forced to conform by combined pressure from industry organizations, market forces, regulatory agencies and, ultimately, punitive tax measures.

Trends and Implications

A trend toward sustainable development of the Earth's resources has been gathering strength in recent decades, reflecting grow-ing concern for maintenance of environmental quality. Such concern is of direct relevance to tourism where protection and enhancement of the resource base, and an enriched social and cultural environ-ment, are fundamental considerations. Evidence is emerging in the tourism indus-try of heightened awareness of the need for more sustainable modes of operation, and a commitment to practice environmental management.

The trend toward sustainable tourism development, while variable and frag-mented, can be seen as sequential and incremental. As the initial focus in the 1970s on ecologically sustainable develop-ment broadened to include sociocultural and economic considerations, the relevance to tourism gained increasing acceptance. Recognition by significant elements in the tourism industry of an obligation for improved environmental performance ensued, in response to the expectations of a more discerning community and clientele, and clear endorsement by public agencies of the sustainability imperative.

Although the strength and continuity of commitment by the tourism industry to environmental sustainability have been questioned, the need to maintain and rein-force the trend toward sustainable forms of development is undeniable. This, in turn, has implications for all facets of tourism – policy makers, the industry itself, tourists and affected communities, and tourism globally.

The implication for policy makers is for even more explicit support, from all levels of government, for sustainable tourism and for the environmental management proces-ses which contribute to it. Agreement on standards and environmental codes of prac-tice, encouragement of environmental audits, and education and awareness pro-grammes, are all part of the role of the public sector in striking a balance between regula-tion and self-regulation to reinforce the trend toward sustainable tourism develop-ment.

The implication for the tourism industry is for action to ensure that the message and practice of environmentally sustainable modes of operation reach all levels and scales of tourism activity. Progress toward sustainable tourism development has been most marked among larger firms and orga-nized hotel and accommodation groups. The challenge is to raise the levels of con-cern for the environment, and for environmental best practice, among the smaller more numerous tourism establish-ments, and the service and ancillary components of the industry. What is required is a partnership between industry and government so that barriers to progress can be identified, and offset or removed. Change agents in the form of sanctions and awards for recognition of enhanced environ-mental performance may be effective, when coupled with benchmarking and perform-ance indicators, as forms of peer pressure to achieve. Sanctions, such as denial of accred-itation with industry organizations, and withdrawal of supplies and services for non-compliance, can help convince even small operators to lift their environmental per-formance.

The implication for the tourist market is that a more environmentally aware clientele can be expected to be more discerning and critical in the selection of accommodation and tourist facilities based on demonstrated sound environmental credentials. Already, tourist brochures are displaying symbols denoting levels of environmental excellence and sustainable management. Signage and advertising literature also reflect an aware-ness of the growing importance and influence of the 'green' market in promoting the use of environmentally friendly prod-ucts and materials. Tourists also have an important role to play in demonstrating awareness of the environmental implica-tions of their own activities, as well as in demanding high environmental standards from facilities and operations, and in coop-erating as compatible partners in the interests of sustainable tourism develop-ment.

The implication for tourist destinations is that residential communities exposed to the seasonal influx of visitors can be expec-ted to be more demanding in their insistence on observation of acceptable environmental criteria in the type, location, design and operation of tourism developments. This implies, in turn, a stricter approval regime, and the possibility of withholding or delaying approval where the prospect of long-term sustainability and compatibility with community norms are in doubt. Ultimately, people are the key to sustainable tourism development. Through the political process, most communities can demand higher standards of tourism development and operation, and by working with the tourism sector, can help ensure that standards are maintained. At the same time, the attitude of local residents to tourism and tourists may need to change from indifference or intolerance, to one of welcoming visitors to share the environment they, as stewards, value and enjoy. As with welcoming house guests, the attitude should be 'Ours to Share'.

Globally, the trend in the industrialized world toward increased concern for sustainable forms of tourism, has implications for tourism projects in developing regions. Tourism development in the Third World can expect to be asked to conform to higher (than current) environmental standards, and to satisfy specific expectations regarding economic benefits and social and cultural compatibility. Moreover, as globalization gathers pace, transnational linkages across the tourism industry, along with international bodies such as the World Trade Organization and Green Globe, are likely to be instrumental in ensuring support for sustainable tourism development worldwide.

Conclusion

Tourism is assuming an increasingly prominent place in the global economy, and with this comes the expectation that tourism establishments will be developed and managed at the highest standards of environmental excellence. No longer should tourism be seen as a threat to the environment, but as an instrument of positive environmental change. The pursuit of sustainable forms of tourism can serve as a powerful incentive toward protection and enhancement of the biophysical resource base of tourism regions, along with an enriched social environment and more effective care and concern for culture and heritage. Harnessing the potential for environmental betterment in this way presents an opportunity to view sustainable tourism development from a different perspective. The goal of sustainability implies the provision of harmonious, compatible, and satisfying settings for today's tourists, while ensuring at least the same quality experiences for the tourists of tomorrow. In a rapidly changing world, this represents a significant challenge and calls for a holistic approach with a commitment from all stakeholders – the public and private sector, the tourists, and the communities concerned. Such a commitment will do much to offset the scepticism regarding the prospect of achieving tourism development sustainably.

35

Citizen Participation Trends and their Educational Implications for Natural Resource Professionals

Dennis B. Propst, J. Douglas Wellman, Henry Campa III and Maureen H. McDonough

Background and Purpose

Participation and volunteerism have long characterized American culture (deToqueville, 1945; Langton, 1978). Recent trends in various institutions reflect these characteristics, especially the desire of citizens to participate in important decisions that affect them. For example, the medical profession has witnessed the movement from a physician-centred to an integrated patient–doctor system of health care where individuals share in the responsibility for their own health (Ferguson, 1987; Smith, 1996; Cleary and Edgman-Levitan, 1997).

Another illustration of the trend toward citizen participation in decision making is a redefinition of the role of public administration to one of enhancing representation (Wamsley, 1990). This new role envisions 'a public service that remains subordinate to other actors (the President, Congress and the judiciary) in the governance process, but acts on behalf of the citizenry in a vigorous, autonomous way' by focusing on the agency as a 'special citizen' standing in the place of other citizens, acting for them 'but always consciously responsible to them and acting by their authority' (Wellman and Tipple,

1993, p. 341). Several authors have outlined a new role for natural resource administrators and other professionals as implementers of fair and responsive decision making (Shannon, 1987; Wellman and Tipple, 1989). This role redefinition explicitly acknowledges that public administrators play an important role in the process of citizen participation. They bridge the gap between the organization(s) involved and various publics (King *et al.*, 1998). Furthermore, Fischer (1993) claims that for 'wicked' problems, such as the siting of toxic waste dumps, collaborative citizen–expert inquiry is necessary to finding solutions.

A major barrier to public participation is administrators' lack of confidence regarding the competence and decision making ability of groups of laypersons (Doble and Richardson, 1992). This lack of confidence has been referred to as the 'assumption of lack of competence' (Kaplan, 1995, p. 64) and the 'cult of expertise' (Brunson, 1992, p. 293). Despite this scepticism of some administrators, there is evidence that individuals who lack knowledge of technical scientific issues:

- can quickly learn about their critical

features and choose policy options similar to those chosen by scientists (Ferguson, 1987; Doble and Richardson, 1992);

- are likely to ask the right questions and find novel solutions (Kaplan and Kaplan, 1982); and
- are healthier and more satisfied than their counterparts in purely top-down situations (Kaplan *et al.*, 1996).

In addition, Fortmann's (1990) study of a community protest regarding a timber harvesting plan in California concluded that local protestors, contrary to agency perceptions, were well informed about the specifics of the issue.

The key questions we address are: What should natural resources educators do with the knowledge that the role of public administration is changing toward fostering collaborative decision making and that citizens can learn technical information and make effective and novel decisions? How can the learning environment in higher education be altered to demonstrate the value of citizen participation while simultaneously giving current and future natural resource professionals the knowledge and skills they will need to embrace increasing societal demands for more voice? Our purpose is to challenge those outdoor recreation and natural resource educators who have not already done so, to change the learning environment so that participatory processes and diverse natural resource values become part of the mindset of future professionals. Our objectives in this chapter are:

- to document the nature and extent of the trend toward more citizen participation in outdoor recreation and other natural resource management and planning activities;
- to present recommendations for changing the traditional educational paradigm to accommodate the trend.

Nature and Extent of the Trend in Citizen Participation

Participation has become a buzzword in many fields, yet there is no agreement on what behaviours or activities are meant by the term. For example, McDonough and Wheeler state that definitions of participation in international development projects

> vary along a spectrum anchored at one end by provision of labor for project implementation and at the other by projects where local communities control all project features from objectives to outcomes
> (McDonough and Wheeler, 1998)

Along with definitions, the goals of participation also vary. Participation can be either a means to achieve governmental or institutional goals or an end in itself (Nagel, 1992; Dudley, 1993; Lane, 1995). If participation entails a method of accomplishing externally determined goals (e.g. labour as a cost-saving strategy), then it is a means rather than an end (McDonough and Wheeler, 1998).

When empowerment and capacity building are explicit project goals, participation is an end (Setty 1994; Lane 1995). Participation also can be viewed as a 'hybrid reality', that often includes both means and ends no matter what the original intent (Nagel, 1992). The intent may be that communities or individuals will simply provide labour for projects. Along the way, however, facilitators may find that communities or individuals, once consulted, insist on expressing their views (Nagel, 1992). Conversely, those who aim for community empowerment may find that participation has some practical benefits in accomplishing projects efficiently.

Another way to define participation is according to specific behaviours that reflect the degree of citizen power over decision making (Wandersman, 1979; Wandersman *et al.*, 1987). These behaviours can be arrayed along a spectrum according to the extent of citizen power over decision making about natural resources. The spectrum ranges from participation in outdoor recreation activities at one end (low power) to policy making in planning and management at the other (high power). In between are such behaviours as volunteerism, provision of unsolicited feedback, provision of solicited feedback and a host of other behaviours. At any point along this spectrum, the goal of participation could be either a means or an end.

Outdoor recreation is broadly defined as the voluntary use, understanding, and/or appreciation of natural resources during discretionary time (Ford and Blanchard, 1985). As such, it includes a wide range of active (e.g. cross-country skiing, gardening, golfing) and passive (e.g. a quiet walk, sitting by a pond, viewing birds out of one's window) behaviours. Voluntary participation in natural resource management and planning activities includes tasks in which individuals freely and willingly volunteer their time to provide skills and labour, under the direction of others (e.g. picking up litter, interpretation, trail maintenance). Solicited feedback is the type of public input that natural resource agencies obtain most frequently, most often in the form of public hearings or requests for written comments on draft plans. Feedback solicited in this manner may or may not have any direct influence on decision making. Unsolicited feedback may appear in a variety of oral or written communication forms and requires voluntary effort by the individual. A highly committed level of unsolicited feedback is civil disobedience (Kimmins, 1992; Fischer, 1993). Policy making authority involves the highest level of power and might involve such activities as serving on a formal board, commission or task force.

Empirical evidence of trends in various participatory behaviours across the power spectrum is weak. The exception is outdoor recreation participation, which has been fairly well documented. For example, one nationwide survey found that nearly 95% of all Americans reported engaging in some form of outdoor recreation and that overall growth in outdoor recreation participation (13.4%) exceeded the rate of population expansion between 1982 and 1994 (Cordell et al., 1995).

Independent of increases in various forms of outdoor recreation is the growth in participatory democracy. Participation of the governed in their government is, in theory, the cornerstone of democracy – a revered idea that is vigorously applauded by virtually everyone (Arnstein, 1977). This implies more than just voting on election day. Public participation may serve humanitarian purposes, such as assisting in Red Cross functions or helping to raise money for books for local schools. Participation may also involve acts of self-interest, such as the protest activities of NIMBY ('Not In My Backyard') groups (Kraft and Clary, 1991).

The term 'participatory democracy' is broad and goes by different names in various fields and disciplines. In the natural resources field, terms like 'local level management', 'participatory management', and 'co-management' are used to reflect the trend toward greater user participation in natural resource management (McCay and Jentoft, 1996). Whatever the terminology, the underlying premise is that, more and more, people expect to be able to have a say in governmental decisions that affect them. People want experts to perform certain roles and functions but not necessarily be the ones to prescribe a certain path or regimen. Instead citizens, often acting in their own self-interest (Perloff, 1987), want the experts to provide choices and knowledge of the consequences of those choices, but to leave the actual choice up to the client or participant. If experts and clients disagree, negotiation and resolution of differences are necessary. Once the choice is made, individuals then rely on the experts to do what experts do best – apply their technical skills and knowledge to help groups and individuals attain their chosen outcomes (Propst and McDonough, 1999). In the natural resources professions, this translates into increasing demands to participate in natural resource decision making processes that traditionally were considered the exclusive realm of the experts: planning and management activities. Examples of the trend away from authoritarian natural resource management models include: grassroots environmentalism (Freudenberg and Steinsapir,

1992) and ecosystem management (Maser, 1994; McDonough *et al.*, 1997).

Another example of the trend is 'cooperative resource management', which is exemplified by such activities as:

- governance of a US national park by a board of trustees composed primarily of private citizens (Lins, 1991);
- joint management of communal wildlife areas in Zimbabwe (Saunier and Meganck, 1995); and
- co-management boards consisting of government officials and aboriginal people regarding the allocation of fishing and hunting rights in Canada (Peterson and Johnson, 1995).

A number of additional international examples have been documented (West and Brechin, 1991; McNeely, 1995; Furze *et al.*, 1996; McCay and Jentoft, 1996), but not all would be considered cooperative resource management in the sense that participants do not always have decision making authority.

The evidence and examples of the trend toward more citizen participation in governance and management point to one conclusion: the traditional role of the resource manager as an omniscient, autocratic expert is being challenged in conjunction with challenges to authority-based leadership models across society (Heifitz and Sinder, 1988; Sirmon, 1993). There are at least two fundamental reasons for these challenges.

First, the ability to participate in decisions that affect one's life – to exercise choice based on the knowledge of the consequences of various alternatives – is critical to human psychological health and functioning (Rodin, 1986; Litt, 1988; Zimmerman and Rappaport, 1988). This fundamental human need for a sense of control and the ability to participate can be seen at the macro level in the worldwide movement toward more democratic forms of governance and at the micro level in such aspects of human behaviour as outdoor recreation (Propst and Kurtz, 1989).

The second reason for increases in public participation in the natural resources field is the aversion to the type of government perceived to be distant from the populace it serves. One result of this aversion is a citizenry, with diminished trust in government, which in turn is demanding more accountability from public officials (Parr and Gates, 1989). Another result is the changing role of public administration (Wondolleck, 1988; Wellman and Tipple, 1989; Feeny *et al.*, 1990; Fischer, 1993; Wellman and Tipple, 1993; Roberts, 1997; King *et al.*, 1998). The trend toward decentralization, deregulation, greater local participation in resource management, 'co-management', and 'participatory management' reflects dissatisfaction with purely top-down, autocratic and bureaucratic models of natural resource management (McCay and Jentoft, 1996).

Educational Implications of the Citizen Participation Trend

The first part of this chapter was devoted to documenting the trend toward more demand by citizens to have an active role in decision making in natural resources, outdoor recreation and related areas. In this part of the chapter, the discussion revolves around trying to answer the question, 'so what?' What are the educational and professional development implications of the trend in citizen participation? The major implication is the need to change the learning environment for future outdoor recreation and other natural resources professionals.

How well are we preparing our students (undergraduates, professionally oriented graduate students and working professionals seeking continuing education) to work with members of the public in planning and managing our outdoor recreation estate? We believe there is ample room for improvement. Students leave our programmes reasonably well versed in such things as soils, vegetation, recreation programming and facilities management but less well prepared for the 'wicked' problems inherent in working with the public (Allen and Gould, 1986).

Many things could be done to prepare our graduates better for working with citizens in the management of natural resources and outdoor recreation areas, and faculties around the country are experimenting with creative approaches. For example, one of the coauthors uses 'structured controversy' based on realistic natural resource scenarios (Campa *et al.*, 1996). Before having her students try to determine the best ways to work with private woodlot owners, another of the coauthors takes her communications class to retirement homes and primary schools to talk with senior citizens and children about how they value trees. Increasingly, teaching which involves students in working directly with the various publics or which simulates participatory democracy is being reported in natural resource journals and presented at meetings such as the Biennial Conference on University Education in Natural Resources (Heister, 1998).

Most basic, however, is to reconsider the student learning outcomes we are seeking, not only within natural resources recreation programmes but also in the totality of the student's educational experience. To prepare students to respond constructively to the growing public demands for involvement in planning and management, we need to find ways to complement professional training with liberal education.

A recent publication from the American Association of Colleges and Universities provides a compact and useful statement on 'liberal learning' (Schneider and Shoenberg, 1998). From the 'culture wars' involving the academy and outside critics, from advances in instructional technology, from taxpayer protests based on the stereotype of the professor as someone interested only in research, lazy about teaching and indifferent to students, and from many other sources, a wealth of new programmes and practices in higher education has emerged. According to Schneider and Shoenberg, these innovations are beginning to coalesce into a new conceptual framework that is both contemporary and traditional, and this conceptual framework is linked with new approaches to teaching.

This conceptualization responds to the reality of a changing and knowledge-intensive society. But it also draws directly on those traditions of excellence the academy has long described as 'liberal learning,' ways of approaching knowledge that expand imaginative horizons, develop intellectual powers and judgment, and instill in students the capacity and resolve to exercise leadership and responsibility in multiple spheres of life, both societal and vocational. This conceptualization further includes new ways of talking about the content of a liberal education and new approaches for teaching and learning
(Schneider and Shoenberg, 1998, p. 7)

From their survey of the myriad reform initiatives in the US and around the world, Schneider and Shoenberg distil the following pattern of learning goals:

- *Acquiring intellectual skills or capacities* such as communications skills, quantitative skills, applied ethics and conflict resolution;

- *Understanding multiple modes of inquiry and approaches to knowledge*, effectively supplanting the traditional distribution requirements with guided practice in diverse epistemologies;

- *Developing societal, civic and global knowledge*, with the goal of augmenting the perspective derived from traditional history and 'Western Civilization' courses with the study of cultures removed from the dominant culture by geography or differential power;

- *Gaining self-knowledge and grounded values*, an explicit effort to assist students to understand the sources of their own identity and values as a prelude to understanding others in our increasingly diverse population;

- *Concentration and integration of learning*, which seeks to weave together students' departmental requirements and the general education requirements, as a way of adding meaning and value to both.

As new learning goals are emerging, so are new ways of teaching. The traditional 'presentational approach' to instruction –

the lecture and the instructor-led discussion – features the knowledge and personality of the professor. In the new pedagogies, the learner is the centre of attention, and the role of the instructor shifts towards creating an environment in which students are motivated and guided in their learning (Barr and Tagg, 1995). Among the student-centred forms of pedagogy are cooperative/collaborative learning, experiential learning, service learning, research or inquiry-based learning and integrative learning (e.g. high level, synthesis courses). In all these forms of teaching, students are actively engaged in constructing their own knowledge, and that process usually involves working with peers or with individuals and groups outside the college or university.

We are not advocating total abandonment of the lecture. Lecturing, done well, can be inspirational, can help stretch student understanding beyond the reach of even the most productive group process, and can help to ensure that all students are starting from the same base of knowledge. Problems arise with an over-reliance on lecturing. Not only do passive students learn less well than active students, but we must recognize that the way we conduct our classes may provide powerful models of behaviour. If we present ourselves to our students as omniscient authorities, expecting passive acceptance of our wisdom, future resource management professionals will, understandably, treat the public in the same way. We know from hard experience that this simply will not work; the era of 'Trust us, we're the experts' is over.

Schneider and Shoenberg (1998) characterize the new conception of curriculum and pedagogy as 'relational learning'. According to this conceptualization, a liberally educated person is one who is able to deal responsibly with the growing social pluralism of what philosopher Maxine Greene (1988) has called 'a world lived in common with others':

> Thus colleges and universities must educate not in terms of mind alone but also in terms of a life lived in relationships with

others whose experiences and assumptions may be very different. Faculties are therefore beginning to pay increased attention to the 'civic arts' that lead to an understanding of diversity and to skill in negotiating difficult differences and building communities that respect and acknowledge difference. They are more insistently involving students in an engagement with diversity and equity issues both at home and abroad and in learning experiences that help students develop those capacities and understandings in morally honest and dialogical ways
>
> (Schneider and Shoenberg, 1998, p. 12)

This new conception of curriculum and pedagogy fits well with the emerging challenges of participatory democracy. While content mastery will always be important for natural resource professionals, it must be balanced with the kinds of liberal learning spelled out by Schneider and Shoenberg, if our graduates are to work successfully with diverse publics. As a price for that liberal learning, we must be willing to accept some reduction in content coverage. However, given the rapid obsolescence of much technical knowledge, we must prepare our students for a lifetime of learning, anyway. The notion that we can 'train' people for lifetime careers in 4 or 5 years of undergraduate study is a delusion. What we can do is help them acquire a command of basic principles and the capacity to be lifetime learners. These, combined with the understanding of themselves in relation to others that is implied in liberal education, will serve our students well.

Toward Revising Natural Resource Education

In the first chapter of their book, Campbell and Smith (1997) reproduce the keynote address given by Parker J. Palmer to the 1997 faculty development conference of The Collaboration for the Advancement of Teaching and Learning in Bloomington, Minnesota. In his address, Palmer speaks of

> a movement that is happening all across the

country – a movement toward the renewal of teaching and learning, a movement that cares about students, that cares about the world, a movement that cares about all the connections that this word 'community' suggests to us

(Palmer, 1997, p. 2)

Palmer wants the type of community that allows one's sense of identity to evolve via education versus stifling that identity by saying: 'here's what you are; here's what you should believe; here's what you should think if you want to be like us'. He argues that the educational system of Nazi Germany failed (i.e. the killers were the educated elites of the Third Reich, not illiterate misfits or rabble) because of the absence of 'community, diversity and social accountability'. Both identity and community are essential for natural resources professionals who must engage diverse publics over time. The old 'training' paradigm of natural resource education, to the extent that it focuses on indoctrination, stifles both identity and community.

It is our contention that if we can build connectedness and communities of learning in the classroom, current and future natural resource professionals will be inclined to build communities of interest (Sirmon, 1993; Sirmon *et al.*, 1993) regarding the management of the nation's natural resources. Such communities are critical to the success of many outdoor recreation and natural resource management projects. For example, those who are trying to define and advocate ecosystem management (Maser, 1994; Freemuth, 1996; Yaffee, 1996; Grumbine, 1997; Brussard *et al.*, 1998; Clark *et al.*, 1999) make it clear that human communities must be part of the equation and that power sharing with communities should be a major role of natural resource agencies. Grumbine is clear on this point:

Potential partners never come to the table equal in power. The trick is to make power imbalances explicit and to facilitate equitable power sharing as much as possible. Because professionals are not often trained to either of these tasks, partnership work is challenging

(Grumbine, 1997, p. 44)

To Palmer, learning communities or communal learning does not mean assigning group projects, for such assignments are merely technique: they do not get us closer to understanding how people learn. He argues that students need to know more than today's information. They need to know how to generate new information, check it, critique it, analyse it, draw conclusions and use it to make better decisions. These are the elements of 'learning to learn' that professionals use daily in their careers. To know, learn and teach these elements, he proposes a mini-model of community development in higher education, which he illustrates with the medical school model of McMaster University in Canada. As part of their curriculum, medical students at McMaster interact with living patients, rather than skeletons, trying to understand what is wrong with the patient by talking to the patient, to each other and to a mentor. They do other traditional things, too (lectures, laboratory work, etc.), but they always come back to the core, the reason they are there – to be doctors and help people. Despite the critics, who deplored the loss of content coverage, objective test scores at McMaster have risen since the new curriculum was implemented (Palmer, 1997, p. 11).

Palmer and others who espouse the values of learning communities are talking about much more than isolated assignments in individual courses. They are talking about connecting students with technical content, with each other and with the reality in which they will be asked to apply what they know. A lesson learned at McMaster and at other institutions is that community (not a top-down approach) in higher education makes people smarter faster.

Palmer argues that the learning community approach makes people smarter faster for two reasons. First, reality is communal. In physics, in the Gaia hypothesis, in ecosystem thinking, we are now being told that everything is connected and in service to a larger whole. Secondly, new insights into epistemology indicate that humans know not by distance, or by separating the student from the subject, but by a complicated interplay between the subjective and the objective, perception and reality. Thus, it is not pedagogy *per se* that is critical but understanding the dynamics and the underpinnings of knowing and learning. Connectedness can be achieved by using many different methods.

Therefore, natural resources professionals must be asked not to reduce citizens to their own preconceived, structured, objective ways of thinking and stereotypes, but to interact with and look at them in a new light. Two potential barriers to connectedness are fear and inexperience. Students may be afraid to get deeply connected with their subjects (Palmer, 1997, p. 17). They may lack experience in communicating with members of the public because of their fears. Conversely, they may lack experience because of their fears or because of not being asked to interact directly with potential clients. Whatever the case, educators have the job of getting students to face their fears and build their experiences with their subjects.

In the light of these thoughts about general education and pedagogy, what can we do to prepare our students better for working with the public in natural resource and outdoor recreation planning and management? We offer the following suggestions in hopes of provoking a productive conversation. They are not in any particular order. However, they do reflect the theme of connectedness and community.

Seek connectedness with other disciplines
Throughout the academy, scholars are working with others from different disciplines in their research, but there is little such connection in the teaching and learning enterprise. Historian John Higham offers this metaphor to describe the situation:

> the contemporary academy is like a house in which the inhabitants are looking out of the many open windows gaily chatting with the neighbors, while the doors between the rooms stay closed
> (quoted in Schneider and Shoenberg, 1998, p. 14)

The message this disconnectedness sends students is that all they need is in their degree course. Since two-thirds of all Amer-

ican undergraduates are in pre-professional programmes, this disconnectedness is of great consequence. As Ernest Boyer wrote in *The Undergraduate Experience in America* (1987):

> In many fields, skills have become ends. Scholars are busy sorting, counting, and decoding. We are turning out technicians. But the crisis of our time relates not to technical competence, but to a loss of social and historical perspective, to the disastrous divorce of competence from conscience ... And the values professionals bring to their work are every bit as crucial as the particularities of the work itself
> (quoted in Schneider and Shoenberg, 1998, p. 15)

Seek to connect the major subjects to general education
Simply adding courses in philosophy, history, psychology, sociology and political science to natural resources curriculum is not always feasible. Even if it were feasible, these additions alone may be meaningless. Instead, we must try to find ways of making the general education requirements contribute meaningfully to our students' professional education. Some of this can be done relatively easily, by simply guiding our students' thinking in their specialist subject courses. In our assignments, tests and class discussions, we should seek to reinforce the new learning goals – the multiple ways of knowing – presented above. We can also provide better advice on the choice of general education options. Beyond these steps, we should consider linked courses, learning communities (Palmer, 1997) and other approaches to making explicit connections between the general education requirements and the majors. Many schools have already begun this work through writing across the curriculum programmes (Bishop and Fulwiler, 1997), so the model of interweaving and reinforcing general education courses in the specialist subject courses is not entirely new.

Seek connections within the major
As Lee Shulman of the Carnegie Foundation for the Advancement of Teaching has

argued, we need to begin to make teaching 'community property'. All too often, teaching is one of the most solitary activities in a professor's life. Yet, what happens in one course in the major subject, including both the content and the pedagogy, influences and is influenced by other courses in the major subject. For example, a faculty seeking to elicit higher-order thinking from their students will have an uphill battle if most of their colleagues are teaching for facts and recognition, and a faculty wishing to move toward collaborative learning will struggle to gain student acceptance if everyone else in the department is lecturing.

Seek a more integrated curricular architecture

We need to move away from the distinction between general education and the major, from the sort of thinking that the first two years of college are for liberal education (breadth) while the last two years are for the major specialization (depth). Such a model robs general education of its meaning for the two-thirds of American college students in preprofessional programmes, including most in natural resources and outdoor recreation. At the same time, it steals the richness and human depth of general education away from the majors. Instead, we should seek continuously to bring general education goals before students in their major courses. One way to set the stage for a more integrated curriculum is to begin with first-year seminars. In small classes, students can be encouraged to think broadly about significant issues to help them discover how things are connected in the real world and how all the courses in their programme of study, including both the major courses and the general education courses, are valuable to them as professionals.

Avoid becoming slaves to pedagogy

Palmer (1997) eloquently presents a message that we wish to highlight: *The techniques of teaching are necessary but insufficient.* We do not advocate becoming so obsessed with pedagogy that teachers forget what is really important: 'forming a community of learning' by connecting with students and helping students connect with their own education. The point is to use whatever teaching technique helps facilitate these connections and gives students opportunities to apply what they learn. A given technique is less important than forming connections (Campbell and Smith, 1997, p. xii) and making applications.

Conclusion

Natural resources affect everything humans do and everything humans do affects natural resources. The problem is that individuals are often unaware of human–natural resource interactions and impacts (Kellert and Wilson, 1993; Kellert, 1996). In addition, as the population urbanizes, suburbanizes and exurbanizes, people's attitudes toward natural resources become more diverse. While there is little knowledge difference between rural and urban residents in relation to natural resources, particularly wildlife, there are significant differences in how people believe these resources should be used (Kellert, 1996). The challenge for resource managers of the future is to recognize, acknowledge and balance these conflicting values. One of the coauthors is reminded of his neighbour, an intelligent, caring man, who spends enormous energy and money reconstructing the immediate environment surrounding his 'cabin' in the woods to make it look like a manicured, city park rather than something else – a wildlife sanctuary, or even a pastoral landscape. The same coauthor wonders what his other neighbour, the dairy farmer whose family has farmed the same 600 acres for several generations, thinks when he sees how the exurbanites have transformed the land (the same land that provides him and his family with income) into neat and tidy 5- and 10-acre rural retreats. How can we prepare students to deal with these differences within a context of increased demand for citizen participation?

One thing that we can expect as educators is that students are unfamiliar both with the everyday environment of the natural resource management professional and also with people who live in circumstances with dependencies on natural resources far different from their own. Most of our students are adept at learning the differences between *Quercus rubrum* and *Q. alba*, black ducks and mallards, county parks and national parks, but they remain insulated from the realities of such problems as environmental degradation, social and environmental injustice, competing demands for natural resources, and politics (Wellman, 1995). As students become immersed in their natural resources education, they become even further removed from the everyday lives of ordinary Americans where 'nature' plays a significant role but not in ways ordinarily recognized by traditional resource management (Kaplan, 1995). Trees are central to residential satisfaction in cities (Kaplan and Kaplan, 1989), private gardens are a widespread and critical component of urban greenspace (Lippard, 1997), and everyday experiences with nature, including gardening, birdwatching and strolling through the woods, decrease the stress of cancer patients (Cimprich, 1992). When professors ask for reports, term projects and answers to exam questions about some of these tricky, real issues and experiences, they often get cautious or naïve answers aimed at pleasing the professor and an audience of classmates, many of whom share the same points of view or have the same misconceptions.

So there are two concurrent trends: an increase in the diversity of priorities for natural resources and a subpopulation of future natural resource professionals insulated from the really messy issues they will face after graduation, one of which happens to be figuring out how to incorporate diverse citizen values into natural resource management and planning activities. Then,

we ask for solutions to these messy problems from students who themselves may have only a limited range of experiences with natural resources and diverse citizen values. We assume that natural resources and people and democracy can benefit from active citizen participation in management and planning activities, but, for this assumption to become internalized into the natural resource organizational culture, we have to help students build a knowledge base in and out of the classroom, a knowledge base that permits discourse and debate that are not superficial or contrived, but based upon real experiences. In addition, we must give them 'guided practice' in the art of democratic governance.

How can educators expect future natural resource professionals to facilitate 'direct democracy' (Wellman and Tipple, 1990) or consider the values and views of various publics if students do not begin to learn how before entering the workforce? One way is through the adoption of learning as our primary emphasis in teaching versus conveying lots of information (Barr and Tagg, 1995; Campbell and Smith, 1997). We have tried to provide concrete examples of other ways to answer this question as well. However, we see these recommendations as only the beginning of a conversation that needs to take place across the outdoor recreation and natural resources educational community.

Acknowledgements

We wish to thank Nancy Knap and Steven Bentley, graduate students at Michigan State University, who helped compile and summarize the literature on citizen participation in the first section of this chapter.

36

Trends in the Development of Recreation Services for Youth at Risk

Peter A. Witt and John L. Crompton

Introduction

The problems created by young people dropping out of school, using drugs or alcohol, joining gangs, becoming teenage parents, and/or being involved in antisocial and delinquent acts are widely recognized. These behaviours put children 'at risk' of not growing up to be fully functioning adults, able to earn a living wage and otherwise achieve a fully functioning adulthood. Many agencies – educational, social service, law enforcement, health, recreational, and other youth development agencies – are responding to these issues through targeted prevention and intervention strategies. With the problems created by at-risk youth emerging as a central concern in many communities, there were increasing pressures on the political system to respond throughout the 1990s. Recreation service providers have been called upon to be part of the solution.

Youth Issues in the US

In 1997, there were 69.5 million children in the US below the age of 18, with approximately equal numbers in the 0–5, 6–11 and

12–17 age groups. While not all children engage in behaviours that put them at risk, considerable numbers do.[1]

In 1996, 10% of white, non-Hispanic children lived in poverty, compared with 40% of black children and 40% of Hispanic children. While not all of the precursors to undertaking at risk behaviour are understood, poverty seems to be related to increasing the probability of children being at risk. Children who live in families that are poor are more likely than children in other families to have difficulty in school, to become teenage parents and, as adults, to earn less and be unemployed more.

Children under 17 represent a large segment of the poor population (40%), and children under the age of 6 living in female-householder families are particularly at risk of living in poverty. For example, in 1996, 59% of these children were living below the poverty line, compared with only 12% of children under 6 years old living in married-couple families. A quarter (24%) of all children lived with only their mothers, 4% lived with their fathers and 4% lived with neither parent. Among the factors contributing to the increase in children living with just one parent is the sharp rise in the per-

[1] The statistics in this section are taken from: Federal Interagency Forum on Child and Family Statistics (1998), *America's Children: Key National Indicators of Well-being*. Washington, DC: US Government Printing Office.

centage of all births that were to unmarried mothers. Between 1980 and 1994, the birth rate for unmarried women increased from 29 to 47 per thousand. Although the rate has fallen between 1994 and 1996, it is still at 45 births per thousand. For unmarried women between 15 and 17 years old, the rate was approximately 32 per thousand, up from 21 in 1980.

Smoking cigarettes, and use of alcohol and illicit drugs among teenagers have all increased in the 1990s. These three behaviours put teenagers at considerable risk. For example, smoking cigarettes can cause later health problems; the use of alcohol is associated with motor vehicle accidents, injuries, deaths and with problems in school and in the workplace, fighting and crime; and illicit drugs use has both long-term health and social consequences. The percentage of 8th, 10th, and 12th graders who reported that they smoked cigarettes daily increased between 1992 and 1997. In 1997, the percentage of 8th, 10th and 12th graders reporting smoking daily during the previous 30 days was 9, 18 and 25%, respectively. In 1997, almost one in three 12th graders, one in four 10th graders, and more than one in ten 8th graders reported heavy drinking (i.e. having at least five drinks in a row in the previous 2 weeks). The percentage of students in each of these three grade levels reporting illicit drug use increased substantially between 1992 and 1996 – from 14 to 26% for 12th graders; from 11 to 23% for 10th graders; and from 7 to 15% for 8th graders.

While the rate at which adolescents are victims of violent crimes was actually less in 1996 than in 1980 (33 versus 38 per 1000), young people aged 12–17 are nearly three times more likely than adults to be victims of serious violent crimes. In 1996, 25% of crimes against juveniles involved a juvenile offender.

Trends Leading to Increases in Problematic Youth Behaviours

Attempts to decrease negative behaviours undertaken by young people has led to an increase in efforts to reduce these behaviours through programmes and services offered by schools and other public and private youth serving agencies, including park and recreation departments (PARDs). Concerted efforts by PARDs began in the late 1980s. In a 1993 survey of PARDs, only 28% of agencies that offered these programmes launched them before 1989 (Espericuerta-Schultz *et al.*, 1995). Another 31% of agencies initiated these programmes between 1989 and 1991, while the remaining 41% started targeted programmes after 1991. The recent expansion in programmes that target at-risk youth has been stimulated by several factors, one of which is an increase in gang membership and the problems caused by gangs. For example, the number of gangs in Fort Worth, Texas, increased from 77 to 211 between 1987 and 1992, while gang membership rose from 1316 to 3448. In a national survey, 57% of agencies which targeted programmes for at-risk youth indicated that gangs were perceived to be a problem by residents in their jurisdictions.

Besides gangs, many factors contributed to the emergence of these programmes, but four major stimuli seem responsible for the trend toward greater involvement of PARDs in providing services seem particularly prominent: (i) changed demographics; (ii) emergence of negative youth behaviours in smaller communities; (iii) growth in the number of latchkey children; and (iv) increased high visibility violent incidents.

Changing demographics

The demographics of many major cities significantly changed during the 1980s in the US. The proportion of African Americans, Hispanics and, in some cities, immigrants, increased. In many instances, the age distribution of recent migrants to the inner cities was younger than that of the general population. Typically, inner cities have had high rates of unemployment and a larger percentage of families living below the poverty line. During the late 1980s and early 1990s, many cities reported substantial increases in drug use among young people and violent crime committed by and on youngsters; school dropout rates accelerated, not only among high school students, but also among middle school students; and rates of teenage pregnancy increased. These factors galvanized local residents and political forces to demand solutions to these spiralling societal problems.

Emergence of negative youth behaviours in smaller communities

Thought previously to be confined to 'big cities', many of these same factors began to appear in suburban and smaller communities in the late 1980s and early 1990s.

In both Boulder, Colorado, and Columbus, Mississippi, growing concerns about high poverty levels and unemployment, high drug use and gang activity, and lack of meaningful activities for Housing Authority residents led to the development of recreation and drug education programmes at these sites in 1991. A federal programme sponsored by HUD was initiated that year which made the development of these types of programmes possible.[2] In Scottsdale, Arizona, there was a 44% increase in juvenile crime between 1989 and 1994.

Growth in the number of latchkey children

Problems associated with a lack of adult supervision at home were prevalent in communities of all sizes, due to the growing number of two-wage-earner families and the number of single-parent households. Many localities have developed after-school and summer camp programmes in response to the need for affordable, supervised non-school programmes for children, with some communities also beginning to develop programmes for middle and high school students as well.

Kelso and Longview, Washington, initiated after-school programmes in 1992 in response to concerns about the high number of distress calls received by the police from children who were 'home alone' after school.

A 1993 NBC Dateline segment about latchkey children featured a Tucson, Arizona, single mother who was forced to leave her children home alone while she worked at a minimum wage job. Along with concerns about gang activity and youth violence, the story spurred the expansion of after-school and summer programme efforts which had been initiated in 1989.

Increased high visibility violent incidents

The late 1980s witnessed unprecedented levels of violence involving young people, due in part to increased gang activity and the highly competitive illegal narcotics market. In many communities dramatic events such as drive-by shootings moved the community to implement targeted intervention and prevention strategies.

Although Cincinnati, Ohio, had already established a comprehensive city-wide programme to address youth at-risk problems, in 1993 the city expanded programme efforts in the Winton Hills community as a result of a Federal Bureau of Investigation (FBI) drug raid and a shooting in the neighbourhood.

In Fort Worth, Texas, a 1991 drive-by shooting after a Sunday church service led to the mobilization of at-risk youth and gang intervention efforts. Actions had to be more than putting additional police officers on the street, because, as the Fort Worth Police Chief stated, 'We can't arrest our way out of social problems'. The mayor of Fort Worth offered a trenchant analogy: 'I compare it to smoking and the progress we've made with lung cancer. We didn't get there because we perfected surgery. We got there because we educated people into prevention' (Witt and Crompton, 1996b).

The case studies of park and recreation programmes across the US included in Witt and Crompton (1996b) indicate that, in most instances, that 'something' was the establishment of a task force whose typical charge was to solicit broad community input to enable the identification of all dimensions of

---

[2] Many of the examples in this and the following sections are taken from the case studies presented in Witt and Crompton (1996b).

the problem and its magnitude, recommend actions to alleviate the problem, and coordinate and mobilize community resources so these actions could be undertaken efficiently and effectively. The 1993 national survey indicated that 71% of agencies that targeted at-risk youth had established a community-wide task force (Espericuerta-Schultz *et al.*, 1995).

Task force action plans usually embraced *prevention*, designed to lower the number of children and adolescents engaging in undesirable behaviours in the future, and *intervention*, intended to change the attitudes, behaviour and 'life course' of the individuals causing problems. For example, in 1991, the mayor of Cincinnati, Ohio, formed a Youth Steering Committee, consisting of the directors of a number of municipal departments including the Recreation Commission, to deal with youth problems stemming from 'historical disenfranchisement, poverty, discrimination, inadequate education and skill levels, damaged self-esteem and thwarted aspirations'. The development of a comprehensive approach to youth services, 'Back on the Block', was the result (Witt and Crompton, 1996b).

Implications for the Parks and Recreation Field

Returning to the roots of the parks and recreation movement

In general, park and recreation agencies are beginning to move beyond a 'fun and games' philosophy to one in which recreation programmes serve as vehicles for an agency's objectives for serving at-risk youth (National Recreation and Park Association, 1994; Crompton and Witt, 1997). Thus, Seattle (Washington) PARD's at-risk youth staff do not talk about recreation. Rather they talk of the 're-creation' of human lives. In addition, the definition of what constitutes a recreation programme has been broadened considerably.

- YO! Hott Shotts is a job training pro-

gramme organized by Seattle PARD. It is intended to inspire at-risk youth to take an interest in business and entrepreneurial self-direction.

- Seattle includes specifications in their concession contracts which require concessionaires to hire and train at-risk youth.

- TEEN TEAMWORKS is a summer employment programme for 200 at-risk young people which has been operated by the Minneapolis (Minnesota) Parks and Recreation Board since 1986. Its mission is to offer a positive park maintenance work experience, recreational opportunities and educational sessions to unemployed youngsters aged 14–18.

- Midnight basketball in Kansas City, Missouri, includes a required educational component in which participants are exposed to opportunities for personal development, motivational training, entrepreneurial skills, job interviewing skills, antidrug and other health programmes.

The types of services now being offered are in some ways reminiscent of those which were prominent in the 1950s and 1960s. Jim Colley, Director of the Phoenix (Arizona) Parks, Recreation, and Libraries Department reminds us that during that period

> We did mobile recreation centers, school campus lunch time programs, after-school programs, teen councils, gang outreach programs and so on, but we then we got away from this type of approach to services
> (Witt and Crompton, 1996b)

The Witt and Crompton (1996b) case studies also indicate that many agencies are returning to the mission and objectives that spurred the launching of the public recreation movement in the late 1800s and early 1900s. Public recreation services emerged in response to negative social conditions in major cities. There was a humanistic concern for the welfare of those who found themselves with few resources, places to recreate, and/or skills to undertake recreational activities. Comments made by Jane Addams in 1893 are reminiscent of those made by commentators today:

> The social organism has broken down through large districts of our great cities. Many of the people living there are very poor, the majority of them without leisure or energy for anything but the gain of subsistence. They move often from one wretched lodging to another. They live for the moment side by side, many of them without knowledge of each other, without fellowship, without local tradition or public spirit, without social organization of any kind. Practically nothing is done to remedy this. The people who might do it, who have the social tact and training, the large houses, and the traditions and custom of hospitality, live in other parts of the city. The club-houses, libraries, galleries, and semi-public conveniences for social life are also blocks away
>
> (Addams, 1893, reprinted 1960, p. 4)

In response to this situation, Addams established Hull House, a settlement house in Chicago, Illinois, which was in many respects the precursor of the modern recreation centre. Facilities such as the Columbia Neighborhood Center developed in Sunnyvale, California, are reminiscent of Addams' philosophy and a reaffirmation of the importance of a holistic approach to serving at-risk youth.

Increasing the quantity of services

Recognition of the magnitude of the challenge presented by at-risk youth has sparked a renaissance of interest among some PARDs in providing services for at-risk youth. The prospect for the immediate future is that an increasing number of park and recreation agencies will be involved in developing services in this area, and those already involved will increase their efforts. Three types of approaches are usually taken to deal with youth issues: prevention, intervention or incarceration. PARDs are probably best positioned to provide services that can help prevent risk behaviours from occurring in the first place or to a lesser degree intervening to lessen risk behaviours for young

people who are already undertaking them. Presently, PARDs have virtually no role to play in serving young people who are incarcerated.

PARD prevention efforts have two components: (i) occupying young people in activities such that time and opportunity are not available to undertake risk behaviours, and (ii) using the occupied time to involve youth in constructive activities that can teach the skills necessary to avoid risk behaviours when not in the PARD setting. The potential for the use and abuse of free-time during the after-school, evening, weekend and school holidays has led to increased efforts to find safe and secure environments for children during these 'risky periods'. At the same time, there is increased interest in using the occupied time in a planned purposeful manner to decrease the odds that adolescents will become involved in risk related behaviours, or even decrease the amount of risk behaviours they are already undertaking.

Incorporating youth development and protective factors perspectives

Most youth serving agencies are beginning to take a youth development approach in their efforts to serve better the needs of youth. These approaches include helping young people develop the inner resources and skills they need to cope with pressures that might lead them into unhealthy and antisocial behaviours. Thus, the goal is to promote and prevent, not to treat or remediate. Prevention of undesirable behaviours is one outcome of healthy youth development, but there are others: the production of self-reliant, self-confident adults who can take their place as responsible members of society (Carnegie Council on Adolescent Development, 1992). The youth development emphasizes the positive aspects of how youth serving agencies can work with young people to contribute to these goals. Thus, youth development programmes apply accepted theory and empirical evidence (indicating that such programmes are essential to the healthy development of young adolescents) through interventions designed to help youth build personal resilience. A resilient individual has several attributes: social competence; problem-solving skills; autonomy (sense of self-identity and an ability to act independently and to exert control over his or her environment); and a sense of purpose and of a future. According to the Carnegie Council on Adolescent Development (1992), programmes work on three levels: (i) helping individual young people build the above four characteristics; (ii) ensuring that there is at least one caring, consistent adult in each young person's life; and (iii) developing a sense of security in the lives of all young people.

Conceptualization of protective and resiliency factors have been important to providing an underpinning for youth development work. A large literature has focused attention on identifying protective factors that can 'modify, ameliorate, or alter a person's response to some environmental hazard that predisposes them to a maladaptive outcome' (Rutter, 1985, p. 600). It is hoped that these protective factors will help children develop resilience, which has been defined as the 'capacity for successful adaptation, positive functioning or competence (Masten et al., 1990; Garmezy, 1993), despite high-risk status, chronic stress or following severe trauma' (Egeland et al., 1993, p. 517). This approach changes the paradigm from one that focuses on risks to which children are exposed, to the mechanisms that 'protect' and enable them to be resilient in the presence of risk, and how to teach youth the processes of negotiating risk situations (Rutter, 1990).

Since a number of young people manage to avoid the deviant behaviours exhibited by peers who grew up in the same environment, there has been growing interest in the 'protective factors' that are operative in the lives of 'resilient' youth, which enable them to avoid the negative consequences of multiple risk environments. Protective factors are those facets which impinge on an individual's life space that moderate and/or mitigate the impact of risk on subsequent behaviour and development (Jessor, 1991). Resiliency has been defined as a pattern of successful adaptation following exposure to

biological and psychosocial risk factors and/or stressful life events (Public/Private Ventures, 1994). Protective factors and resilience help at-risk children and adolescents avoid behaviours that compromise health and normal growth, and help them achieve economic self-sufficiency, positive and responsible family and social relationships, and good citizenship (Masten and Garmezy, 1985; Jessor, 1991). The protective factors approach shifts attention from identifying the risks to which children are exposed, to focusing on the protective mechanisms and processes of negotiating risk situations (Rutter, 1990).

Table 36.1 provides a simplified view of Jessor's framework for understanding adolescent risk behaviour. Column A delineates some of the risk conditions to which young people may be exposed through their biological background, social environment, personality and behaviour. Through exposure to these risk factors, the individual is 'at risk of' undertaking one or more risk behaviours (Column C), which in turn can lead to some of the health or life compromising outcomes listed in Column D.

Column B displays the role of protective factors in mediating, insulating and buffering against the risk factors (Rutter, 1985, p. 600). Protective factors include such elements as the youngster knowing there is at least one adult who supports their positive development; the existence of places for youth to spend free time in a positive, productive environment; opportunities for adolescents to learn how to work together in a group and how to resolve conflicts constructively; and the opportunity to be around other young people who are demonstrating positive conventional behaviour.

Developing protective factors is central to promoting positive youth development in risk environments. PARDs clearly have the potential to structure and design programmes to facilitate many of these protective factors as outcomes. A recent study by Gambone and Arbreton (1997) identified seven programme elements that PARDs and other youth serving agencies should use as part of a youth development approach which focuses on enhancing the

Table 36.1.   The relationship between risk factors, risk behaviour and health/life compromising outcomes.

(A) Risk factors	☞	(B) Protective factors	☞	(C) Risk behaviours	☞	(D) Health/life compromising outcomes

Poverty
Illegitimate
Opportunity models for deviant
  behaviour
Low perceived life chance
Low self-esteem
Risk-taking propensity
Poor school work
Latchkey situations (due to single-
  parent families or two-wage-
  earner families)
		Interested and caring adults
		Neighbourhood resources
		School and club
		  involvement
		High control against
		  deviant behaviour
		Models for conventional
		  behaviour
		Positive attitudes toward the
		  future
		Value on achievement
		Ability to work with others
		Ability to work out conflicts
		Sense of acceptance
		Church attendance
		Quality schools
		Cohesive family
				Illicit drug use
				Drunk driving
				Tobacco use
				Delinquency
				Truancy
				Unprotected sex
						School failure
						Legal trouble
						Low work skills
						Unemployability
						Disease/illness
						Early childbearing
						Social isolation
						Depression/suicide
						Lack of motivation

Adapted from the *Adolescent Risk Behaviour Model* (Jessor, 1991).

resilience of young people. These elements were: opportunities that enable young people to develop a sense of safety; challenging and interesting activities; settings and experiences that help youngsters develop a sense of belonging; social support from adults; opportunities for youth input and decision making; opportunities for young people to develop leadership skills; and opportunities for youngsters to undertake volunteer and community service activities.

Most youth serving agencies are increasingly defining their mission in terms of the potential of their programmes for increasing protective factors. Federal juvenile justice programmes are also defining outcomes of their efforts in terms of the ability of programmes to supply the structural elements necessary to develop these protective factors, as well as by the extent to which they decrease such risk behaviours as dropping out of school or using drugs.

The protective factors approach has been successfully used in the development and

evaluation of a number of evaluation studies of recreation programmes for at-risk youth. For example, Witt and his students (see Witt, 1997; Witt and Baker, 1999) have conducted evaluations of a number of programmes for the Austin (Texas) PARD. Using a Protective Factors Scale developed by Witt *et al.* (1996), programmes have been shown to increase various protective factors as a result of youngsters participating in programmes that have used the protective factors model to develop programming elements.

Although programmes are being developed, it is not always clear what future role PARDs seek to play in dealing with young people in our communities, including at-risk youth. Most departments appear to operate without an underlying theory that would link youth needs with the goals and objectives of specific programmes. What appears to be missing is an understanding of the underlying dynamics of child and adolescent development and what park recreation services have to contribute to

these processes. While the benefits movement spearheaded by the National
Recreation and Park Association (NRPA)
has tried to define a list of potential impacts
of PARD programmes, as yet there is no great
commitment at the local park and recreation
department level to move beyond rhetoric to
create a theory of practice and action necessary for programmatic efforts.

Integrating PARDs and other youth development agencies

PARDs are also having to redefine how they
fit within the overall system of youth development services provided by other youth
serving agencies (e.g. boys' clubs, girls'
clubs, YMCAs, YWCAs). In a similar manner, in areas such as after-school
programmes, park and recreation agencies
need to become proactive in working out
schemes with schools in terms of their
respective roles and responsibilities. PARDs
are very comfortable with the idea of providing safe and secure environments for
children and youth during the afternoon and
early evening. However, beyond keeping
kids safe, there is often no clear articulation
of the role on the part of PARDs. The consequence of this lack of role definition is that
nationally and in many communities
PARDs are being left out of the debate, and
in many cases the processes that are planning service systems to meet the needs of
children and young people. Many of the
other agencies involved in these processes
do not recognize PARDs as key players in
prevention and intervention efforts. In some
cases, such as the movement to increase
available after-school services, communities
have been trying to link several goals
together, e.g. by using the after-school hours
as an additional period for increasing academic performance through the
involvement of students in enrichment
activities and tutoring. In addition, in some
cases, efforts are being made to use models
developed in the after-school hours as one
element in an overall plan for school reform.
Whether the goal is increasing academic
performance or school reform, in many
cases, schools and PARDs do not see these
goals as central to their mission. Thus, there

is a real danger of PARDs being left out of
some of the better financed, politically viable, and more highly visible after-school
programme efforts.

Increasing PARDs understanding of programming impacts

Even if the goals that PARDs are trying to
achieve are stated, not enough is known
about the connection between participation
in particular programmes and specific outcomes. While some information is available
documenting specific programme outcomes
(e.g. Scott *et al.*, 1996), we still do not know
enough about the programme elements that
bring about these outcomes. Consequently,
many programmes are planned without
much evidence that they really work or that
the elements that make up a programme are
applicable to achieving the desired outcomes.

Finding additional funding

Future resources for at-risk youth programmes may come from three sources:
redirecting resources from other recreational programmes, additional
appropriations from legislative bodies, or
additional reliance on external partners.
The first option is, of course, likely to be
resisted by the users of programmes from
which funds are reallocated, and perhaps
also by staff who may perceive a loss of
personal power. Lowering service standards
for existing client groups frequently leads to
political protest. Opposition from staff to
changes in emphases may occur since the
changes may threaten an individual's status,
area of expertise or self-confidence. Thus,
reallocation of resources is likely to occur
only when a programme's life cycle nears its
end and when turnover of staff occurs. This
is likely to be a gradual process.

Reluctance to raise tax rates means that if
any additional appropriations are made,
they are likely to be small. On the other
hand, the critical nature of the at-risk youth
issues means that some cities have become
increasingly willing to earmark additional
funds for programmes to serve this portion
of the population.

Providing evidence of programme impacts

In order to justify tax increases for at-risk youth services to their constituents, legislators have to be provided with evidence that these programmes are effective, hence the current interest in developing evaluation measures which provide this evidence. Evaluating whether programmes have reached their goals is crucial to continued funding. Systematic evaluation procedures, unfortunately, have not been instituted by most agencies.

In a follow-up to the national survey of 120 agencies offering at-risk youth programmes, approximately 30% of the sample indicated that they undertook no evaluation of their programmes (Witt et al., 1995). The remaining respondents were categorized along a continuum of data sophistication. Thirteen percent of the agencies used mainly participation data, the least sophisticated form of evaluation; approximately 14% undertook some effort to collect testimonials or case studies; 19% used surveys to obtain participant, parent or other stakeholders' input about programme quality or outcome; 20% used or planned to use crime statistics as an indicator of programme impact; and only 4% had undertaken any form of evaluation utilizing a pre-post study of changes in such indicators as school grades, test scores, leisure related attitudes or behaviour.

These data suggest that increased efforts are needed by recreation and park agencies to build evaluation procedures into their programme development efforts. Several examples of this process have been utilized with some success. For example, representatives of eight universities and 12 cities have joined together to undertake evaluations of selected programmes for at-risk youth (Witt and Crompton, 1996a). In addition, Allen et al. (1998b) have worked with selected cities to apply Benefits-Based Management (BBM) principles to programmes for at-risk youth and evaluate the impact of these programmes. Both projects have received funding from the National Recreation and Park Association and the National Recreation Foundation. Yet to occur are analyses that place a cost on each crime (and the costs

of prosecuting and incarcerating guilty individuals associated with them) and document the amount of money saved by any drop in crime rates which appear to be related to the programme.

Educating future professionals

Colleges and university programmes, along with in-service and continuing education efforts sponsored by PARDs must supply current and future professionals with a greater understanding of youth development principles and benefits management programming techniques (Allen et al., 1998a). Professionals who seek to work in this field need an understanding of their role beyond the 'fun and games' mentality present in many current park and recreation programmes. They need to know when and how to create partnerships with other youth serving agencies, how to undertake meaningful programme evaluations, and how to raise funds to support programmes beyond the amounts supplied by city governments. In essence, park and recreation professionals must be helped to see their responsibilities differently and to have the necessary tools to deal with changing job responsibilities.

Concluding Comments

The human services view of recreation and parks as practiced in many urban communities places the recreation and park movement at a crossroads. One path travels down the narrow road of traditionally defined, segmented activities based on economic values; the other path leads to a multi-disciplinary community services approach that places recreation, parks and amenities in the center of the urban policy debate

(Foley and Pick, 1995, p. 70)

Many recreation and park agencies are returning to the roots of the profession by investing more resources in providing programmes for at-risk children and adolescents. The service priorities of responsive recreation and park agencies are shaped by external forces which they cannot control, but to which they must adapt. In the late 1970s and throughout the 1980s, the external political forces directed that an agency's primary concern should be to increase efficiency or to 'do more with less'. This was accomplished by reducing an agency's tax subsidy, while maintaining or expanding its range of offerings. This resulted in focusing on target markets with the ability and willingness to pay prices high enough to cover most service costs, and reducing resources invested in high subsidy programmes.

Since the late 1980s, political forces have continued to stress reducing tax subsidies, but with a priority emphasis 'to do something about' juvenile crime and delinquency. Explosive, high-profile incidents involving young people have grown exponentially in recent years, and each horrific event directs more political attention to this issue. Recreation programmes have been viewed by some as a means through which these problems may be addressed.

Despite being labelled by some critics as 'wasteful social spending' and 'politically motivated, nonpriority spending', recreation programmes have been embraced as one means to address problems associated with high-risk youth. Smith (1991) noted the cost benefits in her report to the Carnegie Council on Adolescent Development.

> The provision of community recreation services is a good investment. Participation in organized recreation provides for the constructive use of free time and develops skills for the management of discretionary time and thereby reduces the need for, and the costs of, providing other governmental and social services that deal with the management of anti-social behaviors after they occur
>
> (Smith, 1991, p. ii–iii)

Repositioning, however, takes time. Agencies that have focused for a decade or more on middle-class target markets, cannot immediately reorient staff and resources to serving at-risk young people. Unfortunately today's youth, and indeed society, cannot wait.

37

So What? Implications of Trends for Management, Public Policy, Marketing and Planning

William C. Gartner and David W. Lime

This final chapter has three sections. The first consists of 72 trends taken from the chapters in this book, organized according to the six topical sections (Parts I–VI). The second section discusses the meaning and implications of the trends. The third section concludes this chapter, and the book, by listing 79 of the important trend implications according to the categories of policy, planning, management and operations.

Major Trends Concerning Leisure, Recreation and Tourism

Society

- A new definition of family continues to emerge, brought on by: men and women delaying age of first marriage, greater percentage of children born to unmarried women, and smaller percentage of divorced women and men remarrying. The 'traditional family' is becoming less of a model for recreation and tourism programming.
- There is more variety in work situations brought on by: the narrowing education gap between women and men, an increase in telecommuting options, an increasing average working week, and

the majority of the new work force being women and minority groups.

- The dominant influence in market system ideology coupled with changing personal value systems has led to democratization of travel consumption (mass tourism).
- The rise in the number of recreation services and programmes for at-risk youth has been brought on by: the growth in the number of latchkey children, emergence of negative youth behaviour in smaller communities, and the increased visibility of violent incidents involving young people.
- Women will continue to form a growing population in recreation, which will mean challenges for managers striving for equality and inclusiveness.
- Issues addressed in outdoor recreation research continue to evolve to meet societal interests and needs.
- Planning is becoming more inclusive of the values incorporated into the planning process.
- Planning has moved away from simplistic, carrying-capacity-based paradigms to those more focused on management of desired social and biophysical conditions.

- Retirees will demand a much richer range of social activities and learning opportunities than previous senior citizens have.
- There is increased citizen demand for government accountability and for personal input into decisions affecting them and their communities.

Resources

- Most federal, state and local land agencies have recently experienced flat to slightly decreasing current dollar budgets for recreation acquisition and management.
- Federal land agencies are experiencing reductions in professional staffing for recreation.
- Federal land agencies are increasingly relying on volunteers to carry out day-to-day site maintenance and customer interface activities.
- Federal land agencies are rapidly expanding the application of various fee structures.
- Federal land having inadequate access (due to increased restrictions by adjacent private landowners) will increase.
- Local growth has been focused toward athletic fields, ball courts, passive recreation spaces and parks versus recreation centres and water sites.
- The private sector is expanding its role as a supplier of outdoor recreation goods, services, travel and sites in the US.
- Overall, developed recreation opportunities on public land are increasing.
- There is an increased move toward urban casino development.
- There is an explosion in supply of cultural attractions, which is rapidly outpacing the growth in demand.

Participation

- Even though individual activity participation levels may not be growing, expenditures for these activities may show substantial increases.
- Four of the fastest growing activities are birdwatching, hiking, backpacking and primitive camping.

- Hunting remains the most popular activity pursued on private lands.
- There is increased participation in technology-driven, adventure activities such as snow skiing/snowboarding, canoeing/kayaking, cycling.
- There is moderate growth in family-oriented activities such as camping and swimming.
- There is slowing growth resulting in decreased participation (compared to population growth) in hunting, horse riding, and fishing.
- Travellers are going in search of exotic, unfamiliar, and unpredictable situations and destinations.
- There is an increased legal presence of casinos in various parts of the world. During the last half on the 1990s the legalization of new casinos has dramatically slowed down but there has been a continuing expansion of other forms of casino-style gaming (e.g. slot machines in bars, taverns and arcades).
- There is an increase in positive public attitudes regarding casino gaming as a legitimate form of entertainment.
- The growth trend of number, size and diversity of festivals will continue well into the 21st century.
- Travellers are becoming more interested in improving themselves intellectually, emotionally and physically, than they are in goals such as making money, getting promoted at work, or acquiring clothes, houses and cars.
- There will be continued growth in cultural tourism demand, stimulated by higher levels of education and a thirst for knowledge.
- A blurring of the distinction between high and popular culture, and between culture and economy, has been fuelling the growing supply of attractions and events.

Evaluation and valuation

- There will be increased biophysical impacts due to recreation (e.g. impacted trees, damaged vegetation and bare ground, exposed and compacted soils, disturbed wildlife and contaminated waters).

- Researchers and practitioners are searching for situation-specific tourist typologies to serve specific marketing objectives. It is believed that an infinite number of tourist typologies exist rather than one universal mould.
- There is an increased demand for tourism economic impact information.
- Recreation research has evolved from primarily empirically based studies of visitor characteristics and use patterns to more theoretically based studies of visitor behaviour and the underlying meanings of outdoor recreation.
- The research-based literature in outdoor recreation has been synthesized to develop a number of conceptual frameworks that are useful for integrating multiple studies, and ultimately guiding further research and management.
- The synergistic effects of an accumulating body of research have developed a strong theoretical understanding of a number of important issues in outdoor recreation.
- There is increased use of the following economic valuation methods: revealed preference or actual behaviour methods, contingent valuation, contingent behaviour, combining revealed and stated preference methods.
- The empirical estimate of the economic value of camping, picnicking, motorboating and hiking have increased over time.
- Analysis of quantitative impacts tends to take precedence over analysis of qualitative impacts.
- Since measurement and analyses of social impacts is complex, case studies predominate and theory development has been slow to emerge.
- Social impacts studies tend to adopt a reductionist and linear model, ignoring complex interactions among entities involved in a development project.

Development

- There is an increase in the number of foreign nationals working in recreation/tourism enterprises in many countries.
- Globalization of world financial markets has greatly increased the mobility of capital allowing tourism development projects to appear throughout the developing world.
- In effect, the world has become a smaller place where the line between domestic and international tourism and services becomes blurred.
- There will be new rural tourism market opportunities caused by a swing away from resort destinations.
- Travellers are looking for destinations which provide a better balance between humans and nature.
- More attention has been given to collaborative tourism planning, development and promotion in general, as well as to tourism planning integrated within a community or regional planning process.
- Private enterprises are becoming more involved with tourism in developing countries.

Management and operations

- There is, especially in Europe, substantial evidence of consolidation occurring among tour operators.
- Information technology has been used to: reduce customer waiting time, meet customer information needs and improve accuracy of operations.
- As methods for gathering public input and analysing this input improve, a better understanding of the relationship between visitors, communities and the resource will emerge.
- There is an increased use of improved monitoring frameworks (LAC, VERP) and protocols by resource managers. This is occurring at a slow rate.
- There will be an increase in the quality and quantity of low-impact visitor education programmes.
- Partnerships between public land agencies and private organizations are increasing.
- State land agencies are moving toward more year-round operation. Lodges on state land have rapidly increased.
- Destination differences are becoming far less important than the undeniable

pleasures that placeless holidays bring. Exterior strangeness and differences have been minimized by injecting large amounts of familiarity into foreign settings.

- The types of planning settings confronted by recreation, tourism and protected area planners have moved from tame problems to wicked problems and messes.
- There is a growing linkage between recreation, tourism and protected area planning and broader social policy goals (e.g. preserving our cultural and natural heritage, enhancing economic opportunity, increasing family cohesiveness, reduced crime and greater educational opportunity).
- There is more integration of tourism considerations in national park planning and vice versa.
- Planning is moving away from standards-based decisions and cookie cutter solutions to needs-based resolutions tailored to the needs of individual situations.
- Information technology is increasingly the basis for new resort products and service.
- Information technology may reduce the necessary number of employees.
- Information technology is being used to integrate customer experiences with multiple vendors.
- Resort Internet sites are increasingly being used to provide guest education.
- Recreation resource management theory is moving away from management of inputs and outputs toward identifying, measuring, and managing beneficial outcomes (benefit-based management).
- There is widespread endorsement and the incorporation of a proactive environmental dimension into corporate strategic planning and business management that is being termed sustainable development.
- There is a growing commercialization of cultural tourism, through the creation of commercial cultural tourism products and the provision, distribution and sale of information on cultural products.

- Social impact research tends to focus on internal aspects of a system under study, and often ignores the boundary-spanning nature of impacts.
- There are an increasing number of programmes and services offered by public and private agencies for at-risk youth.

The above trends and their corresponding implications can be examined from a variety of perspectives. Some trends indicate a decreasing supply of the 'right' resources expected to increase in demand. Supply solutions are mixed but presently do not include much expansion of the public resource base. As will be discussed, the private sector will increasingly be expected to satisfy unmet demand, in a variety of ways. In the middle section of this chapter we try to discuss the various implications of the trends presented in this book from demand/supply, market fragmentation, information technology, human resources, private sector ascendancy and knowledge acquisition perspectives.

Demand and supply

Demand for recreation and tourism experiences is expected to increase in the coming years. In Chapter 1 we discussed projections for global tourism arrivals. It would not be unexpected to realize annual percentage increases in the range of 4–5%. Similarly many of the authors in this book project increasing levels of recreationists for the foreseeable future. What will these increases mean for people who are on the front lines and expected to deal with the increases?

First we cannot expect the demand to be evenly distributed according to the proportional breakdowns we see today. Tourist arrivals are expected to shift more toward developing countries except for North American destinations, which are expected to gain market shares. As Teigland points out, travel in Europe by Europeans may already be at a maximum as the number of leisure days available to the general public is not expected to increase. Given the historic importance of holidays to the Europeans, the roof may have already been reached. Richards also sounds a cautionary note about the continued focus on heritage/ cultural attractions that are a major part of the attraction package for Europe. If, as Richards indicates, heritage/cultural attractions may have reached market saturation, additional supply increases will only serve to spread the market thinner and increase competition between destinations heavily invested in this market.

Examples of what might be in store for Europe are found in other places in the world. According to Eadington, the 1990s has seen more casino development, worldwide, than at any other time in history. Similar supply increases are recorded for the festival/event market (Getz). What this means for destinations relying on attractions that may have reached, or be close to reaching, market saturation is that their effective market area will shrink and at some point will primarily serve only a local market. Those destinations that retain or gain competitive advantage will invest heavily in attraction development and rejuvenation. By doing so a large market area (e.g. in the case of Las Vegas, the world) will be maintained but at a substantial investment in attraction development with accompanying infrastructure. This is a high-risk development strategy which only a few destinations will be able to adopt. Other destinations will have to explore product diversity strategies to increase market area.

As discussed in Chapter 1, shifts in tourist arrivals are expected to favour developing countries more than developed. Keller points to the low input factor costs (e.g. labour, land) in developing countries as one indication of a comparative advantage for the developing world. However, input factor costs alone will not be responsible for any market shift. Developing countries have extensive problems providing an adequate infrastructure for tourism to flourish. Wahab points out the need for more focused tourism policy by developing countries if they are to capture any of the demand building for the type of experiences they offer.

The supply of land available for recreational activity has been increasing since the 1960s (this is particularly evident in the US, for example, due to its large land base) but

access is diminishing (Cordell). Public land surrounded by private land is becoming increasingly harder to access as more private land is posted (a legal statement printed on signs 'No Trespassing') each year. On available public land and adjacent service communities conflict between user groups and, user groups and management continue to increase. With more people using public lands, biophysical resources will continue to decline in quality (Cole). Similarly, communities in demand by tourists and recreationists will also experience increasing levels of conflict between local residents and guests (Van der Stoep). Although not a complete response to immediate problems, the monitoring of users, resource conditions and management actions is seen as one way to address problems as they arise (McCool and Patterson, Anderson *et al.*, Stokowski, Hammit and Schneider).

Market fragmentation

It is clear from the authors that leisure, recreation and tourist markets are becoming increasingly fragmented. Nickerson and Black discuss the importance of women in the labour force and how this may impact the types of leisure activities demanded by this emerging market power. Henderson details some of the changes brought on by decades-old policy in the US that made a variety of sports and recreation pursuits increasingly available to women. Experiences gained while growing up should translate into more market power and demands for different experiences. Pollock and Williams discuss a specific type of recreation/tourism activity, health and wellness, and they emphasize the need to develop more specialized programmes for those seeking this type of experience.

As the population ages, health services tied to recreation and travel will assume even greater importance. Even with mature recreation pursuits, such as hunting, market awareness will be the key to success. Brown *et al.* point out that the numbers of hunters in the US has held relatively stable for quite a few years. However, though overall numbers may not be increasing, the same cannot be said for the amount of money spent on the activity. Expenditures have gone up substantially in the last decade as new equipment, using new materials, is constantly being introduced and marketed by manufacturers. The investment in research to develop these new products is substantially underscoring again, how difficult it is becoming to compete for available consumers even when long-term projections show rather significant increases in the market base.

An increasingly fragmented market also is underscored by the contribution from Hutchison. He points out that although the US is undergoing a period of substantial diversification in ethnic affiliation, the majority of leisure research continues to focus on the dominant white, majority population. Even studies that include different ethnic groups usually relegate ethnicity to a long list of explanatory variables in a demand equation, often citing discredited theories as the basis for any ensuing discussion of research findings.

On the supply side, research is also expected to assume greater importance. Mention was made above of the decreasing supply of land available for recreation. Assuming more land will be added to the available supply, the question then becomes what type of land? Land, unlike money, is not fungible. As we increasingly recognize that leisure and tourism markets are becoming more fragmented, or that we are now able to identify more fragmentation in the market, the 'right' type of land will be more important than simply more land. Understanding the benefits sought by leisure publics (Anderson et al., Peterson) or tourists' preferences (Dolnicar and Mazanec) should raise the status and importance of research and facilitate management and policy making.

Market fragmentation is seen as an advantage for small scale businesses that do not have the capital to reach out to mass markets. Buhalis underscores this as he argues that small or medium size businesses will have the opportunity to compete with their larger competitors through the Internet. Communication technology is expected to level the playing field for all firms. Yet Čavlek sounds a cautionary note as she

examines the consolidation efforts during the last decade in the European tour market. Through vertical integration tour companies are more able to control product and/or exert pressure on product suppliers in destination areas. Owning or controlling means of transport and destination accommodations should serve to reduce or eliminate any communication technology that the Internet brings to the marketplace. However, given the increased market fragmentation that exists, small- or medium-size firms should still be able to cater to a select share of the overall market.

The demand for individual travel and recreation products for the discerning customer should increase (Buhalis, Teigland). Dann also addresses this issue in a somewhat different vein. He argues that the more advertising promotes place difference to appeal to a certain market, the more it loses its appeal as others copy successful promotional campaigns.

Information technology

Advances in information and communication technology have important implications for how products are packaged and sold. In addition to those mentioned above, customer service is expected to become much more specialized. Firms that adopt technology-driven customer service programmes are expected to reap the dual outcomes of increasing visitor satisfaction by providing the right products at the right time while reducing labour requirements for providing the products (Perdue). One of the major challenges facing the private sector is how to integrate all the various databases available to a leisure provider so the service component of the business does not get stalled by information overload. Consultants or firms with a proclivity for performing this challenging task should prosper most.

Human resources

Many of the trend implications noted above translate into a need for better trained personnel. The human resource component will not be replaced by using communication technology but instead be transformed by it. Employees will have to have computer savvy and especially in some areas (e.g. travel agencies) reduce emphasis on selling product and increase their skills for selling information services. A greater awareness of customer needs combined with an ability to utilize rapidly changing communication technology will be a requirement for success in the marketplace.

Change in the human resource requirements will not only affect how touristic products are sold but will affect all levels of management for the provision of leisure services. Propst *et al.* and Siehl discuss the trend toward greater citizen participation in management decisions affecting recreation and natural areas. New teaching methods in university courses, including modelling of real life situations, are needed if managers are going to be able to stay on top of this trend. Lifelong learning courses also will be in demand as managers increasingly rely on researchers for data needed for informed decisions and they must be able to communicate the research findings in a way that can be absorbed by an ever more vigilant and discerning public (Hammitt and Schneider). Lifelong learning is a given as society comes to terms with rapidly changing technology, diversity of user groups in the marketplace and new types of conflict, some brought on by the use of new toys that have yet to be invented.

Society

Societal issues will turn more to recreation and leisure providers for some of the answers. Witt and Crompton, for example, focus on one specific area, youth at risk, and discuss ways in which some of the problems associated with a changing society can be dealt with through targeted leisure programming. Nickerson and Black, and also Henderson, deal with societal change and suggest that all aspects of society will need to recognize the changes taking place and initiate new ways of dealing with a much more complex, integrated social mix in the recreation/leisure field.

Private sector ascendancy

The private sector appears to be the big winner for the provision of products and services to many different aspects of the recreation, leisure and tourism markets as the new millennium dawns. A number of authors underscore this implication in a variety of ways. Cordell and Betz question whether the recent rise in user fees for entrance to public areas will exclude lower income socioeconomic classes. LaPage suggests partnerships as a means to help with funding, infrastructure development and educational programming. He suggests that the potential for public/private partnerships to 'improve stewardship, accountability, consensus building, and the organizational structure for public land management agencies is just beginning to be realized'. Long and Lane suggest more partnerships to help rural areas develop their tourism potential. Pigram suggests that one way to achieve sustainable tourism development is through the use of partnerships. 'Green' policies should be worked out in collaboration between public policy makers and private sector providers in a more relaxed regulatory regime. Fletcher and Wanhill suggest that a worldwide movement to adopt market-based systems puts more control into the hands of private providers with less policy control being exerted by the public sector. Yet Wahab suggests that the public sector, in developing countries, must elevate tourism policy to a higher level. Keller echoes this sentiment when he argues that destinations must become more sophisticated if they are to continue to prosper.

The ascendancy of the private sector as evidenced by more market-based policies (e.g. fee increases and new fees) and a greater role, via partnerships, in the provision of what historically has been under public sector control (e.g. park products and services) has so far been viewed as a good thing. Yet a note of caution needs to be interjected. As previously discussed, conflicts among different user groups, and between citizens and managers, over decisions is expected to increase. Who will decide the outcome of these disagreements? Will it be a public agency empowered to represent all citizens or it will be a private sector-dominated public agency that is more concerned over the bottom line and less over the provision of services to all? Will national tourism organizations (NTOs) abandon their mandate to deal with environmental and sociocultural issues instead focusing their entire effort on marketing and economic concerns? There have been questions raised about the 'good' NTOs do for local people when what they are promoting may not be authentic to local conditions or the desires of destination citizens (Dann). Will these concerns be addressed by an NTO that considers its mandate one of increasing economic impact to support its private sector partners? These questions and more will be increasingly raised as the private sector assumes more control over the provision of all aspects of recreation, leisure and tourism services in the coming years.

Knowledge acquisition

A number of authors focused on recent advances in the acquisition of knowledge. As mentioned, Manning argues that recreation research is coming of age as it gains respect and credibility through advances in methods and establishment of theoretical base. The same can be said of tourism research. In the area of economic impacts, Smith and Erkkila discuss impact methodology. Erkkila argues that the ease of desktop computing and the use of more sophisticated models makes economic impact modelling more user friendly for input into the policy and planning process. Smith discusses recent advances in developing methods (i.e. satellite accounts) that enable planners to put tourism economic impact estimates on a par with traditional industry sectors. These advances, focusing on economic impact, reinforce the earlier discussion that the private sector is assuming more power in the leisure, recreation and tourism areas. Indeed Van der Stoep laments the relative absence of sophisticated models for measuring sociocultural impacts.

According to Manning, recreation and by inference tourism research (see also Dolnicar and Mazanec), has come of age. New conceptually grounded methods, the establishment of a sound theoretical base, and respect for findings are indications of a mature field. It is not surprising then that so many authors suggested more research is needed to solve some identified problems. In fact this was the one implication that seemed to be almost universal. However, new research methods and lines of inquiry will have to take on even greater importance if many of the implications discussed in this book are going to be dealt with in an informed, professional manner.

Implications for Management, Public Policy, Planning and Marketing

The above discussion addresses some of the concerns regarding the implications of leisure, recreation, and tourism trends identified by the authors in this book. This last section concludes with a litany of the various implications found in the book. Some have been addressed above, some are new to the discussion. The following implications are presented randomly in bullet form with no formal discussion, apart from which appears in the preceding section, as to what they might mean. As the reader reviews the list, we are confident they will begin to form in their minds an idea of how many of us will live and play in the next century. If considered in conjunction with the mega-trends discussed in the opening chapter (e.g. population growth, increasing urbanization, environmental pressure) it should become clear that we are in for a profound change in how we deal with the recreation and tourism of tomorrow.

Management

- Management will have to remain cognizant of the benefits visitors attain and do not attain.
- Management objectives should consider multiple variables that can be used to identify which leisure opportunities might have the greatest likelihood of aiding visitors in attaining their desired beneficial outcomes.
- Increased training is needed for employees dealing with advanced technology.
- As the world population increases, biophysical impacts from leisure,

recreation and tourism will grow, necessitating a high level of 'management professionalism'.

- Monitoring of biophysical and social impacts concerning recreation, leisure and tourism will have to become a high priority.
- Because of shifting leisure use patterns and the trend toward increased biophysical and social impact, management strategies will have to confine, contain and concentrate use.
- Pressure on the leisure infrastructure and for places to recreate will increase.
- There will be more and new types of conflicts as interest groups diversify and compete for access rights to participate in activities and experiences incompatible with other recreation groups.
- Resource management will become more difficult due to the number and diversity of recreational users.
- Management issues such as equitable access, fees, reservation systems and information distribution will be a challenge and will need attention.
- Domestic and international tourism to natural areas will grow, bringing with it increased management and visitor pressure, but also economic opportunity.
- Greater citizen participation in management of recreation and natural areas means major changes for education of outdoor recreation and other natural resource professionals.

Marketing

- Small to medium-sized businesses can compete on a more equitable level with larger concerns.
- More market fragmentation as consumers choose travel experiences they want.
- More knowledgeable consumers means opportunities for specialized businesses.
- Increasing consolidation means new entrants will have a tough time.
- Businesses will have to become more focused on which customers they are attracting.
- Promotional differences lose their difference the more they are employed in advertising.

- Growing awareness that NTO literature may not be authentic to local people.
- Number of casinos may shrink market area, losing their tourism importance.
- Because it will be difficult to elevate an event to an international level (due to competition) most will be local or regional. It will be necessary to cultivate a mix of events for destinations and adopt a diversification strategy. Consideration to spreading events across geography and season should be undertaken.
- Global communication systems make price transparency common.
- Destinations must become more sophisticated with all units in the destinations working together.
- Marketing will become more effective and sophisticated.
- An implication of the time and monetary constraints on single working parents, particularly women in family situations where the father is absent, is that children will have fewer opportunities to participate in outdoor recreation.
- Due to an increase in women going to college and having careers rather than children, there will be large increases in the number of women pursuing outdoor recreation and travel opportunities.
- Creation of departments devoted to information technology and guest/ employee satisfaction should be considered.
- There will be a move away from a focus on inputs and outputs to an emphasis on beneficial outcomes.
- Health tourism opens new opportunities for development as health focus has generally been ignored in North America.
- Globalization will reduce available leisure time in Europe.

Planning

- Certain parts of the distribution system will change (i.e. travel agency/ transform to service).

- New methods allow for even more complex market segmentation analysis.
- Holiday style segmentation can identify segments by motives and combine this with expenditure/length of stay data.
- Apart from Las Vegas, which has established itself as a unique world attraction, most other casino developments can no longer use tourism development as a major reason for legalization.
- New information technology advances provide for more input in the policy and planning process.
- To avoid negative visitor responses, research ' ... determining the relationships between situational, psychological, and managerial conflict conditions and outdoor recreation visitor stress-coping responses is essential to conflict management'.
- More integrated tourism planning needed, especially in developed countries.
- The market will grow for rural tourism products.
- New ways of planning for the future and problem management will have to continue to evolve as collaborative management 'take precedence over model building and scientific analysis ... '.
- Linking planning for recreation, protected areas, and tourism will require consideration of the goals, purposes and functions of these three units to achieve benefits for all.
- Tourism will have to take on more holistic attitudes rather than purely focusing on a narrow functional promotional emphasis.
- Integration of ideas and methods of supplying goods and services will be an important, but difficult, job for planners.
- While dealing with planning methods, agencies will have to move away from simple cookie cutter methods and use more dynamic paradigms.
- New economic estimation and monitoring methods allow the measurement of a variety of impacts including the comparison of tourism activity to regular business cycle.

- Mega-trends and short-term processes may converge to provide specific place instability. Managers need to be flexible.
- Globalization will affect the rich versus poor schism, leading to a small group choosing expensive destinations and a larger one looking for more value.
- More packaging of goods and services is essential to meeting the needs of an increasingly fragmented market.
- Communities will have to integrate and work well together in the development and identification of their resources. They will also have to work in concert with outside interests to create an industry that respects the needs and goals of the involved community, as well as those of the external stakeholders.
- There needs to be more research and evaluation directed at programme planning and outcomes in order to reach specific programme goals.

Policy

- Urbanization will erode support for some traditional outdoor pursuits such as hunting.
- Vertical integration means consolidation in the destinations as well.
- Better trained and higher quality staff will be needed to keep the recreation/leisure and tourism sectors growing.
- Because budgets across the board for public lands remain flat or shrinking, and demand for outdoor recreation is rising, managing organizations are looking for ways to increase their financial resource base. One way for this to be accomplished is through the use of fee programmes. The implication of this is that access may become an issue, particularly for lower economic classes. The major implications, in fact, of all outdoor recreation supply as defined by available lands, be they federal, state, local or private, is one of decreasing access.
- NTOs may be promoting difference as a counterpoint to tour operators who promote sameness. It is in the best inter-

est of some operators to de-emphasize difference as they can then play destinations off against each other.

- More private sector control of all aspects of the recreation/leisure and tourism market will occur.
- Developed countries are at a disadvantage in terms of labour costs and recruitment of workers.
- Traditional tourism countries are losing market share and find themselves at a disadvantage on price.
- Future research must be expanded to consider the activities of other (white and non-white) ethnic subgroups.
- Parks are moving toward partnering with other groups to help with funding, infrastructure, and education, among other things. To respond to this, parks 'should consider restructuring, and rethinking their strategies in ways that will facilitate the growing demand for participation and partnering'.
- More national and provincial/regional rural tourism policies will be formulated.
- Recreation research will continue to grow in importance, acceptance, credibility and status.
- Marketing of recreation will have to account for a growing number of specific demographic subgroups that have specific ideas about recreation.
- Closer collaboration between researchers and management and more continuing education of managers is needed to meet tomorrow's fragmented demand for recreation/tourism products.
- Closer government–industry linkages will take on greater importance for the provision of services.
- Collaboration between the various sectors of the tourism industry in a more relaxed regulatory regime is one option in pursuing higher environmental standards.
- More explicit support, from all levels of government, for sustainable tourism and for the environmental management processes which contribute to it. Yet, governments are getting looser with private sector control.
- There will be a shift from treating sick-

ness to staying well, which may conflict with the medical services market.
- There will be an increasing need for quality control in provision of health tourism services.
- New learning goals and ways of teaching, such as actual interaction with the public and active course work modelling real-life situations, rather than passive lectures, are emerging to meet the needs of a profession increasingly involved with public participation.
- More supply than demand, population more educated and interested, blurring lines between high and popular culture, make developing cultural tourism policy very difficult.
- Interest groups build awareness of issues that translate into policy actions, forcing public agencies to constantly adjust.
- Rapid change is inevitable but policy over the years has consistently built up the recreation resource. If it is enough or how we treat it and protect it are highly volatile and debatable issues.
- Tourism Satellite Accounts (TSAs) represent a revolution in how governments track and view tourism – most significant statistical change to affect how tourism is viewed.
- Need more of a longitudinal focus as well as broader contextual detail when designing recreation/tourism research studies.
- Social impact assessment models need to assess secondary or indirect impacts and cumulative effects over time and space.
- As tourism development increases in the developing world there is a need for inter-ministerial bodies with a full time secretariat.
- Park and Recreation Departments and schools need to get together and agree upon goals, or the Park and Recreation Departments will be left out of some of the better ... after-school programmes.
- There needs to be more research and evaluation directed at programme planning and outcomes in order to reach specific programme goals.

References

Ackoff, R.L. (1974) *Redesigning the Future: a Systems Approach to Societal Problems*. John Wiley and Sons, New York.

Adamowicz, V., Louviere, J. and Williams, M. (1994) Combining revealed and stated preference methods for valuing environmental attributes. *Journal of Environmental Economics and Management* 26(3), 271–292.

Adams, J. (1930) Diminishing returns in modern life. *Harpers* 160, 529–537.

Adams, M. (1997) *Sex in the Snow: Canadian Social Values at the End of the Millennium*. Viking, Toronto.

Addams, J. (1893; Reprinted 1960) The subjective necessity for social settlements. In: *Philanthropy and Social Progress*. Books for Libraries Press, Freeport, New York, pp. 1–26.

Aderhold, P. (1996) Urlaubreisen 1970-1994. Ausgewälte Zeitreihen. Die reiseanalyse. Forschungsgemeinschaft Urlaub und Reisen e.V. (F.U.R.) Hamburg.

Ajzen, I. (1988) *Attitudes, Personality, and Behavior*. Dorsey, Chicago, Illinois.

Ajzen, I. (1991) Benefits of leisure: a social psychological perspective. In: Driver, B.L., Brown, P.J. and Peterson, G.L. (eds) *Benefits of Leisure*. Venture Publishing, State College, Pennsylvania, pp. 411–417.

Ajzen, I. and Driver, B.L. (1991) Prediction of leisure participation from behavioral, normative and control beliefs: an application of the theory of planned behavior. *Leisure Sciences* 13, 185–204.

Ajzen, I. and Fishbein, M. (1972) Attitudes and normative beliefs as factors influencing behavioral intentions. *Journal of Personality and Social Psychology* 21, 1–9.

Ajzen, I. and Madden, T.J. (1986) Prediction of goal-directed behavior: attitudes, intentions and perceived behavioral control. *Journal of Experimental Social Psychology* 22, 453–474.

Albert, H. (1957) Theorie und prognose in den sozialwissenschaften. Reprinted in: Topitsch, E. (ed.) *Logik der Sozialwissenschaften*. Kiepenheuer Witsch, Köln, pp. 126–143.

Alldredge, R. (1973) Some capacity theory for parks and recreation areas. *Trends* 10, 20–29.

Allen, G.M. and Gould, E.M. Jr. (1986) Complexity, wickedness and public forests. *Journal of Forestry* 84(4), 20–24.

Allen, L., Harwell, R., Stevens, B. and Paisley, K. (1998a) *Benefits-based Management of Recreation Services*. National Recreation and Park Association, Ashburn, Virginia.

Allen, L., Stevens, B., Harwell, R., Paisley, K. and Less, M. (1998b) *Benefits-based Management Demonstration Project Technical Report*. Clemson University, Clemson.

Allen, L.R. (1991) Benefits of leisure services to community satisfaction. In: Driver, B.L., Brown, P.J. and Peterson, G.L. (eds) *Benefits of Leisure*. Venture Publishing, State College, Pennsylvania, pp. 331–350.

Allen, L.R. (1996) Benefits-based management of recreation services. *Parks and Recreation* 31(3), 64–76.

Allin, C.W. (1982) *The Politics of Wilderness Preservation*. Greenwood Press, Westport, Connecticut.

American Association of University Women (1991) *Shortchanging Girls, Shortchanging America: Executive Summary*. AAUW, Washington, DC.

American Forestry Association (1980) *Key to the Future: Renewable Natural Resources. Report on the 1980 National Conference on Renewable Natural Resources*. American Forestry Association, Washington, DC.

Americans Facing More Problems Balancing W/F, New Study to Show (1998) *The National Report on Work & Family* 11(4), 39.

Anderson, D. and Brown, P. (1984) The displacement process in recreation. *Journal of Leisure Research* 16, 61–73.

Anderson, D. and Schneider, I. (1993) Using the Delphi Process to identify significant recreation research-based innovations. *Journal of Park and Recreation Administration* 11, 25–36.

Anderson, D., Leatherberry, E. and Lime, D. (1978) *An Annotated Bibliography on River Recreation.* USDA Forest Service General Technical Report NC-41.

Anderson, D., Lime, D. and Morrissey, W. (1995) A continuing education program to upgrade knowledge and skill levels of professional natural resources staff. *Journal of Natural Resources and Life Sciences Education* 24(2), 125–132.

Anderson, D., Lime, D. and Wang, T. (1998) *Maintaining the Quality of Park Resources and Visitor Experiences: A Handbook for Managers.* St Paul, Minnesota, University of Minnesota Cooperative Park Studies Unit.

Anderson, D.H. and Stein, T.V. (1997) *Community Benefits Study: Itasca and Tettegouche State Parks.* (Technical Report) University of Minnesota, Department of Forest Resources, St Paul, Minnesota.

Andersson, A. (1987) *Culture, Creativity and Economic Development in a Regional Context.* Council of Europe Press, Strasbourg.

Andestad, G. (1994) Linking pleasure with health: the development of health resorts as venues for health promotion. Unpublished Masters Thesis, School of Community and Regional Planning, University of British Columbia, Vancouver.

Apgar, M., IV (1998) The alternative workplace: changing where and how people work. *Harvard Business Review* 76(3), 121–137.

Archdale, G., Stanton, R. and Jones, G. (1992) *Destination Databases: Issues and Priorities.* Pacific Asia Travel Association, San Francisco.

Archer, B. and Fletcher, J.E. (1988) The tourist multiplier. *TJoros* 7, 6–10.

Archer, B. and Fletcher, J. (1996) The economic impact of tourism in the Seychelles. *Annals of Tourism Research* 23, 32–47.

Archer, B.H. (1977) *Tourism Multipliers: the State-of-the-Art.* University of Wales Press, Cardiff.

Archer, B.H. (1978) The uses and abuses of multipliers. In: Gearing, C., Swart, W. and Var, T. (eds) *Planning for Tourism Development*, Praeger, New York, pp. 115–131.

Aristotle *c.* 320 BC (1955) The Nichomachean Ethics. In: Bronstein, D.J., Krikorian, Y.H. and Wiener, P.P. (eds) *Basic Problems of Philosophy.* Prentice-Hall, Englewood Cliffs, New Jersey.

Arnold, M.L. and Shinew, K.J. (1998) The role of gender, race, and income on park use constraints. *Journal of Park and Recreation Administration* 16.

Arnstein, S.R. (1977) A ladder of citizen participation. In: Marshall, P. (ed.) *Citizen Participation Certification for Community Development.* National Association of Housing and Redevelopment Officials, Washington, DC, pp. 40–49.

Ashor, J., McCool, S. and Stokes, G. (1986) Improving wilderness planning efforts: application of the transactive planning approach. In: *Proceedings – National Wilderness Research Conference: Current Research.* USDA Forest Service General Technical Report INT-212, 424–431.

Augustyn, M. (1998) National Strategies for Rural Tourism Development and Sustainability. *Journal of Sustainable Tourism* 6(3), 191–209.

Baghwati, J. (1998) The capital myth. *Foreign Affairs* 77(33), 7ff.

Bailey, S.M. (1993) The current status of gender equity research in American schools. *Educational Psychologist* 28(4), 321–339.

Barham, L.J., Gottlieb, B.H. and Kelloway, E.K. (1998) Variables affecting Managers' willingness to grant alternative work arrangements. *The Journal of Social Psychology* 138(3), 291–303.

Barr, R.B. and Tagg, J. (1995) From teaching to learning: a new paradigm for undergraduate education. *Change* November/December, 13–25.

Barro, R.J. and Sala-i-Martin, X. (1995) *Economic Growth.* McGraw-Hill, New York.

Barry, D.J. (1998) Cape Cod National Seashore, off road vehicle use. *Federal Register* 63, 9143–9149.

Bass, J.M., Ewert, A. and Chavez, D.J. (1993) Influence of ethnicity on recreational and natural environment use patterns: managing recreation sites for ethnic and racial diversity. *Environmental Management* 17, 523–529.

Bates, G. (1935) The vegetation of footpaths, sidewalks, cart-tracks, and gateways. *Journal of Ecology* 23, 470–487.

Baum, T. (1994) The development and implementation of national tourism policies. *Tourism Management* 15(3), 185–192.

Baumol, W.J. (1991) *Productivity and American Leadership. The Long View.* The MIT Press, Cambridge, Massachusetts.

Bayfield, N.G. and Lloyd, R.J. (1973) An approach to assessing the impact of use on a long distance footpath – the Pennine Way. *Recreation News Supplement* 8, 11–17.

Becker, G.S. (1965) A theory of the allocation of time. *The Economic Journal LXXV* (299), 493–517.

Becker, H.A. (1995) Generations and value change. In: de Moor, R. (ed.) *Values in Western Societies.* Tilburg University Press, Le Tilburg.

Beeler, C.S. (1999) Local government recreation and park agencies. In: Cordell, H.K. (ed.) *Outdoor Recreation in American Life: a National Assessment of Demand and Supply Trends.* Sagamore Publishing, Champaign, Illinois, pp. 124–130.

Bendavid-Val, A. (1983) *Regional and Local Economic Analysis for Practitioners.* Praeger, New York.

Bengston, D. and Xu, Z. (1993) Impact of research and technical change in wildland recreation: Evaluation of issues and approaches. *Leisure Sciences* 15, 251–272.

Berger, B. (1962) The sociology of leisure: some suggestions. *Industrial Relations* 1, 31–45.

Bergstrom, A., Clark, R., Hogue, T., Iyechad, T., Miller, J., Mullen, S., Perkins, D., Rowe, E., Russell, J., Simon-Brown, V., Slinksi, M., Snider, B.A. and Thurston, F. (1995) *Collaboration Framework: Addressing Community Capacity.* National Network for Collaboration, http://www.cyfernet.org/nnco/framework.html

Bergstrom, J.C. and Cordell, H.K. (1991) An analysis of the demand for and value of outdoor recreation in the United States. *Journal of Leisure Research* 23(1), 67–86.

Berkowitz, E., Kerin, R., Rudelius, W. and Crane, F. (1991) *Marketing: First Canadian Edition.* Irwin, Homewood, Illinois.

Bernard, M. (1987) Leisure-rich and leisure-poor: leisure life styles among young adults. *Leisure Sciences* 10, 131–49.

Berry, L. and Parasuraman, A. (1997) Listening to the customer: the concept of a service quality information system. *Sloan Management Review*, 39.

Betz, C.J. and Cordell, H.K. (1998) Outdoor recreation supply in the United States: a description of the resources, data, and other information sources. Unpublished report. USDA Forest Service, Southern Research Station, Outdoor Recreation and Wilderness Assessment Group, Athens, Georgia.

Betz, C.J., English, D.B.K. and Cordell, H.K. (1999) Outdoor recreation resources. In: Cordell, H.K. (ed.) *Outdoor Recreation in American Life: a National Assessment of Demand and Supply Trends.* Sagamore Publishing, Champaign, Illinois, pp. 39–182.

Bhutan Tourism Corporation (n.d.) *Bhutan. Land of the Thunder Dragon* (catalogue). Bhutan Tourism Corporation, Thimphu.

Bialeschki, M.D. (1992) 'We said, why not?' A historical perspective on women's outdoor pursuits. *Journal of Physical Education, Recreation, and Dance* 60(1), 52–55.

Bialeschki, M.D. and Walbert, L.K. (1998) You have to have some fun to go along with your work: the interplay of race, class, gender, and leisure in the industrial new south. *Journal of Leisure Research* 30.

Binswanger, H. and Ruttan, V. (1978) *Induced Innovation: Technology, Institutions and Development.* The Johns Hopkins University Press, Baltimore, Maryland.

Bishop, R.C. and Heberlein, T.A. (1979) Measuring values of extra-market goods: are indirect measures biased? *American Journal of Agricultural Economics* 61(December), 926–930.

Bishop, W. and Fulwiler, T. (1997) The braiding of classroom voices: learning to write by learning to learn. In: Campbell, W.E. and Smith, K.A. (eds) *New Paradigms for College Teaching.* Interaction Books, Edina, Minnesota, pp. 37–49.

Bitner, M.J., Booms, B.H. and Tetreault, M.S. (1996) The service encounter: diagnosing favorable and unfavorable incidents. In: Rust, R.T., Zahorik, A.J. and Keiningham, T.K. (eds) *Readings in Service Marketing*, Harper Collins, New York, pp. 263–282.

Blahna, D. (1992) Comparing the preferences of black, Asian, Hispanic, and white fishermen at Moraine Hills State Park, Illinois. In: *Proceedings of the Symposium on Social Aspects and Recreation Research.* USDA Forest Service General Technical Report PSW-132, 42–44.

Blahna, D. and Yonts-Shepard, S. (1989) Public involvement in resource planning: toward bridging the gap between policy and implementation. *Society and Natural Resources* 2, 209–221.

Blake, R.R., Shepard, H.A. and Mouton, J.S. (1964) *Managing Intergroup Conflict in Industry.* Gulf, Houston, Texas.

Blamey, R.K. (1995) Citizens, consumers, and contingent valuation: an investigation into respondent behavior. PhD Dissertation. The Australian National University, Canberra, Australia.

Blank, U. (1989) *The Community Tourism Industry Imperative: The Necessity, The Opportunities, Its Potential*, Venture Publishing, State College, Pennsylvania.

Block, P. (1993) *Stewardship – Choosing Service Over Self-interest.* Berrett-Koehler Publishers, San Francisco, California.

Blum, R.W. (1991) Global trends in adolescent health. *The Journal of the American Medical Association* 265(20), 2711–2720.

Bockstael, N. and McConnel, K. (1981) Theory and estimation of the household production function for wildlife recreation. *Journal of Environmental Economics and Management* (September), 199–214.

Bockstael, N. and McConnel, K. (1983) Welfare measurement in the household production framework. *American Economic Review* 73(4), 806–814.

Bollman, R.D. and Bryden, J.M. (eds) (1997) *Rural Employment: an International Perspective*. CAB International, Wallingford, UK.

Bolton, R. (1991) Regional econometric models. In: Bodkin, R.G., Klein, L.R. and Marwah, K. (eds) *A History of Macroeconometric Model-building*. Edward Elgar, Northampton, Massachusetts, pp. 451–477.

Bonink, C. (1992) Cultural Tourism Development and Government Policy. MA Dissertation, Rijksuniversiteit Utrecht.

Boo, E. (1990) *Ecotourism: The Potentials and the Pitfalls*. World Wildlife Fund, Washington, DC.

Boorstin, D. (1987) *The Image. A Guide to Pseudo Events in America*. 25th anniversary edition. Atheneum, New York.

Bord Failte (1998) *Ireland. Live a Different Life* (catalogue). Irish Tourist Board, Dublin.

Borrie, W.T. and Roggenbuck, J.W. (1995) Community based research of an urban recreation application of benefits-based Management. In: Chavez, D.J. (tech. coord.) *Proceedings of the Second Symposium on Social Aspects of Recreation Research*, February 23–25, 1994, San Diego, California. PSW-GTR-156, USDA Forest Service, Pacific Southwest Research Station, pp. 159–163.

Borrie, W.T., McCool, S.F. and Stankey, G.H. (1998) Protected area planning principles and strategies. In: Lindberg, K., Wood, M.E. and Engeldrum, D. (eds) *Ecotourism: a Guide for Planners and Managers*. The Ecotourism Society, North Bennington, Vermont, 2, 133–154.

Bos, H. (1994) The importance of mega-events in the development of tourism demand. *Festival Management and Event Tourism*, 2, 55–58.

Bowker, J.M. and Leeworthy, V.R. (1998) Accounting for ethnicity in recreation demand: a flexible count data approach. *Journal of Leisure Research* 30.

Bowles, R.T. (1981) *Social Impact Assessment in Small Communities: an Integrative Review of Selected Literature*. Butterworth & Co., Toronto, Canada.

Boyer, E.L. (1987) *College: the Undergraduate Experience in America*. Harper and Row, New York.

Branch, K., Hooper, D.A., Thompson, J. and Creighton, J. (1984) *Guide to Social Assessment: a Framework for Assessing Social Change*. Westview Press, Boulder, Colorado.

Brass, J.L. (ed.) (1995) *Community Tourism Assessment Handbook*. Oregon State University, Western Rural Development Center, Corvallis, Oregon.

Braun, B.M. (1992) The economic contribution of conventions: the case of Orlando, Florida. *Journal of Travel Research* 30(3), 32–37.

Bray, R. (1996) Market segments: the package holiday market in Europe. *Travel and Tourism Analyst* 4, 54–60.

Briassoulis, H. (1991) Methodological issues: tourism input-output analysis. *Annals of Tourism Research* 18, 485–495.

Britton, S. (1991) Tourism, capital and place: towards a critical geography of tourism. *Environment and Planning D: Society and Space* 9, 451–478.

Brock, B.J. (1994) Recreation programming tips for the '90s family: demographics and discoveries. *Journal of Physical Education, Recreation, and Dance* 65(6), 64–68.

Brown, F. (1998) *Tourism Reassessed. Blight or Blessing?* Butterworth-Heinemann, Oxford.

Brown, G. and Harris, C.C. (1992) The U.S. Forest Service: toward the new resource management paradigm? *Society and Natural Resources* 5, 231–245.

Brown, L. and Flavin, C. (1999) *A New Economy for a New Century, in State of the World 1999*. W.W. Norton & Company, New York.

Brown, P., Driver, B. and McConnell, C. (1978) The opportunity spectrum concept in outdoor recreation supply inventories: Background and application. In: *Proceedings of the Integrated Renewable Resource Inventories Workshop*. USDA Forest Service General Technical Report RM-55, 73–84.

Brown, P.J. (1984) Benefits of outdoor recreation and some ideas for valuing recreation opportunities. In: Peterson, G.L. and Randall, A. (eds) *Valuation of Wildland Resource Benefits*. Westview Press, Boulder, Colorado, pp. 209–220.

Brown, P.J. and Haas, G.E. (1980) Wilderness recreation experiences: the Rawah case. *Journal of Leisure Research* 3, 229–241.

Brown, T., Churchill, G. and Peter, J. (1993) Improving the measurement of service quality. *Journal of Retailing* 69(1), 127–139.

Brown, T.L. (1995) Wildlife recreation trends in the U.S. and Canada. In: *Proceedings, Fourth International Outdoor Recreation and Tourism Trends Symposium and the 1995 National Recreation Resources Planning Conference*. University of Minnesota, St Paul, Minnesota, pp. 527–530.

Brown, T.L. and Connelly, N.A. (1994) Predicting demand for big game and small game hunting licenses: the New York experience. *Wildlife Society Bulletin* 22, 172–178.

Brown, T.L., Decker, D.J. and Enck, J.W. (1995) *Preliminary Insights about the Sociocultural Importance of Hunting and Trapping.* HDRU Series 95-2. Human Dimensions Research Unit, Department of Natural Resources, Cornell University, Ithaca, New York.

Brown, V. (1996) Heritage, tourism and rural regeneration: the Heritage Regions Programme in Canada. *Journal of Sustainable Tourism* 4(3), 174–182.

Brown, W., Singh, A. and Castle, E. (1964) *An Economic Evaluation of Oregon Salmon and Steelhead Sport Fisheries.* Technical Bulletin 78. Oregon Agricultural Experiment Station, Corvallis, Oregon.

Brown, W.B. and Nawas, F. (1973) Impact of aggregation on the estimation of outdoor recreation demand functions. *American Journal of Agricultural Economics* 55, 246–249.

Brundtland, C.H. (Chair), United Nations Commission on Environment and Development (1987) *Our Common Future*, Oxford University Press, Oxford.

Bruns, D. (1993) Using social information for park and recreation management. In: Anderson, D.H., Lime, D.W. and Morrissey, W. (coord.) *Outdoor Recreation Management in the 90s.* Continuing education shortcourse conducted at the University of Minnesota, St Paul, Minnesota.

Bruns, D. (1995) New paradigms for outdoor recreation and tourism management in government. In: Thompson, J.L., Lime, D.W., Gartner, B. and Sames, W.M. (compilers) *Proceedings of the Fourth International Outdoor Recreation and Tourism Trends Symposium and the 1995 National Recreation Resources Planning Conference*, University of Minnesota Press, St Paul, Minnesota, pp. 425–430.

Bruns, D., Driver, B.L., Lee, M.E., Anderson, D.H. and Brown, P.J. (1994) Pilot tests for implementing benefits-based management. Paper presented at The Fifth International Symposium on Society and Resource Management, Fort Collins, Colorado.

Brunson, M. (1992) Professional bias, public perspectives and communication pitfalls for natural resource managers. *Rangelands* 14(5), 292–295.

Brunson, M. and Shelby, B. (1993) Recreation substitutability: a research agenda. *Leisure Sciences* 15, 67–74.

Brussard, P.F., Reed, J.M. and Tracy, C.R. (1998) Ecosystem management: what is it really? *Landscape and Urban Planning* 40, 9–20.

Bryan, H. (1977) Leisure value systems and recreational specialization: the case of trout fishermen. *Journal of Leisure Research* 9, 174–187.

Buhalis, D. (1993) Regional Integrated Computer Information Reservation Management Systems as a strategic tool for the small and medium tourism enterprises. *Tourism Management* 14, 5, 366–378.

Buhalis, D. (1994) Information and telecommunications technologies as a strategic tool for small and medium tourism enterprises in the contemporary business environment. In: Seaton, A. *et al.* (eds) *Tourism – The State of the Art*. John Wiley and Sons, Chichester, pp. 254–275.

Buhalis, D. (1995) The impact of information telecommunication technologies on tourism distribution channels: implications for the small and medium sized tourism enterprises' strategic Management and Marketing. University of Surrey PhD Thesis, Department of Management Studies, Guildford.

Buhalis, D. (1997) Information technologies as a strategic tool for economic, cultural and environmental benefits enhancement of tourism at destination regions. *Progress in Tourism and Hospitality Research* 3(1), 71–93.

Buhalis, D. (1998a) Strategic use of information technologies in the tourism industry. *Tourism Management* 19(3), 409–423.

Buhalis, D. (1998b) The future of tourism: Information technology. In: Cooper, C. *et al.* (eds) *Tourism: Principles and Practices.* Addison Wesley Longman, Harlow, UK 423–465.

Buhalis, D. (2000) Marketing the competitive destination of the future. *Tourism Management* 21(1), 97–116.

Buhalis, D. and Cooper, C. (1998) Competition vs co-operation: Small and medium sized tourism enterprises at the destination. In: Laws, E. *et al.* (eds) *Embracing and Managing Change in Tourism.* Routledge, London, 324–347.

Buhalis, D. and Main, H. (1998) Information technology in small and medium hospitality enterprises: strategic analysis and critical factors. *International Journal of Contemporary Hospitality Management* 10(5), 198–202.

Buhalis, D. and Schertler, W. (eds) (1999) *Information and Communication Technologies in Tourism.* Springer-Verlag, Wien.

Buhalis, D., Tjoa, A.M. and Jafari, J. (eds) (1998) *Information and Communication Technologies in Tourism.* Springer–Verlag, Wien.

Bulgaria Ministry of Trade and Tourism (n.d.) *Culture Bulgaria. Just Unique* (catalogue). Bulgaria Ministry of Trade and Tourism, Sofia.

Bulmer-Thomas, V. (1982) *Input-output Analysis in Developing Countries: Source, Methods and Applications*. John Wiley and Sons, New York.

Bumpass, L.L., Raley, R.K. and Sweet, J.A. (1995, August) The changing character of stepfamilies: implications of cohabitation and nonmarital childbearing. *Demography* 32(3), 425–437.

Burdge, R. (1974) The state of leisure research. *Journal of Leisure Research* 6, 312–319.

Burdge, R. (1983) Making leisure and recreation research a scholarly topic: views of a journal editor, 1972–1982. *Leisure Sciences* 6, 99–126.

Burdge, R., Buchanan, T. and Christensen, J. (1981) A critical assessment of the state of outdoor recreation research. In: *Outdoor Recreation Planning, Perspectives, and Research*. Kendall-Hunt, Dubuque, Iowa, pp. 3–10.

Bureau of Land Management (1987) *Final Environmental Impact Statement and Wilderness Recommendations for the Shoshone-Eureka Resource Area*. US Department of the Interior, Battle Mountain District, Nevada.

Burns, P. and Holden, A. (1995) *Tourism. A New Perspective*. Prentice Hall, London.

Burt, B. (1995) *Fodor's Healthy Escapes*. Fodor's Travel Publications, New York.

Burton, H. (1971) *The Ski Troops*. Simon and Shuster, New York.

Burton, J.W. (1990) *Conflict: Resolution and Prevention*. St Martin's, New York.

Bushnell, R.C. and Hyle, M. (1985) Computerized models for assessing the economic impact of recreation and tourism. In: Probst, D.B. (ed.) *Assessing the Economic Impacts of Recreation and Tourism*. USDA Southeastern Forest Experiment Station, Asheville, North Carolina, pp. 46–51.

Busser, J.A., Hyams, A.L. and Carruthers, C.P. (1996) Differences in adolescent activity participation by gender, grade, and ethnicity. *Journal of Park and Recreation Administration* 14.

Butler, R. (1993) Tourism – an evolutionary perspective. In: Nelson, J., Butler, R. and Wall, G. (eds) *Tourism and Sustainable Development*. University of Waterloo Press, Waterloo, pp. 27–41.

Butler, R., Hall, M.C. and Jenkins, J. (eds) (1998) *Tourism and Recreation in Rural Areas*. John Wiley and Sons, Chichester.

Butler, R.W. (1980) The concept of a tourist area cycle of evolution: implications for management of resources. *Canadian Geographer* 24(1), 5–12.

Bywater, M. (1990) Spas and health resorts in the EC. *EIU Travel and Tourism Analyst* 6, 52–67.

Bywater, M. (1993) The market for cultural tourism in Europe. *Travel and Tourism Analyst* 6, 30–46.

Bywater, M. (1998) Who owns whom in the European travel industry. *Travel and Tourism Analyst* 3, 41–59.

Cabot, A., Thompson, W. and Tottenham, A. (eds) (1993) *International Casino Law*, 2nd edn. Institute for the Study of Gambling and Commercial Gaming, University of Nevada, Reno.

Caff, D.S. and Williams, D.R. (1993) Understanding the role of ethnicity in outdoor recreation experience. *Journal of Leisure Research* 25.

Cairncross, A. (1969) Economic forecasting. *Economic Journal* 79, 797–812.

Calcote, S., Friedman, L., Gaiptman, S. and Roberts, R. (1994) Benefits and challenges of tourism (ch. 2) In: Calcote, S., Friedman, L., Gaiptman, S. and Roberts, R. (eds) *Rural Tourism Handbook*. US Travel and Tourism Administration, Department of Commerce, Washington, DC, pp. 7–10.

Callicott, J.B. and Mumford, K. (1997) Ecological sustainability as a conservation concept. *Conservation Biology* 11(1), 32–40.

Carr, D.S. and Williams, D.R. (1993) Understanding the role of ethnicity in outdoor recreation experiences. *Journal of Leisure Research* 25(1), 22–38.

Cameron, T. (1992) Combining contingent valuation and travel cost data for the valuation of nonmarket goods. *Land Economics* 68, 302–317.

Campa, H., Millenbah, K.F. and Ferreri, C.P. (1996) Lessons learned from fisheries and wildlife Management: using constructive controversies in the classroom. In: Propst, D. (ed.) *Proceedings: First Biennial Conference on University Education in Natural Resources*. College of Agricultural Sciences, Pennsylvania State University, University Park, Pennsylvania, pp. 235–244.

Campbell, C. (1994) *Gambling in Canada: the Bottom Line*. School of Criminology, Simon Fraser University, Vancouver.

Campbell, W.E. and Smith, K.A. (eds) (1997) *New Paradigms for College Teaching*. Interaction Books, Edina, Minnesota.

Canadian Parks Partnership (1994) *Biennial Report*. Calgary, Alberta.

Canadian Parks and Recreation Federation (1997) *The Benefits Catalogue*. Canadian Parks and Recreation Association, Gloucester, Ontario.

Cardozo, C. (1992) Mind spas. *Harper's Bazaar* 125(3362), 140–145.

Carnegie Council on Adolescent Development (1992) *A Matter of Time: Risk and Opportunities in the Nonschool Hours*. Carnegie Corporation of New York, New York.

Carroll, M.S. (1988) A tale of two rivers: comparing NPS–local interactions in two areas. *Society and Natural Resources* 1(4), 317–333.

Cathelat, B. (1985) *Styles de vie*. Vols 1 & 2. Editions d'organisation, Paris.

Catton, W., Jr (1971) The wildland recreation boom and sociology. *Pacific Sociological Review* 14, 330–357.

Čavlek, N. (1998) *Turoperatori i Svjetski Turizam*. Golden Marketing, Zagreb, pp. 188–193.

Čavlek, N. (1999) *Tour Operators and International Tourism a translation from Turoperatori I Sujetski Turizam*, 1998. Golden Marketing, Zagreb.

Cesario, F.J. and Knetsch, J.L. (1976) A recreation site demand and benefit estimation model. *Regional Studies* 10(March), 97–104.

CFLI (Canadian Fitness and Lifestyle Institute) (1994a) *Health Promotion at Work: Results of the 1992 National Workplace Survey*. Canadian Fitness and Lifestyle Institute, Ottawa.

CFLI (Canadian Fitness and Lifestyle Institute) (1994b) *Active Living in the Workplace: Results of the 1992 National Workplace Survey*. Canadian Fitness and Lifestyle Institute, Ottawa.

Chalmers, J. (1987) *Wish You Were Here? 50 of the Best Holidays*. Queen Anne Press, London.

Chappelle, D.F. (1985) Strategies for developing multipliers useful in assessing economic impacts of recreation and tourism. In: Probst, D.B. (ed.) *Assessing the Economic Impacts of Recreation and Tourism*. USDA Southeastern Forest Experiment Station, Asheville, North Carolina. pp. 1–6.

Charney, A. and Leones, J. (1997) A structural flaw in IMPLAN's induced effects identified through multiplier decomposition. *Journal of Regional Science* 37, 1–15.

Chavez, D. (1996a) Mountain biking: direct, indirect, and bridge building management styles. *Journal of Park and Recreation Administration* 14, 21–35.

Chavez, D. (1996b) *Mountain Biking: Issues and Actions for USDA Forest Service Managers*. USDA Forest Service Research Paper PSW-226.

Chavez, D., Winter, P. and Baas, J. (1993) Recreational mountain biking: a management perspective. *Journal of Park and Recreation Administration* 11, 29–36.

Checkland, P. and Scholes, J. (1990) *Soft Systems Methodology in Action*. John Wiley and Sons, Chichester.

Cheng, A., White, T., Hacker, J. and Ellefson, P. (1993) Managing public forests in a shared-power world: The integration of conflict Management principles into USDA-Forest Service planning and Management. Minnesota Agricultural Experimentation Station Paper 20, 820. St Paul, Minnesota.

Cherlin, A.J. and Furstenberg, F.F. (1994) Stepfamilies in the United States: a reconsideration. *Annual Review of Sociology* 20, 359–382.

Choi, K.-S. (1998) Development situation and policy programs for the rural tourism in Korea. In: *Proceedings of the International Seminar on Rural Tourism*. Korean Academy of Tourism Agriculture, Choonchun, Korea.

Christiansen, E. (1998) The United States 1997 gross annual wager. Supplement to *International Gaming and Wagering Business Magazine*, August.

Christiansen, E. and Brinkerhof-Jacobs, J. (1997) Gambling and entertainment. In: Eadington, W.R. and Cornelius, J.A. (eds) *Gambling: Public Policies and the Social Sciences*. Institute for the Study of Gambling and Commercial Gaming, University of Nevada, Reno, pp. 11–48.

Cimprich, B. (1992) A theoretical perspective on attention and patient education. *Advances in Nursing Science* 14(3), 39–51.

Clark, C. (1999) *Changes in Leisure Time: the Impact on Tourism*. World Tourism Organization, Madrid.

Clark, R. and Stankey, G. (1979) *The Recreation Opportunity Spectrum: A Framework for Planning, Management, and Research*. USDA Forest Service Research Paper PNW-98.

Clark, R.N., Stankey, G.S. and Kruger, L.E. (1999) From new perspective to ecosystem Management: a social science perspective on forest Management. In: Aley, J., Burch, W.R., Conover, B. and Field, D. (eds) *Ecosystem Management: Adaptive Strategies for Natural Resources Organizations in the 21st Century*. Taylor & Francis, Philadelphia, Pennsylvania, pp. 73–84.

Clawson, M. (1959a) The crisis in outdoor recreation. *American Forests* 65, 22–31, 40–41.

Clawson, M. (1959b) *Methods of Measuring the Demand for and Value of Outdoor Recreation*. Resources for the Future, Washington, DC.

Clawson, M. (1983) *The Federal Lands Revisited*. Resources for the Future, Washington, DC.

Clawson, M. and Knetsch, J. (1963) Outdoor recreation research: some concepts and suggested areas of study. *Natural Resource Journal* 3, 250–275.

Clawson, M. and Knetsch, J.L. (1966) *The Economics of Outdoor Recreation*. The Johns Hopkins University Press, Baltimore, Maryland.

Cleary, P. and Edgman-Levitan, S. (1997) Health care quality: incorporating consumer perspectives. *Journal of the American Medical Association* 278, 1608–1612.

Cline, R. (1997) Investing in technology. *Lodging Hospitality* 2, 45–47.

Cohen, E. (1972) Toward a sociology of international tourism. *Social Research* 39, 164–182.

Cohen, E. (1978) The impact of tourism on the physical environment. *Annals of Tourism Research* 2, 215–237.

Cohen, E. (1979) A phenomenology of tourist experiences. *Sociology* 13, 179–201.

Cohen, E. (1984) The sociology of tourism: approaches, issues, and findings. *Annual Review of Sociology* 10, 373–392.

Cohen, E. (1988) Authenticity and commoditization in tourism. *Annals of Tourism Research* 15, 467–486.

Cole, D.N. (1983a) *Assessing and Monitoring Backcountry Trail Conditions.* Research Paper INT-303. USDA Forest Service, Intermountain Research Station, Ogden, Utah.

Cole, D.N. (1983b) *Monitoring the Condition of Wilderness Campsites.* Research Paper INT-302. USDA Forest Service, Intermountain Research Station, Ogden, Utah.

Cole, D.N. (1989a) *Wilderness Campsite Monitoring Methods: a Sourcebook.* General Technical Report INT-259. USDA Forest Service, Intermountain Research Station, Ogden, Utah.

Cole, D.N. (1989b) *Low-impact Recreational Practices for Wilderness and Backcountry.* General Technical Report INT-265. USDA Forest Service, Intermountain Research Station, Ogden, Utah.

Cole, D.N. (1993) *Campsites in Three Western Wildernesses: Proliferation and Changes in Condition over 12 to 16 Years.* Research Paper INT-463. USDA Forest Service, Intermountain Research Station, Ogden, Utah.

Cole, D.N. (1994) Backcountry impact management: lessons from research. *Trends* 31(3), 10–14.

Cole, D.N. (1995) Wilderness management principles: science, logical thinking or personal opinion? *Trends* 32(1), 6–9.

Cole, D.N. (1997) Recreation management priorities are misplaced – allocate more resources to low-use wilderness. *International Journal of Wilderness* 3(4), 4–8.

Cole, D.N. and Hall, T.E. (1992) *Trends in Campsite Condition: Eagle Cap Wilderness, Bob Marshall Wilderness, and Grand Canyon National Park.* Research Paper INT-453. USDA Forest Service, Intermountain Research Station, Ogden, Utah.

Cole, D.N. and Stankey, G.H. (1997) Historical development of Limits of Acceptable Change: conceptual clarifications and possible extensions. In: *Limits of Acceptable Change and Related Planning Processes: Progress and Future Directions,* USDA Forest Service, Missoula, Montana.

Cole, D.N., Petersen, M.E. and Lucas, R.C. (1987) *Managing Wilderness Recreation Use: Common Problems and Potential Solutions.* General Technical Report INT-230. USDA Forest Service, Intermountain Research Station, Ogden, Utah.

Cole, D.N., Watson, A.E. and Roggenbuck, J.W. (1995) *Trends in Wilderness Visitors and Visits: Boundary Waters Canoe Area, Shining Rock, and Desolation Wildernesses.* Research Paper INT-483. USDA Forest Service, Intermountain Research Station, Ogden, Utah.

Coleman, R.A. (1977) Simple techniques for monitoring footpath erosion in mountain areas of northwest England. *Environmental Conservation* 4, 145–148.

Colfer, J.P. and Colfer, A.M. (1978) Inside Bushler Bay: lifeways in counterpoint. *Rural Sociology* 43(2), 204–220.

Commonwealth Department of Tourism (1994) *Rural Tourism Strategy.* CDT, Canberra.

Cooper, C. (1992) The life cycle concept and strategic planning for coastal resorts. *Built Environment* 18, 57–66.

Cooper, C. and Jackson, S. (1989) Destination life cycle: the Isle of Man case study. *Annals of Tourism Research* 15, 377–398.

Cordell, H.K. (1999) *Outdoor Recreation in American Life: a National Assessment of Demand and Supply Trends.* Sagamore Publishing, Champaign, Illinois.

Cordell, H.K., Bergstrom, J.C., Hartmann, L.A. and English, D.B.K. (1990) *An Analysis of the Outdoor Recreation and Wilderness Situation in the United States: 1989–2040.* GTR RM-189. USDA Forest Service, Rocky Mountain Forest and Range Experiment Station, Fort Collins, Colorado.

Cordell, H.K., Bergstrom, J.C., Teasley, R.J. and Maetzold, J.A. (1998) Trends in outdoor recreation and implications for private land management in the East. In: Keys, J.S., Goff, G.R., Smallidge, P.J., Grafton, W.N. and Parkhurst, J.A. (eds) *Proceedings, Natural Resources Income Opportunities for Private Lands.* University of Maryland Cooperative Extension Service, College Park, Maryland, pp. 4–10.

Cordell, H.K., Lewis, B. and McDonald, B.L. (1995) Long-term outdoor recreation participation trends. In: Thompson, J.L., Lime, D.W., Gartner, B. and Sames, W.M. (compilers) *Proceedings of the Fourth International Outdoor Recreation and Tourism Trends Symposium.* College of Natural Resources and Minnesota Extension Service, University of Minnesota, St Paul, Minnesota, pp. 35–38.

Cordell, H.K., McDonald, B.L., Lewis, B., Miles, M., Martin, J. and Bason, J. (1996) United States of America. In: Cushman, G., Veal, A.J. and Zuzanek, J. (eds) *World Leisure Participation: Free Time in the Global Village.* CAB International, Wallingford, UK.

Corfu Tourism Promotion Board (n.d.) *Corfu. Discover the Difference* (catalogue). Corfu Tourism Promotion Board, Corfu Town.

Cortese, C.F. and Jones, B. (1977) The sociological analysis of boom towns. *Western Sociological Review* 8(1), 76–90.

Cornwall, G. and Burns, B. (1992) The greening of Canada. In: Edwards, F. (ed.) *Environmental Auditing. The Challenge of the 1990s.* Banff Centre for Management, University of Calgary, Banff, pp. 1–6.

Craik, J. (1997) The culture of tourism. In: Rojek, C. and Urry, J. (eds) *Touring Cultures. Transformations of Travel and Theory.* Routledge, London, pp. 113–136.

Crandall, R. and Lewko, J. (1976) Leisure research, present and future: who, what, where. *Journal of Leisure Research* 8(3), 150–159.

Creighton, J.L. (1983) The use of value: public participation in the planning process. In: Creighton, J.L. (ed.) *Public Involvement and Social Impact Assessment.* Westview Press, Boulder, Colorado, pp.143–161.

Crick, M. (1994) *Resplendent Sites, Discordant Voices. Sri Lankans and International Tourism.* Harwood Academic Publishers, Chur.

Crispell, D. (1996, August) Family futures. *American Demographics* 18(8), 13–14.

Crompton, J.L. (1979) Motivations for pleasure vacation. *Annals of Tourism Research* 6, 408–424.

Crompton, J.L. (1995) Economic impact analysis of sports facilities and events: eleven sources of misapplication. *Journal of Sport Management* 9, 14–35.

Crompton, J.L. and McKay, S.L. (1994) Measuring the economic impact of festivals and events: some myths, misapplications and ethical dilemmas. *Festival Management and Event Tourism* 2, 33–43.

Crompton, J.L. and Witt, P.A. (1997) Repositioning: the key to building community support. *Parks and Recreation* 32(10), 80–90.

Crouch, G.I. (1994) The study of international tourism demand. A review of findings. *Journal of Travel Research* 33(1), 12–23.

Crouch, G.I. (1995) A meta-analysis of tourism demand. *Annals of Tourism Research* 22(1), 103–118.

Crouch, G.I. and Shaw, R.N. (1994) International tourism demand. A meta-analytical integration of research findings. In: Johnson, P. and Thomas, B. (eds) *Choice and Demand in Tourism.* Mansell Publishing Limited, London.

Dabholkar, D. (1994) Technology based service delivery: a classification scheme for developing marketing strategies. *Advances in Services Marketing and Management* 3, 241–272.

Dahl, A. (1996) Measuring the unmeasurable. *Our Planet* 8(1), 29–33.

Daigle, J. (1993) *Bibliography of Forest Service Recreation Research: 1983–1992.* USDA Forest Service General Technical Report NE-180, Northeastern Forest Experiment Station, Randor, Pennsylvania.

Dalton, D.R. and Mesch, D.J. (1990) The impact of flexible scheduling on employee attendance and turnover. *Administrative Science Quarterly* 35 (2), 370–388.

Dana, S. (1957) *Problem Analysis: Research in Forest Recreation.* US Department of Agriculture, Washington, DC.

Dann, G. (1977) Anomie, ego-enhancement and tourism. *Annals of Tourism Research* 4, 184–194.

Dann, G. (1988) Images of Cyprus projected by tour operators. *Problems of Tourism* XI (3), 43–70.

Dann, G. and Potter, R. (1994) Tourism and postmodernity in a Caribbean setting. *Cahiers du Tourisme,* serie C, no. 185.

Darden, W. and Darden, D. (1976) A study of vacation life styles. In: *Travel and Tourism Research Association, Proceedings of the 7th Annual Conference,* TTRA, Salt Lake City, Utah, pp. 231–236.

Dargitz, R.E. (1988) Angling activity of urban youth: factors associated with fishing in a metropolitan context. *Journal of Leisure Research* 20.

Darling, F.F. (1967) A wider environment of ecology and conservation. *Daedalus* 96(4), 1003–1019.

Davidson, R. and Maitland, R. (1997) *Tourism Destinations.* Hodder & Stoughton, London.

Davis, R.K. (1963) Recreation planning as an economic problem. *Natural Resources Journal* 3(2), 239–249.

de Cauter, L. (1995) *Archeologie Virginian de Kick.* Virginian Halewijck, Leuven.

Decker, D.J. and Connelly, N.A. (1990) The need for hunter education in deer management: insights from New York. *Wildlife Society Bulletin* 18, 447–452.

Decker, D.J., Brown, T.L., Driver, B.L. and Brown, P.J. (1987) Theoretical developments in assessing social Values of wildlife: Toward a comprehensive understanding of wildlife recreation. In: Decker, D.J. and Goff, G.R. (eds) *Valuing Wildlife: Economic and Social Perspectives.* Westview Press, Boulder, Colorado.

Deer and Deer Hunting (1998) *1998 Media Kit.* Krause Publications, Iola, Wisconsin.

de Kadt, E.J. (ed.) (1979) *Tourism: Passport to Development?* Oxford University Press, New York.

Dennis, S. (1988) Incorporating public opinion surveys in national forest land and resource planning. *Society and Natural Resources* 1, 309–316.

Denver Service Center (1993) *Special Report – VERP: a Process for Addressing Visitor Carrying Capacity in the National Park System.* National Park Service, Denver, Colorado.

Department for Culture, Media and Sport (1999) *Tomorrow's Tourism.* DCMS, London.

Department of Industry, Science and Tourism (1997) *Coastal Tourism. A Manual for Sustainable Development.* Department of Industry, Science and Tourism, Canberra.

de Tocqueville, A. (1945) *Democracy in America.* Knopf, New York. Phillips Bradley (translator).

DeVoto, B. (1953) Let's close the national parks. *Harpers* 207, 49–52.

Die Reiseanalyse RA 99 – Urlaub + Reisen, Erste Ergebnisse (1999) F.U.R. Forschungsgemeinschaft Urlaub und Reisen e.V., Hamburg, pp. 1–4.

Dietz, T. (1987) Theory and method in social impact assessment. *Sociological Inquiry* 57(1), 54–69.

Ding, P. and Pigram, J. (1995) Environmental audits: an emerging concept in sustainable tourism development. *Journal of Tourism Studies* 6(2), 2–11.

Ditton, R., Loomis, D. and Choi, S. (1992) Recreation specialization: re-conceptualization from a social worlds perspective. *Journal of Leisure Research* 24, 33–51.

Dixon, R. and Thirlwall, A.P. (1975) A model of regional growth differences along Kaldorian lines. *Oxford Economic Papers* 27, 201–214.

Doble, J. and Richardson, A. (1992) You don't have to be a rocket scientist … *Technology Review* 1, 51–54.

Dolnicar, S. (1997) *Urlaubserwartungen der Sommergäste in Österreich – Eine psychographische Taxonomieerstellung mittels neuronaler Netzwerkverfahren.* Service-Fachverlag, Vienna.

Dolnicar, S., Grabler, K. and Mazanec, J.A. (1999) A tale of three cities: perceptual charting for analysing destination images. In: Woodside, A.G., Crouch, G.I., Mazanec, J.A., Opperman, M. and Sakai, M.Y. (eds) *Consumer Psychology of Tourism, Hospitality, and Leisure.* CAB International, Wallingford, UK, pp. 39–62.

Domestic Policy Council Task Force on Outdoor Recreation Resources and Opportunities (1988) *Outdoor Recreation in a Nation of Communities: Action Plan for Americans Outdoors.* US Government Printing Office, Washington, DC.

Dortch, S. (1997) American weights in. *American Demographics.* June.

Douglass, R.W. (1999) History of outdoor recreation and nature-based tourism in the United States. In: Cordell, H.K. (ed.) *Outdoor Recreation in American Life: a National Assessment of Demand and Supply Trends.* Sagamore Publishing, Champaign, Illinois, pp. 15– 24.

Dovers, S.R. and Handmer, J.W. (1993) Contradictions in sustainability. *Environmental Conservation* 20(3), 217–222.

Driver, B. (1972) Potential contributions of psychology to recreation resources management. In: *Environment and the Social Sciences: Perspectives and Applications.* American Psychological Association, Washington, DC, pp. 233–48.

Driver, B. (1996) Benefits-driven management of natural areas. *Natural Areas Journal* 16, 94–99.

Driver, B., Brown, P., Stankey, G. and Gregoire, T. (1987) The ROS planning system: evolution, basic concepts, and research needed. *Leisure Sciences* 9, 201–212.

Driver, B.L. (1977) *Item Pool for Scales Designed to Quantify the Psychological Outcomes Desired and Expected from Recreation Participation.* USDA Forest Service Rocky Mountain Forest and Range Experiment Station, Fort Collins, Colorado.

Driver, B.L. (1992) The benefits of leisure. *Parks and Recreation*, November, 18–25, 75.

Driver, B.L. (1994) The benefits-based approach to amenity resource policy analysis and management. Unpublished paper.

Driver, B.L. (1997) The defining moment of benefits. *Parks and Recreation*, December, 38–40.

Driver, B.L. and Brown, P.J. (1975) A social-psychological definition of recreation demand, with implications for recreation resource planning. In: US Department of Interior, Bureau of Recreation and National Academy of Sciences (eds) *Assessing Demand for Outdoor Recreation*, US Government Printing Office, Washington, DC, pp. 64–88.

Driver, B.L. and Brown, P.J. (1978) The opportunity spectrum concept and behavioral information in outdoor recreation resource supply inventories: a rationale. In: Lund, C. *et al.* (eds), *Integrated Inventories of Renewable Natural Resources*: Proceedings of the January workshop at Tucson, Arizona, Publication RM – 55, USDA Forest Service, Rocky Mountain Forest and Experiment Station, Fort Collins, Colorado, pp. 24–31.

Driver, B.L. and Bruns, D. (1999) Concepts and use of the benefits approach to leisure. In: Burton, T.L. and Jackson, E.L. (eds) *Leisure Studies: Prospects for the Twenty-first Century.* Venture Publishing, State College, Pennsylvania.

Driver, B.L. and Tocher, R. (1983) Toward a behavioral interpretation of recreational engagements, with implications for planning. In: Driver, B.L. (ed.) *Elements of Outdoor Recreation Planning*, The University of Michigan Press, Ann Arbor, Michigan, pp. 9–31.

Driver, B.L., Nash, R. and Haas, G. (1985) Wilderness benefits: A state-of-knowledge review. In: Lucas, R. (ed.), *Proceedings – National Wilderness Research Conference: Issues, State-of-knowledge,*

Future Directions. GTR INT-220. USDA Forest Service, Intermountain Research Station, Ogden, Utah, pp. 294–319.

Driver, B.L., Brown, P.J. and Peterson, G.L. (eds) (1991a) *Benefits of Leisure.* Venture Publishing, State College, Pennsylvania.

Driver, B.L., Brown, P.J. and Peterson, G.L. (1991b) Research on leisure benefits: an introduction to this volume. In: Driver, B.L., Brown, P.J. and Peterson, G.L. (eds), *Benefits of Leisure*, Venture Publishing, State College, Pennsylvania, pp. 3–11.

Driver, B.L., Tinsley, H.E.A. and Manfredo, M. (1991c) Results from two inventories designed to assess the breadth of the perceived psychological benefits of leisure. In: Driver, B.L., Brown, P.J. and Peterson, G.L. (eds) *Benefits of Leisure.* Venture Publishing, State College, Pennsylvania, pp. 263–286.

Driver, B.L., Dustin, D., Baltic, T., Elsner, G. and Peterson, G.L. (1996) *Nature and the Human Spirit: Toward an Expanded Land Management Ethic.* Venture Publishing, State College, Pennsylvania.

Duane, T.P. (1997) Community participation in ecosystem management. *Ecology Law Quarterly* 24, 771–798.

Duda, M.D. (1993) *Factors Related to Hunting and Fishing Participation in the United States.* Responsive Management, Harrisonburg, Virginia.

Duda, M.D., Bissell, S.J. and Young, K.C. (1998) *Wildlife and the American Mind.* Responsive Management, Harrisonburg, Virginia.

Dudley, E. (1993) *The Critical Villager: Beyond Community Participation.* Routledge, New York.

Dunn, W. (1993) *The Baby Bust: a Generation Comes of Age.* Ithaca, New York, *American Demographics* Books.

Dustin, D.L. and Goodale, T.L. (1997) The social cost of individual 'benefits'. *Parks and Recreation* 32(7), 20–22.

Dwyer, J. (1993) Outdoor recreation participation: an update on blacks, whites, Hispanics, and Asians in Illinois. In: *Managing Urban and High-Use Recreation Settings.* USDA Forest Service General Technical Report NC-163, pp. 119–121.

Dwyer, J., Kelly, J. and Bowes, M. (1977) *Improved Procedures for Valuation of the Contribution of Recreation to National Economic Development.* Water Resources Centre Report no. 128. University of Illinois, Urbana-Champaign.

Dwyer, J.F. and Gobster, P.H. (1992) Recreation opportunity and cultural diversity. *Parks and Recreation* 27(9), 22–32, 128.

Dwyer, J.F. and Hutchison, R. (1990) Outdoor recreation participation and preferences by Black and White Chicago households. In: Vining, J. (ed.) *Social Science and Natural Resource Recreation Management.* Westview Press, Boulder, Colorado, pp. 49–67.

Dwyer, L. and Forsyth, P. (1998) Economic significance of cruise tourism. *Annals of Tourism Research* 25, 393–415.

Eadington, W.R. (1999) The economics of casinos. *Journal of Economic Perspectives* 13(3).

Eadington, W.R. and Redman, M. (1991) Economics and tourism. *Annals of Tourism Research* 18(1), 41–56.

Eagly, A.H. and Chaiken, S. (1993) *The Psychology of Attitudes.* Harcourt Brace College Publishers, Fort Worth, Texas.

Echelberger, H., Gilroy, D. and Moeller, G. (comp) (1983) *Recreation Research Publications Bibliography,* 1961–1982. USDA Forest Service, Washington, DC.

Eco, U. (1986) *Travels in Hyperreality. Essays.* Harcourt, Brace, Jovanovich, San Diego.

Edgell, D. (1990) *International Tourism Policy.* Virginian Nostrand Reinhold, New York.

Edgell, D. (1988) Viewpoints: Barriers to international travel. *Tourism Management* (March), 63–66.

Edlin, G. and Golanty, E. (1985) *Health and Wellness: a Holistic Approach,* 2nd edn. Jones and Bartlett, Boston.

Edwards, A. (1985) *International Tourism Forecasts to 1995.* Special report no. 188. The Economist Intelligence Unit, London.

Edwards, A. (1992) *International Tourism Forecasts to 2005.* Special report no. 2454. The Economist Intelligence Unit, London.

Egeland, B., Carlson, E. and Sroufe, L.A. (1993) Resilience as a process. *Development and Psychopathology* 5(4), 517–528.

Egypt National Council on Productivity and Economic Affairs (1997) *Report of Tourism Policy in Egypt.*

Eisenberg, D., Kessler, R.C., Foster, C., Norlock, F.E., Calkins, D.R. and Delbanco, T.L. (1993) Unconventional medicine in the United States: prevalence, costs and patterns. *New England Journal of Medicine* 328(4), 246–252.

Elliot, J. (1997) *Tourism, Politics and Public Sector Management.* Routledge, London.

Emmer, R., Tauck, C., Wilkinson, S. and Moore, R. (1993) Marketing hotels using Global Distribution Systems. *The Cornell Hotel Restaurant Administration Quarterly* 34(6), 80–89.

Employers must provide flexible schedules for dual-career couples (1998) *The National Report on Work and Family* 11(2), 17.

Enck, J. (1998) Human Dimensions Research Unit, Cornell University.

Enck, J.W. (1996) Deer-hunter identity spectrum: a human dimensions perspective for evaluating hunting policy. PhD dissertation, Cornell University, Ithaca, New York.

Endangered Species Act (1973) Act of December 28, 1973 (P.L. 93–205, 87 Stat. 884, as amended; 16 U.S.C. 1531–1536, 1538–1540).

Entergy Corporation (1992) *Community Development Handbook*. Entergy Corporation, New Orleans, Louisiana.

Enzensberger, H.M. (1996) Reminiszenzen an den Überfluss. Der alte und der neue Luxury. *Der Spiegel* 51(16.12.96), 108–118.

Erickson, P.A. (1994) *A Practical Guide to Environmental Impact Assessment*. Academic Press, San Diego, California.

Erkkila, D.L. and Penney, C. (1994) Tourism impact estimation methods. University of Minnesota Tourism Center, St Paul.

Espericuerta-Schultz, L., Crompton, J.L. and Witt, P.A. (1995) A national profile of the status of public recreation services for at-risk children and youth. *Journal of Park and Recreation Administration* 13(3), 1–26.

Estonian Tourist Board (n.d.) Estonia. *The Baltic Country with a Difference* (catalogue) Estonian Tourist Board, Tallinn, Estonia.

Evenson, R. (1999) Agricultural productivity growth. Paper presented at the Vernon W. Ruttan Recognition Symposium. Department of Applied Economics, University of Minnesota, St Paul, Minnesota.

Everhart, W. (1972) *The National Park Service*. Praeger, New York.

Faulkner, B. and Raybould, M. (1995) Monitoring visitor expenditures associated with attendance at sporting events: an experimental assessment of the diary and recall methods. *Festival Management and Event Tourism* 3, 73–81.

Fayos-Sola, E. (1996) Tourism policy, a midsummer night's dream. *Tourism Management* 17(6), 405–412.

Federal Interagency Forum on Child and Family Statistics (1998) *America's Children: Key National Indicators of Well-Being*. US Government Printing Office, Washington, DC.

Feeny, D., Berkes, F., McCay, B.J. and Acheson, J.M. (1990) The tragedy of the Commons: twenty-two years later. *Human Ecology* 18(1), 1–19.

Ferguson, T. (1987) Health in the information age: sharing the uncertainty. *Whole Earth Review* Winter, 130–133.

Fessenmaier, D. and Fessenmaier, J. (1993) *Helping Rural Communities Prepare for Economic Development, Assessing and Developing Tourism Resources*, Illinois Laboratory for Community and Economic Development, University of Illinois, Urbana-Champaign, Illinois.

Fick, G. and Ritchie, J.R.B. (1991) Measuring service quality in the travel and tourism industry. *Journal of Travel Research* 30(2), 2–9.

Field, D. and Cheek, N. Jr. (1974) A basis for assessing differential participation in water-based recreation. *Water Resources Bulletin* 10, 1218–1227.

Finsterbusch, K., Llewellyn, L.G. and Wolf, C.P. (eds) (1983) *Social Impact Assessment Methods*. Sage Publications, Beverly Hills, California.

Fischer, K.W. (1993) Citizen participation and the democraticization of policy expertise: from theoretical inquiry to practical cases. *Policy Sciences* 26(3),165–187.

Fisher, R.J. (1994) Generic principles for resolving intergroup conflict. *Journal of Social Issues* 50, 47–66.

Fleming, W.R. and Toepper, L. (1990) Economic impact studies: relating the positive and negative impacts to tourism development. *Journal of Travel Research* 29(1), 35–42.

Fletcher, J.E. (1989) Input-output analysis and tourism impact studies. *Annals of Tourism Research* 16, 514–529.

Flora, C.B. (1997) Innovations in community development. In: *Rural Development News*. North Central Regional Center for Rural Development, Ames, Iowa.

Flora, J., Spears, L., Swanson, J., Flora, L. and Weinberg, M. (1992) *Rural Communities: Legacy and Change*. Westview Press, Boulder, Colorado.

Floyd, D.W., Germain, R. and ter Horst, K. (1996) A model for assessing negotiations and mediation in forest resource conflicts. *Journal of Forestry* 94, 29–33.

Floyd, M., Gramann, J. and Saenz, R. (1993) Ethnic factors and the use of public outdoor recreation areas: the case of Mexican-Americans. *Leisure Sciences* 15, 83–98.

Floyd, M.F., Shinew, K.J., McGuire, F.A. and Noe, F.P. (1994) Race, class, and leisure activity preferences: marginality and ethnicity revisited. *Journal of Leisure Research*. 26, 158–73.

Floyd, M.F., Outley, C.W., Bixler, R.D. and Hammitt, W.E. (1995) Effects of race, environmental preference and negative affect on recreation preferences. *Abstracts From the 1995 National Recreation and Park Association Symposium on Leisure Research*, 88.

Flynn, G. (1996) Hallmark cares. *Personnel Journal* 75(3), 50–60.

Foley, J. and Pick, H. (1995) Healthy cities: Survival strategies for recreation and parks. *Parks and Recreation* 30(4), 68–72.

Foley, M. (1996) Cultural Tourism in the United Kingdom. In: Richards, G. (ed.) *Cultural Tourism in Europe*. CAB International, Wallingford, UK, pp. 283–309.

Forbes, M. (1996) *Creating Customers: Marketing to Today's Transforming Travelers*. The Forbes Group/Travel Information Resources, Charlotteville, Virginia.

Ford, P. and Blanchard, J. (1985) *Leadership and Administration of Outdoor Pursuits*. Venture, State College, Pennsylvania.

Forester, J. (1989) *Planning in the Face of Power*. University of California Press, Berkeley, California.

Formann, A.K., Mazanec, J.A. and Oberhauser, O.C. (1979) *Numerische Klassifikationsprobleme in 'großen' Datensätzen der demoskopischen Marktforschung: Ein numerischer Methodenvergleich von Latent Class- und Cluster-Analyse*. Arbeitspapiere der absatzwirtschaftlichen Institute der Wirtschaftsuniversität Wien. Orac, Vienna.

Forrester Research (1998) On-line forecast revenues for America (www.forrester.com).

Fortmann, L. (1990) The role of professional norms and beliefs in agency-client relations of natural resource bureaucracies. *Natural Resources Journal* 30(2), 361–380.

Fost, D. (1996, March) The lost art of fatherhood. *American Demographics* 18(3), 16–19.

Frechtling, D.C. (1994a) Assessing the economic impacts of travel and tourism – introduction to travel economic impact estimation. In: Ritchie, J.R.B. and Goeldner, C. (eds) *Travel, Tourism, and Hospitality Research*, 2nd edn. John Wiley and Sons, New York, pp. 359–365.

Frechtling, D.C. (1994b) Assessing the economic impacts of travel and tourism – measuring economic benefits. In: Ritchie, J.R.B. and Goeldner, C. (eds) *Travel, Tourism, and Hospitality Research*, 2nd edn. John Wiley and Sons, New York, pp. 367–391.

Freemuth, J. (1996) Emergence of ecosystem Management: reinterpreting the gospel? *Society and Natural Resources* 9, 411–417.

Freitag, R. (1999) Leisure Time. WTO News/Feb–Mar. 1999. http://www.world-tourism.org/newslett/febmar99/leisure.html

French, T. (1998) The future of Global Distribution Systems. *Travel and Tourism Analyst* (3), 1–17.

Freudenberg, N. and Steinsapir, C. (1992) Not in our backyards: the grassroots environmental movement. In: Dunlap, R.E. and Mertig, A.G. (eds) *American Environmentalism: the U.S. Environmental Movement (1970–1990)*. Taylor and Francis, Washington, DC, pp. 27–38.

Freudenburg, W.R. (1986) Social impact assessment. *Annual Review of Sociology* 12, 451–478.

Freyer, W. (1998) Tourismus – Einführung in die Fremdenverkehrsökonomie, 6th edn. R. Oldenbourg Verlag, München, Wien, pp. 218–227.

Friedmann, J. (1987) *Planning in the Public Domain: From Knowledge to Action*. Princeton, New Jersey, Princeton University Press.

Frisby, W. and Getz, D. (1989) Festival Management: a case study perspective. *Journal of Travel Research* 28(1), 7–11.

Frissell, S. and Stankey, G. (1972) Wilderness environmental quality: search for social and ecological harmony. In *Proceedings of the Society of American Foresters Annual Conference*, Hot Springs, Arkansas. Society of American Foresters, Bethesda, Maryland, pp. 170–183.

Frissell, S.S. (1978) Judging recreation impacts on wilderness campsites. *Journal of Forestry* 76, 481–483.

Furstenberg, F.F. and Kate, N.T. (1996) The future of marriage. *American Demographics* 18(6), 34–41.

Furze, B., DeLacy, T. and Birckhead, J. (1996) *Culture, Conservation and Biodiversity: the Social Dimension of Linking Local Development and Conservation through Protected Areas*. John Wiley & Sons, Chichester.

FVW International (1998a) Deutsche *Veranstalter in Zahlen – Beilage zur FVW International* 28, 1–34.

FVW International (1998b) Europäische *Veranstalter in Zahlen – Beilage zur FVW International* 13, 1–23.

Gambia Ministry of Tourism and Culture (The) (1995) *The Gambia. The Smiling Coast* (catalogue) The Gambia Ministry of Tourism and Culture, Banjul.

Gambone, M.A. and Arbreton, A.J.A. (1997) *Safe Havens: the Contributions of Youth Organizations to Healthy Adolescent Development*. Public Private Ventures, Philadelphia.

Gaming Board for Great Britain (1998) *Report of the Gaming Board for Great Britain, 1997–98.* HM Stationery Office, London.

Garfield, D. (ed.) (1997) *Partners in Tourism: Culture and Commerce.* American Association of Museums, Washington, DC.

Garmezy, N. (1993) Vulnerability and resilience. In: Funder, D.C., Park, R.D., Tomlison-Keesey, C. and Widaman, K. (eds) *Studying Lives Through Time: Approaches to Personality and Development.* American Psychological Association, Washington, DC, pp. 377–398.

Gartner, W. (1996a) Community tourism development. In: *Tourism Development: Principles, Processes, and Policies.* Van Nostrand Reinhold, New York, pp. 265–306.

Gartner, W. (1996b) *Tourism Development: Principles, Processes, Policies.* Van Nostrand Reinhold, New York.

Gartner, W. and Hunt, J.D. (1988) A method to collect detailed tourist flow information. *Annals of Tourism Research* 15, 159–165.

Gee, C.Y. (1996) *Resort Development and Management*, 2nd edn. Educational Institute of the American Hotel and Motel Association, East Lansing, Michigan.

Gee, C.Y., Loke, M. and Ikeda, G. (1994) *Opportunities for the Development of Health-Related Tourism in Hawaii.* School of Travel Industry Management, University of Hawaii, Honolulu.

Getz, D. (1986) Models in tourism planning: towards integration of theory and practice. *Tourism Management* 7(1), 21–32.

Getz, D. (1991) *Festivals, Special Events, and Tourism.* Virginian Nostrand Reinhold, New York.

Getz, D. (1992) Tourism planning and the destination life cycle: the case of Niagara Falls. *Annals of Tourism Research* 19(4), 752–770.

Getz, D. (1993a) Case study: marketing the Calgary Exhibition and Stampede. *Festival Management and Event Tourism: an International Journal* 1(4), 147–156.

Getz, D. (1993b) Corporate culture in not for profit festival organizations. *Festival Management and Event Tourism: An International Journal* 1(1), 11–17.

Getz, D. (1997) *Event Management and Event Tourism.* Cognizant Communication Corp., New York.

Getz, D. (1998) Information sharing among festival managers. *Festival Management and Event Tourism: An International Journal* 5(1/2), 33–50.

Getz, D. and Frisby, W. (1988) Evaluating management effectiveness in community-run festivals. *Journal of Travel Research* 27(1), 22–27.

Getz, D. and Page, S. (1997) Conclusions and implications for rural business development. In: Page, S. and Getz, D. (eds) *The Business of Rural Tourism: International Perspectives.* International Thomson Business Press, London.

Gill, A. and Williams, P. (1994) Managing growth in mountain tourism communities. *Tourism Management* 15(3), 212–220.

Girard, K. (1998) Telecommute leaves road less traveled. *Computerworld* 32(10), 49–50.

Gobster, P. (1998) Explanations for minority 'underparticipation' in outdoor recreation: a look at golf. *Journal of Park and Recreation Administration* 16.

Godbey, G. (1997) *Leisure and Leisure Services in the 21st Century.* Venture Publishing, State College, Pennsylvania.

Goedhart, S. (1997) 'New Producers' in Cultuurtoerisme. MA Thesis, Tilburg University.

Goldblatt, J. (1997) *Special Events: Best Practices in Modern Event Management.* Virginian Nostrand Reinhold, New York.

Goodall, B. (1995) Environmental audits: a tool for assessing the environmental performance of tourism firms. *Geographical Journal* 161(1), 29–37.

Goodrich, J.N. (1994) Health tourism: a new positioning strategy for tourist destinations. In: Uysal, M. (ed.) *Global Tourist Behavior.* Haworth Press, Binghampton, pp. 227–238.

Goodrich, J.N. and Goodrich, G.E. (1991) Health care tourism. In: Medlik. S. (ed.) *Managing Tourism.* Butterworth-Heinemann, Oxford, pp. 107–114.

Goold, M. and Sommers Luchs, K. (1996) *Managing the Multibusiness Company.* Routledge, London and New York, pp. 1–8.

Government of Andorra, Ministry of Tourism and Culture (1998) *Andorra. The Pyrenean Country* (catalogue) Government of Andorra, Ministry of Tourism and Culture, Andorra.

Graburn, N. (1989) Tourism, the sacred journey. In: Smith, V. (ed.) *Hosts and Guests. The Anthropology of Tourism.* 2nd edn. University of Pennsylvania Press, Philadelphia, pp. 21– 36.

Graefe, A., Vaske, J. and Kuss, F. (1984) Social carrying capacity: an integration and synthesis of twenty years of research. *Leisure Sciences* 6, 395–431.

Graefe, A.R., Kuss, F.R. and Vaske, J.J. (1990) *Visitor Impact Management: a Planning Framework*, vol. 2. National Parks and Conservation Association, Washington, DC.

Graham, S., Goldblatt, J. and Delpy, L. (1995) *The Ultimate Guide to Sport Event Management and Marketing.* Irwin, Chicago.

Gramann, J. (1982) Toward a behavioral theory of crowding in outdoor recreation: an evaluation and synthesis of research. *Leisure Sciences* 5, 109–126.

Gramann, J., Floyd, M. and Saenz, R. (1993) Outdoor recreation and Mexican American ethnicity: a benefits perspective. In: Ewert, A., Chavez, D. and Magill, A. (eds), *Culture, Conflict, and Communication in the Wildland-Urban Interface*. Westview Press, Boulder, Colorado, pp. 69–84.

Granger, A. (1996) Promoting health for better or for worse. *BCMA News*, February, 3–4.

Greene, M. (1988) *The Dialectic of Freedom*. The Teachers College Press, New York.

Griffin, N. (1995) The spa industry. *Spa Management*, July–August, 4–9.

Grubb, H. and Goodwin, J. (1968) *Economic Evaluation of Water Oriented Recreation in the Preliminary Texas Water Plan*. Texas Water Development Board no. 84. Dallas, Texas.

Grumbine, R.E. (1994) What is ecosystem management. *Conservation Biology* 8(1), 27–38.

Grumbine, R.E. (1997) Reflections on 'what is ecosystem management?' *Conservation Biology* 11(1), 41–47.

Grümer, K.-W. (1993) Gesellschaftliche Rahmenbedingungen für Mobilität/Tourismus/Reisen. In: Hahn, H. and Kagelmann, H.J. (eds) *Tourismuspsychologie und Tourismussoziologie. Ein Handbuch zur Tourismuswissenschaft*. Quintessenz Verlag. Hamburg.

Gulliford, A. (1989) *Boomtown Blues: Colorado Oil Shale, 1885–1985*. University Press of Colorado, Niwot, Colorado.

Haas, G., Driver, B. and Brown, P. (1980) Measuring wilderness recreation experiences. In: *Proceedings of the Wilderness Psychology Group*. Wilderness Psychology Group, Durham, New Hampshire, pp. 20–40.

Hack, S. (1998) Arabian knights. *Conde Nast Traveler*, November, 226–237, 281–285, 296–302.

Haigh, N. (1993) *The Precautionary Principle in British Environmental Policy*. Institute for Environmental Policy, London.

Haley, R.J. (1968) Benefit segmentation: a decision-oriented research tool. *Journal of Marketing* 32, 30–35.

Hall, C. and Weiler, B. (1992) Introduction: what's special about special interest tourism? In: Weiler, B. and Hall, C. (eds) *Special Interest Tourism*. Belhaven Press, London, pp. 1–14.

Hall, C.M. (1994) *Tourism and Politics*, John Wiley, London.

Hall, D. and O'Hanlon, L. (eds) (1998) *Rural Tourism Management: Sustainable Options*. Scottish Agricultural College, Auchincruive.

Hall, M. (1992) *Hallmark Tourist Events*. Belhaven, London.

Halman, L. and Pettersson, T. (1995) Individualization and value fragmentation. In: de Moor, R. (ed.), *Values in Western Societies*. Tilburg University Press. Tilburg.

Hamilton, J. (1972) Tourism and its effects on the national economy. *IUOTO Travel Research Journal*.

Hammitt, W.E. (1988) The spectrum of conflict in outdoors recreation. In: Watson, A. (ed.) *Outdoor Recreation Benchmark 1988: Proceedings of the National Outdoor Recreation Forum*. USDA Forest Service General Technical Report SE-52, pp. 439–450.

Hammitt, W.E. and Cole, D.N. (1998) *Wildland Recreation: Ecology and Management*, 2nd edn. John Wiley & Sons, New York.

Hammitt, W.E. and Patterson, M.E. (1991) Coping behavior to avoid visitor encounters: its relationship to wildland privacy. *Journal of Leisure Research* 23(3), 225–237.

Hampton, B. and Cole, D. (1988) *Soft Paths*. Stackpole Books, Harrisburg, Pennsylvania.

Hanefors, M. and Larsson, L. (1993) Video strategies used by tour operators. What is really communicated? *Tourism Management* 14(1), 27–33.

Hanemann, M. (1984) Welfare evaluations in contingent valuation experiments with discrete responses. *American Journal of Agricultural Economics* 66(3), 332–341.

Hardin, G. (1968) The tragedy of the commons. *Science* 162, 1243–1248.

Hart, C., Casserly, G. and Lawless, M. (1984) The product life cycle: how useful? *Cornell Hotel and Restaurant Administration Quarterly* 25(3), 54–63.

Hartmann, L. and Overdevest, C. (1990) Race, ethnicity, and outdoor recreation participation: A state-of-the-knowledge review and theoretical perspective. In: *Proceedings of the 1989 Southeastern Recreation Research Conference*. University of Georgia, Athens, Georgia, pp. 53–63.

Hauser, P. (1962) Demographic and ecological changes as factors in outdoor recreation. In: *Trends in American Living and Outdoor Recreation: Report to the Outdoor Recreation Resources Review Commission no. 22*. US Government Printing Office, Washington, DC, pp. 27–59.

Hawkes, S. and Williams, P.W. (eds) (1993) *The Greening of Tourism: From Principles to Practice – a Casebook of Best Environmental Practice in Tourism*. Centre for Tourism Policy and Research, Simon Fraser University, Burnaby.

Hawking, S. (1980) Is the end in sight for theoretical physics? (Inaugural Lecture). Reprinted in:

Hawking, St. (1993) *Black Holes and Baby Universes and Other Essays*. Bantam, Toronto, pp. 42–61.

Hays, R.L. (1997) *Beyond Command and Control*. North American Wildlife and Natural Resource Conference, The Wildlife Society.

Heath, R.P. (1997) Life on Easy Street. *American Demographics* 19(4), 33–38.

Heberlein, T. and Shelby, B. (1977) Carrying capacity, values, and the satisfaction model: a reply to Greist. *Journal of Leisure Research* 9, 142–148.

Heberlein, T.A. and Thomson, E. (1997) The effects of hunter-education requirements on hunting participation and recruitment in the United States. *Human Dimensions of Wildlife* 2(1), 19–31.

Heifitz, R.A. and Sinder, R.M. (1988) Political leadership: managing the public's problem solving. In: Reich, R.B. (ed.) *The Power of Public Ideas*. Harvard University Press, Cambridge, Massachusetts, pp. 179–205.

Heister, C.G. (compiler) (1998) *Proceedings of the Second Biennial Conference on University Education in Natural Resources*. Utah State University, College of Natural Resources Logan, Utah.

Hellevik, O. (1996) Nordmenn og det gode liv. Norsk Monitor 1985–1995. Universitetsforlaget. Oslo.

Hendee, J. (1971) Sociology and applied leisure research. *Pacific Sociological Review* 14, 360–368.

Hendee, J. and Stankey, G. (1973) Biocentricity in wilderness management. *Bioscience* 23, 535–538.

Hendee, J.C., Stankey, G.H. and Lucas, R.C. (1978) *Wilderness Management*. USDA Forest Service, Washington, District of Columbia. Miscellaneous publication no. 1365.

Henderson, K. (1990) The meaning of leisure for women: an integrative review of the research. *Journal of Leisure Research* 22, 228–243.

Henderson, K. (1994a) Theory application and development in recreation, parks and leisure research. *Journal of Park and Recreation Administration* 12, 51–64.

Henderson, K.A. (1994b) Perspectives on analyzing gender, women, and leisure. *Journal of Leisure Research* 26, 119–137.

Henderson, K.A. (1996a) Feminist perspectives on outdoor leadership. In: Warren, K. (ed.) *Women's Voices in Experiential Education*. Kendall/Hunt Publishing Company, Dubuque, Iowa, pp. 107–117.

Henderson, K.A. (1996b) Just recreation for girls and women. *Journal of Physical Education, Recreation, and Dance* 67(2), 45–46.

Henderson, K.A. (1997) Just recreation: ethics, gender, and equity. *Journal of Park and Recreation Administration* 15(2), 16–31.

Henderson, K.A. (1999) Should gender-specific programs, such as all women courses, be offered in adventure education? Yes. In: Wurdiger, S. and Potter, T. (eds) *Controversial Issues in Adventure Education*. Kendall Hunt, Dubuque, Iowa. pp. 247–253.

Henderson, K.A. and Bialeschki, M.D. (1990–91) Ecofeminism: recreation as if nature and woman Mattered. *Leisure Information Quarterly* 17(1), 1–5.

Henderson, K.A. and Bialeschki, M.D. (1995) The status and career development of women in leisure services. *Journal of Park and Recreation Administration* 13(1), 26–42.

Henderson, K.A., Bialeschki, M.D., Shaw, S.M. and Freysinger, V.J. (1996) *Both Gains and Gaps*. Venture Publishing, State College, Pennsylvania.

Hendricks, J. and Burdge, R. (1972) The nature of leisure research: a reflection and comment. *Journal of Leisure Research* 4, 215–217.

Hensdill, C. (1998) Hotels technology survey. *Hotels*, February.

Herbert, D.T. (ed.) (1995) *Heritage, Tourism and Society*. Mansell, London/New York.

Hierta, E. (1996) Staying afloat. *National Parks*, March/April 1996, pp. 41–46.

Hill, R., Baird, A. and Buchanan, D. (1999) Aborigines and fire in the wet tropics of Queensland: Ecosystem Management across cultures. *Society and Natural Resources* 12, 205–224.

Hirsch, J.S. (1994) Of luxury and losses. *Wall Street Journal*, 22 April, 1994.

Hirschman, A.O. (1958) *The Strategy of Economic Development*. Yale University Press, New Haven.

Hobbs, D. (1987) Why save rural America. In: *A New Agenda for Rural America, Conference Proceedings*. University of Minnesota Cooperative Extension, St Paul, Minnesota.

Hof, M. and Lime, D. (1997) Visitor experience and resource protection framework in the national park system: Rationale, current status, and future direction. In: *Proceedings – Limits of Acceptable Change and Related Planning Processes: Progress and Future Directions*. USDA Forest Service General Technical Report INT-371, Utah Rocky Mountain Research Station, Ogden, pp. 29–36.

Hoffman, L.W. (1989) Effects of maternal employment in the two-parent family. *American Psychologist*, 44, 283–292.

Hollinshead, K. (1993) The truth about Texas. Unpublished PhD thesis, Texas A&M University.

Hollinshead, K. (1998) Tourism, hybridity, and ambiguity: the relevance of Bhabha's 'Third Space' cultures. *Journal of Leisure Research* 30.

Holmes, L. (1999) Special report – Leading UK travel groups, *TTG Europa ITB Daily* (in press).

Horgan, M. (1995) An analysis of the current spa and resort operations in the USA. Unpublished paper prepared for the International Spa and Fitness Association. International Spa and Fitness Association, Washington, DC.

Howe, G., McMahon, E. and Propst, L. (1997) Balancing nature and commerce in gateway communities. The Conservation Fund and the Sonoran Institute. Island Press, Washington, DC.

Hsieh, Sh., O'Leary, J.T. and Morrison, A.M. (1992) Segmenting the international travel market by activity. *Tourism Management* 13, 209–223.

Hudson, L., Griffin, J. and Watt, H.P. (1998) *A Plan for Les Cheneaux; Where Nature, Economy and Community Come Together*, Les Cheneaux Economic Forum, Cedarville, Michigan.

Hughes, J.M. and Lloyd, R.D. (comp) (1977) *Outdoor Recreation: Advances in Application of Economics*. USDA Forest Service, Washington, DC. General Technical Report WO-2. March.

Hutchison, R. (1988) A critique of race, ethnicity, and social class in recent leisure-recreation research. *Journal of Leisure Research* 20, 10–30.

IHRA (International Health and Recreation Association) (1997) *American Sports Data Health Club Report*. International Health and Recreation Association, Washington, DC.

Inglehart, R. (1977) *The Silent Revolution*. Princeton University Press, Princeton.

Inglehart, R. (1990) *Culture Shift in Advanced Industrial Society*. Princeton University Press, Princeton.

Inskeep, E. (1991) *Tourism Planning: An Integrated and Sustainable Development Approach*, Virginian Nostrand Reinhold, New York.

International Events Group (1995) *IEG's Complete Guide to Sponsorship*. Chicago.

International Festivals Association (n.d.) *Event Trends in the 90's*. IFA, Port Angeles, Washington.

International Hotels Environmental Initiative (1992) *Environmental Management for Hotels*. Butterworth-Heinemann, London.

International Union for the Conservation of Nature (1980) *World Conservation Strategy*. International Union for the Conservation of Nature, Gland.

Irwin, P.N., Gartner, W.C. and Phelps, C.C. (1990) Mexican/Anglo cultural differences as recreation style determinants. *Leisure Sciences* 12, 335–348.

Iso-Ahola, S. (1986a) Concerns and thoughts about leisure research. *Journal of Leisure Research* 18, iv–x.

Iso-Ahola, S. (1986b) A theory of substitutability of leisure behavior. *Leisure Sciences* 8, 367–389.

I-SPA (International Spa Association) (1995) Unpublished conference material handouts. International Spa Association, Washington, DC.

Jackson, E.L. and Henderson, K.A. (1995) Gender-based analysis of leisure constraints. *Leisure Sciences* 17, 31–51.

Jacob, G.R. (1977) Conflict in outdoor recreation: the search for understanding. *Utah Tourism and Recreation Review* 6, 1–5.

Jacob, G.R. and Schreyer, R. (1980) Conflict in outdoor recreation: a theoretical perspective. *Journal of Leisure Research* 12, 368–380.

Jacobs, M. (1995) Sustainability and community. *Australian Planner* 32(3), 109–115.

Jakes, P., Dwyer, J. and Carr, D. (1998) Demonstrating the Value of a social science research program to a natural resource Management agency. In: *Proceedings of the 1997 Northeastern Recreation Research Symposium*. USDA Forest Service General Technical Report NE-241, pp. 228–233.

Jakes, P., Gregersen, H., Lundgren, A. and Bengston, D. (1990) Emerging issues in forest Management and use. *Journal of Forestry* 88, 25–34.

Janiskee, R. (1994) Some Macroscale growth trends in America's community festival industry. *Festival Management and Event Tourism: an International Journal* 2(1), 10–14.

Janiskee, R. (1996) The temporal distribution of America's community festivals. *Festival Management and Event Tourism: an International Journal* 3(3), 129–137.

Jefferson, A. and Lickorish, L. (1988) *Marketing Tourism*. Longman, Harlow.

Jenkins, C. (1992) Tourism in Third World Development, Inaugural Lecture. University of Strathclyde.

Jensen, M.E., Bourgeron, P., Everett, R. and Goodman, I. (1996) Ecosystem management: a landscape ecology perspective. *Water Resources Bulletin* 32(2), 203–216.

Jessor, R. (1991) Risk behavior in adolescence: a psychosocial framework for understanding and action. *Journal of Adolescent Health* 12, 597–605.

Johnson, C., Bowker, J., English, D. and Worthen, D. (1997a) *Theoretical Perspectives of Ethnicity and Outdoor Recreation: A Review and Synthesis of African-American and European American Participation*. USDA Forest Service General Technical Report SRS-11.

Johnson, C., Horan, P. and Pepper, W. (1997b) Race, rural residence, and wildland visitation: examining the influence of sociocultural meaning. *Rural Sociology* 62, 89–110.

Johnson, C.Y. and Bowker, J.M. (1999) On-site wildland activity choices among African American and white Americans in the rural South: implications for Management. *Journal of Park and Recreation Administration* 17.

Johnson, C.Y., Bowker, J.M., English, D.B.K. and Worthen, D. (1998) Wildland recreation in the rural South: an examination of marginality and ethnicity theory. *Journal of Leisure Research* 30, 101–120.

Johnson, D.G. and Sullivan, J. (1993) Economic impacts of civil war battlefield preservation: an ex-ante evaluation. *Journal of Travel Research* 32(1), 21–29.

Johnson, R.L. and Moore, E. (1993) Tourism impact estimation. *Annals of Tourism Research* 20, 279–288.

Johnson, R.L., Obermiller, F. and Radtke, H. (1989) The economic impact of tourism sales. *Journal of Leisure Research* 21(2), 140–154.

Jones, A. (1998) Black concern for the environment: myth and reality. *Society and Natural Resources* 11.

Jones, H. (1993) Pop goes the festival. *Marketing Week* 16(23), 24–27.

Jordan, C.R. (1991) Parks and recreation: More than fun and games. In: Driver, B.L., Brown, P.J. and Peterson, G.L. (eds) *Benefits of Leisure*, Venture Publishing, State College, Pennsylvania, pp. 365–368.

Jordan Tourism Board (1998) *Jordan. Where Adventure Awaits You* (catalogue). Al Favar Press, Amman.

Jurowski, C., Uysal, M. and Williams, D.R. (1997) A theoretical analysis of host community resident reactions to tourism. *Journal of Travel Research* Fall, 3–11.

Kacapyr, E. (1996) Are you middle class? *American Demographics*. October.

Kaldor, N. (1970) The case for regional policies, *Scottish Journal of Political Economy* 17, 337–348.

Kamakura, W.A. and Novak, Th.P. (1992) Value-system segmentation: exploring the meaning of LOV. *Journal of Consumer Research* 19, 119–32.

Kaplan, R. (1995) Informational issues: a perspective on human needs and inclinations. In: Bradley, G.A. (ed.) *Urban Forest Landscapes: Integrating Multidisciplinary Perspectives*. University of Washington Press, Seattle, Washington, pp. 24–43.

Kaplan, R. and Kaplan, S. (1989) *The Experience of Nature: a Psychological Perspective*. Cambridge University Press, Cambridge.

Kaplan, R. and Norton, D. (1992) The balanced scorecard: measures that drive performance. *Harvard Business Review*, January–February.

Kaplan, S. and Kaplan, R. (1982) *Cognition and Environment: Functioning in an Uncertain World*. Ulrich's, Ann Arbor, Michigan.

Kaplan, S.H., Greenfield, S., Gandek, B., Rogers, W.H. and Ware, J.E. Jr. (1996) Characteristics of physicians with participatory decision-making styles. *Annals of Internal Medicine* 124, 497–504.

Kärcher, K. (1996) The four Global Distribution Systems in the travel and tourism industry. *Electronic Markets* 6(2), 20–24.

Kärcher, K. (1997) *Reinventing Package Holiday Business*. Deutscher Universitäts Verlag, Berlin.

Kash, D.E. and Ballard. S. (1987) Academic and applied policy studies: a comparison. *American Behavioral Scientist* 30(6), 597–611.

Kaspar, C. (ed.) (1995) Jahrbuch der Schweizerischen Tourismuswirtschaft 1994/95. Institut für Tourismus und Verkehrswirtschaft and der Hochschule St.Gallen. St.Gallen.

Keller, K. (1990) Mountain bikes on public lands: a manager's guide to the state of the practice. Bicycle Federation of America.

Keller, P. (1996) Globalisation and tourism. *AIEST* 38, 8–19.

Keller, P. (1998) Scope and limits of destination Marketing. *AIEST* 40, 9–22.

Keller, P. and Koch, K. (1995) Globalisation and tourism. *La Vie économique* 5, 16–22.

Keller, P. and Smeral, E. (1997) Increased international competition and structural changes: what are the responsibilities of European governments? *WTO World Tourism Organisation*, Salzburg.

Kellert, S.R. (1996) *The Value of Life: Biological Diversity and Human Society*. Island Press, Washington, DC.

Kellert, S.R. and Wilson, E.O. (eds) (1993) *The Biophilia Hypothesis*. Island Press, Washington, DC.

Kelly, J. (1980) Outdoor recreation participation: a comparative analysis. *Leisure Sciences* 3, 129–154.

Kelly, J.R. (1987) *Recreation Trends: Toward the Year 2000*. Management Learning Laboratories Ltd, Champaign, Illinois.

Kelly, J.R. (1997) Changing issues in leisure-family research – again. *Journal of Leisure Research* 29(1), 132–134.

Kent-Lemon, N. (1984) Significant influences on the United Kingdom casino industry since 1960. *The Annals of the American Academy of Political and Social Sciences: Gambling and the Social Sciences* 474, 72–79.

Kim, C., Scott, D., Thigpen, J.F. and Kim, S. (1998) Economic impact of a birding festival. *Festival Management and Event Tourism* 5, 51–58.

Kimmins, H. (1992) *Balancing Act: Environmental Issues in Forestry.* UBC Press, Vancouver, British Columbia.

King, C.S., Feltey, K.M. and Susel, B.O. (1998) The question of participation: toward authentic public participation in public administration. *Public Administration Review* 58(4), 317–326.

Kingman-Brundage, J. (1989) The ABCs of Service System Blueprinting. In: Bitner, M.J. and Crosby, L.A. (eds) *Designing a Winning Service Strategy.* American Marketing Association. Chicago.

Klobus-Edwards, P. (1981) Race, residence, and leisure style: some policy implications. *Leisure Sciences* 4, 95–112.

Knight, R.L. and Gutzwiller, K.J. (eds) (1995) *Wildlife and Recreationists: Coexistence Through Management and Research.* Island Press, Covello, California.

Knopf, R.C. (1990) From Management to Marketing: a necessary evolution in wilderness policy. In: Lime, D.W. (ed.) *Managing America's Enduring Wilderness Resource,* Proceedings of the Conference, Minnesota Extension Service, University of Minnesota, St Paul, Minnesota, pp. 641–645.

Knopf, R.C., Peterson, G.L. and Leatherberry, E.C. (1983) Motives for recreational river floating: relative consistency across settings. *Leisure Sciences* 5, 231–235.

Knopp, T. and Caldbeck, E. (1990) The role of participatory democracy in forest management. *Journal of Forestry* 5, 13–18.

Knopp, T.B. and Tyger, J.D. (1973) A study of conflict in recreational land use: snowmobiling versus ski-touring. *Journal of Leisure Research* 5, 6–17.

Knutson, B., Stevens, P., Wullart, C., Patton, M. and Yokoyama, F. (1990) LODGSERV: a Service Quality Index for the Lodging Industry. *Hospitality Research Journal* 14(2), 277–283.

Kohonen, T. (1982) Self-organized formation of topologically correct feature Maps. *Biological Cybernetics* 43, 59–69. Reprinted 1988. In: Andersen, J.A. and Rosenfeld, E. (eds) *Neurocomputing: Foundations of Research.* MIT Press, Cambridge, Massachusetts, pp. 511–521.

Kohonen, T. (1984, 3rd edn, 1988) *Self-organization and Associative Memory.* Springer, New York.

Kohonen, T. (1990) The self-organizing Map. In: Proceedings of the IEEE, 78(9), 1464–1480. Reprinted 1992 in: Mehra, P. and Wah, B.W. (eds) *Artificial Neural Networks: Concepts and Theory.* IEEE Computer Society Press, Los Alamitos, pp. 359–375.

Kohonen, T. (1997) *Self-organizing Maps,* 2nd edn. Springer Series in Information Sciences, Berlin-Heidelberg.

Kooyman, M.E. (1990) Stress busters. *Business and Economic Review* 36(3), 7–9.

Korea National Tourism Organization (n.d.) *Welcome to Korea* (catalogue). Korea National Tourism Organization, Seoul.

Kotler, P., Haider, D. and Rain, I. (1993) *Marketing Places.* The Free Press, New York.

Kotler, P., Bowen, J. and Makens, J. (1999) *Marketing for Hospitality and Tourism,* 2nd edn. Prentice Hall, Upper Saddle River, New Jersey.

Kottke, M. (1988) Estimating economic impacts of tourism. *Annals of Tourism Research* 15, 122–133.

KPMG (1998) Europe gets wired: a survey of Internet use in Great Britain, France and Germany [www.kpmg.co.uk/direct/industry/ice/ewired/inderx.html].

Kraft, M. and Clary, B.B. (1991) Citizen participation and the NIMBY syndrome: public response to radioactive waste disposal. *Western Political Quarterly* 44(2), 299–328.

Kramer, S. (1991) *Europäische Life-Style-Analysen zur Verhaltensprognose von Konsumenten.* Dr Kovac, Hamburg.

Kretzmann, J.R. and McKnight, J.L. (1993) *Building Communities from the Inside Out,* Northwestern University, Center for Urban Affairs and Policy Research, Evanston, Illinois.

Kreutzer, R. (1991) Länderübergreifende Segmentierungskonzepte – Antwort auf die Globalisierung der Märkte. *Jahrbuch der Absatz- und Verbrauchsforschung* 37, 4–27.

Krippendorf, J. (1987) *The Holiday Makers. Understanding the Impact of Leisure and Travel.* Heinemann, Oxford.

Kroeber-Riel, W. (1992) *Konsumentenverhalten,* 5th edn. Vahlen, Munich.

Krugman, P. and Obstfeld, M. (1991) *International Economics: Theory and Policy.* Harper Collins, New York.

Krumpe, E. and McCool, S.F. (1997) Role of public involvement in the Limits of Acceptable Change wilderness planning system. In: *Limits of Acceptable Change and Related Planning Processes: Progress and Future Directions,* USDA Forest Service Intermountain Research Station, Missoula, Montana.

Kuentzel, W. and McDonald, C. (1992) Differential effects of past experience, commitment, and lifestyle dimensions on river use specialization. *Journal of Leisure Research* 24, 269–287.

Kuentzel, W.F. and Heberlein, T.A. (1992) Cognitive and behavioral adaptations to perceived crowding: a panel study of coping and displacement. *Journal of Leisure Research* 24(4), 377–393.

Kuentzel, W.F., Robertson, R.A. and Ramaswamy, V.M. (1996) A time-series comparison of Vermont and New Hampshire travel trends. In: Thompson, J.L., Lime, D., Gartner, B. and Sames, W.M. (eds)

Proceedings of the Fourth International Outdoor Recreation and Tourism Trends Symposium, May 14–15, 1995. University of Minnesota. St Paul, Minnesota.

Kuralt, C. (1985) *On the Road With Charles Kuralt.* Ballantine Books, New York.

Kuss, F., Graefe, A. and Vaske, J. (1990) *Visitor Impact Management: a Review of Research.* National Parks and Conservation Association, Washington, DC.

Lalonde, M. (1974) *A New Perspective on the Health of Canadians: a Working Document.* National Health and Welfare Canada, Ottawa.

Lamar, M. and Donnell, R. (1987) *Hunting: The Southern Tradition.* Taylor Publishing, Dallas, Texas.

Lambkin, M. and Day, G. (1989) Evolutionary processes in competitive markets: beyond the product life cycle. *Journal of Marketing* 53 (July), 4–20.

Lan, Z. (1997) A conflict resolution approach to public administration. *The Public Administration Review* 1, 1–9.

Lance, A.N., Baugh, I.D. and Love, J.A. (1989) Continued footpath widening in the Cairngorm Mountains, Scotland. *Biological Conservation* 49, 201–214.

Landrum, N.C. (1999) America's State Parks – an end-of-century assessment. In: Cordell, H.K. (ed.) *Outdoor Recreation in American Life: a National Assessment of Demand and Supply Trends.* Sagamore Publishing, Champaign, Illinois, pp. 112–115.

Landry, C. and Bianchini, F. (1995) *The Creative City.* Demos, London.

Landsorganisasjonen (1998) Arbeidstid i et nytt årtusen. LO. Oslo (In Norwegian).

Lane, B. (1994a) Sustainable rural tourism strategies: a tool for development and conservation. In: Bramwell, B. and Lane, B. (eds) *Rural Tourism and Sustainable Rural Development.* Channel View Publications, Clevedon.

Lane, B. (1994b) What is rural tourism? *Journal of Sustainable Tourism* 2, 7–21.

Lane, J. (1995) Nongovernmental organizations and participatory development: the concept in theory versus the concept in practice. In: Nelson, N. and Wright, S. (eds) *Power and Participatory Development: Theory and Practice.* Technology Publications, London, pp. 73–99.

Langholz, J. (1998) Exploring the effects of alternative income opportunities on rainforest use: some insights from Guatemala's Maya Biosphere Reserve. *Society and Natural Resources* 11, 139–150.

Langton, S. (1978) *Citizen Participation in America.* Lexington Books, Lexington, Massachusetts, 125 pp.

LaPage, W.F. (1994a) *Partnerships for Parks: 'To Form a More Perfect Union' – A Handbook for Building and Guiding Park Partnerships.* National Association of State Park Directors, Tallahassee Florida.

LaPage, W.F. (1994b) Self-funding state parks – the New Hampshire experience. *Parks* 4(2), 22–27. IUCN, Protected Areas Programme, Gland, Switzerland.

LaPage, W.F. (1995) Parklands as paradox: the search for logic in the public's parklands. *Journal of Park and Recreation Administration* 13(4), 1–12.

Lapierre, J. (1991) A proposal for a satellite account and information system for tourism: unpublished discussion paper. National Accounts and Environment Division, Statistics Canada, Ottawa.

Lapierre, J. and Hayes, D. (1994) The tourism satellite account. *National Income and Expenditure Accounts, Second Quarter,* xxxiii–lvii. Statistics Canada, Ottawa.

Lash, S. (1990) *Sociology of Postmodernism.* Routledge, London.

Lavery, P. (1993) Outbound Markets – UK Outbound. *Travel and Tourism Analyst* 3, 20–34.

Lazarus, R. and Folkman, S. (1984) *Stress, Appraisal and Coping.* Springer Publishing, New York.

Lea, J. (1988) *Tourism and Development in the Third World.* Routledge, London.

Ledgerwood, C., Crotts, J. and Everett, A. (1998) Antecedents of employee burnout in the hotel industry. *Progress in Tourism and Hospitality Research* 4, 31–44.

Lee, K.N. (1993) *Compass and Gyroscope: Integrating Science and Politics for the Environment.* Island Press, Washington, DC.

Lee, M.E. and Driver, B.L. (1996) Benefits-based Management: a new paradigm for Managing amenity resources. In: *Second Canada/U.S. Workshop on Visitor Management in Parks, Forests, and Protected Areas,* May 13–16, 1992. University of Wisconsin, Madison, pp. 1–22.

Leistritz, F.L. and Murdock, S.H. (1981) *The Socioeconomic Impact of Resource Development: Methods for Assessment.* Westview Press, Boulder, Colorado.

Leitch, J.A. and Leistritz, F.L. (1985) Techniques for assessing the secondary impact of recreation and tourism. In: Probst, D.B. (ed.) *Assessing the Economic Impacts of Recreation and Tourism.* USDA Southeastern Forest Experiment Station, Asheville, North Carolina. pp. 23–27.

Leones, J., Colby, B. and Crandall, K. (1998) Tracking expenditures of the elusive nature tourists of Southeastern Arizona. *Journal of Travel Research* 36(3), 56–64.

Leopold, A. (1934) Conservation economics. *Journal of Forestry* 32, 537–544.

Levin, L. (1987) Every silver lining has a cloud: the limits of health promotion. *Social Policy* 18(1), 57–60.

Levitt, T. (1965) Exploit the product life cycle. *Harvard Business Review* 11, 81–94.

Librarian of Congress (1962) *Outdoor Recreation Literature: a Survey: Outdoor Recreation Resources Review Commission Study Report 27*. US Government Printing Office, Washington, DC.

Lickorich, L. (1991) Developing a single European policy. *Tourism Management* 12(3), 178–184.

Liddle, M. (1997) *Recreation Ecology*. Chapman & Hall, London.

Lime, D. (1972) Behavioral research in outdoor recreation management: an example of how visitors select campgrounds. In: *Environment and the Social Sciences: Perspectives and Applications*. American Psychological Association, Washington, DC, pp. 198–206.

Lime, D. (1977) Principles of recreation carrying capacity. In: *Proceedings of the Southern States Recreation Research Applications Workshop*. Asheville, North Carolina, pp. 122–134.

Lime, D. (1985) Who uses rivers for recreation and what of the future? In: *National River Recreation Symposium Proceedings*. Louisiana State University, Baton Rouge.

Lime, D. and Stankey, G. (1971) Carrying capacity: maintaining outdoor recreation quality. In *Recreation Symposium Proceedings*. USDA Forest Service, pp. 174–184.

Lime, D.W., Thompson, J.L. and Anderson, D.H. (1994) Why do people float rivers and how long do the benefits last? In: *Rivers Without Boundaries: Proceedings of the second biennial American River Management Society symposium on river planning and Management, April 18–22, 1994, Grand Junction*, Colorado. American River Management Society, Missoula, Montana, pp. 135–142.

Lindberg, K., McCool, S.F. and Stankey, G.H. (1997) Rethinking carrying capacity. *Annals of Tourism Research* 24(2), 461–464.

Lindsay, J.L. (1980) Trends in outdoor recreation activity conflicts. In: *Proceedings of the 1980 National Outdoor Recreation Symposium*. USDA Forest Service General Technical Report NE-57, Broomall, Pennsylvania, 1, 215–221.

Lins, S.A. (1991) Community development and the National Park Service: examples of cooperation in Boxley Valley, Arkansas, and Ebey's Landing, Washington. *Small Town* July–August, 4–11.

Lipman, G.H., Savignac, A.E. and Strong, J.F. (1996) *Agenda 21 for the Travel and Tourism Industry: Towards Environmentally Sustainable Development*. World Travel and Tourism Council, London.

Lippard, L.R. (1997) *The Lure of the Local: Senses of Place in a Multicentered Society*. The New Press, New York.

Lithuanian Tourist Board (1997) *Lithuania. Baltic Hospitality at its Best* (catalogue). R. Paknys Publishing, Vilnius.

Litt, M. (1988) Self-efficacy and perceived control: cognitive mediators of pain tolerance. *Journal of Personality and Social Psychology* 54(1), 149–160.

Little, W. and Noe, F.P. (1984) A highly condensed description of the thought process used in developing visitor research for southeast parks. US Department of the Interior, National Park Service, Southeast Regional Office, Atlanta, Georgia.

Littrell, M.A. (1997) Shopping experiences and Marketing of culture to tourists. In: Robinson, M., Evans, N. and Callaghan, P. (eds) *Tourism and Culture: Image, Identity and Marketing*. Centre for Travel and Tourism, University of Northumbria, pp. 107–120.

Long (1998) National Rural Tourism Foundation Information Piece. University of Colorado, Boulder, Colorado.

Long, P., Clark, J. and Liston, D. (1994) *Win, Lose or Draw? Gambling With America's Small Towns*. The Aspen Institute, Washington, DC.

Loomis, J. and Shrestha, R. (1998) *Update to the Resources Program and Assessment (RPA) Values*. Dept. of Agricultural and Resource Economics, Colorado State University, Fort Collins, Colorado.

Loomis, J., Rosenberger, R. and Shretha, R. (1998) *Using META Analysis as a Recreation Benefit-Transfer Protocol: Guidance and Results*. Dept. of Agricultural and Resource Economics, Colorado State University, Fort Collins, Colorado.

Loomis, J.B. (1993) *Integrated Public Lands Management: Principles and Applications to National Forests, Parks, Wildlife Refuges, and BLM Lands*. Columbia University Press, New York.

Lord, R. (1997) New media will rip apart the travel business. *Revolution* (Sept.), 34–39.

Lovelock, C. (1996) *Services Marketing*, 3rd edn. Prentice Hall, Upper Saddle River, New Jersey.

Loveman, G.W. (1998) Employee satisfaction, customer loyalty, and financial performance: An empirical examination of the service profit chain in retail banking. *Journal of Service Research* 1(1), 18–31.

Lowyck, E., Langenhove, L.V. and Bollaert, L. (1992) Typologies of tourist roles. In: Johnson, P. and Thomas, B. (eds) *Choice and Demand in Tourism*. Mansell, London, pp. 13–32.

Lozada, M. (1997) Balancing act. *Techniques*, 72(1), 14–26.

Lucas, R. (1964) *The Recreational Capacity of the Quetico-Superior Area*. USDA Forest Service Research Paper LS-15.

Lucas, R. (1966) The contribution of environmental research to wilderness policy decisions. *Journal of Social Issues* 22, 117–126.

Lucas, R.C. (1985) *Visitor characteristics, attitudes, and use patterns in the Bob Marshall Wilderness complex, 1970–1982.* Research Paper INT-345. USDA Forest Service, Intermountain Research Station, Ogden, Utah.

Lundberg, K. and Johnson, R.L. (1997) The economic values of tourism's social impacts. *Annals of Tourism Research* 24, 90–116.

Lundgren, A. (ed.) (1996) *Recreation Fees in the National Park Service – Issues, Policies and Guidelines for Future Action.* St Paul, Minnesota: University of Minnesota Cooperative Park Studies Unit.

Lundgren, A. and Lime, D. (1997) Overview of a 1997 National Park Service monitoring study to obtain visitor reactions to the Recreational Fee Demonstration Program. Final Report to National Park Service. University of Minnesota, Department of Forest Resources and Cooperative Park Studies Unit, St Paul, Minnesota.

Lux, T.P. and Migliaccio, J.N. (1994) Successful marketing to a four generation marketplace. Spectrum, January–February, 6–9.

Luxembourg Ministry of Tourism (n.d.) *Luxembourg. Small and Beautiful* (catalogue) Interpub', Luxembourg.

MacCannell, D. (1976) *The Tourist: A New Theory of the Leisure Class.* London: Macmillan.

MacCannell, D. (1989) *The Tourist. A New Theory of the Leisure Class.* 2nd edn. Schocken Books, New York.

MacCannell, D. (1992) *Empty Meeting Grounds. The Tourist Papers.* Routledge, London.

Machlis. G. and Harvey, M. (1993) The adoption and diffusion of recreation research programs: a case study of the visitor services project. *Journal of Park and Recreation Administration* 11, 49–65.

Madrigal, R. and Kahle, L.R. (1994) Predicting vacation activity preferences on the basis of value-system segmentation. *Journal of Travel Research* 32, 22–28.

Mak, J. (1989) The economic contribution of travel to state economies. *Journal of Travel Research* 28(2), 3–5.

Maki, W. (1997) Accounting for local economic change in regional I-O modeling. *Journal of Regional Analysis and Policy* 27, 95–109.

Malaysia Tourism Promotion Board (1988) *Malaysia. Moving On* (catalogue). Malaysia Tourism Board, Kuala Lumpur.

Manfredo, M.J., Driver, B.L. and Brown, P.J. (1983) A test of concepts inherent in experience based setting Management for outdoor recreation areas. *Journal of Leisure Research* 15, 263–283.

Manidis Roberts Consultants (1997) Developing a tourism optimization management model (TOMM), a model to monitor and manage tourism on Kangaroo Island, South Australia. Surry Hills, New South Wales, Manidis Roberts Consultants.

Manning, R. (1979) Strategies for managing recreational use of national parks. *Parks* 4, 13–15.

Manning, R. (1985) Crowding norms in backcountry settings: a review and synthesis. *Journal of Leisure Research* 17, 75–89.

Manning, R. (1986a) Density and crowding in wilderness: search and research for satisfaction. In: *Proceedings – National Wilderness Research Conference: Current Research.* USDA Forest Service General Technical Report INT-212, pp. 440–448.

Manning, R. (1997) Social carrying capacity of parks and outdoor recreation areas. *Parks and Recreation* 32, 32–38.

Manning, R. (1999) *Studies in Outdoor Recreation.* Oregon State University Press, Corvallis, Oregon.

Manning, R., Jacobi, C., Valliere, W. and Wang, B. (1998) Standards of quality in parks and recreation. *Parks and Recreation* 33, 88–94.

Manning, R. and Lime, D. (1996) Crowding and carrying capacity in the national park system: toward a social science research agenda. In: *Crowding and Congestion in the National Park System: Guidelines for Management and Research.* St Paul, Minnesota: University of Minnesota Agricultural Experiment Station Publication 86, 27–65.

Manning, R. and Wang, B. (1998) Social science in the national park system: an assessment of visitor information. *Park Science* 18, 1, 16–17.

Manning, R., Lime, D., Hof, M. and Freimund, W. (1995a) The visitor experience and resource protection process: the application of carrying capacity to Arches National Park. *The George Wright Forum* 12, 41–55.

Manning, R., Lime, D., Hof, M. and Freimund, W. (1995b) The carrying capacity of national parks: theory and application. In *Proceedings of the Conference on Innovations and Challenges in the Management of Visitor Opportunities in Parks and Protected Areas.* University of Waterloo, Waterloo, Canada, pp. 9–21.

Manning, R., Lime, D. and McMonagle, R. (1995c) Indicators and standards of the quality of the visitor experience at a heavily-used national park. In: *Proceedings of the 1994 Northeastern Recreation Research Symposium.* USDA Forest Service General Technical Report NE 198, pp. 24–32.

Manning, R., Lime, D., Freimund, W. and Pitt, D. (1996a) Crowding norms at frontcountry sites: a visual approach to setting standards of quality. *Leisure Sciences* 18, 39–59.

Manning, R., Lime, D. and Hof, M. (1996b) Social carrying capacity of natural areas: theory and application in the U.S. National Parks. *Natural Areas Journal* 16, 118–127.

Manning, R.E. (1986b) *Studies in Outdoor Recreation: Search and Research for Satisfaction*. Oregon State University Press, Corvallis, Oregon.

Manning, W.D. and Smock, P.J. (1997) Children's living arrangements in unmarried-mother families. *Journal of Family Issues* 18(5), 526–545.

Margherio, L. (1997) *The Emerging Digital Economy*. US Dept. of Commerce, Washington, DC.

Marion, J.L. (1991) Developing a natural resource inventory and monitoring program for visitor impacts on recreation sites: a procedural manual. Natural Resources Report NPS/NRVT/NRR-91/06. USDI National Park Service, Denver, Colorado.

Marion, J.L. (1994) An assessment of trail conditions in Great Smoky Mountains National Park. Research/Resources Management Report. USDI National Park Service, Atlanta, Georgia.

Marion, J.L. (1995) Capabilities and management utility of recreation impact monitoring programs. *Environmental Management* 19, 763–771.

Marion, J.L. and Cole, D.N. (1996) Spatial and temporal variation in soil and vegetation impacts on campsites. *Ecological Applications* 6, 520–530.

Marion, J.L. and Sober, T. (1987) Environmental impact management in a wilderness area. *Northern Journal of Applied Forestry* 4, 7–10.

Marion, J.L., Roggenbuck, J.W. and Manning, R.E. (1993) Problems and practices in backcountry recreation Management: A survey of national park service managers. Natural Resources Report NPS/NRVT/NRR-93/12. USDI National Park Service, Denver, Colorado.

Marks, S.A. (1991) *Southern Living in Black and White: Nature, History, and Ritual in a Carolina Community*. Princeton University Press, Princeton, New Jersey.

Martin, D. (1995) An importance/performance analysis of service providers' perceptions of quality service in the hotel industry. *Journal of Hospitality and Leisure Marketing* 3(1), 5–16.

Martin, W. (1986) Measuring and improving your service quality. *The Cornell Hotel and Restaurant Administration Quarterly* 26(4), 80–87.

Martin, W.E., Gum, R.L. and Smith, A.H. (1974) *The Demand for and Value of Hunting, Fishing, and General Rural Outdoor Recreation in Arizona*. Agricultural Experiment Station Technical Bulletin 211. University of Arizona, Tucson.

Martinetz, T. and Schulten, K. (1994) Topology representing networks. *Neural Networks* 7, 507–522.

Martinetz, T., Berkovich, St. G. and Schulten, K. (1993) 'Neural gas' network for vector quantization and its application to time-series prediction. *IEEE Transactions of Neural Networks* 4, 558–569.

Maser, C. (1994) *Sustainable Forestry: Philosophy, Science and Economics*. St Lucie Press, Delray Beach, Florida.

Mason, M.A. and Mauldon, J. (1996) The new stepfamily requires a new public policy. *Journal of Social Issues* 52(3), 11–28.

Masten, A.S. and Garmezy, N. (1985) Risk, vulnerability and protective factors in developmental psychopathology. In: Lahey, B.B. and Kazkin, A.E. (eds) *Advances in Clinical Child Psychology* 8. Plenum Press, New York, pp. 1–52.

Masten, A.S., Best, K.M. and Garmezy, N. (1990) Resilience and development: contributions from the study of children who overcome adversity. *Journal of Child Psychological Psychiatry* 29, 745–764.

Mathieson, A. and Wall, G. (1982) *Tourism: Economic, Physical and Social Impacts*. Longman Scientific & Technical, Harlow, Essex, UK.

Matthews, H. (1978) *International Tourism, a Political and Social Analysis*, Schenkman Publishing Company, Massachusetts.

Matulef, M.L. (1988) Community development: a national perspective.

Mazanec, J. (1980) Deterministische und probabilistische Klassifikation in der Konsumverhaltens-forschung: Ein empirischer Anwendungsversuch der Quervalidierung clusteranalytischer Verfahren für qualitative Daten mit der Latent Class-Analyse. In: Fandel, G. (ed.) *Operations Research Proceedings 1980*. Springer, Berlin-Heidelberg- New York, pp. 296–305.

Mazanec, J.A. TRN, http://leisure.wu-wien.ac.at/software/

Mazanec, J.A. (1984) How to detect travel market segments: a clustering approach. *Journal of Travel Research* 23, 17–21.

Mazanec, J.A. (1995) Positioning analysis with self-organizing maps, an exploratory study on luxury hotels. *The Cornell Hotel and Restaurant Administration Quarterly* 36, 80–95.

Mazanec, J.A. and Zins, A. (1992) EUROSTYLES and SOCIO-TARGETS as guest segments: selected findings, a brief outline of the EUROSTYLES typology. *Revue de Tourisme* 2/1992, 5–8.

Mazanec, J.A. and Zins, A. (1993) Tourist behavior and the new European life style typology: exploring the managerial relevance for tourism marketing. In: Theobald, W. (ed.) *Global Tourism: the Next Decade*. Butterworth-Heinemann, Oxford, pp. 199–216.

McAfee, R.R. and McMillian, J. (1997) Electronic markets. In: Kalakota, R. and Whinston, A.B. (eds) *Readings in Electronic Commerce*. Addison Wesley, Reading, Massachusetts, pp. 293–309.

McAvoy, L.H. and Dustin, D.L. (1983) Indirect versus direct regulation of recreation behavior. *Journal of Park and Recreation Administration* 1, 12–17.

McCay, B.J. and Jentoft, S. (1996) From the bottom up: participatory issues in fisheries management. *Society and Natural Resources Journal* 9(3), 237–250.

McClintock, M. (1996) Why women's outdoor trips. In: Warren, K. (ed.) *Women's Voices in Experiential Education*. Kendall/Hunt Publishing Company, Dubuque, Iowa, pp. 18–23.

McConnell, K.E. (1977) Congestion and willingness to pay: a study of beach use. *Land Economics* 53, 187–195.

McCool, S.F. and Ashor, J.L. (1984) *Politics and Rivers: Creating Effective Citizen Involvement in Management Decisions*. 1984 National River Recreation Symposium, College of Design, Louisiana State University, Baton Rouge, Louisiana.

McCool, S.F. and Cole, D.N. (comp) (1997) *Proceedings –Limits of Acceptable Change and Related Planning Processes: Progress and Future Directions*. General Technical Report INT-371. USDA Forest Service, Intermountain Research Station, Ogden, Utah.

McCool, S.F. and Lucas, R.C. (1990) Managing resources and people in wilderness: accomplishments and challenges. In: Lime, D.W. (ed.) *Managing America's Enduring Wilderness Resource: Proceedings of the Conference*. Minnesota Agricultural Experiment Station, St Paul, Minnesota, pp. 64–75.

McCool, S.F. and Stankey, G.H. (1986) *Planning and Social Change: Responding to the Revolution in Recreation Demand*. World Congress, International Union of Forest Research Organizations, Llubljana.

McCool, S.F. and Watson, A.E. (comp) (1995) *Linking Tourism, the Environment, and Sustainability*. Proceedings of a Special Session at the 1994 National Recreation and Park Association Congress, Minneapolis, Minnesota. Intermountain Research Station, USDA Forest Service, Ogden, Utah (Gen. Tech. Rpt. INT-GTR-323).

McDonald, J. and Hutchison, I. (1986) Minority and ethnic variation in outdoor recreation participation. A literature review: the President's Commission on Americans Outdoors. S-41-S-51, US Government Printing Office, Washington, DC.

McDonough, M.H. and Wheeler, C.W. (1998) *Toward School and Community Collaboration in Social Forestry: Lessons from the Thai Experience*. US Agency for International Development, Washington, DC.

McDonough, M.H., Smith, P.D. and Propst, D.B. (1997) Public participation in ecosystem Management planning: Can the net be widened? McIntire-Stennis Project Proposal no. 1432, Department of Forestry, Michigan State University, East Lansing, Michigan.

McFarlan, D. (ed.) (1989) *The Guinness Book of Records 1990*. Industria Grafica, Barcelona.

McKercher, B. and Robbins, B. (1998) Business Development Issues affecting Nature Based Tourism Operators in Australia. *Journal of Sustainable Tourism* 6(2), 173–188.

McLaughlin, W.J. and Paradice, W.E.J. (1980) Using visitor preference information to guide dispersed winter recreation management for cross-country skiing and snowmobiling. In: *Proceedings of the North American Symposium on Dispersed Winter Recreation*. Office of Special Programs, Education Series 2–3, University of Minnesota, St Paul, Minnesota, pp. 64–70.

McLean, D. (1999) Trends in visits to state parks. In: *Outdoor Recreation in American Life: a National Assessment of Demand and Supply Trends*. Sagamore Publishing, Champaign, Illinois, 284–287.

McMillen, J. and Eadington, W.R. (1986) The evolution of gambling laws in Australia. *The Journal of International and Comparative Law* 8(1).

McMullin, S.L. and Nielsen, L.A. (1991) Resolution of natural resource allocation conflicts through effective public involvement. *Policy Studies Journal* 19, 553.

McNair, D. (1993) 1993 RPA Recreation Values Database. USDA Forest Service, Washington, DC.

McNeely, J.A. (ed.) (1995) *Expanding Partnerships in Conservation*. Island Press, Washington, DC.

Meadows, D. and Meadows, D. (1972) *Limits to Growth*. Universe Books, New York.

Medjuck, S., Keefe, J.M. and Fancey, P.J. (1998) Available but not accessible: an examination of the use of workplace policies for caregivers of elderly kin. *Journal of Family Issues* 19(3), 274–300.

Medlik, S. and Middleton, V.T.C. (1973) Product formulation in tourism. *Tourism and Marketing* 13, 267–279.

Meinecke, E. (1928) *A Report Upon the Effects of Excessive Tourist Travel on the California Redwood Parks*. California State Printing Office, Sacramento, California.

Meis, S. and Lapierre, J. (1995) Measuring tourism's economic importance – a Canadian case study. *Economic Intelligence Unit Travel and Tourism Analyst* 2, 78–91.

Meyersohn, R. (1969) The sociology of leisure in the United States: introduction and bibliography, 1945–1965. *Journal of Leisure Research* 1, 53–68.

Miers, D. (1996) Objectives and systems in the regulation of commercial gambling. In McMillen, J. (ed.) *Gambling Cultures: Studies in History and Interpretation.* Routledge, London and New York, pp. 288–311.

Mill, R.C. and Morrison, A.M. (1985) *The Tourism System.* Prentice-Hall, Englewood Cliffs, New Jersey, pp. 406–407.

Miller, J.M. (1992) *Deer Camp.* Massachusetts Institute of Technology, Cambridge, Massachusetts and Vermont Folklife Center, Middlebury, Vermont.

Miller, R.E., Polenske, K.R. and Rose, A.Z. (1989) *Frontiers of Input-Output Analysis.* Oxford University Press, New York.

Miller, T. and McCool, S.M. (1998, May) Stress and coping in recreational settings: a transactional approach. In: *Seventh International Symposium on Society and Resource Management, Abstract Proceedings.* Columbia, Missouri.

Milne, S.S. (1987) Differential multipliers. *Annals of Tourism Research* 14, 509–515.

Milon, J.W., Mulkey, W.D. and Efferbrock, M.J. (1982) Regional impact analysis and recreation multipliers. *Review of Regional Science* 12(3), 11–21.

Minnesota Department of Natural Resources (MN DNR) (1997) Tettegouche State Park Management Plan. Division of Parks and Recreation, St Paul, Minnesota.

Minnesota Department of Natural Resources (MN DNR) (1998) Itasca State Park Management Plan. Division of Parks and Recreation, St Paul, Minnesota.

Minogue, K. (1985) Democracy. In: Kuper, A. and Kuper, J. (eds) *The Social Science Encyclopedia.* Routledge & Kegan Paul. London.

Mitchell, L. (1969) Recreational geography: evolution and research needs. *Professional Geographer* 21, 117–119.

Mitchell, R. and Carson, R. (1989) *Using Surveys to Value Public Goods: the Contingent Valuation Method.* Resources for the Future, Washington, DC.

Mitchell, S. (1995) The next baby boom. *American Demographics* 17 (10), 22–31.

Mitten, D. (1986) Women's outdoor programs need a different philosophy. *The Bulletin of the Association of College Unions-International* 54(5), 16–19.

Mitten, D. and Dutton, R. (1996) Outdoor leadership considerations with women survivors of sexual abuse. In: Warren, K. (ed.), *Women's Voices in Experiential Education,* Kendall/Hunt Publishing Company, Dubuque, Iowa, pp. 130–140.

Mo, Ch-M., Howard, D.R. and Havitz, M.E. (1993) Testing an international tourist role typology. *Annals of Tourism Research* 20, 319–335.

Mogelonsky, M. (1995) Happy workers, lower costs. *American Demographics* 17(7), 30–36.

Molotch, H. (1988) The rest room and equal opportunity. *Sociological Forum* 3(1), 128–132.

Moncrief, L. (1970) Trends in outdoor recreation research. *Journal of Leisure Research* 2, 127–130.

Monteiro, S. and Rowenczyk, C. (1992) Les Vacances des Francais. Tendances Conques et resultats. Institut National de la Statistique et des étydes Economiques (INSEE) Paris.

Monteson, P.A. and Singer, J.L. (1992) Turn your spa into a winner. *Cornell Hotel and Restaurant Quarterly* 33 (June), 37–44.

Morey, E. (1994) *Two RUM's Uncloaked.* Department of Economics, University of Colorado, Boulder, Colorado.

Morgan, W.P. (1994) Physical activity, fitness and depression. In: Bouchard, C., Shephard, R.J. and Stephens, T. (eds) *Physical Activity, Fitness and Health, International Proceedings and Consensus Statement.* Human Kinetics, Champaign, Illinois, pp. 851–867.

Morris, B. (1996) The future of retirement – its not what you think. *Fortune,* August,19, 22–28.

Morris, B. (1997) Home-office heaven – and hell. *Fortune* 135(5), 82–83.

Morris, C. (1956) *Varieties of Human Value.* University of Chicago Press, Chicago, Illinois.

Morrow, S. (1997) *The Art of the Show.* International Association for Exposition Management, Dallas, Texas.

Mowforth, M. and Munt, I. (1998) *Tourism and Sustainability,* Routledge, London.

Mueller, E. and Gurin, G. (1962) Participation in Outdoor Recreation: Factors Affecting Demand Among American Adults. Outdoor Recreation Resources Review Commission Study Report 20. US Government Printing Office, Washington, District of Columbia.

Muller, H. (1997) The thorny path to sustainable tourism development. In: France, L. (ed.) *The Earthscan Reader in Sustainable Tourism.* Earthscan Publications, London.

Mundt, J.W. (1993) *Reiseveranstaltung.* R. Oldenburg Verlag, München, Wien, pp. 57–58.

Murdock, S.H., Backman, K. and Hoque, M.N. (1991) The implications of change in population size and composition on future participation in outdoor recreational activities. *Journal of Leisure Research* 23.

Murphy, P. (1994) Tourism and sustainable development. In: Theobald, W. (ed.) *Global Tourism. The Next Decade.* Butterworth-Heinemann, Oxford, pp. 274–279.

Murphy, P.E. (1985) *Tourism: A Community Approach.* Methuen, New York.

Murphy, P.E. (1988) Community driven tourism planning. *Tourism Management*, June, 96–97.

Murray, J. (1995) Festivals and events in Nova Scotia: a development strategy for the 90's. Paper presented at the TTRA Canadian Chapter annual conference.

Myrdal, G. (1957) *Economic Theory and Underdeveloped Regions*. Duckworth, London.

Nagel, W. (1992) *Policy and Practice of Community Participation in the U.S. Agency for International Development*. US Agency for International Development, Washington, DC.

Nahrstedt, W. (1993) Leisure Policy in Germany. In: Bramham, P., Henry, I., Mommaas, H. and von der Poel, H. (eds), *Leisure Policies in Europe*. CAB International. Wallingford, UK.

National Academy of Sciences (1969) *A Program for Outdoor Recreation Research*. National Academy of Sciences, Washington, DC.

National Advisory Commission on Civil Disorders (1970) Kerner Commission Report: Grievances. In: *Recreation and Leisure Service for the Disadvantaged*. Lea and Febiger, Philadelphia, Pennsylvania, pp. 41–48.

National Gambling Impact Study Commission (1999) Native American gaming. Staff report.

National Park Service, USDI (1994) National Park Service Strategic Plan – Vision. US Department of the Interior, NPS, Washington, DC.

National Park Service, USDI (1995a) Draft General Management Plan and Environmental Impact Statement for Grand Canyon National Park, Arizona. US Department of the Interior. March.

National Park Service, USDI (1995b) *The Visitor Experience and Resource Protection Implementation Plan: Arches National Park*. USDI, National Park Service, Denver Service Center, Colorado.

National Park Service, USDI (1997a) Draft Yosemite Valley Implementation Plan and Supplemental Environmental Impact Statement for Yosemite National Park, California. US Department of the Interior. September.

National Park Service, USDI (1997b) *VERP: The Visitor Experience and Resource Protection (VERP) Framework – a Handbook for Planners and Managers*. Denver, Colorado: Denver Service Center.

National Park Service, Northeast Field Area, USDI (1996) Partnership Network – an Ambassador's Guide to park partnerships in the Northeast US Philadelphia, Pennsylvania.

National Recreation and Park Association (1994) *Beyond Fund and Games: Emerging Roles of Public Recreation*. National Recreation and Park Association, Arlington, Virginia.

National Sporting Goods Association (1999) *The Sporting Goods Market in 1999*. National Sporting Goods Association, Mt Prospect, Illinois.

National Task Force on Tourism Data (1987) *Tourism Satellite Account: Working Paper No. 3*. Statistics Canada, Ottawa.

National Tourism Organization of Serbia (1998) *Serbia. Landscape Painted from the Heart* (catalogue). National Tourism Organization of Serbia, Belgrade.

Nepal Department of Tourism (1998) *Nepal. A World of its Own* (catalogue) Nepal Department of Tourism, Kathmandu.

Nevitte, N. and Inglehart, R. (1995) North American Value Change and Integration. Lessons from Western Europe? In: de Moor, R. (ed.) *Values in Western Societies*. Tilburg University Press, Tilburg.

New Families, Old Values? Changes in the family structure (1993) *The Futurist*. 27(1), 45–46.

New Zealand Tourist Board (1995) *Product Development Opportunities for Asian Markets*. New Zealand Tourist Board, Wellington.

Nickerson, N.P. and Nickerson, R.E. (1998) Economic impacts of Going-to-the-Sun Road reconstruction: Montana and 'Glacier Area' impacts. Institute for Tourism and Recreation Research, The University of Montana, Missoula, Montana.

Nickerson, R. (1998) Understanding the personal onsite beneficial experiences of Minnesota State Park visitors. PhD dissertation, University of Minnesota, St Paul, Minnesota.

Nickerson, R., Anderson, D.H., Perger, B., Pierskalla, C. and Johnson, W. (1997a) 1993 Study of visitor experiences and benefits at Forestville/Mystery Cave State Park. Final Report to Minnesota Department of Natural Resources, Division of Parks and Recreation, St Paul, Minnesota.

Nickerson, R., Anderson, D.H., Perger, B., Pierskalla, C. and Johnson, W. (1997b) 1993 study of visitor experiences and benefits at Itasca State Park (Tech. report) University of Minnesota, Department of Forest Resources, St Paul, Minnesota.

Nickerson, R., Anderson, D.H., Perger, B., Pierskalla, C. and Johnson, W. (1997c) 1993 study of visitor experiences and benefits at Tettegouche State Park (Tech. report) University of Minnesota, Department of Forest Resources. St Paul, Minnesota.

Nickerson, R., Anderson, D.H., Perger, B., Pierskalla, C., Johnson, W. and Hagerty, K. (1998a) 1993 Fall study of visitor experiences and benefits at Tettegouche State Park. Final Report to Minnesota Department of Natural Resources, Division of Parks and Recreation, St Paul, Minnesota.

Nickerson, R., Anderson, D.H., Perger, B., Pierskalla, C., Johnson, W. and Hagerty, K. (1998b) 1993 Study of visitor experiences and benefits at Interstate State Park. Final Report to Minnesota Department of Natural Resources, Division of Parks and Recreation, St Paul, Minnesota.

Nickerson, R., Anderson, D.H., Perger, B., Pierskalla, C., Johnson, W. and Hagerty, K. (1998c) 1993 Study of visitor experiences and benefits at St. Croix State Park. Final Report to Minnesota Department of Natural Resources, Division of Parks and Recreation, St Paul, Minnesota.

Nigerian Tourism Development Corporation (n.d.) *Nigeria. A Land of Cultural Diversity* (catalogue). Wuse, Abuja.

Nilsson, O.S. and Solgaard, H.S. (1995) The changing consumer in Denmark. *International Journal of Research in Marketing* 12, 405–416.

Nitsch, B. and Virginian der Straaten, J. (1995) Rural tourism development: using a sustainable development approach. In: Coccossis, H. and Nijkamp, P. (eds) *Sustainable Tourism Development*. Avebury/Ashgate, Aldershot/Vermont.

NTA (National Tour Association) (1997) *Market Assessment Plan for the Future Senior Market: A Tour Operator Survival Guide for the Next Generation of Seniors*. National Tour Association, Market Development Council. Lexington.

NTS (National Travel Survey) (1995 and 1997) Full year results of national travel survey (NTS) Marked report from US. Travel Data Center and the Travel Industry Association of America. Washington DC. See also Statistical Abstract of the Unites States (1998) (under Parks, Recreation and Travel).

Nyberg, K. (1995) Changes in tourism demand – the Swedish Case. *The Tourist Review* 1/95, 53–57.

Obermair, K. (1998) *Future Trends in Tourism*. University of Vienna.

Oboler, S. (1995) *Ethnic Labels, Latino Lives: Identity and the Politics of (Re)Presentation in the United States*. University of Minnesota Press, Minneapolis, Minnesota.

Observer (1996), 8th December.

O'Connor, P. (1995) *Using Computers in Hospitality*. Cassell, London.

O'Connor, P. (1999) *Electronic Information Distribution in Tourism and Hospitality*. CAB International, Wallingford, UK.

OECD (Organization for Economic Cooperation and Development) (1973) *Tourism Policy and International Tourism in OECD Member Countries*. Organization for Economic Cooperation and Development, Tourism Committee, Paris.

OECD (Organization for Economic Cooperation and Development) (1991) *Manual on Tourism Economic Accounts*. Tourism Committee, Document OCDE/GD (19)82. Organization for Economic Cooperation and Development, Tourism Committee, Paris.

OECD (Organization for Economic Cooperation and Development) (1992) *Business and Jobs in the Rural World*. OECD, Paris.

OECD (Organization for Economic Cooperation and Development) (1992 and 1996) Tourism Policy and International Tourism in OECD Member Countries, Paris.

OECD (Organization for Economic Cooperation and Development) (1994) Tourism Strategies and Rural Development. In: *Tourism Policy and International Tourism*. OECD, Paris.

OECD (Organization for Economic Cooperation and Development) (1995a) *Niche Markets as a Rural Development Strategy*. OECD, Paris.

OECD (Organization for Economic Cooperation and Development) (1995b) *Niche Markets and Rural Development – Workshop Proceedings and Policy Recommendations*. OECD, Paris.

OECD (Organization for Economic Cooperation and Development) (1998a) *Maintaining Prosperity in an Aging Society*. Paris.

OECD (Organization for Economic Cooperation and Development) (1998b) *A Tourism Satellite Account for OECD Countries*. October 7, 1998. Organization for Economic Cooperation and Development, Tourism Committee, Paris.

Okotai, T. (1980) Research requirements of tourism in the Cook Islands. In: Pearce, D. (ed.) *Tourism in the South Pacific, Proceedings of UNESCO Tourism Workshop*. Rarotonga, pp. 169–170.

O'Leary, J. (1999) International tourism in the United States. In: *Outdoor Recreation in American Life: A National Assessment of Demand and Supply Trends*. Sagamore Publishing, Champaign, Illinois, 294–298.

O'Leary, J.T. and Lang, C. (1995) International trends in the development of heritage policies and programs. In: *Proceedings of the 4th International Outdoor Recreation and Tourism Trends Symposium – 1995 National Recreation Resource Planning Conference*, St Paul, Minnesota.

O'Leary, J.T. and Siehl, G.H. (1992) *Trends in Outdoor Recreation: a Review of the Trends Symposium*. Paper presented at the 1992 Fourth North American Symposium on Society and Resource Management. Madison, Wisconsin.

Oliver, R. (1997) *Satisfaction: a Behavioral Perspective on the Consumer*. McGraw Hill, New York.

Omi, P. and Winant, H. (1994 [original edition, 1986]) *Ethnic and Racial Formation in the United States*, 2nd edn. Routledge, New York.

Opaschowski, H.W. (1996) Tourismus. Systematische Einführung – Analysen und Prognosen. Leske+Budrich. Opladen.

Oppermann, M. (1998) Destination threshold potential and the law of repeat visitation. *Journal of Travel Research* 37(Nov), 131–137.

Orbeta-Heytens, A. (1995) A market survey of non spa-goers in 48 continental United States. Masters Thesis Monograph, Cornell University, Ithaca, New York.

Outdoor Recreation Resources Review Commission (1962) *Outdoor Recreation for America*. US Government Printing Office, Superintendent of Documents, Washington, DC.

Owens, P.L. (1985) Conflict as a social interaction process in environment and behavior research: the example of leisure and recreation research. *Journal of Environmental Psychology* 4, 243–259.

Oxford English Dictionary (1994) On-line edition: http://www.lib.uwaterloo.ca/weboed/html.

Palmer, P.J. (1997) The renewal of community in higher education. In: Campbell, W.E. and Smith, K.A. (eds) *New Paradigms for College Teaching*. Interaction Books, Edina, Minnesota, pp. 1–17.

Parasuraman, A., Zeithaml, V. and Berry, L. (1985) A conceptual model of service quality and its implications for future research. *Journal of Marketing* 49, 41–50.

Parasuraman, A., Berry, L. and Zeithaml, V. (1993) More on improving service quality measurement. *Journal of Retailing* 69(1), 140–147.

Parks and Recreation Federation of Ontario (1992) *The Benefits of Parks and Recreation: a Catalogue*. Canadian Parks and Recreation Association, Gloucester, Ontario.

Parr, J. and Gates, R. (1989) Assessing community interest and gathering community support. In: Propst, D.B. (ed.) *International City Management Associations, Partnerships in Local Governance: Effective Council Manager Relations*. International City Management Association, Washington, DC, pp. 122–135.

Parsons, D.J. (1979) The recovery of Bullfrog Lake. *Fremontia* 7(2), 9–13.

Parsons, D.J. (1983) Wilderness protection: an example from the southern Sierra Nevada, USA. *Environmental Conservation* 10, 1–8.

Parsons, D.J. and MacLeod, S.A. (1980) Measuring impacts of wilderness use. *Parks* 5(3), 8–12.

Pawelko, K., Drogin, E. and Graefe, A. (1997) The influence of recreationists' cultural or ethnic background upon their river recreation experiences. In *Proceedings of the 1996 Northeastern Recreation Research Symposium*. USDA Forest Service General Technical Report NE-232, pp. 49–54.

Pearce, D. (1989) *Tourist Development*. Longman Scientific and Technical, Harlow, Essex.

Pearce, P.L., Moscardo, G. and Ross, G.F. (1996) *Tourism Community Relationships*. Elsevier Science, New York.

Pearlin, L.I. and Schooler, C. (1978) The structure of coping. *Journal of Health and Social Behavior* 19, 2–21.

Peppard, J. (ed.) (1993) *IT Strategy for Business*. Pitman, London.

Perloff, R. (1987) Self interest and personal responsibility redux. *American Psychologist* 42(1), 3–11.

Perroux, F. (1955) Note sur la nation de 'pole de croissance, *Cahiers de L'Institut de Science Economique Appliquée*, series D, no. 8.

Perry, R., Dean, K. and Brown, B. (1986) *Counterurbanization: International Case Studies*. Geo Books, Norwich.

Perryman, M.R. and Schmidt, J.R. (1986) *Regional Econometric Modeling*. Kluwer-Nijhoff, Boston, Massachusetts.

Peterson, D.L. and Johnson, D.R. (eds) (1995) *Human Ecology and Climate Change: People and Resources in the Far North*. Taylor and Francis, Washington, DC.

Peterson, G.L. and Williams, J.M. (1999) Access to National Forest land. In: Cordell, H.K. (ed.) *Outdoor Recreation in American Life: a National Assessment of Demand and Supply Trends*. Sagamore Publishing, Champaign, Illinois, pp. 42–44.

Peterson, G.L., Driver, B.L. and Gregory, R. (1988) *Amenity Resource Valuation: Integrating Economics with Other Disciplines*. Venture Publishing, State College, Pennsylvania.

Petzoldt, P. (1974) *The Wilderness Handbook*. Norton & Co., New York.

Phillip, S.F. (1993) Racial differences in perceived attractiveness of tourism destinations, interests, and cultural resources. *Journal of Leisure Research* 25(3), 290–304.

Phillip, S.F. (1998a) Race and gender differences in adolescent peer group approval of leisure activities. *Journal of Leisure Research* 30, 214–234.

Phillip, S.F. (1998b) Race, gender, and leisure benefits. *Journal of Leisure Research* 19.

Pigram, J. (1996) Best practice environmental Management and the tourism industry. *Progress in Tourism and Hospitality Research* 2(344), 261–272.

Pigram, J. and Wahab, S. (1997) Sustainable tourism in a changing world. In: Wahab, S. and Pigram, J. (eds) *Tourism Development and Growth*. Routledge, London, pp. 7–32.

Pirfman, E. (1988) The effects of a wilderness challenge course on victims of rape in locus-of-control, self-concept, and fear. Doctoral dissertation, University of Northern Colorado.

Plant, J. (ed.) (1989) *Healing the Wounds: the Promise of Ecofeminism*. New Society Publishers, Philadelphia, Pennsylvania.

Plog, S. (1973) Why destinations rise and fall in popularity, *Cornell H.R.A. Quarterly*, November, 3–16.

Plog, S.C. (1974) Why destination areas rise and fall in popularity. *The Cornell Hotel and Restaurant Administration Quarterly* 14, 55–58.

Plog, S.C. (1991) *Leisure Travel: Making it a Growth Industry … Again!* John Wiley & Sons, New York.

Plog, St.C. (1990) A carpenter's tool: an answer to Stephen L. J. Smith's review of psychocentrism/allocentrism. *Journal of Travel Research* 28, 43–45.

Poland National Tourism Promotion Agency (1998) *Poland. The Natural Choice* (catalogue) Poland National Tourism Promotion Agency, Warsaw.

Polders, B. (1988) Legalizing gambling as a weapon to combat illegal gambling in the Netherlands. *Nevada Review of Business and Economics* 12(1), 31–33.

Pomeroy, R.S., Uysal, M. and Lamberte, A. (1988) An input-output analysis of South Carolina's economy: with special reference to coastal tourism and recreation. *Leisure Science* 10, 281–291.

Poon, A. (1988) Tourism and information technologies. *Annals of Tourism Research* 15, 531–549.

Poon, A. (1993) *Tourism, Technology and Competitive Strategies*. CAB International, Wallingford, UK.

Porter, M. (1990) *The Competitive Advantage of Nations*. Free Press, New York.

Preister, K. (1989) The theory and management of tourism impacts. *Tourism Recreation Research* 14(1), 15–22.

Prentice, R. (1993) *Tourism and Heritage Attractions*. Routledge. London.

President's Commission on Americans Outdoors (1986) *Report and Recommendations to the President of the United States*. US Government Printing Office, Washington, DC.

President's Commission on Americans Outdoors (1987a) *Americans Outdoors: the Legacy, the Challenge* (with case studies), Sec. 4, Chap. 1. Island Press, Washington, DC.

President's Commission on Americans Outdoors (1987b) *Report and Recommendations to the President of the United States*. Government Printing Office, Washington, DC.

President's Council on Recreation and Natural Beauty (1968) *From Sea to Shining Sea*. Government Printing Office, Washington, DC.

Price, M.F. (1992) Patterns of the development of tourism in mountain environments. *GeoJournal* 27(1), 87–96.

Propst, D.B and Kurtz, M.E. (1989) Perceived control/reactance: a framework for understanding leisure behavior in natural settings. *Leisure Studies* 8, 241–248.

Propst, D.B. and McDonough, M.H. (1999) Role of manager and visitor self-interest in wilderness management: Nordhouse Dunes and the limits of acceptable change (manuscript submitted to *International Journal of Wilderness*), University of Idaho, Wilderness Research Center, Moscow, Idaho.

Pruitt, D.G. and Rubin, J.Z. (1986) *Social Conflict*. Random House Publishers, New York.

Public Land Law Review Commission (1970) *One Third of the Nation's Land*. Government Printing Office, Washington, DC.

Public/Private Ventures (1994) *Community Ecology and Youth Resilience: a Report to the Annie E. Casey Foundation*. Public/Private Ventures, Philadelphia, Pennsylvania.

Purdy, K.G., Decker, D.J. and Brown, T.L. (1989) New York's new hunters: influences from beginning to end. HDRU Series 89-3. Cornell University, Department of Natural Resources, Ithaca, New York.

Quinn, J. (1995) The productivity paradox is false: information technology improves service performance. *Advances in Services Marketing and Management* 5(247), 71–84.

Randall, A. (1983) The problem of Market failure. *Natural Resources Journal* 23, 131–148.

Rasell, E. and Appelbaum, E. (1998) Nonstandard work arrangements: a challenge for workers and labor unions. *Social Policy* 27(2), 31–37.

Real, T. (1997) Looking good: how cultural tourism has changed the face of North American travel destinations. In: Robinson, M., Evans, N. and Callaghan, P. (eds) *Tourism and Culture: Image, Identity and Marketing*. Centre for Travel and Tourism, University of Northumbria, Newcastle upon Tyne, pp. 171–184.

Redekop, D. (1997) *Travel Forecast 2000. Twenty-One Questions for the 21st Century*. Canadian Tourism Research Institute, Ottawa.

Reid, D. (1995) Retirement Living in Elliot Lake-Canada. In: *Niche Markets as a Rural Development Strategy*. OECD, Paris.

Reiling, S., Cheng, H. and Trott, C. (1992) Measuring the discriminatory impact associated with higher recreational fees. *Leisure Sciences* 14, 121–137.

Reilly, E.M. (1997) Telecommuting: putting policy into practice. *HR Focus*, 72(9), 5–6.

Republic of Turkey, Ministry of Tourism (1998) *Turkey. A Gateway to Paradise*. Gokce Ofset, Ankara.

Republique d'Haiti, Secretaire d'Etat au Tourisme (n.d.) *Haiti. Unique* (catalogue) Republique d'Haiti, Secretaire d'Etat au Tourisme, Port au Prince.

Resnick, J. (1997) What makes flex work? (managing flexible work arrangements). *HR Focus*, 74(4), 31.

Resources for the Future (1983) *Outdoor Recreation for America, 1983*. Resources for the Future, Washington, DC.

Revolution in Family Life (1990) *The Futurist* 24(5), 53–55.

Rey, S.J. (1997) Integrating regional econometric and input output models: an evaluation of embedding strategies. *Environment and Planning A 29*, 1057–1072.

Rhode, D.L. (ed.) (1990) *Theoretical Perspectives on Sexual Difference*. Yale University Press, New Haven, Connecticut.

Richards, G. (1996a) *Cultural Tourism in Europe*. CAB International, Wallingford, UK.

Richards, G. (1996b) European cultural tourism: Trends and future prospects. In: Richards, G. (ed.) *Cultural Tourism in Europe*. CAB International, Wallingford, UK, pp. 311–333.

Richards, G. (1996c) Production and consumption of European cultural tourism. *Annals of Tourism Research* 23, 261–283.

Richardson, H.W. (1985) Input-output and economic base multipliers: looking backward and forward. *Journal of Regional Science* 25, 607–661.

Richmond, C. (1991) As their health improves, British broaden their quest for alternative health care. *Canadian Medical Association Journal* 144(7), 912–914.

Richter, R. (1989) *The Politics of Tourism in Asia*, 1989. University of Hawaii Press.

Riddick, C., DeSchriver, M. and Weissinger, E. (1984) A methodological review of research in Journal of Leisure Research from 1978 to 1982. *Journal of Leisure Research* 16, 311–321.

Riordan, C. (1990) *Girls and Boys in School: Together or Separate?* Teachers College Press, New York.

Ritchie, B. and Goeldner, C. (eds) (1994) *Travel, Tourism and Hospitality Research: a Handbook for Managers and Researchers*, 2nd edn. John Wiley & Sons, New York.

Rittvo, S.M. (1997) Planning casinos that complement the urban mosaic. In: Eadington, W.R. and Cornelius, J.A. (eds) *Gambling: Public Policies and the Social Sciences*. Institute for the Study of Gambling and Commercial Gaming, University of Nevada, Reno, pp. 331–350.

Ritzer, G. (1996) *The McDonaldization of Society: an Investigation into the Changing Character of Contemporary Social Life*. Pine Forge Press, Thousand Oaks, California.

Ritzer, G. (1998) Sociological enlightenment: through synthesisme or through eclecticism? Paper delivered at the conference *Sociologists on Postmodemism and Postmodemity*, Amsterdam, 12 February.

Ritzer, G. and Liska, A. (1997) 'McDisneyization' and 'post-tourism': complementary perspectives on contemporary tourism. In: Rojek, C. and Urry, J. (eds) *Touring Cultures. Transformations of Travel and Theory*. Routledge, London, pp. 96–109.

Roberts, N. (1997) Public deliberation: an alternative approach to crafting policy and setting direction. *Public Administration Review* 57(2), 124–132.

Roberts, N.S. (1995) Wilderness as therapy for women. *Parks and Recreation (Research Update)* 30(5), 26–32.

Roberts, N.S. and Drogin, E.B. (1993) The outdoor recreation experience: factors affecting participation of African American women. *Journal of Experiential Education* 16(1), 14–18.

Roberts, N.S. and Drogin, E.B. (1996) *Attitudes and Experiences of Women of Color in the Outdoors*. A paper presented at the NRPA Leisure Research Symposium (abstract in Proceedings), Kansas City, Missouri.

Roberts, N.S. and Henderson, K.A. (1997) Women of color in the outdoors: culture and meanings. *Journal of Experiential Education* 20(3), 134–142.

Robertson, R. (1992) *Globalisation: Special Theory and Global Culture*. Sage, London.

Robertson, R.A. and Regula, J.A. (1994) Recreation displacement and overall satisfaction: a study of central Iowa's licensed boaters. *Journal of Leisure Research* 26, 174–181.

Robinson, M. and Boniface, P. (eds) (1999) *Tourism and Cultural Conflicts*. CAB International, Wallingford, UK.

Robson, W. (1997) *Strategic Management and Information Systems: an Integrated Approach*. 2nd edn. Pitman, London.

Rodin, J. (1986) Aging and health: effects of sense of control. *Science* 233, 1271–1276.

Rogers, E. (1962) *Diffusion of Innovations*. Free Press, New York.

Roggenbuck, J., Williams, D. and Bobinski, C. (1992) Public-private partnership to increase commercial tour guide's effectiveness as nature interpreters. *Journal of Park and Recreation Administration* 10(2), 41–50.

Roggenbuck, J.W. (1992) Use of persuasion to reduce resource impacts and visitor conflicts. In: Manfredo, M.J. (ed.) *Influencing Human Behavior: Theory and Applications in Recreation,*

Tourism, and Natural Resources Management. Sagamore Publishing, Champaign, Illinois, pp. 149–208.

Rojek, C. (1993) *Ways of Escape: Modern Transformations in Leisure and Travel.* MacMillan, Basingstoke.

Rojek, C. (1997) Indexing, dragging and the social construction of tourist sights. In: Rojek, C. and Urry, J. (eds) *Touring Cultures. Transformations of Travel and Theory.* Routledge, London, pp. 52–74.

Rojek, C. and Urry, J. (1997) *Touring Cultures: Transformations of Travel and Theory.* Routledge, London.

Rolston, H., III (1981) Values in nature. *Environmental Ethics* 3(2), 113–128.

Rolston, H., III (1985) Valuing wildlands. *Environmental Ethics* 7, 23–42.

Rolston, H., III (1991) Creation and Recreation: Environmental benefits and human leisure. In: Driver, B.L., Brown, P.J. and Peterson, G.L. (eds) *Benefits of Leisure*, Venture Publishing, State College, Pennsylvania, pp. 365–368.

Rolston, H., III (1994) *Conserving Natural Value.* Columbia University Press, New York.

Rose, S. and Larwood, L. (1988) Charting women's careers: current issues and research. In: Rose, S. and Larwood, L. (eds) *Women's Careers: Pathways and Pitfalls.* Praeger Publishing Co., New York, pp. 3–24.

Rosen, C. (1999) Business Travel News (www.btnonline.com).

Rosenberg, M.J. (1967) Cognitive structure and attitudinal effect. In: Fishbein, M. (ed.) *Readings in Attitude Theory and Measurement.* John Wiley & Sons, New York, pp. 325–340.

Rosenthal, D.H., Loomis, J.B. and Peterson, G.L. (1984) Pricing for efficiency and revenue in public recreation areas. *Journal of Leisure Research* 16(3), 195–208.

Ross, G. (1997) Career stress responses among hospitality employees. *Annals of Tourism Research* 24, 41–51.

Rossman, M. (1994) *Multicultural Marketing: Selling to a Diverse America.* American Management Association, New York.

Rostow, W.W. (1971) *The Stages of Economic Growth.* Cambridge University Press, New York.

Round, J.I. (1983) Non-survey techniques: a critical review of the theory and the evidence. *International Regional Science Review* 8, 189–212.

Runge, C.F. (1987) Induced agricultural innovation and environmental quality: the case of groundwater regulation. *Land Economics* 63(3), 249–258.

Runge, C.F. (1999) Stream, river, delta: induced innovation and environmental values in economics and policy. University of Minnesota, Department of Applied Economics, St Paul, Minnesota.

Rural Development Commission (1992) *Tourism in the Countryside.* Rural Development Commission, London.

Russel, C. (1995) The baby boom turns 50. *American Demographics* 17(12), 22–33.

Rust, R. and Oliver, R. (1994) Service quality: insights and managerial implications from the frontier. In: Rust, R. and Oliver, R. (eds) *Service Quality: New Directions in Theory and Practice.* Sage Publications, Thousand Oaks, California, pp. 1–20.

Rust, R.T., Zahorik, A.J. and Kenningham, T.L. (1996) *Service Marketing.* Harper Collins, New York.

Ruttan, V. (1971) Presidential address: technology and the environment. *American Journal of Agricultural Economics* 53(5), 707–717.

Rutter, M. (1990) Psychosocial resilience and protective mechanisms. In: Role, J., Masten, A., Cached, D., Nuechterlein, C.K. and Weintraub, S. (eds) *Risk and Protective Factors in the Development of Psychopathology*, pp. 181–214. Cambridge University Press, Cambridge.

Rutter, M. (1985) Resilience in the face of adversity: protective factors and resistance to psychiatric disorder. *British Journal of Psychiatry* 147, 598–611.

Ryan, C., Smee, A., Murphy, S. and Getz, D. (1998) New Zealand events: a temporal and regional analysis. *Festival Management and Event Tourism: an International Journal* 5(1/2), 71–83.

Sahlberg, B. (1996) The structure and dynamics of tourism – the Swedish Case. Paper presented at the 31th Tourist Research Centre. Bergen, 16–19 May.

Said, E. (1991) *Orientalism. Western Conceptions of the Orient.* Penguin, Harmondsworth.

Salem, G. (1986) Gender equity and the urban environment. *Urban Resources* 13(2), 3–8.

Santayana, G. (1896) *The Sense of Beauty.* Reprinted by Dover in 1955. Charles Scribner's Sons, New York.

Saunier, R.E. and Meganck, R.A. (eds) (1995) *Conservation of Biodiversity and the New Regional Planning.* Organization of American States and the IUCN – The World Conservation Union, Washington, DC.

Schleicher, T.D., Anderson, D.H. and Lime, D.W. (1994) Techniques to monitor social conditions in the Cuyahoga Valley National Recreation Area – Report 2: Visitor data and information to implement the VERP planning process: Ohio and Erie Canal Towpath Trail. National Park Service Cooperative Studies Unit, University of Minnesota, St Paul, Minnesota.

Schmidhauser, H. (1992) The distinction between short and long holidays. *Revue de Tourisme*. AIEST, 2, 10–13.

Schmidhauser, H. (1995) Die Reiseziele der Schweizer 1980–1992 nach Altersklassen. Trend zur Globalisierung – Aufholen der Ältern – Abkehr der Jugendlichen von Europa. In: Kaspar, C. *Jahrbuch der Schweizerischen Tourismuswirtschaft 1994/95*. St Gallen.

Schneider, C.G. and Shoenberg, R. (1998) *Contemporary Understandings of Liberal Education*. American Association of Colleges and Universities, Washington, DC.

Schneider, I., Anderson, D. and Jakes, P. (1993) *Innovations in Recreation Management: Importance, Diffusion, and Implementation*. USDA Forest Service General Technical Report NC-155, North Central Forest Experiment Station, St Paul, Minnesota.

Schneider, I.E. (1995) Summary results of experimental forest user focus groups. Unpublished report, Clemson University, Clemson, South Carolina.

Schneider, I.E. and Hammitt, W.E. (1995) Visitor response to outdoor recreation conflict: a conceptual approach. *Leisure Sciences* 17, 223–234.

Schreiber, A. (1994) *Lifestyle and Event Marketing*. McGraw-Hill, New York.

Schreiner, E.S. and Moorhead, B.B. (1979) Human impact inventory and management in Olympic National Park backcountry. In: Ittner, R., Potter, D., Agee, J. and Anschell, S. (eds) *Proceedings, Recreational Impact on Wildlands*. USDA Forest Service, Pacific Northwest Region, Portland, Oregon, pp. 203–212.

Schreyer, R. (1990) Conflict in outdoor recreation: the scope of the challenge to resource planning and Management. In: Vining, J. (ed.) *Social Science and Natural Resource Recreation Management*. Westview Press: Boulder, Colorado, pp.13–31.

Schreyer, R., Knopf, R.C. and Williams, D.R. (1984) Reconceptualizing the motive/environment link in recreation choice behavior. In: Stankey, G.H. and McCool, S.F. (eds), *Symposium on Recreation Choice Behavior*, GTR INT-184, USDA Forest Service, Intermountain Research Station, Ogden, Utah, pp. 9–18.

Schutz, A. (1944) The stranger: an essay in social psychology. *American Journal of Sociology* 49(6), 495–507.

Schwartz, J. (1992) Is the baby boomlet ending? *American Demographics* 14(5), 9.

Scott, D., Witt, P.A. and Foss, M.G. (1996) Evaluation of the impact of the Dougherty Arts Center's Creativity Club on children at-risk. *Journal of Park and Recreation Administration* 14(3), 41–60.

Scott, M.J., Belzer, D.B., Nessie, R.J., Schultz, R.W., Stokowski, P.A. and Clark, D.C. (1987) The Economic and Community Impacts of Closing Hanford's N-Reactor and Nuclear Materials Production Facilities. Prepared for the US Department of Energy, Contract DE-AC06-76 RLO 1830. Battelle Memorial Institute, Pacific Northwest Laboratory, Richland, Washington.

Scottish Tourist Board (and British Tourist Authority) (1998) *Scotland. Where to Go and What to See* (catalogue) Scottish Tourist Board, Edinburgh.

Searns, R.M. (1995) The evolution of greenways as an adaptive urban landscape form. *Landscape and Urban Planning* 33(1), 65–80.

Secretary-General, World Tourism Organization (1983) Report of the Secretary-General on the execution of the general programme of work for the period 1982–1983, Addendum B.5.2.1, 'Determination of the importance of tourism as an economic activity within the framework of the national accounting system.' Paper presented to the Fifth Session of the General Assembly, New Delhi, p. 1.

Selanniemi, T. (1996) *Matka Ikuiseen Kesaan. Kulttuuriantropologinen Nakokulma Suomalaisten Etelanmatkailuun (A Journey to the Eternal Summer. The Anthropology of Finnish Sunlust Tourism)*. Suomalaisen Kirjallisunden Seura, Helsinki.

Selin, S. (1998) The promise and pitfalls of collaborating. *Trends* 35(1), 9–13.

Selin, S. and Chavez, D. (1995a) Developing a collaborative model for environmental planning and Management. *Environmental Management* 19(2), 189–195.

Selin, S. and Chavez, D. (1995b) Developing an evolutionary tourism partnership model. *Annals of Tourism Research* 22(4), 844–856.

Selin, S. and Myers, N. (1995) Correlates of partnership effectiveness: the coalition for unified recreation in the Eastern Sierra. *Journal of Park and Recreation Administration* 13(4), 37–46.

Selin, S.W. and Darrow, K. (1995) Partnerships: providing new solutions in outdoor recreation and tourism. In: *Proceedings of the Fourth International Outdoor Recreation and Tourism Trends Symposium and the 1995 National Recreation Resources Planning Conference*, pp. 445–447. University of Minnesota, St Paul, Minnesota.

Selin, S.W., Schuett, M.A. and Carr, D.S. (1997) Has collaborative planning taken root in the national forests? *Journal of Forestry* 95(5), 25–28.

Selwyn, T. (1993) Peter Pan in South-East Asia. Views from the brochures. In: Hitchcock, M., King, V. and Parnwell, M. (eds) *Tourism in South-East Asia*. Routledge, London, pp. 117–137.

Sem, J. (1994) Tourism development decision models. In: Workshop Notebook of *Communities in*

Economic Transition: a Multiregional Conference on Rural Economic Development, Columbus, Ohio (co-sponsored by NCRCRD, NERCRD, ES-USDA, and the Farm Foundation).

Sen, A.K. (1977) Rational fools: a critique of the behavioral foundations of economic theory. *Philosophy and Public Affairs* 6, 317–344.

Senge, P. (1990) *The Fifth Discipline: the Art and Practice of the Learning Organization*. Doubleday, New York.

Setty, E.D. (1994) *Participatory Rural Development in Asia: a Critical Analysis*. Inter-India Publications, New Delhi, India.

Shannon, M.A. (1987) Forest planning: learning with people. In: Miller, M.L., Gale, R.P. and Brown, P.J. (eds) *Social Science in Natural Resource Management Systems*. Westview Press, Boulder, Colorado, pp. 233–252.

Shannon, M.A. (1991) *Ecosocial Systems in an Evolving Policy Context*. Ecosystem Management in a dynamic society. Department of Forestry and Natural Resources, Purdue University, West Lafayette, Indiana.

Shannon, M.A. (1992) Foresters as strategic thinkers, facilitators, and citizens. *Journal of Forestry* 90, 24–27.

Shaull, S.L. and Gramann, J.H. (1998) The effect of cultural assimilation on the importance of family-related and nature-related recreation among Hispanic Americans. *Journal of Leisure Research* 30.

Shaw, S. (1994) Gender, leisure, and constraint: toward a framework for the analysis of women's leisure. *Journal of Leisure Research* 26, 8–22.

Shaw, S. (1995) On taking a stand on gender issues: is neutrality possible? In: Fain, G.S. (ed.) *Leisure and Ethics: Reflections on the Philosophy of Leisure*, (vol. 2). American Association for Leisure and Recreation, Reston, Virginia, pp. 274–291.

Sheehy, G. (1995) *New Passages: Mapping Your Life Across Time*. Random House, Toronto.

Shelby, B. and Heberlein, T. (1986) *Carrying Capacity in Recreation Settings*. Oregon State University Press, Corvallis, Oregon.

Shelby, B. and Vaske, J.J. (1991) Using normative data to develop evaluative standards for resource Management: a comment on three recent papers. *Journal of Leisure Research* 23(2), 173–187.

Shelby, B., Brown, T. and Baumgartner, R. (1992) Effects of streamflows on river trips on the Colorado River in Grand Canyon, Arizona. *Rivers* 3, 191–201.

Sheldon, P. (1993) Destination Information Systems. *Annals of Tourism Research* 20(4), 633–649.

Sheldon, P. (1997a) Information Technologies for Tourism. CAB International, Wallingford, UK.

Sheldon, P. (1997b) *Tourism Information Technology*. CAB International, Wallingford, UK.

Sherif, M. (1958) Superordinate goals in the reduction of intergroup conflict. *The American Journal of Sociology* 63, 349–356.

Shinew, K., Floyd, M., McGuire, F. and Noe, F. (1995) Sex, race, and subjective social class and their association with leisure preferences. *Leisure Sciences* 17, 75–89.

Siehl, G.H. (1988) Developments in outdoor recreation policy since 1970. In: Watson, A. (comp), *Outdoor Recreation Benchmark 1988: Proceedings of the National Outdoor Recreation Forum*. Gen. Technical Report SE-52, pp. 10–21. USFS Southeastern Forest Experiment Station, Asheville, North Carolina.

Sileo, L. (1988) Preview Travel Post IPO: Why Wall Street loves Internet Travel. *The PhoCusWright Insighter* 1(5), May 11, [www.phocuswright.com/ptstory.html].

Simmel, G. (1950) The stranger. In: Wolff, K. (ed.) *The Sociology of Georg Simmel*. Free Press, Glencoe.

Simmons Market Research Bureau (1994) *Simmons 1994 Study of Media and Markets*. Simmons Market Research Bureau, New York.

Sirmon, J.M. (1993) National leadership. In: Berry, J.K. and Gordon, J.C. (eds) *Environmental Leadership: Developing Effective Skills and Styles*. Island Press, Washington, DC, pp. 165–185.

Sirmon, J.M., Shands, W.E. and Liggitt, C. (1993) Communities of interest and open decision-making. *Journal of Forestry* (91)7, 17–21.

Slover, B.L. (1995) *A Music of Opinions: Collaborative Planning for the Charles C. Deam Wilderness*. 1995 SERR Conference, Chattanooga, Tennessee.

Slovenian Tourist Board (n.d.) *Welcome to Slovenia* (catalogue) Slovenian Tourist Board, Ljubljana.

Smeral, E. (1994) Tourismus 2005. Entwicklungsaspekte und Szenarien für die Tourismus- und Freizeitwirtschaft. Wirtschaftsverlag, Ueberreuter.

Smith, A.J., Walker, J. and Clurman, A. (1997) *Rocking the Ages: the Yankolovich Report on Generational Marketing*. Harper Collins, New York.

Smith, C. (1991) *Overview of Youth Recreation Programs in the United States*. Carnegie Council on Adolescent Development, Washington, DC.

Smith, C. and Jenner, P. (1998) Tourism and the Internet. *Travel and Tourism Analyst* 1, 62–81.

Smith, R.C. (1996) *The Patient's Story: Integrated Patient-Doctor Interviewing*. Little, Brown and Company, Boston, Massachusetts.

Smith, S.L.J. (1990a) A test of Plog's allocentric/psychocentric model: evidence from seven nations. *Journal of Travel Research* 28, 40–43.

Smith, S.L.J. (1990b) Another look at the carpenter's tools: a reply to Plog. *Journal of Travel Research* 28, 50–51.

Smith, S.L.J. (1994) The tourism product. *Annals of Tourism Research* 21, 582–595.

Smith, V.K. and Desvousges, W. (1986) *Measuring the Benefits of Water Quality*. Kluwer, Boston, Massachusetts.

Smith, V.K. and Kaoru, Y. (1990) Signals or noise? Explaining the variation in recreation benefit estimates. *American Journal of Agricultural Economics* 72(2), 419–433.

Smith, V.L. (1989 [original edition 1977]) *Hosts and Guests: the Anthropology of Tourism*, 2nd edn. The University of Pennsylvania Press, Philadelphia, Pennsylvania.

Sofield, T. and Li, F. (1997) Rural tourism in China: development issues in perspective. In: Page, S. and Getz, D. (eds). *The Business of Rural Tourism: International Perspectives*. International Thomson Business Press, London.

Solomon, C.M. (1996) Flexibility comes out of flux. *Personnel Journal* 75(6), 34–41.

Solow, R.M. (1956) A contribution to the theory of economic growth. *Quarterly Journal of Economics* 70, 65–94.

Sorg, C. and Loomis, J. (1984) Empirical Estimates of Amenity Forest Values: a Comparative Review. General Technical Report RM-107. Rocky Mountain Forest and Range Experiment Station, USDA Forest Service, Fort Collins, Colorado.

Spiselman, A. (1995) Visionary Ritz-Carlton takes TQM to new level. *Hotels*, October, 45–46.

Stamps, S. and Stamps, M. (1985) Race, class, and leisure activities of urban residents. *Journal of Leisure Research* 17, 40–56.

Stankey, G. (1989) Solitude for the multitudes: managing recreational use in wilderness. In *Public Places and Spaces*. Plenum Press, New York, pp. 277–299.

Stankey, G. and Lime, D. (1973) *Recreational Carrying Capacity: an Annotated Bibliography*. USDA Forest Service General Technical Report INT-3.

Stankey, G. and Manning, R. (1986) Carrying capacity of recreation settings. In: *A Literature Review: the President's Commission on Americans Outdoors*. US Government Printing Office, Washington, DC, pp. M-47-M-57.

Stankey, G.H. (1973) *Visitor Perception of Wilderness Recreation Carrying Capacity*. USDA Forest Service Research Paper INT-142, Intermountain Forest and Range Experiment Station, Ogden, Utah.

Stankey, G.H., Cole, D.N., Lucas, R.C., Petersen, M.E. and Frissell, S.S. (1986) *The Limits of Acceptable Change (LAC) System for Wilderness Planning*. General Technical Report INT-176. USDA Forest Service, Intermountain Research Station, Ogden, Utah.

Stankey, G.H., McCool, S.F., Clark, R.N. and Brown, P.J. (1999) Institutional and organizational challenges to Managing natural resources for recreation: a social learning model. In: Burton, T. and Jackson, E. (eds) *Leisure Studies at the Millenium*. Venture Publishing, State College, Pennsylvania.

Stansfield, C.A. (1969) Recreational land use patterns within an American seaside resort. *Tourist Review* 24(4), 128–136.

State of the Industry Report (1998) *Demographics of consumers*. http://www.outdoorlink.com/infosou...ustry/state.industry.sect.1.3.html

Statistics Canada (1996) *Historical Labour Force Statistics* (Catalogue 71–201) Ottawa: Supply and Services Canada.

Statistics Canada, Income and Expenditure Accounts Division (1998) *Feasibility study: The Provincial Tourism Satellite Accounts*. Statistics Canada, Ottawa.

Stedman, R.C. and Decker, D.J. (1996) Illuminating an overlooked hunting stakeholder group: non-hunters and their interest in hunting. *Human Dimensions of Wildlife* 1(3), 29–41.

Stegner, W. (1962) *Wolf Willow: a History, a Story and a Memory of the Last Plains Frontier*. Viking Press, New York.

Stein, T.V. (1994) A benefits based approach to recreation management on Bureau of Land Management lands in Colorado. Masters thesis, Northern Arizona University, Flagstaff, Arizona.

Stein, T.V. (1997) Understanding how rural community stakeholders value and benefit from natural landscapes. PhD dissertation, University of Minnesota, St Paul, Minnesota.

Stein, T.V. and Anderson, D.H. (1998) Community benefits study: Itasca and Tettegouche State Parks. Technical Report, University of Minnesota, Department of Forest Resources, St Paul, Minnesota.

Stein, T.V. and Lee, M.E. (1995) Managing recreation resources for positive outcomes: an application of benefits-based management. *Journal of Park and Recreation Administration* 13(3), 52–70.

Stein, T.V., Anderson, D.H. and Thompson, D. (1999) Identifying and managing for community benefits in Minnesota state parks. *Journal of Park and Recreation Administration* 17(4), 1–19.

Stephens, L.S. (1996) Will Johnny see daddy this week? An empirical test of three theoretical perspectives of postdivorce contact. *Journal of Family Issues* 17(4), 466–495.

Stevens, B. and Rose, A. (1985) Regional input-output methods for tourism impact analysis. In: Probst, D.B. (ed.) *Assessing the Economic Impacts of Recreation and Tourism.* USDA Southeastern Forest Experiment Station, Asheville, North Carolina, pp. 16–22.

Stevens, P., Knutson, B. and Patton, M. (1995) DINESERV: a tool for measuring service quality in restaurants. *Cornell Hotel and Restaurant Administration Quarterly* 36(2), 56–60.

Stokowski, P.A. (1996) *Riches and Regrets: Betting on Gambling in Two Colorado Mountain Towns.* University Press of Colorado, Niwot, Colorado.

Stynes, D.J. and Stewart, S.I. (1991) The impacts of the grand traverse resort on the local community: a case study. Department of Park and Recreation Resources, Michigan State University, East Lansing, Michigan.

Sumner, E. (1936) *Special Report on a Wildlife Study in the High Sierra in Sequoia and Yosemite National Parks and Adjacent Territory.* US National Park Service Records, National Archives, Washington, DC.

Swain, R. (1996) Leave no trace (LNT) – outdoor skills and ethics program. *International Journal of Wilderness* 2(3), 24–26.

Swan, T.W. (1956) Economic growth and capital accumulation, *Economic Record* 32, 334–361.

Syria Ministry of Tourism (n.d.) *Syria. Cradle of Civilization* (catalogue) Salhani Establishment, Damascus.

Szyrmer, J. (1989) Trade-off between error and information in the RAS procedure. In: Miller, R., Polenske, K. and Rose A. (eds) *Frontiers of Input-Output Analysis.* Oxford University Press, New York, pp. 258–78.

Tanaka, J. (1997) There's no place like home, unless it's the office. *Newsweek* 130(1), 14–15.

Tanzania Tourist Board (n.d.) *Tanzania. The Land of Kilimanjaro and Zanzibar* (catalogue) Selling Africa, Amersham.

Taylor, C.N. and Bryan, C.H. (1987) Social impact assessment in New Zealand resource management. In: Miller, M.L., Gale, R.P. and Brown, P.J. (eds) *Social Science in Natural Resource Management Systems.* Westview Press, Boulder, Colorado, pp. 109–122.

Taylor, P. (1991) The precautionary principle and the prevention of pollution. *ECOS* 124, 41–46.

Taylor, S. (1997) Assessing regression based importance weights for quality perceptions and satisfaction judgements in the presence of higher order and/or interaction effects. *Journal of Retailing* 73(1), 135–159.

Tax, S. and Stuart, I. (1997) Designing and implementing new services: the challenge of integrating service systems. *Journal of Retailing* 73(1), 105–134.

Teasley, R.J., Bergstrom, J.C., Cordell, H.K., Zarnoch, S.J. and Gentle, P. (1999) Private lands and outdoor recreation in the United States. In: Cordell, H.K. (ed.) *Outdoor Recreation in American Life: A National Assessment of Demand and Supply Trends.* Sagamore Publishing, Champaign, Illinois, pp. 183–218.

Teigland, J. (1990) The Norwegian holidays in the 1970- and 1980'ies. Norwegian Institute for Nature Research. Oppdragsmelding 30. Lillehammer (In Norwegian).

Theroux, P. (1985) *Sunrise with Seamonsters* Penguin, Harmondsworth.

Thomas, G., Farrell, M.P. and Barnes, G.M. (1996) The effects of single-mother families and nonresidential fathers on delinquency and substance abuse in black and white adolescents. *Journal of Marriage and the Family* 58, 884–894.

Thompson, J.D. and Tuden, A. (1987) Strategies, structures and processes of organizational decision. In: Thompson, J.D., Hammond, P.B., Hawkes, R.W., Junker, B.H. and Tuden, A. (eds) *Comparative Studies in Administration.* Garland Publishing, New York, pp. 197–216.

Thompson, W. (1988) The Dutch gamble: a strategy for the expansion of legalized casino gambling in the Netherlands. *Nevada Review of Business and Economics* 12(1), 34–42.

TIA (Travel Industry Association) (1997) *Travel & Interactive Technology: a Five Year Outlook.* Travel Industry Association of America, Washington, DC.

Toth and Brown (1997) Racial and gender meanings of why people participate in recreational fishing. *Leisure Sciences* 19.

Tourism Council of Australia (1998) *Code of Sustainable Practice.* Australian Tourist Commission, Canberra.

Tourism Development Report (1999) Ecklein Communications, Novato, California, 2(5)

Towner, J. (1985) The Grand Tour: a key phase in the history of tourism. *Annals of Tourism Research* 12, 297–333.

Towner, J. (1996) *An Historical Geography of Recreation and Tourism in the Western World, 1540–1940.* John Wiley & Sons, Chichester.

Travel Industry Association of America (1997) Tourism Works for America. Washington, DC.
Travel Industry Association of America Newsletter (1991) Washington, DC.
Treyz, G.I. (1995) Policy analysis applications of REMI economic forecasting and simulation models. *International Journal of Public Administration* 18, 13–42.
Treyz, G.I., Rickman, D.S. and Shao, G. (1992) The REMI Economic-Demographic Forecasting and Simulation model. *International Regional Science Review* 14, 221–253.
Trinidad and Tobago Tourism and Industrial Development Company (n.d.) *Trinidad and Tobago. Come to Life* (catalogue). Trinidad and Tobago Tourism and Industrial Development Company, Port of Spain.
Troland, T. (1997) Outlook on shifts in demographic Markets. In: *Travel Industry Association Marketing Outlook Forum*. Cleveland, Ohio.
Truitt, L., Teye, V. and Farris, M. (1991) The role of computer reservation systems: international implications for the tourism industry. *Tourism Management* 12(1), 21–36.
Tunisian National Tourist Office (n.d.) *Unique Tunisia* (catalogue) Tunisian National Tourist Office, London.
Turismo Andaluz (1998) *Andalucia. There's Only One* (catalogue) Costa del Sol Patronato de Turismo, Malaga.
Turner, A. (1995) Tourism Council of Australia. In: Harris, R. and Leiper, N. (eds) *Sustainable Tourism. An Australian Perspective*. Butterworth-Heinemann, Oxford, pp. 76–79.
Turner, L. and Ash, J. (1975) *The Golden Hordes: International Tourism and the Pleasure Periphery*. Constable, London.
Tyrrell, T.J. (1985) Data consideration in assessing economic impacts of recreation and tourism. In: Probst, D.B. (ed.) *Assessing the Economic Impacts of Recreation and Tourism*. USDA Southeastern Forest Experiment Station, Asheville, North Carolina, pp. 40–45.
Udall, S.L. (1990) Pausing at the pass: reflections of a native son. In: *Beyond the MythicWest*. Peregrine Smith Books, Salt Lake City, Utah.
Uganda Tourist Board (n.d.) *Uganda. The Pearl of Africa* (catalogue) Selling Africa, Amersham.
Uhlik, K.S. (1995) Partnership, step by step: a practical model of partnership formation. *Journal of Park and Recreation Administration* 13(4), 13–24.
United Nations (1973) *Elements of Tourism Policy in Developing Countries*. UNCTAD, New York.
United Nations (1994) International Commission on Peace and Food, Uncommon Opportunities.
University of Missouri, Department of Recreation and Park Administration, University Extension (1978) *Tourism USA: Guidelines for Tourism Development*, University of Missouri, Department of Recreation and Park Administration, University Extension, Columbia, Missouri.
University of Missouri, Department of Recreation and Park Administration, University Extension (1986) *Tourism USA: Guidelines for Tourism Development*, University of Missouri, Department of Recreation and Park Administration, University Extension, Columbia, Missouri.
Urry, J. (1990) *The Tourist Gaze. Leisure and Travel in Contemporary Societies*. Sage, London.
Urry, J. (1995) *Consuming Places*. Routledge, London.
US Bureau of the Census (1992) Households, families, and children: a thirty year perspective (Current Population Reports, Series P23, no. 181) US Government Printing Office, Washington, DC.
US Bureau of the Census (1993) Poverty in the United States. (Current Population Reports, Series P-60, no. 185.) Government Printing Office, Washington, DC.
US Bureau of the Census (1994) The diverse living arrangements of children: Summer 1991. (Current Population Reports, Series P-70, no. 38) Government Printing Office, Washington, DC.
US Bureau of the Census (1997) America's Children at Risk. *Census Brief*, CENBR/97-2, www.census.gov.
US Bureau of the Census (1998) Increase in at-home workers reverses earlier trend, *Census Brief*, CENBR/98-2, www.census.gov.
USDA Forest Service (1998) Final Environmental Impact Statement: Proposed Improvement and Development at Sugarbush Resort. Rutland, Vermont: Green Mountain National Forest. June.
US Department of Commerce, International Trade Administration (1998) International Visitors (Inbound) and U.S. Residents (Outbound) (1988–1997) On web site: http://tinet.ita.doc.gov/view/f-1997-06-001/index.html
US Department of the Interior (1974–1992) *Federal Recreation Fee Report*. US Department of the Interior, National Park Service, Washington, DC.
US Department of the Interior, National Park Service (1997) The visitor experience and resource protection (VERP) framework: A handbook for planners and Managers. USDI National Park Service, Denver Service Center, Denver, Colorado.
US Department of the Interior, Bureau of Land Management (1998) Ruby Canyon/Black Ridge Integrated Resource Management Plan. US Department of the Interior, Bureau of Land Management, Grand Junction, Colorado.

US Fish and Wildlife Service (1997) 1996 national survey of fishing, hunting, and wildlife-associated recreation. Arlington, Virginia.

US General Accounting Office (1997) *A Profile of the Indian Gaming Industry.* GAO/GGD-97-91.

US National Park Service (1994) *National Park Service Strategic Plan* Vision. USNPS, Washington, DC.

US National Park Service, Northeast Field Area (1996) *Partnership Network – an Ambassador's Guide to Park Partnerships in the Northeast US* Pennsylvania.

Uzzell, D. (1984) An alternative structuralist approach to the psychology of tourism Marketing. *Annals of Tourism Research* 11, 79–99.

van den Berghe, P.L. (1993) Cultural impact of tourism. In: Khan, M.A., Olson, M.D. and Var, T. (eds) *Encyclopedia of Hospitality and Tourism.* Van Nostrand Reinhold, New York, pp. 619–628.

Van Doren, C. and Heit, M. (1973) Where it's at: a content analysis and appraisal of the *Journal of Leisure Research. Journal of Leisure Research* 5, 67–73.

Van Doren, C.S. and Lollar, S.A. (1985) The consequences of forty years of tourism growth. *Annals of Tourism Research* 3, 469.

Van Hoff, H., Collins, G. Combrink, T. and Verboten, M. (1995) Technology needs and perceptions: an assessment of the United States lodging industry. *Cornell Hotel and Restaurant Administration Quarterly* 36(5), 64–70.

Var, T. and Quayson, J. (1985) The multiplier impact of tourism in the Okanagan. *Annals of Tourism Research* 12, 497–514.

Vaske, J., Donnelly, M. and Shelby, B. (1992) Establishing management standards: selected examples of the normative approach. In *Defining Wilderness Quality: the Role of Standards in Wilderness Management – a Workshop Proceedings.* USDA Forest Service General Technical Report PNW-305, pp. 23–37.

Vaughan, W. and Russell, C. (1982) Valuing a fishing day: an application of a systematic varying parameters model. *Land Economics* 58(4), 450–463.

Veal, A.J. (1989) Leisure, life styles and status. *Leisure Studies* 8, 141–53.

Veblen, T. (1899) (1994) *The Theory of the Leisure Class.* Dover Publications, New York.

Velazquez Cortes, T. (1996) Designing artifice for touring illusions: an analysis of visitor approaches to tourist attractions. MA Thesis, Programme in European Leisure Studies, Tilburg University.

Verdoorn, P.J. (1949) Fattori che regolano lo sviluppo del producttivita del lavoro. *L'Industria* 1, 3–10.

Vining, J. and Schroeder, H.W. (1989) The effects of perceived conflict, resource scarcity, and information bias on emotions and environment. *Environmental Management* 13, 199–206.

Virden, R.J. and Knopf, R.C. (1989) Activities, experiences and environmental settings: A case study of recreation opportunity spectrum relationships. *Leisure Sciences* 11, 159–176.

Vlitos-Rowe, I. (1995) *The Impact of Technology on the Travel Industry.* Financial Times Management Reports, London.

Wagar, J. (1964) *The Carrying Capacity of Wildlands for Recreation.* Forest Science Monograph 7, Society of American Foresters, Washington, DC.

Wagar, J. (1968) The place of carrying capacity in the Management of recreation lands. In: *Third Annual Rocky Mountain-High Plains Park and Recreation Conference Proceedings.* Fort Collins, Colorado: Colorado State University.

Wagar, J.A. (1966) Quality in outdoor recreation. *Trends in Parks and Recreation* 3(3), 9–12.

Wagner, J.E. (1997) Estimating the economic impacts of tourism. *Annals of Tourism Research* 24, 592–608.

Wahab, S. (1974) *Elements of State Policy on Tourism.* Italgraphica, Torino, Italy.

Wahab, S. (1993) Government's role in strategic planning for tourism. In: *VNR's Encyclopedia of Tourism and Hospitality,* pp. 746–753. Virginian Nostrand Rheinhold, New York.

Wahab, S. and Pigram, J. (eds) (1997) *Tourism, Development and Growth.* Routledge, London.

Waitt, G. (1999) Naturalizing the 'primitive': a critique of marketing Australia's indigenous people as 'hunter-gatherers.' *Tourism Geographies* 1, 1–21.

Wales Tourist Board (and British Tourist Authority) (1998) *Wales. Land of Nature and Legend* (catalogue) Wales Tourist Board, Cardiff.

Wall, G. (1997) Sustainable tourism – unsustainable development. In: Wahab, S. and Pigram, J. (eds) *Tourism, Development and Growth.* Routledge, London, pp. 33–49.

Walle, A. (1994) The festival life cycle and tourism strategies: the case of the Cowboy Poetry Gathering. *Festival Management and Event Tourism: An International Journal* 2(2), 85–94.

Walsh, R., Johnson, D. and McKean, J. (1992) Benefit transfer of outdoor recreation studies, 1968–1988. *Water Resources Research* 28(3), 707–713.

Walsh, R. and Olienyk, J. (1981) *Recreation Demand Effects of Mountain Pine Beetle Damage to the Quality of Forest Recreation Resources in the Colorado Front Range.* Department of Economics, Colorado State University, Fort Collins, Colorado.

Walsh, R.G. and Gilliam, L.O. (1982) Benefits of wilderness expansion with excess demand for Indian peaks. *Western Journal of Agricultural Economics* 7, 1–12.

Walsh, R.G., Peterson, G.L. and McKean, J.R. (1989) Distribution and efficiency effects of alternative recreation funding methods. *Journal of Leisure Research* 21(4), 327–347.

Wamsley, G.L. (1990) *Refounding Public Administration.* Sage, Newbury Park, California.

Wandersman, A. (1979) User participation in planning environments: a conceptual framework. *Environment and Behavior* 11(4), 465–482.

Wandersman, A., Florin, P., Friedmann, R. and Meier, R. (1987) Who participates, who does not and why? An analysis of voluntary neighborhood organizations in the US and Israel. *Sociological Forum* 2, 534–555.

Wandless, E.G. (1943) *The Story of the Rubber Life Raft.* New York Rubber Corporation, New York.

Wang, N. (2000) *Tourism and the Ambivalence of Modernity.* Pergamon, Oxford.

Wanhill, S. (1994) Appraising tourism projects. In: Seaton, A.V. *et al.* (eds) *Tourism: the State of the Art,* John Wiley & Sons, Chichester.

Wanhill, S. (1997) Peripheral area tourism: a European perspective. *Progress in Tourism and Hospitality Research* 3, 47–70.

Ward, F. (1987) Economics of water allocation to instream uses in a fully appropriated river basin: evidence from a New Mexico wild river. *Water Resources Research* 23(2), 381–392.

Wardell, D. (1998) The impact of electronic distribution on travel agents. *Travel and Tourism Analyst* (2), 41–55.

Warner, M. (1997) Working at home – the right way to be a star in your bunny slippers. *Fortune* 135(4), 165–168.

Warren, K.J. (1990) The power and promise of ecological feminism. *Environmental Ethics* 12, 125–146.

Washburne, R. (1978) Black under-participation in wildland recreation: alternative explanations. *Leisure Sciences* 1, 175–189.

Washburne, R. and Wall, P. (1980) *Black-White Ethnic Differences in Outdoor Recreation.* USDA Forest Service Research Paper INT-249.

Watson, A., Williams, D. and Daigle, J. (1991) Sources of conflict between hikers and mountain bikers in the Rattlesnake NRA. *Journal of Park and Recreation Administration* 9, 59–71.

Weber, R.E. (1986) Regional econometric modeling and the New Jersey state model. In: Perryman, M.R. and Schmidt, J.R. (eds) *Regional Econometric Modeling.* Kluwer-Nijhoff, Boston, Massachusetts, pp. 13–39.

Wedel, M. and Kamakura, W.A. (1998) *Market Segmentation, Conceptual and Methodological Foundations.* Kluwer, Boston.

Wellman, J.D. (1995) Masters education and the art of recreation management. *Trends* 32(4), 28–30.

Wellman, J.D. and Tipple, T.J. (1990) Public forestry and direct democracy. *The Environmental Professional* 12, 77–86.

Wellman, J.D. and Tipple, T.J. (1993) Governance in the wildland-urban interface: a normative guide for natural resource managers. In: Ewert, A.W., Chavez, D.J. and Magill, A.W. (eds) *Culture, Conflict and Communication in the Wildland-Urban Interface.* Westview Press, Boulder, Colorado, pp. 337–347.

Wells, W.D. (1974) *Life Style and Psychographics.* AMA, Chicago.

Wells, W.D. and Tigert, D.J. (1971) Activities, interests and opinions. *Journal of Advertising Research* 11, 27–35.

Werthner, H. (1998) *IFITT Workshop on Open Issues and Challenges in IT and Tourism.* Innsbruck, Austria, September.

Werthner, H. and Klein, S. (eds) 1999 *Information Technology and Tourism: a Challenging Relationship.* Springer-Verlag, Vienna.

West, G.R. (1993) Economic significance of tourism in Queensland. *Annals of Tourism Research* 20, 490–504.

West, G.R. (1995) Comparison of input–output, input–output + econometric and computable general equilibrium impact models at the regional level. *Economic Systems Research* 7(2), 209–227.

West, P. (1989) Urban regional parks and black minorities: Subculture, marginality, and interracial relations in park use in the Detroit metropolitan area. *Leisure Sciences* 11, 11–28.

West, P.C. and Brechin, S.R. (1991) *Resident Peoples and National Parks: Social Dilemmas and Strategies in International Conservation.* University of Arizona Press, Tuscon, Arizona.

Westover, T. (1989) Perceived crowding in recreational settings: an environment-behavior model. *Environment and Behavior* 21, 258–276.

Wheatcraft, S. (1989) Strategic planning for tourism, government view. In: Witt, S. and Moutinho, L. (eds) *Tourism Marketing and Management Handbook.* Prentice Hall, Englewood Cliffs, New Jersey.

Wheeller, B. (1993) Sustaining the ego. *Journal of Sustainable Tourism* 1(2), 121–129.

White House Conference on Travel and Tourism (1995) *Cultural Tourism in the United States.* National Endowment for the Arts, Washington DC.

Whitiam, G. (1993) Who goes to spas? *Cornell Hotel and Restaurant Quarterly* 34(5), 3–15.

WHO (World Health Organization) (1946) Constitution. World Health Organization, New York.

Whyte, L.B. and Shaw, S.M. (1994) Women's leisure: an exploratory study of fear of violence as a leisure constraint. *Journal of Applied Recreation Research* 19(1), 5–21.

Wicks, B. (1995) Celebrating festivals of the future. *Trends* 20 (2), 12–19.

Wicks, B. and Schultz, W. (1995) Assessing issues that will impact the festival and special event industry in the next five to ten years. Paper presented at the research symposium, annual conference of the International Festivals and Events Association conference, Vancouver.

Widdekind, L. (1995) *Human Powered Outdoor Recreation: State of the Industry Report 1995.* The Outdoor Recreation Coalition of America, Washington, DC.

Williams, B.A. and Matheny, A.R. (1995) *Democracy, Dialogue, and Environmental Disputes: the Contested Languages of Social Regulation.* Yale University.

Williams, P.W., Andestad, G., Pollock, A. and Dossa, K.B. (1996) Health spa travel markets: Mexican long-haul pleasure travellers. *Journal of Vacation Marketing* 3(1), 11–31.

Wilson, K. (1998) Market/industry confusion in tourism economic analyses. *Annals of Tourism Research* 25, 803–817.

Wilson, W.J. (1980 [1978]) *The Declining Significance of Race*, 2nd edn. University of Chicago Press, Chicago, Illinois.

Wilton, D. (1998) *Recent Developments in Tourism, as Revealed by the National Tourism Indicators, Research Report 1998–1.* Canadian Tourism Commission, Ottawa.

Witt, P.A. (1997) *Evaluation of the Totally Cool, Totally Art Program, Austin Parks and Recreation Department.* Texas A&M University, College Station, Texas.

Witt, P.A. and Baker, J. (1999) The Get R.E.A.L. Roving Leader Program. *Parks and Recreation* (in press).

Witt, P.A. and Crompton, J.L. (1996a) The at-risk youth recreation project. *Journal of Park and Recreation Administration* 14(3), 1–9. This paper was reproduced with some modifications in (1997), *Parks and Recreation* 32(1), 54–61.

Witt, P.A. and Crompton, J.L. (1996b) *Recreation Programs That Work for at-Risk Youth: the Challenge of Shaping the Future.* Venture Publishing, State College, Pennsylvania.

Witt, P.A., Garteiser, M. and Crompton, J.L. (1995) Status of the evaluation of recreation programs for at-risk youth. Unpublished paper. Department of Recreation, Park and Tourism Sciences, College Station, Texas.

Witt, P.A., Baker, D.A. and Scott, D. (1996) *The Protective Factors Scale.* Unpublished manuscript. Texas A&M University, College, Texas.

Wondolleck, J. (1996) Incorporating hard-to-define values into public lands decision making: a conflict management perspective. In: Driver, B.L., Dustin, D., Baltic, T., Elsner, G. and Peterson, G. (eds) *Nature and the Human Spirit: Toward an Expanded Land Management Ethic.* Venture Publishing, State College, Pennsylvania, pp. 257–262.

Wondolleck, J.M. (1988) *Public Lands Conflict and Resolution: Managing National Forest Disputes.* Plenum, New York.

Woods, J. (1992) Building or adding a spa to hotels and resorts is an exercise calling for experienced help. *Florida Hotel and Motel Journal*, May, 20–29.

World Bank (1998) *Global Economic Prospects and the Developing Countries*, Washington, DC.

World Commission on Environment and Development (1987) *Our Common Future.* Oxford University Press, Oxford.

World Travel and Tourism Council (1995) *The WTTC Report – Research Edition: Travel and Tourism.* World Travel and Tourism Council, London.

WTO (World Tourism Organization) (1988) *Guidelines for the Transfer of New Technologies in the Field of Tourism.* World Tourism Organization, Madrid.

WTO (World Tourism Organization) (1993a) *Sustainable Tourism Development: Guide for Local Planners.* WTO, Madrid.

WTO (World Tourism Organization) (1993b) *Tourism Development and the Responsibility of the State.*

WTO (World Tourism Organization) (1994a) *Global Distribution Systems in the Tourism Industry.* World Tourism Organization, Madrid.

WTO (World Tourism Organization) (1994b) *Recommendations on Tourism Statistics.* World Tourism Organization, Madrid.

WTO (World Tourism Organization) (1995a) Agenda 21 for the Travel and Tourism Industry.

WTO (World Tourism Organization) (1995b) Budgets and Marketing Plans of National Tourist Administrations.

WTO (World Tourism Organization) (1995c) L'impact des nouvelles technologies dans la distribution touristique, Committee of Affiliate Members, World Tourism Organisation, Madrid.

WTO (World Tourism Organization) (1995d) Seminar on Global Distribution Systems Tourism and New Information Technologies, 18 October, Cairo, World Tourism Organisation, Madrid.

WTO (World Tourism Organization) (1996) *International Tourism Statistics*. WTO, Madrid.

WTO (World Tourism Organization) (1997) *International Tourism: a Global Perspective*, Gee, C. and Fayos-Sola (eds) WTO, Madrid.

WTO (World Tourism Organization) (1998a) Global tourism forecasts to the year 2000 and beyond. *Tourism 2020 Vision*, Revised, WTO, Madrid.

WTO (World Tourism Organization) (1998b) *Tourism Satellite Account*, draft 4. World Tourism Organization, Madrid.

WTO (World Tourism Organization) (1999) *Tourism Highlights 1999*. WTO, Madrid.

Wu, Z. (1996) Childbearing in cohabitational relationships. *Journal of Marriage and the Family* 58, 281–292.

Yaffee, S.L. (1996) Ecosystem Management in practice: the importance of human institutions. *Ecological Applications* 6(3), 724–727.

Yankelovich, D. (1991) *Coming to Public Judgment: Making Democracy Work in a Complex World*. Syracuse University Press, Syracuse, New York.

Yiannakis, A. and Gibson, H. (1992) Roles tourists play. *Annals of Tourism Research* 19, 287–303.

Youell, R. (1994) *Leisure and Tourism*. Pitman Publishing, London, pp. 11.1–11.32.

Young, R.A. and Kent, A.T. (1985) Using the theory of reasoned action to improve understanding of recreation behavior. *Journal of Leisure Research* 17(2), 90–106.

Yuan, M. and Moisey, R.N. (1992) The characteristics and economic significance of visitors attracted to Montana wildlands. *Western Wildlands* 18(3), 20–24.

Yuan, M.S. and McEwen, D. (1989) Test for campers' experience preference differences among three ROS setting classes. *Leisure Sciences* 11, 177–185.

Zanders, H. and Harding, S. (1995) Changing work values in Europe and North America. Continents and occupations compared. In: de Moor, R. (ed.) *Values in Western Societies*. Tilburg University Press, Le Tilburg.

Zeithaml, V.A. and Bitner, M.J. (1996) *Services Marketing*. McGraw Hill, New York.

Zhou, D., Yanagida, J.F., Chakravorty, U. and Leung, P. (1997) Estimating economic impacts from tourism. *Annals of Tourism Research* 24, 76–89.

Zimmerman, M.A. and Rappaport, J. (1988) Citizen participation, perceived control and psychological empowerment. *American Journal of Community Psychology* 16, 5–750.

Zins, A. (1998) *Gästebefragung Österreich – Österreich Bericht Wintersaison 1997/98*. ÖGAF, Vienna.

Zukin, S. (1991) *Landscapes of Power: From Detroit to Disney World*. University of California Press, Berkeley.

Zukin, S. (1996) *The Cultures of Cities*. Blackwell, Oxford.

Zuzanek, J. (1992) Culture-tourism partnership: from rags to riches? In: Fleischer-van Rooijen, C.A.M. (ed.) *Spatial Implications of Tourivm*. Geo Pers, Groningen, pp. 105–118.

Index